Human-Computer Interaction Series

T0138141

Human-Computer Interaction is a multidisciplinary field focused on human aspects of the development of computer technology. As computer-based technology becomes increasingly pervasive - not just in developed countries, but worldwide - the need to take a humancentered approach in the design and development of this technology becomes ever more important. For roughly 30 years now, researchers and practitioners in computational and behavioral sciences have worked to identify theory and practice that influences the direction of these technologies, and this diverse work makes up the field of human–computer interaction. Broadly speaking it includes the study of what technology might be able to do for people and how people might interact with the technology. In this series we present work which advances the science and technology of developing systems which are both effective and satisfying for people in a wide variety of contexts. The human–computer interaction series will focus on theoretical perspectives (such as formal approaches drawn from a variety of behavioral sciences), practical approaches (such as the techniques for effectively integrating user needs in system development), and social issues (such as the determinants of utility, usability and acceptability).

For further volumes:
http://www.springer.com/series/6033

John M. Carroll
Editor

Creativity and Rationale

Enhancing Human Experience by Design

Springer

Editor
John M. Carroll
College of Information Sciences and Technology
The Pennsylvania State University
University Park, PA, USA

ISSN 1571-5035
ISBN 978-1-4471-6093-9   ISBN 978-1-4471-4111-2 (eBook)
DOI 10.1007/978-1-4471-4111-2
Springer London Heidelberg New York Dordrecht

Springer is part of Springer Science+Business Media (www.springer.com)

Contents

Contributors

Mark Aakhus Department of Communication, School of Communication and Information, Rutgers, The State University of New Jersey, New Brunswick, NJ, USA

Phillip J. Ayoub College of Information Sciences and Technology, The Pennsylvania State University, University Park, PA, USA

Eli Blevis Human-Computer Interaction Design, School of Informatics and Computing (SoIC), Indiana University–Bloomington, Bloomington, IN, USA

Stacy M. Branham Center for Human-Computer Interaction, Virginia Tech, Blacksburg, VA, USA

Bo Brinkman Department of Computer Science and Software Engineering, Miami University, Oxford, OH, USA

Simon J. Buckingham Shum Knowledge Media Institute, The Open University, Milton Keynes, UK

Janet E. Burge Department of Computer Science and Software Engineering, Miami University, Oxford, OH, USA

Winslow Burleson School of Computing, Informatics, and Decision Systems Engineering, Arizona State University, Tempe, AZ, USA

Linda Candy Creativity & Cognition Studios, School of Software, Faculty of Engineering and IT, University of Technology, Sydney, Australia

John M. Carroll Center for Human-Computer Interaction, College of Information Sciences and Technology, The Pennsylvania State University, University Park, PA, USA

Aldo de Moor CommunitySense, Tilburg, The Netherlands

Umer Farooq Microsoft Corporation, One Microsoft Way, Redmond, WA, USA

Gerhard Fischer Center for LifeLong Learning and Design (L3D), Department of Computer Science and Institute of Cognitive Science, University of Colorado, Boulder, CO, USA

Gabriela Goldschmidt Faculty of Architecture and Town Planning, Technion - Israel Institute of Technology, Haifa, Israel

Steve Harrison Center for Human-Computer Interaction, Virginia Tech, Blacksburg, VA, USA

Brian Magerko Digital Media Program, School of Literature, Communication, and Culture, Georgia Institute of Technology, Atlanta, GA, USA

Raymond McCall Department of Planning and Design, University of Colorado, Denver, CO, USA

D. Scott McCrickard Center for Human-Computer Interaction, Virginia Tech, Blacksburg, VA, USA

Anders I. Mørch InterMedia, University of Oslo, Oslo, Norway

Rosalie J. Ocker College of Information Sciences and Technology, The Pennsylvania State University, University Park, PA, USA

Irene J. Petrick College of Information Sciences and Technology, The Pennsylvania State University, University Park, PA, USA

Matthew J. Prindible KIT Digital, New York, NY, USA

Albert M. Selvin Verizon Information Technology, White Plains, NY, USA

Knowledge Media Institute, The Open University, Milton Keynes, UK

Frank Shipman Center for the Study of Digital Libraries, Department of Computer Science, Texas A&M University, College Station, TX, USA

Alistair Sutcliffe Manchester Business School, University of Manchester, Manchester, UK

John C. Thomas Software Productivity Research Group, IBM T. J. Watson Research Center, Yorktown Heights, NY, USA

Priyamvada Tripathi School of Computing, Informatics, and Decision Systems Engineering, Arizona State University, Tempe, AZ, USA

Shahtab Wahid Center for Human-Computer Interaction, Virginia Tech, Blacksburg, VA, USA

Jing Wang Center for Human-Computer Interaction, College of Information Sciences and Technology, The Pennsylvania State University, University Park, PA, USA

Chapter 1
Creativity and Rationale: The Essential Tension

John M. Carroll

Abstract Creativity and rationale comprise an essential tension in design. They are two sides of the coin; contrary, complementary, but perhaps also interdependent. Designs always serve purposes. They always have an internal logic. They can be queried, explained, and evaluated. These characteristics are what design rationale is about. But at the same time designs always provoke experiences and insights. They open up possibilities, raise questions, and engage human sense making. Design is always about creativity. This book presents a set of research papers addressing the topic of creativity and rationale in software design. This introductory chapter presents an account of the workshop and review process through which the papers were developed, and thumbnail summaries of the individual papers.

Keywords Creativity • Rationale • Design • Design rationale • Software design • Essential tension

1.1 Introduction

Creativity and rationale connote two faces of design that are sometimes viewed as complementary, or even opposed: envisioning new worlds through intuitive strokes of innovation versus analyzing reasons and tradeoffs to guide the development of new artifacts and systems. Because it is frequently the case that different practitioners and researchers, and different design disciplines, prize one or the other more highly, there is not only a contrast, but also a lack of integration between creativity and rationale.

J.M. Carroll (✉)
Center for Human-Computer Interaction and College of Information Sciences and Technology,
The Pennsylvania State University, University Park, PA 16802, USA
e-mail: jmcarroll@psu.edu

J.M. Carroll (ed.), *Creativity and Rationale: Enhancing Human
Experience by Design*, Human–Computer Interaction Series,
DOI 10.1007/978-1-4471-4111-2_1, © Springer-Verlag London 2013

Yet looking at the two, it also seems they are indivisible: What would be the point of building and/or using rationale in design if doing so were to result in anything other than greater creativity? And almost analogously, what good would be served by cultivating or purporting creativity that could never be interrogated, understood, or deliberately improved and applied, never be explained or conveyed to colleagues, never be passed on to students?

This is most definitely *not* to say that the only reason for rationale in design is to enhance creativity, or that sources of creativity that cannot be explicitly articulated (put into words) have no value. Rather, it is to say that designers and design researchers should want rationales and rationale practices that enhance creativity, and should want to be able to understand and to explain their use of creativity to students, to clients, to users, and to other stakeholders.

It is not hard to state how creativity and rationale could fail to have a mutually facilitative relationship. Rationale can easily become an obsession of documentation and formalization, excessively detailing issues, arguments, and alternatives to an extent or in a manner that no one would ever want to revisit, let alone create in the first place. And indeed, rationale practices are often cited as exemplifying a classic rationalist *mis*understanding of what design is about and how it moves forward. Rationale practices that suffocate design by enforcing a tedious documentation burden could appropriately be regarded as undermining possibilities for creativity.

But creativity has its challenges as well. It is sometimes characterized as necessarily arcane, inherently ineffable, and slightly (or even primarily) mystical. But this attitude unambitiously conflates the nuance and intellectual rigor required to pose and investigate subtle questions with reluctance to pose questions at all. It makes it a point of definition (or perhaps religion) that creativity cannot be fathomed or explained simply. It is true that such a view of creativity would have few or no implications for understanding, teaching, or practicing design. But we are not forced to this view. Perhaps, like learning, emotion, sociality, and other characteristically human capacities, creativity is embedded in activity, difficult to isolate for analysis, but quite real and principled.

Ironically, and tragically, research on creativity may have inadvertently vindicated the tendency toward know-nothing views of creativity by considering it in austere generality, and (perhaps as a result) producing fairly ethereal and obvious characterizations, for example, the somewhat underwhelming chestnut that creative activity requires both divergent and convergent thinking.

Given how easy it is to imagine, or just to see in the world, that creativity and rationale can have little to offer one another, it becomes all the more interesting to ask whether and how creativity and rationale can have mutually facilitative interactions.

1.2 A Workshop on Creativity and Rationale in Software Design

A diverse group of designers and design researchers met at Penn State University, June 15–17, 2008, to exchange perspectives and approaches, to articulate and develop new research ideas and hypotheses, and to reconsider and reconstruct prior work and results toward new research directions.

The workshop included thought leaders from several software design research communities, such as human–computer interaction design, sociotechnical systems design, requirements engineering, information systems, and artificial intelligence: Mark Ackerman, University of Michigan; Eli Blevis, Indiana University; Janet Burge, Miami University of Ohio; John Carroll, The Pennsylvania State University; Fred Collopy, Case Western Reserve University; John Daughtry, The Pennsylvania State University; Umer Farooq, The Pennsylvania State University; Gerhard Fischer, University of Colorado; Jodi Forlizzi, Carnegie-Mellon University; Batya Friedman, University of Washington; John Gero, George Mason University; Steve Harrison, Virginia Tech; Sal March, Vanderbilt University; Raymond McCall, University of Colorado; Rosalie Ocker, The Pennsylvania State University; Colin Potts, Georgia Institute of Technology; Mary Beth Rosson, The Pennsylvania State University; Al Selvin, the Open University and Verizon; Alistair Sutcliffe, University of Manchester; and Deborah Tatar, Virginia Tech.

The workshop premise was that creativity and rationale should not be opposed worldviews, and that coordinating them and integrating them is a key to having more effectively reflective design practices, and absolutely essential to a serious science of design. Discussions of design in the computer and information science and engineering (aka CISE) disciplines are highly compartmentalized. In software engineering, design is often discussed as if it were nearly algorithmic, whereas in human-computer interaction it is sometimes treated as nearly ineffable art. At a finer level, critical concepts like *rationale* and *creativity* are understood in multiple incompatible ways. Thus, rationale can be a designer's inchoate intent, an analyst's inference about overall intent or significance, a comprehensive representation of the design process (e.g., IBIS; Kunz and Rittel 1970), or a detailed (e.g., propositional) representation of consequences for various sorts of users (elaborated by empirical results; Moran and Carroll 1996). Similarly, creativity can refer to the personal experience of being creative (e.g., flow; Csikszentmihalyi 1996; or eudaimonic well-being; Ryan and Deci 2001), it can refer to the novelty of strategies and practices employed in design as problem solving, it can refer purely operationally to the proportion of novel ideas generated, or it can refer to the novelty of artifacts and other embodied products (cf. innovation; von Hippel 1988).

The workshop started with seven orienting questions:

1. When and how can design rationale evoke creativity in design? For example, does/can design rationale function differently (more effectively) in end-user design, participatory design, pair programming/agile design, or open source design communities?
2. When and how can design rationale fail to evoke, or even undermine, creativity?
3. How can the construction of design rationale be construed and experienced as a creative activity? And how can this be enhanced?
4. What tools and methods for rationale can support or enhance the creativity of design products? For example, how much structure should design rationale tools provide/impose to maximize creative outcomes (e.g., contrast QOC, gIBIS, and design blogs).
5. How might valuing the creativity of rationales inspire new forms of design rationale? What would be characteristics of such new forms of rationale?

6. How can design rationale be used in the classroom to motivate and instruct students about reflection, idea generation, and evaluation?
7. What are useful models, theories, and frameworks for understanding and managing the relationship between rationale and creativity in design?

We specifically eschewed starting from definitions: That is such a formulaic workshop activity after all, and can implicitly filter out diversity in positions. But definitions of course crept in. To understand the relationships between creativity and rationale in design, perhaps one must fix a conception of design, creativity and rationale, at least to some extent.

We characterized design as involving the construction of frames or worlds within which designers work. The scope of this construction is broader than merely an artifact. It encompasses the designer's values and intentions, assumptions and knowledge about people and their activity, and the palette of materials and components that can be incorporated.

We characterized design as inherently iterative, that is, iterative beyond the prescriptive sense of "design one to throw away." New purposes, new requirements emerge from a design as soon as it is embodied, and continue to emerge as people (i.e., users) appropriate and adapt the design within their own activities. One way this was put was to say that software "changes the world." Another way was to say that new artifacts change people's expectations and values.

Another way this was described was using the task–artifact cycle: the notion that a design (artifact) responds to activities (tasks) in the world, directly transforming them in some ameliorative manner (i.e., achieving requirements), but also, most likely, introducing other transformations (creating new unanticipated affordances, and perhaps unfortunate side-effects).

We characterized creativity in design as playfulness, pursuing surprise, and unexpected outcomes. Another aspect of creativity in design is empathy: The exercise of putting oneself into the role of another. Another is liminality: Thinking and acting on the border between two contrasting concepts or rules, such as a rapid switching between convergent and divergent modes of thinking.

We characterized rationale in a variety of ways. One was to consider it a design representation: a way of presenting a design that contrasts with other ways (e.g., sketching, software prototypes), and resultingly evokes descriptive tensions (and perhaps creativity).

Rationale can be prospective (i.e., generated within design activity, as an enabling part of design work) or retrospective (i.e., generated after design activity, perhaps even after the design is embodied and in use). This distinction is important because retrospective design rationale can only evoke creativity for subsequent design work. And conversely, one cannot get the retrospective benefit of perspective and reflection just by "capturing" prospective rationale in situ.

We also characterized the role of rationale in design in a variety of ways. Most basically, rationale is a kind of documentation. This is actually a complex and problematic concept. For example, it is clear that there are many possible rationales for any feature, for any decision taken. Which rationale is to be codified? Rationale could be documented at many levels of detail: Should it be relatively sketchy, focusing on key ideas and issues, or should it be highly detailed?

Thinking of rationale as documentation also raises division-of-labor questions such as whose job is it to capture the rationale, whose job is it to validate the rationale, whose job is it use rationale created by someone else. These cost–benefit tradeoff questions arise whenever a workflow involves people extrinsically tasked to create value for others in an organization.

Rationale as documentation might of course limit creativity (see above) by anchoring thought, and limiting divergence or risk taking. But it could also evoke creativity by framing the design world in terms of the issues and choices that are being managed, and perhaps doing this in multiple ways. In other words, codifying the disciplined part of the designer's world might make it easier to problematize the parts of the world that are codified, by labeling them, but it could also make it easier to problematize the parts that are not yet codified, by contrasting them against the provisional frame.

But there are other ways to see rationale. For example, the discussions among stakeholders presenting, analyzing, and perhaps contesting, assumptions, decisions, values, roles, processes, and so on are also rationale. This is Rittel's (Kunz and Rittel 1970) democratic conception of many authors contributing to making an argument space more visible for all.

Indeed, focusing on design as a potentially—and perhaps even typically—collaborative task changes the way one might characterize the activity of creating and using rationale. After all, collaborators must continuingly create common ground. This is never a matter of once and done. As the shared activity develops, as assumptions and commitments are made as interim outcomes are obtained, collaborators must make these things public at least to the extent required to allow effective coordination of individual contributions.

For example, Minneman (1991) reported that part of design collaboration is reaching agreement about issues that will not be discussed again (at least for some span of time). This is a highly specialized area of common ground management, and one that design rationale could support, just by providing a language to cordon off areas of discussion and debate.

Like most workshops, this one ended up posing, but leaving open, many questions and identifying projects that ought to be undertaken, but have not yet been started. For example, if rationale can support creativity in design through reframing, that is, through helping designers see their design world in alternative ways, what specific properties of rationales can facilitate this function, what are the rules and heuristics of rationales that provoke insights? One future project we articulated was identifying cases where rationale evoked ideas that had not been raised before in a given design process. What are kinds of ideas are they? What kinds of rationale evoked them? What were the design process circumstances in which they were evoked?

1.3   This Book

A key objective of the workshop was to facilitate longer-term processes of scholarly interaction, and the development of more refined proposals, analyses, and results. One result is this volume in the Springer Series on Human-Computer Interaction, presenting 19 chapters developed from presentations and discussions at the Creativity and Rationale in Software Design workshop and from ensuing interactions with colleagues in the HCI research community.

Creativity is evoked by articulated tensions in goals and interpretations. Rationale can help to articulate tensions in design, and thereby energize creativity. A key thread through the book is an examination of the roles that codifications of design ideas and interactions can play in evoking creativity. In "Critical Conversations: Feedback as a Stimulus to Creativity in Software Design," Raymond McCall analyzes interactions among designers and other stakeholders as integrating ideation and evaluation, through both reflection and situated cognitive analysis, to provide feedback about consequences of design decisions that challenges designers to devise new ideas. McCall argues that exploiting the full potential of critical conversations requires rationale methods that are better integrated with software tools.

Gabriela Goldschmidt in "A Micro View of Design Reasoning: Two-Way Shifts Between Embodiment and Rationale" describes an analysis of data from the Delft Protocols investigating the distribution and sequential dependencies of design argumentation addressing the embodiment of designs (for example, their physical form) and the rationale for designs (evaluation of design decisions). She examined an individual designer's protocol as well as a design team protocol, and found that embodiment and rationale arguments occurred with equal frequency, and are highly interleaved. She concludes that interplay between the two modes is instrumental in producing creative design outcomes.

Linda Candy, in "Evaluating Creativity," draws upon studies of participant engagement in the domain of interactive digital arts. She analyzes four key dimensions of interaction among of the act of creation, its outcomes, and their implications for users: The capabilities of creators (dispositions, abilities, and experiences of people that enable creative activity); the processes enacted by both artist/creators and audience/participants, as well as the interactions between participant experience and continuing development of the interactive digital artwork; the products of the creative process, that is, features and properties of the artifacts, installations and performances of the interactive digital artwork; and the contexts of creation, formative interaction with participants, public performance and so forth each of which constrain and enable creativity in myriad ways.

Alistair Sutcliffe, in "Integrating Design Representations for Creativity," investigates the notion that tension between alternative design embodiments can be a source of creativity. He argues that the concurrent use of scenarios, prototypes and models can evoke creativity by juxtaposing complementary cognitive affordances.

"Achieving Both Creativity and Rationale: Reuse in Design with Images and Claims," by Scott McCrickard, Shatab Wahid, Stacy Branham and Steve Harrison, addresses the technical issue of reuse: Designs are almost never *ab initio*; they typically are based upon prior designs. McCrickard et al. operationalize rationale through inspiring imagery and explicit enumeration of trade-offs implicit in a design, and they investigate how to encourage the reuse of rationale toward better designs and greater creativity.

Anders Mørch, in "Predecessor Artifacts: Evolutionary Perspectives on a Reflective Conversation with Design Materials," discusses the historical character of design, examining the roles of predecessor artifacts in design processes. Predecessor artifacts often embody the problem statement for successor artifacts. They serve as props for articulating adaptations that later may become the successor design. At any point in time, predecessor artifacts are used with their successors as backup systems or alternatives. In these roles, predecessor artifacts both embody and evoke elaboration of rationale and reflection on designs.

Designers need to articulate and push boundaries. They need to know where boundaries are, and rationale organizes design spaces to indicate boundaries. But designers also need to explore and push boundaries to help identify opportunities for creative innovations. Eli Blevis describes the PRInCiPleS (Predispositions, Research, Insights, Concepts, Prototypes, Strategies) design framework as a methodological tool for mediating and more explicitly integrating analysis and synthesis in design work. He illustrates the framework with the example of designing for sustainable food practices.

The chapters by Janet Burge and Bo Brinkman and by Jing Wang, Umer Farooq and John M. Carroll continue this theme, examining the role of rationale in the development of creative design professionals, specifically with respect to identifying boundaries. Burge and Brinkman, in "Using Rationale to Assist Student Cognitive and Intellectual Development," address the challenge students experience when they first encounter problems for which there is more than one "right" answer. They found that introducing students to design rationale techniques helped them consider multiple alternatives and to reflect on reasons for choosing a particular alternative.

In "Does Design Rationale Enhance Creativity?" Wang et al. studied the design processes and outcomes of student teams in an advanced software engineering course. They found that greater use of design rationale by teams was correlated with more creative outcomes. In particular, they found that the comprehensiveness of tradeoff analysis and the feasibility of design alternatives in the rationales were critical to enhancing novelty, persuasiveness, and insightfulness of the designs.

Much creativity arises within organizations and collaborative teams. The social validation of ideas by communities helps to differentiate creativity from merely novelty. But social interactions are also complex. In "Promoting Group Creativity in Upstream Requirements Engineering," Rosalie Ocker examines this topic by focusing on negative intergroup social processes associated with status differentials, in-group bias, and majority influence, which are known to undermine group creativity. She shows how group support system tools that incorporate design rationale can promote creativity.

Farooq and Carroll, in "Supporting Awareness in Creative Group Work by Exposing Design Rationale," address the level of small design teams and the challenge of maintaining team activity awareness in producing a creative collective outcome. For example, team members must monitor the development of key ideas across the team in order to be able to coordinate their own contributions, and to communicate with their teammates. Farooq and Carroll investigate the consequences of sharing rationales around work activities through status updates in a collaborative environment to support overall team awareness.

Brian Magerko, in "Studying Humans to Inform Interactive Narrative Technology" describes empirical studies of human gamemasters in tabletop roleplay and of performers in improvisational theater. The goal of the research is to identify the strategies and rationales that guide these creative practices in order to develop effective computational agents for interactive narrative technology (INT) systems.

In "Improvisation in the Cloud: Devised Theatre in Support of Problem Finding," Irene Petrick, Phillip Ayoub and Matthew Prindible examine improvisation in organizational contexts. They specifically focus on organizations addressing innovation the new context of cloud computing, and the shift away from strictly in-house design. They argue that one consequence of the emerging cloud paradigm is that problem finding and improvisational thinking has become more critical. They analyze a devised theatre metaphor to help design teams better engage improvisation.

Albert M. Selvin, Simon J. Buckingham Shum, and Mark Aakhus, in "The Practice Level in Participatory Design Rationale: Studying Practitioner Moves and Choices," present a theory of practice, and analytical tools, to identify some of the creative dimensions in expert practice when constructing design rationale visualizations in meetings. It looks especially at moments when design rationale practitioners encounter obstacles, or anomalies interfere with the smooth unfolding of the intended process. By examining the actions that practitioners take at such moments, experiential phenomena such as sense making, improvisation, aesthetics, and ethics can be observed and discussed.

In "Managing Conflict in Information System Design Stakeholder Conferences: The Role of Transparency Work," Mark Aakhus analyzes a case of collaborative design decision-making facilitated by iterative publication and adjustment of rationales to maintain the group's coherence and effectiveness, a technique he called "fashioning-a-record". The facilitation technique involved persuasion to help members maintain a sense of commitment and participation in a worthwhile activity.

In "Mining Creativity Research to Inform Design Rationale in Open Source Communities," Burleson and Tripathi investigate the role of rationale in open source communities. This is an interesting paradigm of software and do-it-yourself development with respect to creativity, since membership in open source communities is voluntary. Winslow Burleson and Priyamvada Tripathi describe practices of these organizations that cultivate informal rationale, specifically enabling them to codify knowledge from recent project activities and to apply that knowledge in future projects.

The chapters by Aldo de Moor and John Thomas explore the use of patterns, schematic summaries of effective approaches to real problems, as a semi-formal notation for codifying the lessons of innovative design. In "Creativity Meets Rationale: Collaboration Patterns for Social Innovation," de Moor discusses the collaborative design of social innovations. He characterizes the social actors in three design cases and their use of roles, tools, and workflows through articulating design patterns. The idea is that patterns can make complex design practices more understandable and appropriable to a wide range of stakeholders, and thereby enhance participation, sense making, and effectiveness of collaboration communities.

Thomas, in "Patterns for Emergent Global Intelligence," presents several design patterns focused on the initial stages of system development. He argues that patterns are an effective method of creating, organizing and disseminating design knowledge for individuals, groups and communities of practice.

Gerhard Fischer and Frank Shipman, in "Collaborative Design Rationale and Social Creativity in Cultures of Participation," address the succession of cultural paradigms, from a *consumer culture,* in which people are users and relatively passive with respect to designs, toward *cultures of participation,* in which users are designers and redesigners. In this view, it is possible, indeed necessary, for design rationale to be articulated by and accessible to anyone and everyone. Moreover, it is permitted, indeed expected, that everyone's creative contributions can be heard and considered in addressing the widest variety of contemporary design problems. Fischer and Shipman argue that the emergence of cultures of participation provides new ways to reconcile creativity and design rationale.

Thomas Kuhn (1979) wrote "Like artists, creative scientists must occasionally be able to live in a world out of joint" (p. 79). He called this the essential tension: Research always produces anomalies between theoretical concepts and empirical data; the possibility of crisis and breakdown is always present. A routine problem from one perspective can be a crippling counterexample from another. Faced with significant crisis, scientific communities may engage in what Kuhn calls extraordinary science, in which fundamental assumptions are questioned, conventions are abandoned, and innovative practices become routine.

Describing, developing, and fully enjoying the linkages between creativity and rationale in software design will entrain essential tension. Perhaps we are now at the threshold of a period extraordinary science. Indeed, Kuhn's notion seems appropriate for what has recently been called "a science of design" for software-intensive systems (Freeman and Hart 2004). Surely, a science of design would have to be extraordinary; it would have to question assumptions, innovate, reorient and recreate itself. The tensions between relatively discursive, qualitative, and conceptual social-behavioral art and science, and relatively formal, quantitative, and device-oriented computer science and software engineering are inherent and abiding. We must recruit it as an intellectual resource and not (only) experience it as a source of interdisciplinary conflict. Further and finally, I think people are indeed attracted to software design in part because it is exciting to live in a world out of joint, and to participate in a perpetually extraordinary endeavor.

Acknowledgements The Creativity and Design Rationale in Software Design workshop was supported by the US National Science Foundation (IIS 0742392). Earlier version of the chapters by Raymond McCall, Alistair Sutcliffe, Burge and Brinkman, Ocker, Wang et al., and Selvin et al. appeared in a special issue of *Human Technology: An Interdisciplinary Journal on Humans in ICT Environments* in May 2010. Earlier versions of the chapters by McCrickard et al., Farooq and

Carroll, Burleson and Tripathi, and Fischer and Shipman appeared in a special issue of *Human Technology: An Interdisciplinary Journal on Humans in ICT Environments* in August of 2011. I am grateful to Pertti Saariluoma, Editor-in-Chief of the journal at that time, and to Barbara Crawford, Managing Editor of the journal, for their help and support in these special issue projects. I am grateful to the members of the workshop who helped me develop this introductory chapter.

References

Csikszentmihalyi, M. (1996). *Creativity: Flow and the psychology of discovery and invention.* New York: Harper Perennial.

Kuhn, T. (1979). *The essential tension: Selected studies in scientific tradition and change.* Chicago: University of Chicago Press.

Kunz, W., & Rittel, H. W. J. (1970, July). *Issues as elements of information systems* (Working Paper No. 131). Studiengruppe fur Systemforschung, Heidelberg. Germany. Also available on-line from the Institute for Urban and Regional Development, University of California, Berkeley at http://iurd.berkeley.edu/sites/default/files/wp/131.pdf

Minneman, S. L. (1991). *The social construction of a technical reality: Empirical studies of group engineering design practice.* Unpublished doctoral dissertation, Stanford University, California, USA, Department of Mechanical Engineering.

Moran, T. P., & Carroll, J. M. (Eds.). (1996). *Design rationale: Concepts, techniques, and use.* Hillsdale: Erlbaum.

Ryan, R. M., & Deci, E. L. (2001). On happiness and human potentials: A review of hedonic and eudaimonic well-being. *Annual Review of Psychology, 52*, 141–166.

von Hippel, E. (1988). *The sources of innovation.* New York: Oxford University Press.

Chapter 2
Critical Conversations: Feedback as a Stimulus to Creativity in Software Design

Raymond McCall

Abstract Three decades of creating software to support design rationale showed the author that rationale processes can promote generation of novel ideas by promoting critical conversations among designers and other project participants. Critical conversations intertwine ideation and evaluation, using feedback about consequences of decisions to challenge designers to devise new ideas. Such conversations take two forms. The first is discussion involving feedback from speculation about consequences of design decisions for implementation and use. The second is discussion involving feedback from actual experiences of implementation and use of the software being designed. The former is purely a process of reflective discourse, the latter a process of situated cognition involving both action and reflective discourse. Thus, the former is pure argumentation, the latter situated argumentation. Exploiting the full potential of critical conversations for creative design requires rethinking rationale methods and integrating them into software supporting implementation and use.

Keywords Creativity • Software • Design • Rationale • Feedback • Situated cognition • Action • Reflection • Planning • Reflective practice • Design reasoning • Argumentative approach • Wicked problems

2.1 Introduction

This article presents a picture of how feedback-driven rationale processes promote creativity in software design. This picture derives from my three decades of experience in creating software supporting the documentation and use of issue-based

R. McCall (✉)
Department of Planning and Design, University of Colorado, Denver, CO 80309, USA
e-mail: Mccall@Colorado.EDU

J.M. Carroll (ed.), *Creativity and Rationale: Enhancing Human
Experience by Design*, Human–Computer Interaction Series,
DOI 10.1007/978-1-4471-4111-2_2, © Springer-Verlag London 2013

rationale for design, that is, the type of rationale pioneered by Horst Rittel (Kunz and Rittel 1970). This picture is not meant to portray all the ways creativity takes place in design, but it does seek to portray crucial processes that have been largely omitted from other accounts of rationale and creativity, especially the former.

To discuss how rationale promotes creativity in software design, it is useful to define some basic terms. In this chapter *software design creativity* refers to the generation of innovative, high-quality ideas for the design of software. The term *ideation* refers to generation of ideas, especially novel ideas, for artifact design. The term *evaluation* refers to determination of the value of such ideas. *Feedback* refers to any information about consequences of design decisions that a designer gets from external sources, such as persons or situations. These are narrow definitions, but they serve the purposes of this chapter. Note that the definition of software design creativity involves both ideation and evaluation.

The picture presented here is based on a number of notions that contrast with ideas advocated by others. First of all, it takes a *process-oriented view of rationale*, while many proposed rationale approaches either eschew process orientation—for example, the question, options, and criteria (QOC) approach (MacLean et al. 1996)—or provide only a rationale schema with no indication of processes for eliciting and recording the schematized rationale—such as the decision representation language (DRL; Lee 1991).

Second, the picture created here is prescriptive in that it not only seeks to record design processes but also to improve them. In particular, it seeks to increase the use of rationale processes that improve design creativity. Not all rationale approaches are prescriptive (Dutoit et al. 2006); some are purely descriptive and seek only to record rather than to change what designers think and do, such as QOC (though they might unintentionally improve design).

Third, the picture presented here is based on the view that intertwining ideation and evaluation is a powerful method for promoting creativity. Yet there is much literature both on creativity and on rationale that treats ideation and evaluation as separate phases, that is, not intertwined. Of particular importance here is that Rittel (1966) saw no role for the intertwining of ideation and evaluation in design.

Finally, this chapter takes the view that creativity is enhanced if design and its rationale are considered not merely as planning for future action—for example, implementation and use—but also as a type of situated cognition in which design is shaped by feedback resulting from action. Yet, Rittel, who pioneered the field of design rationale, viewed design strictly as planning, in the sense of thinking before acting (Rittel 1966); he saw rationale as documentation of this preparatory thinking. Most existing approaches to rationale appear to share this view, since they provide no account of rationale being generated in response to actions taken.

The picture presented here of how rationale processes promote creativity in software design can be summarized as follows. Intertwining ideation and evaluation promotes creativity in software design because feedback about consequences of design decisions challenges designers to devise new ideas. This intertwining takes two basic forms. The first involves discussion among designers in which verbal evaluations of proposed ideas prompt them to devise new ideas. The second and more important involves situated cognition in which feedback resulting from actions, especially the actions of implementation and use, prompts designers to devise new ideas.

The commitment to using feedback-driven, critical conversations to promote creativity has crucial implications for rationale methods used in software projects. One implication concerns the type of processes that are modeled. Currently, none of the rationale methods that deal with design decision making explicitly models the ways in which evaluative feedback leads to the generation of new design ideas. When rationale methods cannot model these processes, they not only cannot promote them but may actually discourage them. A second implication concerns the sources of design rationale. Current approaches concentrate almost exclusively on rationale from design discussion (planning). This is sufficient to allow rationale based on speculative reasoning and the experience of previous projects, but not sufficient to allow rationale based on feedback from actions.

The picture of software creativity as being promoted by feedback-driven critical conversations extends and generalizes Schön's (1983) portrayal of design as a conversation with the situation. It is argued here that Schön's notion of design as both reflection and action provides a better picture of the role of rationale in design than Rittel's. While Rittel saw design as purely argumentation, Schön's theory implies that design is what we might call *situated argumentation*, that is, argumentation informed by feedback from action. Yet Schön's theory by itself covers only a small subset of the situated argumentation that stimulates creativity in software creation. Extending his theory produces a more complete picture of how rationale processes promote creative design. Ironically, extending his theory involves adding ideas of collaborative and participatory design advocated by Rittel.

The following sections of this chapter expand on the above-stated ideas. The next section explains the background and motivation for the ideas presented here. The section following that explains the prescriptive and process-oriented approach used here to analyze rationale and creativity. I then look at the relationship between ideation and evaluation in both rationale processes and creative processes. I also contrast views of design as planning for action versus as situated cognition. After that, I identify implications for rationale processes that support creativity in software design. Finally, I summarize the conclusions of this chapter and look at ideas for future work.

2.2 Historical Background

Rittel (Kunz and Rittel 1970) pioneered the field of design rationale with his work on Issue-Based Information Systems (IBIS). As a student of Rittel's, I devised a new approach to IBIS called Procedural Hierarchy of Issues (PHI; McCall 1979, 1986, 1991) and began a series of software projects aimed at using PHI to improve the quality of designed artifacts. These projects revealed previously unforeseen potentials and limitations of rationale in design. In particular, they showed how the generation of novel ideas for software can be supported by processes in which the consequences of design ideas are identified. This chapter describes what these projects revealed about the connections between rationale and creativity.

The PHI-based projects created the following software:

- PROTOCOL (McCall 1979), a text-only hypertext system that elicited rationale from users in PHI form
- MIKROPLIS (McCall 1989; McCall et al. 1984), text-only hypertext supporting user-controlled authoring and navigation of PHI rationale
- JANUS (McCall et al. 1990b; Fischer et al. 1996), a system for kitchen design using loosely coupled subsystems for 2D computer-aided design (CAD), knowledge-based critiquing, and hypermedia for delivery of PHI rationale
- PHIDIAS (McCall et al. 1990a, c,1994,), a system for the design of buildings using a unified hypermedia substrate to implement 3D CAD and knowledge-based agents as well as the authoring and delivery of PHI rationale augmented with images and video
- HyperSketch (McCall et al. 1997, 2001), a pen-based system for designing buildings by creating linked collections of hand-drawn sketches.

The later systems were designed using lessons learned from the earlier ones. These projects were stages in a larger project meant to find out (a) how rationale can help designers create better artifacts and (b) what software support is needed for such use of rationale.

In addition to documenting rationale for design of physical artifacts, all of the above-listed systems except JANUS were also used to document rationale for their own design. The experiences of this documentation effort revealed that the ways in which new ideas emerged involved processes not described anywhere in the rationale literature. In particular, the creative rationale processes in our projects were not supported either by Rittel's (Kunz and Rittel 1970) IBIS or my PHI method. Furthermore, our creative processes were incompatible with parts of Rittel's theory about design processes and problems. This article looks at these differences and their implications for rationale approaches and software supporting creative software design.

The above-listed projects changed my understanding of rationale processes and creativity. To understand how, I should begin by describing what that understanding was at the start. Simply put, it was based on Rittel's (1972) ideas about (a) the need for an argumentative approach to design, and (b) how IBIS was to help achieve that goal. Rittel's advocacy of an argumentative approach was based on his theory that design problems are "wicked problems" (WPs; Rittel and Webber 1973). By this he meant that they are ill-defined and ill-behaved in a variety of ways that, for example, go far beyond the difficulties of "ill-structured problems" (Simon 1973). WPs systematically violate conditions required for use of rigorous scientific method to understand and solve them. Rittel (1972) therefore called for a collaborative and participatory approach that involved stakeholders in defining requirements and evaluating proposed designs. Instead of relying on the unexplained judgments of "experts," however, he called for a process in which the reasoning of designers was open to inspection and criticism by others. This implied the need for an argumentative approach, that is, an approach in which all of design was treated as argumentation about design decisions.

Rittel used the term *argument* with the meaning of explicit reasoning, and not with the colloquial English meaning of heated verbal disagreement, as in, "We had an argument about who was to blame" (Rittel, 1977, personal communication). In other words, he used the word *argument* with the meaning it has in his native German language as well as in philosophical discourse in English. Unfortunately, his intentions were often misunderstood by his American students. In the later years of his life, he told his colleague, Jean-Pierre Protzen, that because of this he wished he had called his approach *deliberative* rather than *argumentative* (Protzen, 1992, personal communication).

Further promoting misunderstanding was the fact that, despite Rittel's insistence that the term *argument* was not a reference to disagreement, he felt that controversy was an intrinsic part of design and that forceful debate was the most valuable type of design discussion. He devised IBIS not as a general means of handing all argumentation in design but rather as a way of handing disagreement through debate. IBIS centered on the discussion of issues, but Rittel (1980) defined IBIS' issues as controversial design questions. All other design questions he labeled "trivial issues," and excluded them from IBIS discourse.

These days, all issue-based approaches to design rationale, as well as similar approaches like QOC and DRL, have abandoned Rittel's exclusive focus on controversy and adversarial argumentation. Rittel's focus on controversy, however, is more than an interesting historical footnote, because it apparently led him and others to neglect the collaborative, constructive argumentation described here as a driving force of design creativity.

To clarify discussion, it is useful to briefly describe IBIS and to explain how PHI differs from it. IBIS was intended both as a method for discussing issues and as a means for documenting the discussion. For each issue, participants in the design propose possible answers, called *positions*. Arguments for and against the positions are then given, along with arguments for and against other arguments. Finally, an issue is *resolved* by deciding which position to accept. Issues are linked to each other by various relationships to form a connected graph called an *issue map*. In Rittel's (personal communication, 1975, 1980) version of IBIS, the inter-issue relationships included *logical-successor-of, temporal-successor-of, more-general-than, similar-to* and *replaces*.

IBIS provided no way of grouping issue-based discussions to represent higher levels of granularity in design processes. Thus, for example, the widely used description of design as being divided into larger-scale processes of analysis, synthesis, and evaluation (Lawson 2005) could not be expressed in IBIS. This was no accident. Rittel (1975, personal communication) was deeply suspicious of such higher levels of granularity. In particular, he argued that the belief in large-scale phases of design, such as analysis, synthesis, and evaluation, was the hallmark of the first-generation approach to design, which he judged a failure and sought to replace with a second-generation based on an argumentative approach (Rittel 1972). He insisted that the only sensible level of description of design process was in terms of its *microstructure*—that is, the level of issue-based discourse (Rittel, 1975, personal communication).

Of course, it can be argued that analysis and synthesis might also be found at the microstructural level for the generation of positions on issues. And evaluation is certainly part of IBIS. Perhaps the generation of positions could be divided into processes of analysis and synthesis. Unfortunately, IBIS provided no account of any processes for devising positions. It may well be, therefore, that its picture of the microstructure of design is not complete.

PHI was meant to implement Rittel's argumentative approach more fully than IBIS by including noncontroversial issues and using a better structure for discussion. To accomplish the latter, PHI replaced the inter-issue relationships of IBIS with two types of *dependency relationships*: *serves* and *leads-to*. The former indicates that the resolution of one issue influences the resolution of another, while the latter indicates that the resolution of an issue influences the relevance of another. In PHI, a single *root issue* represents the project as a whole. Since all other issues are resolved in order to resolve the root issue, they serve the root issue directly or indirectly. PHI modeled design rationale as a *quasi-hierarchy* of issues connected by serves relationships, that is, a directed acyclic graph with some added cycles.

PHI showed the structure of discussion more completely than IBIS. In particular, its serve relationships provided a way of grouping issue discussions to represent higher levels of granularity of design process structure. These relationships also enabled representation of detailed processes by which positions on issues were devised—including processes of ideation—something not possible with IBIS. While PHI did not use terms such as *synthesis*, *analysis*, and *evaluation* to label its process structures, it did enable the representation of such processes at many different levels of granularity in issue-based discussion.

Because the quasi-hierarchical structure of PHI is far more orderly than the "spaghetti" structure of IBIS (Fischer et al. 1996), it enabled a substantial increase in the number of issues dealt with in a project. Rittel suggested that, for practical reasons, IBIS should deal with no more than 35 issues (Rittel, 1975, personal communication). But most of the dozens of PHI projects undertaken since 1976 involved more than 250 issues.

The initial goal of the series of software projects described above was to extend the use of PHI to all aspects of design, thus demonstrating Rittel's point that the entire design process was nothing but argumentation. A virtue of attempting to create software that achieves such a grand goal is that the attempt can produce feedback from reality that challenges the assumptions on which the goal is based. This is precisely what happened.

2.3   A Prescriptive and Process-Oriented Approach

The central topic of this chapter is the way in which rationale processes promote creative software design. More specifically, this chapter identifies processes of rationale generation that reflect software life cycle processes that lead to the generation of important, new ideas for software design. In addition, this chapter aims both to analyze and to promote such processes. Doing these things is impossible without using a rationale modeling approach that can represent the processes of interest. In other words, it is necessary to use a process-oriented approach to describe rationale in software creation.

Using a process-oriented approach to describe how rationale promotes creativity limits which rationale approaches can be used. This is because these approaches differ in the degree to which they model process. Most approaches can be broadly categorized as structure oriented or process oriented (Lee and Lai 1996). Structure-oriented approaches make no attempt to record the temporal order in which rationale is generated in design. They only record the logical relationships between statements, e.g. that one statement argues against another. Process-oriented approaches record the temporal order, meaning the history, of the rationale generation, for example that an argument arose in response to another statement.

Many approaches to rationale are structure oriented. For example, the authors of the QOC approach (MacLean et al. 1996) are adamant that QOC in no way records the manner in which rationale statements arise during design. The proponents of DRL (Lee and Lai 1996) generally make no claims about design processes, but they insist that DRL does not deal with processes by which solution ideas are generated, meaning ideation. Certain applications of IBIS and PHI have also been structure oriented (McCall 1991). In particular, the domain-oriented issue bases created using PHI (McCall et al. 1990b) and used in JANUS and PHIDIAS give no indication of the processes in which rationale is generated.

Relatively few rationale approaches are explicitly process oriented. IBIS is process oriented in its original form (Kunz and Rittel 1970; Rittel and Noble 1989) and in the form used by Conklin, Begeman and Burgess-Yakemovic (Conklin and Begeman 1988; Conkin and Burgess-Yakemovic 1996). In addition, when PHI is used to document individual design projects, it typically is used in a process-oriented manner that records the history of rationale creation. Carroll and Rosson (1992) used a very different type of process-orientation. Their rationale approach centers on the processes represented in usage scenarios. More specifically, it documents "claims," that is, user evaluations of the pros and cons of system features, as the users go through such scenarios. I refer to this approach here as *scenario-claims analysis* (SCA).

While process-oriented rationale contains temporal information not found in structure-oriented rationale, structure-oriented rationale generally requires more work to create. The reason is that process-oriented rationale is documented in the order and wording in which it is stated. Structure-oriented rationale must be edited to exhibit its logical structure and eliminate temporal information. Advocates of the structured approach, such as the authors of QOC, argue that it is worth spending the extra time to design the rationale statements and structure because it facilitates understanding (MacLean et al. 1996).

Since my analysis is process-oriented, it must employ process-oriented rationale methods. As is explained in the next section, the experiences that led to the understanding of how rationale relates to design creativity involved a series of projects that designed software supporting PHI and used it to document the software design.

It seems only appropriate, therefore, to use PHI as the primary basis here for the analysis of rationale processes that support creativity in software design. But, since my analysis attempts to show how feedback from users promotes design creativity, SCA (Carroll and Rosson 1992) also has a crucial role to play.

2.4 Ideation and Evaluation: From Separation to Intertwining

2.4.1 Ideation and Evaluation in Design Rationale

In most approaches to design rationale—IBIS, QOC, and DRL being well-known examples—ideation takes the form of the generation of alternatives for decisions. In IBIS and its PHI variant, decision alternatives are *positions* and the things to be decided are *issues*. It should be noted, however, that not all issues in PHI deal with decisions about features of the artifact being designed. Any question arising in design is considered an issue, including questions about facts, goals, concept definitions, causes of problems, and effects of decisions. None of these other types of issues involve ideation as it is defined above.

QOC differs from IBIS in that it *only* deals with decisions about features of the artifact being designed, that is, decisions that involve ideation. In QOC the decision alternatives are called *options* and the things to be decided are called *questions* (MacLean et al. 1996). DRL is quite similar to QOC in many respects, but its decision alternatives are simply called *alternatives*, while things to be decided are called *decision problems*. From the examples that Lee (1991) gives, it appears that DRL's decision problems are identical to QOC's questions and thus deal exclusively with decisions about features of the artifact. As mentioned above, however, Lee and Lai (1996) make a point of stating that DRL does not represent ideation processes.

Evaluation in most rationale approaches is done by identifying pros and cons of decision alternatives. In IBIS and PHI this is done by stating arguments for or against the alternatives (positions), while both QOC and DRL perform evaluation by assessing how well the alternatives satisfy given criteria (called *goals* in DRL). In these and other approaches, the evaluation can be augmented by the stating of arguments that support or attack the statements of the pros and cons.

2.4.2 The Separation of Ideation from Evaluation

2.4.2.1 The Separation of Ideation and Evaluation in Approaches to Creativity

Literature on creativity frequently emphasizes the value of completing ideation before evaluation begins. The main argument for this phased approach is as follows. Criticizing ideas as they are generated inhibits the elicitation of new ideas, especially innovative ideas, which can sound risky and are often vulnerable to attack as first stated. Fear of being attacked can make people reluctant to propose creative ideas; so evaluation should be postponed until after ideas are generated.

The well-known creativity-enhancing methods known as brainstorming (Osborn 1963) and lateral thinking (de Bono 1973) focus on ideation. In both cases, it is treated as separate from evaluation. In fact, both methods have explicit prohibitions on evaluation during ideation, so as not to inhibit the free flow of ideas. In brainstorming, this prohibition is called "suspension of judgment" (Michalko 2006) or "withholding criticism" (Osborn 1963). In defending this prohibition in lateral thinking, de Bono (1973, p. 7) explains, "One is not looking for the *best* approach but for as many *different* approaches as possible." He even adds, "In the lateral search for alternatives these do not have to be reasonable" (p. 7). Both approaches emphasize quantity over quality, in the belief that quantity leads to novelty. The writings of Osborn and de Bono have been very influential; thus many other creativity techniques come with warnings about not evaluating ideas as they are generated.

2.4.2.2 The Separation of Ideation and Evaluation in Rationale Research

Rittel's (Kunz and Rittel 1970) work on IBIS has also been influential. Conklin and his colleagues have done extensive work with IBIS (Conklin and Begeman 1988; Conklin and Burgess-Yakemovic 1996). And PHI (McCall 1979), of course, is a revision of IBIS. In addition, the Potts and Bruns (1988) approach to rationale is a revision of IBIS with the goal of fitting it better to software engineering. DRL is a revision of Potts and Bruns (Lee 1991) and RatSpeak (Burge and Brown 2006) is revision of DRL for software engineering—ironically, one that restores some features of IBIS. QOC (MacLean et al. 1996) was devised entirely separately from IBIS yet strongly resembles DRL. While there are many deviations from Rittel's approach, few of them stray far from it.

Because of Rittel's influence, it is important to understand his ideas about the relationship between ideation and evaluation in design. Simply put, Rittel saw no need to intertwine them. This is reflected in the following statement in which he briefly describes a phased model of how designers attack a decision task:

> A designer first tries to develop a set of alternative courses of action, then to figure out their potential outcomes and their likelihood, and then to evaluate them, finally to decide in favor of one of them. (Rittel 1966, p. 13)

In this statement, the ideation part corresponds to the phrase, "to develop a set of alternative courses of action." Evaluation corresponds to the phrase, "to figure out their potential outcomes and their likelihood, and then to evaluate them."

Rittel further states that he sees design as, "an alternating sequence of two kinds of basic mental activities" (Rittel 1966, p. 17), the first kind being ideation, which he describes as follows:

> Initially, a phase of "generating variety": the search for a set of relevant possibilities which might solve the problem at hand. (This is the process of developing ideas. It ends with a set of alternatives which contain at least one element.) (Rittel 1966, p. 17)

The second kind consists of evaluation and selection, which he describes as follows:

This is followed by a phase of "reducing variety": the alternatives are evaluated for their feasibility and desirability, and a decision is made in favor of the most desirable, feasible alternative ... (Rittel 1966, p. 17)

Because of these statements, from an article published 4 years before his first paper on IBIS, it should not be surprising that ideation and evaluation became incorporated into IBIS as separate processes: first, generation of positions, and then argumentation to evaluate the already-generated positions.

Rittel's commitment to separating ideation and evaluation appears to be mirrored in other rationale approaches that, like IBIS, center on the evaluation of alternatives for design decisions. Thus, for example, none of these other approaches contains a type of link that could be used to indicate that an alternative was suggested by an evaluation of another alternative or that any alternative is an improvement on another alternative. The latter is important for the simple reason that the notion of improvement implies evaluation. In short, there is no sign of any connection between ideation and evaluation in any of the major approaches for modeling rationale about design decisions. Whether intentional or not, all of these approaches, like IBIS, give the impression that ideation and evaluation are in no way intertwined. This similarity might not be entirely due to Rittel's influence, however, because many early theories of design (Alexander 1964; Jones 1970; Simon 1969) exhibited a similar separation of ideation and judgment.

2.4.3 The Intertwining of Ideation and Evaluation in Design Discussion

MIKROPLIS (McCall 1989; McCall et al. 1984) was the first PHI project to reveal the intertwining of ideation and evaluation in design discussion. Whereas its predecessor, the PROTOCOL project (McCall 1979), had only a single designer, MIKROPLIS had a team of people involved in its design. Much of their discussion was documented. Because users of PROTOCOL had complained about not having control over the order in which it elicited rationale, MIKROPLIS was aimed at giving users control over display and input. This led to discussion of many issues of user interaction.

While MIKROPLIS team membership changed over its 5-year history, it included at various points people with solid knowledge of IBIS theory and applications. These included Wolfgang Schuler (Schuler and Smith 1990), Barbara Lutes-Schaab (Lutes-Schaab et al. 1985), Harald Werner (Reuter and Werner 1984) and Wolf Reuter (1983). Reuter, in particular, had a decade of IBIS experience when he joined the project.

As we documented discussions of the MIKROPLIS design team, differences emerged between our rationale and the adversarial rationale that Rittel (1980, pp. 7, 8) wrote about. Discussions in our team had a fundamentally different character from the clash of worldviews that IBIS was meant to deal with. Rather than being adversarial, our discussions were generally cooperative and collaborative. This is not to say that proposed ideas were not subjected to strong criticism, but the thrust of this criticism was constructive and there was a general openness to it by the group. This was also characteristic of teams in the later PHI projects.

One strong pattern that emerged in group discussion was that new ideas often arose out of evaluations of proposed ideas. While the response to criticism of (arguments against) a proposed idea (i.e., position) was sometimes to argue against it, often the response was to accept the criticism and propose a new or modified position. The adversarial argumentation that Rittel wrote of featured an uncompromising defense of positions; the collaborative argumentation in our teams featured a general willingness to rethink positions. Where adversarial argumentation responded to criticism with rebuttal, our collaborative argumentation responded with creative ideation. Thus, while the former tended to separate ideation from evaluation, the latter intertwined them.

One of the forms that the intertwining commonly took was arguments that proposed better positions. Such arguments would typically identify an undesirable consequence of a proposed position and then immediately suggest a new or revised position that avoided that consequence. In fact, it seemed that the inclusion of the new position at the end of an argument was, in effect, a demonstration that its criticism was constructive. Thus, new positions were contained within arguments on old positions. Unfortunately, neither IBIS nor PHI recognized such combined utterances, because neither recognized intertwining. The following simple example, taken from a project we did a few years ago, shows how a new position, indicated in italics, arose in an argument critical of an existing position:

ISSUE: What programming technology should we use to create our 3D, Web-based, educational game for Mars exploration?

POSITION: Flash CS4, using open-source Papervision3D for the 3D graphics.

ARGUMENT FOR: Flash has 98% browser penetration. The new version of ActionScript runs up to 10 times faster, and Papervision3D looks promising.

ARGUMENT AGAINST: The problem is that existing approaches to Flash 3D, such as Papervision3D, cannot make use of the GPU. This will prevent us from creating the complex graphics we need for the game. *It would be better to use a technology that doesn't have these limitations—such as Java. That way we could use Java3D or JOGL for the 3D graphics.*

Intertwining took many other forms as well. Sometimes complex negotiations would take place between the person who proposed an idea and those who criticized it. These sometimes turned into mini design projects, each with the goal of devising ways of overcoming negative consequences of a proposed idea. Often these discussions were aimed at "rescuing" a flawed proposal by figuring out how to defuse its undesirable consequences.

It was not just criticism of an idea that produced new ideas. Some arguments approved of the basic idea behind a position but advocated taking it further. Such arguments often had the form, "If you're going to do that, why not go all the way and do X."

Design ideas often went through considerable evolution as a result of many iterations of critical argumentation and revision. These tended to be long, critical conversations among the team members. Sometimes there were creative breakthroughs during meetings. Sometimes discussions dead-ended but breakthroughs occurred between meetings.

The MIKROPLIS project showed me that critical conversations promoted creativity in design. Since then I have seen this pattern of creative argumentation in a wide variety of design discussions, both in PHI-based projects and in other projects that made no use of rationale methods. It seems that the hallmark of successful collaborative discourse is the revision of ideas based on feedback from argumentative evaluation.

In retrospect, it is clear that our documentation of such creative discussions was inadequate. When a new position on an issue was generated in response to an argument, we simply connected the argument to the position with an argument-for link. When an argument contained a new position, we would extract the position and record it separately as a position linked to a revised version of the argument that omitted the statement of the position. The problem with this approach was that inspection of the documented rationale revealed no evidence of the intertwined processes by which ideas had in fact been generated. While we were in theory using a process-oriented approach to rationale, in fact we were misrepresenting the processes involved. This was because PHI had unwittingly inherited IBIS's built-in separation of ideation from evaluation—in the form of link types that treated arguments only as *responses to* rather than *generators of* positions. As a consequence, the impression that our documented rationale gave was that positions were generated intuitively and immediately as direct responses to stated issues and that the only role of arguments was to evaluate previously generated positions. There was no real indication that argumentation had played a crucial role in ideation.

The intertwining of ideation and evaluation in discussions among designers turned out to be merely one of a number of ways in which such intertwining promotes creative design. Discovery of other ways was made possible by a profound change in our understanding of the nature of design. The change was from Rittel's (1966) view of *design as planning* to Schön's (1983) view of *design as situated cognition*. This change in perspective solved major problems we encountered in creating the PHIDIAS software (McCall et al. 1990a, c, 1994). The following section begins by looking at the differences between these two views and their implications for the role of rationale in design. It then describes the problems we encountered and explains how these led us to adopt Schön's point of view.

2.5   Design: From Planning to Situated Cognition

The term *situated cognition* is used with a number of different meanings. It is used here in the behavioral sense of "a transactional process of transforming and interpreting materials in the world" (Clancey 1997, p. 23). It is in this sense of the term that we can say that both Suchman (1987) and Schön (1983) have written about situated cognition.

2.5.1 Two Views of Design

There are two fundamentally different views of design: as planning and as situated cognition. The former sees design as reasoning that precedes action, the latter as reasoning intertwined with and informed by action. The implication of the former is that design rationale is the documentation of the thinking and discussion of designers preparing for the actions of implementation and use. The implication of the latter is that design rationale is the documentation not only of planning by designers but also of (a) the feedback from actions that challenges design decisions, and (b) the creative thinking of designers in response to such challenges. The situated cognition viewpoint thus sees design as an intertwining of ideation and action-based evaluation. To date, the literature on all rationale methods except SCA (Carroll and Rosson 1992) has dealt exclusively with rationale as planning.

2.5.1.1 Rittel's View of Design as Planning

Rittel clearly viewed design as planning, not as situated cognition. He declared, "Designing means thinking before acting," and he described design as a process of devising a plan (Rittel 1966, p. 13). In fact, Rittel used the terms *designing* and *planning* interchangeably and saw design as a phase that is completed before feedback from action is available:

> The distinctive property of designing lies in the—frequently very long—interval between the design process (i.e., the construction of the plan) and the 'feedbacks'—the effects of the execution of the plan. (Rittel 1966, p. 14)

This lack of feedback implies that designers cannot test their ideas in real-world settings:

> …there is not the opportunity to approach solutions by trial and error; there is nothing like experimentation with real situations. (Rittel 1966, p. 14)

Therefore, designers must rely solely on their imaginations to determine the consequences of their ideas:

> As a result of these characteristics, the designer operates in a world of imagination. He has to anticipate, to guess, to judge what *might* happen if a certain contemplated action will be carried out. (Rittel 1966, p. 14)

The picture that Rittel paints is of design as speculative reasoning aimed at the production of a plan. In other words, Rittel's notion of design as purely a process of argumentation is a direct consequence of his view of design as planning.

2.5.1.2 Schön's View of Design as Situated Cognition

Schön's (1983) theory of design as reflective practice provides a fundamentally different view. Schön saw design as an alternation between an intuitive process he called *knowing-in-action* and a type of reasoning he called *reflection-in-action*. With knowing-in-action, the designer is engaged in performing a task without conscious reflection. With reflection-in-action, the designer stops acting and instead reflects on how to perform the task at hand. A designer cannot simultaneously engage in both knowing-in-action and reflection-in-action.

Knowing-in-action proceeds until a breakdown occurs. This happens when intuitive performance produces unexpected feedback from the situation at hand. In other words, there is a breakdown in the designer's expectations. Schön describes this by saying "the situation talks back" (1983, p. 131). A breakdown results when something goes wrong, but it also results when something unexpectedly good happens. Breakdowns occur when intuitive action produces either problems or opportunities that intuition cannot deal with. At this point, the designer switches to reflection-in-action to reason about how to deal with the unexpected results. If and when reflection is successful, the designer resumes knowing-in-action.

Reflective practice is repeated alternation between knowing-in-action and reflection-in-action. Schön describes the designer as engaging in an ongoing "conversation with the situation" (1983, p. 76). This is a view of design as a type of situated cognition, in that it sees design reasoning as intertwined with and informed by action.

Reflective practice models design as an intertwining of ideation and evaluation. When the situation "talks back," the "backtalk" is evaluative feedback that reveals consequences of the actions taken. The purpose of the resulting reflection-in-action is to devise new ideas for how to act; in other words, the purpose of reflection-in-action is ideation. Putting new ideas into action with knowing-in-action is how the designer resumes "talking to the situation." This eventually results in more "backtalk" that again triggers reflection that results in further ideation—and so forth.

2.5.1.3 Implications of the Two Views

To Rittel (1966), design is nothing but explicit reasoning, that is, argumentation; to Schön (1983), design is both explicit reasoning and intuitive action. Rittel's view implies that rationale can represent all design processes; Schön's view implies that it cannot. For Rittel design is reasoning in preparation for action in an external environment; for Schön design is reasoning triggered and motivated by action in an external environment. Rittel portrays design as a conversation among designers, Schön as a "conversation" between designers and a situation. As my colleagues, students, and I implemented Rittel's view of design in software, experiences in implementing and using prototypes ultimately led to rejecting Rittel's view of design as planning, in favor of Schön's view of design as situated cognition.

2.5.2   From Viewing Design as Planning to Viewing It as Situated Cognition

2.5.2.1   Limitations of MIKROPLIS

Towards the end of the MIKROPLIS project (McCall 1989; McCall et al. 1984) in 1984–1985, user testing revealed two major shortcomings. One was that it did not solve the *rationale capture problem*, that is, the reluctance of designers to document their rationale. We originally thought this problem resulted from the copious and tedious secretarial work involved in documenting rationale. MIKROPLIS successfully eliminated most such work. Unfortunately, this merely revealed the enormity of the cognitive overhead in rationale capture. The other shortcoming was that when MIKROPLIS was used to design buildings, its users created rationale that failed to deal with decisions about the forms of the buildings. Without representing and editing these forms graphically, there was apparently no way for users to make decisions about them.

2.5.2.2   Ideas for PHIDIAS

In 1985 my colleagues and I began designing PHIDIAS (PHI-based Design Intelligence Augmentation System; McCall et al. 1990a, c, 1994) by extending MIKROPLIS. The new functionality supported design ideas aimed at overcoming the two major limitations of MIKROPLIS.

The first idea was for PHIDIAS to use *domain-oriented issue bases* to mitigate the capture problem (McCall 1990a). Such an issue base is a collection of the issues, positions and arguments commonly occur in a design domain—for instance, the design of a given type of building. The main goal was to reduce the work of creating a project issue base by "priming the pump" with a generic issue base for a domain— for example, design of lunar habitats—that could be tailored to a specific project— such as the design of a specific lunar habitat for four astronauts. In addition to alleviating the capture problem, domain-oriented issues bases could help designers by providing useful design information.

The second idea was to have PHIDIAS enable decision making about building forms by adding functionality for CAD graphics. We created this functionality but failed to foresee that attempting to incorporate form-making into PHI would lead us to abandon Rittel's (1966) view of design as nothing but argumentative planning.

2.5.2.3   Unexpected Problems in Creating PHIDIAS

We had no difficulty creating domain-oriented issue bases and integrating them into PHIDIAS, and these issue bases greatly reduced the work of creating a project-specific issue base. Unfortunately, they were not effective in providing student designers with useful information. Since students did not know what information was and was not in the system, they did not know whether searching for information would pay off. As a consequence, they often searched for information that was not in the system, got frustrated and then stopped searching for any information. This was especially unfortunate, because the system had information that could have saved them from many of the mistakes they made in design.

We also successfully implemented basic CAD functionality, but we ran into profound difficulties in attempting to integrate CAD graphic editing into the interface for rationale creation. The problem was conceptual, not technical. It resulted from apparent conflicts between the activities of form making and verbal reasoning. To solve this problem we attempted to study how student designers reasoned about form making. This attempt was repeatedly frustrated. Asking students to document their own reasoning while they drew building forms produced little or no plausible rationale. Sending others in to document the rationale of designers also produced no significant results. They would explain their rationale right up to the moment they started drawing, at which point they would not talk about what they were doing. We did succeed in getting one talented student to record a think-aloud protocol about his form making over 6 weeks. Unfortunately, he felt that reasoning aloud had interfered with his ability to design; so he redid the entire design over a weekend without recording any rationale. So, while we made excellent progress on implementing CAD functionality in PHIDIAS, we made no real progress integrating form-making into rationale. This prevented us from completing the PHIDIAS interface.

2.5.2.4   CRACK

The solutions to the problems that PHIDIAS had encountered became obvious when I saw a demo of the CRACK (CRitiquing Approach to Cooperative Kitchen design) system created by Anders Morch under the supervision of Gerhard Fischer (Fischer and Morch 1988). Fischer had been investigating the use of domain-oriented construction kits for design (Fischer 1987; Fischer and Lemke 1988). A *construction kit* is a set of graphical building blocks that can be dragged and dropped into a workspace. He found that while such kits greatly facilitated the creation of designs, these designs were often functionally flawed. He concluded that construction kits had to be supplemented with some way of avoiding design mistakes. For this purpose, Fischer proposed using what he termed *knowledge-based critics* to guide design with construction kits. Morch's master's thesis implemented Fischer's ideas in the kitchen design domain, in which Morch had previously done some commercial work.

CRACK featured a CAD graphics editor for creating kitchen floor plans using a kitchen construction kit featuring such domain-level building blocks as walls, windows, doors, counters, stoves and sinks. This kit provided a direct and intuitive way for users to construct kitchen floor plans. Since each building block had an assigned domain-level meaning, knowledge-based critics could determine whether a constructed floor plan satisfied or violated rules of kitchen design. If rules were violated during the construction of a layout, critiquing messages popped up on the screen to tell the user which rules had been broken. For example, if a stove were placed where pans could be hit by an opening door, then the designer got a message saying that the stove should not be located next to a door.

CRACK was intended not to enforce its rules, for example, as an expert system would, but rather to empower the user to decide whether to accept or reject them. Unfortunately, it was often difficult for users to decide whether to break rules. I suggested that this was because such decisions required knowledge of the rationale underlying the rules. I therefore proposed the addition of a hypertext subsystem containing rationale for the rules of kitchen design in the form of a PHI-based, domain-oriented issue base. The decision was made to create a successor to CRACK that did just that. The successor was called JANUS (McCall et al. 1990b; Fischer et al. 1996), after the Roman god with two faces, because it had both a form-construction interface and an argumentation interface.

2.5.2.5 JANUS and PHIDIAS

From the perspective of the PHIDIAS project, the notion of coupling PHI hypertext to a CRACK-type interface was a revelation. It offered in one stroke a solution to two problems plaguing the PHIDIAS project. First of all, it showed how users could be alerted to the existence of useful information in a PHI issue base while they worked on a design problem. Secondly, it suggested that rather than attempting to integrate the editing of CAD graphics into the editing of a PHI hyperdocument, the solution was to have two separate interfaces—a form construction interface and an argumentation interface—and switch between these using critics. So as JANUS was constructed by Morch, my programming team constructed a similar coupling of CAD form-construction and argumentation in PHIDIAS. User testing showed that both systems successfully supported use of rationale to inform construction of floor plans.

2.5.2.6 From Argumentative Planning to Reflective Practice

It was not immediately clear that the new systems challenged Rittel's (1966) theory of design as argumentative planning. Awareness of that challenge first surfaced when Morch wrote a working paper proposing that JANUS supported two different modes of designing: *constructive design* and *argumentative design*. At first, I balked at that distinction, which was heresy from the Rittelian perspective. But the failed attempts to integrate form-construction into PHI ultimately led me to abandon the notion that form making is purely an argumentative process. Morch's names for the two design modes were therefore put in the title of our first paper on the new type of system (Fischer et al. 1989).

Not long after this it became clear that the failure in integrating form-construction into PHI and the success of our dual-interface approach both fit Schön's (1983) ideas

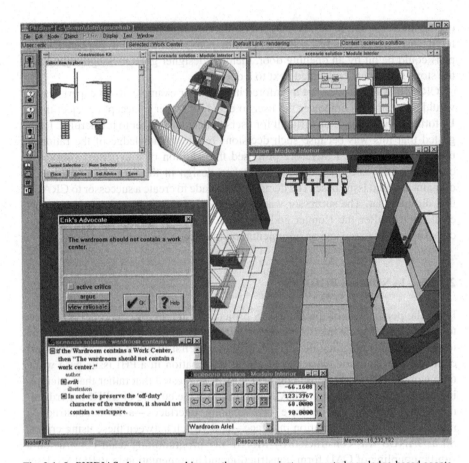

Fig. 2.1 In PHIDIAS, designers working on the same project can create knowledge-based agents called *advocates*, which are critics that lobby for design principles that they believe in. In this figure, Patrick violated an advocate created by Erik, and thus received a critiquing message. Patrick has opted to view Erik's rationale for the advocate

about reflective practice. Constructive design with construction kits corresponded to knowing-in-action, critiquing corresponded to breakdowns, and argumentative design with PHI hypermedia corresponded to reflection-in-action. So we came to see JANUS and PHIDIAS as unintended demonstrations of the correctness of Schön's theory of design—a theory fundamentally incompatible with Rittel's.

While at first Schön's theory was merely a retrospective explanation for the success of our systems, later it became the central driving principle behind the design of PHIDIAS and HyperSketch (McCall et al. 1997, 2001). PHIDIAS implemented a variety of additional ways in which the existence of breakdowns could be detected by the system (McCall and Johnson 1997) or volunteered by users of the system (McCall 1998). An example of the former is shown in Figs. 2.1 and 2.2. Here, knowledge-based agents are created by system users as advocates

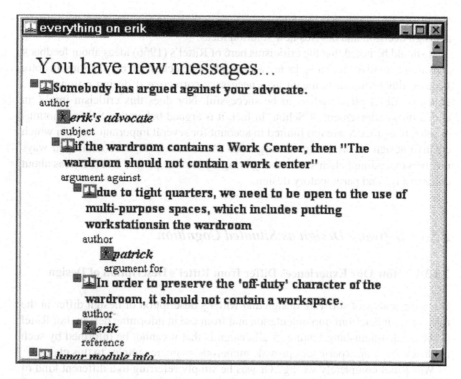

Fig. 2.2 Patrick argued against the rationale for Erik's advocate, so Erik was notified and sent the argument. He was then given the option to participate in an issue-based discussion with Patrick about whether the advocate should be violated

of their opinions in a collaborative design environment. Then when other designers use the system, they are alerted if they construct design features that conflict with any of these advocate agents, as in Fig. 2.1. They also have the opportunity to view and argue with the rationale for the advocate. If a designer argues against the advocate agent, the designer who created it is alerted to this fact and offered the chance to discuss this situation with the designer who disagreed with the advocate. The resulting online discussion can be recorded in the form of issue-based argumentation, as in Fig. 2.2.

Other research driven by Schön's ideas inquired into what sorts of interfaces were needed for intuitive knowing-in-action. HyperSketch (McCall et al. 1997, 2001) explored intuitive form construction through computer-supported sketching. This was in response to architecture students who complained that construction kits inhibited their intuitive exploration of building forms.

Schön's (1983) theory of design as situated cognition shows another way in which ideation and evaluation are intertwined. Previously we saw this only in argumentative design discussion; now we see it when argumentation is coupled with action. Furthermore, this intertwining can be seen as promoting creative ideation.

When a critic reveals that something is wrong with the design, the designer rethinks a design decision and devises new solution ideas.

It should be noted that the criticisms here of Rittel's (1966) ideas about feedback and argumentative planning in no way imply a rejection of his theories in toto. Instead, this criticism is meant as a necessary corrective if design rationale, the field that Rittel pioneered, is to be successful. Nor does this criticism imply an unqualified endorsement of Schön. In fact, it is argued below that Schön's notions of reflective practice are too limited to account for several important ways in which creative design involves situated cognition. Accounting for these additional ways involves extending Schön's notions by bringing into the picture Rittel's ideas about collaborative and participatory design.

2.5.3   Software Design as Situated Cognition

2.5.3.1   How Our Experiences Differ from Rittel's Description of Design

Our experiences of software design and Rittel's description of design differ in the roles of feedback from implementation and from use in informing design. For Rittel (1966), a distinguishing feature of all design is that it cannot be informed by such feedback. Yet our experiences provide numerous counterexamples to this claim.

Was Rittel completely wrong? Or was he simply referring to a different kind of design than we engaged in? His arguments against learning from feedback suggest the latter. Consider the following statement from the article that he wrote with Webber about *wicked problems*:

> One cannot build a freeway to see how it works, and then easily correct it after unsatisfactory performance. Large public-works are effectively irreversible, and the consequences they generate have long half-lives. Many people's lives will have been irreversibly influenced, and large amounts of money will have been spent—another irreversible act. (Rittel and Webber 1973, p. 163)

Rittel (1966) claims that his theory applies to all types of design, yet the above-stated argument depends on properties found in some types of design but not others. In particular, the argument applies to large-scale design projects with large costs and large consequences. The specific example used, a freeway, represents an infrastructural level of design, meaning a very low-level of structure—*infra* meaning *below* in Latin (Hoad 1996). Designing such a large-scale physical artifact might indeed be, as Rittel claimed, a one-shot operation in which feedback from implementation and use plays no role. Nevertheless, this does not imply that it plays no role in other levels of design.

If one substitutes a "high-level" artifact, such as a piece of furniture, into the Rittel-Webber argument, the credibility of that argument collapses. For example, an industrial designer can in fact build a chair to see how it works. If its performance is unsatisfactory, for example, if it is uncomfortable or structurally unsound, the designer can easily correct the bad design. Furthermore, its consequences are unlikely to have long half-lives. If any consequences are irreversible, they are unlikely to be severe and can be restricted to a small group of users who test the chair before it is made available to the public. The costs of redesigning and re-implementing the chair are likely to be small compared to profits made from selling thousands of well-designed chairs. In other words, feedback from implementation and use *can* play a significant role in the design of chairs and other "high-level" artifacts.

Difference in level, however, cannot explain all the differences between the design of software and the design of the sorts of low-level, large-scale artifacts that Rittel focused on. The design of new buildings and freeways generally might not involve learning from feedback about implementation and use, yet it is hard to find any level of software design that cannot learn from such feedback. The implementation and use of working prototypes and early versions play crucial roles in shaping the design of new operating systems, new browsers, and new rich Internet applications—three very different levels of software design. There are no comparable roles for usable prototypes or early versions of buildings or freeways.

Another limitation of Rittel's theory is that it ignores the redesign of artifacts. It is a truism that buildings and cities evolve over decades through many episodes of redesign (Brand 1994). Such redesign is often informed by implementation and use. Successful software at all levels also goes through many episodes of redesign that are informed by feedback from implementation and use of previously released versions.

Our PHI-based software projects contained many cases where the design was changed in the middle of being implemented. The design of the PHIDIAS interface between PHI rationale and CAD graphic construction of form is the most conspicuous example of this. Current work by software engineers on iterative and incremental design also has this character. To be sure, software engineering for years militated against changes in decisions about requirements and design, because they were so costly. But in recent years, software engineers have become increasingly open to such changes.

2.5.3.2   How Feedback from Implementation Led to New Design Ideas

Over the history of the MIKROPLIS and PHIDIAS projects, a single type of phenomenon dominated the generation of design ideas: the repeated discovery of new affordances that arose as unplanned side-effects of implementing required design features. These discoveries influenced the design of the software in two ways. One was in suggesting ideas for the architecture of the system; the other was in leading us to re-evaluate and revise the requirements for the system.

Over the 18 years of the projects, the system architecture that emerged was a radically simple and integrated hyperbase management system (HBMS) with an operator-algebraic, functional language called PHIQL (PHIDIAS Hypermedia Inference and Query Language). This HBMS was coupled with subsystems for display of a wide range of multimedia data, including text, vector graphics, images, and video, together with subsystems for editing text and vector graphics. We came to call this a *hyperCAD architecture*.

The way in which ideas for PHIDIAS' architectural features emerged shows how feedback from implementation can shape the design of system architecture. For example, when we decided we needed to represent and edit vector graphics, the obvious approach was to buy or build a separate 3D graphics system and add it to the architecture. I started to do just that, but my knowledge of the implementation details of the graph-handling functionality of MIKROPLIS led to the insight that it could be used for scene graphs as well as textual networks. Once this new affordance of the MIKROPLIS system was discovered, it became clear that utilizing this affordance would make it possible to link any text to any vector graphic object in the system—thus enabling PHI-based discussion of all graphical objects and configurations. In other words, knowledge of implementation details led to discovery of an unplanned affordance of an existing system, which in turn led to the insight that exploiting this affordance served the goals of the larger project in ways that had not been foreseen. Here, both knowledge of implementation details and the affordances of those details provided feedback from implementation that led to the generation of design ideas.

As it turned out, once we had designed a system architecture that implemented scene graphs in the HBMS, additional unplanned affordances emerged as direct consequences of this decision. For example, since PHIQL could now construct arbitrary displays of linked text and vector graphics, it became trivial to construct in PHIDIAS the catalogues of completed designs that existed in JANUS—something which had previously been of interest to us but too far down on our priorities to appear in our system requirements. Using PHIQL and scene graphs also made it possible and easy to create a catalogue of reusable subassemblies, something that did not exist in JANUS. Though we had never before thought of creating such a catalogue, we quickly realized it would be a very useful feature for a designer. So we added this and a catalogue of completed designs to our list of system requirements.

The integrated hyperCAD architecture emerged as a consequence of repeated discovery of unplanned affordances. Over the history of the PHIDIAS project, we frequently found that desired new functionality could best be implemented by exploiting affordances of the existing system rather than by adding new code that implemented the functionality from scratch. It was a more efficient use of our time and knowledge, and it tended in turn to produce still more affordances. We kept discovering that we were able to generate valuable new functionality almost for free. We began talking not only of what we wanted the system to be but also of what the system itself "wanted to be"—a metaphorical way of referring to new affordances produced as side effects of implementation. This sort of metaphor, which anthropomorphizes the artifact being designed and treats it is if it were a partner in discussion, has been used by a number of well-known (building) architects, most famously Louis Kahn (Twombly 2003). It is closely related to Schön's (1983) reference to the situation "talking back."

There are dozens of other examples of how feedback from implementation shaped the architecture of PHIDIAS and led to the addition of new system requirements, far more than there is room here to describe. While this sort of feedback was the most frequent source of new design ideas, many of the more profound ideas emerged in feedback about system use.

2.5.3.3   How Feedback from Use Led to New Design Ideas

Our PHI-based software projects contained a number of important cases where feedback from use led to new design ideas. These included the following:

- Users of PROTOCOL complained about lack of control of the order in which issues were dealt with. This led to the design of MIKROPLIS as a system where users had complete control over the order of rationale input and display.
- Use of MIKROPLIS indicated that it had not solved the rationale capture problem. This led to the use of domain-oriented issue bases in JANUS and PHIDIAS.
- Tests of MIKROPLIS users attempting building design determined that they failed to deal with decisions about the building form. This led to the inclusion of CAD graphics in the redesigned version of MIKROPLIS that came to be called PHIDIAS.
- Tests of users of domain-oriented issue bases in PHIDIAS showed that they had difficulty finding useful information in these issue bases. This contributed to the use of critics in PHIDIAS to identify and retrieve useful issue-based information.

There were numerous other examples during all of our software projects. One early example of this happened in 1982 with the very first MIKROPLIS prototype. MIKROPLIS had originally been designed as a query-based retrieval system, but tests with users revealed this approach to be inadequate. In particular, almost all users of the system kept pointing to individual texts displayed on the screen and saying something like, "How do I find the information about this?" We repeatedly showed users how to use queries to find such information, but they continued to have difficulties. I finally got the idea of enabling them to place the cursor on the desired text and instruct the computer to traverse a link associated with that text— something roughly comparable to clicking on a link in a Web page. At the time we had no graphical user interfaces, so I had the user move the cursor to the text with the arrow keys and then press the Enter key to signal the computer to perform link traversal. Once we had implemented this feature, all users rapidly adopted this as the favored mode of interacting with the system. This was the first inkling we had of what was to become the future of interacting with hyperdocuments: clicking on links. The crucial point is that without feedback from users, we would not have come to this idea on our own.

Another example came from having design students use PHIDIAS to construct building forms. Many complained that construction kits were too restrictive and not sufficiently intuitive, especially since using construction kits in realistic projects requires browsing through many menus and panels of information to find the objects the designer wants to place in the scene. In response to these complaints, we created functionality for pen-based drawing and creating hyperdocuments of linked drawings (McCall et al. 1997).

2.5.4 Extending Schön's Theory to Feedback from Implementation and Use

Schön's (1983) theory of reflective practice does not cover the sort of situated cognition in which feedback from implementation and use challenges a designer to revise the design of software. This is because Schön's theory only deals with action in the sense of the purely intuitive process he calls knowing-in-action. According to reflective practice the designer is in this process when feedback occurs that produces a breakdown and a switch to reflection-in-action. There are a number of features of this account that do not fit crucial cases of situated cognition in software design. First of all, actions do not have to be intuitive to produce feedback that leads designers to rethink the design of the system. The actions of implementation and use may well involve complex combinations of knowing-in-action and reflection-in-action. In any case, the mental states of the implementers or the users are not relevant here. Nor is it relevant what mental state the designer is in when feedback arrives; the designer could be acting, reflecting, just browsing the web, or eating a sandwich. The only thing that matters is that the feedback produces surprises and that these constitute a breakdown of the designer's expectations about the consequences of design ideas—either in the form of unexpected problems or unexpected opportunities. In such cases, the breakdowns will challenge the designer to rethink the design of the system and come up with new ideas that solve the problems or exploit the opportunities.

If we simplify Schön's model of reflective practice, we can make it general enough to cover all the cases. Rather than talking of knowing-in-action and reflection-in-action, we can talk simply of action and reflection. We can then say that in all cases of design as situated cognition *action* produces *feedback* that results in a *breakdown of expectations*, and that this promotes *reflection* aimed at the generation of new design ideas (ideation) to deal with the source of the feedback.

We can further modify Schön's model to account for critical conversations in argumentation among designers. Here a designer proposes an idea to a group of participants and gets feedback from them in the form of critiques of the idea. These critiques are only based on *speculations about the consequences* of the proposed design idea but are still capable of causing a breakdown in the expectations of the designer who proposed it. Such a breakdown then leads that designer—and others participating in the discussion—to reflect on how to revise the proposed idea or to devise a new idea. Here we have feedback, breakdown, reflection and the generation of new ideas without any actions of any kind. And yet this type of critical conversation bears a clear resemblance to reflective practice.

2.6   Implications for Rationale That Promotes Design Creativity

2.6.1   Critical Conversations That Promote Creativity in Software Design

This chapter has identified three processes in which the intertwining of ideation and evaluation promotes creativity in software design. When design ideas are evaluated, this evaluation can produce feedback that challenges designers to generate new ideas that improve the quality of the design. The three processes are as follows:

- The intertwining of ideation and evaluative argumentation in design discussion
- The intertwining of the action of software implementation with reflection on the feedback from implementation
- The intertwining of the action of use with reflection on the feedback from use

The first process involves purely argumentative conversation. The second and third involve types of situated cognition that do not precisely fit Schön's (1983) model of reflective practice but which, nevertheless, can be described as designers' conversations with situations.

Rittel's (1972) idea about the importance of involving implementers and users in participatory collaboration with designers comes into play in creative design of software—but in a way that Rittel did not anticipate. While he envisioned participation as taking the form of argumentative discussion, understanding design as situated cognition leads to us to extend this participation to the provision of feedback by implementers and users about the actual consequences of implementation and use of the software being designed.

2.6.2   What Rationale Needs to Do to Support Critical Conversations

Critical conversations are rationale processes that help designers to be more creative. Since they are processes, a rationale approach that recognizes and promotes them is by definition process oriented. Since these processes are for the purpose of improving design, the rationale approach is by definition prescriptive. To support the evaluation that promotes ideation, a rationale approach must represent how evaluations promote ideation. It must represent the evaluations and the ideas they lead to. It must also provide links that show which ideas were generated in response to which evaluations. Any approach to rationale that aims to support the full range of design creativity must encourage and document the generation of evaluative feedback from (a) design discussion, (b) implementation, and (c) use. To do this, it must capture rationale containing this feedback from designers, implementers and users. It must also support the communication of this rationale to designers. If feedback from action conflicts with feedback from the pure argumentation, it is likely that the former should trump the latter—since evidence and experience trump speculation. Because of this, documented feedback should always indicate whether its source is argumentative discussion, implementation, or use. In addition, the author of the feedback should always be indicated so that follow-up conversations can be established.

Decision-centric approaches to rationale, such as IBIS (Kunz and Rittel 1970) and PHI (McCall 1979, 1986, 1991), are unlikely to be sufficient for collecting feedback from implementation and use, because such methods only model the design process as a coherent whole. A rationale method, such as SCA (Carroll and Rosson 1992), is highly preferable for collecting feedback from use, because it models use processes as coherent wholes. It can thus systematically enumerate use situations and the feedback resulting from them in a way that decision-centric approaches simply cannot match. However, what needs to be done is to more closely integrate approaches like SCA with decision-centric rationale.

An open question is how the feedback from implementation should be collected. Should it be treated as a decision-centric rationale process or should a special method be developed? Whatever is done needs to be capable of systematically enumerating the feedback from implementation and it needs to be integrated with the decision-centric rationale for design.

2.7 Conclusions and Future Work

Methods for rationale elicitation and documentation can promote creativity in software design by recognizing and promoting feedback-driven critical conversations in software projects. Critical conversations are rationale discussions in which the ideation, meaning the generation of design ideas, is intertwined with evaluation of those ideas in the sense that feedback from evaluation challenges designers to devise new ideas. There are three main types of such conversations:

- purely argumentative design discussions where designers get feedback from the speculative reasoning of other design participants,
- discussions where designers get feedback from implementers about the consequences of implementation of the software being designed, and
- discussions where designers get feedback from users about the consequences of use of the software being designed.

The first of these corresponds to Rittel's (1972) view of design as purely a process of argumentation, but it goes beyond the argumentative discussions that IBIS supports. The other two view design as a process in which argumentation is situated in the context of action that motivates and informs it. To maximize the potential of rationale to promote creative software design, we must move beyond Rittel's view of design rationale as *pure argumentation* and see it also as *situated argumentation*.

Considerable work needs to be done in revising approaches to rationale to support the critical conversations described above. Decision-centric rationale methods, such as IBIS and PHI, have to be revised to represent the intertwining of argumentative evaluation and idea generation. The changes made to represent this intertwining in pure argumentation will provide a basis for further changes needed to support situated argumentation in the context of implementation and use. In addition to modifying decision-centric approaches, usage-centric approaches to rationale such as SCA (Carroll and Rosson 1992) need to be utilized as ways of systematically obtaining feedback from use situations. Research also needs to be done to determine how best to support the capture and communication of feedback from implementation. Finally, work needs to be done on integrating these various approaches to rationale.

A crucial lesson of the JANUS (McCall et al. 1990b; Fischer et al. 1996) and PHIDIAS (McCall et al. 1990a, c; McCall et al.) projects is that both delivery and capture of rationale need to be integrated into the software that supports action. This means that rationale functionality should be integrated into the tools for modeling and implementing software. It also suggests that rationale capture may need to be integrated into the software artifacts being designed to enable feedback from actual use.

References

Alexander, C. (1964). *Notes on the synthesis of form.* Cambridge, MA: Harvard University Press.

Brand, S. (1994). *How buildings learn: What happens after they're built.* London: Phoenix Illustrated.

Burge, J. E., & Brown, D. C. (2006). Rationale-based support for software maintenance. In A. Dutoit, R. McCall, I. Mistrik, & B. Paech (Eds.), *Rationale management in software engineering* (pp. 273–296). Heidelberg: Springer.

Carroll, J. M., & Rosson, M. B. (1992). Getting around the task-artifact cycle: How to make claims and design by scenario. *ACM Transactions on Information Systems, 10,* 181–212.

Clancey, W. J. (1997). *Situated cognition: Human knowledge and computer representations.* Cambridge, UK: Cambridge University Press.

Conklin, E. J., & Begeman, M. (1988). gIBIS: A hypertext tool for exploratory policy discussion. *ACM Transactions on Information Systems, 6,* 303–331. New York: ACM.

Conklin, E. J., & Burgess-Yakemovic, K. C. (1996). A process-oriented to design rationale. In T. P. Moran & J. M. Carroll (Eds.), *Design rationale: Concepts, techniques, and use* (pp. 393–427). Mahwah: Lawrence Erlbaum and Associates.

de Bono, E. (1973). *Lateral thinking: Creativity step by step.* New York: Harper Colophon.

Dutoit, A. H., McCall, R., Mistrik, I., & Paech, B. (2006). Rationale management in software engineering: Concepts and techniques. In A. H. Dutoit, R. McCall, I. Mistrik, & B. Paech (Eds.), *Rationale management in software engineering* (pp. 1–43). Heidelberg: Springer.

Fischer, G. (1987, April). An object-oriented construction and tool kit for human-computer communication. In R. Beach (Ed.), *Computer graphics* (Vol. 21, No. 2, pp. 105–109). New York: ACM.

Fischer, G., & Lemke, A. (1988). Construction kits and design environments: Steps toward human problem-domain communication. *Human-Computer Interaction, 3,* 179–222. Hillsdale: L. Erlbaum Associates.

Fischer, G., & Morch, A. (1988). CRACK: A critiquing approach to cooperative kitchen design. In *Proceedings of the international conference on intelligent tutoring systems* (pp. 176–185). New York: ACM.

Fischer, G., McCall, R., & Morch, A. (1989). Design environments for constructive and argumentative design. In K. Bice & C. Lewis (Eds.), *Proceedings of the SIGCHI conference on human factors in computing systems, CHI'89* (pp. 269–275). New York: ACM.

Fischer, G., Lemke, A. C., McCall, R., & Morch, A. I. (1996). Making argumentation serve design. In T. P. Moran & J. M. Carroll (Eds.), *Design rationale: Concepts, techniques, and use* (pp. 267–321). Mahwah: Lawrence Erlbaum Associates.

Hoad, T. F. (Ed.). (1996). *Oxford concise dictionary of English etymology.* New York: Oxford University Press.

Jones, J. C. (1970). *Design methods: Seeds of human futures.* New York: Wiley-Interscience.

Kunz, W., & Rittel, H. W. J. (1970). Issues as elements of information systems (Working Paper 131). Institute for Urban and Regional Development, University of California, Berkeley.

Lawson, B. (2005). *How designers think: The design process demystified* (4th ed.). Burlington: Architectural Press (Elsevier).

Lee, J. (1991). Extending the Potts and Bruns model for recording design rationale. In *Proceedings of the 13th International Conference on Software Engineering (ICSE 13)* (pp. 114–125). New York: ACM.

Lee, J., & Lai, K.-Y. (1996). What's in design rationale? In T. P. Moran & J. M. Carroll (Eds.), *Design rationale: Concepts, techniques, and use* (pp. 21–51). Mahwah: Lawrence Erlbaum Associates.

Lutes-Schaab, B., McCall, R., Schuler, W., & Werner, H., (1985). MICROPLIS – ein Textbank-Management-system [MICROPLIS – a Textbase Management System]. Bericht, [Report], Heidelberg, Germany: Gesellshaft für Information und Dokumentation (GID), Sektion für Systementwicklung (SfS), [Society for Information and Documentation, Section for Systems Development].

MacLean, A., Young, R. M., Belotti, V. M. E., & Moran, T. P. (1996). Questions, options and criteria. In T. P. Moran & J. M. Carroll (Eds.), *Design rationale: Concepts, techniques, and use* (pp. 53–106). Mahwah: Lawrence Erlbaum and Associates.

McCall, R. (1979). *On the structure and use of issue-systems in design.* Unpublished doctoral dissertation, University of California, Berkeley. (Available from University Microfilms International, Ann Arbor Michigan.)

McCall, R. (1986). Issue-serve systems: A descriptive theory of design. *Design Methods and Theories, 20,* 443–458, San Luis Obispo: The Design Methods Group.

McCall, R. (1989). MIKROPLIS: A Hypertext system for design, *Design Studies, 10,* 228–238, London: Butterworth.

McCall, R. (1991). PHI: A conceptual foundation for design hypermedia. *Design Studies, 12,* 30–41, London: Butterworth.

McCall, R. (1998). World wide presentation and critiquing of design proposals with the Web PHIDIAS System. In S. van Wyck & S. Seebohm (Eds.), *Digital design studios: Do computers make a difference? Proceedings of the 1998 conference of the Association of Computer Aided Design in Architecture (ACADIA 98)* (pp. 254–265). Quebec City: Association for Computer Aided Design in Architecture.

McCall, R., & Johnson, E. (1997). Using argumentative agents to catalyze and support collaboration in design. *Automation in Construction, 6,* 299–309, Amsterdam: Elsevier.

McCall, R., Lutes-Schaab, B., & Schuler, W. (1984). An information station for the problem solver: System concepts. In *Proceedings of the first international conference on application of mini- and microcomputers in information, retrieval and libraries* (pp. 111–118). North-Holland: Amsterdam.

McCall, R., Bennett, P., Oronzio, P., Ostwald, J. L., Shipman, F. M., & Wallace, N. F. (1990a). PHIDIAS: A PHI-based design environment integrating CAD graphics into dynamic hypertext.

In R. A. Streitz & J. Andre (Eds.), *Hypertext: Concepts, systems, and applications* (pp. 152–165). Cambridge, UK: Cambridge University Press.

McCall, R., Fischer, G., & Morch, A. (1990b). Supporting reflection-in-action in the JANUS design environment. In M. McCullough, W. Mitchell, & P. Purcell (Eds.), *The electronic design studio: Architectural education in the computer era* (pp. 247–259). Cambridge, MA: MIT Press.

McCall, R., Ostwald, J. L., Shipman, F. M., & Wallace, N. F. (1990c). The PHIDIAS hyperCAD system: Extending CAD with hypermedia. In *From research to practice: Proceedings of the 1990 conference of the Association for Computer Aided Design in Architecture (ACADIA 90)* (pp. 145–156). Big Sky: Association for Computer Aided Design in Architecture.

McCall, R., Bennett, P., & Johnson, E. (1994). An overview of the PHIDIAS hyperCAD system. In A. C. Harfmann & M. Fraser (Eds.), *Proceedings of the 1994 conference of the Association for Computer Aided Design in Architecture (ACADIA '94)* (pp. 63–76). Saint Louis: Association for Computer Aided Design in Architecture.

McCall, R., Johnson, E., & Smith, M. (1997). HyperSketching: Design as creating a graphical hyperdocument. In R. Junge (Ed.), *Proceedings of the 7th international conference of Computer Aided Architectural Design Futures (CAAD Futures 1997)* (pp. 849–854). Dordrecht: Kluwer Academic.

McCall, R., Vlahos, E., & Zabel, J. (2001). Conceptual design and HyperSketching: Theory and Java prototype. In B. de Vries, J. van Leeuwen, & H. Achten (Eds.), *Computer-aided architectural design futures 2001 (CAAD Futures 2001)* (pp. 285–297). Dordrecht: Kluwer Academic.

Michalko, M. (2006). *Thinkertoys: A handbook of creative-thinking techniques* (2nd ed.). Berkeley: Ten Speed Press.

Osborn, A. F. (1963). *Applied imagination: Principles and procedures of creative problem solving.* New York: Scribner.

Potts, C., & Bruns, G. (1988). Recording the reasons for design decisions. In *Proceedings of the 10th international conference on software engineering* (pp. 418–427). Washington, DC: IEEE Computer Society Press.

Reuter, W. D. (1983). Thesen und Empfehlungen zur Anwedung von Argumentativen Informationssystemen [Theses and recommendations for the application of argumentative information systems]. Stuttgart: Institut für Grundlagen der Planung, Universität Stuttgart, Arb. Ber. A-84-4.

Reuter, W. D., & Werner, H. (1984). Zusammenstellung und Beschreibung von Anwendungsfaellen Argumentativer Informationssysteme [Compilation and description of applications of argumentative information systems]. Stuttgart: Institut für Grundlagen der Planung, Universität Stuttgart, Arb. Ber. A-84-4.

Rittel, H. W. J. (1966, April). Some principles for the design of an educational system for design. In: *Education for architectural technology* (pp. 1–46). Also available as Reprint 54, Institute of Urban and Regional Development, University of California, Berkeley.

Rittel, H. W. J. (1972, October). On the planning crisis: Systems analysis of the "first and second generations". In Bedrifts Okonomen, No. 8 (pp. 390–396). Also available as Reprint 107, Institute of Urban and Regional Development, University of California, Berkeley.

Rittel, H. W. J. (1980). APIS: A concept for an argumentative planning information system (Working Paper 324). Institute of Urban and Regional Development, University of California, Berkeley.

Rittel, H. W. J., & Noble, D. (1989). Issue-based information systems for design (Working Paper 492). Institute of Urban and Regional Development, University of California, Berkeley.

Rittel, H. W. J., & Webber, M. (1973). Dilemmas in a general theory of planning. In: *Policy Sciences* 4 (pp. 155–169). Amsterdam: Elsevier Scientific Publishing. Also available as Reprint 86, Institute of Urban and Regional Development, University of California, Berkeley.

Schön, D. (1983). *The reflective practitioner: How professionals think in action.* New York: Basic Books.

Schuler, W., & Smith, J. B. (1990). Author's argumentation assistant (AAA): A hypertext-based authoring tool for argumentative texts. In A. Rizk, N. Streitz, & J. Andre (Eds.), *Hypertext: Concepts, systems and applications* (pp. 137–151). Cambridge, UK: Cambridge University Press.

Simon, H. A. (1969). *The sciences of the artificial.* Cambridge, MA: The MIT Press.

Simon, H. A. (1973). The structure of ill-stuctured problems. *Artificial Intelligence, 4,* 181–202. Amsterdam: Elsevier.

Suchman, L. (1987). *Plans and situated actions: The problem of human–machine communication.* Cambridge, UK: Cambridge University Press.

Twombly, R. (2003). *Louis Kahn: Essential writings.* New York: W.W. Norton & Co.

Chapter 3
A Micro View of Design Reasoning: Two-Way Shifts Between Embodiment and Rationale

Gabriela Goldschmidt

Abstract This chapter is based on the assumption that because designing (of tangible artifacts) is aimed at specifying configurations and properties of entities, designers must manipulate forms and shapes and they must resort to visual reasoning to do so. Visual reasoning in designing is seen as the interplay between two modes of reasoning: embodiment and rationale, such that the one supports and continues the other in order to arrive at a result that is novel and valid in terms of all the requirements it is to satisfy. We use protocol analysis to explore the bond between embodiment and rationale reasoning modes at two levels of cognitive operation – that of the design move and that of the argument that is its building block. We conclude that the two modes of reasoning are equi-present in designing; they describe a binary system characterized by high-frequency shifts between embodiment and rationale.

Keywords Design argument • Design move • Embodiment • Rationale • Shift • Visual reasoning.

3.1 Introduction

Is there such a thing as visual reasoning, as opposed to 'regular' reasoning? The question brings to mind the (now rather obsolete) imagery debate, in which proponents defended, propositional *or* pictorial views of mental imagery (Block 1981; Tye 1991). According to Margaret Boden, all reasoning is of a kind, i.e. computational *tout court*, and attempting to single out visual reasoning is, in this view,

G. Goldschmidt (✉)
Faculty of Architecture and Town Planning, Technion – Israel Institute of Technology,
Haifa 32000, Israel
e-mail: gabig@technion.ac.il

futile at best.[1] fMRI-based research has proved that mental imagery does indeed rest on pictorial grounds, i.e. it has shared properties with vision (e.g., Ganis et al. 2004). That reasoning in general is not contingent on visualization is quite clear: many abstract concepts can be reasoned about with no recourse to visualization. However, when spatial configurations or two and three dimensional shapes and forms are the objects of reasoning, images are involved that must be figuratively represented to be reasoned about. Some of the properties of such shapes and forms, like size, color, texture etc., are equally best represented visually. As observed by Argiris (1981) in the case of architectural design: "Architectural thinking can be divided into things that can only be drawn and things that can only be talked about." (620). Representations may be internal, as in mental imagery, or external, such as live and inanimate physical entities, or various kinds of drawings and other pictorial repre- sentations. In tasks that require communication with others, mental imagery is inadequate not only because of the inability to share it, but also due to its significant inherent limitations (i.e., inaccuracy, fast fading, etc.; see e.g., Kosslyn 1996). Even in private, individuals very often feel the need to transcend and extend the representational powers of mental imagery by using external representations while reasoning during problem-solving. In designing,[2] where one must by definition reason about properties of forms and shapes, imagery is commonly complemented, amplified and surpassed by using external visual displays, often self-generated in the form of drawings, especially sketches (e.g., Do and Gross 2001; Goldschmidt 1991; Fish 2004; Fish and Scrivener 1990; Suwa and Tversky 1996). Drawings produced by designers, and sketches in particular, "talk back" to the designer; the feedback they provide is essential in making further design steps (Goldschmidt 2003). We propose that reasoning that is heavily reliant on shape, form and their properties may be termed 'visual reasoning', regardless of the medium of represen- tation involved.

According to Sloman (1996) we are endowed with two independent (but inter- acting) cognitive systems, each dedicated to one mode of reasoning: one associative and similarity-based, the other symbolic and rule-based. The associative system makes use of visuals when relevant (as in design); the rule-based system specifies rationale. In chess, for example, there is evidence that pattern recognition and rational 'forward search' are deeply entangled (Linhares et al. 2012); this may suggest a similar entanglement of systems in other instances of problem-solving and thinking. In this chapter we are interested in design reasoning where visual displays in the form of sketches are commonly generated and contemplated in the process of preliminary, conceptual design, as fortifications of internal imagistic representations. We shall propose a binary reasoning system in which *embodi- ment* is representative of a tangible aspect (or aspects) of the entity that is being

---

[1] Personal communication, Vienna, April 6, 1994.

[2] *Design* in this chapter refers to physical design only, such as architectural, industrial, or graphic design.

designed, which is constantly coupled with a validating concept, *rationale*, or raison d'être. At the same time every expression of rationale is likewise matched with an instance of embodiment, such as an illustration, instantiation, example, or explicit description of physical properties, represented externally or internally. We shall show that the one has no existence without the other: a causal relationship appears to exist between embodiment and rationale, which is responsible for a nearly perfect balance between both modes in design reasoning. We maintain that this balanced relationship is inherent in effective design reasoning, and is one of the prerequisites for creative designing.

    We start with a theoretical exposition of design reasoning, followed by empirical work based on the 'Delft Protocols', which pertain to the design of a bicycle rack for a given backpack, to be attached to a specific bicycle. Two protocols were generated, one of an individual designer and another of a team of three designers. All designers were experienced professionals and the design sessions, under equal conditions, lasted two hours each. For further details see Cross et al. (1996). All examples in this chapter are likewise taken from the Delft Protocols.

3.2   Analyzing the Process of Designing: Moves and Arguments

When solving well-defined and well-structured problems, one is not expected to justify the solution that is reached; at most, one is asked to retrace one's steps, so as to explain how the solution was arrived at. The case of ill-defined and ill-structured problems, to which design problems belong, is different. More than one solution is possible and sometimes a large number of very different solutions may be equally acceptable and similarly valued (Simon 1973). When presenting a solution to a design problem one is always required to accompany it with a justification. The justification is meant to establish the appropriateness and demonstrate the advantages of that particular solution vis a vis any number of alternative solutions to the problem (that the problem-solver has not chosen although they may have been considered earlier in the design search). Because of the complexity of most design problems and the need to reach a good fit among the components of a design solution, it is almost impossible to postpone thinking of justifications until the complete design solution is in place. Rather, designers constantly look for congruence between their candidate partial solutions and corresponding design goals, requirements, and constraints (Pahl et al. 2007). In other words, designers *reason* about the actions they take such that at any given moment there is a rational explanation for the goodness of those actions in terms of the appropriateness of the design choices. Indeed, it would not be exaggerated to claim that design education, as carried out in the studio, is largely aimed at training students to so reason while engaged in designing. Acquiring the kind of reasoning that is typical of designing (Cross 2006) is by no means a trivial feat. The difficulty dwells in the need to deal with a large number of different issues (e.g., in the case of architecture, climatic and environmental concerns, topography, functional needs, structural requirements, social and cultural values, budgetary issues and more) in the framework of one unified design solution. Within this framework, the rationale for every single response to a partial problem must be in good agreement (Alexander (1964) used the term 'good fit') with responses to the various other partial problems.

Sometimes an explicit request to specify the design rationale for accepting (or rejecting) a certain proposal is voiced (Ball et al. 2001). For example, in a design session in which a bicycle rack is being designed (Delft Protocols), several parallel ideas are being inspected; on one occasion, a team-member asks: "...should we like break down a rationale for our killing off some of these ideas...?" In another instance, a team-member asks: "[what is the] design rationale?" Reasoning about designing is not an activity apart, which lies outside of designing and closely follows it: it is part and parcel of designing. Designing means generating and manipulating forms, shapes and configurations and reasoning about their properties in terms of their congruence with goals and requirements, both predetermined and those generated or modified on the fly. This notion is critical to our inquiry in this chapter and we hope to clarify it in the sections that follow.

Once a design task is put forth, a problem-solving process is initiated in which solutions are sought while problems are being framed and reframed (Schön 1984). Since design problems are, as mentioned earlier, typically ill-defined and/or ill-structured, this process takes the form of a search. The search is conducted in a design space (Woodbury and Burrow 2006) that combines problem and solution spaces respectively (Dorst and Cross 2001), regulated by the design world in which the designer operates, i.e., prevailing cultural and professional norms, the designer's personal set of values, repertoire and skills, and the context in which the task is set (Schön 1983). The dimensions of the search-space are proportional to the degree of novelty and creativity of the task: with increased novelty, the space is extended and enlarged to encompass new explorations and plausible solutions (Habraken 1985; Rosenman and Gero 1993).

3.2.1 Units of Analysis: Moves and Arguments

Within the search space, the designer navigates by making design *moves*. A design move, analogous to a chess move, is an act that transforms the state of the design search in some measure. It may be, but does not have to be, a decision, nor even a tentative assertion; it may be a question regarding an aspect of the emerging design, a side comment, or a request for information. A move is the smallest perceivable and semantically coherent unit of operation that the designer makes (the average duration of a move is approximately seven seconds; see for example Baya (1996). A move consists of between a few words and a few sentences; often it is one sentence). Semantically incomplete sentences such as 'OK', 'yeah', 'emm' are not counted as moves and are removed from the protocol for the purpose of its analysis. To get a better sense of what we are talking about, let us consider a move (move 32), verbally expressed, made by a designer who is a member of the team engaged in the design of the bicycle rack:

> 32 "cos it would be nice I think I mean just from a positioning standpoint if we've got this frame outline and we know that they're [clients] gonna stick with that you can vacuum form a tray or a"

Most design moves are composite – they are made of smaller units of thought, which we call *arguments*. An argument is a single statement that is syntactically (but not necessarily semantically) complete, but does not necessarily constitute a complete move, or a design operation of any kind. Arguments are the building blocks of moves. Some succinct moves are composed of a single argument; others comprise several arguments, usually no more than two or three, and rarely more than five. The argument is our second, smaller unit of analysis (in our data moves by team members and by an individual designer comprise, on average, 1.50 and 1.74 arguments, respectively).

Move 32 (above) is composed of four arguments:

32.1 cos it would be nice I think I mean just from a positioning standpoint
32.2 if we've got this frame outline
32.3 and we know that they're gonna stick with that
32.4 you can vacuum form a tray or a

In what follows, we shall briefly discuss design reasoning at the level of moves, by way of also introducing a more detailed discussion of design reasoning at the level of arguments, in which we explore the relationship between the embodiment and rationale modes of reasoning.

3.3   Design Reasoning at the Level of Moves

The design sessions in the experiment reported here lasted 2 h. The protocol of each session was divided into segments defined by the contents of the design activity, typically lasting several minutes each. In many cases wherein a cognitive exploration is the aim, it is both unnecessary and too laborious to analyze a long protocol in its entirety and researchers choose significant segments for analysis. Chosen segments are then parsed into moves: depending on its length a segment may contain somewhere between 15 and 100 moves. In most protocol studies the moves (or other units of analysis) are then coded using a scheme of categories that the researchers establish as per the objectives of the study (e.g., Ericsson and Simon 1984/1993; Gero and McNeill 1998; Purcell et al. 1996). This enables them to determine the frequencies of appearance and priorities of certain categories of moves and compare them across designers and design situations.

In our case, we are interested in the question: how does the designer construct the design rationale, along with the embodiment of the candidate design solution, along the design search? Given that the design problem is largely ill-defined, we must assume that the search is wide and often unstructured at least to some degree, and that the designer may resort to information from totally unpredictable sources, in any domain at all, and in a sequence that may be highly random, to reason about the emerging design. In the early phases of the search the designer may be considering several solution directions; much of what is being considered is tentative and may be dropped in favor of more promising solution directions. Therefore, our interest in this study dwells in the mechanisms of reasoning rather than the categories of information, and we do not code the moves. In previous studies we dwelt particularly on links among moves, based on contents. A network of links, notated in a designated representation called *linkograph*, is very telling of the nature of reasoning in a particular segment. We maintain that the frequency of links is correlated with the quality, and creativity, of the design process and outcome (Goldschmidt 1996). In particular, we can identify moves that are especially rich in links to other moves; those are called critical moves. Their positioning in the sequence and their percentage in the move 'population' have been shown to be of high significance in terms of understanding design reasoning (e.g., Cross 1997; Goldschmidt 1996; Goldschmidt and Tatsa 2005; Goldschmidt and Weil 1998; Kan and Gero 2008; van der Lugt 2000).

Linkography is a potent analytic tool and the insights we can derive from looking at link networks are important to a better understanding of design cognition. Indeed, we maintain that linking moves to each other is a key prerequisite for fruitful design thinking. However, in this study we focus on rationale and embodiment and it is more appropriate, for this purpose, to refine the analysis and work with a smaller unit of analysis, namely the argument. As we shall see, this impacts moves as well.

3.4 Design Reasoning at the Level of Arguments: Embodiment and Rationale

Let us return to move 32 which, as we have already noted, is composed of four arguments. Are these arguments all of a kind? If we suspect they are not, what criteria should we use to differentiate them? Keeping in mind that we wish to concentrate on what distinguishes creative design reasoning from 'general' reasoning in problem-solving, we now bring into the analysis the visual dimension of design activity and reasoning. In the kinds of design we address in this chapter, the objective of the process of designing is to come up with at least one design proposal that ultimately specifies the designed entity in terms of its form(s) and function(s) at a certain level of precision and detail. This process is almost always marked by the production of visual representations, mostly rough sketches, from which the designer infers information and feedback that can be reasoned about. As discussed earlier, the final design proposal is – when presented – accompanied by a rationale, stressing the advantages that should make us prefer it to other plausible proposals. Since the rationale is being built up step by step as the process of designing proceeds, it is logical to assume that reasoning about emerging configurations and their properties, referred to as embodiment, are matched with reasoning about the corresponding rationale. The designer examines the compatibility of the tentative embodiment with requirements and desires (e.g., cost effectiveness, ease of manufacturing, sustainability, novelty, aesthetic value, cultural significance and so on). The process is not linear and en route designers may side-track and generate alternative ideas and possible solutions or partial solutions, which they explore and reason about before accepting or rejecting them. The question we ask is therefore: is there a discernible pattern of design reasoning, in terms of the arguments that are being voiced? In particular, we would like to know how arguments concerning embodiment relate to arguments holding the rationale for choosing a form, a shape and physical properties thereof, explicitly or implicitly. We propose the following taxonomy of design argument modalities:

Embodiment (E) Arguments of this modality directly address physical properties of
   form or shape, usually, but not always, as represented in a figure drawn (sketched)
   on paper as part of the design activity and/or described verbally.
   Example: "if we've got this frame outline"
Rationale (R) Arguments of this modality present a direct rationale for favoring or
   rejecting specific forms or physical objects with specific properties.
   Example: "cos it would be nice I think I mean just from a positioning standpoint"
Embodiment/Rationale (ER) In these hybrid arguments, Embodiment and Rationale
   cannot be pulled apart (at a finer grain of analysis, which is not attempted here,
   it should be possible to subdivide them into the two parent modalities). We
   acknowledge these arguments and include them in our analyses.
   Example: "you can vacuum form a tray or a"
Comment (C) These arguments are general statements that cannot be seen as direct
   expressions of rationale, but which are part of the discussion regarding the
   designed entity or design in general.
   Example: "emm gravity, gravity"

   Chosen segments of verbal design protocols are thus parsed into moves, and then into arguments. Sketches are used to help interpret the verbalizations. On rare occasions we come across verbalizations that cannot be considered design arguments, such as jokes, general statements or incomplete expressions (e.g., "whatever the tray"). They are not acknowledged as arguments and are withdrawn from the analysis. When there is no agreement among coders regarding the modality of an argument, no modality can be assigned.[3] Such arguments are also withdrawn from the analysis. ER (Embodiment/Rationale) and C (Comment) arguments are a little tricky. For the sake of simplicity, since we are interested in Embodiment versus Rationale arguments, we aggregate the arguments into two major consolidated

---

[3] Unless otherwise noted, codes are assigned by three coders; when at least two coders agree on the same coding, it is assigned.

Table 3.1 Distribution of embodiment and rationale arguments

Segment	No. arguments	% E	% R	
T-32	101	54.5	45.5	
T-37	95	62.1	37.9	
I-19	72	45.1	54.9	
I-23	33	50.0	50.0	
Team average		58.2	41.8	p=0.067
Individual average		46.7	53.3	p=0.242

T Team, *I* Individual

groups as follows: all E arguments and 50% of the ER arguments are grouped into the Embodiment category. All R, all C and 50% of the ER arguments are grouped into the Rationale category. We can now proceed to analyze our protocols at the level of moves and arguments, and explore shifts between the E and R modes of reasoning. Based on our view of design reasoning in the preceding sections, we put forth the following hypotheses regarding the frequency and modality shifts of arguments of the two (consolidated) modalities in a typical conceptual design session (sample thereof):

Hypothesis 1 There is no difference between the number of arguments of the embodiment modality and the number of arguments of the rationale modality.

Hypothesis 2 There is no difference between the number of moves starting with an embodiment argument and the number of moves starting with a rationale argument.

Hypotheses 3 There are frequent modality shifts between the last argument of a move and the first argument of the subsequent move, in both directions: from E to R and from R to E.

We have coded four sequences of arguments from the Delft Protocols. Two were generated by the team (T) over a total of 9 min, and two by the individual designer (I), lasting 12 min in total. The total number of arguments produced in these sequences is 196 by the team, and 105 by the individual. Table 3.1 summarizes the argument modality distribution in the four segments we have inspected. Note that in the segments in question the team makes roughly twice the number of arguments made by the individual. In teamwork, where natural conversation flows fast, design moves tend to be significantly shorter than in an individual's think-aloud verbalization.[4] The speed of production, however, has no proven effect on the nature and pattern of reasoning. The number of arguments is, in both cases, sufficiently large to qualify as a statistically valid sample of the phenomenon we are investigating.

Table 3.1 shows that as hypothesized (hypothesis 1), there is a nearly perfect balance between embodiment and rationale arguments in typical design reasoning.

---

[4] In the segments analyzed here, team-members generated an argument every 2.8 s, whereas the individual took 6.9 s to produce an argument.

We compare the two modalities once for the team and once for the individual. The team makes on the average 58.2% E arguments and 41.8% R arguments and since $p > 0.05$, we conclude that for the team hypothesis 1 is confirmed. The individual designer makes 46.7% E arguments and 53.3% R arguments and since $p > 0.05$, we conclude that for the individual, too, hypothesis 1 is confirmed, this time with even more confidence.

These results assert that in the design sessions we have analyzed, for every E argument a designer makes, regardless of whether the work is carried out individually or by a team, a R 'counter argument' is also advanced. The opposite is also true: for every R argument voiced, an E counterpart argument is brought forth. In other words, arguments of both modalities even each other out. We have obtained similar results in other studies concerning shorter protocol segments of architectural design sessions (Goldschmidt 1991) and graphic advertisement design (unpublished), as well as another, shorter, sequence from the Delft protocols (Goldschmidt 1997).[5]

We have established that designers make an equal number of embodiment and rationale arguments, but this in itself does not yet certify that rationale and embodiment reasoning are inseparably enmeshed in designing. One could theorize that a designer might first manipulate a configuration, or embodiment, and only once it has been brought to a certain degree of completion, look for a supporting rationale for it. Or conversely, that a designer could possibly work on specifying all the requirements that a not-yet-existent configuration should satisfy, before generating the embodiment. Looking at our data reveals that not even the slightest shred of evidence exists in support of such a theory. The longest string of sequential arguments of the same modality contains 13 arguments (moves 4–7, Team segment 37, in which 12 arguments are coded E and one ER). This sequence, generated over 35 s, is exceptionally long. Most sequences of same-modality arguments are much shorter. Interestingly, practically all longer strings of same modality arguments are embodiment arguments. Since most sketching activity typically accompanies the generation of E arguments, a possible explanation of the inequality between E and R arguments in long same-modality strings, may have to do with the length of time necessary for the production of sketches. Sequences of same-modality arguments vary in length, then, from 1 to 13 (sequences of same 'root' modality arguments, before consolidation, are shorter; the longest includes eight arguments).

At this point we turn our attention to moves. We return to moves because unlike arguments, which are complete entities syntax-wise, moves are also semantically complete entities. We would like to know with what kinds of arguments moves are initiated: what modalities are involved and consequently: is there a balance between moves starting with E and R modes of reasoning? Table 3.2 presents the data pertaining to the modalities of arguments at the heads of moves. The findings prove that in the case of the individual, we get the same number of E and R arguments at the

---

[5] In these studies a single experimenter coded the arguments. As mentioned earlier, in the current study three coders determined the final assignment of codes.

Table 3.2 Embodiment and rationale arguments at heads of moves

Segment	No. moves	% starting with E	% starting with R	
T-32	64	58.6	41.4	
T-37	61	59.0	41.0	
I-19	42	50.0	50.0	
I-23	19	47.4	52.6	
Team average	125	58.8	41.2	p=0.044
Individual average	61	49.2	50.8	p=0.05

T Team, *I* Individual

beginnings of moves. The team is less 'perfect': there is a slight but statistically significant difference in favor of E arguments at the beginnings of moves.

We therefore conclude that moves, which are logical entities, have an almost equal chance of beginning with E or R modes of reasoning. Hypothesis 2 is therefore partially confirmed: it is true for the individual but not quite for the team.

3.5   Embodiment-Rationale Shifts

If we had found long strings of arguments within which modalities shift from E to R and vice versa after every argument, we would have taken this to prove our claim that the two modes of reasoning are inextricable. This is not quite the case, although shifts in modality occur very frequently in our samples. In this section we look closely at these shifts, from E to R and from R to E.

We looked at arguments at heads of moves, and compared their modality with that of the last argument of the previous move. There are four possibilities: in the first two, there is no shift in modality, that is, a move ends with an E argument and the subsequent move starts with an E argument, or: a move ends with a R argument and the subsequent move starts with a R argument. When there is a shift in modality, there are again two possibilities: a move ends with an E argument and the subsequent move starts with a R argument, or: a move ends with a R argument and the subsequent move starts with an E argument. Table 3.3 summarizes the count.

The results in Table 3.3 show that on the average, in roughly half the cases a new move boasts a modality shift at its head argument, as compared to the last argument of the previous move, or otherwise put: we discern a shift every other move. This is of course not as clear-cut as a shift with every new move, but such an extreme condition probably exists only in theory. Interestingly, there is no difference between the frequency of shifts from E to R and shifts from R to E. We shall comment on this finding in our conclusions.

We may thus state that hypothesis 3 was confirmed, contingent on a definition of 'frequent shifts'. To help arrive at such a definition, we establish a measure called Shift Index.

Table 3.3 Distribution of modality sequences at heads of moves

| Segment | % E→E | % R→R | Modality shifts | |
			% E→R	% R→E
T-32	27.0	12.7	27.8	32.5
T-37	30.0	13.3	27.5	29.2
I-19	26.8	31.7	22.0	19.5
I-23	16.7	16.7	33.3	33.3
Team average	28.5	13.0	27.6	30.9
Individual average	23.7	27.1	25.5	23.7
T+I average	26.9	17.6	26.9	28.6

T Team, *I* Individual

Table 3.4 Shift Index (S.I.): All arguments, and at heads of moves

Segment	S.I. argument modality (all)	S.I. argument modality (heads of moves)
T-32	0.65	0.44
T-37	0.48	0.36
I-19	0.44	0.36
I-23	0.49	0.53
Team average	0.57	0.40
Individual average	0.47	0.44
T+I average	0.52	0.42

T Team, *I* Individual

3.5.1   Shift Index

Shift Index (S.I.) is a value obtained by dividing the number of shifts in a given segment into the number of relevant units, i.e. arguments or moves. As stated above, in the most perfect of all possible worlds we should obtain S.I. = 1.0, which means a shift every time a new argument/move is generated. But since reasoning in design (not unlike all other domains) is not perfect, we do not obtain this value for the Shift Indexes we have calculated. Table 3.4 lists the S.I. values for our protocol segments, once for arguments, and once for heads of moves.

If we look at the average values, our overall Shift Index is almost S.I. = 0.5 which, as stated above, means that roughly every other unit of reasoning comes into the world after the designer has switched his or her attention from embodiment to rationale, or vice versa. It is hard to sharply define the range that qualifies as 'frequent shifts', but it is reasonable to assume that any value between 0.5 and 1.0 can definitely be thought of as 'frequent'. Accordingly we reaffirm that hypothesis 3 was confirmed.

3.5.2 Creativity and Multi-Modal Reasoning in Design

We have now established the rhythm at which embodiment and rationale sequences of reasoning are generated. It is useful to compare our findings with those of a study by Akin and Lin (1996) that is based on the same Delft Protocols that provided our data (individual designer). In their study, Akin and Lin developed an activity-based model of the design process. The coding categories assigned the activities the designer was engaged in to three main groupings: Examining, Drawing, and Thinking.[6] The duration of each activity unit was measured and for the three activities was on average 25.4, 22.2, and 19.8 s respectively. Activities were carried out unaccompanied, or in overlap with one or two of the other activities. The most intriguing cases where those Akin and Lin call "triple-modes", i.e., where all three activities occurred simultaneously. Such units were longer and lasted 35.3 s on average, which is the equivalent of 5.2 arguments, or three moves, in our study (individual designer). Then they identified all instances in the protocol in which design decisions were made (hundreds of decisions), and singled out some as Novel Design Decisions (NDD). In the main portion of the protocol they found eight such NDDs. Design Decisions were then correlated with the findings regarding activities. The correlation showed that NDDs occur "while triple-mode activities are almost exclusively present" and statistically, this correlation's probability is shown to be beyond pure chance (ibid., 57–58). Although Akin and Lin's work has different goals than ours, and their results cannot be directly mapped onto our concerns, it seems possible to conclude from their work that hybrid reasoning in designing, i.e. simultaneous multi modal reasoning (triple, in their taxonomy), is crucial for significant (novel) design progress. The activity modes they stipulate, Exploring, Drawing and Thinking can be seen as roughly reminiscent of our embodiment and rationale argumentation, or reasoning.

Although the grain of analysis in the two studies is different – we work at a finer grain (the argument and the move are shorter than any of the units used by Akin and Lin) – we still may, using appropriate caution, conclude that Akin and Lin's findings support our basic conception. Akin and Lin recorded two NDDs in the time span that corresponds to our segment 23, and no NDD in what is our segment 19. We can confirm, based on previous studies, that the individual designer made an important breakthrough in segment 23 (Goldschmidt 1996). If we direct our attention to the S.I.s in Table 3.4 we notice that indeed, segment 23 has a much higher S.I. (heads of moves), compared to segment 19 (0.53 vs. 0.36 respectively). This may indicate that the S.I. value goes up with the rigorousness of the design

---

[6] We have reservations concerning the differentiation between these activities, but we report Akin and Lin's study in the spirit in which it was undertaken.

search and its productivity (see also Goldschmidt 1991). In other words, the frequency of shifts in reasoning modes may be a good indicator of a productive process of design problem-solving. The E-R bond, then, is not only ubiquitous in design reasoning, but its strength, as measured by shift frequencies, joins indicators like the frequency of links among moves in assessing the quality and creativity of the design process.

3.6   In Conclusion

This study encompasses a limited set of data, and to be conclusive more experiments need to be performed. However, the results are clear-cut and are supported by a number of additional preliminary studies; moreover, the data is sufficiently large for the viable statistical analysis that was presented. We are therefore confident in presenting our conclusions. We have shown that an embodiment-rationale bond permeates design reasoning at all levels (arguments, moves). Designers generate equal numbers of E and R arguments, and similar numbers of moves start with either mode of reasoning. Furthermore, we have shown that the design search is characterized by frequent shifts between E and R arguments and we find that every other move begins with an argument the modality of which differs from that of the last argument in the preceding move. These findings are in line with other analyses of design reasoning (Akin and Lin 1996) and with studies that stress the faculty of visual reasoning and its importance in tasks that require the manipulation of forms and shapes (even in literary thinking; see for example Stern 2000). Visual thinking, and in particular imagery, is often believed to be indispensable in creative thinking and problem solving (of which design is a paramount example). We have shown that rationale, rather than being a 'thing apart', is part and parcel of reasoning in design thinking, which is largely visual.

This chapter does not deal with software design directly; software is embodied as sequences of program expressions, interactions among modules or objects, flows of control and data, and so on. More concretely, software is embodied in user interface displays of a programming environment, in the activities of programmers, and ultimately in user experiences. All the same, I speculate that the findings of this chapter can be extended to conform to other design domains, including software design. The following very short protocol vignette[7] from a conversation between two programming students working on a preliminary characterization of an information system gives us more than a subtle hint; they talk about external physical as well as internal logic characterization. Much more

---

[7] The protocol in question was recorded by graduate students Eran Toch and Yael Yariv as part of a term paper in the course *Cognitive aspects of the design process* at the Technion, in March 2005.

research is needed to validate this claim, but at least we have an indication, albeit only anecdotal at this point.

Student A Right, here too. Oh, you changed this from... I missed the moment at which you changed it [from physical]. It seems to me that we want only the physical, really.
Student B Want what?
Student A The external SRM. It seems to me that we want only the physical.
Student B No. We want both the physical and the logic, internal.
Student A Why? Here... OK.

We would like to stress the finding that no 'directionality' was found in the modality shifts. In other words, as many moves start with an E argument after a R argument, as there are moves that begin with a R argument after an E argument. We take this finding to indicate that the creative search in design is compiled of flexible small steps that lean on 'educated' associative thinking and not on prescriptive rules. The designer may proceed by wanting to do *x* because it helps reach goal *y*; but alternatively, he or she may also progress by wanting to achieve goal *y*, and therefore implementing action *x*. The ability to go in either direction is vastly important because of the flexibility it affords without any loss of focus. Rationale, then, is a component of creative design at any level of the design process: there is no creativity without rationale, just as there is no novelty and originality without embodiment.

Acknowledgements The research for this chapter was supported by a grant from the fund for the promotion of research at the Technion, hereby gratefully acknowledged. A preliminary version of this work was published under the title "Is a figure-concept binary argumentation patterns inherent in visual design reasoning?" in the proceedings of *International Conference on Visual and Spatial Reasoning in Design: Computational and Cognitive Approaches*, Bellagio, 177–205, 2001.

References

Akin, Ö., & Lin, C. (1996). Design protocol data and novel design decisions. In N. Cross, H. Christiaans, & K. Dorst (Eds.), *Analysing design activity* (pp. 35–64). Chichester: Wiley.
Alexander, C. (1964). *Notes on the synthesis of form*. Cambridge, MA: Harvard University Press.
Argiris, C. (1981). Teaching and learning in design settings. In W. L. Porter & M. Kilbridge (Eds.), *Architecture education study* (pp. 551–660). New York: Consortium of East Coast Schools of Architecture/Andrew W. Mellon Foundation.
Ball, L., Lambell, N., Ormerod, T., Slavin, S., & Mariani, J. (2001). Representing design rationale to support innovative design reuse: A minimalist approach. *Automation in Construction, 10*, 663–674.
Baya, V. (1996). *Information handling behavior of designers during conceptual design: three experiments*. PhD dissertation, Department of Mechanical Engineering, Stanford University, Stanford.
Block, N. (1981). *Imagery*. Cambridge, MA: MIT Press.
Cross, N. (1997). Creativity in design: Analyzing and modeling the creative leap. *Leonardo, 30*(4), 311–317.
Cross, N. (2006). *The designerly ways of knowing*. London: Springer.
Cross, N., Christiaans, H., & Dorst, K. (Eds.). (1996). *Analyzing design activity*. Chichester: Wiley.

Do, E. Y.-L., & Gross, M. D. (2001). Thinking with diagrams in architectural design. *Artificial Intelligence Review, 15*, 135–149.

Dorst, K., & Cross, N. (2001). Creativity in the design process: Co-evolution of problem-solution. *Design Studies, 22*(5), 425–437.

Ericsson, K.A., & Simon, H.A. (1984/1993). *Protocol analysis: Verbal reports as data*, Cambridge, MA: MIT Press.

Fish, J. (2004). Cognitive catalysis: Sketches for a time-lagged brain. In G. Goldschmidt & W. L. Porter (Eds.), *Design representation* (pp. 151–184). London: Springer.

Fish, J., & Scrivener, S. (1990). Amplifying the mind's eye: Sketching and visual cognition. *Leonardo, 23*, 117–126.

Ganis, G., Thompson, W. L., & Kosslyn, S. M. (2004). Brain areas underlying visual mental imagery and visual perception: An fMRI study. *Cognitive Brain Research, 20*, 226–241.

Gero, J. S., & McNeill, T. (1998). Analysis of design protocols. *Design Studies, 19*(1), 21–61.

Goldschmidt, G. (1991). The dialectics of sketching. *Creativity Research Journal, 4*(2), 123–143.

Goldschmidt, G. (1996). The designer as a team of one. In N. Cross, H. Christiaans, & K. Dorst (Eds.), *Analysing design activity* (pp. 65–91). Chichester: Wiley.

Goldschmidt, G. (1997). Capturing indeterminism: Representation in the design problem space. *Design Studies, 18*(4), 441–455.

Goldschmidt, G. (2003). The backtalk of self-generated sketches. *Design Issues, 19*(1), 72–88.

Goldschmidt, G., & Tatsa, D. (2005). How good are good ideas? Correlates of design creativity. *Design Studies, 26*(6), 593–611.

Goldschmidt, G., & Weil, M. (1998). Contents and structure in design reasoning. *Design Issues, 14*(3), 85–100.

Habraken, N. J. (1985). *The appearance of the form*. Cambridge, MA: Awater Press.

Kan, J. W. T., & Gero, J. S. (2008). Acquiring information from linkography in protocol studies of designing. *Design Studies, 29*(4), 315–337.

Kosslyn, S. M. (1996). *Image and brain: The resolution of the imagery debate*. Cambridge, MA: MIT Press.

Linhares, A., Freitas, A. E. T. A., Mendes, A., & Silva, J. S. (2012). Entanglement of perception and reasoning in the combinatorial game of chess: Differential errors of strategic reconstruction. *Cognitive Systems Research, 13*, 72–86.

Pahl, G., Beitz, W., Feldman, J., & Grote, K. H. (2007). *Engineering design: A systematic approach* (3rd ed.). London: Springer.

Purcell, T., Gero, J. S., Edwards, H., & McNeill, T. (1996). The data in design protocols: The issue of data coding, data analysis in the development of models of the design process. In N. Cross, H. Christiaans, & K. Dorst (Eds.), *Analysing design activity* (pp. 225–252). Chichester: Wiley.

Rosenman, M. A., & Gero, J. S. (1993). Creativity in design using a design prototype approach. In J. S. Gero & M.-L. Maher (Eds.), *Modeling creativity and knowledge-based creative design* (pp. 11–138). Hillsdal: Erlbaum.

Schön, D. A. (1983). *The reflective practitioner*. New York: Basic Books.

Schön, D. A. (1984). Problems, frames and perspectives on designing. *Design Studies, 5*(3), 132–136.

Simon, H. A. (1973). The structure of ill structured problems. *Artificial Intelligence, 4*, 181–201.

Sloman, S. A. (1996). The empirical case for two systems of reasoning. *Psychological Bulletin, 119*(1), 3–22.

Stern, J. (2000). *Metaphor in context*. Cambridge, MA: MIT Press.

Suwa, M., & Tversky, B. (1996). What architects see in their design sketches: implications for design tools. In *Human factors in computing systems, in CHI'96 conference companion* (pp. 191–192). New York: ACM.

Tye, M. (1991). *The imagery debate*. Cambridge, MA: MIT Press.

van der Lugt, R. (2000). Developing a graphic tool for creative problem solving in design groups. *Design Studies, 21*(5), 505–522.

Woodbury, R. F., & Burrow, A. L. (2006). Whither design space? *AIEDAM, 20*, 63–82.

Do, E. Y.-L., & Gross, M. D. (2001). Thinking with diagrams in architectural design. *Artificial Intelligence Review*, 15, 135–149.

Dorst, K., & Cross, N. (2001). Creativity in the design process: Co-evolution of problem and solution. *Design Studies*, 22(5), 425–437.

Eastman, C. M., Simon, H. A. (1968/1985). Protocol analysis. *Urban type structure*. Cambridge: MIT Press.

Fish, J. (2004). Resonance, cognition and creativity. In B. Goldschmidt & W. L. Porter (Eds.), *Design representation* (pp. 151–165). London: Springer.

Fish, J., & Scrivener, S. (1990). Amplifying the mind's eye: Sketching and visual cognition. *Leonardo*, 23, 117–126.

Garza, G. Thompson, W. L., & Kosslyn, S. M. (2002). Brain areas underlying visual mental imagery and visual perception. *Cognitive Brain Research*, 20, 226–241.

Goel, A. & Scott, J. (1989). Analysis of design problem solving. *Design Studies*, 10(1), 54–71.

Goldschmidt, G. (1991). The dialectics of sketching. *Creativity Research Journal*, 4(2), 123–143.

Goldschmidt, G. (1994). The designer as a team of one. In J. A. Cross, H. Christiaans, & K. Dorst (Eds.), *Analysing design activity* (pp. 65–91). Chichester: Wiley.

Goldschmidt, G. (1997). Capturing indeterminism: Representation in the design problem space. *Design Studies*, 18(4), 441–455.

Goldschmidt, G. (2003). The backtalk of self-generated sketches. *Design Issues*, 19(1), 72–88.

Goldschmidt, G. & Tatsa, D. (2005). How good are good ideas? Correlates of ideation quality. *Design Studies*, 26(6), 593–611.

Goldschmidt, G. & Weil, M. (1998). Contents and structure in design reasoning. *Design Issues*, 14(3), 85–100.

Thomson, M. (1983). The appreciation of the poem. Cambridge, MA: Harvard Press.

Kavakli, M., & Gero, J. S. (2002). Acquiring information concurrently with perception: A picture richer of visual imagery. *Design Studies*, 22(4), 313–434.

Kosslyn, S. M. (1994). *Image and brain: The resolution of the imagery debate*. Cambridge, MA: MIT Press.

Liikkanen, L. A., Pieters, A. E. T. A., Mendez, A., & Silva, J. G. (2012). Entanglement of perception and reasoning in the comprehension of visual-difficult content of language recurrences. *Cognitive Science*, 2, 15–35.

Pahl, G., Beitz, W., Feldhusen, J., & Grote, K. H. (2007). *Engineering design* (3rd ed.). London: Springer.

Purcell, A. T., Gero, J. S., Edwards, H., & McNeill, T. (1996). The data in design protocols: The issue of data coding, data analysis in the development of models of the design process. In K. Cross, H. Christiaans, & K. Dorst (Eds.), *Analysing design activity* (pp. 225–252). Chichester: Wiley.

Schön, D. A., & Wiggins, G. (1992). Kinds of seeing and their functions in designing. *Design Studies*, 13(2), 135–156.

Schön, D. A., & Wiggins, G. (1992). Kinds of seeing and their functions in designing. *Design Studies*, 13(2), 135–156.

Schön, D. A. (1983). *The reflective practitioner*. New York: Basic Books.

Suwa, M., & Tversky, B. (1997). What architects and students perceive in their design sketches: A protocol analysis. *Design Studies*, 18(4), 385–403.

Suwa, M., Gero, J. S., & Purcell, T. (1998). Macroscopic analysis of design process based on a scheme for coding designers' cognitive actions. *Design Studies*, 19(4), 455–483.

Simon, H. A. (1973). The structure of ill-structured problems. *Artificial Intelligence*, 4, 181–201.

Stellan, S. A. (1996). The cognitive cost for two systems of representing. *Psychological Bulletin*, 120(4), 3–22.

Stenning, K. (2000). *Seeing reason: Image and language in learning to think*. Oxford: Oxford University Press.

Suwa, M., & Tversky, B. (1996). What architects see in their design sketches: Implications for design tools. In *Human factors in computing systems* (pp. 191–192). New York: ACM.

Tye, M. (1991). *The imagery debate*. Cambridge, MA: MIT Press.

van der Lugt, R. (2000). Developing a graphic tool for creative problem solving in design groups. *Design Studies*, 21(5), 505–522.

Woodbury, R. F., & Burrow, A. L. (2006). Whither design space? *AI EDAM*, 20, 63–82.

Chapter 4
Evaluating Creativity

Linda Candy

Abstract This chapter explores the concept of evaluation and its potential contribution to creativity. The particular focus is on evaluation within those areas of creative practice where the interaction between human beings and digital systems is a central goal. A multi-dimensional model of creativity is introduced that provides a holistic framework for evaluating the actors and elements in creativity. The approach is informed by studies arising from practice-based research, a form of research adopted by creative practitioners for whom the artifact, for example an artwork, is a central concern. The domain from which the ideas and examples are derived is the interactive digital arts, a vibrant, emerging field that affords rich opportunities for interaction design to explore criteria for evaluation arising directly from designing interactive systems that engage people in creative ways.

Keywords Creativity • Evaluation • Reflection-in-action • Design rationale • Interactive art

4.1 Introduction

In many walks of life, creativity is seen as a desirable 'something' that can be beneficial to organizations as well as to individual people and groups. Creativity is highly valued because we believe that it can deliver significant advantages such as gaining a leading edge in business or establishing the basis for a lifetime of satisfaction and even happiness. That creativity is "a good thing" is rarely disputed and yet, when we start to try to be more precise about we mean by creativity, it soon

L. Candy (✉)
Creativity & Cognition Studios, School of Software, Faculty of Engineering and IT,
University of Technology, Sydney, Australia
e-mail: linda@lindacandy.com

J.M. Carroll (ed.), *Creativity and Rationale: Enhancing Human
Experience by Design*, Human–Computer Interaction Series,
DOI 10.1007/978-1-4471-4111-2_4, © Springer-Verlag London 2013

becomes apparent that there are many different views as to what it is. Many careers and businesses have been founded on the notion that it is possible both to define and to promote creativity as an achievable activity. However, if we make claims that it is possible to enhance creativity, we need first to be clear about what exactly we are aiming for: in other words, what do we mean by creativity? Whilst much is known about creativity from research, and the outcomes of creative practice, what is less well known, or perhaps less talked about, is the role of evaluation in creativity. Even more problematic than defining an agreed view of creativity, is the question of whether creativity can be measured and, if so, how can that be achieved?

Evaluation in creative practice is an entirely different matter to that which takes place in a research context, where the generation of new knowledge is as much a part of the expected outcomes as the production of a novel design or artifact. Depending on the particular context or domain conditions, criteria for evaluation may be established prior to or arise during the creative process, may be implicit or explicit, may be shared within a collaborating group or known only to an individual creator. Whichever is the case there are many varied situations where evaluation is both necessary and important to the production of a successful outcome. There is a clear differentiation between judging the worth of a finished artifact and evaluating the creative thinking process. In the first case, this form of evaluation is open to all comers if the finished outcome is made available to a wider constituency. In the second case, the decision-making is within the individual or team and is not usually generally available to outsiders. This is where evaluation meets rationale for, in order to uncover the evaluation process, there is a need for detailed documentation of the decisions taken and the reasons why certain choices were made over others. The contribution of documented rationale also extends to a description of the objects, artifacts and the products that arise from the creative process.

Evaluation in creativity and design rationale are connected by the notion of reflection-in-action. Reflection-in-action that is documented, in field diaries, sketchbooks and logs as part of everyday creative practice, can act as a trace of the generation of new ideas and the exploration of options leading to decision-making in the development of an interactive system. In the interactive arts, practitioner researchers are developing methods for exploring the implications of their artifacts for creative engagement using documented reflective practice in combination with studies of participant engagement. This has provided insights into the creative process that have contributed to our understanding of the interaction between the act of creation, its outcomes and their implications for users.

The chapter explores the concept of evaluation and the way that it can contribute to our understanding of creativity. The particular focus is on evaluation within those areas of creative practice where the interaction between human beings and digital systems is a central goal. The approach is informed by studies arising from practice-based research, a form of research adopted by creative practitioners for whom the artifact, for example an artwork, is a central concern. Evaluating creativity in this context implies being able to characterize meaningfully the particular phenomena we call 'creativity'. In taking this view it becomes clear that the way in which creativity is scoped shapes the frameworks and criteria for evaluation that are used. The domain context from which the ideas and examples are derived is the interactive digital arts, a vibrant, emerging field that affords rich opportunities for exploring questions arising directly from the design of interactive systems that aim to engage people in creative ways.

The ideas and examples that follow are based upon a series of practice-based research studies carried out at the Creativity and Cognition Studios, the University of Technology, Sydney and Beta Space, at the Powerhouse Museum, Sydney, Australia. An evaluation matrix was developed from the audience participation research (Candy and Bilda 2007, 2009). This has been extended to a multi-dimensional model of creativity that proposes a holistic framework for evaluating the actors and elements in creativity. A Multi-dimensional Model of Creativity and Evaluation is described and example criteria for evaluation proposed.

4.2 Creativity and Creativity in Design

This section provides an overview of creativity and creativity in design that draws upon the authors' previous work in the area (Candy 1997; Candy and Edmonds 1994, 1995, 1996, 2002a) and key writings that have informed the multi-dimensional view of creativity proposed in this chapter.

That creativity is a complex human phenomenon is undoubtedly true and this gives rise to a belief that it is too difficult to analyze and inaccessible to evaluation in any measurable sense. Nevertheless, many researchers have dedicated their professional lives to trying to define the fundamentals of this elusive but richly rewarding aspect of human life. Whilst much is known about it, and it is widely believed to be essential to individual wellbeing and the cultural health of local communities and nation states alike, it continues to be contested ground. This is an inevitable result of the sheer range and diversity of creative works emerging from the arts, design, architecture, engineering, science and all fields of endeavor that involve making physical artifacts and products as well as generating new ideas and knowledge. Within each field there are norms and procedures that have taken many years to establish but which are continually being revisited and reworked by the respective communities of expertise to suit the demands of an ever-changing world. In these circumstances, it would be overly optimistic to expect agreement about the exact nature of the creative act within a domain, let alone across the many diverse fields that have claims on creativity.

Creative practitioners in music, visual arts, dance, design etc., make artifacts, install interactive environments, give performances and exhibit the fruits of their creative work to the world at large. Because the outcomes of their efforts are visible to all, as distinct from the largely hidden cognitive mind processes that are necessary to the realization of these outcomes, the public debate as to what is truly creative often centers on artifacts and performances. People with many varied levels of knowledge and experience may take different views of whether or not something is truly 'creative', based upon their appreciation of a particular outcome such as an artwork. However, whilst the creative artifact is clearly important, it has never been enough to help us fully understand the complex, interwoven and interdependent dimensions of creativity.

4.2.1 Creativity Research

In research communities, approaches to the study of creativity differ in three main respects: (1) the type of research design, whether experimental, psychometric, observational etc. (2) the focus of the research, whether on human attributes cognitive processes or features of creative outcomes, and (3) the type of information that is used for the basis of evidence, by which is meant whether the time frame is present (real-time observation) or past (historical data) and whether the situation is artificial (laboratory) or natural (real world settings). There are significant differences in the way that the subject has been studied. Sternberg (1999) presents a variety of approaches by leading researchers in their respective fields. In recent times, there have been advances in our understanding of the nature of creativity and a growing consensus that features can be identified that distinguish creative thinking from everyday routine thinking. Weisberg is a notable dissenter (Weisberg 2006) from the more commonly held view that creative cognition has characteristics such as divergent thinking, problem finding and incubation that distinguish it from routine structuring, planning and problem solving (e.g. Finke et al. 1992; Cross et al. 1996).

Studies of the personalities and attributes of people, indicates that there are certain traits that seem to be indicators of greater creative potential. Creative attributes that have been investigated include: independent attitudes, a diverse range of interests, a rejection of external controls, high confidence levels, intrinsic or extrinsic motivation and risk taking inclinations (Collins and Amabile 1999). Conversely, low confidence, risk avoidance and fear of criticism imply poor potential for breaking barriers and moving beyond conventional thinking. Amabile uses results from motivational and organizational research to support the development of models and instruments for assessing incentives and obstacles to creativity in the work place (Amabile 1985).

The creative process has frequently been studied in its "small acts" such as identifying how incubation takes place by way of laboratory experiments. Alternatively, creativity may be seen in the larger scale, where all issues, including the creative outcome itself, are considered (Partridge and Rowe 1994). A variant on this approach is to examine creative work (as defined by the creative outcomes) in terms of the totality of the person's activities. Creativity looked at this way can be considered to be characteristics (e.g. mental operations such as memory, recognition, intelligence etc.) that are combined in an exceptional way so as to maximize their effectiveness (Perkins 1981). The traits might be extended to include basic cognitive capabilities, values, motivations and strategies. Gardner describes creativity as the human capacity regularly to solve problems or to fashion products in a domain, in a way that is initially novel but ultimately acceptable in a culture. Based on his theory of multiple intelligences, he categorizes different types of human intelligence as well as the kinds of creativities associated with them and the sources of such creative activities. He also believes that "creativity is most likely to be fostered by a transformative atmosphere" (Gardner 1989: 14). If 'atmosphere' is important to creativity, this implies that context matters and it is necessary to include it in any creativity model.

In relation to the context in which creativity operates, a number of factors have been identified which bring people centered and contextual factors together. Contextual factors include the physical environment, the home and workplace, the conditions of the field or domain, as well as the social and cultural dimensions. Lubart has concluded that creativity is context dependent and that we need to be aware of cross-cultural differences. Western culture values production and originality above seeking inner truths in the way that many Eastern cultures do. They also differ greatly in relation to the recognition given to outstanding individual work over collective endeavor (Lubart 1999). However, although the context has been increasingly recognized as important to creativity, in the main, socially and culturally defined influences have received less attention than people and process areas. Contextual influences on creativity include access to physical and intellectual resources, rewards and incentives and culturally defined value systems including legal regulations and organizational constraints. In studies of art and technology collaboration, the role of the physical and technical environment proved to be critical. Without the ready availability of flexible software and hardware platforms, organizational support and access to expertise, the possibilities of producing innovative outcomes would have been seriously limited (Edmonds et al. 2005). In addition, opportunities for studying audiences and designing innovative interactive systems are enhanced significantly if they take place in appropriate public settings (Reeves 2011).

One identifiable issue that divides opinion about the nature of creativity, and thereby influences attitudes to its evaluation, is the role of the unconscious, inspired mind versus the conscious, rational mind. The unconscious mind school of thinking has given rise to many assumptions about the nature of creativity. It is sometimes characterized as indefinable but evidently beautiful and surprising. This view often comes with a warning that as soon as rational thought is introduced, it can interfere with the creative process. By contrast, those who believe in the power of the conscious mind are more open to the possibility that there is a systematic way of understanding creativity. Scientific models inevitably follow this second view given that they embody an implied assumption that all natural phenomena can ultimately be revealed, described, shared and challenged.

These diametrically opposite positions can be traced back to Plato's concept of divine inspiration and Aristotle's claims for the action of the deliberative, rational mind. From the Renaissance, the rational thinkers began to prevail and we have inherited those patterns of thought. Nevertheless, it is fair to say that particularly in popular culture, and also within the creative arts, the mystery of unconscious mind still has strong residual power. Those of the scientific school have to admit that we are far from having a definitive account of human creativity in all its dimensions, let alone are able to agree a predictive model. This has become all the more so since the initial primary focus on creative cognition has begun to given way to a wider view of creativity that includes complex socio-cultural influences.

When we take a broad view of the research and practice in creativity, it soon becomes clear that there is no simple pathway to a complete picture. For a full understanding, it is essential to take account of many factors that influence the process and its outcomes, from the creator's personal attributes and cognitive style, to social influences, environmental constraints and cultural values. By bringing together three dimensions of the creativity spectrum: creative attributes, creative process and creative context, we can start to scope the ways in which those factors promote or hinder the manifestation of creative behavior and outcomes. In design in particular, the role of creativity has its own domain specific interests and the resulting research has been influenced by those factors.

4.2.2 Creativity in Design

A number of key contributions to creativity in design research and our understanding of its many elements have been made. In a useful analysis, Williams, Ostwald and Askland structure the discussion of creative design research around Rhodes' four category scheme (Rhodes 1961) for studies of creativity (Williams et al. 2010, chapter 1). They also make the point that the association of designing with ill-defined or 'wicked' problems has heavily influenced creative design research. Because design involves the development of new artifacts and products, and, frequently, the problems are complex, it is assumed that creativity is an inherent part of the process. Much of the focus of design research is on the designer as problem solver or solution finder. This focus, whilst not ignoring personal attributes and environmental and social factors altogether, has meant that the predominant view of creativity is that it is a thinking process required to generate novel ideas to produce innovative solutions, and that this in itself defines the creative designer.

It is worth noting that design is also seen in many areas as being primarily concerned with the conceptual and structural aspects of a problem that, once solved, does not necessarily carry over into the making process, usually the remit of construction engineers and others. This has implications for how the role of the artifact and the influence of the making process, is perceived in certain areas of design research. It might also partly explain why practice-based research approaches in which the artifact plays a central role have yet to penetrate design research. The role of the artifact in the creative process in the digital arts differs fundamentally because the designer and implementer of the physical, or indeed virtual, artifact is often the same person. This does, of course, depend upon the scale of the system under development and, where it requires multiple levels of expertise, collaboration is commonplace. Nevertheless, the artist is usually deeply involved in the craft aspects of the work from carving wood to software programming required; this includes elements of the overall design such as drawings, specifications, scenarios and prototypes (Edmonds 2007; Candy and Edmonds 2002b, 2011).

4.2.3 Can Creativity Be Evaluated?

The question of whether or not it is really possible to evaluate creativity may be answered in different ways. There is no consensus about this issue one way or the other amongst researchers in creativity and even less amongst creative practitioners. In interactive digital arts, evaluation is on the research agenda and has given rise to questions as to how we should consider the nature of creativity in this context. Should we judge creativity by the way participating audiences respond or behave, or by the features of the artworks themselves, or by the abilities of the creators to make such art? An important question is whether it is possible to establish realistic measures for evaluating creativity that can be agreed amongst the relevant stakeholders and also be applied to many scenarios involving interactive art systems.

The answer to the first question often depends upon the particular conceptual framework or definition of what creativity is. Those who believe that creativity is impossible to define because it is inaccessible to direct observation (e.g. locate accurately in the brain) are likely to be most skeptical about the feasibility of evaluation. Others believe that the observed phenomena of creativity in action and the outcomes of the process provide some access to what happens; those holding this view are usually more open to the possibilities of evaluation. The visible externalization of people's creative work expressed as artworks or system designs are part of the evidence that can be evaluated. In the case of interactive art systems, the participant behavior and responses can be accessed using an appropriate research methodology.

4.3 Evaluation

The word 'evaluation' is used to characterize and assess subjects of interest in a wide range of enterprises, including the arts, sciences, government, health care, and other services. In the context of the subject matter of this chapter, it is used to describe assessing and judging the value or worth of a particular idea or artifact both during the creative process and afterwards. Whether the process is systematic or ad hoc, evaluation depends upon criteria and measures that are situated and domain specific. This evaluation covers a range of possible processes that involve ascertaining the value or worth of a thing or an event or situation or a person: for example: judging whether or not a person is suitable to be awarded an art commission on the basis of track record; or assessing the performance of a system by assigning a grade or score; or appraising of the value of a set of organizational procedures against competing programs. Evaluation in this last sense can include a comparison of effects against goals and strategies by examining original objectives and assessing what was accomplished. It can be formative, by which is meant taking place during the lifetime of a project, with the intention of improving the strategies, functions and outcomes. It can also be summative, drawing lessons from a completed project that can be compared with other similar types.

Whatever the context, evaluation is always tailored to the approach, needs, purpose and methodology of that context. This means that it involves exercising judgments based on criteria that are either established prior to, or during the design process. To evaluate successfully may necessitate the systematic collection and analysis of data needed to make decisions. On the other hand, expert judgment can often be exercised without recourse to such studies because it is founded upon many years of experiential knowledge.

Evaluation is fundamental to the creative process. However, it is rarely given the prominence it deserves in the general discourse that comprises creativity research and practice. Indeed for many creative practitioners, the very word 'evaluation' suggests something too systematic or even 'scientific' to sit comfortably with the complexities and uncertainties of creativity. Nevertheless, evaluation is a key activity in creativity that involves exercising judgments based on criteria that are established prior to or during the actual designing and making process. For evaluation to contribute to a successful outcome, the practitioner needs to have the necessary information including constraints on the options under consideration.

The practice-based research conducted by practitioner researchers is documented in the book, *'Interacting: Art, Research and the Creative Practitioner'* (Candy and Edmonds 2011). The concept of creative engagement and experiential principles for designing systems that stimulate such creative engagement is new thinking in interaction design that illustrates how the digital interactive arts can contribute to interaction design and HCI (Bilda 2011). From this work, a matrix of creativity evaluation categories, criteria and measures was developed (Candy and Bilda 2009). The matrix for evaluating creativity represents three standpoints: the capabilities of the creator, the audience, or more accurately, participant, experiences, and the features of the interactive systems as artworks. This initial matrix has been extended to include creative processes for both creator and audience participant (i.e. working practices and interaction experiences) and contextual factors in the form of the physical and technical environment in which the creative acts and events take place, including the influence of physical and technical resources and real world constraints. In the model of creativity described later evaluation plays a pivotal role.

4.3.1 Evaluation and Human-Computer Interaction

Evaluation is the key to improving design processes, design of new technologies and human-computer interaction. Evaluation studies are well established in the field of Human-Computer Interaction (HCI) as well as interaction design contexts in general. The studies include evaluation of how new technologies are used in the workplace, evaluation of interactive experiences such as web design, interactive products and evaluation of design activities in order to improve the quality and efficiency of a design process and to develop support tools for creative designing. In the history of HCI, 'interaction' was primarily studied through effectiveness and efficiency of a system and has been measured by focusing on usability, user's understanding, the number of errors users' make, and the amount of time required to complete a task. However, for some time, there has been an awareness that quantitative methods that seek to assign precise metrics through usability mea-surement such as that prescribed in ISO9241 standards (e.g. Bevan and MacLeod 1994) are inappropriate. Even before the extension of user experience through new forms of interactive systems, there were doubts. Later on, Saul Greenberg and Bill Buxton summarized these limitations (Greenberg and Buxton 2008) and Gilbert Cockton argued that usability should be replaced by a 'value-based' approach (Cockton 2008).

That task-oriented evaluation techniques do not satisfy interactive art experi-ence evaluation objectives has been understood in the art and technology world for some time (Candy and Edmonds 2002a, b). It was clear early on to some HCI researchers working at the boundaries of interaction design, creativity and art that, in order to address creativity support, it is necessary to question familiar approaches such as predictive, well-defined task hierarchies and usability measures of efficiency and effectiveness. The move towards evaluation frameworks that involve non-predictive, open-ended activities operating in situated scenarios and subject to behavioral rather than performance measures has been ongoing for some time but is only more recently become apparent to the mainstream because of the significant transformation that interactive art brings to user experiences. Recent trends in HCI research have begun to focus on fun, pleasure, goodness and beauty (Hassenzahl 2004; Jordan 2000; Tractinsky et al. 2000) as experiential goals. For example, Hassenzahl argued that evaluation should take the role of affect and emotions into account to better understand people's experience of technology (Hassenzahl 2004).

The evaluation of user, or rather, participant, experience of interactive artworks often involves measurement of aesthetic appreciation and the various engagement qualities which are dependent on personal traits, motivations, expectations, emotions and cognitive states of the audience. Those experiences that involve open-ended activity tend towards the creative end of human activity and, as such, are hardly ever measurable in quantitative ways. From what we know about the way creativity works, we need to apply evaluation methods and tools that reveal creative cognition such as exploratory thinking, problem finding, parallel ways of thinking and a vari-ety of cognitive styles. Audience or participant experience evaluation is conducted using several methods such as direct and lateral observations in the context of expe-rience, contextual enquiries (interviews with the audience during their experience of an interactive system) and/or expert workshops (where experts are invited to experi-ence and discuss an interactive system). These methods can help the interaction designer to understand to what extent user/viewer expectations are met and how to further develop the interaction design.

4.3.2   Evaluation, Design Rationale and Reflective Practice

Evaluation is a key activity in creative design that can be revealed through documentation from design rationale. The introduction of rationale has been an important contribution to the quest for clarity and traceability in design decision-making. Design rationale may be thought of as structured records of design that support the understanding of decisions taken and allow designers to give better informed reconsideration to them at a later stage.

A software system can be viewed as an artifact that embodies implicit theoretical constructs that are realized as functional and operational requirements (Carroll and Campbell 1989). Structures are chosen because of their ability to achieve the intended functionality, and such choices may be evaluated against various criteria. During the design process, the ideas are modified and there is a clarification and refinement of intended functions and features. There may be additional factors arising from the context of the project that affect the way the design is carried out: for example the need to keep sight of general applicability whilst meeting the domain specific requirements, or the influence of the given hardware platform and software tools. Whatever the situation, the relationship between designers' decision making and the design outcome is not necessarily transparent and this is can be a problem when it comes to system maintenance. The explicit listing of decisions made during a design process, and the reasons why those decisions were made provides a means to record and communicate the reasoning and justification behind a design decision, including alternatives considered and constraints that affected the decision-making including why alternatives were rejected. The successful application of design rationale to software system design can provide a form of communication of intent from the designer to those who are to maintain the system.

My previous work in design rationale led to some caution as to its viability for designing creativity support systems (Candy 1993). The experience of design rationale in practice was that creative designing was disrupted by the required analytic considerations. The designing we observed was strongly synthetic in character, based upon models of known systems and experimentation with new functions and features during the implementation process. The rationale that did emerge was for the most part a rationalization of design decisions rather than a true account of the process as it unfolded. The observation of the design process and its outcomes led us to conclude that design rationale as applied in the form used, did not necessarily support the creative design process (Candy and Edmonds 1993). Thus, it was argued that whilst design rationale might be valuable as a post hoc method for communicating between different stages of the design process, other methods were needed to facilitate communication and sharing during that process.

In order to communicate the rationale for those decisions, the first step is to articulate them in a sharable form. A promising approach to the externalization of decision-making during the design process is being explored within practice-based research in the creative arts in the form of documented reflective practice. The approach builds upon a normal part of creative practice whereby practitioners draw and note ideas, designs and options in their sketch and notebooks. In this way, the documentation of tentative ideas and how they are worked into firmer proposals through testing and evaluation is a familiar and integral part of creativity. In practice-based research, documented reflective practice and empirical studies are frequently brought together (Candy 2011).

Seeking an understanding of the decision making process is a critical aspect of creative work. For the practitioner, creating a work and then reflecting on the process and outcome, is a pathway to understanding how to progress the work further. Indeed the process of making an artifact can facilitate a form of 'thinking-in-action'. The role of 'reflection-in-action', first proposed by Donald Schön (1983), has proven to be effective in supporting this process. Schön's ideas have been influential because he located research enquiry within practice itself and asserted the value of practitioner knowledge as having distinctive contributions to make to professional capabilities. He recognized that what he referred to as 'technical rationality' was inadequate for improving professional development and thereby challenged existing orthodoxies in research traditions. His concept of 'reflection-in-action' provides a plausible explanation for how the practitioner makes explicit some of the tacit knowledge (Polyani 1966) embedded in action and, thereby, learns how to act differently. In later work, Schön described the reflective design process in terms of 'seeing->drawing->seeing'. In making a drawing, the designer externalizes an emerging idea through the identification of patterns, and in doing so, is able to construct a meaning beyond the patterns themselves. Thus, by creating something it becomes possible to design "as a reflective conversation with the materials of the situation" (Schön 1992: 5). In a similar sense, when an artist creates something and reflects upon it, the process is a form of 'seeing' again. Reflective practice in creativity involves multiple iterations, which can be summed up as: 'creating ->reflecting->creating again->reflecting again'. There is, moreover, an important extra dimension to reflective creative practice when the practitioner researcher chooses to take an empirical route to new understandings. By adding a principled enquiry stream to reflective practice, based on gathering and analyzing observations of interactive works live with participating audiences, the process becomes one of 'creating->reflecting->creating again->investigating->creating again ...'.

There are notable differences in the way 'reflection-in-action' has been incorporated into creative practice compared to professional practice more generally. This is because a major part of the creative process involves taking actions towards creating an entity that stands separate from the insights gained from the reflections themselves. This entity or artifact has its own integrity and value quite apart from the insights. The development of an artifact may draw upon, even embody, the insights obtained by looking back at the recorded reflections but it is, nevertheless, part of an externalized reality that invites a different kind of response. Thus, documented reflective practice, as an integral part of creative practice, provides an opportunity to reveal idea generation and decision-making in explicit ways. If part of the practitioner's normal working practice it can support the process of identifying a rationale. That rationale can, in turn, contribute to evaluation.

4.4   Dimensions of Creativity and Evaluation:
A Multi-dimensional Model

The model of creativity described in this section and shown in Fig. 4.1 below is informed by previous work in creativity research from which a multi-dimensional perspective on creativity arose. The earliest classification of the elements of creativity that comes closest to it is that by Rhodes in which studies that address: (1) cognitive and behavioral aspects, (2) personal attributes, expertise and skills, (3) outcomes such as designs and artifacts, and (4) environmental conditions: the 4Ps scheme of Process, Person, Product and Press (Rhodes 1961). This kind of representation of creativity is holistic and multi-dimensional. It is intended to act as a larger framework within which it is possible to adopt a narrower focus of attention whilst, at the same time, acknowledging that this is not the totality of creativity. This approach serves the requirements of evaluation well in that it is then easier to identify criteria and measures that apply in different ways to the different aspects of creativity.

The Multi-dimensional Model of Creativity and Evaluation (MMCE) shown in Fig. 4.1 has four elements: people, process, product and context. The MMCE Model represents four key aspects of creativity in the interactive digital arts. More broadly, it could equally be seen to be applicable to emerging forms of interactive system design envisaged by Hassenzhal and others mentioned previously.

The elements of the model and corresponding features that can be evaluated against each are presented in Table 4.1 below.

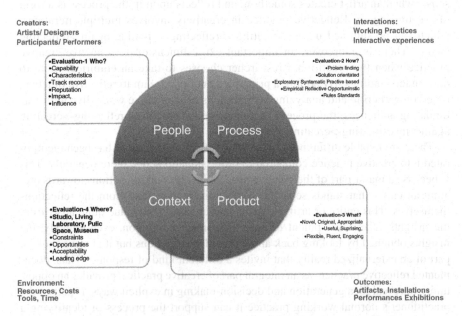

Creators:
Artists/ Designers
Participants/ Performers

Interactions:
Working Practices
Interactive experiences

•Evaluation-1 Who?
•Capability
•Characteristics
•Track record
•Reputation
•Impact,
•Influence

•Evaluation-2 How?
•Prolem finding
•Solution orientated
•Exploratory Syntematic Practive based
•Empirical Reflective Opportuninstic
•Rules Standards

People   Process

Context   Product

•Evaluation-4 Where?
•Studio, Living
Laboratory, Pulic
Space, Museum
•Constraints
•Opportunities
•Acceptability
•Leading edge

•Evaluation-3 What?
•Novel, Original, Appropriate
•Useful, Suprising,
•Flexible, Fluent, Engaging

Environment:
Resources, Costs
Tools, Time

Outcomes:
Artifacts, Installations
Performances Exhibitions

Fig. 4.1 Model of creativity and evaluation: creators, interactions, outcomes, environment

Table 4.1 Categories of creativity: actors and elements with evaluation measures: criteria, qualities, value

Categories in creativity	Actors and elements	Instances	Feature descriptors	Outcomes	Criteria, qualities, values to measure
People – who is involved?	Creators	(i) Designer, artist	Imagination, artistry, expertise, skill experience, intention, reputation	(ii) Participant, performer	Profile, demographic, motivation, skills, experience, curiosity commitment
Process – how is it done?	Interactions	(i) Working practices	Inspirational, solution driven, goal oriented, problem solver, systematic, exploratory, reflective, risk taking	(ii) Interactive behaviors	Opportunistic, adventurous, curious, cautious, expert, knowledgeable, experienced
Product – what comes out?	Outcomes	(i) Artifacts, installations	Novel, original, surprising, compelling, adaptable, aesthetically pleasing, effective	(ii) Performances, experiences	Immediate, engaging, purposeful, enhancing, exciting, disturbing
Context – where does it happen and with what?	Environments	(i) Studio, living laboratory (ii) Public spaces, museums	Physical space, light, technical facilities, rules, costs, time resources, effort, organizational constraints/support	(i) Prototypes (ii) Exhibitions	Design quality, usable, convincing, adaptable, effective, innovative, transcendent

Table 4.1 shows four interrelated and interdependent elements: who? how? what? where? with associated feature descriptors. It also indicates the kinds of characteristics or traits we might expect to find in people, processes, products and the context of creativity in interactive digital art. Against each of these it is possible to identify measures of evaluation such as criteria, qualities, values. The precise measures for evaluation are set by the specific context: for example, for the awarding of prizes of excellence in a given field, the focus of attention is quite likely to be on the outcomes and people involved rather than the process or contextual factors.

4.5 Actors and Elements for Evaluating Creativity

4.5.1 People as Creators: Who Is Involved in Creativity?

There are two categories of people who play different parts in the creation of the interactive artwork or art system: the artist or designer and the participant or performer. These actors have different but interrelated roles depending upon the kind of interactive work or installation. The creator artist initiates the work or project and establishes the design features, functions and intended qualities of the art system to be created. In interactive artworks, it is not always possible to predict the behavior and nor it is desirable in most cases, because the intention is usually to enable the participant audience to have an influence on the way it behaves visually, sonically or otherwise. The participant might also be a dancer whose movements are captured in such a way as to create images and sounds dynamically. Of course, it is the artist's vision that sets the parameters within which the participant or performer operates and these can be tightly or loosely defined depending on his or her intentions. Thus the participant role as creator depends upon the opportunities provided by the artist to engage in interaction that is some way affects the physical manifestation of the artwork.

4.5.1.1 Studies Related to Creator Capability

There have been many studies of people in creativity research and the results are interesting to consider as general indicators of attributes of creativity potential. However, where the situation is novel and previously unexplored, as in the case of interactive art, our understanding of the people involved whether as artist creators or participant creators, is new territory. It is also a field where interdisciplinary collaboration is almost always the norm. Therefore, if we are to understand what forms of creator capability matter here, studies of collaboration are essential.

In the COSTART art-technology collaboration project, studies were carried out which identified creator characteristics according to three dimensions: cognitive style, knowledge and communication. It was then possible to see which features were present in the creator collaborations. Success factors were then identified on the basis of the evaluation of outcomes and participant opinion. For example, communication attributes such as mutual openness, shared language, continuous rather than intermittent, exchange, mutual flexibility and reciprocal affirmation of one another were all positive indicators of a successful creative collaboration. Cognitive style, a term used to denote thinking and making as revealed by external behavior and self evaluation, involved such features as exploratory versus goal-oriented thinking, complementary roles and skills and a blend of traditional and digital methods (see Candy 2002, chapter 4 'Collaboration', pp. 56–66, for a detailed account). Phalip's study of filmmakers and composers confirmed the critical role of communication skills in creative collaboration (Phalip 2011).

In her studies of collaboration in the creation of interactive art systems, Zhang analyzed the communication patterns of inter-disciplinary work. She identified five modes of communication pattern: face-to face, proposal assisted (i.e. project specification), computer-assisted, interactive artifact assisted and drawing assisted. These findings provided the basis for evaluating the role of computer-mediated communication in a creative context. She found that the use of mediation tools varied a great deal over time and that strategies were needed to select the most effective support tool at a given stage in the process (Zhang and Candy 2007a, b; Zhang 2011). Another study by Leggett discovered that participants could be divided into two persona categories: the 'quickie' people used ready to hand prompts for maximum speed whereas the 'explorer' personas took time to add to their knowledge and experience of the system. Having differentiated in this way, he was able to observe different kinds of interaction behavior according to the system affordances. In this way, he linked cognitive style to interaction style (Leggett 2011).

These studies illustrate the range of results that arise from practice-based research studies carried out by practitioners working in creative technologies. An interesting feature of practice-based research is the way in which practitioners use results from empirical studies to inform and evaluate subsequent creative products (Edmonds and Candy 2010).

4.5.1.2 Evaluating People as Creators: Artists, Designers, Participants, Performers

What might be the role of evaluation in respect of people as creators? Although this is a difficult and often sensitive business, there is no doubt it is a form of evaluation that is frequently carried out with varying degrees of visibility. Track records are evaluated by funding bodies when people bid for prizes or commissions or grants. Juries and selection panels for awarding prizes rely heavily upon the evaluation of people's ability to be creative. This usually takes place in conjunction with appraisal of previous works and so people and product are commonly evaluated together. In certain circumstances, other factors, such as regional distribution, may also be taken into account, and in this way, factors outside the control of the individual or group applicant may play a part.

What ever the situation, evaluation according to whether or not the person (or team) who creates works demonstrates particular skills, knowledge and creative sensibilities is a necessary part of assessment for the distribution of funds to support creative work. The creator must be able to demonstrate an ability to create an outstanding work where subject matter, artistic ideas and technique are combined well to produce a coherent outcome. He or she must be able to demonstrate an ability to make work that is exploratory, creative and imaginative. Interesting ideas are presented in intelligent and surprising ways. Key features that might be considered in the visual arts in particular, are capabilities in: composition and interpretation, content selection, ideas and techniques, artistic expression and individual responsiveness.

Some examples of how these capabilities can be expressed as criteria follow.
Criteria for evaluating creator capability:

1. The creator must be able to demonstrate an ability to create an artistic outcome where subject matter, ideas and technique are combined well to produce a coherent outcome.
2. The creator must be able to demonstrate an ability to make work that is exploratory, creative and imaginative. Interesting ideas are presented in intelligent and surprising ways.
3. In respect of Composition and Interpretation, the creator must be able to demonstrate the ability to:

   • Select subject matter that is appropriate to a given theme
   • Manipulate ideas and techniques in a coherent manner
   • Express ideas visually (visual communication)
   • Respond in an individual and personal way

The People as Creators category can yield information about the potential of the artist creator based on prior performance and expertise. However, these kinds of criteria are less appropriate when it comes to evaluating the role of the participant creator, something that might be necessary only in limited circumstances such as suitability to perform highly skilled dance. It might also be a factor in research undertaken by creator artists or designers who are seeking the participation of people with particular abilities and experience to suit the requirements of a particular project.

4.5.2 Process as Interactions: How Does Creativity Take Place?

The second category, Process, is concerned with understanding how different types of creators work creatively. For the artist/designer this involves consideration of how an individual's working practices lead to the creation of an artifact and for the participant/performer, the way they interact and the experience it entails. There is likely to be interaction between the participant interaction and the ongoing development of the work by the artist. Understanding participant or performer behavior or response may involve more than casual observation by the artist seeking to develop the work further in the light of interactive experience. Interaction can occur in any number of different ways or styles and participant actions and the feedback can be designed to be minimal or ornamental, for example. We can apply evaluation concepts to "the nature of interaction itself" and not just to the appearance of the objects that facilitate it (Boden 2010: 217). Examples of the properties that Boden identifies as pertaining to the aesthetics of interaction are predictability and 'attributability' (to what extent is the audience able to detect that they are causing change). In relation to predictability and 'attributability', she notes that artists differ in the degree of awareness expected of the participant audience.

> Some interactive artists say that the changes in the computerized product/environment should be clearly attributable by the human person (i.e. the audience) to his/her actions. The artists may or may not deem it acceptable for this 'attributability' to dawn slowly on the person concerned, as opposed to being near-instantly recognizable... (Boden 2010: 219).

This implies that establishing criteria for evaluation of an interactive experience will inevitably depend upon the artist's intentions for the work. Such criteria might be very different for a museum or galley curator aiming to evaluate the interactive experience from the audience's perspective. In evaluating interactive experience, practitioners in the interactive arts have turned to practice-based research to develop a deeper level of understanding about participant experience for a discussion of approaches and methods (Candy 2011, chapter 2).

4.5.2.1 Studies Related to Interactive Experience

In the world of participative interactive art, understanding the process aspects is central to creative practitioners and researchers in the field. The experience of an art system has many dimensions according to the purposes of the artists. That experience can be immediate and short lived or subtle and long term depending upon the nature of the works. HCI as a discipline has much to gain from learning from the studies conducted in this area.

The results discussed in the following section are drawn from studies of ten newly created interactive art systems by practitioner researchers involving many public and expert participants. Systematic evaluations conducted over 2 years has led to an accumulation of knowledge about audience behavior and interactivity, which has advanced our understanding of the nature of interaction between participants and interactive systems. This form of a systematic analysis enabled the researchers to better understand participants' behavioral patterns, emotions and thinking processes in relation to different outcomes of the creative process. A 'Creative Engagement Model' was the culmination of this work (Bilda et al. 2008). This is a model based on a definition of an interactive experience as a reflective and transformative dialogue between the audience and the interactive art system. It represents interaction modes and phases of audience behavior in relation to different kinds of art works. From the knowledge accrued, Bilda, as an interaction designer, was able to transform the descriptions of audience engagement into experience design principles. These guides to designing interactive systems are intended to achieve engaging and creative experiences (Bilda 2011). The guidelines can also be expressed as criteria for evaluation of creative engagement.

A discussion follows in which criteria for evaluation are proposed.

4.5.2.2 Evaluating Process as Interactions: Working Practices, Interactive Experience

Interaction with Interactive art systems are particularly interesting in that, not only do people exhibit different kinds of behavior faced with different examples of works but the works themselves change in response to audience presence. By adopting appropriate observational methods, it is possible to assess the degree and quality of engagement that participants have with different works.

If an interactive work excites immediate attention and appears to elicit playful behavior, we can say that the work has the quality of immediate engagement. If, having obtained the audience's attention, people continue to interact with the work for a given length of time we can say there is sustained engagement. If, as the audience attention declines with familiarity and the passing of time, the work changes unexpectedly leading to renewed interest, then a transformation may take place. This also depends on how the audience interprets the change. If the unexpected change in the system is seen as frustrating, there might be no further engagement. On the other hand, the audience may welcome the unexpected change as a positive challenge and embrace this as a new way to look at the same work. At this point there is a high possibility that audience experience will be transformed. We call this transformation in the experiential paradigm creative engagement. Creative engagement is sustainable and rewarding for the audience. It often makes the experience a 'memorable' one, rather than a 'pretty' one.

Criteria for evaluation can be expressed as follows:

1. For a work to be deemed engaging, the participant should exhibit observable responses. There are likely to be different levels of engagement depending on whether or not the audience has had prior experience of this kind of artwork or installation or similar.
2. The participant responses demonstrate active engagement in three ways: Immediate, Sustained or Creative. The categories are defined as follows:
   - *Immediate* engagement: the work grabs immediate attention and yet is not so mundane as to create boredom.
   - *Sustained* engagement: the work must excite curiosity in the and also be accessible to a general audience.
   - *Creative engagement*: the work must excite immediate attention and encourage an audience to interact with it in a playful/purposeful way. As attention declines with familiarity and time, changes take place in the work that renew audience engagement.

If unexpected change leads to frustration in the participants, engagement is negative and therefore not creative; if unexpected change leads to positive attitudes in audience, a transformation takes place that defines nature of creative engagement. Any assessment of creative engagement is more complex than the above suggests and requires an understanding of audience psychology and behavior, as people move through different levels of experience. There are two indicators for assessment: (1) behavioral change and (2) conceptual change. Participants often demonstrate observably different behavior before and after the unexpected change in the system. They may describe their tactical changes to interact with the unexpectedness. The behavior change observed in real time should be confirmed with participant's retrospective reports or with in-depth post-experience interviews. Participants may demonstrate a conceptual transformation in time. This is a shift in how they understand and interact with the system, from the beginning of their experience to the now. It is possible to track this change by comparing how participants describe the work in the beginning and at the end of their experience. These two descriptions must be distinctive. Another way of assessing conceptual change is to take the point where participants describe the system anthropomorphically: e.g. by ascribing decisions to the system's choice.

4.5.3 Product as Artifacts: What Are the Outcomes of Creativity?

The third category is that of the product of the creator's process. These are various depending on the genre (e.g. sound, visual imagery, performance, hybrid forms). There are many ways to evaluate the artifacts, installations and performances. The creator's own evaluation may be carried out through informal reflection or documented reflection-in-action or evaluation studies based upon practitioner defined theoretical frameworks. Peer group critique or the art historian's longer view also can be used to places the work in the context of other work in the genre.

4.5.3.1 Studies Related to Outcomes: Artifacts, Performances, Experiences

Studies have shown that designing and implementing interactive art systems can engage audiences in a creative way. Edmonds describes how categories of interaction have evolved during his exploration of the implications of creating artworks that are dynamic, responsive, ambient etc. (Edmonds 2010, 2011). He also shows how interaction itself has evolved into the notion of participant experience. Artworks can be evaluated in terms of whether they embody features that are 'attracting', 'sustaining' or 'relating' to an audience. Taking this further, a number of studies of participant experience of interactive artworks were carried out in order to understand whether that experience relates to the artist/designer's intentions (Bilda et al. 2006).

Costello also analyzed creator behavior in her practice-based research on play enhancing art systems. She combined knowledge from the literature on play with evidence from her participant interaction studies to derive a set of interaction design strategies for creating playful art systems. The aim was to create interactive works that embodied features identified in the 'pleasure framework' (Costello 2007) such as the participants' ability to experience discovery, danger, fantasy, camaraderie, subversion etc. This framework was used during conceptual development to create a picture of the type of pleasures she wanted her new artworks to evoke. The resulting new works were then evaluated in terms of whether or not they met the criteria derived from the framework (Costello 2011). Note that Costello's product evaluation was carried out against criteria based on participant response. However, there are other types of criteria that may be drawn from domain knowledge based on qualities of the particular genre as discussed in the next section.

4.5.3.2 Evaluating Product as Outcomes: Artifacts, Installations, Performances

Evaluation according to the result or outcome of creativity such as works of art and performances, can be divided into two main categories: those that are perceived to be creative to the individual concerned and those which have been recognized as historically significant over the passage of time, according to Boden's two types of creativity: 'P'-creative or 'H'-creative (Boden 1990). If, on the other hand, the work is being judged as an entrant in a competition, the criteria for evaluation will necessarily appraise its intrinsic qualities against other comparable works.

Typical features for judging artworks include composition, aesthetic, affect, content, and technique.

Criteria for evaluation can be expressed as follows:

- the composition of work should be coherent, exhibit shape and balance between order and complexity.
- the work should exhibit outstanding visual and sound qualities in color, line and form.
- the work should be pleasing, challenging, exciting, original etc.
- the content should be appropriate and effective for the chosen subject matter
- the execution should demonstrate high quality technique that fits the form.

Such criteria are very general in themselves and whilst they might be adaptable to fit interactive systems, they could be seen to be inadequate for the sheer range and diversity of the genre. It is interesting, therefore, to consider how criteria for judging the digital arts are specified by the Prix Ars Electronica, an international competition for Cyber Arts and the foremost event of its kind today. Ars Electronica has served as an interdisciplinary platform for those who use the computer as a medium for implementing and designing creative projects at the interface of art, technology and society. The Interactive Art category is dedicated to interactive works in all forms and formats, from installations to performances.

Entries are judged by a Jury of experts in the order of their arrival and according to the following categories:

- Aesthetics
- Originality
- Excellence of execution
- Compelling conception
- Innovation in technique of the presentation

At the top of the agenda is artistic quality in the development and design of the interaction as well as a harmonious dialog between the content level and the interaction level—that is, the inherent principles of interaction and the interfaces that implement them. Of particular interest is the sociopolitical relevance of the interaction as manifested by its innate potential to expand the scope of human action. Jurors look for innovative technological concepts blended with outstanding and effective design.

The Prix Ars Electronica today has directed its aims towards larger goals than simply rewarding individuals and groups for their efforts. It has used the prize giving and the evaluation criteria it specifies, to encourage the production of art projects that aim to enhance human existence. The quest for bettering human life through the digital arts is a powerful indication of the growing potential of the field to propose new models for improved ways of using energy and resources; new concepts and ideas for a world that has become more mobile and more globalized; measures and projects designed to enable broader access to and participation in the possibilities afforded by today's Information Society (Prix Ars Electronica 2012). Thus the role of evaluation in creative endeavor has demonstrable practical benefits.

4.5.4 Context as Environment: Where Does Creativity Take Place?

Context embraces a range of factors in the environment that could be expected to influence, inform and shape the nature of the creator's process and products. Of the many dimensions of context for creativity referred to previously, the physical and technical settings have great significance for the interactive arts. Context here includes the physical spaces in which the action takes place: the private studio, the more public 'living laboratory' and open public spaces such as galleries and museums. The artist's studio is a private space where much of what goes on is hidden from general view whereas interactive art in public spaces is open and accessible to many including the public at large. The opportunities for evaluating what takes place depend upon many factors, in particular, the modus operandi of the creator or creative team. The advent of living laboratories is a half way house which allows interactions between works and participants to be assessed by artists and researchers (Muller et al. 2006).

4.5.4.1   Studies Related to Context as Environment

The role of the environment in which creativity takes place is a largely under researched area. And yet, the influence of the particular kind of physical space is critical to the way the creator works and the availability of resources such as technical facilities and materials can have a significant effect on what is possible. Defining what makes an appropriate environment for interactive art research presents interesting challenges. An environment for interactive art research requires more than technical facilities and programming expertise if it is to meet the needs of the creative practitioner and the curators seeking to present innovative, and sometimes complex, installations to the general public. Where the goal is to create interactive works that engage the audience in the artwork itself, this adds to the complexity of task that can only be addressed by working within a particular kind of environment.

For the COSTART artist in residencies, an environment of technical and human resources was established in a university where a multiplicity of different skills and knowledge was available across faculties. An important proviso was that, that unlike the PAIR artist residencies at Xerox PARC (Harris 1999), the artists were assigned the role of creative directors of the projects. This created a different ethos whereby, instead of being visitors who could take the opportunity of existing technologies to develop their work on the back of existing work by others, the aim was to create art forms and develop innovative technologies in tandem, the first acting as inspiration for the second. Thus, it was argued, environments for creativity need to be established on the basis of true partnership collaboration where an ethos of openness and flexibility operated within a well-structured organizational framework. The resource needs were very variable and therefore had to be adaptable to the particular requirements of the creators' aspirations (Edmonds et al. 2005).

The recognition that digital technologies have transformed the expectations of museum visitors has driven change for curators of such environments. Beta_Space at The Powerhouse Museum, Sydney, represented an innovative solution to the need for spaces for exploring artistic concepts, creating art systems and evaluating experiences with real audiences. Its origins and the course of its rich and varied interactive art exhibitions are described by two curators Turnbull and Connell working at the leading edge of curatorial practice (Turnbull and Connell 2011). These curators explore the innovative idea, still barely known in the wider art world, of an interaction space that is both a studio and a living laboratory where artistic research and public exhibitions take place and are evaluated. The 'living laboratory' (Muller et al. 2006) for creating and evaluating interactive art with a range of audiences as participants, has become a model for a new kind of environment for engaging people in interactive experiences. The initiative gave rise to many challenges which could be seen as the basis for establishing similar environments and from which criteria for evaluation could be derived. The model acts as a "hybrid space of change" (Turnbull and Connell 2011: 93) where the change is within museum culture and conventions, a way of breaking rules in such a manner as to reveal to the organization what successful and innovative partnerships could offer. In placing novel interactive systems into such an environment for evaluation by the public involves challenges of a kind that do not arise in academic laboratory settings. The environment for creativity is both physical and technical and can afford great opportunities for novel and exciting new works to be created. At the same time, these opportunities may conflict with established conventions. Turnbull and Connell discuss how setting up Beta-Space in a museum with long traditional practices was a challenge. Not only were well-established house rules a barrier to be overcome, there was also a need to manage the expectations of staff.

4.5.4.2 Evaluating Context as Environment: Studio, Living Laboratory, Public Spaces

When defining the criteria for evaluating a context for creativity, the physical environment is a key element. In addition, managing expectations and deploying scarce resources in the face of other competing calls must be taken into account.

Establishing a workable living laboratory for interactive art and evaluation involved setting down acceptance criteria for assessing whether or not a new interactive art system was ready to be deployed. These included:

- degree of robustness of the art system in expectation of heavy public use
- appropriate accessibility in respect of type of audience (e.g. children)
- adherence to safety and house rules required by the museum
- impact of other coinciding exhibits (sound, noise, light impacts)
- attention to participant orientation and training
- attention to art system maintenance by creator and technical support

Evaluation on these lines yields information that can inform the design of future environments for interactive participative art in public museums.

4.6 Measuring Creativity

The notion of 'measuring' usually connotes deriving numerical values that can be used to test or compare something according to a set of agreed standards. Galileo's famous advice to "Count what is countable, measure the measurable and what is not measurable, make measurable" is at the heart of scientific research methodology. This immediately raises the question as to whether or not creativity, looked at in a holistic human centered sense, is potentially a measurable phenomenon. In turn, this requires an approach to measurement that recognizes the limitations of standard reductionist approaches (Sydenham 2003). If we are to be able to demystify creativity and, in doing so, contribute to new knowledge about the nature of creativity, we need to apply strategies for generating clear and unambiguous data that can be turned into meaningful information. From meaningful information, we can then derive understandings related to the context of use, the outcome of which might take the form of a coherent model. Applying appropriate measures of creativity can be seen as a necessary basis for generating reliable understandings about creativity and therefore, providing a stronger basis for evaluating its worth. Measurement is, therefore, fundamental to evaluation, where evaluation implies comparing different phenomena with claims to creativity.

One strategy for deriving meaningful information about creativity is based on collecting observable data about human behavior where creative products are involved or the process itself is identified as creative. We may derive measures of creative activities by undertaking a longitudinal involvement in the process of creation and in the situations where creative engagements occur. The data collection methods include first hand, direct observation of events, generating reports of behavior, making informed judgments, referring to histories of events and participants, comparing the current situations and outcomes with historical records as well as the current trends, movements. The aim is to arrive at a rich set of 'observable' data, which can be used to derive a "ranking" of the originality of the person, process, and the product.

Observation as a method for data collection raises issues as to its reliability in creativity evaluation. Data from observing creativity depends upon the interpretation of what the individual observer sees. Hence the advantage of multiple observers and video data that can be analyzed by different researchers. Overall, it is fair to say that this form of creativity research is a description of either the end product or the process that is shaped by a collective knowledge and interpretation.

Some researchers in the creativity domain study examples of human creative process and products using in-depth case study method. Being involved in creative practices, observing creative processes and engagements in different places at different times, understanding the creative process better and improving judgments over time can provide "stories" of creativity measurement. We refer to it as a 'story' because each measurement is a case in itself with the people, processes, its creative context and artifact(s). Because each case is unique, one measurement method may not apply to the other story/case. Given this is so, if measurements may not apply across cases, in what sense can we call this a measurement?

In traditional scientific method, measurements must provide consistent results across different cases at different times and that is why they are taken over and over to verify the previous measurements or to reach an average value (with an acceptable standard deviation) for a series of measurements. Meanwhile, the factors, which affect the measurement, have to be controlled rigorously so that researchers can explain why variations (in measurements) occur. However, in order to 'measure' creativity, we have to conduct research outside of controlled laboratory conditions, and cannot rely on fixed criteria that can be applied to all cases. The shifting ground and the ever-changing contexts often renders consistency out of reach.

If the term 'measurement' does not match what we are doing within the creativity domain, then why do we still use this word? The reason is that we consider that creativity is, nevertheless, accessible to systematic study, including by the creative practitioners themselves using the reflective processes discussed above. From our research, we have some evidence that there are factors, conditions and other phenomena that occur every time we observe creativity. Many of these factors and possibilities have led to the emergence of computational creativity and development of creativity support tools (Boden 1998; Shneiderman 2002; Shneiderman et al. 2006). Although these kinds of repeatable conditions and factors are not as easy to demonstrate as those in scientific measurements of non-human systems, still we see enough evidence to start a discussion about criteria for creativity measurement. From this starting point, we aim to stimulate a discussion and, in time, further research about whether creativity can be made more measurable.

4.7 Conclusions

In HCI, historically, the focus has been on people as users deploying task oriented systems. The criteria for evaluation has largely been in terms of ease of use, task efficiency and effectiveness- usability. However, attributes such as speed and productivity are, for the most part, meaningless in the context of creative interactive experience. Whether an action is successful or unsuccessful depends on whether the intended result is achieved. However, for understanding the experiences with an artwork, whether an action is deemed to be accurate or quick is unlikely to be an appropriate measure of success. Measuring success is more likely to be dependent on factors such as whether or not the system has engaged the audience in a playful or immersive way or whether it has elicited curiosity or excitement or concentrated attention and so on.

Evaluation as conceived in this chapter is a way of investigating creativity in terms of people, process, product and context as represented in the multi-dimensional model of creativity and evaluation proposed. Studies have given rise to findings that in turn can inform the practice of creators and researchers. These findings can be expressed as criteria for evaluation that in turn can be applied to the evaluation of new works. This approach characterizes the way that many practitioners work in the interactive arts. In the context of creative practice, successful evaluation depends upon documented reflection-in-action and on-action about the development of new works as well as studies of participant engagement. This process supports the externalization of design rationale and constitutes an important contribution to the ongoing development and maintenance of innovative interactive systems. Evaluation in creativity, as represented in the MMCE model described in this chapter, sits within a broader conception of design rationale than one often encounters in the literature. Practice-based research in the interactive digital arts indicates that externalizing design rationale in this way, can contribute to the enhancement of creative processes and products. It can also make visible the constraints and affordances of contexts which might otherwise be taken as givens. Taken further, the model could have wider implications for interaction design in many domains.

Acknowledgements The author is profoundly grateful to the artists and researchers who worked at the Creativity and Cognition Studios, University of Technology and Beta-Space, The Powerhouse Museum, Sydney. Special thanks are due to Dr Zafer Bilda for his important contribution to the creativity evaluation model through his studies of interactive art experience and the development of the Creative Engagement Model.

References

Amabile, T. M. (1985). Motivation and creativity: Effects of motivational orientation on creative writing. *Journal of Personality and Social Psychology, 48*, 393–399.

Bevan, N., & Macleod, M. (1994). Usability measurement in context. *Behaviour and Information Technology, 13*, 132–145.

Bilda, Z. (2011). Designing for audience engagement. In L. Candy & E. Edmonds (Eds.), *Interacting: Art, research and the creative practitioner* (pp. 163–181). Oxfordshire: Libri Publishing.

Bilda, Z., Costello, B., & Amitani, S. (2006). Collaborative analysis framework for evaluating interactive art experience. *International Journal of CoDesign, 2*(4), 238–255.

Bilda, Z., Candy, L., & Edmonds, E. A. (2008). Designing for creative engagement, in interaction design and creative practice special issue. *Design Studies, 29*(6), 525–540.

Boden, M. A. (1990). *The creative mind: Myths and mechanisms*. London: George Weidenfeld and Nicolson Ltd.

Boden, M. A. (1998). Creativity and artificial intelligence. *Artificial Intelligence, 103*(1–2), 347–356.

Boden, M. A. (2010). Aesthetics and interaction. In: *Creativity and art: Three roads to surprise* (Chapter 11, pp. 210–234). Oxford: Oxford University Press.

Candy, L. (1993, August). Hypothetical design in the perfect world: Observations on design rationale in knowledge support systems development. In *5th International Conference on Human-Computer Interaction* (p. 222). Poster Sessions: Abridged Proceedings, Orlando.

Candy, L. (1997). Computers and creativity support: Knowledge, visualization and collaboration. *Knowledge Based Systems, 10*(1), 3–13.

Candy, L. (2002). Collaboration. In L. Candy, & E. Edmonds (Eds.), *Explorations in art and technology* (Chapter 4, pp. 56–66). London: Springer.

Candy, L. (2011). Research and creative practice. In L. Candy & E. Edmonds (Eds.), *Interacting: Art, research and the creative practitioner* (pp. 33–59). Oxfordshire: Libri Publishing.

Candy, L., & Bilda, Z. (2007, June). Understanding and evaluating creativity. In *Creativity and cognition 2007*. Washington, DC/New York: ACM Press.

Candy, L., & Bilda, Z. (2009, October). Understanding and evaluating creativity. In *Creativity and cognition 2009*. UC Berkeley/New York: ACM Press.

Candy, L., & Edmonds, E. A. (1993). Collaborative design in system development: What place for design rationale? In *AAAI-93 Workshop Program, Working Notes on the 11th National Conference on Artificial Intelligence* (pp. 283–285). Washington, DC: American Association for Artificial Intelligence.

Candy, L., & Edmonds, E. A. (1994). Artefacts and the designer's process: Implications for computer support to design. *Journal of Design Sciences and Technology, 3*(1), 11–31.

Candy, L., & Edmonds, E. A. (1995). Creativity in knowledge work: A process model and requirements for support. In H. Hassan, & C. Nicastri (Ed.), *Proceedings OZCHI'95, HCI A Light into the Future*. New York: ACM Press.

Candy, L., & Edmonds, E. A. (1996). Creative design of the lotus bicycle: Implications for knowledge support system research. *Design Studies, 17*(1), 71–90.

Candy, L., & Edmonds, E. A. (2002a). Modeling co-creativity in art and technology. In T. T. Hewett & T. Kavanagh (Eds.), *Proceedings of the fourth international conference on creativity and cognition* (pp. 134–141). New York: ACM Press.

Candy, L., & Edmonds, E. A. (2002b). *Explorations in art and technology*. London: Springer.
Candy, L., & Edmonds, E. A. (2011). *Interacting: Art, research and the creative practitioner*. Oxfordshire: Libri Publishing.
Carroll, J. M., & Campbell, R. L. (1989). Artifacts as psychological theories: The case of human-computer interaction. *Behaviour and Information Technology, 8*(4), 247–256.
Cockton, G. (2008). Revisiting usability's three key principles. In *CHI08 extended abstracts in CHI2008*. New York: ACM.
Collins, M. A., & Amabile, T. M. (1999). Motivation and creativity. In R. J. Sternberg (Ed.), *Handbook of creativity* (pp. 297–312). Cambridge: Cambridge University Press.
Costello, B. (2007). A pleasure framework. *Leonardo, 40*(4), 370–371.
Costello, B. (2011). Many voices, one project. In L. Candy & E. A. Edmonds (Eds.), Interacting: Art, research and the creative practitioner (pp. 182–194). Oxford: Libri Publishing.
Cross, N., Christiaans, H., & Dorst, K. (1996). Introduction: The Delft protocols workshop. In N. Cross, H. Christiaans, & K. Dorst (Eds.), *Analysing design activity* (pp. 1–14). Chichester: Wiley.
Edmonds, E. A. (2007). The art of programming or programs as art. In H. Fujita & D. Pisanelli (Eds.), *Proceedings of the 6th new trends in software methodologies, tools and techniques (SoMeT_07)* (pp. 119–125). Washington, DC: Ios Press.
Edmonds, E. A. (2010). The art of interaction. *Digital Creativity, 21*(4), 257–264.
Edmonds, E. A. (2011). Art, interaction and engagement. In L. Candy & E. Edmonds (Eds.), *Interacting: Art, research and the creative practitioner* (pp. 228–241). Oxfordshire: Libri Publishing.
Edmonds, E. A., & Candy, L. (2010). Relating theory, practice and evaluation in practitioner research. *Leonardo Journal, 43*(5), 470–476.
Edmonds, E. A., Candy, L., Fell, M., Pauletto, S., & Weakley, A. (2005). The studio as laboratory: Combining creative practice and digital technology research. *International Journal of Human-Computer Studies Special Issue on Creativity and Computational Support, 63*(4), 452–481.
Finke, R. A., Ward, T. B., & Smith, S. M. (1992). *Creative cognition: Theory, research and application*. Cambridge, MA: MIT Press.
Gardner, H. (1989). *To open minds*. New York: Basic Books, Inc.
Greenberg, S., & Buxton, B. (2008). Usability evaluation considered harmful (some of the time). In *Proceedings of CHI2008*. New York: ACM Press.
Harris, C. (1999). *Art and innovation: The Xerox PARC artist-in-residence program*. Cambridge, MA: MIT Press.
Hassenzahl, M. (2004). The interplay of beauty, goodness, and usability in interactive products. *Human-Computer Interaction, 19*(4), 311–318.
Jordan, P. W. (2000). *Designing pleasurable products*. London: Taylor & Francis.
Leggett, M. (2011). Memory, schema and interactive video. In L. Candy & E. Edmonds (Eds.), *Interacting: Art, research and the creative practitioner* (pp. 282–294). Oxfordshire: Libri Publishing.
Lubart, T. I. (1999). Creativity across cultures. In R. J. Sternberg (Ed.), *Handbook of creativity*. Cambridge, UK: Cambridge University Press.
Muller, L., Edmonds, E., & Connell, M. (2006). Living laboratories for interactive art, in CoDesign. *International Journal of Co-Creation in Design and the Arts 2*(4), 195–207. Taylor & Francis Group, UK.
Partridge, D., & Rowe, J. (1994). *Computers and creativity*. Oxford: Intellect.
Perkins, D. N. (1981). *The mind's best work*. Cambridge: Harvard University Press.
Phalip, J. (2011). Creative communication in film scoring. In L. Candy & E. Edmonds (Eds.), *Interacting: Art, research and the creative practitioner* (pp. 136–149). Oxfordshire: Libri Publishing.
Polyani, M. (1966). *The tacit dimension*. New York: Doubleday & Company Inc.
Prix Ars Electronica: http://www.aec.at/prix/en/. Accessed 23 Feb 2012.
Reeves, S. (2011). *Designing interfaces in public settings*. London: Springer.
Rhodes, M. (1961). An analysis of creativity. *The Phi Delta Kappan, 42*, 305–310.

Schön, D. A. (1983). *The reflective practitioner: How professionals think in action*. New York: Basic Books. (Reprinted Aldershot: Ashgate Publishing Ltd., 1991, 2003)

Schön, D. A. (1992). Designing as reflective conversation with the materials of a design situation. *Knowledge-Based Systems, 5*(1), 3–14.

Shneiderman, B. (2002). Creativity support tools. *Communications of the ACM, 45*(10), 116–120.

Shneiderman, B., Fischer, G., Czerwinski, M., Resnick, M., Myers, B., Candy, L., Edmonds, E., Eisenberg, M., Giaccardi, E., Hewett, T., Jennings, P., Kules, B., Nakakoji, K., Nunamaker, J., Pausch, R., Selker, T., Sylvan, E., & Terry, M. (2006). Creativity support tools: Report from a U.S. National Science Foundation sponsored workshop. *International Journal of Human-Computer Interaction, 20*(2), 61–77.

Sternberg, R. J. (Ed.). (1999). *Handbook of creativity*. Cambridge, UK: Cambridge University Press.

Sydenham, P. H. (2003). Relationship between measurement, knowledge and advancement. *Measurement, 34*, 3–16.

Tractinsky, N., Adi, S. K., & Ikar, D. (2000). What is beautiful is usable. *Interacting with Computers, 13*(2), 127–145.

Turnbull, D., & Connell, M. (2011). Prototyping places: The museum. In L. Candy & E. Edmonds (Eds.), *Interacting: Art, research and the creative practitioner* (pp. 79–93). Oxfordshire: Libri Publishing.

Weisberg, R. W. (2006). *Creativity: Understanding innovation in problem solving, science, invention and the arts*. Hoboken: Wiley.

Williams, A., Ostwald, M. J., & Askland, H. H. (2010). *Creativity, design and education*. NSW: Australian Learning & Teaching Council, Sydney, Print National.

Zhang, Y., & Candy, L. (2007a). An in-depth case study of art- technology collaboration. In *Proceedings of creativity and cognition 2007* (pp. 53–62). New York: ACM Press.

Zhang, Y., & Candy, L. (2007b). A communicative behaviour analysis of art-technology collaboration. In M. J. Smith & G. Salvendy (Eds.), *Proceedings of the 12th international conference on human-computer interaction, 2007* (pp. 212–221). Beijing: Springer.

Zhang, Y. (2011). Investigating collaboration in art and technology. In L. Candy & E. Edmonds (Eds.), *Interacting: Art, research and the creative practitioner* (pp. 122–135). Oxfordshire: Libri Publishing.

Chapter 5
Integrating Design Representations for Creativity

Alistair Sutcliffe

Abstract This chapter argues that the influence of design rationale on creativity is best achieved by concurrent use of scenarios, prototypes and models. A framework of cognitive affordances is introduced to discuss the merits and limitations of each representation. The chapter concludes by discussing how different representations might complement each other in creative scenario-based design.

Keywords Scenarios • Prototypes • Cognitive affordances • Design representations

5.1 Introduction

It is often argued that creative design is best supported by examples of good design, thought probes, and stimulating artifacts (Cross 2000; Gaver et al. 2003). In contrast, the methodical engineering approach to design emphasizes a systematic process, models, and the reuse of design knowledge, criticizing less systematic approaches as "craft" (Dowell and Long 1998). Design rationale may provide a middle ground between the two approaches as an easy-to-use notation that can stimulate creativity while preserving some of the generality and rigor of models. I will investigate the contributions that different design representations can make to the creative design process from the viewpoint of cognitive reasoning processes. The relative merits of design rationale, scenarios, models, and prototypes are investigated in terms of their roles in the design process and cognitive affordances.

A. Sutcliffe (✉)
Manchester Business School, University of Manchester, Manchester, UK
e-mail: ags@man.ac.uk

J.M. Carroll (ed.), *Creativity and Rationale: Enhancing Human Experience by Design*, Human–Computer Interaction Series, DOI 10.1007/978-1-4471-4111-2_5, © Springer-Verlag London 2013

The integrated use of different representations will be illustrated by the scenario-based requirements analysis method (SCRAM; Sutcliffe and Ryan 1997). SCRAM advocates a combination of design rationale, scenarios, and early proto-types as a means of effective requirements analysis and design exploration. More recently we have used a merge of SCRAM and scenario-based design (Carroll 2002) with a similar combination of design representations in eScience health informatics domains (Sutcliffe et al. 2007). The following section of this chapter describes the properties of different design representations. Next, I discuss how the representations can support creative reasoning, with the following section elaborat-ing the theme by investigating cognitive affordances. Then I review how representa-tions can be integrated into the design requirements discovery process. Integration is illustrated with the SCRAM method, followed by a brief review of other approaches to creative design support. The chapter concludes by reviewing the potential for juxtaposing different design representations for creative design, as well as requirements specification of systems.

5.2   Design Representations

This section reviews the role of the more common design representations in creative design from a human–computer interaction (HCI) perspective and from the more analytic view of software engineering.

5.2.1   Scenarios

One of the key distinctions between scenarios and any model is that the former are grounded examples of specific experience, whereas models are more abstract repre-sentations of phenomena in the real world. Unfortunately, the term *scenario* has been abused in the literature and a large number of definitions exist (see Rolland et al. 1998). Indeed, much of the scenario literature, especially in the software engineering tradition (Kaindl 1995), is in fact describing event–sequence traces through state tran-sition models. In object-oriented design it becomes difficult to distinguish between use cases, alternative paths through use cases, and scenarios, which are just another path through a use case (Cockburn 2001; Graham 1996; Jacobson et al. 1992).

Scenarios have several roles in design; according to Carroll, one of these is a "cognitive prosthesis," or an example to stimulate the designer's imagination. Scenarios and other techniques, such as claims, are lightweight instruments that guide thought and support reasoning in the design process (Carroll 2002). Carroll has articulated several different roles for scenarios in the design process, including envisionment for design exploration, requirements elicitation, and validation (Carroll 1995). Usage scenarios illustrate problems for analysis and initiating or visioning scenarios stimulate design of a new artifact, while projected use scenarios describe future use of an artifact that has been designed (Sutcliffe and Carroll 1998). Scenarios can promote creative reasoning by stimulating examples and vivid illustration of real-life problems.

One problem with scenarios is that extreme examples might bias reasoning towards exceptional and rare events, or towards the viewpoint of an unrepresentative stakeholder. These biases are an acknowledged weakness of scenarios; however, some proposed scenarios are deliberately exceptional to provoke constructive thought (Djajadiningrat et al. 2000). Although scenarios are useful as cognitive probes for design, this is not their only role.

Scenarios arguably are the starting point for all modeling and design, and contribute to several parts of the design process. For instance, Potts (1999) has advocated scenarios to validate or check the acceptability of designs. The process of generalization inevitably loses detail, and the analyst has to make judgments about when unusual or exceptional behaviors are omitted, or explicitly incorporate them in task models as branches in action sequences. Hence one criticism that can be leveled at scenarios is that gathering detail comes at the price of effort in capturing and analyzing a "necessary and sufficient" set of scenarios.

5.2.2   Models

A prime role of models, either in the HCI tradition of task modeling or in software engineering (e.g., use cases, class diagrams, activity sequence diagrams, UML, etc.), has been to specify the system and represent the problem space to support design reasoning.

One criticism of models is that they do not capture the richness of interaction that occurs in the real world, compared with scenario narratives that concentrate on contextual description (e.g., Kuutti 1995; Kyng 1995). For instance, software engineering and task models may be criticized for not representing the relationships between agents, activity, and organizational structures, although these concepts are described in sociotechnical system design frameworks such as ORDIT (Eason et al. 1996). Meanwhile, a more comprehensive modeling language can be found in the i* requirements engineering method that analyzes the dependencies between agents, tasks, goals, and resources (Mylopoulos et al. 1999; Yu 1993). Models can expose design dilemmas and inconsistencies and thereby support the generation of creative solutions; however, how well models expose problems depends on the clarity of their notations and the reasoning mechanisms associated with the model. Models show an abstract view of problems so they might be accused of having a narrow scope of phenomena and omit detail, whereas scenarios might be able to represent phenomena in more detail, but they do so in an ad hoc manner and leave the responsibility of generalization to the analyst. Of course, models can be used with scenarios, and this theme is elaborated later in this chapter.

5.2.3 Design Rationale

The essence of design rationale (DR) is to represent argumentation and knowledge within the design process. Hence DR can be viewed as models that are specialized to represent the problem space for decision making, including evidence for evaluating alternative designs. Various forms of DR have appeared since their genesis in Toulmin's argumentation semantics, notably issue-based information systems and the diagrammatic form gIBIS (Conklin and Begeman 1988), which represents issues (design problems to be solved), alternatives (possible solutions), and evidence that supports or detracts from each alternative. The most influential HCI variant of DR recapitulates the semantics as questions (design problem), options, and criteria (QOC; MacLean and McKerlie 1995; MacLean et al. 1991). DR can also be used to express generalizable knowledge accumulated during iterative design. Psychological DR, or claims (Carroll and Rosson 1992), uses a simpler semantic representation of the claim (problem statement), a solution (expressed as an artifact/design pattern), and arguments divided into upsides and downsides. Claims may be used to support reasoning during the design process (Carroll 2002) or present reusable knowledge by recording the results of evaluation, including the problem that motivated a general design principle—called a claim—with trade-offs expressed as upsides and downsides (Carroll 2000; Sutcliffe and Carroll 1999). When DR is used to support the design process, the trade-off concerns for a claim about DR representations might invite comparison of the cost of representing the design space versus the advantage gained in more effective reasoning. The juxtaposition of alternatives is a key affordance for creative reasoning. For collaborative decisions, DR diagrams can function as a shared representation to focus discussion, although the costs may well outweigh the benefits. The uptake of DR in industry has been slow. When representing reusable knowledge, the benefits of DR may be potentially larger, but reuse depends on an effective knowledge management and retrieval system.

5.2.4 Prototypes

This category includes a variety of design representations, ranging from paper (or computer-based) storyboards to mock-ups/concept demonstrators with limited scripted functionality and prototypes with a partial software implementation. Prototypes stimulate creative design because they engage the user (designer) with the material of the product, be that software or hardware. Experimentation becomes part of the implementation unless a rigorous specification in detail of the implementation process is adopted, as practiced in software engineering. The prototype artifacts all result from the creative design process and, unlike models and DR, show the user concrete aspects of a design. Prototypes, mock-ups, and storyboards are probably the most common ways of representing the problem space for creative design exploration. This applies not only in software-related products but also in many other areas of creative design. The variation between the techniques lies in the media used (paper, video, computer media, interactive software), the cost of production, and the fidelity and extent of the representation of the intended design. While very early creative brainstorming may be used to map out a space of ideas and concepts, once these have been prioritized, design realization becomes necessary to progress the user–designer dialogue. The power of the prototype lies in anchoring the focus of discussion in a concrete example, and stimulating user reaction to specific features.

5.3 Representations and Reasoning Pathologies

In this section, the merits of different representations are reviewed in light of how they can stimulate and support creative design. Scenarios use language and concepts that are readily accessible to users and domain experts, whereas tasks and other conceptual models are expressed in a specialized language that users have to learn. Because scenarios invoke specific memory schema associated with experience or similar stories, they help to recruit specific knowledge (Carroll 2000; Sutcliffe 2002). This tunes our critical faculties, since detail tends to provide more subject matter to detect inconsistencies and errors when we reason about models and specifications.

In contrast, models are harder to comprehend because they represent abstract generalizations. While people naturally form categorial abstractions of physical things (Rosch et al. 1976), we are less efficient at forming categories of abstract concepts and functions (Hampton 1988). Unfortunately, formation of conceptual-functional categories is a necessary part of the generalization process, so users can find reasoning with simple conceptual models, such as data flow diagrams, difficult (Sutcliffe and Maiden 1992). Once learned, models become memory schema that represent abstract concepts removed from everyday experience, so their effectiveness depends on how well connected they are to more specialized memory schema representing scenario-based knowledge. The importance of the connection becomes clear when we try to validate models. Without any connection to specialized knowledge, I can accept the validity of the general concept simply because it has a wide scope of meaning. For example, I might accept the proposition that < all birds can fly > as a true type definition of the class < birds > in the absence of more specific knowledge of penguins, kiwis, rheas, ostriches, and dodos. Models therefore need to be integrated examples and scenarios and, furthermore, cannot exist profitably without them; indeed, human categorial memory is probably an integration of abstract models and specific examples (Lakoff and Johnson 1999).

While scenarios might be effective in grounding reasoning, their downsides lie in reasoning biases and partial mental model formation. Confirmation bias is a well-known weakness of human reasoning (Johnson-Laird and Wason 1983). We tend to seek only positive evidence to support hypotheses, so scenarios can be dangerous in supplying us with minimal evidence to confirm our beliefs. While problem statement scenarios and anti-use cases (Alexander 2002) can counteract confirmation bias, we need to be wary of this downside. Another potential pathology is encysting, more usually described by the saying "can't see the wood for the trees." Since scenarios are detailed, they can bias people away from the big picture of important design issues and towards obsession with unnecessary detail. Models exist to counteract this pathology. Partial mental model formation is another weakness when we test hypotheses without sufficient reasoning (Simon 1973). Scenarios can encourage this pathology by reassuring us that we have covered all aspects of the problem with a small number of scenarios. This exposes the Achilles heel of scenario-based reasoning: It is difficult, if not nearly impossible, to be confident that a necessary and sufficient set of scenarios has been gathered to escape from the partial mental model problem.

Prototypes and other concrete design realizations share many of the same pathologies with scenarios, such as encysting and confirmation bias, since users might be prone to accepting a design to please the designer. This may be critical when the power relationships give designers a de facto authority over users, which they should strive to avoid. Groups of users may also be prone to suppress criticism of a design and agree with the consensus, following a group-think bias. However, prototypes do afford concrete representations and detail that users can react to, as well as anchoring discussion to specific issues/features, which can facilitate users' participation in the creative design process.

Many of the same criticisms can be leveled at DR as a genre of models. Although DR represents the decision space with specific issues in some detail, arguments may make little sense without the background knowledge contained in other representations. Also, DR may bias problem exploration by presenting a ready-made set of alternatives. Furthermore, unless the author of the DR diagram is careful, the diagram can embed biases from the author's viewpoint in the relationships between the alternatives and supporting/detracting evidence (Karsenty 1996; Sutcliffe 2002; Sutcliffe and Ryan 1997).

5.4   Affordances and Representations

While analysis of general properties of representations can provide some insight into their potential contribution towards supporting design, a more detailed view is necessary to unpack the nature of cognitive affordances. The term *affordance* was borrowed by Norman (1999) from Gibson's concept of physical features that suggested or afforded intuitive understanding, for instance, cliffs suggest the danger of falling. As Norman realized, when the concept of affordances is applied to design features, the meaning of the term becomes more complex, since it has to account for the general suggestibility of the external form towards some purposeful use and the cognitive internalization of the external form into an individual's plan of action; for example, a slider control on a user interface suggests movement of the control itself that then changes another component, such as panning a display.

A useful distinction, therefore, is to examine the external appearance of a representation (or design) and its integration into action plans after people have

Fig. 5.1 In the gIBIS design rationale, the +or − signs denote arguments that either support or hinder a particular alternative

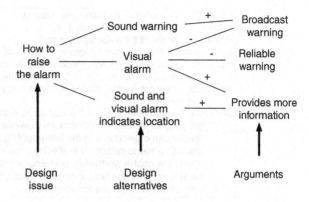

Fig 5.2 The QOC (questions, options, criteria) form of design rationale, applied to trade-offs between representations to support creative design

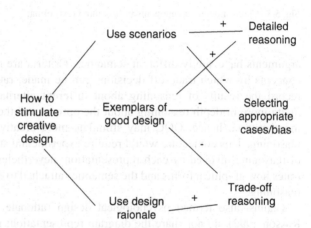

interpreted its meaning. To illustrate this line of inquiry, I will compare three exemplars of design rationale: gIBIS, QOC, and claims. The first two have a similar external form but differ in their semantics. Claims, in contrast, have a different (text-based) external form and semantics.

gIBIS diagrams, as illustrated in Fig. 5.1, have a simple tree/network structure that can be traced from the root node representing the issue, to the branches (two or more design/solution alternatives), and then to leaf nodes representing supporting arguments. The graphical form intuitively suggests composition and relationships, as do most hierarchy diagrams. The semantics of the diagram nodes are easily explained so the representation can be used to trace relationships from the issues through each alternative solution to the supporting (or detracting) arguments. Thus the representation "affords" comparison of alternative solutions by pathway tracing. Furthermore, the external representation reduces working memory loading since different pathways can be reviewed at will.

QOC (see Fig. 5.2) has a similar graphical notation, so the diagram also affords pathway tracing of questions or different design options. However, criteria and

```
Claim ID:    Colour-coded Telegraphic Display
Author:      Singley, M.K.; Carroll, J.M.
Artifact:    MoleHill tutor -Goalposter tool
Description: A colour-coded telegraphic display of goals
Upside:      Provides persistent feedback on the correctness of
             actions, as well as access to further information
Downside: Learners must learn the display's feature-language
             and controls
Scenario: The presentation of individual goals in the window is
             telegraphic, several words at most. However, the
             learner can expand any of the telegraphic goals
             (through a menu selection) to display a fuller explanation
             of why the goal is worthwhile pursuing or not. Thus
             the system provides both shorthand feedback on
             correctness and access to further help.
```

Fig. 5.3 Claim showing components in structured text format

arguments have subtly different semantics. Criteria are more terse and represent concepts by which trade-off decisions can be made, rather than arguments that record the results of reasoning about different alternatives. Criteria therefore invite more in-depth reasoning about the options and their relationship to one or more criteria; hence, QOC may stimulate more creative thought by provoking reasoning. This conjecture would require experimental study to assess the quality of reasoning invoked by each representation; nevertheless, the comparison illustrates how graphical forms and the semantics attached to diagrams might influence reasoning.

Claims, also termed psychological design rationale by Carroll (Carroll and Rosson 1992), do not share the diagram representation; instead, formatted text is used to illustrate the structure of a claim (see Fig. 5.3). The basic components of claims are (a) the claim (essentially a design principle); (b) upside and downside trade-offs that may arise from application of the claim; (c) a scenario of use; and (d) an artifact illustrating a design that embeds the claim. The juxtaposing of alternatives has been moved from alternative designs to the assessment criteria or arguments. Claims present essentially only one design alternative and then positive and negative arguments about its merits. While DR provides more structured arguments, claims use the combination of a design solution (a generalized design principle) with examples of use illustrated in scenarios and artifacts. Claims may therefore stimulate creative thought by the challenge posed from the general assertion about a design treatment (the claim), concrete illustrations of its interpretation and use, and the results of previous design experience recorded in the upsides and downsides. Design patterns (Borchers 2001) follow a similar format with forces, scenarios and illustrations of exemplar design for the pattern.

So how do other representations compare with the affordances of DR? Models share diagrammatic notation with DR but have many more morphologies and semantics, ranging from the simple (e.g., use case diagrams) to the very complex

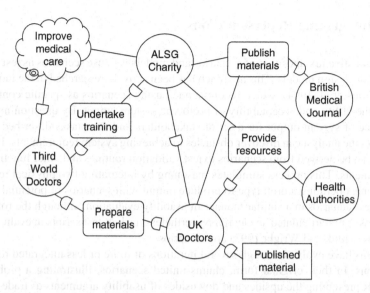

Fig. 5.4 An i* strategic dependency model illustrating complex modeling. The *circles* denote agents, *boxes* are resources, *rounded boxes* are goals, and *clouds* are quality goals. The *D* symbols stand for "depends on" relationships

(e.g., i* requirements modeling language; Yu 1993). It is notable that most semiformal modeling notations rely on a restricted number of graphical formats that afford intuitive interpretations, namely hierarchies (task models, class diagrams), networks (data flow diagrams, activity sequence diagrams), and timelines (Gantt charts, interaction diagrams). Complexity arises when diagram notations become overloaded with symbols to represent a large variety of relationships and objects, as illustrated in Fig. 5.4.

Scenarios, in contrast, use natural media (text and image) for representing concrete examples of experience. Prototypes also represent concrete examples of designs as physical artifacts, with storyboards and mock-ups providing representations of the physical form early in the design process.

Cognitive affordances therefore emerge from intuitive understanding or representations in a variety of media, coupled with reasoning about the content of those representations. DR and models provide abstract representations of knowledge and design trade-offs to support creative reasoning, while scenarios and prototypes give grounded examples from which to abstract more general principles. However, creative thought should generate innovative designs, but these need to be based on general principles; otherwise, design is limited to a craft-style incremental improvement of specific examples (Dowell and Long 1998). I argue that a combination of representations is the most productive way to stimulate creative design, a challenge addressed in the next section.

5.5   Integrating Representations

One productive juxtaposition of scenarios and models is to use scenarios as test data to validate design models. This approach has been actively researched in the inquiry cycle (Potts et al. 1994), which recommended using scenarios as specific contexts to test the utility and acceptability of prototype system output. By questioning the relevance of system output for a set of stakeholders and their tasks described in a scenario, the analyst can discover obstacles to achieving system requirements. Input events can be derived from scenarios to test validation routines and other functional requirements. This process stimulates reasoning by integrating two physical representations, operating a prototype to produce output with scenarios of potential use. HCI uses scenarios in a similar manner in usability evaluation, although the role of scenarios is not articulated so clearly. Nevertheless, task or test scripts in evaluation methods (Monk and Wright 1993) are scenarios.

Claims have evolved through several iterations of more or less integrated representations. In their original form, claims united scenarios, illustrating a problem with DR presenting the upsides and downsides of usability arguments as trade-offs for applying a design principle with a concrete example of an implementation. Claims are situated in a context by a scenario of use and the artifact that helps designers understand how to apply usability arguments. Since claims have a domain-specific anchor in the artifact context, insight into more general design implications and trade-offs may be gained if they can be integrated with models.

By associating claims in this manner, the designer can have the best of both worlds. Claims with their associated artifacts and scenarios provide grounded examples of design advice while models represent a more general context within which to consider the implications of the design decision. This view of claims is similar to the schema of patterns that recommend that design advice is presented in the context of a motivating problem, and with an example of its application (Borchers 2001). Although patterns do have a clause that indicates the range of problems the design advice can be applied to, this scoping is ad hoc. Advocates of patterns propose relationships between individual patterns constructed into a hypertext-like pattern network or language (Alexander et al. 1977) to set the context. Unfortunately, pattern languages tend to be incomplete. Claims have been integrated with models that may be specific to the application, or generalized models of tasks to stimulate reuse of knowledge (Sutcliffe and Carroll 1999); see Fig. 5.5.

The scope of the claim is defined by models that may be related to particular applications, for example, task models, class diagrams for a telephone fault-finding application, or more generic models capturing a range of applications (e.g., generic models of diagnostic tasks, including fault finding). One of the problems with integrating claims with models and other arguments lies in the complexity of the number of representations, which in turn necessitates further guidance about how the representations may be combined in the design process. More elaborate representations therefore run into the criticism leveled at the engineering approach: The complexity of models and process advice militates against the creative freedom

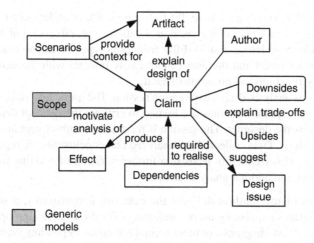

Fig. 5.5 An extended claims schema, associating claims with reusable generic models and supporting arguments

necessary in design. In the following section, I introduce the SCRAM method, which attempts to tread a middle path between creative use of multiple representations and a systematic approach.

5.5.1   The SCRAM Method

The SCRAM method (Sutcliffe and Ryan 1997) for analyzing the requirements for interactive systems provides one way forward for integrating representations. The approach is based on integrating three representations:

Prototypes or concept demonstrators provide a designed artifact that users can react to;

Scenarios, in which the designed artifact is situated in a context of use, thereby helping users relate the design to their work/task context;

Design rationale, where the designer's reasoning is deliberately exposed to the user to encourage user participation in the decision process.

The representations are combined with a method to provide process guidance, composed of advice on setting up sessions, and more detailed guidance on fact acquisition and requirements validation. The method consists of the following phases:

1. Initial requirements capture and domain familiarization. This is conducted with conventional interviewing and fact-finding techniques to gain sufficient information to develop a first-concept demonstrator.
2. Specification and development of the concept demonstrator. I define a concept demonstrator as a very early prototype with limited functionality and interactivity,

so it can only be run as a script to illustrate a typical task undertaken by the user. *Scripts* illustrate a scenario of typical user actions with effects mimicked by the designer. Concept demonstrators differ from prototypes in that no real functionality is implemented and the user cannot easily interact with the demonstrator since many functions are not implemented.

3. Requirements analysis-design exploration session. The users involved in the initial requirements capture interview are invited to critique the concept demonstrator and interview the designer. The session is recorded for subsequent analysis.
4. Session analysis. Data collected are analyzed and conclusions are reported back to the users. This frequently leads to a further iteration of revising the concept demonstrator and another analysis session.

The end point of the method delivers the concept demonstrator, a set of analyzed DR diagrams expressing users' preferences for different design options, and specifications as text, diagrams, or more formal notations, depending on the designer's choice. In addition, video of the analysis sessions is available for requirements traceability analysis.

The walkthrough method employs scenario scripts that describe an imaginary work situation for the user and a typical key task. The session is started with an introduction and verbal summary of the situation described in the scenario narrative, for example, "Imagine you are in your office and a production order arrives ...". One developer operates the concept demonstrator while the explainer-rapporteur asks questions at key points in the demonstration script.

At key points in the sequence, a designed response to a requirement is illustrated. This is best explained by reference to the example used for the validation, which is covered later. Figure 5.6 illustrates a screen dump from a shipboard emergency management system. The user's requirement is for timely and appropriate information to support decision making. The operational steps accompanying Fig. 5.6 are

User: identify the hazard location
System: shows location of fire
User: sound alarm
User: find location of fire-fighting crews
System: displays crew information and location on the diagram
User: decide appropriate instructions to give to crew
System: displays a checklist of actions.

The key point in the task is how to instruct the emergency team on where to go and how to deal with the hazard, in this case a fire. The concept demonstrator illustrates one design option. Alternative solutions expressed in a DR format are illustrated in Fig. 5.7. The user's attention is drawn to the design options, in this case providing complete information for decision support. The first option displaying comprehensive information is illustrated with the demonstrator; this is followed by option 2, provision of more restricted but relevant information for the task, by identifying the team nearest the fire; and then the final option to give the emergency team autonomy and broadcast the location of the fire. The users are asked to rate each option and consider the trade-off criteria. The diagram also functions as a

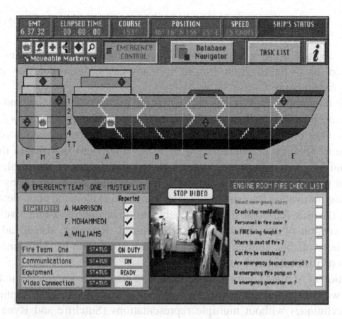

Fig. 5.6 Concept demonstrator showing the "show emergency teams and hazard location" design option for the Muster emergency teams task

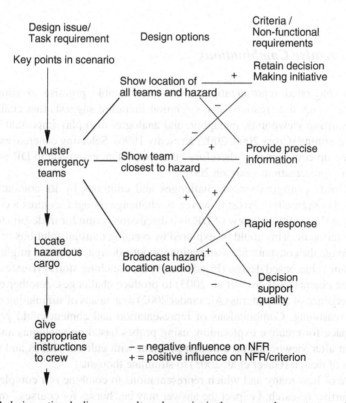

Fig. 5.7 A design rationale diagram used as a key point in the concept demonstrator script

recording medium, since ranking of options, additional ideas, and notes can be scribbled on top of the diagram. Indeed, in many cases, discussion may promote redrawing the diagram.

The DR diagram is used as a shared artifact to promote discussion, and gesture is used where possible to illustrate differences between the options by pointing to the screen. One obvious problem is bias towards the option implemented in the demonstrator. This can be counteracted by using storyboard sketches of the other options and by more vigorous critiquing by the developers of the implemented version. In particular, use of the criteria is a powerful way of promoting critical thought. The motivation for using design rationale is to explore the possible solution space with the user. Rationale diagrams enable this to be done cost-effectively, since only one version of the demonstrator is produced. However, should additional resources be available, alternative versions of the artifact can be implemented and both versions illustrated at the key point.

Evaluation of SCRAM demonstrated that more detailed requirements and design feedback were captured using the method than with conventional requirements analysis techniques without multiple representations (Sutcliffe and Ryan 1997). The method also stimulated creative reasoning about new design solutions through the process of critiquing the concept demonstrator and alternative solutions that were presented.

5.5.2   Creative Combinations

Although integrated representations show considerable promise in stimulating design reasoning, the creativity and cognition literature suggests that challenging content, shifting viewpoints, metaphor, and analogies also play important roles in creative reasoning (Cross 2000, 2002; Karsenty 1996). Selecting concrete examples and setting up contrasts may therefore be an important extension to DR and integration of representations (Buxton 2007).

DR affords configuration of challenges and contrasts by its comparison of trade-offs between alternatives; however, to challenge thought requires a considerable shift in the traditional view of DR as a discussion forum for trade-offs to active design of rationale. This could be explored by creating unusual solutions or criteria that challenge the conventional assumptions about a design. Contrasts might be borrowed from value-based design (Friedman 1997), sketching stories (Buxton 2007), or extreme characters (Gaver et al. 2003) to produce challenges. Another example is the emergence of antipatterns (Alexander 2002) as a means of stimulating counterintuitive reasoning. Combinations of representation and content could provide a design space for creative exploration, using probes based on analogies and metaphors that alter viewpoints on a design problem with cultural probes and unusual examples of design (Gaver et al. 2003) to stimulate thought.

Choice of how many and which representations to combine is a complex question for further research. I expect the answer may be "horses for courses," meaning, for wide-ranging creative design with green-field applications, sketches, storyboards, and scenarios (Buxton 2007; Moggridge 2006) may be the best choice, although as Nigel Cross (2002) noted, expert designers still reuse basic knowledge in the form of "first principles." Such knowledge could be passed on as DR or claims. In more constrained contexts, creative reasoning may be better supported with more detailed representations, models, and specifications (Kaindl 1995; Paterno 1999). Although multiple representations were effective in SCRAM (see previous section), there were limits; I did not integrate models with the other representations, since the management of artifacts, DR, and scenarios within one session was already complex. A future view on the representation creativity problem may be to evaluate how representations contribute to the "common ground" (Clark 1996) between the parties in design conversations. Representations need to promote shared understanding between the parties according to their prior knowledge and the design problem in hand.

5.6   Creative Combinations in the Design Process

This section reviews the fit of creative design representations in the design process more generally. Creativity is particularly important in the early phases of the design process when the users' requirements may not be clear, and furthermore users need help from designers to explore the space of possible solutions. Early phases of development in user-centred design employ iterative cycles of design exploration and user evaluation, gradually refining the design to converge on a solution acceptable to users' needs. Experience in the ADVISES project (Sutcliffe et al. 2011; Thew et al. 2009) which developed visualizations and decision support tools for epidemilogists demonstrated the potential for creative exploration of the design space with users, by integration of storyboards, scenarios and cut-down design rationale as claims, as illustrated in Fig. 5.8.

Prototype, scenarios, personae and storyboards are commonly used representations. Software engineering adopted a similar approach, especially in the agile tradition (Beck 1999) where iterations of prototypes are combined with "stories", essentially scenarios of use. More traditional software engineering approaches, such as the Rational Unified Process, use informal diagrams (use cases) to record the overall scope of a system, in combination with more formal specifications, such as class and activity sequence diagrams. The soft systems methodology (Checkland 1981) follows an informal modeling and analytic approach to discovering problem-oriented requirements. Informal diagrams and sketches, which may be referred to as domain models or rich pictures (Checkland 1981) are used to support creative exploration of problems.

When the solution space needs to be explored, workshops and focus groups are used in HCI and other design traditions. For example, the KJ brainstorming method, named after its inventor Jiro Kawakita, and Rapid Applications Development (DSDM Consortium 1995) advocate use of workshops to explore

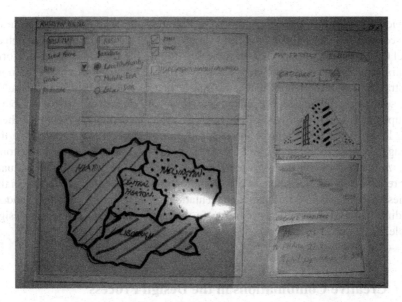

Fig. 5.8 Storyboard and claim from the ADVISES project used to explore design ideas for visualisations to support statistical analysis of epidemiological data. *Claim*: integrated representations (*maps, graphs* and *tables*) help analysis because the user can easily cross reference information between the representations. *Upsides*: users can scan maps and graphs to see associations; maps and graphs can be combined with query sliders so dynamic changes can be seen. *Downsides*: visual complexity may confuse users; many representations makes details hard to see

requirements and design solutions, combining lists and informal maps of the problem space, mock-ups and storyboards as means of stimulating creative thought, although these methods also offer little systematic guidance. Scoping requirements and generating design ideas is achieved by discussion with all the stakeholders and documenting the high-level system goals on post-it notes or lists. Notes can be grouped during collaborative discussion either manually or on electronic whiteboards and then ideas can be prioritized by voting. Recording goals and high-level solutions tends to focus users' attention on where the boundaries of the system investigation should lie, and helps to identify an initial scope for the system. Design rationale can play an important role is integrating ideas, goals and prioritization arguments.

Integrating representations is an important means of stimulating creative exploration of problems and solutions in several design approaches. However, one area where little guidance exists and further research is necessary concerns the transitions between idea generation, prioritizing and trade-off analysis, and refication of ideas. Ideas recorded in semantic terms as notes, lists and informal models are quick to create and process. Design rationale can help to integrate ideas with arguments to support trade-off analysis. However, the implications of ideas may not be understood until they have been reified as storyboards or prototypes. How to optimally manage the transition between the breadth of ideas created by brainstorming in semantic mode and the depth of understanding produced by more physical embodiment of those ideas is an open question.

5.7 Conclusions

The argument advocated in this chapter is that the constructive tension between different types of representation is productive since they have different affordances for abstract reasoning and detailed critiquing. Unfortunately, there are obstacles in the way of using multiple representations, even though many advocate them in HCI and software engineering (Mylopoulos et al. 1999; Paterno 1999; Sutcliffe 2000). In reality, it is difficult to get practitioners to accept complex representations, and even simple ones get misused and customized to individuals' needs. Take MacLean et al.'s (1991) QOC variant of DR as an example. This is a simple representation of a design question, alternative solutions, and evaluation criteria for the solutions. However, QOC has been difficult to introduce into new communities of practice (MacLean and McKerlie 1995), and similar problems have been encountered with the gIBIS (Conklin and Begeman 1988) version of DR (Buckingham Shum 1996; Sutcliffe and Ryan 1997). Carroll, in his more recent work, has simplified claims (Carroll 2000; Rosson and Carroll 2001), abandoning complex formatting. Claims are presented as simple design principles, in association with a motivating scenario and occasionally an artifact. In terms of process, Carroll advocates a more creative view of design, with scenarios playing roles of "thought prostheses" and challenges for design.

So is there a synthesis for the model-analytic and creative-exploration approaches to design? A partial answer is acknowledging the "horses for courses" argument. A differentiation between formal model-analytic and creative-exploratory design approaches will always be necessary for applications that range between safety critical, on the one hand, and those oriented toward entertainment, education, and general commerce on the other. So different combinations of design presentations have contributions to make in different phases of design and design contexts. Scenarios and prototypes can stimulate thought and provoke argument on detail, whereas models give the wider, more abstract context for design reasoning. DR can provide the link between the two, although its effectiveness in supporting decision making or just documenting the result is an open question. Finally, design representations enable knowledge to be reused effectively in a generalized form as models, claims, principles, and guidelines.

Combinations of representations using prototypes, scenarios, and claims are advocated in scenario-based design (Carroll 2002), and these have been successfully applied in eScience applications (Thew et al. 2008, 2009), as well as in Carroll's development of collaboration tools for eCommunity applications (Carroll and Rosson 1996). SCRAM integrated DR with scenarios and early prototypes and this proved to be an effective combination for critiquing designs and stimulating further design ideas (Sutcliffe and Ryan 1997). Prototypes with scenarios and formatted question lists have been successfully applied in requirements analysis (Sutcliffe et al. 2005) which, while not using DR explicitly, did present issue lists and alternatives to provoke design reasoning. The scenario presenter tool evolved from earlier research on automated support for design reasoning with tools that produced question prompts linked to specific locations in a scenario or use case, thus giving more active support for design reasoning (Sutcliffe et al. 1998). A combination of scenarios, prototypes, and lightweight design representations appears to have evolved in several research strands suggesting that combining representations has some utility.

The more general question that requires considerable future research is how juxtaposing contrasts in the content can augment the combination of different representations. Challenges to reasoning from usual content are known to induce creative reasoning; however, how such content can be produced for specific situations is not clear. Seeding the design environment with stimulating content (Fischer 1996) assumes considerable insight into future problems. Although premade solutions might inhibit creative reasoning if designers just take the easy option of reusing previous solutions, cognitive probes in the forms of personae and extreme characters (Djajadiningrat et al. 2000) can stimulate thought. In future work I will use common ground (Clark 1996) as a theoretical framework for exploring cognitive probes and DR, as well as a combination of representations to support creative design reasoning.

References

Alexander, I. (2002). Initial industrial experience of misuse cases in trade-off analysis. In *Proceedings of RE-02 IEEE joint international conference on requirements engineering* (pp. 61–70). Los Alamitos: IEEE Computer Society Press.

Alexander, C., Ishikawa, S., & Silverstein, M. (1977). *A pattern language*. Oxford: Oxford University Press.

Beck, K. (1999). *Extreme programming explained: Embracing change*. New York: Addison-Wesley.

Borchers, J. (2001). *A pattern approach to interaction design*. Chichester: Wiley.

Buckingham Shum, S. (1996). Analyzing the usability of a design rationale notation. In T. P. Moran & J. M. Carroll (Eds.), *Design rationale: Concepts, techniques and use* (pp. 185–215). Hillsdale: Lawrence Erlbaum Associates.

Buxton, W. (2007). *Sketching user experiences: Getting the design right and the right design*. Amsterdam: Elsevier.

Carroll, J. M. (Ed.). (1995). *Scenario-based design: Envisioning work and technology in system development*. New York: Wiley.

Carroll, J. M. (2000). *Making use: Scenario-based design of human-computer interactions*. Cambridge, MA: MIT Press.

Carroll, J. M. (2002). Making use is more than a matter of task analysis. *Interacting with Computers, 14*, 619–627.

Carroll, J. M., & Rosson, M. B. (1992). Getting around the task-artifact framework: How to make claims and design by scenario. *ACM Transactions on Information Systems, 10*, 181–212.

Carroll, J. M., & Rosson, M. B. (1996). Developing the Blacksburg Electronic Village. *Communications of the ACM, 39*, 69–74.

Checkland, P. (1981). *Systems thinking, systems practice*. Chichester: Wiley.

Clark, H. H. (1996). *Understanding language*. Cambridge, UK: Cambridge University Press.

Cockburn, A. (2001). *Writing effective use cases*. Boston: Addison-Wesley.

Conklin, J., & Begeman, M. L. (1988). gIBIS: A hypertext tool for exploratory policy discussion. *ACM Transactions on Office Information Systems, 64*, 303–331.

Cross, N. (2000). *Engineering design methods: Strategies for product design*. Chichester, UK: Wiley.

Cross, N. (2002). Creative cognition in design: Processes of exceptional designers. In *Proceedings of the 4th conference on creativity and cognition* (pp. 14–19). New York: ACM Press.

Djajadiningrat, J. P., Gaver, W. W., & Frens, J. W. (2000). Interaction relabelling and extreme characters: Methods for exploring aesthetic interactions. In D. Boyarski & W. A. Kellogg (Eds.), *Conference proceedings: DIS2000 designing interactive systems: Processes, practices methods and techniques* (pp. 66–71). New York: ACM Press.

Dowell, J., & Long, J. L. (1998). A conception of the cognitive engineering design problem. *Ergonomics, 41*, 126–139.

DSDM Consortium. (1995). *DSDM consortium: Dynamic systems development method*. Farnham: Tesseract Publishers.

Eason, K. D., Harker, S. D. P., & Olphert, C. W. (1996). Representing socio-technical systems options in the development of new forms of work organisation. *European Journal of Work and Organisational Psychology, 5*, 399–420.

Fischer, G. (1996). Seeding, evolutionary growth and reseeding: Constructing, capturing and evolving knowledge in domain-oriented design environments. In A. G. Sutcliffe, D. Benyon, & F. Van Assche (Eds.), *Domain knowledge for interactive system design; Proceedings: TC8/WG8.2 conference on domain knowledge in interactive system design* (pp. 1–16). London: Chapman & Hall.

Friedman, B. (Ed.). (1997). *Human values and the design of computer technology*. Cambridge, UK: Cambridge University Press.

Gaver, W. W., Beaver, J., & Benford, S. (2003). Ambiguity as a resource for design. In V. Bellotti, T. Erickson, G. Cockton, & P. Korhonen (Eds.), *CHI 2003 conference proceedings: Conference on human factors in computing systems* (pp. 233–240). New York: ACM Press.

Graham, L. (1996). Task scripts, use cases and scenarios in object oriented analysis. *Object-Oriented Systems, 3*, 123–142.

Hampton, J. A. (1988). Disjunction in natural categories. *Memory and Cognition, 16*, 579–591.

Jacobson, I., Christerson, M., Jonsson, P., & Overgaard, G. (1992). *Object-oriented software engineering: A use-case driven approach*. Reading: Addison Wesley.

Johnson-Laird, P. N., & Wason, P. C. (1983). *Thinking: Readings in cognitive science*. Cambridge, UK: Cambridge University Press.

Kaindl, H. (1995). An integration of scenarios with their purposes in task modelling. In G. M. Olson & S. Schuon (Eds.), *Designing interactive systems: DIS 95 conference* (pp. 227–235). New York: ACM Press.

Karsenty, L. (1996). An empirical evaluation of design rationale documents. In *Proceedings of CHI'96 conference: Human factors in computing systems* (pp. 150–156). New York: ACM Press.

Kuutti, K. (1995). Workprocess: Scenarios as a preliminary vocabulary. In J. M. Carroll (Ed.), *Scenario based design* (pp. 19–36). New York: Wiley.

Kyng, M. (1995). Creating contexts for design. In J. M. Carroll (Ed.), *Scenario based design* (pp. 85–108). New York: Wiley.

Lakoff, G., & Johnson, M. (1999). *Philosophy in the flesh: The embodied mind and its challenge to western thought*. New York: Basic Books.

MacLean, A., & McKerlie, D. (1995). *Design space analysis and user-representations* (Technical Report EPC-1995-102). Cambridge, UK: Xerox Research Centre Europe.

MacLean, A., Young, R. M., Bellotti, V., & Moran, T. P. (1991). Questions, options and criteria: Elements of design space analysis. *Human-Computer Interaction, 6*, 201–250.

Moggridge, B. (2006). *Designing interaction*. Cambridge, MA: MIT Press.

Monk, A. G., & Wright, P. (1993). *Improving your human-computer interface: A practical technique*. Boston: Prentice Hall.

Mylopoulos, J., Chung, L., & Yu, E. (1999). From object-oriented to goal-oriented requirements analysis. *Communications of the ACM, 42*, 31–37.

Norman, D. A. (1999). *The invisible computer: Why good products can fail, the personal computer is so complex, and information appliances are the solution*. Cambridge, MA: MIT Press.

Paterno, F. (1999). *Model-based design and evaluation of interactive applications*. Berlin: Springer.

Potts, C. (1999). ScenIC: A strategy for inquiry-driven requirements determination. In *Proceedings: 4th IEEE international symposium on requirements engineering* (pp. 58–65). Los Alamitos: IEEE Computer Society Press.

Potts, C., Takahashi, K., & Anton, A. I. (1994). Inquiry-based requirements analysis. *IEEE Software, 11*, 21–32.

Rolland, C., Ben Achour, C., Cauvet, C., Ralyte, J., Sutcliffe, A. G., & Maiden, N. A. M. (1998). A proposal for a scenario classification framework. *Requirements Engineering, 3*, 23–47.

Rosch, E., Mervis, C. B., Gray, W., Johnson, D., & Boyes-Braem, P. (1976). Basic objects in natural categories. *Cognitive Psychology, 7*, 573–605.

Rosson, M. B., & Carroll, J. M. (2001). *Usability engineering: Scenario-based development of human computer interaction*. San Francisco: Morgan Kaufmann.

Simon, H. A. (1973). The structure of ill-structured problems. *Artificial Intelligence, 4*, 181–201.

Sutcliffe, A. G. (2000). Bridging the communications gap: Developing a lingua franca for software developers and users. In *Actes du XVIIIe Congres: INFORSID* (pp. 13–32). Toulouse: Inforsid.

Sutcliffe, A. G. (2002). *User-centred requirements engineering*. London: Springer.

Sutcliffe, A. G., & Carroll, J. M. (1998). Generalizing claims and reuse of HCI knowledge. In H. Johnson, L. Nigay, & C. Roast (Eds.), *People and computers XIII; Proceedings: BCS-HCI conference* (pp. 159–176). Berlin: Springer.

Sutcliffe, A. G., & Carroll, J. M. (1999). Designing claims for reuse in interactive systems design. *International Journal of Human-Computer Studies, 50*, 213–241.

Sutcliffe, A. G., & Maiden, N. A. M. (1992). Analysing the novice analyst: Cognitive models in software engineering. *International Journal of Man-Machine Studies, 36*, 719–740.

Sutcliffe, A. G., & Ryan, M. (1997). Assessing the usability and efficiency of design rationale. In S. Howard, J. Hammond, & G. Lindgaard (Eds.), *Proceedings: Human computer interaction INTERACT-97* (pp. 148–155). London: Chapman and Hall.

Sutcliffe, A. G., Maiden, N. A. M., Minocha, S., & Manuel, D. (1998). Supporting scenario-based requirements engineering. *IEEE Transactions on Software Engineering, 24*, 1072–1088.

Sutcliffe, A. G., Gault, B., & Maiden, N. A. M. (2005). ISRE: Immersive scenario-based requirements engineering with virtual prototypes. *Requirements Engineering, 10*, 95–111.

Sutcliffe, A. G., Thew, S., Venters, C., De Bruijn, O., NcNaught, J., Proctor, R., & Buchan, I. (2007). ADVISES project: Scenario-based requirements analysis for e-science applications. In *Proceedings of UK All Hands Conference on e-Science, Nottingham*. Available on CD-ROM.

Sutcliffe, A. G., Thew, S., & Jarvis, P. (2011). Experience with user-centred requirements engineering. *Requirements Engineering, 7*, 1–14.

Thew, S., Sutcliffe, A. G., De Bruijn, O., McNaught, J., Procter, R., Venters, C., & Buchan, I. (2008). Experience in e-science requirements engineering. In *Proceedings: 16th IEEE international requirements engineering conference* (pp. 277–282). Los Alamitos: IEEE Computer Society Press.

Thew, S., Sutcliffe, A. G., Procter, R., De Bruijn, O., McNaught, J., Venters, C., & Buchan, I. (2009). Requirements engineering for e-science: Experiences in epidemiology. *IEEE Software, 26*(1), 80–87.

Yu, E. S. K. (1993). Modelling organisations for information systems requirements engineering. In S. Fickas & A. C. W. Finkelstein (Eds.), *Proceedings: 1st international symposium on requirements engineering* (pp. 34–41). Los Alamitos: IEEE Computer Society Press.

Chapter 6
Achieving Both Creativity and Rationale: Reuse in Design with Images and Claims

D. Scott McCrickard, Shahtab Wahid, Stacy M. Branham, and Steve Harrison

Abstract Although designers seek to create designs that are novel, most are based in some part on previous work. However, formal methods for design rationale reuse are dismissed as too inhibiting to the creative process. In this chapter we argue for the reuse of rationale as a central activity in design, and explore how this can be used as part of the creative process. Specifically, we examine how claims, paired with representative images, can stimulate the creative process while providing a bridge to rationale reuse. We present a design approach in which images and claims are presented together, supporting reuse in design activities like storyboarding. An evaluation revealed the careful interplay between creativity and rationale reuse, illustrating how they can complement each other during the design process. Our work serves to demonstrate that an appropriate design activity can be used to leverage creativity with the use of rationale.

Keywords Reuse • Creativity • Rationale • Claims • Images

6.1 Introduction

The formal and mechanized nature of many design rationale methods may seem a hindrance to the creative process, inhibiting the natural flow of ideas that is so important to groundbreaking concepts. However, by ignoring the lessons learned by others, a designer may risk lacking the knowledge to put forward potentially creative ideas. In this chapter we explore ways to present design rationale that help

D.S. McCrickard (✉) • S. Wahid • S.M. Branham • S. Harrison
Center for Human-Computer Interaction, Virginia Tech, 2202 Kraft Drive,
Blacksburg, VA, USA
e-mail: mccricks@cs.vt.edu; swahid@cs.vt.edu; sbranham@cs.vt.edu; srh@cs.vt.edu

J.M. Carroll (ed.), *Creativity and Rationale: Enhancing Human Experience by Design*, Human–Computer Interaction Series, DOI 10.1007/978-1-4471-4111-2_6, © Springer-Verlag London 2013

stimulate the creative process, while providing at the appropriate time a bridge to design rationale. In particular, we consider how the representation of images—a familiar construct in many creative activities—encourages designers to generate novel ideas as a first instinct, with the rationale enabling the desire to justify, compare, and build toward a solution.

One important approach to leveraging design rationale is appropriate knowledge reuse, wherein previously created artifacts are considered in the design process toward creating a design that might be an improvement over a prior solution. Many practitioners exercise knowledge reuse informally by basing new solutions on old experiences: Products developed previously could be used in new ways, distinct ideas can be connected together, or evolutions of previous products can be made possible through technological advances. When new products are created, designers tend to naturally reuse techniques of the past—providing impetus behind an often-ignored need to gain and even build on what has been used before (Whittaker et al. 2000).

New designs built with formal design rationale approaches show promise in enabling designers to think deeply about the trade-offs presented in each design decision towards lowering costs (Bias and Mayhew 2005) and improving usability (Wania 2008). Prior efforts within interface development communities have investigated ways of facilitating the reuse of various components, often rooted in design knowledge capture (Borchers 2000; Hughes 2007; Landay and Borriello 2003; Sutcliffe and Carroll 2000). However, constraints placed in design rationale systems, such as formalized structures and processes, can hamper the effectiveness of creative workers (Horner and Atwood 2006).

Creative ideation is often seen as beneficial since it can spark new directions with the potential to lead to interesting and novel designs. Quality creative ideas balance novelty with appropriateness (Bias and Mayhew 2005; Amabile et al. 1996), often with a role for appropriate information acquisition and selection. Even though there are many avenues to creative design, it is essential to consider how well the generated ideas fit with the intended design.

In this chapter, we put forth the position that those engaged in design may benefit from both creative ideation and rationale-based reasoning centered around reusable features. Although new ideas might lead to fresh ways of thinking about technology, we believe that their value may be increased when grounded in reasoning acquired through previous efforts. Creativity and rationale are not, a priori, opposing forces, but rather could be made complementary when encapsulated in appropriate design artifacts. We reason that lightweight rationale buffered by rich pictures and an engaging storyboarding activity may be one solution to this challenge.

Therefore, we explore the role of creativity and rationale in reuse with emphasis on the *claim*—a form of rationale capturing a feature and its design tradeoffs (Carroll and Kellogg 1989). We articulate the advantages of leveraging rationale, but also acknowledge the need to ease its reuse in design. Thus, we investigate the nature of creativity, leading to the role that *imagery* can carry out in aiding claims reuse. In an effort to further explore this space, we created domain-specific cards that merge imagery and claims together. We also present one technique, a design activity in which these cards are used to construct storyboards, and reflect on the role of creativity and rationale during reuse.

6.2   Rationale and Reuse

When practitioners approach design problems in search for answers, they rely on internalized reasoning as well as the reuse of past experiences and solutions. Formal rationale reuse methods try to mimic and improve upon these aspects of design with more explicit, externalized representations of knowledge. As digital or physical artifacts, reusable design rationale units provide focus points for dialectic collaboration and offer generalized solutions for contextualized consideration. Moreover, they open opportunities for design knowledge to traverse the gap of time and space between teacher and pupil, or between peers with different perspectives.

History includes many methods for capturing and associating knowledge, toward making it more accessible to researchers. As stores of knowledge grew in the early part of the twentieth century, visionaries like Paul Otlet (Wright 2007) and Vannevar Bush (1945) presented grand schemes for capturing, linking, and accessing knowledge. Their focus was not merely on classifying collections of books, but on identifying the core knowledge units within them that appropriately capture the essence of the contribution.

Design rationale emerged from the inherent bounded rationality of design thinking and wicked nature of design problems (Rittel and Webber 1973; Simon 1996). These notions were encapsulated in the issue-based information system (IBIS) model of design argumentation, which structures discourse by design topic, issues, arguments, and questions of fact that are raised in design dialogue (Kuntz and Rittel 1970). MacLean et al.'s (1991) questions, options, and criteria (QOC) presents a more formal design rationale model, encompassing questions about the design space, alternative design options, and criteria for selecting the solution. In a less formal representation, case studies capture the key rationale that results in observed design outcomes (Borchers 2000; Harvard Business School, n.d.).

Perhaps the component most commonly associated with reuse in interface design is the pattern (Borchers 2000; Landay and Borriello 2003; Lin and Landay 2008; van Duyne et al. 2007; Yahoo! Developer Network, n.d.). Originally proposed by Alexander et al. (1979) for the design of buildings and towns, patterns are reusable design knowledge components. They include information such as context of use, conflicting forces, and potential solutions—components that incorporate design rationale. Pre-patterns are forms of patterns used in emerging design domains (Saponas et al. 2006).

Similar to the pattern or case study, but of a different scale, is the claim. First introduced by Carroll and Kellogg (1989), claims document the psychological effects of user interface features in context. Although claims were initially proposed as disposable knowledge units (e.g., Carroll and Kellogg 1989; Rosson and Carroll 2002), they have since been identified to be of appropriate granularity for reuse (Payne et al. 2003; Sutcliffe and Carroll 2000). Through these transitions, the claim has taken on differing shapes and sizes. In this chapter, we focus on its simplest form: a feature coupled with usability tradeoffs (Fig. 6.1).

Some claims, as illustrated by our example in Fig. 6.1, are based upon scientific findings (Greenberg and Rounding 2001). Others may be generated by designers

Fig. 6.1 An example claim
with a feature, upsides, and
downsides

> ## Organizing information items using a collage metaphor
>
> + *overlapping items indicate relative age of content*
> + *accommodates a wide range of different types of information*
> - *layered content may require users to move several items to uncover others*
> - *lack of organization may hinder efforts to find items*

based upon experience or intuition. The contextualized nature of a claim's creation may alter the relevance and meaning of upsides and downsides when claims are reused in new design situations. Although these characteristics may result in varying claim quality, there is an important contribution beyond explicit transfer of design knowledge. Claims motivate design reasoning, particularly because they call attention to trade-offs and encourage designers to increase positive impacts (Rosson and Carroll 2002). In addition, claims documented by one designer in a unique design situation may provide an outsider's perspective to future designers that interact with that claim. Claims, then, are not just about an explicit hand-off of expert knowledge; they are instead about designer engagement with external perspectives in a user-centered, trade-offs-oriented mindset.

Claims, like patterns, are discrete units of design knowledge. One salient departure is the structure and depth of information captured in each rationale unit. Where a single pattern may fill a dozen pages (van Duyne et al. 2007) and consist of many different parts, such as a synopsis, background, problem, solution, forces, and evidence (Saponas et al. 2006), a claim in its basic form encapsulates a feature description with its design trade-offs (Rosson and Carroll 2002). Although we acknowledge patterns can emerge in different sizes, we submit claims as a viable alternative to patterns since their difference in structure may make claims designer digestible—quick to read, comprehend, and act upon (Carroll and Kellogg 1989).

Claims may be informally and quickly drawn up in the heat of design situations with minimal interruption to design activities. Of course, the test of whether or not designers actually capitalize on this opportunity relies upon sufficient designer buy-in to design rationale reuse; we believe it can be achieved with the framing of an appropriate design activity. Hence, we find claims one suitable form of rationale because they have the potential to both provide insight at design prototyping time as well as capture lessons learned in situ that may be passed on to designers in different times, places, and contexts.

Although design rationale played a larger role earlier, it is now true that design rationale is not widely used (Carroll 2003), in part because it is prone to capture, retrieval, and usage limitations during design (Horner and Atwood 2006). Keeping this in mind, we acknowledge that claims are also subject to potential negative consequences. When faced with a large collection of claims, it can be burdensome and time consuming for designers to investigate claims because of their textual nature—necessitating quick recognition of the essence of claims. It is also quite possible that a designer might have a different view of the feature, but this may potentially influence or eliminate a designer's independent consideration of what the impact of the artifact might be and how it may be used. Designers need to think for themselves to further develop their own understanding of an artifact instead of immediately being exposed to the bias of the claim itself. Only then can a claim serve to challenge designers' own understanding of the artifact. Creating a claim can encourage designers to think for themselves and draw on their own experiences. However, a source of inspiration for new features that might go hand in hand with the existing claims would benefit designers greatly. A new way to represent claims that can inspire designers through creative means is needed to reduce the negative impact during reuse.

6.3 Creativity Supporting Reuse

Creativity has long been a trait sought in design process—it is the source of new ideas, new products, and new hope for human discovery. And yet, researchers are still working to describe and explain the creativity phenomenon. Creative acts can even take on many different forms (Harrison and Tatar 2008). The result is a varied set of equivocal conceptions of creativity and an abundance of questions yet unanswered. Definitions of creativity range from the creative process (e.g., Amabile 1983; Hogarth 1980; Osborn 1963; Shneiderman 2000; Sonnenburg 2004; Wallas 1926), to the creative person (e.g., Guilford 1950; Lubart 2005), to the creative product (e.g., Amabile 1982; Boden 1994). As human–computer interaction (HCI) researchers, our concern with creativity is twofold: Not only are we deeply engaged with questions of how technology can enhance creative endeavors, but—and this second obligation often goes neglected—we also are invested in supporting creativity in our usability design processes. The latter of these is a key focus of this work.

There is a common misunderstanding about the definition of creative products: It is often assumed that creative products must only satisfy the singular criterion of novelty. Certainly, a creative idea must be new, at least to the immediate creators (Bias and Mayhew 2005), but that is not sufficient. Creative ideas must also exhibit appropriateness (Amabile et al. 1996). That is, the idea must solve a problem, be useful and usable, and otherwise satisfy measures of quality.

Generating creative ideas can be considered as the reuse of existing knowledge to elicit new knowledge: "Although cases of insight do occur, more often than not creative thought calls for information acquisition and the selection of appropriate concepts for understanding this information" (Mumford 2000, p. 315). Furthermore, creativity is often the result of the fusion of existing knowledge from disparate domains: "Creative novelty springs largely from the rearrangement of existing knowledge—a rearrangement that is itself an addition to knowledge. Such rearrangement reveals an unsuspected kinship between 'facts long known but wrongly believed to be strangers to one another'" (Kneller 1965, p. 4). Recombinations of existing knowledge can sometimes be viewed as crossing boundaries between fields to apply an analogous solution to a new problem (Thomas et al. 2002). These types of recombinations can sometimes be achieved through lateral thinking techniques, whereby diverse stimuli are used to initiate novel connections (De Bono 1990).

Another important aspect of creativity is its temporal span; it is a staged process that can vary from moments to days in duration. One of the foundational models, conceived by Wallas (1926), includes the transition of an individual through four sequential phases: preparation, incubation, illumination, and verification. Preparation is marked by the gathering of existing information and domain knowledge in response to a motivating problem; it is a period during which the creator "reads, notes, discusses, questions, collects, explores" (Kneller 1965, p. 48). During incubation, the knowledge gained through preparation is left to steep and the problem, perhaps, is even forgotten altogether. In a moment of unconsciously driven illumination, the creator happens upon a novel solution. In the final phase, verification, the implications of the speculative solution are consciously considered and revised for appropriateness. More recent constructions of the creative process (e.g., Amabile 1983; Hogarth 1980; Osborn 1963; Shneiderman 2000; Sonnenburg 2004; Wallas 1926) still include these foundational phases at an abstracted level.

In this staged process, idea illumination and idea verification are separate phases and may take place one before the other (as formalized in Osborn's 1963, brainstorming process). With respect to user-centered HCI design, we consider this an opportunity to balance images (i.e., rich stimuli that may aid idea generation) and reusable design rationale (i.e., a cognitive tool that may aid idea assessment) in a combined artifact-based activity. We propose that, by presenting images first, the initial focus will be placed on the creation of novel ideas without immediate attention to whether ideas fit both the novel and appropriate constraints. And, presenting rationale second may allow novel ideas to be explored before being reigned in by rationale in the assessment of appropriateness. The next two sections explore reusable rationale and images, respectively, as complementary components for enabling the creative process.

Pictures, images, and sketches have been incorporated in a number of creative design activities for their ability to stimulate divergent thinking. In creative writing, picture "sparks" are used to help inspire a new story direction (Kellaher 1999). Trend cards, each comprising a short textual fact about a target market and related picture, are used in industry to stimulate brainstorming sessions (Smith 2009). The Creative Whack Pack (von Oech 2008) and Thinkpak (Michalko 2006) use sketches and images to encourage creative problem finding and problem reframing. Picture-based artifacts that promote creativity are also beginning to appear in HCI design methods in the form of product example pictures (Herring et al. 2009) and cards that capture values (Nathan et al. 2009). Most existing image-centric creative design activities are strong on brainstorming and idea generation, but do not focus on issues of appropriateness and rationale.

In this chapter, we consider images of system features or of symbols thereof not only because this fits the granularity of our chosen unit of design rationale, but also because features may be an appropriate unit for sparking creative ideation. We believe that pictures of system features—objects and symbols captured as moments in rich context—are evocative stimuli that may provide a platform for lateral thinking. This type of thinking spawns novel connections between stimuli—pictures of features—and the problem domain. Furthermore, a pool of diverse feature pictures spread out on a surface such that most are visible at the same time has potential to provide opportunities for novel recombination and rearrangement of existing ideas. Finally, because the visual nature of pictures allows them to be seen and understood in little more than an instant, it may allow designers to flow fluidly between ideas as they "read" each image, thus supporting the preparation and incubation stages of creative ideation.

6.4 Image and Claim Reuse in Storyboarding

Storyboards are visual narratives that include actors engaging in a series of actions toward a common goal. Typically, they consist of multiple panels made of pictures and an accompanying narrative that illustrates a temporal progression. Key aspects of a storyboard are the portrayal of time, the inclusion of people and emotions, the inclusion of text, and the level of detail (Truong et al. 2006). Used by those involved in the creation of movies, cartoons, and commercials, they are powerful tools for thinking through and presenting the most important aspects of a narrative (Finch 1973; Hart 1999).

In HCI, storyboards have been used in the design process to illustrate how users may interact with a system (Buxton 2007; Sharp et al. 2007). Primarily used in early prototyping phases, storyboards in this domain describe the user's interaction with a system over time through a series of graphical depictions, often sketches, and units of textual narrative. Storyboards have been used to help understand the flow of the interaction scenario, to eliminate costly elements of a design, and even to decide how to pitch ideas to others (Buxton 2007; Rosson and Carroll 2002).

Reuse has been supported in the storyboarding process, both formally and informally. The earliest storyboards of films and cartoons used reusable components of characters (Finch 1973). Storyboarding tools such as SILK (Landay and Myers 1995), DENIM (Newman et al. 2003), and DEMAIS (Bailey and Konstan 2003) facilitate storyboarding to create prototypes early in design and support reuse through cutting, copying, and pasting of images within and between storyboards. As in our process, the Damask storyboarding tool leverages the reuse of patterns, although the authors acknowledge that the size of many patterns made them difficult to understand (Lin and Landay 2008).

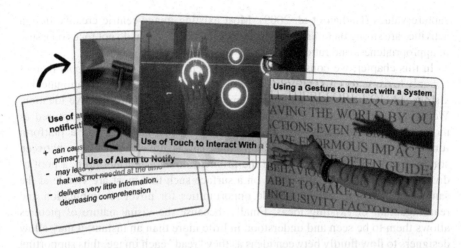

Fig. 6.2 Card fronts have pictures with labels to represent features, and card backs present textual claims with user-centered trade-offs

In our process, we seek to leverage and combine prior work in design rationale, creative inspiration through images, and storyboarding through an image-centric artifact set. Each artifact is presented in the form of a card depicting a feature through an image and label on the front and an associated claim on the back (see Fig. 6.2). We chose to place representative images and brief titles on the front of each card with the expectation that artifacts would be quickly recognized and designers would gain inspiration from the artifacts. In so doing, we expect that they would first consider broad possibilities of how the artifact could be used in design before being influenced by the claim on the back. However, the claim could serve as a gateway to formal design rationale, encouraging designers to consider the validity of their ideas in light of the rationale.

To explore this area, we are developing a method to facilitate the creation of storyboards by reusing premade artifacts for the creation of notification systems, tools that allow users to monitor information in dual-task situations (McCrickard et al. 2003). Our initial work led us to investigate the use of these cards in design sessions, where we asked groups of three to utilize the artifacts in creating a proto-type of a notification system (Wahid et al. 2009). Twenty-one graduate students were gathered to take part in seven sessions for the study. In each design session, the participants were presented with one unique problem and asked to create an appropriate notification system. Some of the design problems we assigned involved notifying nuclear plant operators of changing core temperatures, passengers in airports of flight status changes, commuters of empty parking lot spots while driving, theme park visitors of ride wait times, and students of empty spots for classes they wish to register for.

All participants were actively engaged in conducting HCI research or enrolled in a graduate HCI course at the time of the study. Their familiarity with storyboarding and claims varied. Because we target our artifacts to novice designers as well, we preferred to recruit novice designers at this stage of our investigation. Here, we report on our observations of the balance of creativity and rationale centered about the cards.

Novice designers engaged in this design activity work to familiarize themselves with the set of cards, decide on what cards might be useful for the system they wish to prototype, and construct a storyboard by placing cards together. When needed, they created their own cards to incorporate new ideas. Our observations of this activity have allowed us to understand better how these cards are able to encourage designers to balance novel ideation and grounded reasoning. We provide below some examples from design sessions we ran showing how these cards impacted the construction of storyboards and provided opportunity for creative ideas along the way.

The use of imagery proves to be an important segment of the activity since it is a springboard for new ideas. One way in which imagery does this is by making ideas ready at hand. It enables quick digestion and recognition of reusable ideas, so much so that designers often find themselves considering all of the cards as potential candidates for their design—something often not the case when features must be read in the form of plain text. By making more features available to designers for ready consideration, we vastly expand the design space considered for assimilation in a design session. The pictures support, to a degree, universally understood communication of its direct message, the feature, and provide designers the space to incorporate the appropriate cards into their storyboard.

On the other hand, pictures also support different messages and interpretations of their contents. This proves to be another advantage of using imagery: inspiring the designers to think of other artifacts that might not have been considered, potentially leading to novel ideas. In many of our design sessions, we observed participants thinking of new ideas while viewing the images that were unrelated to the nature of the artifact the image presented. For example, we observed a group that reinterpreted a card about relating preexisting user knowledge to a notification generated by a system. The image used for this card was a picture of a chat window showing the chat history. A participant in the group looking at the card chose to focus on the message timestamp that was contained within the chat window and proposed that the timestamp be a feature incorporated into their storyboard. The timestamp happened to be a part of the image, but was not necessarily there to illustrate the idea of the card. This serves to demonstrate that images can potentially inspire ideas that are beyond that of the claims themselves, leading to creative, divergent thinking patterns as well as a new source of knowledge to capture and store.

Images also afforded a platform for idea combination and domain transcendence–both tenets of creativity. Being that the pictures—which were taken in diverse times and places—all came together on a single table top, unique comparisons and couplings became possible and even natural. Participants placed pictures side by side for comparison and on top of one another for combination. As an example of feature combination, one group discussed joining a large-screen public display with a peripheral display to create a less distracting and user-driven source of information.

Although the features we presented to participants were of the same domain (notification systems), we believe that there is promise in presenting an even more diverse set of images to designers to enable novel combinations.

The textual claims on the back of the cards serve as important ways for designers to consider the utility of the reusable ideas and to gauge how appropriate they are. Whenever designers need more information or have doubts about how to use an artifact, claims serve as a way of describing the artifact and its utility. The claim trade-offs play a vital role in allowing designers to decide whether the artifact should be used in a design. Designers turn to the textual claim when debating the impact of a feature—especially high-impact negative ones that they may not have realized. In one instance, we observed a designer become aware of a claim's downside articulating that a notification generated by the system might be missed by the user. The designer immediately found another card that might mitigate the effects of this downside. Claim trade-offs also aid in deciding between cards when alternatives present themselves. The advantage in having the textual claim is that it can provide designers with rationale-based design concerns that they have possibly not thought of to challenge or counter their own interpretation of the card—providing an alternative perspective to the consideration of the card. Ultimately, the presence of textual claim information makes the designers more aware of the need to consider carefully the reasons for including a feature in a design.

Creating new cards to capture new ideas in the form of pictures and claims is also an important part of the activity. In the sessions we ran, three new cards were created. Although we found that cards are often created as a result of an idea that was inspired by another card, it would be hard to identify whether it is solely because of the image or whether the associated claim played a role as well. For instance, a group decided to create a new card based on a card about graphical information because they wanted to create a system that also incorporated geospatial location, and therefore created a new card about geospatial representation of information. The group drew a picture of a map with various points of interest within it and created a claim that was largely a more specified version of the claim used for graphical information. Their need to refer to the other card demonstrated that they wanted to maintain the same level of scope, making it generic and trying not to overspecify the card so that its potential reuse would not be restricted. Thus, the authoring of the claim was influenced by the claims that were already around them. Although we see that new ideas can arise, we notice that these ideas are often grounded in other artifacts that inspired the designers. Even though creative thought inspired by the graphical information imagery provided a springboard for knowledge capture, the rationale ensured the designers considered the consequence of the new feature. The burdens of creating a new card in terms of content might have been lowered by introducing a simple card structure, but we noticed that other factors, such as the designers' own knowledge and confidence in themselves, influenced whether a card was created.

Ultimately, the storyboard is constructed by choosing relevant cards, sequencing them according to a determined task flow, and then writing an accompanying narrative or scenario for each segment of the storyboard to solve the given design

Fig. 6.3 An example of a storyboard created by reusing the cards. The narrative serves to bring context and integrate the cards together

problem (see Fig. 6.3). We acknowledge the final product of this activity is not a traditional storyboard since it does not enforce sketching. However, elements such as actors and the portrayal of time are still embodied within the narrative.

The construction process is also a careful interplay between creativity and rationale. Designers engage in exploring new ways to combine and order cards to create new functionality. For example, a new notification method could be created by combining a card about a blinking light with an audio notification card—leading them to either place the cards side by side or on top of each other. At the same time, their combined use is analyzed through the claims and further discussion on its potential effects. It is important to note that designers go beyond the individual cards and also focus on the system as a whole—testing out creative new task flows that result from a new sequence of artifacts. Although the participants chose the cards they felt were relevant to their goals, further investigation would be needed to understand which cards are prioritized depending on the given design problems and the eventual quality of the storyboards.

We believe that the nature of combined imagery and rationale is a primary factor in facilitating designers in brainstorming and considering consequences at the same time. Reusing ideas of the past may be beneficial, but the application of these ideas in new ways and forms may bring out potentially innovative solutions.

6.5 Conclusions

Supporting reuse is an important step in bringing together creativity and rationale. To support the types of creative sparks we observed, a corpus of rationale is needed so that there can be a ready source of inspiration and a variety of creative ways of combining them. We acknowledge that identifying new rationale can be beneficial, but believe that a preexisting, reusable set, especially at the start of a project, can serve these goals more effectively.

Even if reuse were to be supported, one could perceive that reuse, as a central tenet to design, can lead to uncreative and uninspired outcomes. However, this perception may be changed with the incorporation of mechanisms that inspire creative thought. In working toward this goal, careful thought must be put into the design of the reusable artifact and how those artifacts might interact with each other because that is where the creativity will most likely percolate. Although further investigation of our technique is needed, the combination of rationale and creativity for reuse seems to be a step toward provoking designers into creating innovative solutions and create a fresh source of knowledge that can be stored for others to reuse later.

Putting such a vision into practice requires that we identify appropriate mechanisms to capture rationale, inspire creativity, and construct meaningful prototypes. Claims are uniquely structured to capture knowledge in a designer-digestible manner to support reuse, and appropriate images associated with the claims summarize the message while facilitating ideation and reinterpretation. Because of their structure, they can be authored easily with limited effort—reducing the burdens associated with formal capture of rationale.

These knowledge-capture and presentation mechanisms (claims and images) must come together through a meaningful design activity. In our case the activity happens to be storyboarding, but other prototyping activities might prove to be equally useful. Because storyboarding is a creative and fun way to illustrate both visually and textually the task flow of a new system, it leverages both the visual images through early innovative bursts while encouraging deeper reflection in the authoring of accompanying text. Designers perform the early creative stages in their design by identifying options, then exploring and conceptualizing solutions— but the claims provide a basis for scientifically sound solution verification and production.

At this point, this work is taking steps to set the stage for design by reuse by assessing the benefits of incorporating creativity and rationale together. One future direction is to assess the quality of the designs that are produced as a result of the activity. Another future effort must explore how the process of brainstorming before storyboard construction can be improved through appropriate designer exposure to images and claims. Early exposure to images without rationale might inspire designers to interpret the images in very different ways, leading to a larger pool of possible insights. When designers are exposed to the associated rationale later, they may weigh the utility of their ideas against the recorded argumentation.

References

Alexander, C., Isikawa, S., & Silverstein, M. (1979). *A pattern language: Towns, buildings, construction*. New York: Oxford University Press.

Amabile, T. M. (1982). The social psychology of creativity: A consensual assessment technique. *Journal of Personality and Social Psychology, 43*, 997–1013.

Amabile, T. M. (1983). The social psychology of creativity: A componential conceptualization. *Journal of Personality and Social Psychology, 45*, 357–376.

Amabile, T. M., Collins, M. A., Conti, R., Phillips, E., Picariello, M., Ruscio, J., & Whitney, D. (1996). *Creativity in context: Update to the social psychology of creativity*. Boulder: Westview Press.

Bailey, B., & Konstan, J. A. (2003). Are informal tools better? Comparing DEMAIS, pencil and paper, and authorware for early multimedia design. In *Proceedings of the 2003 SIGCHI conference on human factors in computing systems* (CHI '03, pp. 313–320). New York: ACM Press.

Bias, R. G., & Mayhew, D. J. (2005). *Cost-justifying usability*. San Francisco: Morgan Kaufmann.

Boden, M. A. (1994). *Dimensions of creativity*. Cambridge, MA: MIT Press.

Borchers, J. O. (2000). A pattern approach to interaction design. In *Proceedings of the conference on designing interactive systems* (DIS '00, pp. 369–378). New York: ACM Press.

Bush, V. (1945). As we may think. *The Atlantic Monthly, 176*(1), 101–108.

Buxton, B. (2007). *Sketching user experiences: Getting the design right and the right design*. San Francisco: Morgan Kaufmann.

Carroll, J. M. (2003). *HCI models, theories, and frameworks: Toward a multidisciplinary science*. San Francisco: Morgan Kaufmann.

Carroll, J. M., & Kellogg, W. A. (1989). Artifact as theory-nexus: Hermeneutics meets theory-based design. In *Proceedings of the 1989 SIGCHI conference on human factors in computing systems* (CHI '89, pp. 7–14). New York: ACM Press.

De Bono, E. (1990). *Lateral thinking*. Harmondsworth: Penguin.

Finch, C. (1973). *The art of Walt Disney: From Mickey Mouse to the Magic Kingdom*. New York: Harry Abrams.

Greenberg, S., & Rounding, M. (2001). The notification collage: Posting information to public and personal displays. In *Proceedings of the 2001 SIGCHI conference on human factors in computing systems* (CHI '01, pp. 514–521). New York: ACM Press.

Guilford, J. (1950). Creativity. *American Psychologist, 5*, 444–454.

Harrison, S., & Tatar, D. (2008, June). *"It's just a rationale!": Creativity in the formation and application of design rationale*. Paper presented at the workshop on creativity and rationale in software design, University Park, PA, USA.

Hart, J. (1999). *The art of the storyboard: Storyboarding for film, TV, and animation*. Amsterdam: Focal Press.

Harvard Business School (n.d.). Faculty & research cases. Retrieved August 4, 2011, from http://www.hbs.edu/research/publications/cases.html

Herring, S. R., Chang, C. C., Krantzler, J., & Bailey, B. P. (2009). Getting inspired! Understanding how and why examples are used in creative design practice. In *Proceedings of the 2009 SIGCHI conference on human factors in computing systems* (CHI '09, pp. 87–96). New York: ACM Press.

Hogarth, R. M. (1980). *Judgement and choice: The psychology of decision*. Chichester: Wiley.

Horner, J., & Atwood, M. E. (2006). Design rationale: Rationale and the barriers. In *Proceedings of the Nordic conference on human-computer interaction* (NordiCHI '06, pp. 341–350). New York: ACM Press.

Hughes, M. (2007). A pattern language for user assistance. *Interactions, 14*(1), 27–29.

Kellaher, K. (1999). *101 picture prompts to spark super writing: Photographs, cartoons, art masterpieces to intrigue, amuse, inspire every writer in your class*. New York: Scholastic Professional Books.

Kneller, G. F. (1965). *The art and science of creativity*. New York: Holt, Rinehart and Winston.

Kuntz, W. R., & Rittel, H. W. J. (1970). *Issues as elements of information systems* (Technical Report No. 131). Berkeley: Institute of Urban and Regional Development, University of California.

Landay, J. A., & Borriello, G. (2003). Design patterns for ubiquitous computing. *IEEE Computer, 36*(8), 93–95.

Landay, J. A., & Myers, B. A. (1995). Interactive sketching for the early stages of user interface design. In *Proceedings of the 1995 SIGCHI conference on human factors in computing systems* (CHI '95, pp. 43–50). New York: ACM Press.

Lin, J., & Landay, J. A. (2008). Employing patterns and layers for early-stage design and prototyping of cross-device user interfaces. In *Proceedings of the 2008 SIGCHI conference on human factors in computing systems* (CHI '08, pp. 1313–1322). New York: ACM Press.

Lubart, T. (2005). How can computers be partners in the creative process: Classification and commentary on the special issue. *International Journal of Human Computer Studies, 63*, 365–369.

MacLean, A., Young, R., Bellotti, V., & Moran, T. (1991). Questions, options, and criteria: Elements of design space analysis. *Human Computer Interaction, 6*, 201–250.

McCrickard, D. S., Chewar, C. M., Somervell, J. P., & Ndiwalana, A. (2003). A model for notification systems evaluation: Assessing user goals for multitasking activity. *Transactions on Computer-Human Interaction, 10*, 312–338.

Michalko, M. (2006). *Thinkertoys*. Berkeley: Ten Speed Press.

Mumford, M. D. (2000). Managing creative people: Strategies and tactics for innovation. *Human Resource Management Review, 10*, 313–351.

Nathan, L., Friedman, B., & Hendry, D. (2009). Sustainably ours: Information system design as catalyst: Human action and environmental sustainability. *Interactions, 16*(4), 6–11.

Newman, M., Lin, J., Hong, J., & Landay, J. A. (2003). DENIM: An informal web site design tool inspired by observations of practice. *Human Computer Interaction, 18*, 259–324.

Osborn, A. F. (1963). *Applied imagination: Principles and procedures of creative thinking*. New York: Scribner.

Payne, C., Allgood, C. F., Chewar, C. M., Holbrook, C., & McCrickard, D. S. (2003). Generalizing interface design knowledge: Lessons learned from developing a claims library. In *Proceedings of the international conference on information reuse and integration* (pp. 362–369). Washington, DC: IEEE Computer Society.

Rittel, H. W. J., & Webber, M. M. (1973). Dilemmas in a general theory of planning. *Policy Sciences, 4*, 155–169.

Rosson, M. B., & Carroll, J. M. (2002). *Usability engineering: Scenario-based development of human-computer interaction*. San Francisco: Morgan Kaufmann.

Saponas, T. S., Prabaker, M. K., Abowd, G. D., & Landay, J. A. (2006). The impact of pre-patterns on the design of digital home applications. In *Proceedings of the conference on designing interactive systems* (pp. 189–198). New York: ACM Press.

Sharp, H., Rogers, Y., & Preece, J. (2007). *Interaction design: Beyond human-computer interaction*. West Sussex: Wiley.

Shneiderman, B. (2000). Creating creativity: User interfaces for supporting innovation. *Transactions on Computer-Human Interaction, 7*, 114–138.

Simon, H. A. (1996). *The sciences of the artificial*. Cambridge, MA: MIT Press.

Smith, S. (2009, May 1). Mobile + Social + Future: M4Change DC [Web log post]. Retrieved from http://www.changeist.com/changeism/2009/5/1/mobile-social-future-m4change-dc.html

Sonnenburg, S. (2004). Creativity in communication: A theoretical framework for collaborative product creation. *Creativity & Innovation Management, 13*, 254–262.

Sutcliffe, A. G., & Carroll, J. M. (2000). Designing claims for reuse in interactive systems design. *International Journal of Human Computer Studies, 50*, 213–241.

Thomas, J. C., Lee, A., & Danis, C. (2002). Creativity and interface: Enhancing creative design via software tools. *Communications of the ACM, 45*(10), 112–115.

Truong, K. N., Hayes, G. R., & Abowd, G. D. (2006). Storyboarding: An empirical determination of best practices and effective guidelines. In *Proceedings of the conference on designing interactive systems* (pp. 12–21). New York: ACM Press.

van Duyne, D. K., Landay, J. A., & Hong, J. I. (2007). *The design of sites: Patterns for creating winning web sites*. Upper Saddle River: Prentice Hall.

von Oech, R. (2008). *A whack on the side of the head*. New York: Hachette Book Group.

Wahid, S., Branham, S. M., Cairco, L., McCrickard, D. S., & Harrison, S. (2009). Picking up artifacts: Storyboarding as a gateway to reuse. In *Proceedings of the IFIP TC.13 conference on human-computer interaction* (pp. 528–541). New York: Springer.

Wallas, G. (1926). *The art of thought*. New York: Harcourt, Brace & World.

Wania, C. (2008). *Examining the impact of an information retrieval pattern language on the design of information retrieval interfaces*. Unpublished doctoral dissertation, Drexel University, Philadelphia, PA, USA.

Whittaker, S., Terveen, L., & Nardi, B. A. (2000). Let's stop pushing the envelope and start addressing it: A reference task agenda for HCI. *Human Computer Interaction, 15*, 75–106.

Wright, A. (2007). *Glut: Mastering information through the ages*. Ithaca: Cornell University Press.

Yahoo! Developer Network (n.d.). Design pattern library. Retrieved August 4, 2011, from http://developer.yahoo.com/ypatterns

Chapter 7
Predecessor Artifacts: Evolutionary Perspectives on a Reflective Conversation with Design Materials

Anders I. Mørch

Abstract Donald Schön described designing as a reflective conversation with the materials of a situation, and proposed a phenomenological account of designing. Ray McCall proposed an extension and generalization of Schön's model that more easily allows for computer support. Building on the work of Schön and McCall, this chapter adopts an evolutionary perspective on the design process and proposes "predecessor artifacts" as a new concept for understanding the reflective conversation with design materials. Predecessor artifacts emerge in creative activities and they encapsulate design history. The concept is applied to software design. Based on a literature survey, experimental prototyping, and empirical analyses in two user organizations, three types of predecessor artifacts are explored: (1) reusable design material, (2) alternative functionality, and (3) reusable design concepts. A goal with PAs is to understand design reuse in software applications from a phenomenological viewpoint.

Keywords Evolving artifacts • Design theory • Human-centred design • Predecessor artifact • Reflective conversation • Resemblance relation • Reusable design • Software design • User-participation

7.1 Introduction

Exploring predecessor artifacts (PAs) and how they are related to creativity and rationale is the aim of this chapter. Two claims are made: (1) Predecessor artifacts add a historical dimension to the reflective conversation with design materials (Schön 1983, 1992), and (2) connecting an artifact with its predecessor artifacts provides new opportunities for creative interactions with the artifact.

A.I. Mørch (✉)
InterMedia, University of Oslo, Oslo, Norway
e-mail: anders.morch@intermedia.uio.no

J.M. Carroll (ed.), *Creativity and Rationale: Enhancing Human Experience by Design*, Human–Computer Interaction Series, DOI 10.1007/978-1-4471-4111-2_7, © Springer-Verlag London 2013

7.1.1 Predecessor Artifacts and Creativity

Wittgenstein (1967) used the notion of "language game" to describe language use by analogy to how games are played and made sense of. He said that all games have common features, but no one feature is found in all games. Wittgenstein's point was that things, which may be thought to be connected by features shared by all, might in fact be connected by a series of overlapping similarities that are present to various degrees. This form of connecting things, referred to as *family resemblance*, was modeled after how members of a family relate to each other according to traits (visible properties): build, features, color of eyes, gait, temperament, etc. For example, a person may have one or more common features with a relative; they may share strong or weak traits, and the traits may change during the person's lifetime. This reveals a more dynamic relationship structure among things than what is common in software design and object-oriented analysis and design. Schön adopted this language into the domain of architectural design in order to understand the intertwining of drawing and talking, calling it a language for doing architecture (Schön 1983, p. 81), and Pelle Ehn adopted the same language for information systems design with end users, emphasizing the mutual learning of two different language games, one for designers and the other for users (Ehn 1988). The language game metaphor goes beyond formal methods in software by tapping into the richness of human experience and the myriads of ways of connecting reusable things. This is the approach to creativity advocated in this chapter.

7.1.2 Predecessor Artifacts and Rationale

Design rationale has been defined as a method of designing an artifact that makes explicit the reasons for its design (Moran and Carroll 1996). One way to organize design rationale is by distinguishing a process-oriented approach from a product-oriented approach (McCall 2010). The process-oriented approach (Conklin and Burgess-Yakemovic 1996; McCall 1991) is about capturing the argumentation or "design history" behind the artifact (a computer interface, a building, a neighborhood plan, etc.), which is a form of documentation that includes the alternatives considered during the design process, the chosen and the rejected alternatives. The historical sequence of the process is significant. The product-oriented approach is about analyzing the structure and nature of the artifacts (i.e. exploring the space of alternative artifacts) not its process of creation and development (MacLean et al. 1991).

A PA is special form design rationale that combines aspects of the process-oriented and product-oriented approaches. A PA is a rejected alternative (a product) that represents a snapshot in the history of a current artifact (the process). Furthermore, a predecessor artifact is represented by a "link" in a current artifact, which can be a role assigned to it or an emergent property (physical trace, symbolic reminder).

For example, when a new tool incorporate features of one or more existing tools, or when a new innovation makes older tools obsolete, or when a new tool appears on the market even though multiple alternatives are available, predecessor artifacts emerge. The process that leads to a predecessor artifact is a complex one that cannot be predicted in advance and includes creative acts of users, innovative system building, and often involving considerable efforts in engineering, management and marketing. For example, Apple's touch and gesture features of the iPhone with its easy-to-use interface for interacting with software components (apps) is an example of a new tool that has transformed competing tools into predecessor artifacts (i.e. other smartphones that were in the market at the time the iPhone was introduced in 2007 as well as the technology the iPhone is based on). Three kinds of predecessor artifacts are differentiated and discussed in this chapter based on analyses of evolving artifacts in a variety of domains: (1) reusable design material (traces of PAs), (2) alternative functionality (actual PAs), and (3) reusable design concepts (reminders of PAs).

Previous research in reusable design rationale has addressed reuse based on a cognitive framework, e.g. indexing, retrieving, understanding, and modifying prior design knowledge (e.g. Ball et al. 2001). The early stages of the reuse process (indexing and retrieving) appear differently from a phenomenological point of view. The 'here and now' of the present situation (features of a current artifact in use) becomes the center of an evolutionary design process, and reusable design rationales are associated with traces and reminders of previous artifacts in new designs.

The chapter is organized as follows. It starts with identifying some open issues in Donald Schön's theory of reflective conversation with design materials, in particular accounting for evolutionary design and computer support. Three cases in software design provide empirical support for the claims, each highlighting a unique role of predecessor artifacts in evolutionary development. The findings are discussed in terms of creativity and rationale. The chapter ends with suggestions for further work, including a method for deepened analysis of artifacts in design situations and design-based models of human learning and development.

7.2 Designing as a Reflective Conversation with Design Materials

Schön coined the expression "designing as reflective conversation with the materials of a situation" (1983, p. 78). He presented his theory to the design community in the "Reflective Practitioner" (Schön 1983), and later discussed implications for computer support and artificial intelligence in an article based on a conference keynote talk in 1992 (Schön 1992). Drawing on empirical studies in a range of different design situations, Schön profiled his theory as a generic design process that was characterized by complexity, and "because of this complexity, the designers moves tend, happily or unhappily, to produce consequences other than those intended," and the designer "responds to the situation's back-talk" (Schön 1983, p. 79). The complexity of the situation is partly a result of incomplete information in the beginning of a design process and the multiple interpretations a designer makes of the situation. Additional information appears as "back-talk" or feedback from the design, to which the designer responds by reflection-in-action, modifications, and reinterpretations (Schön 1983). Observation of designers in a variety of situations (professional and novice) and domains (e.g. architecture, town planning, management, psychotherapy) provided the data to support his claims.

There are two aspects of the reflective conversation model that are mentioned by Schön, but not addressed by him specifically: computer support and evolutionary design (Schön 1992). This will be elaborated in the remainder of the chapter.

McCall proposed an adaptation of Schön's model that more easily allows for computer support; combining reflective conversation with design rationale and referred to as *critical conversation* (McCall 2010). McCall and his colleagues developed computer support for critical conversations based on the procedural hierarchy of issues (PHI) method (McCall 1991). It is the historical dimension (process orientation) of design rationale that is added to the reflective conversation model. This implies that a designer considers the alternative issues, positions, and their arguments as they occur during the design process, in effect intertwining two distinct phases of design, *ideation* (the generation of design ideas) and *evaluation* (feedback from the uncompleted design that challenges the designer to devise new ideas). McCall claims that separating ideation from evaluation is one of the shortcomings of the past work on design rationale that goes back to the work of Rittel (1972), McCall's mentor and the inventor of issue-based information systems (IBIS). Schön's theory, however, provides a clue for their integration. By making a simplified model of the theory, McCall and his colleagues proposed to treat *action* as ideation and *reflection* as evaluation. They further claimed that situational back talk based on computerized feedback could trigger creativity when interacting with a computer-based design environment in certain situations (Fischer 1994). This originated with the Janus system, a computer-based design environment for kitchen design that integrates support for action and reflection in the same system (Fischer et al. 1989; McCall et al. 1990), and a series of systems that both preceded and followed Janus, like Mikroplis and Phidias (McCall 2010).

7.3 Evolving Artifacts

Schön's reflective conversation was not about evolutionary design because reusability of design materials was not a central concern for Schön. His approach to design was to explore creative design (combining design materials in new ways) within the constraints of a realistic design space (defined by task requirements, site properties, etc.). Schön explained that the evolutionary perspective of a design is evident in two ways: (1) a designer can evolve a design by appreciating materials in new ways (Schön used bridge design and jazz improvisation as examples), and (2) design intentions evolve during the design process, which for Schön was a source of problem identification (Schön 1992). These forms of evolutionary design correspond to what this author calls "specific development" or "adaptation," the evolution of an individual artifact (a series of drawings for a new house; the adaptation of a computer application to a user organization, etc.) (Mørch et al. 2009). Schön used the expression "seeing-drawing-seeing" to provide a phenomenological account of this type of evolutionary design (Schön 1992). The work presented here builds on Schön's work by integrating specific development with general development in order to describe predecessor artifacts (PAs) in software design. PAs are concrete artifacts that influence or stimulate a new design and they "reappear" in various forms of expression of the general level information in a new design.

The evolutionary perspective on designing used in this chapter is adopted from the natural sciences as two interdependent processes: (1) the interaction between organism and environment during individual development (adaptation or specific development), and (2) the interaction between specific and general (species) development (generalization and recapitulation). Recapitulation is a mechanism in living organisms for expressing general level information in a new off spring. It provides an analogy for one type of predecessor artifact (physical trace). One example from natural evolution is the gill slits featured in the embryonic development of human infants, serving as the visible remains of a functional organ inherited from a sea-breeding ancestor. The two processes have direct equivalents in the evolution of artifacts: (1) the interaction between a design and its context of use (adaptation or specific development), and (2) the interaction between specific and general development (generalization and predecessor artifacts). In software design, specific development refers to local design and end-user tailoring, e.g. the adaptation of a generic computer application to a user organization, with techniques ranging from workflow modeling to scripting (Mørch 1997). In contrast, general development refers to the work done by professional developers to fix errors and incrementally improve a product at the source code level, and to spawn new products when opportunities arise (Fischer et al. 1994; Mørch et al. 2009). These two processes are often poorly coordinated in software development, resembling the discrepancy of specific and general development in natural evolution.

On the other hand, artifact evolution and natural evolution differ in a number of ways. For example, in the early part of the previous century philosopher Henri Bergson argued that humans co-evolve with their environment in a more constructive manner than natural evolution can explain, and humans can impact evolution by intervention and acts of creative life (Bergson 1911/1993). Human intervention can respond to injustice, seek out areas for improvement, and correct past mistakes. Furthermore, natural organisms evolve by *necessity* (survival and reproduction), whereas artifacts tend to evolve by *convenience* (Basalla 1988), driven by the needs and desires of creative people and the demands of society (simplification, niceties, economic laws like supply and demand, manufacturability, etc.) (Feyerabend and Terpstra 1999; Tomlinson 2008). Therefore, artifacts can evolve along multiple paths that are not constrained by formal relationships; they can be informal as well as formal, which open the way for creative interactions with artifacts, such as appropriation (Carroll 2011), emergence (Seevinck and Edmonds 2008), and perceived resemblance (Mørch 2003) in local design activities. For example Carroll observed in a Blacksburg community-computing project (a virtual world simulating a real place) that users created their own use of the system in ways that was not part of the system's original design rationale.

Simon introduced the notion of evolving artifact in "Sciences of the Artificial" (Simon 1996). Architectural design and software design are examples of this branch of science. The study of artifact evolution at the specific and general levels belongs in the sciences of the artificial. Furthermore, the author, following Carroll (1994), Fischer (1994) and Norman (2008), takes the everyday uses of artifacts as the starting point for design, e.g., an expansive design process triggered by a difficult to use artifact. Previous studies of evolving artifacts include pottery jugs (Basalla 1988), buildings (Brand 1994), everyday tools (Petroski 1992), and computer applications (Carroll and Rosson 1996; Fischer et al. 1994; Mørch 1996). In these studies, design is characterized by incremental improvements of existing artifacts and to resolve the tensions of adaptation and generalization (Mørch et al. 2009). Traces and reminders of predecessor artifacts emerge as a result of these dynamic processes, in particular as a new design reuses material and ideas from previous designs. For example in the ancient African pottery jugs Basalla (1988, p. 107) analyzed, a cord made of organic material served as the first handling mechanism for carrying them. Later it was replaced by a more durable structure formed in clay and built into the jug itself. The original handles became ornamentation in the later series of jugs, serving as a symbolic reminder of the previous ways of using them (Mørch 2003).

Everyday physical artifacts triggered the author's research interest in predecessor artifacts and how they relate to reflective practice, creativity and rationale. Figure 7.1a shows an example of a reusable design material (parts of an old building reused in a new building). Figure 7.1b shows a reusable design concept, "exterior shelter space" or enclosed porch ("svalgang" in Norwegian), which refers to the lightweight structure built around the building's entrance area to protect people from bad weather upon entering, a concept originating in medieval farmhouses in Norway. Coin-operated and wall-plugged telephones represent a third type of predecessor artifact, serving as backup system to mobile phones.

Schön's conceptual framework for reflective conversation does not have a vocabulary for evolutionary design beyond adaptation. Therefore his framework must be augmented to take into account generalization and predecessor artifacts. This is easier with computer-based design environments than paper and pencil techniques because computational artifacts consist of multiple levels of abstraction (e.g. user interface, program code, runtime organization). However, predecessor artifacts are not exclusively tied to computer applications; they are found in all kinds of physical artifacts as illustrated by the motivating examples.

7.4 Research Questions and Methods

The research presented in this chapter is a reinterpretation of data from previous projects the author has been involved in, now with an eye on describing predecessor artifacts. The first project was part of the author's PhD dissertation (1993–1997),

Fig. 7.1 *Left* (**a**): reusable design material (old timber construction in a new house). *Right* (**b**): A reusable design concept ("svalgang," a kind of porch) refined in Storøya kindergarten (Photos from Bærum, Norway)

and demonstrates how end-user tailoring of a generic application (BasicDraw) can create a domain-oriented application (KitchenDesign), revealing PAs as physical traces of old functionality in the new application. The second project is a case study in the organizational implementation of an integrated work and learning platform for a national chain of gasoline stations in Norway (2001–2004), which resulted in existing tools becoming back-up systems (PAs). The third project is an empirical study of the interaction of end-user development and professional development in a software company that develops project-planning tools for the Nordic oil and gas industry. It was a case in a large European project (2006–2011), and revealed a design concept preserved and refined by the company in all its products. The methods used for data collection include experimental prototyping, interviewing, observation, videotaping, and web survey. The analyses reveal three types of predecessor artifacts: (1) reusable design material (project 1), (2) alternative functionality (project 2), and (3) reusable design concept (project 3).

7.5 Reusable Design Material in Application Evolution

The structure for this and the next two sections is: (1) context of case/site, (2) findings from the study, and (3) analysis of results from the point of view of describing predecessor artifacts and their emergence and role in evolutionary application development.

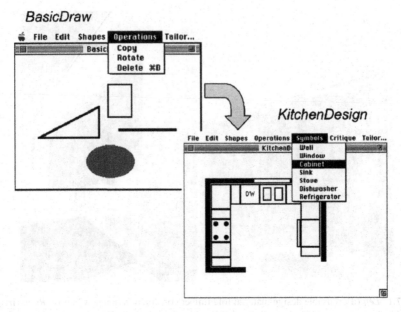

Fig. 7.2 Evolving BasicDraw into KitchenDesign by the tools available in the Tailor menu (customize, integrate, extend). KitchenDesign reuses functionality from BasicDraw, and reveals predecessor artifacts

7.5.1   Context

The goal of this study was to test a hypothesis for the evolutionary development of applications, namely that end-user development tools integrated with a generic application provide the necessary means to evolve the application from one task domain to another (Mørch 1996). Another goal was to bring the inheritance relation between class and subclass in object oriented programming to a more user-oriented level of abstraction (Mørch 1997, 2003).

7.5.2   Findings

We addressed this hypothesis by enabling end users to evolve BasicDraw into KitchenDesign (Mørch 1996). The two screenshots in Fig. 7.2 show before and after stages of this process, which were accomplished with the end-user development (tailor) tools integrated in BasicDraw (Mørch 1997). When using these tools, an end-user developer can modify reusable software functionality (application units) at three different levels of abstraction (user interface, design rationale, and program code).

The menus and shapes in KitchenDesign are subclasses of the menus and shapes in BasicDraw. For example the Symbols menu is a subclass of the Shapes menu. All the kitchen symbols in the work area are subclasses of the rectangle class, with some symbols composed of additional sub-shapes (rectangle, oval, text). The menu items were created in a similar fashion. The operations on the kitchen symbols (e.g. scaling) were realized as specialized methods to extend and constrain the original methods defined in the super-classes (Mørch 1997). The author conducted a video-recorded usability test of BasicDraw with twelve subjects and asked them to perform end-user development modifications to the application, and found that customization and integration were techniques that users could master without much instruction. The extension (writing program code in method bodies), however, required some knowledge of programming and basic skills in object-oriented programming (Mørch 1996).

7.5.3 Analysis

Even though the inheritance relation connected application units at the program code level, e.g. KitchenCabinet class inherits from Rectangle class; it was the resemblance among the application units visible in the user interface that enabled users to understand what reuse could offer them, i.e. *"kitchen cabinet looks like a rectangle."* The basic shapes became, both literally and in effect, predecessor artifacts in the kitchen design symbols. This means that inheritance is reflected at two levels, user interface and program code. The author proposed two types of resemblance relations to model them: perceived resemblance and self-resemblance (Mørch 2003). The first is "inheritance" as perceived by the user and the second is inheritance manifest in the artifact. Self-resemblance is arguable the relation that most faithfully models an application's connection with reusable software functionality (e.g. enabled by inheritance), but perceived resemblance can also be supported by the computer (reusing objects rather than classes).

7.6 Organizational Implementation of an Information Seeking Terminal

7.6.1 Context

A research team from InterMedia participated in the design and organizational implementation of a new information-seeking terminal for the gasoline division of a large oil company (Mørch et al. 2004a; Mørch and Skaanes 2010). This system was delivered as a web portal and installed in retail stations across the country. Participatory design techniques were used during the planning stages and evolutionary prototyping during the portal development stages (Mørch et al. 2004a).

a

b

INFORMATION-SEEKING METHODS BEFORE THE PORTAL (N=34)	
Method	%
Ask a colleague	81
Paper catalogs	58
Staff meetings	50
Call a colleague	38
Post-it notes	19
Call another station	19
Product sheets	19

Fig. 7.3 (a) Prototype of information seeking portal, and (b) information seeking preferences before the portal was introduced

The system contained information about automobile parts, fluids, and hot food preparation procedures, and was meant to serve as an online help system for every-day work (Fig. 7.3a). The portal adoption process lasted for 14 months and data was collected by interviews and a web survey during that period. The use of the system was not mandated, but the station managers encouraged the attendants to use it. Thirty-four respondents completed the survey. Interviews were conducted selected participants across age groups and management levels (Mørch and Skaanes 2010).

7.6.2   Findings

Before the introduction of the portal, the attendants had to make use of a range of resources for accessing information to support their work. The table in Fig. 7.3b gives an overview of these resources, ranked according to frequency of use. Results from the survey showed that 81% of the respondents reported that asking a col-league was the most useful approach when seeking information. Other frequently used resources of information were paper catalogs (58%) and staff meetings (50%). Paper catalogs included vendor specific product manuals containing automobile parts and assembly instructions (Mørch and Skaanes 2010).

After the portal was introduced, 46% of the respondents said they stopped using one or more of the older methods. One of the respondents said: *"It simplifies work to get rid of all the papers scattered around the cash register and to get all this information in one place"* (Mørch and Skaanes 2010). The remaining 54% of the respondents said they continued to use the older methods despite the avail-ability of the portal, and several employees preferred to use the paper catalogs instead of the computerized display in order to find the required information. As one employee said in an interview: *"I am not very good with computers, most of the time it is much faster to use the paper catalogs"* (Mørch et al. 2004a).

According to several of the attendants, it was important to have alternative means for accomplishing daily work. However, the management plans to terminate the production of those methods that are too costly to produce and those that serve only one function.

7.6.3 Analysis

This research project unraveled a complex system of technology and work practice that was comprised of many different tools and resources for information, each associated with a specific generation of work support: browsing a product catalog, using a map book, contacting colleagues, staff meetings, Post-it Notes attached to a display, and a web portal. The attendants would almost always find a way out of a difficult situation when resorting to one of the alternatives. Some of the alternatives would slow down work; others supported on-the-spot problem solving.

At the current stage of technological fluency in the company, removing the sometimes suboptimal alternatives may complicate recovery from a difficult situation and prevent work completion altogether. Many information-seeking methods in the company currently outperform computer-based information seeking. The older technologies serve as predecessor artifacts, providing alternative means to support everyday work, and the age of the user population is an indicator of what type of technology will be preferred. Over time information browsers will improve in quality, making them more efficient for job specific tasks; but equally important older technologies will be serviced less frequently due to the cost of maintaining them and as a result of higher digital competency among the employees.

7.7 Reusable Design Concept in Product Line Development

7.7.1 Context

There is a version incompatibility problem latent in evolutionary application development. A locally adapted version of a system, for example, may be incompatible with a future release as a result of two processes that often are not well coordinated (specific and general development). This issue was addressed by a case study in a small software house (company) to investigate the coordination of specific and general software development (Andersen and Mørch 2009; Mørch et al. 2009). The company develops and sells project-planning tools for the oil and gas industry and provides consultancy services, training, and support for these tools. The company has close relationships with its customers. The researchers from InterMedia were invited into the company to give advice on their knowledge management practices for customer relations. The empirical material consists of interview data and a video recorded meeting with key stakeholders (developers and users).

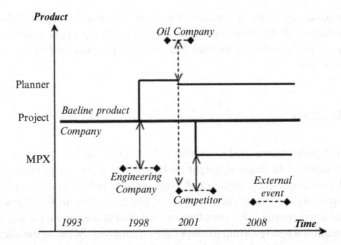

Fig. 7.4 Evolution of a project planing tool (Project) into two specialized products (Planner, MPX) has preserved and refined a design concept that originated in the first (baseline) product

7.7.2 Findings

The company's customers are requested and encouraged to report usability problems and innovative uses; and some of the most skilled users also assist in end-user development (adaptation) of the company's products (Andersen and Mørch 2009). The developers offer communication and information sharing tools for customer interaction, which has been stimulated through long-term relationships (maintenance contracts) and user forums. The main meeting ground is an annual showcase in which customers are invited to communicate with the company's employees.

Understanding the transitions from specific to general development has been one of our research questions (Mørch et al. 2009). The respondents related historical events to some external organizations the company does business with, in particular an oil company and an engineering company. Some of these events led to major changes in the company's product line, including the creation of two new products, Planner and Microsoft Project Extension (MPX). However, most of the external events led to minor changes, producing only gradual improvements and continuation of existing products. Figure 7.4 shows a schematic overview of the factors that have influenced product line development in the company.

A situation where an adaptation for a specific customer led the company to spawn a new product is illustrated in this first excerpt, which was extracted from an interview with one of the company's developers. The developer's view shows that there is a connection between specific and general development, realized when contributions from one customer are incorporated in the product.

Interviewer: Was it an add-on made specifically for Engineering Company?
Respondent: No, it became part of the product. Yes, it started as a patch, what we call a user option.

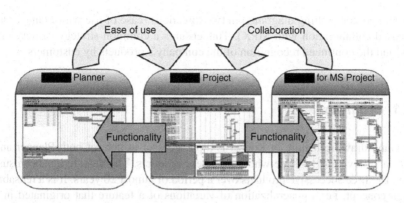

Fig. 7.5 The company's presentation of the relationship between the three products: Planner, Project and MPX (company's extension to MS Project). Planner is a standalone application and MPX a web applicaton

The respondent explains how a major request for change led from "user option" or "patch" and eventually "became part of the product." When a patch, provided for a few customers, is included in a later release cycle of a product, it will become "part of the product" and available to all customers.

The next excerpt is a follow-up question that illustrates the more common situation with regard to adaptation, namely a specific solution for one customer.

Interviewer: So, the rationale for a given upgrade lies with a specific customer, which means that a customer can be a part of setting the standards for what other customers receive?

Respondent: Mm, but if what one customer suggests is far off, then we just make a local adaptation for that specific customer.

The process of incorporating a customer's solution and making it part of the product or spawning new products does not occur very often, because the changes may infringe on property rights. Such changes are mainly initiated by large customers or supported by contracts, such as the engineering company, the oil company and the competitor depicted in Fig. 7.4. In most cases, improvement requests and end-user development activities are responded to by an adaptation, which means a custom-made solution for a single customer created by the company by using patches or user options within the current version of the product.

The idea behind the company's first product (Project) began in 1993. This idea has been preserved and refined in the latest products (Planner & MPX). The first product is, in effect, a template for all subsequent products and the standard against which new products are measured. One consultant was asked to describe what was meant by this and he explained it with a specific example: *"About 4 years ago, we extracted the interactive Gantt drawing part of Project and generated a new low-end bar chart drawing tool named Planner."* Figure 7.5 shows the relationship between the three products. Planner and MPX extend the core design idea of Project (a technique for plotting diagrams) in two directions (ease of use with Planner and increased collaboration with MPX). This ensures a common strategy of development and the continued recognition of the company's products by customers.

7.7.3   Analysis

The Gantt drawing feature of Project is a predecessor artifact of both Planner and MPX, and is visible to those who know these products. This feature has been sustained for three successive products over a period of almost 20 years. It is a reusable design concept, i.e. a generalization of variations of a feature that originated in a specific implementation. The data from the case study shows that customers have proposed some of the features the company has incorporated in their products. The path from adaptation to generalization is complex and subject to multiple factors: proposals for new ideas, acceptance with or without payment, the different stages through which an innovation must pass (user option, patch, build, version, etc.). Only those proposals judged to be "good enough" would pass through the loophole and be taken further; the others will be rejected or will require payment by customers (Andersen and Mørch 2009). There is both intimacy and risk associated with joining forces in generalization: the customers want the best possible tools for their project-planning work, and the company wants to increase revenue and do the things they are good at (writing project planning software). These two processes are tension-laden (e.g. infringe on property rights) and predecessor artifacts emerge in this tension (Mørch et al. 2009), simultaneously addressing specific and general needs. PAs are represented in the specialized products by a reusable design concept important to the company (diagram plotting) that serves as a *reminder* of a feature that was first introduced in an older product (interactive Gantt drawing module of Project).

7.8   Summary and Discussion

Three types of predecessor artifacts have been described in this chapter based on examining data from previous projects:

1. *Reusable design material*: A predecessor artifact is represented by a physical trace of previous functionality (reuse of objects and concrete classes in BasicDraw to create KitchenDesign)
2. *Alternative functionality*: A predecessor artifact becomes a backup system (multiple alternatives to using a computerized information display)
3. *Reusable design concept*: A predecessor artifact is represented by an abstract reminder (an important design concept in Project was preserved and refined across its product line)

7.8.1   Predecessor Artifact as Reusable Design Material

George Herbert Mead, the philosopher and social psychologist, was among the first to recognize that there is a connection between emergence and creativity. When describing emergence he emphasized interaction among the parts and the whole and a reconstructing that is not given in advance, but necessary for seeing more than the sum of parts (Mead and Morris 1934). In the design computing community some researchers have developed a theoretical relationship between emergence and creativity, and define emergence "when a new form or concept appears that was not directly implied by the context from which it arose" (Seevinck and Edmonds 2008, p. 541). For example, two overlapping squares may reveal a triangle, which cannot be found by looking at the squares in isolation. Interactive systems can provide opportunities for creative interaction by exploiting emergence, enabling users to see something new in older things (Seevinck and Edmonds 2008), or to see something "old" in current things as profiled in this chapter. For example, the old wooden beams in the new house displayed in Fig. 7.1a refer to an older farmhouse on the same site, a physical trace of a predecessor artifact. This information provides viewers with an opportunity to learn something new, the evolutionary history of a certain building. At a more general level it points toward a conceptual framework for learning on demand based on phenomenology (the "extended present"). This framework is outside the scope of the present study, and suggests an area for further work.

In the first study, the rectangle was used as an emergent shape in the design units of KitchenDesign (see Fig. 7.2). This type of emergence is called *perceptual emergence* (Seevinck and Edmonds 2008). It is a relationship of two objects (in this case a rectangle and a kitchen cabinet symbol) as perceived by the users. The different abstraction levels of a computer application enable *perceptual* (user interface), *conceptual* (program code), and *physical* (run time organization) emergence. It is arguable program code that provides the most flexible level of reuse for computer applications (i.e. using the class/subclass relation in object-oriented programming), but software components can also provide flexibility in terms of cloning and integration with other components, without accessing source code (Mørch et al. 2004a, b).

A reusable design material can be compared with the design of new buildings by appropriating parts of older buildings and other reusable material in the built environment. For example the Container City in the London Docklands consists of buildings that uses recycled shipping containers for accommodation, resulting in a green and affordable solution to an inner city housing problem (Brand 1994). The original intention of a design may not be preserved when a new design is built from reusable design materials as opposed to when it is based on reusable design concepts. The reuse effect of appropriated software material is manifested in the run time system of an application (objects in memory) and in the user interface (objects on the screen), as well as in the minds of its designers. In program code it is manifested in subclasses (new code) that inherits from super classes (existing code).

7.8.2   Predecessor Artifact as Alternative Functionality

In his early but influential study of computer-supported work in organizations, Gasser (1986) identified a type of work he called *adaptation work*, which was composed of three types of coping with difficult-to-use computers in organizations: fitting, augmentation, and working around. *Fitting* is the strategy of modifying a computer system or changing the structure of work to accommodate a mismatch between workers and technology, i.e. a form of adaptation. *Augmentation* refers to undertaking additional work to make up for an inconsistency in primary work. *Working around* refers to using a computer system in ways it was not intended, or avoiding its use and relying instead on alternative, suboptimal means. One example is *backup systems* (Gasser 1986), which are older technologies one relies on when the main work support fails or becomes temporarily unavailable. An example of a backup system is Post-It notes around a computer display in order to remember difficult operating system commands (see Fig. 7.3a).

A backup system is a type of predecessor artifact that provides alternative functionality, but it is different from the two other types of PAs profiled in this chapter. It is a proper PA, functional artifacts that provide suboptimal but "good enough" alternatives to a new innovation. An example is banking in Norway. Although it is possible to visit a physical bank and make transactions by interacting with a teller, the teller will charge a fee for the service (suboptimal). Internet banking on the other hand is cheaper but requires digital competency. Another example is coin-operated telephones, serving as an alternative to a mobile phone. Most of the time people do not use these telephones, but they can be surprisingly useful when one's mobile phone does not work.

The second case revealed a more subtle form of relation between two artifacts, multiple technologies for supporting information seeking. This is what Suchman referred to as *artful integration*, a hybrid of technology and work practices where technology is comprised of multiple layers of heterogeneous devices, each associated with a specific generation of work support (Suchman 1994). This relationship between two artifacts (new innovation and PA) is also called *perceived resemblance* (Mørch 2003). This refers to a subjective interpretation of the likeness of two artifacts, which may cause dispute regarding the reuse of material or ideas from one to the other (e.g. paper catalogs vs. computerized information displays). The weaker form of relationship has the advantage that the older technologies may coexist and provide alternative work support when the new technology temporarily fails. Despite this, most backup methods are best thought of as the *endangered species* of the evolving artifacts. For example, phone books are gradually disappearing in favour of online services of personal information. A company that wishes to spearhead a modern technology profile, like the one studied in the second case, will often strive towards removal of older technologies even though the older technologies can provide useful alternatives for some employees. It seems that older technologies that cater to multiple ways of use may enjoy a longer life span (e.g. Post-It notes).

7.8.3 Predecessor Artifact as Reusable Design Concept

Ehn applied Wittgenstein's concepts of language game and family resemblance as metaphors to explain the development and use of a newspaper publishing system at the time when typesetting became computerized in Sweden (Ehn 1988). When the system showed family resemblance to something the typesetters already knew well, it stimulated active user participation in the design process and avoided common pitfalls, such as failing to meet user requirements (Ehn 1988). The graphical user interfaces could remind them of previous experiences of type setting. The reusable design in that situation is abstract representations of older typesetting tools and practices associated with new computer-based tools. Due to their abstract nature, these symbolic reminders of PAs are more difficult to capture than the reusable design material described above, but in return they reveal a more durable (space conserving) structure and they apply in more than one situation.

The third study identified predecessor artifacts by analyzing critical events surrounding new releases of a product line spawned by a commercial software house. Familiarity with the original product (Project) made it easier to use the later products (Planner and MPX), and to migrate from one product to the next. This was possible due to the family resemblance evident in the three systems, according to a special technique for displaying diagrams.

Reusable design concepts can be compared with architectural design patterns and archaeological skeuomorphs. Alexander and colleagues have described 250 *design patterns* of buildings and urban spaces (Alexander et al. 1977). Patterns serve as the basic building blocks of problem solving, providing answers to recurring design problems (e.g. How many stories should a building have?). Alexander's pattern language and cataloguing efforts have inspired software engineers, and numerous software design patterns and pattern languages for software systems have been proposed.

A *skeuomorph* is a technical term archaeologists use to denote a non-functional feature of an artifact that was inherited from some precursor artifact (Basalla 1988). The role of skeuomorphs in the evolution of artifacts has been studied in archaeology (Basalla 1988) and architecture of houses (Brand 1994). The notion of skeuomorphs has not yet been widely adopted in software design. As a visible representation of previous functionality at an abstract level, computational skeumorphs can provide an alternative to design patterns for integrating general level design information with software artifacts. This identifies an area for further work.

Seeding, Evolutionary Growth, Reseeding (SER) is a process model for the evolutionary development of software applications by integrating end-user and professional development (Fischer et al. 1994). It postulates that systems that evolve over a sustained time span must continually alternate between periods of unplanned evolutions by end-users (*evolutionary growth*), and periods of deliberate restructuring and enhancement (*reseeding*), involving users in collaboration with skilled software developers. This corresponds roughly to the two interdependent processes of adaptation (evolutionary growth) and generalization (reseeding). However, there are no equivalents of reusable design concepts or predecessor artifacts to account for the transition from one release of a software application to the next in the framework of Fischer et al. (1994).

7.9 Implications for Reflective Conversation with Design Materials

Schön was inspired by the language game metaphor of Wittgenstein when he called reflective conversation (drawing and talking) a language game for doing architecture (Schön 1983). However, Schön did not exploit the full power of the metaphor, since he did not adopt the notion of family resemblance. Wittgenstein (1967) explained the connection of elements in a language game according to the similarity of traits among family members, "sometimes overall similarities, and sometimes similarities of detail." Two forms of resemblance are suggested in order to capture this distinction: *self-resemblance* and *family resemblance*. Sometimes there are *similarities of detail* (self-resemblance); at other times there are *overall similarities* (family resemblances). This allows for a new design or current artifact to be connected with previous designs (PAs) in two different ways, i.e. reuse of material (like in case 1, self-resemblance, well-defined connection) and reuse of concepts (like in case 3, family resemblance, generally accepted but weaker connection). In addition, a third type of connection between a current artifact and PAs was explored in case 2, *perceived resemblance*, which is a subjective likeliness of two things, serving an important function by allowing breakdowns to be resolved by resorting to alternatives. This is a useful distinction for analyzing adaptations of information systems in multiple stages (from design to use), extending the vocabulary of Schön and Ehn. For example it can help to identify a poor organizational implementation of a computer application, or a software design that fails to build on best practice, or an application that fails because it is rejected in favor of simpler alternatives.

Predecessor artifacts can also help the designer to cope with complexity in information-rich environments by addressing the following questions: How does the designer know that information is needed when designing, and when is a piece of information (e.g. design knowledge) relevant to the situation at hand? It is not possible to keep all potentially relevant information in short-term memory; this will lead to information overload. The distinction between known and potentially relevant information was explored in the Janus design environment (Fischer et al. 1989) and operationalized as computer-based back talk (critique) to stimulate reflection-in-action (McCall et al. 1990).

The past work the author has been involved in with regards to Janus has been extended and generalized through the notion of reusable design concepts in this chapter. A reusable design concept is an abstraction (general-level information) originating as a feature in a specific predecessor artifact. An example from the kitchen design domain is the *work triangle*, a concept that refers to the relative position of sink, stove, and refrigerator in a household kitchen. In Janus this concept together with a set of related design principles were implemented in software as critique (condition-action rules) for detecting suboptimal design situations. An application of this was to inform students about the design principles to be resolved in their own designs. In the work presented here the previous work has been generalized to mean "expansive design," identifying in current artifacts emergent properties (traces and reminders) that represent predecessor artifacts.

7.10 Conclusions and Directions for Further Work

This chapter has presented an evolving-artifacts approach to integrate creativity and rationale. The common denominator has been predecessor artifacts (PA) and resemblance relationships to connect PAs with newer artifacts. Schön's theory of reflective conversation with design material provided the starting point for this inquiry, identifying a shortcut in his account of evolutionary design (bypassing generalization and predecessor artifacts). The aim of this study has been to extend the vocabulary of reflective conversation and make it applicable to analyzing software applications that evolve. Three types of PAs were identified and differentiated based on system building efforts and empirical findings from three case studies (*reusable design material, alternative functionality,* and *reusable design concepts*), and three types of resemblance relations based on previous work and literature studies to bring the inheritance relation between class and subclass in object-oriented programming to a user oriented level of abstraction (*self, perceived, and family*), hence proposing a semi-formal approach to software reuse and design. Predecessor artifacts relate to creativity and rationale in the following manner. On one hand a predecessor artifact is a rejected alternative (*product-oriented rationale*) that represents the design history of a current artifact (*process-oriented rationale*). On the other, it is a concrete (physical) trace or abstract (symbolic) reminder in a new artifact (*an emergent property*), and as such can provide opportunities for creative interaction with an artifact, such as enabling users to see a previous version of a tool (a PA) in a new tool, and by repeating the process, the myriads of ways of connecting reusable designs.

This work has implications for discourse analysis methods in design (e.g. interaction analysis), suggesting a dimension of historical artifact analysis to supplement spoken dialogue and body language (deictic references and drawing). It can also provide ideas for design history education in schools of design (e.g. the role of traces and reminders in everyday artifacts), and design-based models of human learning and development in schools of education. In terms of information and computer sciences, this research suggests that some abstract features of today's software tools can be traced back to functional features in some predecessor artifacts. If this relationship can be made durable, it may help to create a tighter connection between program code and design patterns in software projects, and make "software archeology" a new research topic.

This work has not addressed: (1) A fourth type of PA, *disposable artifacts*, older tools of no practical or minimal symbolic value, often removed to reclaim occupied space, and (2) *successor tools*: contrasted with PAs as future tools anticipated and designed by improving the present.

Acknowledgements The author thanks the former InterMedia staff and students who contributed to the research: Camilla Brynhildsen, Bård Ketil Engen, Mari Ann Skaanes, and Ida Tødenes who studied the petrol station workers; and Renate Andersen, Shazia Mushtaq, and Kathrine Nygård who studied the interaction of professional and amateur software developers. Further, the author is grateful for Jack Carroll's invitation to submit this chapter to the Springer volume on creativity and rationale. The author received financial support from the Research Council of Norway (Learning at work project, 2001–2004), and the European Commission's program under Framework 6 (Knowledge practices, KP-Lab, project, 2006–2011).

References

Alexander, C., Ishikawa, S., & Silverstein, M. (1977). *A pattern language: Towns, buildings, construction.* New York: Oxford University Press.

Andersen, R., & Mørch, A. I. (2009). Mutual development: A case study in customer-initiated software product development. In V. Pipek, M. B. Rosson, B. de Ruyter, & V. Wulf (Eds.), *Proceedings 2nd Int'l Symposium on End User Development (IS-EUD 2009), LNCS* (Vol. 5435, pp. 31–49). Berlin: Springer.

Ball, L. J., Lambell, N. J., Ormerod, T. C., Slavin, S., & Mariani, J. A. (2001). Representing design rationale to support innovative design reuse: A minimalist approach. *Automation in Construction, 10,* 663–674.

Basalla, G. (1988). *The evolution of technology.* Cambridge: Cambridge University Press.

Bergson, H. (1993). *Creative evolution.* Lanham: University Press of America (Original published by Henry Holt and Company, New York, 1911).

Brand, S. (1994). *How buildings learn: What happens after they're built.* London: Phoenix Illustrated.

Carroll, J. M. (1994). Making use a design representation. *Communication of the ACM, 37*(12), 28–35.

Carroll, J. M. (2011). Design rationale and appropriation: Providing resources to facilitate creative use. In *Proceedings CHI 2011, Workshop on appropriation and creative use.* New York: ACM.

Carroll, J. M., & Rosson, M. B. (1996). Deliberated evolution: Stalking the View Matcher in design space. In T. P. Moran & J. M. Carroll (Eds.), *Design rationale: Concepts, techniques, and use* (pp. 107–145). Mahwah: Lawrence Erlbaum Associates.

Conklin, E. J., & Burgess-Yakemovic, K. C. (1996). A process-oriented approach to design rationale. In T. P. Moran & J. M. Carroll (Eds.), *Design rationale: Concepts, techniques, and use* (pp. 393–427). Mahwah: Lawrence Erlbaum Associates.

Ehn, P. (1988). *Work-oriented design of computer artifacts.* Stockholm: Arbetslivscentrum.

Feyerabend, P. (1999). In B. Terpstra (Ed.), *Conquest of abundance: A tale of abstraction versus the richness of being.* Chicago: University of Chicago Press.

Fischer, G. (1994). Turning breakdowns into opportunities for creativity. *Knowledge-Based Systems, 7*(4), 221–232.

Fischer, G., McCall, R., & Morch, A. (1989). Janus: Integrating hypertext with a knowledge-based design environment. In *Proceedings Hypertext'89* (pp. 105–117). New York: ACM.

Fischer, G., McCall, R., Ostwald, J., Reeves, B., & Shipman, F. (1994). Seeding, evolutionary growth and reseeding: Supporting the incremental development of design environments. In B. Adelson, S. Dumais, & J. Olson (Eds.), *Proceedings of CHI'94* (pp. 292–298). New York: ACM.

Gasser, L. (1986). The integration of computing and routine work. *ACM Transactions on Information Systems, 4,* 205–225.

MacLean, A., Young, R., Bellotti, V., & Moran, T. (1991). Questions, options, and criteria: Elements of design space analysis. *Human Computer Interaction, 6*(3–4), 201–251.

McCall, R. (1991). PHI: A conceptual foundation for design hypermedia. *Design Studies, 12,* 30–41.

McCall, R. (2010). Critical conversations: Feedback as a stimulus to creativity in software design. *Human Technology: An Interdisciplinary Journal on Humans in ICT Environments, 6*(1), 11–37.

McCall, R., Fischer, G., & Morch, A. (1990). Supporting reflection-in-action in the Janus design environment. In *The electronic design studio* (pp. 247–259). Cambridge, MA: MIT Press.

Mead, G. H., & Morris, C. W. (Eds.). (1934). *Mind, self, and society*. Chicago: University of Chicago Press.

Moran, T. P., & Carroll, J. M. (Eds.). (1996). *Design rationale: Concepts, techniques, and use*. Mahwah: Lawrence Erlbaum Associates.

Mørch, A. (1996). Evolving a generic application into a domain-oriented design environment. *Scandinavian Journal of Information Systems, 8*(2), 63–90.

Mørch, A. (1997). Three levels of end-user tailoring: Customization, integration, and extension. In M. Kyng & L. Mathiassen (Eds.), *Computers and design in context* (pp. 51–76). Cambridge, MA: MIT Press.

Mørch, A. I. (2003). Evolutionary growth and control in user tailorable systems. In N. V. Patel (Ed.), *Adaptive evolutionary information systems* (pp. 30–58). Hershey: IGI Publishing.

Mørch, A. I., & Skaanes, M. A. (2010). Design and use of an integrated work and learning system: Information seeking as critical function. In S. Ludvigsen, A. Lund, I. Rasmussen, & R. Säljö (Eds.), *Learning across sites: New tools, infrastructures and practices* (pp. 138–155). London: Routledge.

Mørch, A. I., Engen, B. K., & Åsand, H.-R. (2004a). The workplace as a learning laboratory: The winding road to e-learning in a Norwegian service company. In A. Clement et al. (Eds.), *Proceedings of PDC'2004* (pp. 141–151). New York: ACM Press.

Mørch, A. I., Stevens, G., Won, M., Klann, M., Dittrich, Y., & Wulf, V. (2004b). Component-based technologies for end-user development. *Communications or the ACM, 47*(9), 59–62.

Mørch, A. I., Nygård, K. A., & Ludvigsen, S. R. (2009). Adaptation and generalisation in software product development. In H. Daniels et al. (Eds.), *Activity theory in practice: Promoting learning across boundaries* (pp. 184–205). London: Routledge.

Norman, D. A. (2008). Workarounds and hacks: The leading edge of innovation. *Interactions, 15*(4), 47–48.

Petroski, H. (1992). *The evolution of useful things*. New York: Vintage Books.

Rittel, H. (1972). On the planning crisis: Systems analysis of the first and second generations. *Bedriftsøkonomen, 8*, 390–396.

Schön, D. A. (1983). *The reflective practitioner: How professionals think in action*. New York: Basic Books.

Schön, D. (1992). Designing as a reflective conversation with the materials of a design situation. *Knowledge-Based Systems, 5*(1), 3–13.

Seevinck, J., & Edmonds, E. (2008). Emergence and the art system 'plus minus now'. *Design Studies, 29*(6), 541–555.

Simon, H. A. (1996). *The sciences of the artificial* (3rd ed.). Cambridge, MA: MIT Press.

Suchman, L. (1994). Working relations of technology production and use. *Computer Supported Cooperative Work, 2*(1–2), 21–39.

Tomlinson, B. (2008). A call for pro-environmental conspicuous consumption in the online world. *Interactions, 15*(6), 42–45.

Wittgenstein, L. (1967). *Philosophical investigations* (3rd ed.). Oxford: Basic Blackwell.

Chapter 8
The PRInCiPleS Design Framework

Eli Blevis

Abstract Some disciplines focus on analytic research and some disciplines focus on synthesis. Design disciplines are interesting because designers need to do both analysis and synthesis tasks. The HCI and design program I presently direct is organized around a framework I have named with the acronym PRInCiPleS, both at the curricular scale and as an organizing device for individual design projects within classes that serves as a kind of design rationale framework. The PRInCiPleS framework is not a scientific framework, but it does have an analogy to an idealized notion of a scientific framework. One of the biggest issues in design pedagogy and practice is how to get students and practicing designers to ensure that analysis leads to synthesis in a sound way and that synthesis follows from analysis in a sound way-that is, the issue of how to bridge the creative, semantic gap between design research and insights and concepts. In much of the curriculum, design research projects are paired with design concept projects in a way that is targeted at addressing this issue by means of iterative practice. Taking a curatorial attitude towards designs constructed according to the PRInCiPleS or indeed other frameworks is an appropriate way to connect notions of creativity to notions of design rationale.

Keywords Design • Creativity • PRInCiPleS design framework • Design challenge based learning (DCBL) • Transdisciplinarity • Transdisciplinary design • Sustainability & food.

E. Blevis (✉)
Human-Computer Interaction Design, School of Informatics and Computing (SoIC),
Indiana University, Bloomington, IN 47408, USA
e-mail: eblevis@indiana.edu

J.M. Carroll (ed.), *Creativity and Rationale: Enhancing Human
Experience by Design*, Human–Computer Interaction Series,
DOI 10.1007/978-1-4471-4111-2_8, © Springer-Verlag London 2013

8.1 Introductory Definitions

PRInCiPleS is an acronym for a design framework. By design framework—especially as distinguished from process, I mean an organizing structure and container for a notion of recording and presenting particular design plans or explanations in terms of (i) analysis frame elements named predispositions, research, insights, and (ii) synthesis frame elements named concept systems, prototypes, and strategies (Fig. 8.1). One of the primary goals—both as design pedagogy and as practice—of recording and presenting design plans or explanations in the PRInCiPleS framework is to ensure that analysis leads to synthesis and that synthesis follows from analysis in a clearly articulated way.

The PRInCiPleS Framework for Design Plans & Explanations

Analysis			Synthesis		
Predisposi-tions	Research ⇩	Insights	Concepts & Concept Systems	Prototypes ⇩	Strategies ⇩
	Observations Literature Collections			Exploratory Appearance Usability	Social Value Technology Enterprise
Predispositions are the things we believe to be true at the outset of a design process or explanation.	Research comes in three forms, namely (i) observations—or primary research, (ii) literature review—or secondary research, and (iii) collections—or knowledge about cultural forms.	Insights are the design issues that arise out of research.	Concepts and systems of concepts are the things, services, communications, or strategies that we envision in response to insights.	Prototypes come in three forms, namely (i) exploratory—or behavioral or low fidelity prototypes, (ii) appearance—or look and feel prototypes, and (iii) usability—or proof of concept or high fidelity prototypes.	Strategies come in three forms, namely (i) social value—or social desirability planning, (ii) technology—or technological feasibility planning, and (iii) enterprise—or economic viability planning.
⇩⇧	⇩⇧	⇩⇧	⇩⇧	⇩⇧	⇩⇧

An Analgous Scientific Framework

Initial hypothesis	Literature search	Reserch hypothesis	Experiment Design	Experiment	Results

Fig. 8.1 Summary of the PRInCiPleS design framework

The letters that play a substantive role in the acronym are easily remembered as the word "principles" from which the word "nile" is removed.

The framework elements are straightforward (Top of Fig. 8.1):

1. Predispositions are the things we believe to be true at the outset of a design process or explanation.
2. Research comes in three forms, namely (i) observations—or primary research, (ii) literature review—or secondary research, and (iii) collections—or knowledge about cultural forms.
3. Insights are the design issues that arise out of research.
4. Concepts and systems of concepts are the things, services, communications, or strategies that we envision in response to insights.
5. Prototypes come in three forms, namely (i) exploratory—or behavioral or low fidelity prototypes, (ii) appearance—or look and feel prototypes, and (iii) usability—or proof of concept or high fidelity prototypes.
6. Strategies come in three forms, namely (i) social value—or social planning, (ii) technology—or technology planning, and (iii) enterprise—or economic planning.

8.2 The PRInCiPleS Framework

As defined and stated above, the PRInCiPleS framework is an organizing structure and container for a notion of recording and presenting particular design plans or explanations in terms of (i) analysis elements named predispositions, research, insights, and (ii) synthesis elements known as concept systems, prototypes, and strategies. The PRInCiPleS framework was not specifically inspired by the literature on design rationale (notably Moran and Carroll 1996), but rather by an oral tradition and practice I learned while teaching off-and-on at The Institute of Design, at IIT in Chicago in the later half of the 1990s, as well as directly by Christopher Alexander's notions of pattern language (Alexander et al. 1977). The PRInCiPleS framework owes to a sense of design as it is understood in broad "traditional design" notions of product design or strategic design planning—neither specific to nor exclusive of human-computer interaction, nor human-centered computing, nor interaction design. This historical account and attributive rigor is repeated and greatly elaborated later in this chapter for those who may be interested, in a section titled "Historical Background and Attributions."

8.2.1 Description by Example: Designing for Sustainable Food Practices

In this section, I give a deliberately simple and somewhat sketchy example to illustrate the content and possible form of a design plan or explanation in the PRInCiPleS framework. The example is deliberately simple in order to serve to articulate the form of explanation in the most general way and one should expect that a design explanation of this form in a practical context would have rather a lot more detail. As a matter of situating what follows in terms of scientific or computing or mathematical notions of formality, kindly understand the the level of discourse in what follows is more along the lines, intents, informality, and scale of a pattern in Alexander's (1977) pattern language. For a more complete example of a design explanation organized according to the PRInCiPleS framework, please see Reed et al. (2005).

As a practical matter, I focus in what follows on the features of the PRInCiPleS framework that are less common in HCI design methods, under the assumption that the reader is already familiar with more common notions of design methods in HCI.

8.2.2 Title

As design explanations have titles, the title of this example is "Designing for Sustainable Food Practices."

8.2.3 Predispositions

Predispositions are the things we believe to be true at the outset of a design process or explanation. These are statements we imagine to be tautological and which frame our initial contentions or understandings of the design context at hand. With respect to designing for sustainable food practices, one predisposition we might have could be:

8.2.3.1 Predisposition One

In western society, most people don't have time to ensure their food is local and healthy.
   and another could be:

8.2.3.2 Predisposition Two

Fast food tastes good, but increases obesity rates in the population.
   Predispositions motivate a design in the first place, and often point to a tension we think we need to resolve—such as the tension between time and eating well with the least environmental impact, or the tension between how certain generally high calorie foods taste and obesity effects. Predispositions are a starting point for an explanation. Importantly, they do not represent a particular position, but rather an attempt to inventory all of the prevailing positions that may motivate a design.

When presenting a design explanation, people in attendance of the explanation will need to see that their individual points of view are represented, even if they are uncomfortable with the points of view of others, and that is the rhetorical point of predispositions as a technique of presentation.

In Fig. 8.1, an analogy between the PRInCiPleS framework and an idealized notion of scientific framework is diagrammed. Predispositions are analogous to the notion of an initial hypothesis in a scientific process. They are a mechanism for stating initial thoughts and tensions which merit further study in the case of science and further design in the case of design. It is important to note that this comparison is only an analogy. The tensions between notions of science and design are discussed in great deal in the design literature. See Cross (2001) for a particular cogent example. The issue is really not much of an issue for the present chapter. The matter is simply understood by noting that design is not strictly science, although it may make use of scientific results and should do so whenever it can.

Finally, the choice of the term Predispositions is inspired in this context by Minsky's (1988) "The Society of Mind." He states *These must be the genes responsible for what we call "human nature"—that is, the predispositions every normal person shares"* (Minsky 1988, p. 310).

8.2.4   Design Research

People often make a distinction between design research—research conducted in order to inform design, and research about design—research conducted to advance understanding of design, methods, and reasoning. In fact, this distinction is not very important and it is hard to strictly separate the two. Moreover, design research and research about design both play a role as both scholarship and practice. These sorts of distinctions are discussed in Blevis et al. (2006), Blevis and Stolterman (2008, 2009), in which a broader literature related to the distinctions between scholarship and practice are described more fully than in this present chapter.

The idea of Research as a framework element in the PRInCiPleS framework is more modest in nature. Although primarily practice oriented, the choice of framework sub-elements is in fact not very different than the necessities one expects in a scholarly research paper. These sub-elements are (i) observations—or primary research, (ii) literature review—or secondary research, and (iii) collections—or curatorial knowledge about cultural forms.

8.2.4.1   Research: Observations

Design research within the PRInCiPleS framework usually requires a certain amount of primary—first hand—observation work. Methods of conducting observations may vary and may include ethnography, surveys, interviews, and so forth—standard fare in HCI. A particular mode of observation research I emphasize is photo-ethnography. For the "Designing for Sustainable Food Practices" example, we have:

Research Observation One

Figure 8.2a shows a photo-ethnographic recording of a market scene. The image uses selective focus to highlight the figures engaged in the transaction. The scene is one of cheerful engagement and speaks to a healthy relationship between people and locally produced food.

Research Observation Two

Figure 8.2b shows a photo-ethnographic recording of a street scene. As a matter of content, this type of photograph speaks to a condition of obesity. The ethics of taking this photograph are a matter of some concern. The photograph is taken in a public place in which people do not have a reasonable expectation of privacy, but it is still prudent to use a mosaic filter to obscure the person's face given the use of this photograph here. The rules that apply to the use of such photographs seem to vary depending on if the photograph is used as un-captioned street photographic Art, or captioned photo-ethnographic research.

Research Observation Three

Figure 8.2c shows a "hot pot" meal cooked at home. It is clearly posed, and even photographic lighting equipment is part of the image. The food appears to be healthy and in fact is locally produced.

Research Observation Four

Figure 8.2d shows modern and older rice cookers sharing counter space in a home. The image was taken as part of an in-home study concerning sustainability and technologies. The owner of the rice cookers kept the old one around, even though the newer one had some improved features, because the old one had been given to her by her mother and held sentimental value as a result. The study in which this image first appeared (Blevis and Stolterman 2007) introduced the notion of personal inventories as a means of understanding why some things have enduring value and others do not, and this image appears as part of that original work.

Photo-ethnography is only one way to do observation design research. The four images characterize a range of approaches. Observations one and two are street scenes. Observation three is staged with friends. Observation four differs from observation two because it is part of an ethics review board approved study which

Fig. 8.2 (**a**) (*Top Left*): Photo-ethnography design research. (**b**) (*Top Right*): The ethical boundaries of photo-ethnography as design research. (**c**) (*Left*): Photo-ethnography design research (Also appears in Choi and Blevis 2011). (**d**) (*Bottom Left*): Photo-ethnography design research (Also appears in Blevis and Stolterman 2007)

engages people by means of interview, as well as by means of documentary photography. The issue of if observation two is research data, design research, or Art is a complex one, which raises genuine ethical issues about the use and handling of such images.

I am privileging photo-ethnography as an observation design research method, since it is less common than many others that are already well known in HCI and since it is one that is key to my own practice.

8.2.4.2 Research: Literature

Design research within the PRInCiPleS framework always requires a certain amount of secondary research—that is, literature review. Doing adequate and conscientious literature review is a matter of some training. The largest problem one faces in working with designers and design students is that they may not have much experience in doing solid literature review. Moreover, they may have learned in grade school to "put things in their own words." This grade school advice is extremely harmful and puts designers and design students at risk of unwittingly engaging in egregious plagiarism. There are a number of things one can tell design students, namely (i) make certain your sources are of high quality, (ii) if you think your idea is new, it probably isn't—do a thorough literature search, (iii) attribute others generously, and (iv) using or re-using work without attribution is plagiarism, whereas attributing others and attributing re-use is scholarship. The most important thing I tell my students is so important that it is worth emphasizing here:

> *Avoid paraphrase, rather quote and attribute.*

And importantly, this advice also appears in Blevis (2010):64, in the form *"Instead of asking students to put things in their own words, ask them to quote and not paraphrase others."*

For the "Designing for Sustainable Food Practices" example, there are several articles that may be referenced, including Choi and Blevis (2010, 2011), Blevis and Coleman Morse (2009), and Hirsch et al. (2010). As a matter of sustainability and more important than any of these is the diagram of Fig. 8.3 taken from the Intergovernmental Panel on Climate Change (IPPC) Summary for Policy Makers (IPPC 2007). This diagram shows the predicted effects of climate change on food supply as well as four other broad sustainability concerns—water, ecosystems, coasts, and health—at various degrees of global average temperature change. The diagram presents the imperative for undertaking design planning for sustainable food practices in a very compelling way. The use of the diagram here illustrates what is meant by the notion that design, while not strictly a science, can and should make use of scientific reporting.

8.2.4.3 Research: Collections

One mode of design research within the PRInCiPleS framework that is not often—if at all—represented in HCI is what I call "collections." By collections, I mean bringing a non-reductive curatorial gaze to the world apropos of the design topic at hand. The idea of collections is to gain an understanding of what is out in the world with

Key impacts as a function of increasing global average temperature change

(Impacts will vary by extent of adaptation, rate of temperature change, and socio-economic pathway)

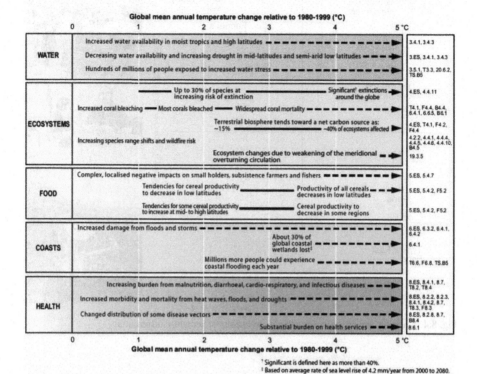

† Significant is defined here as more than 40%.
‡ Based on average rate of sea level rise of 4.2 mm/year from 2000 to 2080.

Figure SPM.2. *Illustrative examples of global impacts projected for climate changes (and sea level and atmospheric carbon dioxide where relevant) associated with different amounts of increase in global average surface temperature in the 21st century [T20.8]. The black lines link impacts, dotted arrows indicate impacts continuing with increasing temperature. Entries are placed so that the left-hand side of the text indicates the approximate onset of a given impact. Quantitative entries for water stress and flooding represent the additional impacts of climate change relative to the conditions projected across the range of Special Report on Emissions Scenarios (SRES) scenarios A1FI, A2, B1 and B2 (see Endbox 3). Adaptation to climate change is not included in these estimations. All entries are from published studies recorded in the chapters of the Assessment. Sources are given in the right-hand column of the Table. Confidence levels for all statements are high.*

Fig. 8.3 Using scientific reporting as design research (Source: IPCC 2007)

a particularly designerly orientation. Photographic essay books like Peter Menzel and Faith D'Aluisio's "Hungry Planet" (Menzel and D'Aluisio 2007) are a form of curatorialism that constitutes designerly observation in a manner that crosses the line between research observations and photographic arts. Each and every image in Menzel's work chronicles some aspect of world culture relevant to our theme of "Designing for Sustainable Food Practices" in a way that is not intended as reducible data, but which is rather more like curated exhibit which may inform design process as much as any technical observation work. Other examples of curatorial gaze include Burtnsky (2005), Ranjan and Ranjan (2010) and Art galleries and museums and any kinds of private collections in general. The idea of collections as design research is an important one and as a matter of creativity and design rationale

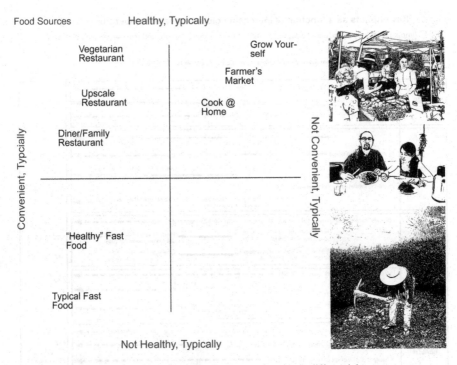

Food Sources   Healthy, Typically

Fig. 8.4 Creating and representing insights by means of semantic differentials

in keeping with this present volume, may be worthy of more attention from the HCI community. Moreover, regarding photographs in particular as the material of design research collections yields a different perspective than the notion of using photographic recording as observation research, one which is germane to designerly visual thinking, a matter taken up in Blevis (2011).

8.2.5 Insights

The idea of the insights framework element is to describe design issues which arise out of the interpretations of the design research and which prompt design concepts. Insights may be confirmations of predispositions, or they may be different owing to the research conducted. As per Fig. 8.1, insights are somewhat analogous to research hypotheses in the sciences—that is, initial hypotheses that have been validated by or modified as a result of secondary research. In the PRInCiPleS framework, insights owe to interpretations of primary observations, secondary literature research, and curatorial collections. There are many ways to represent insights. Prose will do. Figure 8.4 shows a diagrammatic semantic differential—or 2 factor model—for the

"Designing for Sustainable Food Practices" example. This diagrammatic form is a good way to articulate a design space, in this case mapping various meal contexts and food sources in a space defined by a typically convenient to typically inconvenient factor, compared to a typically healthy to typically unhealthy factor. Sometimes, the space that is empty in such a diagram denotes a design opportunity. In the specific case of Fig. 8.4, the space of not convenient and not healthy is rather a circumstance to be rightfully avoided. The insight denoted by Fig. 8.4 is that typical fast food is not typically healthy, but is typically convenient, and that growing food yourself is typically healthy, but not typically convenient, in keeping in this case with the original predispositions. In this particular example, there is a certain amount of subjectivity—sometimes it is possible to be more rigorous than other times depending on the design domain and the quality of the design research conducted and available.

8.2.6 Concepts and Concept Systems

A concept is an idea for a product, communication, or strategy. A concept system is an idea for a system of concepts—products, communications, and strategies—that work together in a coherent way.

Technology, including digital technologies, are not more nor less than materials of concepts, just like any other materials. I ascribe this notion of technologies as materials of design to Erik Stolterman and Harold Nelson (i.e. Nelson and Stolterman 2003). A concept or concept system may also call for eliminating or substituting products, communications, or strategies. Fry (2008) proposes notions of redirective practice—for example, substituting a push lawn mower in place of a gas powered lawn mover, as a matter of sustainable design, and acts of elimination—for example, replacing a lawn with wild flowers or an organic vegetable garden, as a matter of sustainable design. I believe that concepts are always political and need to be constructed in a values-rich way—not just taking values into account, not just adding value, but primarily starting with values and taking on important issues like sustainability, health, equality, and so forth. This belief is in accordance with transdisciplinary notions that values, ethics, and philosophy precede all other design choices—see Max-Neef (2005) and Nicolescu (2002) for compelling accounts of transdisciplinarity, and also Blevis and Stolterman (2009) for an account within HCI. In HCI, Batya Friedman (1997) is noted for advancing issues of the relationship between values and technology. Bonnie Nardi is also known in HCI for values-rich approaches (Nardi and O'Day 1999). In design, Margolin (2002) and Papanek (1984) are good representatives of values-rich orientation. In our program, there is a requirement that concepts and concept systems are constructed in a values-rich way.

Figure 8.5 provides an example for our theme of "Designing for Sustainable Food Practices." Pictured is the very minimal sketch of a concept system for Healthy Food Choices. The diagram shows that the concept system consists of four concepts,

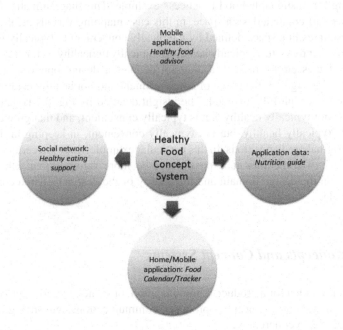

Fig. 8.5 Concept system for healthy food design

namely a healthy food advisor mobile application, a healthy eating support social network, a food calendar/tracker for mobile and home settings, and nutritional guide and other data to support the applications. Clearly there is a lot more detail that needs to be provided to define this concept system, and this figure should be taken as only the barest sketch of an example. Notwithstanding, the important notion is that concept systems should precede concepts, as a matter of designerly approach—that is beginning with a notion of a system to promote healthy food choices precedes the notion of any particular concept in the service of that system.

The types of concepts that one focuses on as a designer determine in some sense the type of designer you are. In our HCI/d program, there are three tracks, namely (i) interaction design—a form of product and communications design, (ii) strategic design planning—a form of strategy design, and (iii) research, scholarship, and creative activity. All of the frame elements of the PRInCiPleS framework may vary depending on focus according to these three tracks, but the framework does apply to all three. Moreover, the most salient differences between the three tracks are at this level of choice of conceptual arenas. I provide the following advice to students in our HCI/d program handbook:

There are three main career goal themes in the program. These are: (i) Interaction Design, (ii) Strategic Design Planning, and (iii) Research, Scholarship, and Creative Activity.

8.2.6.1 Interaction Design

The theme of interaction design will appeal most to those students who want to design products using the materials of digital technologies. If you want to professionally design interfaces, interactive applications, social networking sites, digital products, and so on and so forth, interaction design is the theme for you. In our program, interaction design is always a values-rich theme—we require that everything we design adds genuine and sustainable value to peoples' lives and respects humankind's relationship to the natural environment.

8.2.6.2 Strategic Design Planning

The theme of strategic design planning will appeal most to students who want to start their own design consultancies, or who want to achieve executive level positions and influence in design firms or other firms that make use of digital technologies, or who want to pioneer systemic design innovations for social good. If you want to design strategy from the perspectives of social values, technological insights, and enterprise considerations, strategic design planning is the theme for you.

8.2.6.3 Research, Scholarship, and Creative Activity

The theme of research, scholarship, and creative activity will appeal most to students who are considering a career in scholarship, as a professor or researcher.

8.2.7 Mapping Research to Insights to Concepts

The example of Fig. 8.5 does not really do justice to what is possible in terms of detail for a concept. A ready-at-hand small example of how concepts follow from insights which follow from research, and the corollary—how research leads to insights which lead to concepts, appears in Fig 8.6a, ba. This example does not follow our theme of "Designing for Sustainable Food Practices." It is an example I use as a model solution for a course in HCI and design, which uses an approach to teaching I call Design Challenge Based Learning (DCBL). I have reported on this example in article about DCBL Blevis (2010):

A very common project in introductory HCI classes is to ask students to design a thermostat that illustrates their understanding of the commonly held incorrect mental model many people have of a thermostat as a continuous control rather than the switch that its operational semantics actually denote. The DCBL approach in my treatment recasts this problem, not as a problem of incorrect mental models and thermostat design *per se*, but rather as a design research project about what makes a space comfortable paired with a design concept project about how to use digital

Concept: E-Ink Fabric Wearable Personal Thermostat & Ambient Sensors

The idea of this concept is that a digital thermostat control is woven into the fabric of clothing or worn like a bracelet or as part of a watch. The control travels with the wearer and electronically signals (many tiny transmitter/receiver technologies are available) desired temperature settings to the ambient sensors in whichever environment the wearer occupies at the moment. The environment—home, office, car, train, plane, etc.—adjusts to the needs of its occupants based on reading the desired setting, averaging desired settings when there is more than one person present, or tailoring to specific individual settings where possible, as in—for example—a car equipped with individual climate control settings capabilities. When no one is present in a particular environment, that environment does not need to use as much energy to maintain a temperature and its climate control system can respond accordingly. There are of course details to work out about how fast an environment needs to react to the entrance of a person and to what extent an environment needs to keep a certain temperature when empty in order to respond quickly. These details need to be worked out as a matter of energy use versus convenience and perceived viability of the system.

Research	Insights	Concept
Source [2]	Elimination	Allow individual temperature setting preferences to travel with the person in wearable, reconfigurable forms. Let each location sense the preferences of the people in it and respond systemically by use of environmental sensors rather than interactive devices
Passive climate control green home	Can we eliminate the need for interactivity in climate control systems and still afford comfort while also acting more sustainably?	
Passive | acts of elimination		
Source [3]	Locations	
Dining car	Why do controls need to vary by location? Why are they different in automobiles than in homes?	
Comfortable and absent of digital controls		
Source [1]	Usability	
Digital thermostats	Why are programmable home thermostats so hard to use?	
Variance of control design and interactivity by location | less than thoughtful usability design		

technologies as a material of creating comfortable spaces. My model solution for the design research project describes a passive climate control green home as an example of comfort achieved with minimal energy, a Pullman train dining car as an example of old-world notions of opulence and comfort, and thermostatic climate control devices in a car and a home that are clearly hopelessly complex and unusable (Fig. 8.6b). My model solution for the design concept project describes a wearable encoding of temperature preference and ambient room sensors that enable temperature preferences to follow people rather than be assigned to individual locations (Fig. 8.6a). The description is:

8.2.7.1 Concept: E-Ink Fabric Wearable Personal Thermostat and Ambient Sensors

The idea of this concept is that a digital thermostat control is woven into the fabric of clothing or worn like a bracelet or as part of a watch. The control travels with the wearer and electronically signals (many tiny transmitter/receiver technologies are available) desired temperature settings to the ambient sensors in whichever environment the wearer occupies at the moment. The environment—home, office, car, train, plane, etc.—adjusts to the needs of its occupants based on reading the desired setting, averaging desired settings when there is more than one person present, or tailoring to specific individual settings where possible, as in—for example—a car equipped with individual climate control settings capabilities. When no one is present in a particular environment, that environment does not need to use as much energy to maintain a temperature and its climate control system can respond accordingly. There are of course details to work out about how fast an environment needs to react to the entrance of a person and to what extent an environment needs to keep a certain temperature when empty in order to respond quickly. These details need to be worked out as a matter of energy use versus convenience and perceived viability of the system.

The intermediary step between the research and concept is shown in Fig. 8.10b to include insights about elimination, locations, and usability. This relationship between research and concepts mediated by insights is at least one way to understand a notion of methodological approach to creativity as part of design rationale.

Fig. 8.6 (**a and b**) Research to insights to concepts (Also appears in Blevis 2010)
1. Image source for picture of woman in hallway, automobile and home climate control devices: E. Blevis
2. Source: http://www.flickr.com/photos/jeremylevinedesign/3590460562/ @ 9.14.09 under creative commons license
3. Source: http://www.flickr.com/photos/14589121@N00/2070419285/ @ 8.31.09 under creative commons license
4. Image source for circular arrows: http://www.mattstow.com/circular_arrows.html @ 9.21.09

8.2.8 Prototypes

According to Fig. 8.1, a concept is analogous to an experiment design, and prototypes are analogous to experiments. The HCI literature frequently distinguishes high fidelity and low fidelity prototypes. To these, I add a third kind of prototype, appearance prototypes. Notions of prototypes are well understood in HCI and there is little to add here. Low fidelity or behavioral or exploratory prototypes are designed to push the boundaries of concepts. Appearance prototypes are designed to show the look and feel of a concept. High fidelity prototypes are designed to demonstrate that a concept is technically viable and usable.

For the example of "Designing for Sustainable Food Practices," specifically the concept system shown in Fig. 8.5, we can imagine examples of prototypes as follows.

A low fidelity (or behavioral or exploratory) prototype for the healthy food advisor mobile application might involve an over-the-shoulder study. This would entail following a willing person around pretending to be the application, commenting on food choices the person makes as she or he makes them. One expects that such a prototype would reveal how annoying a healthy food advisor might become to many people and respond to such revelations with design changes. Observations conducted in the service of research to develop insights are distinct from observations conducted to experiment with behavioral prototypes—this point seems obvious, but is often a point of confusion for students.

For an appearance prototype, we might produce relatively high production value visual representations of what the healthy food advisor application will actually look like. At the level of concept system, we might produce communications that enable people to understand the system and its components.

For a usability prototype, we may actually want to program enough of for example, the food tracker/calendar status program or other system elements to be able to conduct a task-directed usability study.

Prototyping—at least low and high fidelity prototyping—is well understood by the HCI community, and there is no need for further treatment here.

8.2.9 Strategies

To complete a design plan or explanation requires producing a strategic diagram of how a concept system may be implemented according to social value, technology, and enterprise concerns. These are not very different than business plans, except that they emphasize social values and technology as well as the economic sustainability of a concept.

Figure 8.7 shows a sketch of a design plan for our theme of "Designing for Sustainable Food Practices." The figure shows that such a plan is developed in terms of level of details, and may in fact be illustrated at the leaf levels. The social value

Strategic design plan:
Sustainable food
system
Level 1

Social values	Y1.Q1	Y1.Q2	Y1.Q3	Y1.Q4	Y2.Q1	Y2.Q2	Y2.Q3	Y2.Q4
Promote possibilities	□	■	○	○	○	○	○	○
Study system effects		□	■		□	■		
Tweak system			□	■		□	■	
Advertise results				□	■		□	■
...								

Technology	Y1.Q1	Y1.Q2	Y1.Q3	Y1.Q4	Y2.Q1	Y2.Q2	Y2.Q3	Y2.Q4
Information architecture	□	■	○	○	○	○	○	○
System elements	□	■	○	○	○	○	○	○
Research and evaluation			□	■		□	■	
Roll outs				□	■		□	■
...								

Enterprise	Y1.Q1	Y1.Q2	Y1.Q3	Y1.Q4	Y2.Q1	Y2.Q2	Y2.Q3	Y2.Q4
Chasm crossing				□	■	○	○	○
Capitalization	□	■	○	○	○			
Promote system		□	■	○	○	○	○	
Create alliances			□	■	○	○	○	○
...								

Level 2

Technology: IA	Y1.Q1	Y1.Q2	Y1.Q3	Y1.Q4	Y2.Q1	Y2.Q2	Y2.Q3	Y2.Q4
Research studies	○	■	■	○	○	○	○	○
Prototype studies			□	■	■	□		
Use case analysis		□	■	○				
Data sourcing			■	□	○			
Object oriented models				□	■	○		
...								

Legend: ○ ongoing activity; ■ primary activity; □ preparation for activity

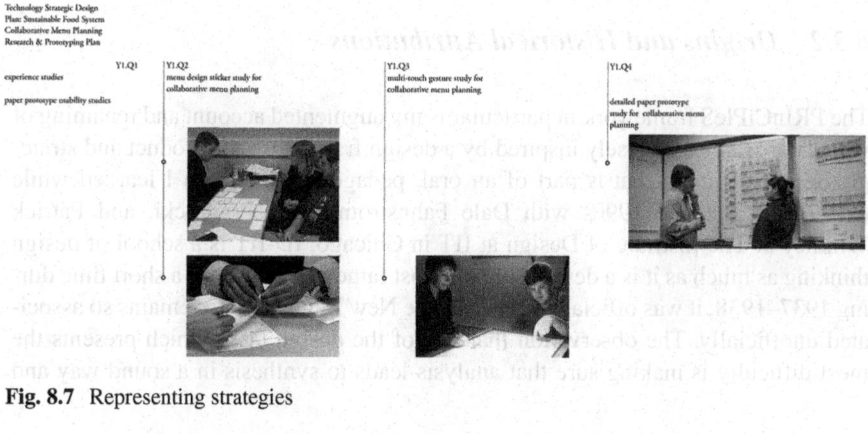

Technology Strategic Design
Plan: Sustainable Food System
Collaborative Menu Planning
Research & Prototyping Plan

	Y1.Q1	Y1.Q2	Y1.Q3	Y1.Q4
experience studies		menu design sticker study for collaborative menu planning	multi-touch gesture study for collaborative menu planning	detailed paper prototype study for collaborative menu planning
paper prototype usability studies				

Fig. 8.7 Representing strategies

plan includes scheduling of activities to promote the health possibilities, study system effects, tweak the system, and advertise results, as examples. The technology plan includes scheduling of activities to create the information architecture, system elements development, beta testing, and roll out, as example activities. The enterprise plan includes scheduling of activities to create alliances with food providers, promote the system, and calculate chasm crossing—the point at which the enterprise becomes economically sustainable, as examples (see Moore 1999). The figure also shows a second level development of a specific activity in the technology plan, expanded to show the detail of activities to create research studies, prototype studies, use case analyses, data sourcing, and object-oriented models, as examples. Finally, a plan for experience studies and paper prototype studies appears in Fig. 8.7 as yet a further, illustrated expansion of the second level technology plan.

8.3 Historical Background and Attributions

8.3.1 Prior and Anticipated Work, Commons Advice

This chapter is closely related to prior and anticipated publications, and as such it requires necessary disclosures and attributions. I—alone and with various others— have described the notion of design plans or explanations and the PRInCiPleS framework here and there over some time, but never before in an archival format. The prior non-archival work which describes design plans or explanations and the PRInCiPleS framework in substantive ways is Blevis (2004), Notess and Blevis (2004), Blevis and Siegel (2005), Reed et al. (2005), Blevis et al. (2008), and Blevis (2010). Kindly note that much of this present chapter will also appear in "Design in the Age of Climate Change" (Blevis and Blevis 2013, anticipated) and that an account of the use of design plans or explanations and the PRInCiPleS framework in design pedagogy will appear in "The Design Habit" (Siegel 2013, anticipated).

8.3.2 Origins and Historical Attributions

The PRInCiPleS framework in particular is my augmented account and renaming of what is or is at least closely inspired by a design framework for product and strategic design planning that is part of an oral, pedagogical tradition I learned while teaching in the late 1990s with Dale Fahnstrom, Greg Prygrocki, and Patrick Whitney at The Institute of Design at IIT in Chicago. ID-IIT is a school of design thinking as much as it is a design school, most famous because for a short time during 1937–1938, it was officially known as the New Bauhaus, and remains so associated unofficially. The observation that one of the design tasks which presents the most difficulty is making sure that analysis leads to synthesis in a sound way and that synthesis follows from analysis in a sound way also owes to this mid 1990s teaching experience at ID, especially to Fahnstrom's, Prygrocki's, and Whitney's insights into design pedagogy.

There are other influences as well, aside from these origins at ID. Nonetheless, as a matter of historical fact and sound scholarship, the origins of the PRInCiPleS framework that occur in large part in the traditions of design planning at ID may not be discounted, and must be so acknowledged by those who use this framework. The importing, adaptation, augmentation, renaming, and refinement of this method into the pedagogical framework that serves as a substantial part of the infrastructure of the HCI/d program I now direct should equally be attributed to the non-archival works I describe above, as well as to a practice which is now in place in the program. Moreover, one of the goals of this chapter is to provide a definitive summary of and reference for this prior mainly non-archival reporting, without the need to refer to these earlier sources.

It may seem that these origins and attributions are described here in a manner more than necessary. I do this because design methods in design schools have somewhat of a guild knowledge status. Consider that (i) in writing about a scholarly abstraction derived from design practice, it is important to appropriately honour the framers of the design of design as it is practiced in design schools, where practice and hard-won experiential knowledge and reflection precede scholarship in some sense and perhaps in another sense are an alternative notion of scholarship worthy of recognition, and (ii) after a decade of graduating students who use the PRInCiPleS framework as an organizing device for design, it is important to provide an alternative to their sometimes less than careful attribution of the framework and its origins by here providing a definitive, archival source to be referenced—one which in turn chronicles and honors the hard won insights of others whose work precedes it.

In the sometimes guild-like context of a design school, notions of design methods and frameworks may sometimes be considered to be intellectual assets and proprietary knowledge. In the context of scholarship—at least in design-oriented HCI—notions of design methods and frameworks are more oftentimes considered to be foundational knowledge that is meant to be widely disseminated, discussed, studied, deployed, and advanced. I write what precedes in this paragraph from personal experience and as a matter of conjecture only—attitudes about proprietary guild knowledge and foundational scholarly knowledge must surely vary widely within both design and HCI. The real point here about design frameworks and methods is that nothing really exists in a vacuum, if one is willing to look around—for example, one of the most widely known design methods in design-oriented HCI is Contextual Design (Beyer and Holtzblatt 1998). In Notess and Blevis (2004), the PRInCiPleS framework is compared to Contextual Design, and here the comparison is tabulated in Fig. 8.8 as presented in that source. There are differences. There are similarities. For a complete explanation, please see Notess and Blevis (2004).

In 2002, Marty Siegel and I founded the Human-Computer Interaction/design (HCI/d) Program at the then new School of Informatics—now, the School of Informatics and Computing—at Indiana University, Bloomington. This program has come to be known as possibly the design-oriented HCI program with a strong

Contextual Design	PRInCiPleS
	predispositions
contextual inquiry	research
work modeling	
consolidation	insights
work redesign	concepts & concept systems
user environment design	
paper prototyping	prototypes
	strategies

Contextual Design Steps		PRInCiPleS Design Framework Elements	
Step	Activities and Deliverables	Element	Description
		predispositions	enumeration of all significant points of view about the population being designed for
contextual inquiry	pairs of design team members observe work practice in the field, co-interpreting data with users	research	data from observations of the target population and/or collected instances of the culture being stud-ied and/or literature review
work modeling	back with the design team, replay the story of what was observed while other team members create diagrammatic models to organize and represent what was observed: sequence model – intents, steps **flow model – movement of work between people in the form of communication or artifacts** **cultural model – pressures, influences and emotions within the work environment** physical model – workspace layout, computer screen layout, network topology, etc. artifact model – objects created or used to accom-plish work		
consolidation	design team looks across multiple sets of models to combine data in a way that shows the larger patterns **without hiding details and differences**	insights	interpretations of the research data that express essential opportunities for improvement of the environment of the target population relevant to the designer's focus and values
work redesign	**design team uses consolidated models to share find-ings with the larger community of stakeholders and** conducts a visioning session to generate ideas for improving users' work; one or more ideas are selected for storyboarding	concepts & con-cept systems	an enumeration of design ideas germane to insights gained from research, organized into systems of concepts that work together coherently to create an improvement in the human condition of the target group
user environ-ment design	a system design is created by walking through a storyboard to identify the main components ("focus areas") of the system and the necessary pathways or connections between them		
paper prototyping	**low-fidelity paper prototypes are generated from the** system design; prototypes are taken back into users' contexts and users "operate" the prototypes to see if **they work better than their current methods;** find-ings from prototype interviews are used to validate **and refine the design**	prototypes	**high (working) and low fidelity (behavioral or ex-**ploratory) and physical (appearance) expressions of selected design concepts, useful for concept explora-tion and refinement
		strategies	a proposal for moving forward, not neglecting busi-ness, technical, or social and ethical issues

Fig. 8.8 Comparison of contextual design steps with PRInCiPleS framework elements (Reproduced from Notess and Blevis 2004)

presence in HCI venues like the ACM SIGCHI, DIS, and CSCW conferences, as well as at design conferences such as DPPI, IASDR, and DRS. From the very first, the PRInCiPleS framework was used as an organizing pedagogical framework, and Marty Siegel and I discussed it at length as a matter of curricular organization. Figure 8.9 shows a sketch of the logical structure of a design plan for a digital music library system of concepts organized in this framework from the very first course

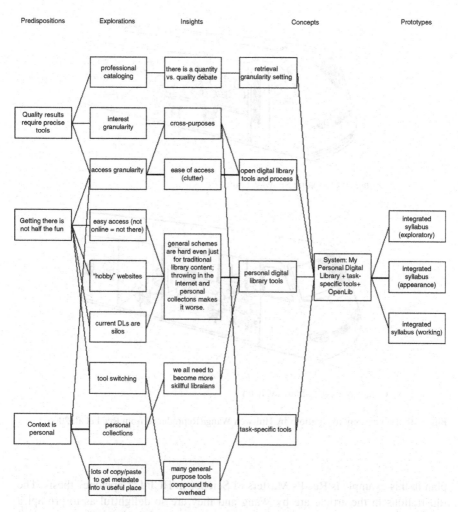

Predispositions   Explorations   Insights   Concepts   Prototypes

Fig. 8.9 Mark Notess' digital music library project (Reproduced from Notess and Blevis 2004)

offered in 2002. The sketch is by Mark Notess, and it is reported also in Notess and Blevis (2004). At the time, the acronym PRInCiPleS was not used *per se,* rather the much more inscrutable acronym PEICPS was used to denote Predispositions, Explorations (a relaxed notion of research—since design research, that is research conducted in the service of design has different emphasis than scholarly research in many people's minds), Insights, Concepts, and Strategies. By 2004, I proposed the acronym PRInCiPleS in response to critical feedback about the inscrutability of PEICPS and the first detailed design plan—concerning sustainability and travel— appears in Reed et al. (2005), to which the reader is referred for a much more elaborate and much better illustrated example than what appears here. The design

Dining and Drinking Subway/Train

Company Skybox Subway/Train

Fig. 8.10 Two concept illustrations by Hui-wen Wang (Reproduced from Reed et al. 2005)

plan in this example is Reed's Masters of Science in HCI/d "Capstone" thesis. The illustrations in the article are by Wang and they are so delightful as to prompt a specific invitation here to the reader to consult that source. Two of Wang's concept illustrations appear in Fig. 8.10.

The notion that the PRInCiPleS framework may be understood as an informal (in the mathematical sense) notion of design as proof is represented by Fig. 8.11a, which shows a logical style sketch of a design plan based on Alexander et al.'s (1977) Shopfront Schools pattern that may possibly annoy logicians for being too informal, and designers for being too formal. In Blevis et al. (2008), the problems of trying to integrate formality (in the mathematical sense) into design curricula are noted. Figure 8.11b shows a more abstract diagram of the kind of relationships expressed in Fig. 8.11a, this time distinguishing presentation order from process order—that is, distinguishing the idea that design plans or explanations may be described in terms of logical connections between the framework elements is primarily a technique of presentation and that in practice, design processes are not so neatly ordered. In practice, one may have a concept before having done adequate research, insights may

Title:
Distributed Learning

…

Predispositions (Viewpoint):
P1: Everyone is entitled to an education
P2: There aren't always enough resources to go around

…

Research-Observations:
P1,P2 ⇨ O1: Some of the townspeople in college towns have never been on the campus; Universities are sequestered from the general public
P1,P2 ⇨ O2: Not everyone can afford to attend the best colleges or universities
P1,P2 ⇨ O3: Internet technologies enable wider distribution of quality materials in the same manner that the introduction of recording technology enabled people to listen to the best performers

…

Insights:
O1 ⇨ I1: To make education accessible to everyone, it's a good idea to move the physical campus into the community with less intimidating artifice
O2,O3 ⇨ I2: To make education accessible to everyone, it's a good idea to distribute it more widely

…

Concepts:
I1 ⇨ C1: Shopfront schools (after Christopher Alexander)
I2 ⇨ C2: Distance education

…

Prototypes:
C1 ⇨ Pr1: Study Sylvan Learning Systems
C2 ⇨ Pr2: Study Existing Distance Education efforts

…

Strategies:
Pr1 ⇨ S1: Evaluate effectiveness of existing Shopfront education enterprises and develop plan for improvement, perhaps integration with other forms of democratization of learning
Pr2 ⇨ S1: evaluate effectiveness of existing distance education enterprises and develop plan for improvement, perhaps integration with other forms of democratization of learning

…

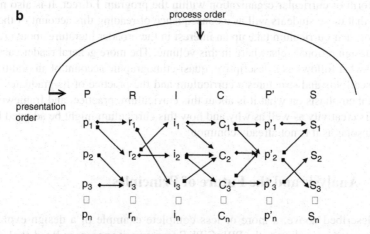

Fig. 8.11 (a) Design explanation example fragment expressed as a frame, based on Christopher Alexander's Shopfront Schools Pattern (Reproduced from Blevis and Siegel 2005). (b) Distinguishing process order and presentation order

arrive after prototyping, and so forth. This observation about ordering in practice is the reason I claim that PRInCiPleS is a framework and not a process.

The relationship between these attempts at formality in design and the design rationale (i.e. Moran and Carroll 1996), and pattern languages (i.e. Alexander et al. 1977), and even ideas like ontological designing (i.e. Winograd and Flores 1986) must be noted. Nowadays, the PRInCiPleS framework is used in the context of our HCI/d program as an informal organizing structure for interaction design and strategic design plans. Based on my experiences at a design school, and now at a school of informatics and computing, I have concluded that rigor should not be taken to be a goal in-and-of-itself. It is at its best a tool of evidence. One hopes for students who are neither afraid of rigor, nor embrace rigor as an end goal. One hopes for students who take rigor as a means of creating evidence for their design plans and explanations, and values-rich design as the end goal. In practice, this is one of the hallmark traits of our best and brightest students.

8.3.3 Purpose

This chapter serves several purposes, namely (i) the purpose of finally chronicling the origins of PRInCiPleS and documenting in an archival way my own present thinking about PRInCiPleS, (ii) as a kind of entre into the world of this notion of a design rationale framework for the many students whom I will ask to read it, and (iii) as an account of how creativity and design rationale are supported structurally within a curriculum and notion of design practice in a way which may appeal to others.

The students to whom I refer above will be asked to read this chapter as a chronicle of and manual for a heretofore primarily oral tradition and practice—that is the use of the PRInCiPleS framework as a notion of design rationale, which serves as one form of curricular organization within the program I direct. It is also my purpose that these students will as a consequence of reading this account of the structure of their curriculum take up an interest in the broader literature about creativity and design rationale elsewhere in this volume. The more general reader can understand what follows as a descriptive, quasi-ethnographic account of an oral tradition that scaffolds and structures a curriculum and the practice of its graduates, with a special emphasis on what it is about this curriculum, practice, and framework that fosters creativity as well as why and how this curriculum might be adopted by others, insofar as it is not already common.

8.4 Analysis and the Future of Principles

As described above, a more or less complete example of a design explanation constructed according to the PRInCiPleS framework appears in Reed et al. (2005). An interesting example of a design explanation based on observations and literature research, insights, and concepts only to support designerly collaborations appears in Wang and Blevis (2004). The students in our HCI/d program maintain a site (www.hcidpeople.com) with links to all of their individual professional, personal sites, and many of these sites contain projects that are structured according to the PRInCiPleS framework with varying degrees of fidelity to the framework. A particular future goal is to curate many examples of the best of this work on our program site, and to see some of it published. Another particular future goal is to see others use and adapt this framework to their own needs and sensibilities and advance the designerly culture within HCI.

Like any treatment that attempts to explain too much with too broad a brush, this account of the PRInCiPleS framework, its origins, and context of use, is likely to cause any particular reader to think of certain under-referencing about certain aspects of what precedes and the need for further comparison between the framework and other notions of design process. The PRInCiPleS framework is not in-and-of-itself a "very big deal," but notions of design processes and frameworks are important. The treatment of PRInCiPleS and its role in a particular curriculum here is more existentially quantified account than universally quantified advice. The relation of PRInCiPleS to other notions of design rationale is material for another chapter or article, possibly written by another author.

More importantly, the publishing and chronicling in a more public way of the many design projects that have been organized according to this framework holds much more utility for the future of the PRInCiPleS framework than do the implications of the framework as a design theoretic construct. This is a curatorial point of view—that collections of design plans or explanations constructed according to the PRInCiPleS framework are themselves a form or genre of design research and that more and more interesting individual such plans or explanations are at least as salient to advancing understanding of design as more and more refinement of the abstract framework. Moreover, I argue that it is the curatorial point of view which is most appropriate to connecting notions of creativity to notions of design rationale. To put it more simply, to understand the relationship between creativity and design rationale, collect more and more examples of design explanations and plans as artifacts of study in-and-of their own right.

References

Alexander, C., Ishikawa, S., & Silverstein, M. (1977). *A Pattern Language*. Oxford: Oxford University Press.

Beyer, H., & Holtzblatz, K. (1998). *Contextual design: Defining customer-centered systems*. San Francisco: Morgan Kaufmann Publishers.

Blevis, E. (2004). What design is matters less than what designs are: Explanations for HCI and design, a case story. In J. Zimmerman, S. Evenson, K. Baumann, & P. Purgathofer. *Workshop on the relationship between design and HCI*. ACM CHI 2004 conference on Human factors and computing systems, Vienna, Austria.

Blevis, E. (2010). Design Challenge Based Learning (DCBL) and sustainable pedagogical practice. *Interactions, 17*(3), 64–69. doi 10.1145/1744161.1744176.

Blevis, E. (2011). Digital imagery as meaning and form in HCI and design: An introduction to the Visual Thinking Backpage Gallery. *Interactions, 18*(5), 60–65.

Blevis, E., & Blevis, S. A. (2013, anticipated) *Design in the age of climate change.* Cambridge, MA: MIT Press.

Blevis, E., & Coleman Morse, S. (2009). Food, dude. *Interactions, 16*(2), 58–62.

Blevis, E., & Siegel M. (2005). The explanation for design explanations. *11th International Conference on Human-Computer Interaction: Interaction Design Education and Research: Current and Future Trends,* Las Vegas, NV.

Blevis, E., & Stolterman, E. (2007). Ensoulment and sustainable interaction design. In *Proceedings of International Association of Design Research Societies Conference (IASDR)* Hong Kong, China: HKPT.

Blevis, E., & Stolterman, E. (2008). The confluence of interaction design and design: From disciplinary to transdisciplinary perspectives. In *Proceedings of 2008 Design Research Society Conference.* Sheffield, UK: Design Research Society. 344/1–12.

Blevis, E., & Stolterman, E. (2009). Transcending disciplinary boundaries in interaction design. *Interactions, 16*(5), 48–51.

Blevis, E., Lim, Y. K., & Stolterman, E. (2006). Regarding software as a material of design. In *Proceedings of WonderGround 2006.* Lisbon: Design Research Society.

Blevis, E., Lim, Y. K., Stolterman, E., & Makice, K. (2008). The iterative design of a virtual design studio. *Techtrends: A Journal of the Association for Educational Communications and Technology, 52*(1), 74–83. Springer, US.

Burtynsky, E. (2005). *Edward Burtynsky: China.* Essays by Ted Fishman, Mark Kingwell, Marc Mayer, and the artist. Göttingen, Germany: Steidl.

Choi, J. H., & Blevis, E. (2010). HCI & sustainable food culture: a design framework for engagement. In *Proceedings of the 6th Nordic conference on human-computer interaction: Extending boundaries (NordiCHI '10)* (pp. 112–117). New York: ACM.

Choi, J. H., & Blevis, E. (2011). Advancing design for sustainable food cultures. In M. Foth, L. Forlano, C. Satchell, & M. Gibbs (Eds.), *From social butterfly to engaged citizen: Urban informatics, social media, ubiquitous computing, and mobile technology to support citizen engagement.* Cambridge, MA: MIT Press.

Cross, N. (2001). Designerly ways of knowing: Design discipline versus design science. *Design Issues, 17*(3), 49–55 (MIT Press).

Friedman, B. (Ed.). (1997). *Human values and the design of computer technology.* Cambridge, UK: Cambridge University Press.

Fry, T. (2008). *Design futuring: Sustainability, ethics and new practice.* London: Berg.

Hirsch, T., Sengers, P., Blevis, E., Beckwith, R., & Parikh, T. (2010). PANEL: Making food, producing sustainability. In *Proceedings of the 28th of the international conference extended abstracts on Human factors in computing systems (CHI EA '10)* (pp. 3147–3150). New York: ACM.

IPCC. (2007). Summary for policymakers. In M. L. Parry, O. F. Canziani, J. P. Palutikof, P. J. van der Linden, & C. E. Hanson (Eds.), *Climate change 2007: Impacts, adaptation and vulnerability. Contribution of Working Group II to the Fourth Assessment Report of the Intergovernmental Panel on Climate Change* (pp. 7–22). Cambridge, UK: Cambridge University Press. (www.ipcc.ch)

Margolin, V. (2002). *The politics of the artificial: Essays on design and design studies.* Chicago: University of Chicago Press.

Max-Neef, M. A. (2005). Foundations of transdisciplinarity. *Ecological Economics, 53*(1), 5–16.

Menzel, P., & D'Aluisio, F. (2007). *Hungry planet: What the world eats.* Random House Digital, Inc.

Minsky, M. (1988). *The society of mind.* New York: Simon and Schuster.

Moore, G. (1999). *Crossing the chasm: Marketing and selling high-tech products to mainstream customers* (Rev. ed.). New York: Harper Business Essentials.

Moran, T. P., & Carroll, J. M. (Eds.). (1996). *Design rationale: Concepts, techniques, and use.* Mahwah: Lawrence Erlbaum Associates, Inc.

Nardi, B., & O'Day, V. (1999). *Information ecology: Using technology with heart.* Cambridge: MIT Press.

Nelson, H., & Stolterman, E. (2003). *The design way—Intentional change in an unpredictable world*. Saddle Brook: Educational Technology.

Nicolescu, B. (2002). *Manifesto of transdisciplinarity*. (Trans. V. Karen-Claire). Albany: SUNY Press.

Notess, M., & Blevis, E. (2004). Comparing human-centered design methods from different disciplines: Contextual design and PRInCiPleS. In *Proceedings of the design research society futureground 2004 conference*. Melbourne: Design Research Society.

Papanek, V. (1984). *Design for the real world: Human ecology and social change* (2nd ed.). Chicago: Academy Chicago Publishers.

Ranjan, A., & Ranjan, M. P. (2010). *Handmade in India: A geographic encyclopaedia of India handicrafts*. New York: Abbeville. http://www.amazon.com/Handmade-India-Geographic-Encyclopedia-Handicrafts/dp/0789120479/ref=sr_1_4?s=books&ie=UTF8&qid=1338930834&sr=1-4

Reed, C., Wang, H. W., & Blevis, E. (2005). Recognizing individual needs and desires in the case of designing an inventory of humanity-centered, sustainability-directed concepts for time and travel. *DPPI 2005 Designing Pleasurable Product Interfaces*. Eindhoven, The Netherlands.

Wang, H., & Blevis, E. (2004). Concepts that support collocated collaborative work inspired by the specific context of industrial designers. *ACM CSCW 2004 conference on Computer Supported Cooperative Work*. Chicago, IL.

Winograd, T., & Flores, F. (1986). *Understanding computers and cognition: A new foundation for design*. New York: Addison-Wesley, Inc.

Chapter 9
Using Rationale to Assist Student Cognitive and Intellectual Development

Janet E. Burge and Bo Brinkman

Abstract One of the questions posed at the National Science Foundation (NSF)-sponsored workshop on Creativity and Rationale in Software Design was on the role of rationale in supporting idea generation in the classroom. College students often struggle with problems where more than one possible solution exists. Part of the difficulty lies in the need for students to progress through different levels of development cognitively and intellectually before they can tackle creative problem solving. Argumentation-based rationale provides a natural mechanism for representing problems, candidate solutions, criteria, and arguments relating those criteria to the candidate solutions. Explicitly expressing rationale for their work encourages students to reflect on why they made their choices, and to actively consider multiple alternatives. We report on an experiment performed during a Data Structures course where students captured rationale.

Keywords Design rationale • Creativity • Student cognitive development

This work was supported by NSF CAREER Award CCF-0844638 (Burge). Any opinions, findings, and conclusions or recommendations expressed in this material are those of the author(s) and do not necessarily reflect the views of the National Science Foundation (NSF).

We would like to thank the students taking the Data Structures course for their willingness to participate in this experiment, and fellow participants in the workshop on Creativity and Rationale in Software Design.

J.E. Burge (✉) • B. Brinkman
Department of Computer Science and Software Engineering, Miami University,
205W Benton Hall, Oxford, OH, USA
e-mail: burgeje@muohio.edu

9.1 Rationale as a Method for Building Creativity and Cognitive Maturity

One of the orienting questions for the National Science Foundation (NSF)-sponsored workshop on Creativity and Rationale in Software Design in 2009 was, "How can design rationale be used in the classroom to motivate and instruct students about reflection, idea generation, and evaluation?" (Daughtry et al. 2009). At the heart of this question is an implicit claim about creativity, that is, "creativity" in software design seems to involve not just idea generation itself, but also the iterative process that moves the designer to reflect, evaluate, and generate more ideas multiple times before committing to a final design.

Carroll's (2009) workshop manifesto, "The Essential Tension of Creativity and Rationale in Software Design," emphasized this by pointing to liminality as a key aspect of the creative design process. The manifesto described liminality as "Thinking and acting on the border between two contrasting concepts or rules, such as rapid switching between convergent and divergent modes of thinking."

We see a direct link between a student's cognitive development and the ability to engage in creative processes. Perry (1970) identified nine positions of development starting with duality, where answers exist for everything and where they can be right or wrong, into multiplicity, where all answers are valid, into relativism, where they begin to evaluate solutions based on the context, and continuing through several levels of commitment, where students can begin to integrate knowledge and make their own choices based on that information.

Students in the first 2 years of college tend to display dualistic and multiplistic tendencies. Though Perry pointed out that most college students are not pure Stage 1 dualists, few students in his study reached even the lowest levels of commitment until their junior year (p. 155). Similarly, Marcia B. Baxter Magolda reported (1992, p. 71) that more than 80% of juniors are "transitional knowers," (those that recognize relativism in some knowledge domains, but are still dualistic in others), and more than 40% of sophomores were still mostly dualistic.

This understanding of the epistemic styles of our students should inform our thinking about teaching design. Dualistic cognition is inherently opposed to the liminal state of mind that is so characteristic of creativity in design. We believe that students who come to a design problem with the attitude that there is a "right answer" to be discovered by analysis will commit to a design without engaging in reflection or iteration. They will commit too early, before they have a chance to be creative. Students in multiplicity or the early stages of relativism may be unable to distinguish between the good designs and poor designs that emerge in their thinking. Some evidence to support these claims can be found in the work of Atman et al. (2005), who showed that senior engineering students spend 2–3 times more time on a design problem than freshman engineering students. This also correlates highly with the quality of the final solution, though their results do not directly address our claim that these effects are due, in part, to student epistemic styles.

We propose that requiring students to generate design rationale prior to implementing their solutions is a mechanism for encouraging reflection and delaying commitment to their initial design choices. Design rationale, the reasons behind decisions made while designing, is a way to represent design alternatives and the deliberation that produced them. In a sense, the rationale can be considered a language of design (Dym et al. 2005); much like sketching (which captures structural aspects of design) or mathematics (which expresses constraints the design must conform to). In the case of rationale, this is a language that captures the design intent and its relationship to the design. The ability to analyze and evaluate design alternatives in terms of their success at achieving design goals (intent) requires higher order thinking skills.

In response to our orienting question, we claim that design rationale help to motivate and instruct students in the creative process by putting off the moment of commitment to a design. The time spent in the liminal phase of design, iterating from idea to evaluation and back, can be lengthened by the use of design rationale. A prospective design rationale (that is, design rationale built before implementation, as a method of exploring possible designs) serves as a way of documenting the designer's process of design.

This lengthening of the time the student spends in ambiguity and reflection should also lead to cognitive development, by forcing the student to experience the kinds of reflection and switching between modes of thought that are characteristic of higher levels of cognition.

In the rest of this chapter we explore more fully the following two questions:

1. What are the links between creativity in design and cognitive level, and how can rationale assist in developing a student's capacities for each?
2. How can we assess whether or not use of rationale has had the intended effect?

In the balance of this first section we explore the first question. First we describe the motivation for teaching creativity in software development, and then expand on our proposition that "liminality" links software design with cognitive development. Next we discuss the use of design rationale as a pedagogical tool for encouraging cognitive development through reflection, and describe some prior applications of rationale to education.

Later in the chapter we describe an experimental assignment we designed based on our ideas, and provide some initial assessments of our approach. In the final two sections we outline areas for future work and other ways that design rationale may be used to stimulate student cognitive development.

9.1.1   Creativity in Software Development

Software development is, at its core, a creative enterprise. Given a problem, there are many possible solutions. For some practitioners, this is what attracts them to the field—software development as an exercise in creative design. For others, especially as college students, the multitude of solutions, where there is often no clear "right" answer, can be a source of frustration. With the many demands on their time, both curricular and extracurricular, there is significant pressure to find the, or a, correct solution in as little time as possible. The skill of being able to understand just enough about the material to come up with an answer serves them well in some of their earlier courses, where a program is correct if it produces the correct set of outputs given a set of inputs. But they run into difficulty in their later courses, where solutions need to be analyzed on multiple dimensions. These difficulties are exacerbated in courses such as Software Engineering and Human–Computer Interaction, where the system design is influenced not only by the technology available but by how people intend to use it.

It is essential that computer scientists, and computer science students, think creatively in order to successfully develop software. Glass (1995) described several aspects of software development where creativity is critical: determining how to translate the customer/business needs into a problem that the software can solve; resolving stakeholder conflicts; designing solutions to new and complex problems; determining test cases; and enhancing existing systems to meet needs that were not initially anticipated by the customer or the developers. A student convinced of a single right answer is likely to either insist that the stakeholder(s) provide this answer (when the stakeholders may not be approaching the problem with an awareness of what is possible with the technology available) or insist that their solution is the only one, or the best one, even if it may not be acceptable to the client.

9.1.2   Liminality, Creativity, and Cognitive Development

The workshop manifesto (Carroll 2009) emphasized three major characteristics of creativity in software design: playfulness, empathy, and liminality. We have chosen to focus on the liminal aspects of creativity because it seems to be the most natural fit for freshman- and sophomore-level courses.

To be sure, many instructors have great luck incorporating playful or empathic approaches in their coursework; many such assignments are presented every year at the SIGCSE (Special Interest Group on Computer Science Education) conference. But, for most students, Data Structures is the first required course that explicitly teaches a set of mathematical tools that can be used to compare one solution to another. Here we are speaking of the use of asymptotic analysis to compare the time and space requirements of data structures. When applied to simple problems, like sorting, such analyses seem definitive: For example, "Randomized Quicksort is more efficient than Insertion Sort." But when designing a data structure for a realistic problem, it is often the case that some operations can only be made fast if other operations are made slow, or if excessive amounts of memory are used, or if auxiliary data structures are used for bookkeeping. This means that, as a data structure is designed, there are many opportunities to shift focus from one operation to another, and to shift from analysis to idea generation and back. The manifesto links this "rapid switching between convergent and divergent modes of thinking" to creativity.

A concrete example will help clarify our point. In the experimental assignment described more fully below, students were asked to design a list-like data structure that needed to support dequeue operations (adding and removing items at the ends) as well as searching by key. One student, in his initial thinking, considered only arrays and linked-lists as possible designs, and selected linked-lists because they support dequeue operations in constant time. Upon evaluation of the designs, however, he discovered that search would be very slow, and so he returned to idea generation and added hash tables as a third design option. Upon evaluating hash tables he discovered that the dequeue operations would be tricky to implement, and returned again to idea generation.

Inspired by this example, we propose that a Data Structures course is a natural place to look for the contrasting concepts that give rise to liminal mental states. In Data Structures we teach the theory of algorithm running times, but also how to actually determine algorithm performance through experiments to confirm (or not!) the theory. We teach the canonical data structures, but we also give students problems for which the canonical data structures are a poor fit. We present the material of the class using diagrams and pseudo-code, but require students to actually write working programs using a real language.

We do not wish to define *creativity* only in terms of liminality, but we feel that much of what is creative about the work of students really arises when they are able to synthesize seemingly incompatible ideas from two apparently opposing or unrelated ways of thinking. In reference to the manifesto (Carroll 2009), we claim that students are best able to "pursue surprise and unexpected outcomes" when they actively embrace and explore the "border between contrasting ideas."

We believe the ability to embrace liminal states and cognitive development are directly linked. Many useful theories of cognitive development might inform this discussion. We have already described the key aspects of Perry's (1970) model, which undergirds much of our thinking in these early sections. In our final section, we also use Bloom's Taxonomy (Bloom 1956), which we found helpful in identifying other pedagogical applications of design rationale. The evidence of Perry (1970, pp. 55–56) and Baxter Magolda (1992, p. 71) suggests that our Data Structures students (who are mostly sophomore computer science majors and junior engineering majors) will still be in transition towards relativism. Baxter Magolda's study showed that more than 40% of sophomores were still noticeably absolute in their thinking, and that very few juniors (less than 10%) are independent thinkers. In Perry's study juniors were rated as being in "commitment" (levels 7, 8 or 9) only about 50% of the time, and for sophomores it was less than 10%.

Students stuck in a dualistic way of thinking are unlikely to discover creative solutions, because they will be satisfied as soon as they identify any "correct" solution. The traps for students in multiplicity or naïve relativism are subtler. At this level, the student is aware that there are many viable solutions, but tends to assume that all are equally good. This can again block creativity because the student chooses a solution somewhat arbitrarily. When students are "stuck" at the lower levels of cognitive development, we suspect that the solution chosen is likely to be routine, familiar, or arbitrary, rather than innovative and creative.

So we propose that there is a link between comfort with liminal mental states and cognitive maturity, and that design activities that cause students to experience rapid switching between contrasting ideas help students to build up both cognitive and creative maturity.

9.1.3   Rationale, Reflection, and Liminality

In the experimental assignment sequence presented in the next section, we used prospective design rationale to encourage student creativity in an individual design task. As mentioned above, a prospective design rationale is one that is created before the design is implemented, as part of the design process. Contrast this with retrospective design rationale, which are written after the design is chosen, and may serve only to document the chosen design. Prospective design rationale fosters both creativity and cognitive development by encouraging, and capturing evidence of, reflection.

Reflection serves an important purpose in both education and in practice. In education, many researchers have proposed a link between reflection and cognitive/epistemic level. Dewey (1933, p. 9) defined reflective thinking as "active, persistent, and careful consideration of any belief or supposed form of knowledge in the light of the grounds that support it and the further conclusions to which it tends." Reflection guides the learning process as evidence is examined and conclusions drawn. Dewey's claim that reflective thinking is necessary when it is not possible to come up with "certain solutions" was the reason why King and Kitchener (2002) chose reflection as the basis for their model of student epistemological development. The reflective judgment model (King and Kitchener 1994) defined seven stages of student epistemological development, broken into three categories: prereflective thinking, quasi-reflective thinking, and reflective thinking.

Schön, in his book *The Reflective Practitioner* (1983), described the need for professionals to move beyond technical rationality, where problem solving is the application of theory, to processes that allow for uncertainty and conflict. He described "knowing-in-action," where practitioners act based on tacit knowledge, and "reflection-in-action," where practitioners reflect on what they are doing as they do it.

Fischer et al. (1991) described how design rationale supports reflection by capturing the designer's knowledge about the situation. Similarly, the iteration between idea generation (divergent thinking) and design selection (convergent thinking) is a reflective process. Design rationale supports both the capture of the alternatives and their exploration by supporting the evaluation of the more promising alternatives and any additional decisions required during their elaboration. In the illustrative example above we saw a student using the process of building design rationale as an opportunity for critical reflection.

We should note, as an aside, that in this study we focus only on the individual design projects, not on teamwork. Though we greatly appreciate the role that rationale can play in capturing and transferring knowledge in a team setting, we believe that the capture of rationale is beneficial even for one individual engaged in an individual design project.

So we claim that design rationale can be used to encourage critical reflection about software design problems. Further, we claim that such critical reflection, if embraced by the student, is likely to lead to greater creativity. Critical reflection and creativity are certainly not the same thing; rather, critical reflection tends to provide grist for creative energies to act upon. Incorrect assumptions tend to act as roadblocks for creativity, but critical reflection helps us to challenge these assumptions. We naturally tend to select designs similar to older successful designs with which we are already comfortable, but critical reflection can cause us to reject familiar solutions that are actually inappropriate.

9.1.4   Prior Work on Rationale in Education

Moran and Carroll's (1996) book included two approaches to using rationale in education. The first was to provide rationale in the form of templates to assist with user interface (UI) design (Casaday 1996). The templates help designers to "ask the right questions" and assist designers with the process by guiding them toward a solution. Carey et al. (1996, p. 375) built a library of "exemplary user-interface designs" along with their rationale so those examples could be used to teach UI design. Other work using rationale in UI design includes using design space analysis (DSA; MacLean et al. 1991); as part of the FLUID (framework for learning user interface design) interactive media system (van Aalst et al. 1995); The work proposed here uses a more general approach (not one aimed at a specific type of design) and supports additional manipulation and evaluation of design criteria, as well as using rationale to assist with the definition and documentation of new designs.

Several software engineering textbooks either teach rationale (Bruegge and Dutoit 2004), or use rationale as explanation for design case studies (Fox 2006). Rationale is also present in the form of "consequences" in the ubiquitous Gang of Four (GoF) design patterns book (Gamma et al. 1995); used both as a reference and as a supplemental textbook.

9.2   Exploring Rationale in a Data Structures Course

In the previous section we claimed that careful use of design rationale by dualistic and multiplistic thinkers should lead them to increases in creativity and cognitive maturity. This theory has implications for how one structures "design" projects for lower-level courses. In this section we will present a first attempt at such an assignment for a Data Structures course, and contrast it with the kinds of design assignments we had used in the past.

Our theory also requires some justification through evidence. We have some initial results based on our evaluation of the work produced by students for our experimental assignment using design rationale. While the experiment was by no means a controlled experiment, nor was it designed to validate our theory (it was, instead, designed to help the students learn), we still are able to report on some tantalizing results that point the direction for future work.

9.2.1 SEURAT and Pugh's Total Design in Data Structures

In the Data Structures course, we chose to use two different methods for capturing prospective design rationale. The first was the rationale management system SEURAT and the second was based on examples from Pugh's (1991) *Total Design*. In order for the reader to understand how we think rationale should be used in undergraduate courses, we must first describe what data these two types of design rationale capture, and how they support decision making.

Let us start with some general observations. Problem solving can be broken into four stages: problem definition and analysis, idea generation, idea evaluation and selection, and implementation of the selected idea (VanGundy 1981). Rationale can support some idea generation techniques, such as brainstorming, by representing alternatives as generated, and attribute listing, a technique developed by Crawford (VanGundy 1981), where attributes listed would be alternatives. Rationale captured in the form of argumentation is especially useful, however, during the evaluation and selection stage by capturing criteria, their relationship to the alternatives, and supporting evaluation. Some of the techniques described by VanGundy (1981) that could be supported by rationale are (a) the advantage–disadvantage approach, enumerating the advantages/disadvantages of each alternative with respect to a predefined set of criteria; (b) the Battelle method (Hamilton 1974; VanGundy 1981), dividing criteria into culling, rating, and scoring in order to narrow the field of alternatives; and (c) reverse brainstorming (VanGundy 1981; Whiting 1958), which is brainstorming on the disadvantages of each alternative. Rationale systems that perform evaluation, such as the software engineering using rationale (SEURAT) system (Burge and Brown 2004), can be considered a type of weighting system (VanGundy 1981), by allowing weights to be assigned to the criteria and using those weights in evaluation.

In this work, we use argumentation-based rationale to capture the idea generation, idea evaluation, and selection stages of problem solving. We used two methods for representing rationale, SEURAT (for one experimental group) and written documents proposed in Pugh's total design methodology (for the other). Both methods require students to list many alternative designs, develop criteria by which to evaluate the designs, perform the evaluation, and select a solution. Both methods, furthermore, require argumentation to back up both the evaluation criteria and the final decision. SEURAT adds the additional capabilities of expressing the rationale in a hierarchical format, showing decisions and subdecisions, as well as providing the capability to calculate a numerical evaluation of the support for each alternative.

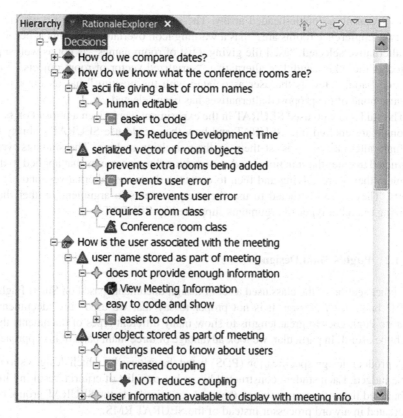

Fig. 9.1 An image of the SEURAT Rationale Explorer, showing the hierarchical view of a structured design rationale

9.2.1.1 Software Engineering Using RATionale (SEURAT)

The SEURAT system (Burge and Brown 2004), is a rationale management system (RMS) originally developed to assist with software maintenance by providing ways that the rationale could be used beyond just its presentation. SEURAT captures rationale as structured argumentation (decision problems, decision alternatives, and arguments) and uses both the structure of the rationale (syntax) and the content (semantics) to inference over the rationale to detect incompleteness (of the rationale) and inconsistency (of the design). The arguments in SEURAT can refer to system requirements, desired qualities, assumptions made, and relationships between alternatives. Figure 9.1 shows some rationale captured in the SEURAT Rationale Explorer. SEURAT stores the rationale in a relational database, allowing the rationales to be shared between multiple users during collaborative decision-making.

Figure 9.1's example shows three decisions, taken from the rationale for a conference room scheduling system. The decisions are displayed using a diamond-shaped icon containing a double-headed arrow. The second decision, "How do we know what the conference rooms are?" has a warning icon overlaid on it. This is because the alternative selected, "ascii file giving a list of room names," is not as well supported as the other candidate alternative, "serialized vector of room objects." The third decision, "How is the user associated with the meeting," has an error icon because none of the proposed alternatives has been selected yet.

The students who used SEURAT in the experiment were given a tutorial on how rationale are entered into SEURAT and how they could use SEURAT's ability to evaluate alternatives to assist them in their decision-making. The students were instructed to enter the functional and nonfunctional requirements that applied to the problem they were solving and then to enter the decisions, alternatives, and arguments. They were instructed to use their requirements in arguments, rather than utilizing the other types of arguments supported by SEURAT.

9.2.1.2 Pugh's Total Design

The other section of the class used a set of design documents based on Stuart Pugh's (1991) book *Total Design*. It is not proper to say that we used "his" documents, because Pugh goes to great lengths to show many different types of documents that might be useful. In particular, we took advantage of three main parts of his approach:

1. A product design specification (PDS) listed the criteria by which designs should be judged. Each student constructed his or her own list of criteria, resulting in a bulleted list with argumentation that was very similar to the SEURAT group, but created in a word processor instead of the SEURAT RMS.
2. A Pugh Matrix was used for idea evaluation. The student created a two-dimensional table in a word processor. Each column corresponded to one of the designs, and each row to one of the criteria from the design specification. The student selected one design to be the "baseline" design, and then each design was compared to the baseline in each criterion. A plus symbol was entered in the table if the design in question was superior to the baseline on that criterion, a minus symbol if it was worse. We also instructed students to enter their arguments in support of their evaluations in each cell.
3. A short essay summarized the idea selection phase and provided arguments in favor of the student's solution, based on the evaluation in the Pugh Matrix. Note that Pugh was very clear that one should not just count up the number of plusses and minuses and then select based on the numerical answer that results. We instructed students to use their evaluation matrix to support their selection process, but to also use common sense.

Pugh's process has many commonalities with SEURAT. Design criteria are explicitly listed, and require argumentation. Designs are evaluated based on the criteria, and arguments supporting those evaluations are captured. The Pugh process supports a quasi-quantitative approach to selecting the final design.

There are major differences as well. On the negative side, SEURAT requires students to learn a new tool (the Rationale Explorer, which is a plug-in for the

Eclipse Integrated Development Environment) instead of using a familiar tool (Microsoft Word). On the positive side, SEURAT forces students to be more careful about linking criteria with design decisions. In the non-SEURAT group, some students used arguments in their Pugh Matrix that had no relationship to their criteria, something that is much harder to do in SEURAT. SEURAT also naturally leads one to represent subdecisions in a hierarchy under the main decisions, much like an outline. The Pugh Matrix places all decisions at the same level.

9.2.1.3   Design in Data Structures Before Design Rationale

For several years we have had design projects in Data Structures similar to the one described here. In the past, however, students simply submitted a retrospective design justification. These documents took a variety of forms, but none of them were particularly formal, and only in very rare cases did the students compose them before implementing their solution. We found the quality of the resulting programs written by the students to be quite disappointing. In particular, there was some anecdotal evidence that students would not consider all of the important design criteria at the start of the project, but focus on only a few. These students tended to select familiar or canonical data structures because they never discovered the trade-offs involved in the real problem until *after* the solution was implemented.

Our feeling was that by introducing design rationale, and specifically prospective design rationale, into the Data Structures course we could cause the students to delay committing to a solution, and give them more opportunities to fully understand the problem.

9.2.2   Data Structures Class Experiment

Our main goal was to explore whether or not rationale could be of benefit to students in 2nd-year computer science coursework. As noted in the manifesto (Carroll 2009), it could be that use of rationale would "limit creativity by anchoring thought"; it could also be that rationale would be viewed as busywork, or that time spent building the rationale would take away time from honest reflection and other creative activities. We expected, however, that students would actually spend more time in reflection if they had to build a full rationale than if they simply had to write a brief essay explaining their choice.

We designed a classroom activity in which students needed to design a solution to a data structures problem based on their understanding of the performance characteristics of various common data structures. The assignment was broken into five steps (see Table 9.1), each of which had its own delivered artifact.

The fifth step of the process is also meant to test whether students overcommit to their chosen solution, and refuse to change when criteria change.

The experimental subjects were 38 students (34 male, 4 female) in an undergraduate course on data structures and data abstraction (most students were in their

Table 9.1 Description of the main problem and stages of the assignment used in the experiment

Problem:	Design a list-like data structure that supports the following operations: Adding and deleting at the head and tail of the list, searching to find the index of the first data item matching a search term, and retrieving an item based on its index in the list
Step 1:	List the criteria that you want your solution to adhere to. For example, do you want to have constant time searching? Do you want to try to minimize time spent coding?
Step 2:	Make a list of possible alternative implementation strategies. For example, a linked list would support all the operations, though not very efficiently. A hash table, on the other hand, can be made to be very efficient, but most students would find implementing it to be too challenging
Step 3:	Create a design rationale expressing the tradeoffs between various alternatives in terms of how well they meet your criteria
Step 4:	Select one of your alternatives, and implement it
Step 5:	Write a paragraph explaining which alternative you would have selected if the "most important" criterion was removed

2nd or 3rd year of college). The difference between the two experimental groups was in Step 3. The first experimental group (henceforth the "SEURAT group") constructed design rationale using the SEURAT system. The second experimental group (henceforth the "Matrix group") used a version of Pugh's total design methodology (Pugh 1991, Section 4.8).

We collected three artifacts from each participant: Their rationale (generated in Steps 1–3), their computer program (generated in Step 4), and their paragraph explaining their response to changing criteria (generated in Step 5). Note that, for the SEURAT group, the rationale could be fully captured in SEURAT, but the rationale for the Matrix group consisted of a list of evaluation criteria (with argumentation), a list of possible designs, and an evaluative matrix (henceforth the "Pugh Matrix"). Table 9.2 provides the metrics used to evaluate both sets of rationale in terms of rationale quality, and Table 9.3 provides the metrics used to evaluate the ideation skills demonstrated.

This first set of metrics, R1–R4, is meant to judge student success on the assignment in terms of their mastery of course objectives, as defined by the instructor. A score of 3 points or 2 points indicates that the student met instructor expectations, 1 or 0 indicates failing to meet expectations.

R1, R2, R3, R5 and R6 evaluate the rationale. R4 evaluates the response to changing criteria, and R7 evaluates the computer program code.

9.2.3 Examples of Student Artifacts and Reflections

In order to make this discussion more concrete, we present some small examples of student work. We will show some examples of creative designs from the experiment, as well as some examples of student argumentation.

Table 9.2 Data structures assignment learning metrics

Metric	Excellent/high (3 pts)	Good/medium (2 pts)	Poor/low (1 pt)
R1: Are all relevant alternatives identified and provided?	The student provides all the relevant alternatives	The student provides most of the relevant alternatives	The student only produces one alternative
R2: Are the criteria appropriately mapped to the alternatives?	The student maps all the criteria to the correct alternatives	The student maps most of the criteria to the correct alternatives	The student does not successfully map criteria to alternatives
R3: Did the student select an alternative based on the rationale?	The student selects an alternative based on the level of support	The student selects some alternatives based on the level of support	The student did not appear to have reasons for making the selection
R4: Did the student change the decision after the criteria change?	The student looks at differences in support levels and changes the decisions	The student sometimes fails to change the decision but instead stays with the initial plan	The student did not acknowledge the effect of changing criteria

Note: Each student received a score between 3 (for excellent) and 0 (for incomplete)

9.2.3.1 What Kind of Creativity Is Expected/Possible in Data Structures?

First, we wanted to provide some examples of creative solutions to the design problem. Recall that the student needed to design a list-like data structure that supports adding to the head and tail, looking up items by index, and searching for the first occurrence of a particular item.

We have already given the start of an example in the Liminality subsection above. Our problem allows for a very wide variety of valid approaches. The most comfortable approaches would have been to use an array (the main data structure used in previous classes) or a linked list (which they had used on the previous assignment). Students had also seen the approach of leaving spare space at both ends of an array to cut down on the time needed for adding and removing items, and hash tables. None of these approaches were optimal for all operations: Linked lists are slow for searching and indexing, arrays are slow for searching, and a naïve use of hash tables would result in either fast searching or indexing (depending on whether one uses the value or the array index as the hash key), but not both. Also, many students considered their own programming abilities when selecting a design, and so leaned toward array- or linked-list-based solutions because these solutions tend to be easier to read, easier to program, and easier to debug.

The most creative students found synergistic combinations of the canonical approaches.

- One student combined arrays with linked-lists to get a solution that had faster indexing, but which was similar enough to the linked-list he had previously written that he felt confident he could complete it correctly. He changed his

Table 9.3 Data structures assignment ideation metrics

R5: Completeness	For each alternative in the following list, the student receives 1 point: Array, Linked List, Vector (or Array-List), Skip List, Hash Table, and Binary Search Tree. These are all of the data structures studied in the class (to that point) that would have been reasonable alternatives for the assignment
	This scale is meant to measure the *quantity* of a student's candidate solutions (Shah et al. 2003). The instructor made a list of all canonical data structures that would have been useful in the assignment, and awarded one point for each. Students did not receive multiple points for minor variations on each data structure, so this scale does not count absolute quantity, but the quantity of "different enough" design candidates
R6: Creativity	For each alternative in the following list, the student receives either 1 point or 0.5 points: Skip List (1 point), Binary Search Tree (1 point), Linked Lists with multi-item nodes (1 point), Extra pointers to speed up list traversal in a linked list (0.5 points), Pre-allocation of nodes for a linked list (0.5 points). These are all of the ideas that students came up with that did not come directly from lecture. Significant ideas received 1 point, and less useful ideas 0.5 points
	This scale is meant to measure the *novelty* of student solutions, and our approach is very similar to that of Shah et al. (2003). In this case the instructor took a list of all design alternatives submitted by students, and eliminated those that appeared in most or all student submissions. The instructor then assigned point values to the remaining novel solutions based on how different the solution approach was from the non-novel approaches
R7: Contest rank	Student solutions were ranked based on three speed tests. These three tests were given to students as part of the assignment description. As part of their analysis, they had to decide how heavily to weight these speed criteria, compared to other criteria such as ease of coding
	This scale is meant to measure the *quality* of student solutions. Students received an ordinal ranking in each speed test, and then final rankings were based on a standard sum of ordinals. So, for example, a student that received 1st in two tests and 3rd in the last (sum of ordinals is 5) would beat a student that placed 2nd in all three tests (sum of ordinals would be 6)

linked-list nodes to contain arrays of length 1,000, which made his index-based lookups several hundred times faster than students with a regular linked list.

- Several students discovered that they could achieve better performance by keeping two separate data structures, one for searching by value and another for index-based lookups. One student had an array and a hash table, and another had two hash tables. One student attempted to combine a binary search tree (something he learned in high school) with an array.
- Two students kept auxiliary pointers to the middle of their linked-lists to speed up index-based lookup. They (and others) had considered skip-lists as a potential design, but eliminated them as an option for being too complicated.

On what grounds do we call these creative solutions? These students all found ways to combine apparently contrasting approaches. This is a form of liminal thinking, and also suggests that they returned more than once to idea generation. There is plenty of room for creativity in data structures classes, because even relatively small problems tend to fit the canonical data structures poorly.

9.2.3.2   Excerpts from Student Rationale and Argumentation

We also want to present a few concrete examples of student use of rationale, and reflections on rationale in our Data Structures course. Our goal here is to briefly indicate to the reader the type of argumentation and rationale that students produced. One should not try to make any general conclusions from the three anecdotes presented here, but instead we feel this should provide a bit of clarity in our discussion of assessment below.

Several students explicitly commented on the way that using rationale affected their performance on the assignment. One student from the SEURAT group said,

> ... I kind of went in biased towards a Doubly Linked list with a Hash Table ... [but] the Hash-backed Array list still came out on top. This is because, while Doubly Linked list has a faster add/remove time, the Array-list has a much faster lookup by index time. ... The design rational helped me visualize. Without this tool, I might not have fully realized that problem until it was too late.

Interestingly, this student's Rationale (see Fig. 9.2) did not take advantage of SEURAT's hierarchical decision-making capabilities, but did make use of its evaluation affordances.

A student in the Matrix group similarly noted that,

> The analysis part of this report helped me pick this option. Doing the analysis allowed me to compare different options with each other to see the advantages and disadvantages of each. In the end the requirements that I found most important to deciding which option to go with included having a very fast way to search through the data structure, and having am [sic] option that was relatively easy to code.

Though the student's argumentation is very brief (see Fig. 9.3), it captures key differences between the various options. The instructor is able to see that the student thought through all the criteria, and had reasons (even if incorrect or naïve) behind the choices made.

Of course, there were some students critical of the use of design rationale. One student in particular commented about SEURAT that,

> My design rational [sic] helped me ... but in the end I don't think I will agree with it. ... I could have figured this process easier by just writing this all out on paper, ... I looked at my decisions and realized what was most important to me in this project, learning about the data structures. (I didn't put this in the calculations, so maybe they would be different...).

What the student is saying here is that he chose not to include his most important decision criteria in his rationale and, as a result, the design rationale did not support

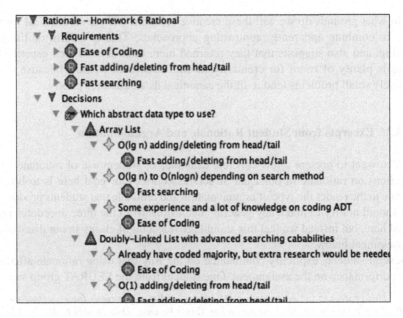

Fig. 9.2 Excerpt from a student's SEURAT rationale

Requirements	Option 4	Option 5
	Array-backed list with doubling approach	*Array-backed list with double and dictionary ADT*
The program is simple to code	Harder than the linked lists	The hardest option to code
The program is commented well	Easy to comment	Easy to comment
addToHead is fast	addToHead is nLog(n) time	addToHead is nlog(n) time
addToTail is fast	addToTail is nlog(n) time	addToTail is nlog(n) time
removeFromHead is fast	removeFromHead is nlog(n)	removeFromHead is nlog(n)
removeFromTail is fast	removeFromTail is nlog(n)	removeFromTail is nlog(n)
Search is very fast	Search is linear	search is constant
The program is robust	Harder than linked lists	Hardest to make robust
The list scales well	Methods do not scale as well as option 3	Search scales well, others methods don't
Finding nth node	time constant	time constant

Fig. 9.3 Excerpt from a student's Pugh Matrix

his eventual decision. Several students struggled because they believed that only technical criteria should be present in design rationale. For a homework project in an undergraduate course, however, the controlling criteria may be completely non-technical, just as in industry. Most students in the course seemed to understand this, and were willing to include nontechnical concerns (like time available to code or educational goals) in their list of criteria.

Table 9.4 Results for student success metrics

		SEURAT	Matrix	Average of both groups
R1: Are all relevant alternatives identified and provided?	%Excellent/high	68	53	61
	%Good/medium	32	37	34
	%Poor/low	0	10	5
R2: Are the criteria appropriately mapped to the alternatives?	%Excellent/high	47	29	38
	%Good/medium	41	35	38
	%Poor/low	12	35	24
R3: Do the students select an alternative based on their rationale?	%Excellent/high	83	79	81
	%Good/medium	6	11	8
	%Poor/low	11	11	11
R4: Do the students change their decision after the criteria change?	%Excellent/high	83	74	78
	%Good/medium	6	5	5
	%Poor/low	11	21	16

Note: $N = 38$, and some columns sum to 99% or 101% due to rounding

9.2.4 Assessing the Results of the Data Structure Design Assignment

The main purpose of this assignment was to stimulate student creativity and critical reflection through the use of design rationale. It will be quite clear to the reader that this was not an experiment designed to validate our theory, but rather a first attempt to put our ideas into practice.

Nevertheless, we provide some assessment of the results of the assignment. We provide some evidence that using a RMS (as opposed to simply written rationale) did not negatively impact student performance. We also tried to gauge the amount of creativity exhibited by students in the project.

9.2.4.1 Experimental Results: Student Success and Rationale

As described above, we evaluated student designs using seven rubrics. The first four rubrics (R1–R4) assessed student success in assignment tasks, and were initially rated on a scale from 0 to 3 independently by the two authors. In cases of disagreement, the authors consulted and reached a consensus rating. Error! Reference source not found. Table 9.4 shows the results for each of the standard scale metrics.

The students showed success as measured by metrics R1, R3, and R4, but were less successful with mapping criteria to alternatives. Lacking a control group, we cannot prove that using design rationale helped students develop their criteria and alternatives, but we can observe that almost all met instructor expectations on these tasks, indicating that the design rationale were not an impediment to the intended learning. From the weak scores on R2 (mapping criteria to alternatives), it appears that students were weakest in the analysis phase of the assignment, which is not surprising for students at this level.

Experimental Results: Comparison of SEURAT
to Matrix Results

The use of Pugh-style matrices is well established in engineering design. We wished to evaluate whether or not using SEURAT in undergraduate classes was a supportable approach. In order to do this, we considered seven hypotheses that compare student performance when using SEURAT to student performance when using the Pugh Matrix method. If students using Pugh matrices did substantially better than students using SEURAT, we might conclude that SEURAT should not be used with younger students. However, this turned out not to be the case: Students using SEURAT performed as well as, or better than, students using Pugh matrices in most tasks.

We used a two-sided Mann-Whitney U test to compare experimental groups (see Table 9.5). Because we have no reason to believe that any of our rubrics would correspond to a normal distribution, we felt that it would be unsound to use, for example, a t-test, because it requires the sampled data to be independent and normally distributed. The Mann-Whitney test does not suffer from this defect because it works by first ranking all samples, and then evaluating the likelihood of there being a marked difference in rank sum between the two experimental groups. More information about Mann-Whitney U tests (also known as Wilcoxon rank sum tests) may be found in statistics textbooks, such as Rice (1995, pp. 402–410). We set our threshold for significance at the $\alpha = 0.1$ level.

We must take some care in interpreting these results. In particular, look at our result for R7. This measures the speed of the student's solution: The instructor gave students some speed-related criteria at the start. Students were free, however, to reject these criteria and instead focus on criteria such as ease of coding, ease of debugging, re-use of code, and other similar criteria that are contrary to high scores in R7.

One major threat to the validity of this assessment is due to the way the experimental groups were assigned; the SEURAT group comprised all students from one section of the course, while the Matrix group composed the other section. The SEURAT group was stronger than the Matrix group as measured by homework grades on assignments other than the experimental assignment. It is possible that higher ability levels of the SEURAT group masked difficulties with using SEURAT that would have been identified if experimental groups were allocated in a more careful way. Furthermore, some have suggested (e.g., Amabile 1983) that technical expertise is a key factor that enables creativity. This would mean that the SEURAT group might be expected to be more creative than the Matrix group, on these sorts of tasks, simply due to their increased technical proficiency.

To try to correct for this problem we computed a best-fit line between each experimental variable (R1–R7) and final homework grade, and then analyzed the residual values that result when subtracting the predicted values from the actual

Table 9.5 Comparison of SEURAT users to matrix users

Alternative hypothesis	N_S	N_M	S_S	S_M	Test result
Students using SEURAT are more likely to present all the relevant alternatives than those using the Pugh method. (R1)	19	19	336	405	Null hypothesis accepted, $\alpha \approx 0.32$
Students using SEURAT are more likely to correctly map criteria to alternatives than those using the Pugh method. (R2)	19	19	322	419	Null hypothesis accepted, $\alpha \approx 0.16$
Students using SEURAT are more likely to select an alternative based on their rationale than those using the Pugh method. (R3)	19	19	369.5	371.5	Null hypothesis accepted, $\alpha \approx 0.98$
Students using SEURAT are more likely to change their selected alterative after criteria change than those using the Pugh method. (R4)	18	19	343.5	359.5	Null hypothesis accepted, $\alpha \approx 0.60$
Students using SEURAT will have a more complete set of alternatives than those using the Pugh method. (R5)	19	19	322.5	418.5	Null hypothesis accepted, $\alpha \approx 0.16$
Students using SEURAT will have a more creative set of alternatives than those using the Pugh method. (R6)	19	19	386	355	Null hypothesis accepted. (Note : this shows a negative correlation) $\alpha \approx 0.66$
Students using SEURAT will do better on instructor-defined performance criteria than those using the Pugh method. (R7)	17	18	246.5	383.5	Null hypothesis rejected, $\alpha \approx 0.05*$

Notes: N_S is the number of samples in the SEURAT group, and S_S is their scaled rank sum. N_M is the number in the Matrix group, and S_M is their scaled rank sum. α is a numerical approximation of the probability of rejecting the null hypothesis when it should be accepted, based on a two-sided Mann–Whitney U test. Note that since the lowest rank is best (1st place is better than 38th place), the *smaller* scaled rank sum indicates better performance
*Statistically significant

values. The residual values essentially tell us how much the student was over- or under-performing on this assignment compared to his or her usual performance in the class. When comparing the groups using these residuals,

- The groups were still not significantly different for rubrics R1, R2 and R4,
- The differences in R5 and R7 were no longer significant, and
- The Matrix group outperformed the SEURAT group in R3 and R6, with levels of $\alpha \approx 0.07$ in both cases

Again, we are not making any strong claims about the validity of this approach, but we felt that in the interest of completeness, as well as fairness to the Pugh method, we should present a grade-corrected version of the results.

Experimental Result: Rationale and Creativity

One other interesting trend is the very strong negative correlation, −0.4906, between R1 (Consider all relevant alternatives) and R6 (Consider a more creative set of alternatives). While we cannot make any claims about statistical significance, this relationship seems an intriguing topic to explore in future research.

We hypothesize that this results from some preconceptions among the study participants about the number of alternatives that the instructor expected them to generate. In particular, the instructor indicated that each student should have "at least 4–5 alternatives."

Some commentators have suggested that rationale might be inherently contrary to creativity (see Carroll 2009). We do not view our results as supporting that claim, because we believe the key problem was the process by which students decided whether or not they had considered "a sufficient variety of alternatives." Students may have been rushing to escape the liminal/undecided state, and so simply stopped when they had four alternatives. We believe that this is not a problem inherent in rationale, but instead a mistake in the instructor's design of the grading rubric for the assignment.

Summary of Claims

Because of the nature of the experiment, we want to be very careful to precisely state what we think our experiment shows. First, our experiment gives some evidence that using a RMS instead of a more traditional (writing) assignment does not negatively impact student learning. Though it now seems obvious that this would be the case, the course instructor initially had serious reservations about using SEURAT in class.

Second, the somewhat weaker scores in evaluating alternatives seem to support our claim that students in the course have not reached the "commitment" stages (levels 7–9) of Perry's (1970) scheme. On the other hand, we would be able to obtain much better data on this topic by giving the subjects appropriate critical thinking inventories, and we should do this in the future.

Third, our results suggest future experiments on rationale and creativity in education must be more careful about the instructions given to students about how to assess their own idea generation process. It appears that the use of rationale did indeed inhibit creativity, but probably primarily as a result of a poorly designed grading rubric, which focused on quantity instead of variety. If our theory, that increasing time spent in a liminal state increases creativity, is correct, then it might make more sense to require students to spend a predetermined amount of time on idea generation, instead of aiming for a predetermined number of ideas.

9.3 Reflections on Verifying the Contribution of Rationale to Creativity in the Classroom

In this chapter we proposed a theory that use of design rationale with 2nd-year computer science students should lead to improved creativity as well as cognitive development. We reported on an experimental assignment that put these ideas into practice in a Data Structures course, and we reported on our assessment of the impact of this intervention on student learning. It is clear, however, that there are many lessons to learn from the first attempt about *how* one ought to try to verify the effects of such an assignment.

First, we wished to make claims about student cognitive levels or epistemologies. At the most basic level, we assumed that students in our class would exhibit some dualistic tendencies, and that few would be contextual or committed knowers. We are particularly interested in how students at different levels of cognitive development respond to the challenge of creating design rationale, but there was no way for us to assess this because we did not collect this data. In the future we are considering applying epistemic inventories, such as Baxter Magolda's (1992) measure of epistemological reflection, as well as attempting to develop an inventory that specifically measures the student's epistemology of knowledge as it relates to software design. We hypothesize that students in transition or multiplicity may view relativism as normal in humanities classes, but not in engineering classes.

It is unlikely, however, that such inventories can directly assess the impact of our intervention on students, even if given as both pretest and posttest. Because students take many courses, most of which aim to increase student cognitive level, it seems unlikely that the effect of our intervention can be teased out from such data. In the future we should directly ask the students questions about why they did what they did and how they made decisions on our particular assignment. The examples of student reflection presented earlier in this chapter were suggestive, but we did not systematically ask students to comment on their processes. So we only have such data for a very small number of students.

Similarly, general-purpose measures of ideation similar to those used by Shah et al. (2003) should be adopted to make our results on creativity more comparable with results presented by other researchers. This would still leave us, however, with the problem of discovering *why* the student produced the set of design ideas that he/she produced. This again requires some qualitative methods that we did not use in our initial assessment. We need to question students, either on paper or through interviews, as to why and when they stopped generating ideas. If, for example, they did not start building their design rationale until the hour before it was due, we should not be surprised that the alternatives discussed were canonical or familiar. An approach similar to the verbal protocol analysis used by Atman et al. (2005) would be most useful.

9.4   Future Work—Rationale Across the Curriculum

The experiment described in this chapter focused on one group of students, those taking the Data Structures course (typically sophomore computer science majors and junior engineering majors). If the goal is to aid student cognitive development, as shown by their progression through the levels of the Perry (1970) scale, appropriate exercises and evaluation measures need to be applied at multiple points throughout the curriculum and, ideally, cognitive development evaluated both as an aggregate over all students and for individual students as they pass through the program.

This would require that the exercises be targeted to specific stages of development. At the earlier stages of their education, students can be presented with the problems, candidate solutions, and the rationale. For example, in a Data Structures course, the students learn many different ways to represent collections of objects. The student focus is often on how to implement these collections. The implementation is certainly important, but since many of these constructs are often supplied with the programming language (and do not require implementation), it is often more important that the students understand why they might choose a particular data structure for a problem, that is, to *analyze* the possible solutions by determining which criteria are relevant to the specific problem. The students' emphasis on the implementation rather than the selection becomes apparent in later classes, where they tend to stick to one or two favorite structures that may or may not be the best choices for the problem at hand. Providing rationale in a form that can be easily understood and manipulated may be a more effective way to teach the students the tradeoffs involved in selecting between data structures. The ability to manipulate the argument criteria can also help the students to explore how changing priorities result in different preferred solutions. Rationale can be presented in a form where the criteria can be manipulated by modifying their relative importance in order to demonstrate how as criteria change, so should the recommended solution.

When the students are comfortable with the idea of multiple alternative solutions, the next step would be to involve them in exercises where the problems and criteria are provided but where the students need to identify (*synthesize*) the candidate alternatives based on what they have learned in class and on their own experience. An example of this would be if students were asked to provide alternative methods for data entry or visualization based on usability criteria that they have learned in an HCI course.

The ability to identify the problems themselves, propose solutions, and define criteria requires *evaluation*—identifying what aspects of the solutions are important to the problem and its context. This is an essential skill in both software requirements analysis and in design. The requirements elicitation process is one of defining the problem and the criteria under which the solution will be evaluated, while the design process involves identifying and selecting solutions to that problem.

The movement from dualism through multiplicity and into relativism and commitment is more of a challenge. Kloss (1994) recommends several strategies to move students from dualism towards relativism that stress the importance of analyzing and structuring different points of view. This requires looking at the alternatives and evidence, including understanding the role of assumptions. As students move from working with the rationale of others to producing rationale themselves, the rationale can serve as both an instructional tool and as a means of assessing their intellectual development.

Table 9.6 lists the levels of the Bloom Taxonomy (1956), how the reflection and rationale approach should support those levels, and how students at different levels of development, as measured by the Perry (1970) scale, would perform on the rationale-supported tasks.

Table 9.6 Relating Bloom's taxonomy, reflection and rationale, and the Perry scale

Bloom	Reflection and rationale	Perry
Knowledge	Given a general decision problem, list and define the alternative solutions, as described in class Example: What data structures can be used to store lists of items?	Students at all levels should be able to do this since it could be directly recalled from their lecture notes
Comprehension	Given a general decision problem, and a set of criteria for making a selection, explain why these criteria are important Example: Why is it important to be able to efficiently remove elements from a list of items? Given a set of alternatives for a general decision problem, differentiate between them (This may require giving the students the criteria) Example: What is the difference between two data structures that store lists of items?	Students at all levels should be able to explain the criteria, but students still in the dualism stage may show biases toward certain alternatives (the "right" one) when differentiating between options and may not explore them in detail
Application	Given a specific decision problem, give a list of possible solutions Example: Given a design that requires sorting and searching a list of items, which data structures could be used to solve it?	Students in dualism may have difficulty providing more than one solution or more than one valid solution
Analysis	Given a specific design problem, provide a list of possible solutions and map those to a set of design criteria Example: Given a design problem that requires sorting and searching a list of items, list the appropriate data structures for storing the items and how they relate to criteria, such as time required to search, time required to add new items, etc.	Students in dualism may have difficulty providing more than one solution or more than one valid solution. If multiple solutions are produced, they may have trouble proposing arguments opposing solutions they have already deemed "correct" or identifying arguments supporting solutions other than the "correct" one
Synthesis	Given a specific design problem, define the criteria that should be used in order to make a decision Example: Given a design problem that requires sorting and searching a list of items, what criteria should be used to evaluate candidate data structures? Which criteria are more important to the specific problem?	This is not clear. Will students in dualism only come up with criteria that apply to their chosen alternative, discarding any criteria that do not support their beliefs? Will students in the multiplicity stage have issues identifying some criteria as being more important than others or will they consider all criteria equally valid?

(continued)

Table 9.6 (continued)

Bloom	Reflection and rationale	Perry
Evaluation	Given a specific design problem, define alternatives and the key criteria, and use this information to select a solution Example: A design problem that requires sorting and searching a list of items, what are the candidate data structures, what criteria apply in evaluating the appropriateness of each data structure to solving the problem, and given those criteria, which solution is the best choice?	Students in dualism are likely to have the same issues listed above, and are likely to have difficulty getting to the evaluation stage. Students in multiplicity may have difficulty in making a selection, even after identifying alternatives and criteria

Three courses in our department curriculum now contain explicit course outcomes regarding analysis of multiple alternatives: CS2 (1st year), Data Structures (2nd year), and Senior Design Project (4th year). Using rationale within these courses will provide an opportunity for studying how rationale can assist in the students' progression from dualism toward the higher levels of development.

9.5   Summary and Conclusions

Students progress through several stages as they gain knowledge and experience. They run into difficulty when they need to operate at higher cognitive levels than they are accustomed to. The ability to make decisions when confronted with uncertainty and ambiguity is important since the problems they will tackle become more realistic and beyond the point where, if they perform the right sequence of actions, they can produce a single correct answer. The ability to synthesize and evaluate solutions becomes critical for problem solving and creativity. Related to this is the need for students to move beyond duality, where there are always right and wrong answers, towards higher levels of thinking where they can begin to analyze the evidence and understand that not all criteria are equally valid in every context.

Our experiment with using two rationale representations, the SEURAT RMS and Pugh's (1991) total design methodology (as part of a writing assignment), indicated that students at the college sophomore level do indeed start out at a fairly low level. The experiment suggests that using the RMS does not inhibit creativity when compared to results using the more traditional writing assignment. Using rationale, however, did not result in a wider variety of ideas. This could be because the students were told how many ideas were required and some may have stopped searching once they achieved their "quota."

While not giving definite answers on rationale's impact on creativity, there were insights to be gained from the use of rationale. The rationale provided insight into student thinking for the instructor to use to assess both the student's understanding of the problem at hand and where they are likely to be in their development along the Perry (1970) scale. Understanding where the students are developmentally, relative to where we want them to go, is important in deciding how to help them progress. Rationale can be a valuable tool in both aiding and assessing that progression.

Our experiment demonstrated that rationale provides a mechanism for students to express the results of the analysis, synthesis, and evaluation required to design solutions to problems and provides assistance during the process. Explicitly expressing rationale for their work encouraged both reflection on why they made their choices and the active consideration of multiple alternatives. This experiment demonstrated that students using rationale considered all reasonable alternatives and were able to select criteria and evaluate alternatives in a way that indicated they were progressing in their intellectual development.

References

Amabile, T. M. (1983). The social psychology of creativity: A componential conceptualization. *Journal of Personality and Social Psychology, 45*, 357–377.

Atman, C. J., Cardella, M. E., Turns, J., & Adams, R. S. (2005). Comparing freshmen and senior engineering design processes: An in-depth follow-up study. *Design Studies, 26*, 325–357.

Baxter Magolda, M. B. (1992). *Knowing and reasoning in college: Gender-related patterns in students' intellectual development.* San Francisco: Jossey-Bass.

Bloom, B. S. (Ed.). (1956). *Taxonomy of educational objectives: The classification of educational goals.* New York: David McKay Company, Inc.

Bruegge, B., & Dutoit, A. H. (2004). *Object-oriented software engineering: Using UML, patterns, and Java* (2nd ed.). Upper Saddle River: Prentice Hall.

Burge, J. E., & Brown, D. C. (2004). An integrated approach for software design checking using rationale. In J. Gero (Ed.), *Design computing and cognition '04* (pp. 557–576). Cambridge, MA: Kluwer Academic.

Carey, T., McKerlie, D., & Wilson, J. (1996). HCI design rationales as a learning resource. In T. Moran & J. M. Carroll (Eds.), *Design rationale: Concepts, techniques, and use* (pp. 373–392). Mahwah: Lawrence Erlbaum Associates.

Carroll, J. M. (2009, June) *The essential tension of creativity and rationale in software design.* Manifesto from the workshop on Creativity and Rationale in Software Design, State College, PA, USA.

Casaday, G. (1996). Rationale in practice: Templates for capturing and applying design experience. In T. Moran & J. M. Carroll (Eds.), *Design rationale: Concepts, techniques, and use* (pp. 351–372). Mahwah: Lawrence Erlbaum Associates.

Daughtry, J., Burge, J., Carroll, J. M., & Potts, C. (2009). Creativity and rationale in software design. *SIGSOFT Software Engineering Notes, 34*(1), 27–29.

Dewey, J. (1933). *How we think.* New York: D.C. Heath and Company.

Dym, C. L., Agogino, A. M., Eris, O., Frey, D. D., & Liefer, L. J. (2005). Engineering design thinking, teaching, and learning. *Journal of Engineering Education, 94*, 103–120.

Fischer, G., Lemke, A. C., McCall, R., & Morch, A. I. (1991). Making argumentation serve design. *Human–Computer Interaction, 6*, 393–419.

Fox, C. (2006). *Introduction to software engineering design.* Boston: Addison-Wesley.

Gamma, E., Helm, R., Johnson, R., & Vlissides, J. (1995). *Design patterns: Elements of reusable object-oriented software.* Reading: Addison-Wesley.

Glass, R. S. (1995). *Software creativity*. Englewood Cliffs: Prentice Hall.

Hamilton, H. R. (1974). Screening business development opportunities. *Business Horizons, 7*(4), 13–24.

King, P. M., & Kitchener, K. (1994). *Developing reflective judgment: Understanding and promoting growth and critical thinking*. San Francisco: Jossey-Bass Publishers.

King, P. M., & Kitchener, K. (2002). The reflective judgment model: Twenty years of research on epistemic cognition. In B. K. Hofer & P. R. Pintrich (Eds.), *Personal epistemology: The psychology of beliefs about knowledge and knowing* (pp. 37–61). Mahwah: Lawrence Erlbaum.

Kloss, R. J. (1994). A nudge is best: Helping students through the Perry scheme of intellectual development. *College Teaching, 42*, 151–158.

MacLean, A., Young, R. M., Bellotti, V. M., & Moran, T. P. (1991). Questions, options, and criteria: Elements of design space analysis. *Human-Computer Interaction, 6*, 201–250.

Moran, T. P., & Carroll, J. M. (Eds.). (1996). *Design rationale: Concepts, techniques, and use*. Mahwah: Lawrence Erlbaum Associates.

Perry, W. G. (1970). *Forms of intellectual and ethical development in the college years: A scheme*. New York: Holt, Rinehart, and Winston.

Pugh, S. (1991). *Total design*. Wokingham: Addison-Wesley Publishing Company.

Rice, J. A. (1995). *Mathematical statistics and data analysis* (2nd ed.). Belmont: Duxbury Press.

Schön, D. A. (1983). *The reflective practitioner*. New York: Basic Books, Inc.

Shah, J. J., Smith, S. M., & Vargas-Hernandez, N. (2003). Metrics for measuring ideation effectiveness. *Design Studies, 24*, 111–134.

van Aalst, J. W., van der Mast, C. A. P. G., & Carey, T. T. (1995). An interactive multimedia tutorial for user interface design. *Computers and Education, 25*, 227–233.

VanGundy, A. B. (1981). *Techniques of structured problem solving*. New York: Van Nostrand Reinhold Company.

Whiting, C. S. (1958). *Creative thinking*. New York: Reinhold.

Chapter 10
Does Design Rationale Enhance Creativity?

Jing Wang, Umer Farooq, and John M. Carroll

Abstract Creativity and rationale are often viewed as two contrasting facets in software design. A lack in recognizing the facilitative relationship between creativity and rationale not only underestimates the benefits designers can obtain from rationale practices, but also confines the approaches that support creativity in software design. Our exploratory study provides empirical evidence of the positive correlation between rationale and creativity. Furthermore, we found that the feasibility of design alternatives and the comprehensiveness of tradeoff evaluation are critical to enhancing novelty, persuasiveness, and insightfulness. We also discuss future directions to further understand how these properties, or rationale quality in general, affects design creativity.

Keywords Design rationale • Creativity • Software design • Collaborative design • Design tradeoffs • Cconvergent thinking • Rationale quality

10.1 Introduction

Creativity is often desirable in design activities. In order to create innovative artifacts, designers and design teams need to generate novel ideas, the originality and usefulness of which should be recognized and appreciated by others. In solving ill-defined complex problems, like software design and development, such creativity can hardly be achieved solely by individuals' one-shot or random thoughts, but requires designers to keep track of what has been done and why that has been done.

J. Wang (✉) • J.M. Carroll
Center for Human-Computer Interaction, College of Information Sciences and Technology,
The Pennsylvania State University, University Park, PA 16802, USA
e-mail: jzw143@psu.edu; jmcarroll@psu.edu

U. Farooq
Microsoft Corporation, One Microsoft Way, Redmond, WA 98052, USA
e-mail: umfarooq@microsoft.com

J.M. Carroll (ed.), *Creativity and Rationale: Enhancing Human Experience by Design*, Human–Computer Interaction Series, DOI 10.1007/978-1-4471-4111-2_10, © Springer-Verlag London 2013

Design rationale can help keep track of those activities and reasons. Moreover, it can provoke designers to analyze and evaluate their design critically. These critical thinking processes are crucial to design creativity. However, we do not advocate capturing every detail of the design process in rationale. Indeed, that extreme form of design rationale is often criticized for the tedious work involved.

Overemphasizing the cost of articulating design rationale will disguise the relationship between rationale and creativity as pure contrast. Instead, by focusing on the benefits of design rationale, the integrative potential between the two may emerge. Therefore, our study aims at bridging the gulf between rationale and creativity in software design by exploring why and how rationale and creativity can be mutually facilitative. Design rationale delineates the assumptions behind the questions in design. It may further stimulate designers to problematize design options and reframe or recreate design. By critically evaluating options, designers may create new possibilities to augment the strength and attenuate the weakness of current options. They may also make more rational decisions by converging on an option. However, such a statement has not been fully verified by theories, or by empirical studies. Our study is an empirical attempt to examine the relationship between rationale and creativity, and, in the long term, to understand how to support creativity by design rationale.

Following the presentation of the conceptual background, we will describe our study's context and design. We then will present the results, followed by an interpretation and discussion of those results and a reflection upon the whole exploratory study. We conclude with a discussion of future work.

10.2 Conceptual Background

Design rationale is often characterized from various perspectives (Shipman and McCall 1997). Instead of recording every detail of design processes, our view of design rationale focuses on reasoning and argumentation. From this perspective, design rationale emphasizes the articulation and representative reasoning underlying design (Fischer et al. 1991; Buckingham Shum and Hammond 1994; Moran et al. 1996). Argumentation-based design rationale attempts to stimulate designers to think and discuss design within a structured or semi-structured representation. For example, in QOC (MacLean et al. 1991), questions are framed to pose key issues in the design, options are proposed as possible alternative solutions to the questions, and criteria are bases for reasoning and evaluating the options so as to choose among them. Argumentation-based design rationale is also illustrated in the task-artifact framework (TAF; (Carroll et al. 2003)), in which tasks are represented as scenarios of use and claim analysis, enumerates the features of a system being used and their upsides and downsides of consequences. Many other endeavors have been invested to capture design rationale with such purpose: for example, an issue-based information system (IBIS; (Kunz and Rittel 1970)) and its variants (gIBIS, (Conklin and Yakemovic 1991); PHI, (Fischer et al. 1991)), three extensions of IBIS (Potts and Catledge 1996), and DRL (Lee and Lai 1991). By adapting notations from these, we will investigate whether and how design rationale facilitates evaluation abilities and critical thinking, and further affects creativity in software design.

The use of argumentation-based design rationale has been investigated in terms of both its benefits and costs (see the review in Buckingham Shum and Hammond (1994)). Despite the distraction and difficulty in externalizing design rationale into one semi-structured form (Fischer et al. 1991; Buckingham Shum 1993b), empirical studies have shown evidence that in the design domain (a) argumentation-based design rationale can facilitate reasoning by augmenting both the product and process (Burgess-Yakemovic and Conklin 1990; Bellotti 1993; Buckingham Shum et al. 1993; Buckingham Shum 1996), and (b) an existing argumentation-based rationale of earlier design is useful for both the owner and others (Conklin and Yakemovic 1991; Buckingham Shum 1993a; McKerlie and MacLean 1994). Studies have indicated that design rationale is particularly beneficial when it is applied to driving construction, to facilitating breadth-first exploration, and to early stages of design when less abstract externalization is required. Other than evaluating design rationale for its usefulness, research on the use of argumentation-based rationale also invested great efforts in the usability of its notation and representation (see the review in Buckingham Shum and Hammond (1994)), which is beyond the scope of this chapter. However, of all the empirical work, none has reported any direct assessment of the quality of design rationale itself that we could build on.

Creativity is also conceptualized in various ways. Although it is sometimes regarded as mythical and unable to be explained, or as a revolutionary innovation that rarely happens, we consider creativity to be embedded in everyday activities and their social contexts (Gardner 1993; Amabile 1996; Csikszentmihalyi 1996), which may have more implications for education and engineering practices. Even from this perspective, creativity can be characterized in many different ways, among which three features were tapped for our study of creativity measurement. Novelty is the most agreed aspect of creativity (Sternberg and Lubart 1991; Mayer 1999; Sternberg 2006). It implies originality, such as new ideas. With regard to its social context, creativity requires the ability to persuade others the value of the work (Sternberg and Lubart 1999) so as to be accepted by the field (Csikszentmihalyi 1999). In our study, persuasiveness as a metric of creativity is assessed by examining the interim product of software design, that is, the rationale documents, with respect to the argumentation elaborated within them. Though insightful thinking cannot guarantee creative design, it is indispensible during the analytical design processes, ensuring powerful critical thinking. Without such scrutiny, novel ideas may not work eventually. The three dimensions of creativity operationalized in our study – novelty, persuasiveness and insightfulness – are expected to demonstrate the three intellectual abilities required to achieve creativity: synthetic ability to see problems in new ways and to escape the bounds of conventional thinking, analytic ability to recognize which of one's ideas are worth pursuing and which are not, and practical-contextual ability, to know how to persuade others of – or to convince other people of – the value of one's ideas (Sternberg 1985).

The connection between design rationale and creativity in our view derives from the role of rationale in evoking critical thinking, which is often conceived as indivisible from creative thinking. In particular, evaluation abilities are crucial to creative thinking. Runco (1992) and Houtz et al. (1979) examined evaluation abilities in creative thinking, and both studies concluded that evaluative abilities play a significant role in creative functioning. Guilford (1967) also assigned an important role to evaluation ability in his models of creative thinking and problem solving.

However, research has been sparse with regard to the integrative potential of rationale and creativity in software design. Ball et al. (2001) proposed that design rationale can provide insights into how best to represent and retrieve design knowledge in order to support innovative design reuse. They developed a design reuse system, Desperado II, to elicit and retrieve design rationale. By comparing the performance of the Desperado group and a control group, they found that the Desperado group considered up to three times as many options per question as the control group, and up to six times as many criteria. They claimed such performances as evidence that Desperado encourages innovative design, even though the increased number of options and criteria were not examined in terms of their quality. Even if it is validated that Desperado can assist in overcoming satisficing tendencies and confirmation biases, their results only demonstrate that the representation of design rationale in Desperado can support creative design better than previous notations. It cannot explain the underpinning relationship between design rationale in general and creativity. Fischer (2004) argued that temporal barriers should be overcome to support social creativity. In a long-term design project, creativity can be supported by recording design rationale with minimal efforts and by providing a search utility to retrieve rationale easily. However, their paper did not provide much detail about empirical validation of this claim.

10.3 Classroom Study

As a preliminary step to explore the relationship between rationale and creativity in software design, we conducted a classroom study that lasted for a whole semester. The design processes involved in such educational setting may not be exactly the same as those of professional designers, for instance, in terms of the process complexities. Nonetheless, the problem-solving practices in our study can still be creative in ways similar to those in professional work settings, especially the roles of reasoning and reflection throughout the entire design process. Moreover, all participants were assigned the same tasks without any other direct manipulation because of the ethical concerns in the educational setting. With particular interest in group collaboration, we asked participants to work on the tasks in groups, while we did not require them to communicate with each other through a particular medium.

Our study context lends itself to directly explore the relationship between rationale and creativity in software design. First, this naturalistic setting allows more flexibility to observe more than one property of design rationale that may influence creativity and to discover multiple ways, if there are any, in which the influences occur. Second, the benefits of articulating rationale on critical and analytical thinking cannot be achieved in a fabricated task that lasts only for a couple of minutes. Participants in our study carried out the task of articulating rationale during their real design practices over the semester.

10.4   Research Questions

As speculated in the workshop manifesto[1] (Carroll 2009), creativity and rationale could have a mutually facilitative relationship. In this empirical study, we focused primarily on one direction of that relationship, that is, the effects of rationale on creativity in software design. More specifically, we wanted to examine whether rationale can play a positive role in enhancing creativity in software design and how. Therefore, we proposed the following research questions to guide our exploration.

10.4.1   Research Questions 1: Does Better Quality Design Rationale Lead to More Creative Software Design?

Design rationale can be classified as prospective and retrospective (Carroll 2009). People have different perspectives and thus different representations and usages of design rationale. From our view, the greatest potential for integrating rationale and creativity is in the activities of constructing and articulating rationale during software design process. Rationale developed in such scenarios can be regarded as prospective because it is generated within the design activities and enables further software development. By creating and capturing rationale themselves, designers can benefit from their own efforts rather than recording the processes for others. Rationale of this kind can facilitate designers framing the problems, evaluating and problematizing alternative solutions, and then approaching the optimal decision. It could also convey the usefulness and value of the design to other people. It may even surface more design options or new design solutions. Therefore, high quality design rationale should enhance designers' reasoning and critical thinking, and thus their creative thinking and creative design. In contrast, retrospective design rationale affects the ongoing design process less and costs more recording efforts.

10.4.2   Research Question 2: What Properties of Design Rationale Are Critical to Enhancing Creativity of Software Design?

Other than demonstrating the facilitative effect of rationale on creativity, the manner in which design rationale can enhance creativity is even more important to design tools that support creative design, improve education in software development, and manage innovation of system development in organizations. Since design rationale

---

[1] This was a workshop on creativity and rationale in software design sponsored by NSF CreativeIT program. It was held at University Park, PA in June, 2008. John M. Carroll wrote a manifesto, "The Essential Tension of Creativity and Rationale in Software Design," for this workshop.

consists of multiple elements involving a variety of quality characteristics, it is plausible to explore what properties of design rationale, with respect to quality, are critical to creative design.

Not every property of design rationale has positive influences on creativity. As the conventional view on the relationship between rationale and creativity implies, there is inevitable tension between these two concepts. Functioning as documentation, rationale may confine creativity by restraining divergence or adventure. Therefore, some properties of rationale may be valued in terms of rationale quality but not promising for fostering creativity.

Additionally, analyzing creativity from process perspective is compelling given our special interest in group collaboration. This research question focuses on the creative abilities of persons involved and creative characteristics of design products. However, design rationale, as a means to communicate and facilitate discourse, may impact the creative design processes of the group. Therefore, we proposed the following research questions with respect to groups' collaborative processes.

10.4.3   Research Question 3: What Properties of Design Rationale Will Enhance Creative Design Processes of the Group?

Other than mutual facilitative correlation, it is also important to understand the causal effect from design rationale to creativity, meaning, why and how design rationale can evoke and foster creativity. Thus investigating creative processes may shed light on an underpinning relationship between the two. Group creativity requires divergent thinking, convergent thinking, shared information and objectives, and reflexivity (Farooq et al. 2005). The first impression of the integrative relationship between rationale and creative processes is that the evaluative thinking evoked by rationale might facilitate reflexivity and convergent thinking of the group. Claims (Lee and Lai 1991; Carroll et al. 2003), criteria (MacLean et al. 1989), or arguments (Kunz and Rittel 1970) motivate designers to examine design options rationally so as to approach the optimal decision. Furthermore, they provide opportunities to amplify strengths and ameliorate weaknesses of the final solution. Prospective rationale can assist groups with planning the design implementation, while retrospective rationale can offer traceable records for designers to ruminate over previous decision making processes or other people's reasoning trajectory so that group members can further refine an old design or create a new one. However, such impression might underestimate the potential of rationale influencing creative processes. By questioning design options with persuasive claims, rationale might inspire more alternative solutions to overcome the downsides of current ones. It may also evoke new ideas by improving designers' understanding of the total problem, or by bringing more opportunities for designers to encounter unexpectedness. Therefore, investigating how rationale affects creative processes other than the final product is needed.

10.4.4   Research Question 4: How Will Sharing Design Rationale Across Groups Influence a Group's Creative Design Processes?

Design rationale is not just used by its creators for the current design practices, but also visited after the design cycle by both its creators and other people outside the design team. Although people are motivated by different purposes to comprehend rationale documents (e.g., reusing and adapting the design, creating new design, or even are not motivated), design rationale makes it possible to communicate with the software designers about what was going on and why. By collaboratively making sense of rationale, designers may reach a shared understanding effectively and acquire insights into their own design problem and possible solutions. Moreover, open information exchange across organizational boundaries is an important determinant of creativity (Woodman et al. 1993; Henry 2004). Design rationale, as one type of information shared between groups, may also augment groups' information sources, introduce flexibility, and open new opportunities. Despite more effort required to take advantage of such rationale, groups will obtain better chances for learning and cooperation. All of the benefits from intergroup sharing of rationale are possible but need to be examined.

10.5   Participants

Participants were undergraduate students majored in computer and information sciences in an advanced object oriented design and software course. The advanced course required prerequisite courses, including one introducing general computer languages and another on a specific computer language (either Visual Basic or C++). Thus all of the participants had basic knowledge and experience to some extent in software design before our study. The course had two sections taught by different instructors. Participants came from both sections and shared the same syllabus and class activities. The 49 students participated in our study by voluntary consent. Three of them are female and the other 46 are male.

10.6   Task Description

The task required participants to solve specific design problems by capturing design rationale and implementing the design by Java. It was integrated into every lab programming assignments of the course over the semester. Each lab assignment specified the goal of design that students should achieve. For example, one assignment asked students to implement a graphical user interface to support a decision model given by the instructor. Students had more than a week to work on each assignment. In the middle of each assignment, they were asked to submit their design rationale as their progress reports, which were counted as part of their grades. After students had turned in their implementation towards the end of each lab, the instructors showed their own solution.

The design problems of each lab assignments allow students to act creatively. Although these assignments are generally close-ended, they do not confine the students' approach to the problems along a single definite path. Therefore, participants had the opportunity and enough flexibility to perform creatively. Furthermore, all of the lab assignments were related to each other, contributing as a component to a complete project. Specifically, the later tasks were supposed to be built upon the earlier ones. This may facilitate students' reuse of prior designs.

We set the submission time of design rationale a few days before that of implementation. We expected this time arrangement could enable design rationale to facilitate students in thinking critically. Based on our hypothesis about the relationship between design rationale and creativity, such prospective design rationale created during design processes should drive the construction as well as augment the reasoning and reflection of its owners. When it is used by other people, it may also have similar benefits for them.

Design rationale documents were specified in a uniform format for all the students of the course. To minimize the overhead of recording rationale, we simplified its representation into four components, including (a) the toughest design problems you are facing or did face, (b) the design alternatives for solving these problems, (c) the pros and cons for each alternative, and (d) what option you are leaning towards (the decision on alternatives). These elements are consistent with those of other methods, such as IBIS (issues, positions and arguments; (Kunz and Rittel 1970)) and QOC (questions, options, and criteria; (MacLean et al. 1991)). Since it was not a topic in the curriculum, the instructors explained what benefits design rationale could bring to software design, such as keeping track of the design state. They further illustrated design rationale by a sample. The sample presented design rationale for a concrete design problem in the format that students were required to use. Because this representation is not highly abstract but rather more narrative, the students did not find difficulty in articulating rationale in this way. Students were already familiar with externalizing design rationale in the way we defined since we did not start our analysis until their third lab assignment.

From the third lab assignment, students also began cooperating on their lab assignments in pairs or triads. Each team had to submit only one design rationale and one implementation for each assignment. No particular medium was specified for their communication and collaboration. They chose teammates by themselves but could not pick the same person more than once. They were also given a short time in class to collaborate with their team member(s) on these assignments. In other words, their initial collaboration was face-to-face, although they also might have communicated virtually sometimes. Such rotated pairing may better motivate students to share design rationale across groups because each student in the group can serve as a boundary object (Fleischmann 2006) between his or her prior and current design. Intergroup information exchange is likely to happen when there are people who have sufficient knowledge of practices of both groups (Henry 2004).

10.7 Data Collection

Data collected in our study comprised two parts: (a) an assessment of design rationale quality and design creativity; and (b) the responses to surveys with respect to design collaboration. The first part was mainly gathered to answer research questions 1 and 2 (i.e., the relationship between rationale quality and design creativity). The second part was used to address research questions 3 and 4 (i.e., the effects of rationale quality on perceived creative processes). Data were sampled from three out of all the lab assignments of the course: one was at the beginning of the semester when they just started to work in teams (i.e., the third lab assignment); one was in the middle of the semester, and the other was at the end. Surveys were disseminated immediately after rationale submission for each of the three lab assignments. The number of respondents varied across the three assignments, based on their own voluntary decision. The assessment on design rationale quality and creativity was conducted with the criteria we developed (see Appendix for details) by two teaching assistants.

To investigate the relationship between rationale quality and design creativity, we developed criteria for evaluating design rationale documents in terms of these two focuses. Design rationale and creativity are each comprehensive concepts with various perspectives. Because, as noted in the previous section, no established evaluation scales can be directly applied in examining our specific data, the three authors brainstormed and decomposed rationale quality and creativity into measurable dimensions, respectively.

Judging rationale quality (six dimensions) encompassed concerns for each element in the design rationale representation we developed, that is, problems, alternatives, tradeoffs, and decision. The overall quality of the rationale as a communication tool was also operationalized as clarity of articulation criteria. Problem identification and definition is critical to all the effort involved in problem-solving activities, determining the level of critical thinking (Henri 1991; Garrison 1992). Given the problem-solving nature of software design, identifying and defining the design problem is are also important in articulating design rationale. These require critical thinking. Moreover, problem-solving influences the quality of other elements in design rationale as well, such as how well the proposed alternatives address the design problem, and whether the decision made is wise. Thus, in our rationale quality evaluation, we asked for judgment on whether the statement of design problem captured a critical issue of the design task (i.e., *toughest design problem identification*). Alternatives are the possible solutions designers generate to tackle the problem. Good alternatives should be able to the design issue as a solution candidate (i.e., *relevance of alternatives* in our evaluation criteria; see Appendix). Furthermore, they should provide not only conceptual guidance but also feasible ideas, since software design is expected to lead to practical results. Therefore, we employed *feasibility of alternatives* in our assessment. Specifically, we customized the definition of feasibility by students' programming ability acquired from the course. Tradeoffs are articulated when designers justify or problematize their alternatives.

Maintaining high quality of tradeoffs requires exploring a wide range of possible consequences of a design alternative. Analysis from a single perspective may bias designers' judgment of an alternative. *Comprehensiveness of tradeoffs* in our criteria aimed at addressing this requirement of rationale quality. One outcome of critical thinking involved in design rationale articulation is the decision, namely the final problem solution to be implemented. The quality of the *decision* indicates the performance of analytical work engaged in design rationale documents. Thus, we included this dimension by asking whether the design alternative selected is the optimal solution in our evaluation criteria. As an artifact for communication purposes, clarity also represents the quality of design rationale. Moreover, clarity implies how thoroughly designers have considered the design problem, alternatives, tradeoffs, and the decision. These metrics were not exhaustive but rather reflected an argumentation perspective that involves critical thinking. Relevance, ambiguities (clarity in our study), practical utility (feasibility in our study), and width of understanding (comprehensiveness in our study) are also identified as critical factors in the model of assessing critical thinking, which was developed by Newman et al. (1997).

The rubrics for evaluating creativity (three dimensions) in the identified problems solutions were adapted from Farooq's (2008) doctoral dissertation. Novelty as a common feature of creative ideas was maintained in the adaptation (i.e., *novelty of alternatives*). *Insightfulness of tradeoffs* was added to our rating dimensions because design rationale has the characteristic of analytical thinking, which was not externalized in the task of Farooq's study. We evaluated creativity by rating rationale documents instead of directly assessing students' code. The underlying assumption for this decision was that the students would solve the problem in the way they stated in their design rationale documents. Furthermore, the overall criteria do not evaluate creativity only from the final product perspective, but also indicate the creative capacity of designers that may not be explicitly codified in their product. For instance, *persuasiveness of tradeoffs* represents the designer's ability to persuade others of the value of his/her design, which is suggested to be an important dimension of creativity (Sternberg and Lubart 1991). The judges who rated the design rationale quality and design creativity were the teaching assistants for the two sections of the course. They were considered to be qualified in several aspects: (a) both had advanced object oriented design experience; (b) they were very familiar with the tasks; (c) they knew the students' design expertise well; and (d) they had the closest interaction with participants, which may have assisted in their understanding and judgment of the students' design processes.

Both judges followed the same procedure to assess the submissions. Prior to implementing the study, we made sure the criteria were appropriate for the context of the course and study and executable for the judges to apply. We walked through the evaluation criteria with the judges, during which they interpreted the rubrics item by item to confirm that their comprehension was consistent with our intention. Then they independently evaluated every document based on their overall impression of the performance of the whole class, with rating scale from 1 (*very poor*) to 5 (*very good*). To prevent the order effect, the judges rated the first half of the students' rationale documents in the order of rationale quality to creativity, and the other half of documents from creativity to rationale quality. In the analysis, we averaged the scores rated by the two judges as the final assessment output.

Surveys were designed to complement our understanding of the collaborative design processes. They consisted of questions with respect to students' perceived creative processes by articulating rationale as well as their use and reflection on previous rationale. These questions were rated on a 9-point Likert scale. We also collected data about some demographic information and personal creative characteristics in the last survey at the end of the semester.

10.8   Results

For the three lab assignments we collected, 27, 28, and 17 design rationale documents submitted by teams, respectively, were rated by judges, while 16, 16, and 14 responses to our surveys by individuals, respectively, were collected. Since participants completed the surveys voluntarily, the number of responses was smaller than the number of design rationale documents that were consented to be analyzed. We conducted regression analysis on both data sets: one set included all 72 average ratings for the progress reports submitted; the other set included all 46 survey responses and the survey participants' progress reports (excluding the assessment scores for the students who did not fill out the surveys). In the analysis, properties of rationale quality were used as independent variables, and properties of creativity and ratings of perceived creative processes were set as dependent variables.

10.8.1   RQ1: Does Better Quality of Design Rationale Lead to More Creative Software Design?

All of the properties of rationale quality significantly positively correlated with the three aspects of creativity as indicated by Pearson correlation analysis. Furthermore, by using multiple regression analysis with stepwise approach, we found that the higher the quality of design rationale, the more creative the design, although the regression models suggested by the two data sets were slightly different. To be specific, for both data sets we performed stepwise regression on the three aspects of creativity the judges rated (i.e., novelty of alternatives, persuasiveness of tradeoffs, and insightfulness of tradeoffs) to select the properties of design rationale that affected these aspects individually. We also coded the lab number as independent variables in regression models to examine whether there was any confounding effect caused by the difference of lab assignments.

Given two judges performed assessment, interrater reliability was also tested on each criterion, as well as the entire rubrics. Comprehensiveness, persuasiveness, and insightfulness of tradeoffs had values of interrater reliability larger than the rule of thumb 0.7 (Cronbach's Alpha = Average Measures Intraclass Correlation Coefficient = 0.839, 0.736, and 0.794, respectively). Additionally, the overall creativity (novelty of alternatives, persuasiveness of tradeoffs, and insightfulness of tradeoffs) had fair interrater reliability (Cronbach's Alpha = 0.686, Average Measures Intraclass Correlation Coefficient = 0.674). The final three measurements did not achieve interrater reliability as high as these, and therefore could be decomposed or clarified more in the future to approach more agreement and consistency.

10.8.2 RQ2&3: What Properties of Design Rationale Are Critical to Enhance Creativity of Software Design and How?

Regression analysis on the first data set indicates that two properties of rationale quality, feasibility of alternatives and comprehensiveness of tradeoffs, are crucial to enhancing design creativity. The first data set does not include any variables measured by survey responses but all the ratings on 72 design rationale documents. We built three models for each aspect of creativity with stepwise regression. Table 10.1 summarizes all these models for predicting the three aspects of creativity on the first data set. The model predicting novelty of alternatives is Novelty = 0.612 * Feasibility +0.238 * Comprehensiveness, $F(2, 69) = 97.88$, $p < .001$, $R^2 = .729$. The model for predicting persuasiveness of tradeoffs is Persuasiveness = 0.361 * Feasibility + 0.620* Comprehensiveness, $F(2, 69) = 202.044$, $p < .001$, $R^2 = .854$. The model for predicting insightfulness of tradeoffs is Insightfulness = 0.254 * Feasibility +0.730 * Comprehensiveness, $F(2, 69) = 166.254$, $p < .001$, $R^2 = .828$. Although the determination of a reliable relationship in this analysis does not imply causality, it will increase our understanding of what properties of design rationale are important to foster creativity.

Moreover, the feasibility of alternatives has a stronger positive relationship with novelty of alternatives ($\beta = 0.612$) than comprehensiveness of tradeoffs ($\beta = 0.238$) according to the values of coefficients in each model above. Conversely, with persuasiveness of tradeoffs and insightfulness of tradeoffs, comprehensiveness of tradeoffs has a stronger relationship than feasibility of alternatives. One reason for such variation can be attributed to the similarity of elements, which means feasibility and novelty are evaluated upon alternatives whereas comprehensiveness, persuasiveness, and insightfulness are evaluated upon tradeoffs.

The Variance Inflation Factor (VIF) values for these multiple regression models are 2.300, which is smaller than 5, indicating that these models do not have multicollinearity problems (O'Brien 2007). That is, individual predictors in the regression model, meaning feasibility of design alternatives and comprehensiveness of tradeoffs, are not redundant or highly correlated. Their coefficient values provide somewhat precise estimate of their effects on the three aspects of creativity.

Furthermore, we tested whether there is any moderation effect or interaction effect of feasibility of design alternatives and comprehensiveness of tradeoffs by centering these two variables. No significant effect was detected.

Table 10.1 Relationship between rationale quality and creativity on the first data set ($N=72$)

Model	Quality of DR (IV 1)	Coefficient 1	Quality of DR (IV 2)	Coefficient 2	Creativity (DV)
1	Feasibility of alternatives	0.612***	Comprehensiveness of tradeoffs	0.238** (p=.001)	Novelty of alternatives
2	Feasibility of alternatives	0.361***	Comprehensiveness of tradeoffs	0.620***	Persuasiveness of tradeoffs
3	Feasibility of alternatives	0.254* (p=.013)	Comprehensiveness of tradeoffs	0.730***	Insightfulness of tradeoffs

Note: Significance level: *** $p<.001$, ** $p<.01$, * $p<.05$

Regression analysis on the second data set also suggests that feasibility of design alternatives and comprehensiveness of tradeoffs are two critical properties of design rationale to enhance creativity in software design. The second data set does not include rating scores on design rationale of students who did not participate in the surveys. Independent variables that entered into the three regression models were slightly different from those in the models shown in Table 10.1. Table 10.2 summarizes the models for predicting the three aspects of creativity on the second data set. The model predicting novelty of alternatives is Novelty $=0.554 *$ Feasibility $+0.228 *$ Comprehensiveness, $F(2, 43) = 94.394$, $p < .001$, $R^2 = .832$. The model for predicting persuasiveness of tradeoffs is Persuasiveness $= 0.295 *$ Feasibility $+0.664 *$ Comprehensiveness, $F(2, 38) = 126.41$, $p < .001$, $R^2 = .869$. The model for predicting insightfulness of tradeoffs is Insightfulness $= 0.297 *$ Decision $+0.746 *$ Comprehensiveness, $F(2, 38) = 122.94$, $p < .001$, $R^2 = .866$. The main difference between results generated from the two data sets is that the independent variable feasibility of alternatives is replaced by decision optimization in the model predicting insightfulness of tradeoffs. However, the significance of the estimated effect from decision is only 0.044, which is not significant enough as compared to more conservative alpha value rather than the default 0.5.

Similarly, neither a multicollinearity problem nor interaction effect has been discovered. The values of VIF for each model are 2.588, 2.588 and 2.902, respectively.

The common structure revealed by both data sets was the positive correlation between comprehensiveness of tradeoffs and creativity. Other than analytical and critical thinking ability, comprehensiveness can be accomplished from knowledge and expertise in related areas. To analyze whether their prior knowledge in software design affected the comprehensiveness of their articulation of tradeoffs, we collected 14 participants' background information in our last survey. According to the results of a nonparametric test, no significant difference was found between students who had prior experience in object-oriented design before the advanced course (mean of comprehensiveness $= 1.71$) and those who did not (mean of comprehensiveness $= 1.92$), nor between students who had built software in their spare time during the previous year (mean of comprehensiveness $= 1.30$) and those who had not (mean of comprehensiveness $= 2.13$).

With respect to the third research question, we conducted regression analysis on variables of rationale quality, creativity, and perceived creative processes. We did not find any significant mediation effect of the perceived creative processes upon the quality of design rationale and the creativity in design, nor did we find any significant relationship between the quality of rationale and creative processes, or between creative processes and creativity.

10.8.3 RQ4: How Will Sharing Design Rationale Across Groups Influence Group's Creative Design Processes?

To investigate the fourth research question about the impacts of sharing rationale across groups on creative processes, we collected participants' ratings on perceived creative processes by revisiting their prior design rationale through these items in

Table 10.2 Relationship between rationale quality and creativity on the second data set ($N=46$)

Model	Quality of DR (IV 1)	Coefficient 1	Quality of DR (IV 2)	Coefficient 2	Creativity (DV)
1	Feasibility of alternatives	0.554***	Comprehensiveness of tradeoffs	0.228** (p=.002)	Novelty of alternatives
2	Feasibility of alternatives	0.295* (p=.013)	Comprehensiveness of tradeoffs	0.664***	Persuasiveness of tradeoffs
3	Decision	0.297* (p=.044)	Comprehensiveness of tradeoffs	0.746***	Insightfulness of tradeoffs

Note: Significance level: *** $p<.001$, ** $p<.01$, * $p<.05$

Table 10.3 Comparison of perceived creative processes between groups with intergroup sharing of rationale ($n=13$) and groups without intergroup sharing of rationale ($n=13$)

Perceived creative processes	Intergroup sharing of rationale	n	Mean	Std. deviation
The pros and cons articulated for our prior labs or projects evoked more design alternatives of my team	0 (not share)	13	5.31	1.49
	1 (shared)	13	6.08	1.04
The pros and cons articulated for our prior labs or projects helped my current team members and me pick the best design solution to our current lab	0 (not share)	13	5.31	1.55
	1 (shared)	13	6.46	1.13

our second and third surveys (The first survey was excluded because students had not yet started working in teams at that time):

1 The pros and cons articulated for our prior labs or projects evoked more design alternatives of my team.
2 The pros and cons articulated for our prior labs or projects helped my current team members and me pick the best design solution to our current lab.

The first question concerns divergent thinking in creative processes, while the second one is about convergent thinking. Both of them were rated on 9-point Likert scale. However, since sharing design rationale across groups was neither an imperative for all students nor controlled for in different groups, we also asked students in the surveys whether they shared their previous design rationale with their current team members.

Twenty-six responses to these questions in total were collected: half of them ($n=13$) did share their prior design rationale with the current group members, while the other half ($n=13$) did not. Table 10.3 presents the descriptive statistics of participants' ratings on their current groups' divergent thinking process and convergent thinking process. According to the mean values of ratings (in the column "Mean"), whether or not they shared their previous design rationale across groups, participants on average felt that they benefited from the rationale of their previous design activities (mean of perceived creative processes > 5). Tables 10.4 and 10.5 show crosstabs for each survey question. They also suggest that most of participants thought sharing design rationale across groups was helpful.

We further examined whether sharing prior rationale affected the creative processes of the group. Results indicate that it affected and only affected groups' convergent thinking and decision making. Because neither set of 13 cases had normal distribution, we compared the perceived creative processes between groups who shared their rationale across groups and those who did not share across groups by conducting nonparametric t-test. According to the results of Mann–Whitney testing, sharing previous design rationale did not have significant effect on a group's divergent thinking (Asymp. Sig. = .202) but did have significant effect on a group's convergent thinking and decision making (Asymp. Sig. = .039). These results suggest that speculating and

Table 10.4 Cross tabulation of intergroup sharing of rationale*perceived divergent thinking

| Count | | The pros and cons articulated for our prior labs or projects helped my current team members and me pick the best design solution to our current lab | | | | | |
		Rating=1	Rating=5	Rating=6	Rating=7	Rating=8	Total
Intergroup sharing of rationale	0 (not shared)	1	7	2	3	0	13
	1 (shared)	0	3	4	3	3	13
Total		1	10	6	6	3	26

Table 10.5 Cross tabulation of intergroup sharing of rationale*perceived convergent thinking

Count		The pros and cons articulated for our prior labs or projects evoked more design alternatives of my team					
		Rating=1	Rating=5	Rating=6	Rating=7	Rating=8	Total
Intergroup sharing of rationale	0 (not shared)	1	6	4	2	0	13
	1 (shared)	0	5	3	4	1	13
Total		1	11	7	6	1	26

communicating with group members on rationale of a related design might assist a group's convergent thinking and decision making. Besides effect on the groups' perceived creative processes, we examined whether such intergroup sharing also affected the quality of rationale and the creativity of the new design. However, no significant difference was found between participants who shared rationale across groups and those who did not. This may indicate that introducing other groups' design rationale would boost their confidence in their consensus but did not make a big difference in real performance. These results will be explained and discussed more in the next section.

10.9 Discussion

Our hypothesis that rationale and creativity in software design are mutually facilitative and potentially integrable is supported by our classroom study results. Moreover, the feasibility of design alternatives and comprehensiveness of tradeoffs are found to be the most critical properties of rationale quality that are positively correlated with novelty of design alternatives, persuasiveness, and insightfulness of tradeoffs. These two properties of design rationale quality involve critical thinking and evaluation ability in different ways. Despite its limitations, our study opens up opportunities to further investigate how to take advantage of design rationale to enhance the effectiveness and creativity of software design.

10.10 Implications

10.10.1 Quality of Design Rationale Facilitates Design Creativity

Our study indicates the positive correlation between rationale and creativity in software design. Although we cannot assert a causal relationship between rationale quality and creativity through our regression analysis, all of the aspects of rationale quality we measured are positive predictors for design creativity. Thus it is plausible to foster design creativity by enhancing the quality of design rationale. The judges might tend to assign similar scores to rationale quality and creativity of each document based on their overall impression of the document. This consistency of individual's judgment can be mitigated by introducing more judges and asking each of them to either assess rationale quality or creativity.

10.10.2 Feasibility and Comprehensiveness of Rationale Enhances Design Creativity

Given the confirmation on their integrative potential, characteristics of rationale quality were examined to help us contemplate on why design rationale can promote creativity and how we can support creativity in software design by design rationale.

Although analysis on the two data sets with different sizes ideally would have shown the same pattern, the results still indicate two critical properties of design rationale that facilitate design creativity: feasibility of design alternatives and comprehensiveness of arguments. By comparing the properties of rationale quality that entered into our final regression models with those that did not, it is not hard to discern that the ones with weak predictability to creativity (i.e., problem identification, relevance of design alternatives and clarity of articulation) are low-level requirements for designers' capacity.

Feasibility of design alternatives may manifest a higher level of designers' capability and the internal evaluation of designers and their groups, which involves their critically selecting the ideas that can be externalized and recorded in their design rationale. Constraints over design space are not always a negative within the creative process; rather constraints are continually applied in good design (Singley and Carroll 1996). They pose finites to the space, directing design turned into product. Additionally, creativity is not just about wild thinking; it requires action and implementation (West 2003). One can hardly operationalize alternatives far beyond one's design knowledge. In this sense, it may also be reasonable to attribute feasibility as one aspect of creativity. Furthermore, creativity, especially divergent thinking, is often mistakenly simplified to represent the number of ideas generated. However, creativity is not only about quantity, but more about quality (Farooq 2008). Emphasizing the feasibility of design alternatives may filter out some spontaneous thoughts, but it can ensure the design is doable. Aligned with the same concern, the grading rubrics provided to students did not require any specific number of design alternatives so that students would not be motivated to generate some invaluable options. Moreover, in general, the assessing feasibility may be biased by the judges' expertise due to the possible gap between judges' and designers' design knowledge, particularly when the design proposals may be executable for designers but beyond judges' skills. However, in our case the judges are teaching assistants who have privileged experience in the course content and design skills. Thus judgment on feasibility in our study should be considered fair and reliable.

Another aspect of rationale quality – comprehensiveness of tradeoffs – consistently contributes as a significant predicator in the six regression models shown in Tables 10.1 and 10.2. Comprehensiveness and correctness decide whether critical reasoning in rationale has positive or negative effect on design (Singley and Carroll 1996). With comprehensive evaluation, designers will not be confined by the downsides of design options but may be able to create new options that can augment the upsides and mitigate the downsides. Comprehensiveness is neither complexity nor detailing every relevant issue. Nevertheless, it is necessary to capture and enumerate each critical issue in design alternatives in order to achieve comprehensiveness. Considering our study context, effects from comprehensiveness on creativity may also likely come from participants' efforts in their work required by achieving comprehensiveness. Even if they are capable of envisioning all of the critical upsides and downsides, designers are normally not motivated to think thoroughly the entire evaluation space and record all considerations. In general, people generally do not make sophisticated analyses to make rational decisions. They would rather just pick one solution candidate that works.

Comprehensiveness also requires adequate knowledge to justify design options. With limited knowledge or expertise, designers may foresee only part of possible consequences, or they may exert all of their efforts on trivial problems but lose sight of the whole picture. The facilitative relationship between comprehensiveness of tradeoffs and creativity may motivate designers to take a more positive attitude toward constructing their design rationale, rather than negatively consider it as overhead, like any other documentation. Furthermore, tradeoffs encompass both pros and cons. Comprehensiveness does not specify a certain portion or weight for each part; even tradeoffs without many cons can be comprehensive. Thus it may provide us more insights to further examine how comprehensiveness of argumentation influences creativity by decomposing argumentation into pros and cons.

10.10.3   Intergroup Rationale Sharing Assists Group's Convergent Thinking

Our analysis on intergroup sharing of design rationale indicates that sharing prior design rationale other than reusing it across groups may facilitate convergent thinking. There are always motivational obstacles that inhibit information flow across organizational boundaries and difficulty in making sense of unfamiliar contexts. Designers may be even more reluctant to revisit their previous or other designers' rationale documents than to create their own for current practices due to the cost of making sense of those documentations. Groups are often not quite motivated to share information with or incorporate information from other groups unless they have specific needs. In our study, the sharing rationale across groups may be less inhibited by those factors. Students maintain a consistent context because they all know the tasks of each lab. Prior design rationale is reusable because posterior lab assignments are built on the design of anterior ones. Moreover, the rotation of group members ensures that each member in a group has adequate knowledge about the rationale created by his or her prior groups. One incentive to revisit previous design is that students were aware of something wrong in their prior design. By explaining their previous design rationale to their current group members, students might have developed shared understanding and common ground, which assisted with their decision making. However, they did not perceive much difference in the process of coming up more alternatives, whether or not they shared their prior rationale. This may have resulted from the superiority of the instructors' solutions to prior lab assignments. In other words, students may only have applied their previous design rationale to prune poor design options to protect themselves from making the same mistakes. They relied more on instructors' previous designs to generate options for current problems. They judged their previous design based on instructors' solutions. As long as they did not discern any significant difference, they will stop exploring other design alternatives. Such satisficing tendencies (Ball et al. 1998; Ormerod et al. 1999) restricted the impact of intergroup sharing of design rationale on groups' divergent thinking. For example, more than one student believed that he or she used the same approach for the next lab assignment as the one for the previous lab because their prior design fit instructors' solution well. Therefore, the motivation for inter-group sharing determines how students reflect on and use their previous design rationale, which is part of their creative design processes. By further investigating the various motivations, we could more precisely understand the effects of sharing design rationale across groups on group creativity.

10.11 Limitations

Our findings are constrained by the characteristic of the task. We did not deploy a direct measurement on the design product (i.e., the code), which arises from the concerns that the lab assignments in our study were relatively close-ended problem solving. In order to obtain a more precise assessment on design creativity, we plan to design more open-ended tasks.

Moreover, our results are limited by our measurement of rationale quality and creativity. Each judge in our study rated both rationale quality and creativity of every rationale document. Thus the positive correlation between rationale quality and creativity may result from the inherent consistency of each individual judge. In the future, we may employ more judges to assess rationale quality and design creativity separately, with each judge rating only one part. This can also balance the individual differences among judges. Alternatively, we can ask judges to qualitatively evaluate the relationship between the design rationales and creativity on the basis of their informed interpretation of rationale quality and creativity. To improve the interrater reliability, we can decompose our assessment criteria and facilitate further discussion on them with all judges.

Additionally, our analysis is confined by the class size. For instance, the required number of cases for stepwise multiple regression should be 40 times the number of independent variables, as recommended by Tabachnick and Fidell (1996). One way to approach a more robust conclusion is to recruit more participants.

10.12 Further Issues

Since our evaluation criteria on rationale quality are not exhaustive, feasibility of design alternatives and comprehensiveness of tradeoffs may not be the only quality facets related to creativity. Other properties we assessed in terms of rationale quality may also predict facets of creativity other than the three (i.e., novelty, persuasiveness, and insightfulness) measured in our study. Nonetheless, the positive correlation between rationale quality and creativity demonstrated in our empirical study connotes rationale articulation as a way to enhance creativity in software development.

This certainly does not imply that documenting design rationale with any approach will necessarily lead to creativity enhancement, but rather inspires the dedication to investigate how to appropriate design rationale and what qualities of rationale should be amplified to support creativity in software development. The rationale qualities facilitating creativity discovered in our study will guide the effort to further elucidate the underpinning reasons why these qualities are critical to enhance design creativity.

The ways that rationale and creativity influence each other need further investigation in collaborative settings. Software design is a complex and ill-defined problem-solving process, which has increasingly demanded collaboration among individuals as the scale of projects grows. To achieve creativity in such situations, it is desired to keep track of the development process. Furthermore, mere individual intellects are hardly sufficient to attain creative design artifacts. Instead, the collective accomplishment will arise from the interaction between and among group members. The role of design rationale in these scenarios may not only involve facilitating individuals' analytic thinking but rather influencing the communication and cooperation processes when rationale is constructed and captured by collective effort. Therefore, it is intriguing and promising to further explore how design rationale articulation affects creative design processes of the group.

10.13 Conclusion and Future Work

When designers think about rationale, they often tend to believe it suffocates design and undermines the possibility of creativity. In this chapter, our study provides empirical evidence to argue that the relationship between rationale and creativity is more than contrast. Instead, rationales and rationale practices can be adapted to enhance creativity in design. Furthermore, based on our assessment of rationale quality and creativity, the feasibility of design alternatives and comprehensiveness of argumentation or tradeoffs have significant positive effects on the novelty of design alternatives, the persuasiveness, and the insightfulness of argumentation. These effects may derive from designers' internal evaluation and critical thinking on design alternatives. They are not bounded by the particular domain in our study (i.e., software design); instead, reasoning and critical thinking can have such effects in any other domain in which they are involved and creativity can happen. Therefore, we can expect that rationale and creativity are mutually facilitative in other domains beyond software engineering and design.

Similarly, our assessment criteria on rationale quality may also be adapted to real-world contexts outside of classrooms. Previous work allows evaluating rationale in terms of their usability by analyzing cognitive costs of different notational forms or in terms of their usefulness by observing their use and narrating anecdotes. Our rubrics provide a quantitative approach to evaluate the quality of design rationale, emphasizing the quality of critical thinking that is related to design creativity. It can be developed to assess real design practices by integrating concerns with organizational factors as well as management issues.

Yet to explain exactly how rationale facilitates creativity and why these two properties are strong predicators, we have to investigate their effects on the creative processes by refining survey questions and collecting more qualitative data. For comprehensiveness, we may also need to look at tradeoffs from pros and cons separately.

Our observation on sharing rationale across groups stimulates us to explore further the various motivations for sharing design rationale and design reuse to understand when to facilitate intergroup sharing. This is worth investigation because design rationale is usually expected to convey the reasoning and decision process of other designers.

In the even longer term, understanding the benefits of design rationale for creativity in software development will inform how to build tools to support creative design.

Acknowledgments This research was supported by John M. Carroll and Umer Farooq's grants NSF SGER IIS-0749172 and NSF CreativeIT Workshop IIS-0742392. We thank instructors of the course in which we implemented our study, Craig Ganoe and John Daughtry, for their assistance in the study design and coordination with participants. We also thank the teaching assistants of the course Ishita Ghosh and Haibin Liu for assessing design rationale documents.

Appendix

Evaluation Criteria

- Quality of Design Rationale ($1 = very\ poor$, $5 = very\ good$)
  Toughest Design Problem Identification: Does the statement of toughest design problem capture a critical issue of this lab?
  Relevance of alternatives: Can the design alternatives solve the problem stated?
  Feasibility of alternatives: Can the design alternatives be implemented by using the technique taught in class?
  Comprehensiveness of tradeoffs (pros and cons): Do the tradeoffs reveal main concerns about each design alternative?
  Decision: Is the design alternative selected the optimal solution?
  Clarity of articulation: Can the report be well understood?
- Creativity of Design
  Novelty of design alternatives: Are the design alternatives novel?
  Persuasiveness of tradeoffs: Are the tradeoffs persuasive?
  Insightfulness of tradeoffs: Do the tradeoffs provide insightful justification of design alternatives?

References

Amabile, T. M. (1996). *Creativity in context*. Boulder: Westview Press.
Ball, L. J., Lambell, N. J., et al. (2001). Representing design rationale to support innovative design reuse: A minimalist approach. *Automation in Construction, 10*(6), 663–674.

Ball, L. J., Maskill, L., et al. (1998). Satisficing in engineering design: Causes, consequences and implications for design support. *Automation in Construction, 7*(2–3), 213–227.

Bellotti, V. (1993). Integrating theoreticians' and practitioners' perspectives with design rationale. In *InterCHI'93: Human factors in computing systems*. New York: ACM Press.

Buckingham Shum, S. (1993a). *QOC design rationale retrieval: A cognitive task analysis and design implication*. Rank Xerox Research Centre Cambridge Laboratory, Cambridge CB2 1AB.

Buckingham Shum, S. (1993b). *QOC design rationale retrieval: A cognitive task analysis and design implication*. Retrieved May 26, 2010, from http://ftp.xrce.xerox.com/Publications/Attachments/1993-105/EPC-1993-105.pdf

Buckingham Shum, S. (1996). Analyzing the usability of a design rationale notation. In T. P. Moran & J. M. Carroll (Eds.), *Design rationale: Concepts, techniques, and use* (pp. 185–215). Mahwah: Lawrence Erlbaum Associates, Inc.

Buckingham Shum, S., & Hammond, N. (1994). Argumentation-based design rationale: What use at what cost. *International Journal of Human Computer Studies, 40*(4), 603–652.

Buckingham Shum, S., MacLean, A., et al. (1993). Summarising the evolution of design concepts within a design rationale framework. *Adjunct Proceedings of InterCHI'93 (Short Papers), Amsterdam*. ACM, New York.

Burgess-Yakemovic, K. C., & Conklin, J. (1990). Report on a development project use of an issue-based information system. In *CSCW'90: Computer supported cooperative work*. New York: ACM Press.

Carroll, J. M. (2009). The essential tension of creativity and rationale in software design. In *Manifesto from the workshop on creativity and rationale in software design*. University Park: College of Information Sciences and Technology, The Pennsylvania State University.

Carroll, J. M., Rosson, M. B., et al. (2003). Design rationale as theory. In *HCI models, theories, and frameworks: Toward an interdisciplinary science* (pp. 531–561). San Francisco: Morgan Kaufmann.

Conklin, E. J., & Yakemovic, K. C. B. (1991). A process-oriented approach to design rationale. *Human Computer Interaction, 6*(3), 357–391.

Csikszentmihalyi, M. (1996). *Creativity: Flow and the psychology of discovery and invention*. New York: HarperCollins Publishers.

Csikszentmihalyi, M. (1999). Implications of a systems perspective for the study of creativity. In R. J. Sternberg (Ed.), *Handbook of creativity* (pp. 313–335). New York: Cambridge University Press.

Farooq, U. (2008). *Supporting creativity: Investigating the role of awareness in distributed collaboration*. PhD. College of Information Sciences and Technology. University Park, The Pennsylvania State University.

Farooq, U., Carroll, J. M., et al. (2005). Supporting creativity in distributed scientific communities. In *Proceedings of GROUP'05, Sanibel Island FL*. New York: ACM Press.

Fischer, G. (2004). Social creativity: turning barriers into opportunities for collaborative design. In A. Clement and P. V. D. Besselaar (Ed.), *Proceedings of the eighth conference on participatory design: Artful integration: Interweaving media, materials and practices* (152–161), Toronto, Ontario, Canada.

Fischer, G., Lemke, A. C., et al. (1991). Making argumentation serve design. *Human Computer Interaction, 6*(3&4), 393–419.

Fleischmann, K. (2006). Boundary objects with agency: A method for studying the design-use interface. *The Information Society, 22*, 77–87.

Gardner, H. (1993). Seven creators of the modern era. In J. Brockman (Ed.), *Creativity* (pp. 28–47). New York: Simon & Schuster.

Garrison, D. R. (1992). Critical thinking and self-directed learning in adult education: An analysis of responsibility and control issues. *Adult Education Quarterly, 42*(3), 136–148.

Guilford, J. P. (1967). *The nature of human intelligence*. New York: McGraw-Hill Companies.

Henri, F. (1991). Computer conferencing and content analysis. In A. R. Kaye (Ed.), *Collaborative learning through computer conferencing: The Najadeen papers*. London: Springer.

Henry, J. (2004). Creative collaboration in organisational settings. In D. Miell & K. Littleton (Eds.), *Collaborative creativity: Contemporary perspectives* (pp. 158–175). London: Free Association Books.

Houtz, J. C., Montgomery, C., et al. (1979). Relationship among measures of evaluation ability (problem solving), creative thinking, and intelligence. *Contemporary Educational Psychology, 4*(1), 47–54.

Kunz, W., & Rittel, H. W. J. (1970). *Issues as elements of information systems*. Berkeley: Institute of Urban & Regional Development, University of California.

Lee, J., & Lai, K. Y. (1991). What's in design rationale? *Human Computer Interaction, 6*(3&4), 251–280.

MacLean, A., Young, R. M., et al. (1989). Design rationale: The argument behind the artifact. In *CHI'89: Human factors in computing systems*. New York: ACM Press.

MacLean, A., Young, R. M., et al. (1991). Questions, options, and criteria: Elements of design space analysis. *Human Computer Interaction, 6*(3), 201–250.

Mayer, R. E. (1999). Fifty years of creativity research. In R. J. Sternberg (Ed.), *Handbook of creativity* (pp. 449–460). New York: Cambridge University Press.

McKerlie, D., & MacLean, A. (1994). Reasoning with design rationale: practical experience with design space analysis. *Design Studies, 15*, 214–226.

Moran, T. P., Carroll, J. M., et al. (1996). Overview of design rationale. In *Design rationale: concepts, techniques, and use* (pp. 1–9). Mahwah: Lawrence Erlbaum Associates, Inc.

Newman, D. R., Johnson, C., et al. (1997). Evaluating the quality of learning in computer supported co-operative learning. *Journal of the American Society for Information Science, 48*(6), 484–495.

O'Brien, R. M. (2007). A caution regarding rules of thumb for variance inflation factors. *Quality and Quantity, 41*, 673–690.

Ormerod, T. C., Mariani, J., et al. (1999). Desperado: Three-in-one indexing for innovative design. In *INTERACT'99: The seventh IFIP conference on human-computer interaction*. Amsterdam: IOS Press.

Potts, C., & Catledge, L. (1996). Collaborative conceptual design: A large software project case study. *Computer Supported Cooperative Work (CSCW), 5*(4), 415–445.

Runco, M. A. (1992). Children's divergent thinking and creative ideation. *Developmental Review, 12*(3), 233–264.

Shipman, F. M., & McCall, R. J. (1997). Integrating different perspectives on design rationale: Supporting the emergence of design rationale from design communication. *Artificial Intelligence for Engineering Design, Analysis and Manufacturing: AIEDAM, 11*(2), 141–154.

Singley, M. K., & Carroll, J. M. (1996). Synthesis by analysis: Five modes of reasoning that guide design. In T. P. Moran & J. M. Carroll (Eds.), *Design rationale: Concepts, techniques, and use* (pp. 241–266). Mahwah: Lawrence Erlbaum Associates, Inc.

Sternberg, R. J. (1985). *Beyond IQ: A triarchic theory of human intelligence*. Cambridge/New York: Cambridge University Press.

Sternberg, R. J. (2006). The nature of creativity. *Creativity Research Journal, 18*(1), 87–98.

Sternberg, R. J., & Lubart, T. I. (1991). An investment theory of creativity and its development. *Human Development, 34*(1), 1–31.

Sternberg, R. J., & Lubart, T. I. (1999). The concept of creativity: Prospects and paradigms. In R. J. Sternberg (Ed.), *Handbook of creativity* (pp. 3–15). New York: Cambridge University Press.

Tabachnick, B. G., & Fidell, L. S. (1996). *Using multivariate statistics*. New York: HarperCollins.

West, M. A. (2003). Innovation implementation in work teams. In P. B. Paulus & B. A. Nijstad (Eds.), *Group creativity: Innovation through collaboration* (pp. 245–276). New York: Oxford University Press.

Woodman, R. W., Sawyer, J. E., et al. (1993). Toward a theory of organizational creativity. *Academy of Management Review, 18*(2), 293–321.

Chapter 11
Promoting Group Creativity in Upstream Requirements Engineering

Rosalie J. Ocker

Abstract The upstream stage of requirements engineering (RE) focuses primarily on determining high-level organizational requirements. Upstream RE provides perhaps the best opportunity to instill creativity into the design process, as it is here where stakeholders figure out what to build. However, how to incorporate creativity into current RE methods remains a fundamental concern. Negative intergroup social processes, such as those associated with status differentials, ingroup bias, and majority influence, can impede group creativity and otherwise negatively impact the upstream RE process. This chapter discuses these issues and suggests how creativity can be promoted using an IBIS design rationale coupled with group support system tools intended to diminish negative social influences between (and within) stakeholder groups.

Keywords Requirements engineering • Social influences • Group support systems • Brainstorming.

11.1 Introduction

The upstream stage of requirements engineering (RE) focuses primarily on determining high-level organizational requirements. The process begins with an often ill-defined, unstructured problem and works towards a feasible problem definition and then to a set of high-level requirements. Determining upstream requirements is typically an intensive collaborative process of communication and negotiation (Holtzblatt and Beyer 1995) among heterogeneous stakeholders, consisting of users, designers,

R.J. Ocker (✉)
College of Information Sciences and Technology, The Pennsylvania
State University, University Park, PA 16802, USA
e-mail: rocker4855@gmail.com

J.M. Carroll (ed.), *Creativity and Rationale: Enhancing Human
Experience by Design*, Human–Computer Interaction Series,
DOI 10.1007/978-1-4471-4111-2_11, © Springer-Verlag London 2013

project sponsors and other effected parties. Each stakeholder group brings its unique perspective to this process; knowledge acquisition, sharing, and integration must be accomplished to develop a mutually shared understanding (Walz et al. 1993).

Upstream RE provides perhaps the best opportunity to instill creativity into the design process (Couger 1996), as it is here where stakeholders figure out what to build. However, how to incorporate creativity into current RE methods remains a fundamental concern as current methods rarely include processes to encourage creativity (Nguyen and Swatman 2006). Furthermore, reaching a stage of shared understanding and eliciting high-level requirements can be laden with negative intergroup social processes such as status differentials, ingroup bias, and majority influence at the expense of minority influence. These social influences can thwart creativity and otherwise negatively impact the upstream RE process.

This chapter seeks to offer insight into how creativity can be encouraged during upstream RE by addressing and diminishing negative social influences between (and within) stakeholder groups. This chapter is organized as follows. The next section reviews individual and group level creativity and discusses how social influences impact creativity. Then group support systems and electronic brainstorming are discussed within the context of social influences. Finally, the IBIS approach to design rationale is discussed. The chapter ends with suggestions for integrating Group Support Systems (GSS) with anonymous electronic brainstorming and anonymous voting into two IBIS based DR approaches.

11.2 Creativity and Social Influences

Creativity is a complex interaction of person and situation that takes places at both the individual and group levels. Creativity at the individual level is a function of antecedent conditions (e.g. home environment), personality, knowledge about the task, motivation and cognitive style/abilities, (Amabile 1988, 1990; Barron and Harrington 1981; Carrol 1985; Guilford 1977). Concerning the latter, a substantial body of research has focused on the divergent production of ideas as the dominant cognitive link to creativity. Divergent thinking progresses away from a problem in a variety of different directions and involves breaking down barriers and restrictions on thoughts. Convergent thinking, on the other hand, involves progression towards a single answer (Thompson 2003). The cognitive processes of fluency, flexibility, originality, and elaboration have been identified as essential to the divergent production of ideas (Guilford 1984). Personality traits associated with creativity include independent thought and judgment, autonomy, persistence, self-confidence, intellectual honesty and an internal locus of control (e.g. Amabile 1988; Barron and Harrington 1981; Woodman and Schoenfeldt 1989).

Creativity at the team level is more likely to occur when the composition of the team includes "stimulating colleagues" (Parmeter and Gaber 1971). Heterogeneous teams comprised of individuals who bring different knowledge, ideas and approaches to problem solving improve teams' creative performance (Hoffman 1959; Hoffman and Maier 1961). Diversity in terms of areas of specialization and work responsibilities are especially relevant to enhanced team creativity.

West (1990) proposes that creative teams operate in an environment of participative safety and foster a climate for excellence. Collaboration which occurs in a non-judgmental and supportive team atmosphere engenders a feeling of interpersonal safety among participants. West reasons that this non-threatening atmosphere promotes creativity as members are more likely to risk proposing new ideas.

A climate for excellence refers to a team atmosphere where there is a mutually shared concern for performance excellence pertaining to a vision or outcome. A tolerance for diversity of opinion and constructive conflict are the hallmarks as opposing opinions are not only offered, but also debated and critiqued by team members (King and Anderson 1990).

11.3 Social Influences

The qualities and characteristics associated with group creativity are influenced by the social conditions and context in which the creative situation occurs. Group level creativity is impacted by a number of factors that come into play when individuals collaborate. These include the member composition of the group, characteristics of the group such as degree of trust and cohesiveness, and group collaboration context (e.g., degree of virtuality or physical distance between group members, means of communication) (Woodman et al. 1993). Interaction between individuals and groups are impacted by social influences. Woodman et al. argue that social influences stemming from cross-level interactions between individuals and groups are critical to understanding enhancers and inhibitors impacting creativity at the group level.

The pervasiveness of social influences within a group is described by Vinacke et al. (1964):

> In a very real sense, any interaction between or among persons can be viewed as a social influence process. It would be hard, certainly, to think of a social setting in which at least one person is not attempting to bring about some desired response in another. Even ordinary conversations have this characteristic (p. 259).

A discussion of social influences which have the potential to impact a group's creativity is presented next. Specifically, status, social identity and ingroup bias, majority influence and minority influence are presented.

11.3.1 Status

A status characteristic is any characteristic that influences a group member's own or others' evaluations and beliefs about the group member. As delineated by Cohen and Zhou (1991),

> Status characteristics can be "diffuse" (i.e., hold over a wide range of situations and performances, or be "specific", i.e., limited to a particular situation, or task. Status characteristics may be external to the interaction or may emerge in the course of task interaction; they may be explicitly relevant to the group task or they may become relevant in the course of interaction.

Gender, race, and military rank are examples of diffuse characteristics that are external to the group interaction. Mathematical ability is a specific status characteristic that is explicitly relevant to solving mathematical problems and may become relevant to a whole range of verbal and nonverbal tasks. (p. 180)

Status characteristics theory (SCT) suggests that individuals *combine* status information of group members to form expectations of their performance (see Wagner and Berger 1993, 1997 for summaries). In this way, status hierarchies are formed within a given group, which result in inequalities in interaction such that higher status individuals initiate and receive more interaction and have more influence than lower-status members. For low status members to attain some level of influence, they must show more evidence of ability than high status members (Biernat and Kobrynowicz 1977).

SCT has relevance for the composition of a given group. It is not the status of the individuals within a group that organizes member interaction, per se. Rather, it is the composition of the group with regard to the status differentials between members (Sell et al. 1992). Moreover, the more divergence between states of a status characteristic (e.g., a team of four males and one female is more divergent than a team of two males and one female), the more impact the status characteristic has on group interaction (Moreland and Levine 1992; Kanter 1977).

A structural approach has also been used to account for behavior due to status differences. The theory of proportional representation posits that the numerical representation of a status type (e.g. race, sex) – that is, the relative numbers of a given status indicator – influences interaction (Kanter 1977). According to Kanter, those in the numerical majority control the group and its culture. Skewed groups are those whose membership has a preponderance of one status type over another. In skewed groups, a member from the non-dominant category experiences feelings of isolation and powerlessness. This leads to behavior by the non-dominant category that tends towards passive and inhibited conduct.

11.3.2 Social Identity and Ingroup Bias

Social categorization theory (Tajfel 1981) and Social Identity Theory (SIT) (Tajfel 1978; Turner 1981; Tajfel and Turner 1986) suggest that people derive social identity primarily from membership in groups (not to be confused with team membership). For example, demographic differences can result in people categorizing themselves into 'us vs. them' groupings. In such situations, positive social identity results when one can make favorable comparisons between the group to which one is a perceived member (i.e., the ingroup) compared to other germane groups to which one is not a perceived member (i.e., the outgroups).

Decades of research indicates that subgroups form due to diversity in terms of demographic attributes (e.g. race, age, sex), psychological differences (e.g. beliefs) and affiliations (for a comprehensive review, see Williams and O'Reilly 1998). Subgroups develop separate identities and exhibit ingroup team bias – increased interaction with and preferential behavior towards members of one's subgroup, reduced

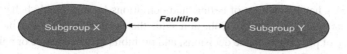

Fig. 11.1 Subgroups divided by a faultine

trust and team cohesiveness, and increased conflict between subgroups – which impairs team effectiveness and performance (e.g. Lott and Lott 1965; O'Reilly et al. 1989; Smith et al. 1994).

A faultline divides a group's members according to one or more attributes (Lau and Murnighan 1998), as depicted in Fig. 11.1. The more attributes that are aligned along the same faultline, the stronger the faultline and the resulting distinction between subgroups. For example, if a team is composed of male engineers and female marketing professionals, it has a stronger faultline than if the engineers and marketers were composed of both males and females. Thus, rather than the amount of diversity within a team, Lau and Murnighan (1998) argue that it is the alignment or correlation (Cramton and Hinds 2005) of member attributes that increases the strength of the division between subgroups.

The configuration of a team has also been shown to create a faultline. For example, when team members are spread across multiple locations, subgroups tend to form according to location, resulting in ingroup bias (Ocker et al., 2011; Panteli and Davison 2005; Polzer et al. 2006). The number of team locations can affect the degree of ingroup bias – for example, teams configured across two locations have been found to exhibit stronger ingroup dynamics compared to teams with three locations. Additionally, when a team includes both co-located members and isolated members, ingroup dynamics can still prevail. Bos et al. (2004) found that co-located members formed one subgroup, while the isolates banded together to form their own subgroup.

11.3.3   Majority Influence

Groups have a need for uniformity of opinion. Moscovici (1974) asserts that this is due to two primary reasons. First, as groups normally have a purpose, the group feels the need to move in a certain direction to achieve that purpose, which is much easier to achieve when group members hold similar opinions. Secondly, groups have a need for a sense of social reality, which is achieved through the validation of one's own judgments and opinions by the other members of the group. To achieve uniformity, groups typically exclude deviance and are unwilling to compromise (Asch 1951; Festinger 1950; Sherif 1935).

Majority influence is a type of social influence centered on conformity, which entails movement in beliefs and behavior toward the group. The act of conforming requires two parties – the majority group and the minority individual or subgroup.

The majority has its own set of beliefs and definitions for acceptable behavior – in essence, its rules and norms. Cohesion with the group reaffirms the belief and acceptance of previously made decisions, and prohibits the acceptance or adherence to other norms. Conformity within the group serves to absorb any deviance by the minority, as deviance is seen as a threat to the majority. The function of conformity is successfully fulfilled when (1) the majority of the group has a well-defined set of norms, responses, and attitudes and (2) the group exerts social pressure on the individual or subgroup that lacks well-established norms. Majority influence prevails when deviant individuals or subgroups re-caste their views or behaviors to conform to those of the group (Moscovici 1974).

In general, research has found that what contributes most to conformity is the existence of unanimous agreement (e.g., Graham 1962; Mouton et al. 1956). Thus, yielding to the majority, although influenced by various factors such as size or shared power of the majority, is credited to the primary influence that a *perceived consistency* of majority opinion has on the minority. It is this attribute which is believed to cause the minority opinion holder to succumb to the majority opinion.

Normalization is the process whereby the "reciprocal influence of group members induces them to formulate or to accept a compromise" (Moscovici 1974, p. 208). Individuals attempt to create an internal reference point – a norm or standard – when an external norm or standard is lacking (Sherif 1935). In considering the case in which the majority of individuals do not have a well-defined norm or solution, Moscovici describes the process of normalization as follows.

> When a number of individuals are confronted by a set of objects or stimuli which they are supposed to judge or a problem which they are supposed to solve and there are no particular norms or rules to govern their behavior, each of the individuals is hesitant and relatively inconsistent. As soon as they begin discussing the situation or making their judgments, each of them becomes aware of the discrepancies among themselves. Since they have no motivation to increase their uncertainty by widening their differences, nor to provoke conflict between themselves, they generally follow the road of compromise. This compromise generally leads to the establishment of an average judgment or response. This is what is called the normalization process… (Moscovici 1974, p. 224).

The development of a norm or standard is due to the need for stability which is provided by a frame of reference within which responses can be organized. Moscovici asserts that the normalization process occurs in order to avoid conflict and disagreement, and therefore is not necessarily a result of cooperation and mutual understanding within the group. Again, convergent, rather than divergent, thinking is prevalent.

11.3.4 Minority Influence

Minority influence describes the situation where minority opinion holders influence the opinions of the majority opinion-holders. Thus, the situation is similar to that of majority influence, however in this case the minority exerts influence on the majority. Conflict and behavioral style are important aspects in the development of minority influence on a group. Moscovici and Nemeth (1974) assert that it is the behavioral style, that is, the "orchestration and patterning of the minority's behavior" that is at the root of the minority's influence (p. 220). They explain,

> It is such behavioral styles that cause the majority to question its own position and consider the possibility that the minority may be correct. When such patterning leads to assumptions that the minority is consistent and certain of its position, that it is objective and unbiased in its judgments, then the minority can be effective (Moscovici and Nemeth 1974, p.220).

Maass and Clark (1984) point out that

> Since Sherif's (1935) and Asch's (1951) early work on conformity, it has become a social psychological truism that individuals tend to yield to a majority position even when that position is clearly incorrect. Conformity became a term nearly equivalent in meaning to social influence. It was not until 1969 that Moscovici and his coauthors pointed out that social influence is by no means limited to a one-direction dependency of the minority on the majority... a consistent minority is able to exert a remarkable degree of influence even when it is not equipped with such characteristics as power, status, competence (Hollander 1964) (Maass and Clark 1984, p. 428).

Nemeth (1986) made a connection between creativity and minority influence. In a series of studies, Nemeth and colleagues found that minority influence stimulates independent and divergent thought, so that issues and problems are considered from more perspectives. This results in group members detecting and exploring not only new solutions, but correct solutions. Nemeth explains the process as follows:

> When the influence source is a minority, the assumption that the minority is incorrect and the disinclination to publicly adopt its position lead to an initial dismissal of the minority viewpoint. However, with consistency and confidence on the minority's part over time, people are stimulated to understand such alternative views (e.g. "how can they be so wrong and yet so sure of themselves?"). As a result, they are stimulated to reappraise the entire situation, which involves a consideration of numerous alternatives, one of which is the position proposed by the minority. As such, the thought processes are marked by divergence and, hence, the potential for detecting novel solutions or decisions. (Nemeth 1986, p. 26)

Nemeth thus offers a reconceptualization of minority influence. "The implications for creativity and decision making, both at the individual and group levels, become considerable" (Nemeth 1986, p. 25).

11.4   Group Support Systems and Brainstorming

Can technology assist in overcoming the negative social influences that can thwart creativity in groups? A recent study indicates the usefulness of group support systems (GSS) in workgroups with distinct social identities (Lim and Guo 2008). A GSS incorporate computer technology with communication and decision processes for the support of group problem solving and decision making activities. Historically, GSS were designed for same-time, same-place meetings where each meeting participant has his/her own computer monitor and keyboard. In these "decision room" GSS, a meeting facilitator assists the group in all activities, from providing technical support to chairing the GSS session and moving the group through a planned agenda.

GSS typically include a toolkit to assist groups in performing their activities. A system might include a planning tool, an electronic brainstorming tool, and various voting tools. For example GroupSystems, arguably the most extensively used and studied GSS, includes a series of tools to support electronic brainstorming for groups. A comparison of traditional and electronic brainstorming provides a good example of how technology and process can alter the affects of social influences on the creative process.

11.4.1 Traditional Brainstorming

As originally devised by Osborn (1963), traditional brainstorming (face-to-face, no technology support) involves four rules designed to reduce negative social influences so as to increase idea generation and group creativity (Osborn 1963). These rules are:

1. Focus on quantity: This rule is based on the axiom that quantity leads to quality. By increasing the number of ideas generated, it is assumed that there is a greater chance of generating a creative and effective solution.
2. Withhold criticism: By withholding criticism, the expectation is that participants will be more likely to submit far-fetched, radical, and even potentially "silly" but potentially stimulating ideas to the group.
3. Welcome unusual ideas: To encourage "out of the box" thinking, participants are encouraged to forego assumptions and look at the problem from new perspectives.
4. Combine and improve ideas: Ideas can be merged to form new, "better" ideas, following the maxim that "$1 + 1 = 3$".

Osborn's claims, that traditional face-to-face brainstorming groups produce more and better ideas than the same number of people working alone, have been refuted time and again (see Mullen et al. 1991, for a review). Two explanations have been offered to explain this phenomenon (Diehl and Stroebe 1987). *Production blocking* occurs when participants must wait to convey their ideas to the group, because another member is speaking. During this waiting period, it is speculated that the silent participants forget their ideas or self-censor, resulting in the loss of a significant number of their ideas. *Evaluation apprehension* stems from a fear of disapproval by others (Cottrell 1972) which results in participants holding back ideas. *Social loafing*, also know as free-riding, is the tendency of participants to put forth less effort in group settings than they would if working individually (Latane, 1981, 1986).

11.4.2 Electronic Brainstorming Using GSS

Using a GSS, electronic brainstorming (EBS) attempts to address the shortcomings of traditional brainstorming by blending a component of the nominal group technique (the ability to generate ideas without interruption) with a component of traditional brainstorming (sharing ideas with other participants). The typical EBS process includes steps for generating ideas, editing ideas, and evaluating ideas in a decision-room type GSS context (Gallupe et al. 1992). Anonymous EBS is a variation which, as the name implies, eliminates the association between a participant and his/her ideas, edits, and evaluations.

When generating ideas, members type an idea into the GSS and hit enter, at which point the idea is disseminated to the group. Members receive others' ideas randomly. In terms of editing ideas, the GSS includes a sort feature that enables members to organize ideas by keywords, and then combine ideas or delete redundant ideas. The evaluation of ideas is typically accomplished by voting. In rank order voting, each participant can individually prioritize the idea list. The GSS then takes these individual rankings and creates a group ranking based on all members' rankings. Any number of votes can occur in an effort to reach consensus on the priority of ideas.

Parallel entry and anonymity are important in addressing the limitations of traditional brainstorming (Connolly et al. 1993). Production blocking is addressed through parallel entry, the ability of participants to simultaneously enter and share ideas. In anonymous EBS, evaluation apprehension and social loafing are reduced because participants share and evaluate ideas without being identified, free from the fear of criticism (given a large-enough pool of participants). Thus, anonymous EBS separates ideas from the status of their proposers, and thus promotes equalized power within the group. Furthermore, the opportunity for minority influence is enhanced, not only by separating ideas from proposers, but also by increasing the opportunity for the minority to be "heard" as there is no opportunity for the majority opinion holders to shut out the minority.

11.5   Design Rationale: IBIS to Support Argumentation

Traditionally design rationale (DR) has been applied to RE, as it epitomizes the "wicked" types of problems addressed by Rittel and Weber (1973). DR provides a structure for focusing discussion among the different stakeholders within a project team. Design rationale originates from two areas: early studies of design activity conducted by Kunz and Rittel (1970) and argumentation as developed by Toulmin (1958). However, Rittel was the first to advocate systematic documentation of design rationale as part of the design process.

Rittel's approach to design reasoning is based on argumentation, and as such is concerned with supporting debate and discussion. Rittel developed a method to represent (a) a network of issues (design questions); (b) selected and reflected answers; and (c) arguments for and against these answers. The outcome of his work was IBIS (Issue-Based Information System) which is a method, not a computerized information system, for supporting the reasoning process required in design and other wicked problems.

The objective of an IBIS discussion is for each of the stakeholders to try to understand the specific elements of each others' proposals. Initially, an unstructured problem area or topic is presented.

About this topic and its subtopics a discourse develops. Issues are brought up and disputed because different positions are assumed. Arguments are constructed in defense or against the different positions until the issue is settled by convincing the opponents or decided by a formal decision procedure (Kunz and Rittel 1970:1–2).

Thus, the discussion unfolds as one tries to persuade others of one's point of view. gIBIS was a prototype software tool for building and browsing IBIS networks (Conklin and Begeman 1988, 1989). gIBIS provided a graphical interface and had a limited GSS capability, allowing several users to contribute to an IBIS discussion synchronously. gIBIS was a software platform used to conduct research on using hypertext, GSS, and rhetorical models to facilitate and capture software system design decisions and their rationale.

The IBIS method makes it "harder for discussants to make unconstructive rhetorical moves, such as 'argument by repetition' and name calling, and it supports other more constructive moves, such as seeking the central issue, asking questions as much as giving answers, and being specific about the supporting evidence of one's viewpoint" (Conklin and Begeman 1988:305). Especially relevant to addressing social influences, users of the IBIS method report that the structure that IBIS imposes on discussions served to expose "axe grinding, hand waving, and clever rhetoric" and that they valued the tendency for assumptions and definitions to be made explicit (Conklin and Begeman 1988:323).

The semi-structured nature of IBIS accounts for some of these advantages (Malone et al. 1986). The IBIS structure does not place any constraint on the writer when it comes to expressibility. At the same time, the reader is provided with the recurrent structure in the textual material that aids both search and comprehension (Conklin and Begeman 1988).

11.5.1 Descriptive and Prescriptive IBIS

As with other DR, an IBIS-based approach can be primarily descriptive or prescriptive (some are a combination of both) (Dutoit et al., 2006). Descriptive approaches aim to portray designers' thinking processes and emphasize the issue-base as a history of the design process; they do not seek to modify designers' reasoning. In contrast, prescriptive approaches seek to improve the design process by improving the reasoning of designers. This is done through a prescribed process to be followed, as the issue-base structure is developed through debate and discussion.

Wisdom is a prescriptive approach that incorporates cognitive mapping tools and IBIS structures (Rooksby et al. 2006). It is intended for use by project stakeholders during the problem definition stage of RE. The Wisdom designers describe the importance of the facilitator:

The effectiveness of a meeting is dependent on the skills of a neutral facilitator (9, 30). The facilitator's objective is to foster procedural rationality, where stakeholders agree that sensible decisions have been made and commit to them. In practice, a facilitator ensures that a meeting remains focused, that the evolving cognitive map accurately reflects the ongoing discussion, that stakeholders get the opportunity to air their views and that the decision process is sensible.

Winwin is an example of a descriptive approach; its main purpose "is to negotiate a set of mutually satisfactory agreements that are foundations to requirements, constraints, and plans of the project." Built on the spiral model (Boehm 1988; Boehm and Kitapci 2006:178), WinWin adds a negotiation front-end to the beginning of each spiral cycle. The negotiation activities consist of (1) identifying key stakeholders, (2) eliciting key stakeholders' "win" conditions and (3) negotiating mutually satisfying "win" conditions between stakeholders. Stakeholders describe their system "goals as 'win' conditions. If everyone concurs, the win conditions become agreements. When stakeholders do not concur, they identify their conflicted win conditions and register their conflicts as issues" (Boehm and Kitapci 2006:180).

11.5.2   Including GSS Tools and Processes

IBIS-based collaborative DR techniques such as Wisdom and Win-Win recognize the importance of eliciting stakeholder input in upstream RE. However, the manner in which stakeholders are included tends toward a utopian view of group interaction, where all participants' viewpoints are encouraged and all participants feel equally valued and willing to share diverse viewpoints, even when they differ from their superiors' views. While there is recognition of the benefits of IBIS to expose "axe grinding" and the like, this does not ensure a non-threatening, collaborative environment.

Thus, the previously discussed negative intergroup social processes (i.e., status differentials, ingroup bias, and majority influence), all of which breed conformity as opposed to creativity, are not recognized by the IBIS-based collaborative DR techniques such as Wisdom and Win-Win. By incorporating GSS tools that such as anonymous sharing and debate of ideas, as well as anonymous voting to prioritize ideas, less dependence is placed on the skills of a facilitator and the benevolence of stakeholder groups. The result is that negative social influences have the potential to be side-stepped. Thus, a group context conducive to a more egalitarian and participative exchange of ideas is promoted, which in turn, is more favorable to group creativity.

References

Amabile, T. M. (1988). A model of creativity and innovation in organizations. In B. M. Staw & L. L. Cummings (Eds.), *Research in organizational behavior* (Vol. 10, pp. 123–167). Greenwich: JAI Press.
Amabile, T. M. (1990). Within you, without you: The social psychology of creativity, and beyond. In M. A. Runco & R. S. Albert (Eds.), *Theories or creativity* (pp. 61–91). Newbury Park: Sage.
Asch, S. E. (1951). Effects of group pressure upon the modification and distortion of judgments. In H. Guetzkow (Ed.), *Groups, leadership, and men*. Pittsburgh: Carnegie Press.

Barron, F. B., & Harrington, D. M. (1981). Creativity, intelligence, and personality. *Annual Review of Psychology, 32*, 439–476.

Biernat, M., & Kobrynowicz, D. (1977). Gender and race-based standards of competence: Lower minimum standards but higher ability standards for devalued groups. *Journal of Personality and Social Psychology, 72*, 44–557.

Boehm, B. (1988). A spiral model of software development and enhancement. *Computer, 21*(5), 61–72.

Boehm, B., & Kitapci, H. (2006). The WinWin approach: Using a requirements negotiation tool for rationale capture and use. In A. H. Dutoit, R. McCall, I. Mistrik, & B. Paech (Eds.), *Rationale management in software engineering*. Berlin: Springer.

Bos, N., Shami, N. S., Olson, J. S., Cheshin, A., & Nan, N. (2004). In-group/out-group effects in distributed teams: An experimental simulation. *CSCW, 6*(3), 429–436.

Carrol, J. B. (1985). *Domains of cognitive ability*. Paper presented at the meeting of the American Association for the Advancement of Science, Los Angeles.

Cohen, B. P., & Zhou, X. (1991). Status processes in groups. *American Sociological Review, 56*, 179–188.

Conklin, J., & Begeman, M. (1988). gIBIS: A hypertext tool for exploratory policy discussion. *ACM Transactions on Office Information Systems (TOIS), 6*(4), 303–331.

Conklin, J., & Begeman, M. L. (1989). gIBIS: A tool for all reasons. *Journal of American Society for Information Science, 40*, 200–213.

Connolly, T., Routhieaux, R. L., & Schneider, S. K. (1993). On the effectiveness of group brainstorming. *Small Group Research, 24*(4), 490–503.

Cottrell, N. B. (1972). Social facilitation. In C. McClintock (Ed.), *Experimental social psychology* (pp. 185–236). New York: Holt, Rinehart & Winston.

Couger, J. D. (1996). *Creativity & innovation in information systems organizations*. Danvers: Boyd & Fraser.

Cramton, C. D., & Hinds, P. J. (2005). Subgroup dynamics in internationally distributed teams: Ethnocentrism or cross-national learning. *Research in Organizational Behavior, 26*, 231–263.

Diehl, M., & Stroebe, W. (1987). Productivity loss in brainstorming groups: Toward the solution of a riddle. *Journal of Personality and Social Psychology, 53*, 497–509.

Dutoit, A. H., McCall, R., Mistrik, I., & Paech, B. (2006). Rationale management in software engineering: Concepts and techniques. In A. H. Dutoit, R. McCall, I. Mistrik, & B. Paech (Eds.), *Rationale management in software engineering* (pp. 1–43). Heidelberg: Springer.

Festinger, L. (1950). Informal social communication. *Psychological Review, 57*, 271–282.

Gallupe, R. B., Dennis, A. R., Cooper, W. H., Valacich, J. S., Bastianutti, L. M., Nunamaker, J. F. (1992). Electronic brainstorming and group size. *Academy of Management Journal, 35*, 350–369.

Graham, D. (1962). Experimental studies of social influence in simple judgment situations. *Journal of Social Psychology, 56*, 245–269.

Guilford, J. P. (1977). *Way beyond the IQ*. Buffalo: Creative Education Foundation.

Guilford, J. P. (1984). Varieties of divergent production. *Journal of Creative Behavior, 18*(1), 1–10.

Hoffman, L. R. (1959). Homogeneity of member personality and its effect on group problem-solving. *Journal of Abnormal and Social Psychology, 58*, 27–32.

Hoffman, L. R., & Maier, N. R. F. (1961). Quality and acceptance of problem solutions by members of homogeneous and heterogeneous groups. *Journal of Abnormal and Social Psychology, 62*, 401–407.

Hollander, E. P. (1964). *Leader, groups, and influence*. New York: Oxford University Press.

Holtzblatt, K., & Beyer, H. R. (1995). Requirements gathering: The human factor. *Communications of the ACM, 38*(5), 31–32.

Kanter, R. M. (1977). Some effects of proportions in group life: Skewed sex ratios and responses to numerical minority women. *The American Journal of Sociology, 82*, 965–990.

King, N., & Anderson, N. (1990). Innovation in working groups. In M. A. West & J. L. Farr (Eds.), *Innovation and creativity at work* (pp. 81–100). Chichester: Wiley.

Kunz, W., & Rittel, H. (1970). Issues as elements of information systems. Working paper no. 131, Institute of Urban and Regional Development, University of California at Berkeley.

Latané, B. (1981) The psychology of social impact. *American Psychologist, 36*, 343–356.

Latane, B. (1986). Responsibility and effort in organizations. In: P. S. Goodman (Ed.), *Designing effective work groups* (pp. 277–304). San Francisco: Jossey-Bass Publishers, Inc.

Lau, D. C., & Murnighan, J. K. (1998). Demographic diversity and faultlines: The compositional dynamics of organizational groups. *Academy of Management Review, 23*, 325–340.

Lim, J., & Guo, X. (2008). A study of group support systems and the intergroup setting. *Decision Support Systems, 45*(3), 452.

Lott, A., & Lott, B. (1965). Group cohesiveness as interpersonal attraction: A review of relationships with antecedent and consequent variables. *Psychological Bulletin, 64*, 259–309.

Maass, A., & Clark, R. D. (1984). Hidden impact of minorities: Fifteen years of minority influence research. *Psychological Bulletin, 95*(3), 428–450.

Malone, T. W., Grant, K., Lai, K.-Y., Rao, R., & Rosenblitt, D. (1986). Semi-structured messages are surprisingly useful for computer-supported coordination. *Proceedings of CSCW'86, MCC/ACM Conference on Computer-Supported Cooperative Work*, Austin, Texas, 102–114.

Moreland, R. L., & Levine, J. M. (1992). The composition of groups. In E. J. Lawler, B. Markovsky, C. Ridgeway, & H. A. Walker (Eds.), *Advances in group processes, 9* (pp. 237–280). Greenwich: JAI.

Moscovici, S. (1974). Social influence I, Conformity and social control. In C. Nemeth (Ed.), *Social psychology, classic and contemporary integrations*. Chicago: Rand McNally.

Moscovici, S., & Nemeth, C. (1974). Social influence II. Minority influence. In C. Nemeth (Ed.), *Social psychology, classic and contemporary integrations*. Chicago: Rand McNally.

Mouton, J. S., Blake, R. R., & Olmstead, J. A. (1956). The relationship between frequency of yielding and the disclosure of personal identity. *Journal of Personality, 24*, 339–347.

Mullen, B., Johnson, C., & Salas, E. (1991). *Basic and Applied Social Psychology, 12*(1), 3–23. Lawrence Erlbaum Associates.

Nemeth, C. J. (1986). Differential contributions of majority and minority influence. *Psychological Review, 93*(1), 23–32.

Nguyen, L., & Swatman, P. A. (2006). Promoting and supporting requirements engineering in creativity. In A. H. Dutoit, R. McCall, I. Mistrik, & B. Paech (Eds.), *Rationale management in software engineering*. Berlin: Springer.

Ocker, R. J., Huang, H., Benbunan-Fich, R., & Hiltz, S. R. (2011). Leadership dynamics in partially distributed teams: An exploratory study of the effects of configuration and distance. *Group Decision and Negotiation, 20*(3), 273–292.

O'Reilly, C., Caldwell, D., & Barnett, W. (1989). Work group demography, social integration, and turnover. *Administrative Science Quarterly, 34*, 21–37.

Osborn, A. F. (1963). *Applied imagination: Principles and procedures of creative problem solving* (Third Rev. ed.). New York, NY: Charles Scribner's Sons.

Panteli, N., & Davison, R. M. (2005). The role of subgroups in the communication patterns of global virtual teams. *IEEE Transactions on Professional Communication, 48*(2), 191–200.

Parmeter, S. M., & Gaber, J. D. (1971). Creative scientists rate creativity factors. *Research Management*, November, 65–70.

Polzer, J. T., Crisp, C. B., Jarvenpaa, S. L., & Kim, J. W. (2006). Extending the faultline concept to geographically dispersed teams: How colocated subgroups can impair group functioning. *Academy of Management Journal, 49*(4), 679–692.

Rittel, H., & Webber, M. (1973). Dilemmas in a general theory of planning. *Policy Sciences, 4*, 155–169.

Rooksby, J., Sommerville, I., & Pidd, M. (2006). A hybrid approach to upstream requirements: Ibis and cognitive mapping. In A. H. Dutoit, R. McCall, I. Mistrik, & B. Paech (Eds.), *Rationale management in software engineering*. Berlin: Springer.

Sell, J., Lovaglia, M. J., Mannix, E. A., Samuelson, C. D., & Wilson, R. K. (1992). Investigating conflict, power, and status within and among groups. *Small Group Research, 35*(1), 44–72.

Sherif, M. (1935). *The psychology of social norms*. New York: Harper & Row.

Smith, K., Smith, K., Olian, J., Sims, H., O'Bannon, D., & Scully, J. (1994). Top management team demography and process: The role of social integration and communication. *Administrative Science Quarterly, 39*, 412–438.

Tajfel, H. (1978). *Differentiation between social groups: Studies in the social psychology of intergroup relations*. London: Academic.

Tajfel, H. (1981). *Human groups and social categories: Studies in social psychology*. Cambridge: Cambridge University Press.

Tajfel, H., & Turner, J. C. (1986). The social identity theory of intergroup behaviour. In S. Worchel & W. G. Austin (Eds.), *Psychology of intergroup relations* (pp. 7–24). Chicago: Nelson.

Thompson, L. (2003). Improving the creativity of organizational work group. *The Academy of Management Executive, 17*(1), 96–109.

Toulmin, S. E. (1958). *The uses of argument*. Cambridge: Cambridge University Press.

Turner, J. C. (1981). The experimental social psychology of intergroup behaviour. In J. C. Turner & H. Giles (Eds.), *Intergroup behaviour* (pp. 66–101). Oxford: Basil Blackwell.

Vinacke, W. E., Wilson, W. R., & Meredith, G. M. (1964). *Dimensions of social psychology*. Chicago: Scott, Foresman and Co.

Wagner, D., & Berger, J. (1993). Status characteristics theory: The growth of a program in theoretical research programs. In J. Berger & M. Zeldich Jr. (Eds.), *Studies in the growth of theory*. Stanford: Stanford University Press.

Wagner, D., & Berger, J. (1997). Gender and interpersonal task behaviors: Status expectation accounts, *Sociological Perspectives, 40*(1–32), 1997.

Walz, D. B., Elam, J. J., & Curtis, B. (1993). Inside a software design team: Knowledge acquisition, sharing and integration. *Communications of the ACM, 36*(10), 63–77.

West, M. A. (1990). The social psychology of innovation in groups. In M. A. West & J. L. Farr (Eds.), *Innovation and creativity at work* (pp. 207–230). Chichester: Wiley.

Williams, K. Y., & O'Reilly, C. A. (1998). Demography and diversity in organizations: A review of 40 years of research. *Research in Organizational Behavior, 20*, 77–140.

Woodman, R., & Schoenfeldt, L. F. (1989). Individual differences in creativity: An interactionist perspective. In J. A. Glover & C. R. Reynolds (Eds.), *Handbook of creativity* (pp. 77–92). New York: Plenum Press.

Woodman, R., Sawyer, J., & Griffin, R. (1993). Toward a theory of organizational creativity. *Academy of Management Review, 18*(2), 292–321.

Chapter 12
Supporting Awareness in Creative Group Work by Exposing Design Rationale

Umer Farooq and John M. Carroll

Abstract When creativity is taken as a long-term, complex, and collaborative activity, support for awareness is required for group members to monitor the development of ideas, track how these ideas became narrowed, and understand how alternatives are being implemented and integrated by colleagues. In this chapter, we investigate the effects of exposing design rationale to convey awareness, specifically activity awareness, in group creativity. Through evaluating a prototype, we investigate status updates that convey design rationale, and to what consequences, in small groups in fully distributed collaboration. We found that status updates are used for a variety of purposes and that participants' comments on their collaborators' status updates provided feedback. Overall, results suggest that participants' awareness about their collaborators' future plans increased over time. Majority of participants found the status updates useful, particularly those with higher metacognitive knowledge. Based on our results, two design strategies for activity awareness are proposed.

Keywords Computer-supported awareness • Status updates • Metacognition • Facebook • Twitter.

U. Farooq (✉)
Microsoft Corporation, One Microsoft Way, Redmond, WA 98052, USA
e-mail: umfarooq@microsoft.com

J.M. Carroll
Center for Human-Computer Interaction, College of Information Sciences and Technology,
The Pennsylvania State University, University Park, PA 16802, USA
e-mail: jmcarroll@psu.edu

J.M. Carroll (ed.), *Creativity and Rationale: Enhancing Human Experience by Design*, Human–Computer Interaction Series, DOI 10.1007/978-1-4471-4111-2_12, © Springer-Verlag London 2013

12.1 Introduction

A fairly typical form of creativity—and perhaps even more important than the isolated lightning bolt—is the relatively long-term and collaborative development of innovative ideas. Researchers have argued in prior work that computer-supported awareness is critical for successful collaborative work, as well as creative work (Farooq et al. 2007).

The concept of awareness in computer-supported cooperative work (CSCW) literature has taken many forms. For example, social awareness (Erickson and Kellogg 1999) involves knowing who else is present in a shared workspace, while workspace awareness (Gutwin et al. 1996) conveys who is doing what in the sense of manipulating shared artifacts. For a detailed review of awareness in CSCW, refer to Schmidt (2002).

More recently, with the adoption of Web 2.0, new social networking media have emerged that incorporate novel ways of providing awareness of people's activities. For instance, Facebook, an on-line social networking site, allows friends to specify what they are doing through status updates. These status updates are broadcasted to one's friends. Twitter is yet another social networking medium that among many functions serves the purpose of keeping friends, family, and colleagues connected through the exchange of quick, frequent answers to one simple question: What are you doing right now?

The notion of providing status updates for informal, nonwork related purposes, such as in social networking media (e.g., Facebook, Twitter), seems to be anecdotally successful in supporting awareness. For example, Farooq et al. (2007) showed that different types of breakdowns in creativity do occur in distributed collaboration and can be supported by designing appropriate awareness mechanisms around status updates.

We thus are motivated to investigate the feasibility, effectiveness, and consequences of such status updates in the context of creative group work. In this chapter, we describe a prototype for updating statuses in collaborative work. We report on a study of small groups using this prototype over an extended period of time to answer the exploratory research question: How can status updates be used in creative group work and with what consequences?

The outline of this chapter is as follows. First, we conceptualize status updates as providing activity awareness in collaborative work. Second, we discuss how our contribution is situated in prior work on status updates in CSCW. Then, based on an existing empirical study, we describe the design of a status update prototype that provides activity awareness in collaborative work. Finally, we present an evaluation of the prototype. We conclude by suggesting implications of our results and future work.

12.2 Exposing Design Rationale as Status Updates to Support Activity Awareness

We are investigating the provision of status updates to convey activity awareness in creative group work. *Activity awareness* is cognizance of other people's intentions, plans, priorities, and understandings with respect to an ongoing endeavor, of the criteria they will use to make decisions and evaluate joint outcomes, of the knowledge, skills, tools, and other resources they can contribute to a joint project, of the social networks they participate in, and of how they can engage others in the shared activity (Carroll et al. 2003, 2006).

By definition (Carroll et al. 2003, 2006), activity awareness is more than a matter of registering the current state information. It transcends synchronous awareness of where a collaborator's cursor is pointing, where the collaborator is looking, and so forth. It involves monitoring and integrating many different kinds of information at different levels of analysis, such as events, tasks, goals, social interactions and their meanings, group values and norms, and more to learn about developing circumstances and the initiatives, reactions, as well as sense making of other people with respect to ongoing and anticipated courses of action. It is continually negotiated, constructed, and enacted throughout the course of a collaborative interaction.

Currently, status updates in social networking media are employed to present general and often lighthearted self-disclosures (e.g., "Joe is glad the semester is over"; "Kathy is craving pizza"). However, one can imagine recruiting the mechanism of status updates for the purpose of supporting activity awareness in collaborative work; thus, a group member might post a status update such as, "Sam is finishing up Section 3 of the heuristic evaluation report." In this application, a status update is specific and activity-oriented. Of course, this single status update is just an excerpt from a presumably more extensive signaling protocol but, even so, it reminds group members of the planning and negotiation that divided up report sections, and of the ensuing steps in the plan. It conveys something about Sam's progress, and about what other group members may need to be doing in order to coordinate with Sam.

In the balance of this chapter, we will refer to status updates that are intended to support activity awareness as *activity updates*. Our perspective on activity updates is that the updates actually constitute design rationale. Each team member keeps his/her partners apprised of that member's activities and reactions through the updates. This puts the partners' actions within the intentional context of what they are trying to do, how they assessed what others are trying to do, and so on. The updates are rationale-in-action, or *situated rationale*, as opposed to more typical case of rationale created after the fact to reconstruct or explain what happened.

12.3   Relation to Prior Literature

Researchers in several CSCW studies have investigated the use of status updates in collaborative contexts. For example, Tickertape (Fitzpatrick et al. 1998) is a lightweight awareness tool to facilitate social interaction between coworkers. The Notification Collage (Greenberg and Rounding 2001) is a full-fledged groupware system that incorporates the notion of activity indicators through a variety of media, such as digital photos and video. The Community Bar (McEwan and Greenberg 2005) extends the Notification Collage by supporting communities in fostering and maintaining ad hoc interaction.

Although there are some similar attributes between our structured activity updates prototype and other systems, there are also significant differences. Primarily, we are studying awareness of longer term activities as intentionally broadcasted by users in the context of fully distributed work, not social settings. For example, Smale and Greenberg (2005) studied status updates among instant messenger clients. Though their study context was not collaborative work, it is interesting to note that some of their communication categories of status updates are similar to ours. In their categorization scheme, "fun" is a type of status update that overlaps with our findings. Particular to our study context, Smale and Greenberg noted that people use status updates to broadcast information without involving chat conversation. This supports the feasibility of recruiting status updates for distributed collaborative work as a natural extrapolation from their original intended use in social networking media.

In their paper, Zhao and Rosson (2009) presented a complementary contribution to our work. They retrospectively investigated why people microblog and its potential impact on informal communication in work environments. Those authors suggested that microblogging may promote informal communication that complements other forms of interaction (e.g., IM, e-mail, phone, face-to-face).

Perhaps the work most related to ours is the study by Rittenbruch et al. (2007). In presenting their model of intentionally enriched awareness, Rittenbruch et al. reviewed and critiqued prior accounts of awareness as ignoring the ways that actors deliberately present themselves and their activity to collaborators. Rittenbruch et al. located intentionally enriched awareness as lying between mere perception of appearances and events and the public communication and explanation of one's activity.

Rittenbruch et al. (2007) focused on notifications of interest and availability for specific activities, such as playing a computer game or going for a coffee. They developed a tool to configure activity-specific polling and notification, enabling users not only to signal their own availability and interest, but to coordinate carrying out the activity with other like-minded users. This tool was used by users who were colocated. Rittenbruch et al. categorized the status notifications as activity indicators and activity inducements. Activity indicator notifications act as invitations to announce that certain activities are about to commence and that fellow users are invited to jointly participate. Activity inducement notifications are statements to convey that people are already engaged in activities.

12.4   Design of Activity Updates

The empirical study that we report in this chapter addresses our overall research question, which we restate as, how can activity updates be used in creative group work and with what consequences? We evaluated a prototype that supports status updates in the context of collaborative work by conveying activity awareness. The design of our prototype is based on the Farooq et al. (2007) study.

12.4.1   Activity Updates as Structured Templates

Farooq et al. (2007) conducted an empirical study of small groups collaborating on a long-term, creative task in a distributed setting. The researchers concluded that members in distributed groups lacked activity awareness that would otherwise be critical not just for successful but also creative collaboration. A design implication emerging from this study was the notion of structured activity updates, whereby team members can enter status updates using predefined activity-centric templates that relate to their current work. An example of a structured activity update would be to allow Sam to fill in the blanks in the following activity-centric template: "Sam is planning to _____." The activity updates are structured in the sense that each group member is presented with a template to update his/her status.

Whereas social networking sites allow users to enter any type of informational update, our proposed updates are activity-centric, that is, they relate to the collaborators' task at hand. By structuring the updates in predefined activity-centric templates, we believe users will be more inclined to think in terms of what they are doing with respect to their immediate task and less inclined to socially loaf and focus on nonwork-related self-disclosures. This is consistent with Malone et al. (1986) finding that semistructured messages can simplify designing systems that (a) help people formulate information they wish to communicate, (b) automatically select, classify, and prioritize information people receive, (c) automatically respond to certain kinds of information, and (d) suggest actions people may wish to take upon receiving certain other kinds of information.

A structured approach to activity updates has its associated trade-offs. For instance, entering activity updates may be too constraining and become an impediment in the users' workflow and creative process. While acknowledging this trade-off, our rationale for keeping the activity updates structured was specifically to make it convenient for users to quickly select from a predefined list of activity templates, rather than ruminating over the nature of their activities.

12.4.2   Types of Activity Updates

Given the rationale for making activity updates structured, the next step was to identify the types of activity updates. We followed an empirical approach to achieve this goal. Based on the data collected from Farooq et al.'s (2007) study, we analyzed the chat communication transcripts to identify the different types of activities that collaborators expressed and shared. The primary researcher in this paper read and reread each chat communication transcript to identify recurring themes related to activities that group members were engaged in consistently. These ten types of activities were then discussed and revalidated with two other researchers engaged in the project. Ten distinct types of activities were identified that would serve as templates for group members to update their status: planning, brainstorming, working, asking, suggesting, summarizing, dividing up work, proofreading, agreeing, disagreeing.

A trade-off to empirically identifying the types of activity updates was that the ten types conveyed activity self-disclosures at different levels of detail and generality. For instance, *working* is a relatively broad activity compared to, say, *proofreading*, which is a very specific activity. We decided not to tweak these empirically based activities (e.g., relabel the activities at a similar level of detail) since, as a secondary research question, it may be interesting to understand how users update activities that vary in granularity. Further, because the ten activity types emerged from a prior study, we took them as first-order, validated approximations to the kinds of activities group members would be engaged in.

12.4.3   Prototype

Based on our analysis, we designed and developed a prototype for structured activity updates (Fig. 12.1). The structured activity updates prototype can be divided into three sections.

In Section 1 (Update Your Activity), users can choose from among the ten activity templates and fill in the blanks to share their activities. The ten activity types were presented in random order. After a user fills in the blank and presses the Update Activity button, the activity updates are displayed in Section 2 of the prototype. In addition to the team's most recent updates, each user's prior activity update is also displayed. We thought that providing a user's previous activity would be useful in contextualizing the current activity.

Section 3 of the prototype provides a mechanism for users to comment on group members' activity updates. Our design rationale was that activity updates could instigate and provoke users to reflect on and possibly respond to group members' activities. By commenting on others' activities, group members could provide feedback and possibly engage in a discourse. For instance, in Figure 1 , Patti commented on Michael's activity update, which led Kristin to agree with Patti's comment.

12.5   Experimental Study

We conducted an empirical study to investigate the use and consequences of structured activity updates. The context was similar to that of Farooq et al.'s (2007) study, where small groups collaborated on a long-term, creative task in a distributed setting.

12.5.1   Research Questions

To answer our overall research question, we formulated specific questions in the following two categories: use of structured activity updates (USE) and consequences

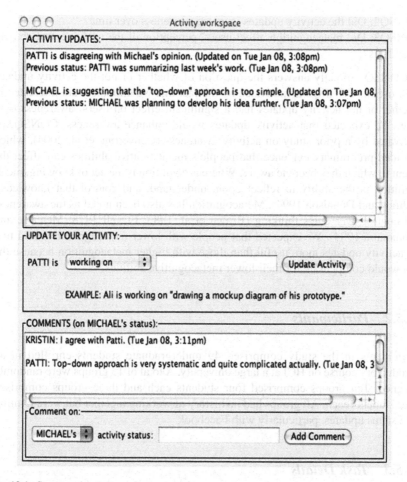

Fig. 12.1 Structured activity updates prototype

of structured activity updates (CONSQ). In the former category (USE), we present results that answer the following three questions:

USE1: How frequently were the different types of activity updates used?
USE2: For what purposes were the activity updates used?
USE3: For what purposes were the activity comments used?

USE1 helps to distill any significant differences in the usage among the ten types of structured activity updates. USE2 and USE3 help in understanding the different ways in which activity updates and comments were used.

In the CONSQ category, we present results that answer the following three questions:

CONSQ1: Did users find the activity updates useful?

CONSQ2: Did the activity updates increase awareness over time?

CONSQ3: Did metacognition affect users' perception of the usefulness of activity updates?

CONSQ1 directly answers the question of whether or not the activity updates were useful. CONSQ2 is motivated by the fact that we ultimately are interested in whether or not activity updates had a significant effect on users' awareness over time. We expected that activity updates would enhance awareness. CONSQ3 is motivated by a prior study on activity awareness (Convertino et al. 2004), which provided preliminary evidence that people's metacognitive abilities can affect the extent to which they become aware. Whereas cognition is the act of knowing, meta-cognition is the ability to reflect upon, understand, and control that knowledge (Schraw and Dennison 1994). Metacognition has also been noted as the awareness and control over one's thinking (Brown et al. 1983; Flavell 1978; Metcalfe and Shimamura 1994). We expected that people with lower metacognition would find the activity updates more useful than those with higher metacognition because the tool would compensate for their lower metacognitive abilities.

12.5.2 Participants

Participants in the study comprised 49 undergraduate students enrolled in an introductory course on HCI at a large university. A total of 13 groups were randomly assigned. Ten groups comprised four students each and three groups comprised three students each. All groups had no history of working together but were familiar with status updates, particularly with Facebook.

12.5.3 Task Details

Each group was instructed to write a formal report exploring design enhancements to Angel, which is the university's course management system that all students must use. The report was to cover functional requirements to enhance the design of Angel's user interface, accompanied with scenarios and storyboards that illustrate the functional requirements. This task was modeled on previously documented tasks (Ocker et al. 1996; Olson et al. 1993) used in distributed collaboration. The instructions emphasized that group members were allowed only to collaborate virtually using the designated shared workspace.

12.5.4 Tools

Group members worked on the collaborative task in a shared workspace called BRIDGE (Ganoe et al. 2003). BRIDGE supports both synchronous and asynchronous

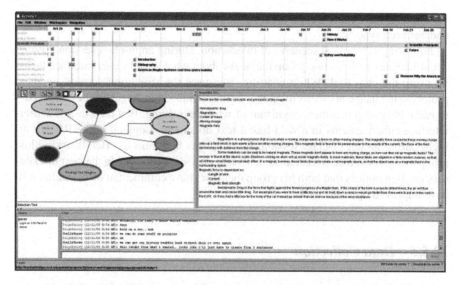

Fig. 12.2 BRIDGE: Basic Resources for Integrated Distributed Group Environments

collaboration. The BRIDGE Java-based client (Fig. 12.2) supports shared editing of documents through replicated objects. Replicated objects are objects that are retrieved by multiple collaborating sessions and whose state is kept synchronized on all clients and the server when any replica is changed. Examples of collaborative tools that were provided in BRIDGE included a persistent chat tool, wiki-based text documents, and drawing editor. The structured activity updates prototype was also provided.

12.5.5   Procedure

All students consented to participate in the experiment. Prior to the experiment, all participants were trained to use BRIDGE. Two in-class sessions, approximately 20 min each, were used for training. Training included using the structured activity updates.

The duration of the experiment was two and a half weeks. Participants collaborated synchronously and asynchronously. Five in-class sessions were used for synchronous collaboration, each lasting approximately 20 min. The participants also collaborated on-line in out-of-class sessions between each of the in-class synchronous sessions. Participants worked in a distributed fashion; the instructor ensured this for the in-class sessions. For out-of-class sessions, we analyzed the chat transcripts for any indicators of face-to-face collaboration (e.g., if one member referred to a face-to-face meeting); we did not find any such indicators.

Because we were interested in studying the use and consequences of the structured activity updates prototype, participants were reminded to update their activity status.

Participants were not compensated for or graded on using the structured activity updates prototype.

Following is a typical scenario of interaction. During an in-class session, "Ben" communicates with his two group members about what Angel's user interface lacks by using the chat tool. While chatting, Ben uses the structured activity updates prototype to change his status to "Ben is brainstorming how Angel can be enhanced" to make his group members cognizant of what he is doing. Ben records a few user interface enhancements in a wiki-based text document. Logging into BRIDGE at night during an out-of-class session, Ben changes his status to "Ben is asking his group members to read his enhancements and provide feedback." In the next in-class session, Ben notices that both his group members have commented on his status and have improved upon his ideas.

12.5.6   Data Collection

When the participants consented at the start of the experiment, we collected background data, such as demographic information. For metacognitive abilities, a previously validated 52-item scale (Kumar 1998) was used.

During the experiment, all interactions in BRIDGE were logged onto the server. For example, communication messages in the chat log and changes to shared data were recorded with time stamps. All activity updates and comments on activity updates were recorded over time.

After each of the five synchronous in-class sessions, participants answered the following statements on a Likert scale of 1 (*strongly disagree*) to 9 (*strongly agree*) related to their level of awareness (LA). These assessments have been previously validated by Convertino et al. (2004):

LA1: I know what my group members have worked on so far.

LA2: I know what my group members will work on next time.

LA3: I could tell what my group members were working on while we were collaborating synchronously.

LA4: I could tell what my group members were working on while we were collaborating asynchronously.

LA5: I found it difficult to tell what work my group members had done after being absent from my team workspace for at least a day.

LA4 and LA5 were not administered following the first synchronous in-class session since the groups had no history of working together on the task. LA2 was not administered after the fifth synchronous in-class session since it was the final group interaction.

After the experiment, participants were asked the following question in relation to the usefulness of the structured activity updates (SAU) prototype: Was the structured activity updates useful? If yes, how was it useful; provide an example.

12.6   Results

Below, we present our results in relation to the six specific research questions (USE and CONSQ) we posed earlier. Each result is followed by a brief discussion.

12.6.1   USE1: How Frequently Were the Different Types of Activity Updates Used?

For each of the 49 participants, we counted the frequency of using each of the 10 activity updates. We also categorized the frequency by synchronous (in-class sessions) and asynchronous (out-of-class sessions) modes of communication. Activity updates were used a total of 511 times, with nearly half split across synchronous (252) and asynchronous (259) updates. These frequencies are summarized in Table 12.1.

We ran a repeated-measures ANOVA to compute any statistically significant differences between the frequencies of the different types of activity updates. The analysis for unequal variances revealed that there were significant differences in the frequencies between the 10 types of activities, $F(1, 48) = 43.071$, $p < 0.001$, though this was a moderate effect size (eta-squared $= 0.473$). Pairwise comparisons for the top four activities revealed that the mean frequency of Working was significantly higher than all other types of activity updates; Planning was significantly different from all except Brainstorming; Brainstorming was significantly different than all except Planning and Proofreading; and Proofreading was significantly different than all except Brainstorming. A similar analysis could not be run against synchronous and asynchronous modes of communication due to sparse data. From Table 12.1, however, it is apparent that in the synchronous mode of communication, the three most frequently used activities in rank order were Working, Brainstorming, and Planning; in the asynchronous mode of communication, the three most frequently used activities were Working, Proofreading, and Planning.

Table 12.1 Frequency of activity updates

Activity type	Total	Sync	Async
Working	170	67	103
Planning	99	54	45
Brainstorming	76	62	14
Proofreading	62	9	53
Agreeing	39	26	13
Suggesting	23	15	8
Asking	20	7	13
Summarizing	10	4	6
Disagreeing	6	4	2
Dividing up work	6	4	2

Discussion. Working was the most frequently used activity update, for which there could be several reasons. Because the structured activity updates prototype was meant to provide activity awareness in the context of work, it seems natural that collaborators would be inclined to select the Working activity to make others aware of their work-related tasks. It is also possible that Working was the type of activity that collaborators most frequently engaged in. The most plausible explanation is that Working is a general adjective that seems to encompass some if not all of the other types of activities, which are more specific in their description. It seems to be the case that semantic granularity plays a vital role in selecting activity updates, a point that we return to toward the end of the chapter.

There was also a disparity in frequencies between the synchronous and asynchronous modes of communication. Two activities particularly stand out. Brainstorming was skewed toward the synchronous mode of communication while Proofreading was skewed toward the asynchronous mode of communication. This is not a surprise. Brainstorming is typically a synchronous activity and proofreading is typically an asynchronous activity.

12.6.2 USE2: For What Purposes Were the Activity Updates Used?

Based on the postexperiment questions (SAU1 and SAU2), we analyzed the responses using qualitative analysis. All 49 participants responded to both questions. We coded the 98 responses with the goal of identifying the different purposes that the activity updates were used for.

A total of 37 distinct phrases were identified as specifying a purpose and thus were open coded (Strauss and Corbin 1998). A total of nine codes emerged from the data that represent different purposes for how the activity updates were used. These purposes are listed in Table 12.2 with a coded phrase (user quote) that illustrates the purpose.

Discussion. The qualitative analysis reveals that activity updates were used in varying ways. Broadcasting one's activity and staying up to date of what one's group members are doing were expected ways of how activity updates would be used. This is similar to how status updates are used in social networking media. However, activity updates also seemed to be used for coordinating work and task dependencies, understanding group progress cumulatively over time, and tracking group member contributions.

12.6.3 USE3: For What Purposes Were the Activity Comments Used?

The actual comments that users expressed in the structured activity updates prototype were analyzed using qualitative analysis. We coded all of the comments with the goal of identifying the different purposes that they expressed.

Table 12.2 Different ways that activity updates were used

Purpose of activity	No. of phrases	Data example
Group member update	13	"Gave a little info on what each member was doing."
Status broadcast	8	"To show my team members what part of the project I was currently working on."
Asynchronous communication	4	"Allowed me to see what each member of my group was working on while I was not logged on."
Group progress	4	"Informed me about my group's progress."
Group member login	2	"I could see who logged in last."
Synchronous communication	2	"When different tasks were going on simultaneously, it was helpful to know who was doing what."
Task coordination	2	"I logged on to finish scenario 1, and saw what other work was necessary."
Member login frequency	1	"Showed how often group members were logging in and making additions."
Timeline	1	"It was helpful as a timeline."

Table 12.3 Different ways that activity comments were used

Purpose of comment	No. of groups	No. of phrases
Feedback	13	292
Coordination	13	55
Encouragement	12	41
Elaboration	11	28
Discourse	9	21
Reminder	7	16
Fun	5	19
Metamorphosis	2	5

We open coded the comments at the group level of analysis for each of the 13 groups so as to understand any dependencies among group members that the comments were referring to.

A total of eight codes emerged from the data that represent different purposes for how the comments were used. These purposes are listed in Table 12.3, accompanied with the following information: the number of groups (No. of groups) that incorporated the particular purpose and the number of phrases (No. of phrases) that were coded.

Feedback was the most frequent purpose for a comment where participants provided feedback to group members, such as, "*Nice job of organizing the list.*" The comments were also heavily used by all groups to coordinate work (e.g., "*We will review each other's sections on Wed.*"), although we distinguish this from Elaboration, which refers to an explication or enhancement of an idea (e.g., "*We should come up with a few more asynchronous ideas!*").

Twelve of the 13 groups moderately used the comments to encourage and support each other (e.g., "*Keep up the good work*"). In nine groups, we noticed that the comments represented a communication discourse similar to a conversation that could have occurred using the chat tool. For example, Greg commented on Katie's status: *"Can you think of any more functional requirements?"*; a few hours later, Ed also commented on Katie's status by following up on Greg's message: *"I'm also trying to figure out some more functional requirements."*

A small number of comments were used to remind group members of deadlines or responsibilities (e.g., *"Make sure to add your pros and cons"*). A small number of comments were also used for nonwork or "fun" purposes (e.g., *"I also like surfing"*) and to reflect on social dynamics during the metamorphosis stage of concluding group work (e.g., *"I have enjoyed working with you and the other group members on this project"*).

Discussion. The qualitative analysis reveals that comments were used in varying ways to support unplanned, brief, and ad hoc communication. The comment feature in the structured activity updates prototype was used not only for the obvious purpose of providing feedback to group members but also served as a secondary mechanism or communication backchannel (Ackerman 2000) to allow group members to coordinate work, encourage and remind each other, and occasionally discuss nonwork topics. Such casual interactions keep individuals informed about each other in social and professional contexts, reinforce social bonds, and make the transition to tightly coupled collaboration easier (Whittaker et al. 1994).

12.6.4   CONSQ1: Did Users Find the Activity Updates Useful?

In the postexperiment question (SAU1), we asked participants whether or not they found the structured activity updates prototype useful. Of the 49 participants, 22 (45%) found the prototype useful, 9 (18%) found it somewhat useful, and 18 (37%) did not find the prototype useful.

Some of the participants expanded on why the structured activity updates prototype was not useful. They expressed that the chat communication tool in BRIDGE served the purpose that was intended by the structured activity updates prototype. Among such responses were the following typical user quotes: *"We communicated what we were doing through the chat function"*; *"This could have automatically been extracted from a chat and displayed"*; *"I could just go into the chat logs and find out the specific task of each person."*

Discussion. There were mixed feelings toward the usefulness of the structured activity updates prototype. Our prior research question (USE2) provides strong evidence that participants used the prototype in varying ways. Directly asking participants about the usefulness of the prototype did not solicit an overwhelming positive response. This may be attributed to the fact that the structured activity updates prototype was not integrated with the chat communication tool. Hence, the design required collaborators to expend extra effort to switch between the structured activity updates prototype and the chat communication tool in order to make effective use of both. Many participants who did not find the prototype useful acknowledged this design shortcoming.

12.6.5   CONSQ2: Did the Activity Updates Increase Awareness Over Time?

We ran a repeated-measures ANOVA to compute any statistically significant differences on each of the five awareness questions (LA1-LA5) over time. There was increased awareness over time for LA2 over the final four in-class sessions: $F(1, 44) = 13.71$, $p < .001$ (eta-squared $= 0.238$). There were no significant differences in the mean rating for LA1, LA3, LA4, or LA5 over time.

Discussion. The result for LA2 implies that the structured activity updates informed group members what their collaborators will work on in the future. This seems to make sense since, in highly interdependent and collaborative tasks, group members require a greater amount of planning to understand what everyone is going to do. LA1, LA3, LA4, and LA5 dealt with understanding what group members already did. The persistent BRIDGE workspace seemed to have provided enough awareness of such an understanding. However, the workspace cannot provide an understanding of what collaborators are going to do next unless such an understanding is externalized by the group members themselves. Such was the case as group members used the structured activity updates to make their collaborators cognizant of what they are going to do.

12.6.6   CONSQ3: Did Metacognition Affect Users' Perception of the Usefulness of Activity Updates?

We conducted a reliability analysis for the 49 responses to the 52-item metacognition questionnaire. The analysis revealed a high value of reliability (Cronbach's alpha $= 0.984$). We then separated the 49 participants into two categories based on their responses of whether they found the structured activity updates prototype useful or not. Thus, we had 31 participants in the "useful" category and 18 participants in the "not useful" category.

We ran a two-sample t-test between the two categories of usefulness (useful, not useful) with metacognition as the dependent variable. The analysis for equal variances revealed no statistically significant difference: $t(47) = -1.53$, $p = 0.133$.

The 52 items in the metacognition questionnaire were then loaded on two factors based on Kumar (1998): metacognitive regulation and metacognitive knowledge. Metacognitive regulation denotes planning, information management, monitoring, debugging, and evaluation. Metacognitive knowledge denotes declarative, procedural, and conditional knowledge. The above two-sample t-test for metacognitive regulation as the dependent variable revealed no statistically significant difference: $t(47) = -0.875$, $p = 0.386$. The same two-sample t-test for metacognitive knowledge as the dependent variable revealed a statistically significant difference: $t(47) = -2.137$, $p < 0.05$. The mean metacognitive knowledge rating for participants who found the structured activity updates prototype useful ($M = 58.76$) was significantly higher than the participants who did not find the prototype useful ($M = 53.92$).

Discussion. The result that participants with higher metacognitive knowledge found the structured activity updates prototype more useful than those with lower metacognitive knowledge seems counterintuitive. One would expect that the prototype would compensate for lower levels of metacognition and thus be more useful to such participants.

According to Flavell (1979), metacognitive knowledge refers to acquired knowledge about cognitive processes, knowledge that can be used to control cognitive processes, as well as knowledge of one's own learning processes. For example, a person may be aware that study session efforts will be more productive in the early morning when everyone is asleep rather than evening when there are many distractions. In this sense, participants with higher levels of metacognitive knowledge can be opportunistic in identifying and leveraging strategies that can help them monitor their progress. In such cases, participants are using their conditional knowledge about when and where it is appropriate to use strategies or, in our case, awareness tools, to enhance their collaborative learning experience. Such an explanation would lend support for our result.

On the other hand, metacognitive regulation implies checking the outcomes of incorporating strategies and ensuring that cognitive goals have been met. In this sense, our prototype did not explicitly support a cognitive goal or outcome but rather the process of reaching a particular goal or outcome. The result that there was no significant difference in the levels of metacognitive regulation would be corroborated by such an explanation.

12.7 Implications for Activity Awareness

In this chapter, we started by posing an exploratory research question: How can activity updates be used in collaborative work and with what consequences? Our study suggests that activity updates—a way of providing activity awareness—can be used for several purposes, increasing awareness of what collaborators will do next over time. Further, activity comments seemed to provide an effective communication backchannel to support ephemeral and infrequent collaboration that is contextually dependent on the activity updates. The results also suggest that users with higher levels of metacognitive knowledge perceive activity updates as more useful than users with lower levels of metacognitive knowledge. In this section, we discuss implications of our results by reflecting on two design strategies for providing activity awareness.

12.7.1 Activity Awareness Can Support Lightweight, Informal Self-Disclosures Through Communication Backchannels

Though the participants were provided with a formal, primary communication channel (chat), the majority of them found activity updates and comments useful during their collaboration. We argue that communication backchannels that allow the expression of lightweight, informal self-disclosures in work contexts can be an effective way to increase activity awareness, particularly to apprise each other of their future cognition.

From previous work in CSCW in work contexts, we know that it is important to provide a communication backchannel. Our study characterizes one type of communication that this backchannel should support, namely, lighthearted and casual meta-activity information. Typical communication backchannels usually demand social responsiveness. For instance, during video conferencing, chat may be used as a backchannel to complement verbal communication. In such a scenario, group members are expected to oblige chat entries and respond in kind. On the other hand, activity updates are an example of an informal communication mechanism, where group members are merely expressing their thoughts on a task that may or may not warrant further explication or response. In this way, activity updates are a lightweight mechanism to express informal activity-related information that has a formal bearing on the group's primary task. Our results suggest that activity updates did indeed provide activity awareness through lightweight, informal self-disclosures, as they were primarily used to update group members of one's progress. Further, comments provided an additional layer of backchannel communication to express feedback on other's work progress over time.

Our design strategy—the provision of activity awareness through lightweight, informal self-disclosures to enrich formal communication mechanisms such as chat—strengthens prior results. In Rittenbruch et al.'s (2007) study, it was discovered that notification and communication are interleaved processes. Our study extrapolates Rittenbruch et al.'s result by implying that activity updates are appropriate to express through notification mechanisms.

The different purposes for which the activity updates were used in our study are much broader and deeper than the two general categorizations of activity indicators or activity notifications as identified by Rittenbruch et al. (2007). For example, we identified nine different ways of how activity updates were used. Because our prototype incorporated the notion of structured activity updates using predefined templates, we were able to explore details of how users coordinated specific types of activities. Further, the activity comments feature was encouraging to the effect of acting as a communication backchannel in distributed work contexts. Our study also raises deeper, theoretical issues of how awareness is related to people's metacognitive abilities, a connection that has not been studied in the above-mentioned literature.

12.7.2   Activity Awareness Can Engage Users at a Metacognitive Level

The dominant approach in CSCW has been to conceptualize awareness mechanisms as engaging users at a cognitive level by making them aware of system-based, event-driven information. For example, knowing where a collaborator's mouse is pointing can indeed facilitate the immediate coordination of manipulating shared artifacts.

Such awareness mechanisms rely on detecting and providing short-term informational states for low-level tasks and subtasks that facilitates users' immediate cognitive goals. Although the provision of such system-based, event-driven information is critical, it is limited to the extent of what people need to, and can be, aware of. Indeed, awareness mechanisms cannot detect and convey people's intentions. In his critique of awareness being construed as a passive process (Dourish 1997), Schmidt (2002) said that passive awareness is restrictive and it prevents users from engaging in practices to align and integrate their distributed but interdependent activities. Rittenbruch et al. (2007) capitalized on this notion to argue for a more intentionally enriched awareness mechanism where users can explicitly characterize and share their own activities.

In this sense, we argue that activity awareness mechanisms should engage users metacognitively. Activity awareness mechanisms should seek to help users regulate their cognition and think explicitly about their design rationale with respect to learning and work goals. By explicitly characterizing and sharing their activity intentions and rationale, users can engage in and think about deeper work-related interactions such as coordinating responsibilities, managing dependencies, resolving conflicts, and so forth. This allows collaborators to be cognizant of each other at the level of activities, a higher-order function of shorter and immediate tasks and subtasks that are merely system-based, event-driven nuggets of information. This design strategy is consistent with our result that, in general, metacognition plays a role in determining the usefulness of awareness mechanisms. Specifically, people with higher metacognitive knowledge seem to be more strongly oriented toward and are interested in being aware of their collaborators' activity. It follows from this result that capitalizing on and effectively using activity awareness mechanisms may also be a metacognitive strategy. This suggests that, in general, awareness mechanisms should not be limited just to system-based, event-driven information of what is currently going on in a shared workspace, but also that awareness should be about providing cognizance of activities that need to be internalized and monitored over time such that users are prompted to strategically regulate their cognition and manage their knowledge in order to better achieve their overall goals collaboratively.

12.8 Discussion and Future Work

As discussed in our results, it is likely that the semantic granularity of the activity types matters. The variability in use of the ten activity types provides some evidence of this. Many issues are raised due to our design choice. For example, did all participants take the ten activity types to mean the same thing? How does the frequency of engaging in a specific activity affect the selection of different activity types? Perhaps most importantly, can circumstances be identified where more general activity types are preferred over more specific activity types, and vice versa? Further studies are required to address these issues comprehensively.

Another important question raised by our study is the design choice of structuring the activity updates. Though participants were not asked to comment on this issue, it seems important to reflect on the level of structure imposed by the predefined activity templates. A system that resembles our design choice of structuring the activity updates is the Coordinator (Winograd and Flores 1986), a large-scale electronic communication system that enlists participants in a coding procedure by using predefined speech acts aimed at making implicit intent explicit. The premise of this procedure was that explicitly identified speech acts are clear, unambiguous, and preferred, because people tend to be vague regarding their own intent and that of others (Suchman 1994). Though the Coordinator was largely cited as a failure, it remains to be empirically determined if structured activity updates are preferred over unstructured activity updates and under what circumstances.

Another interesting area to explore is the relation between activity updates and the design artifact and process. Our study's scope did not include whether or not activity updates helped interpret the design rationale that shaped the artifact. Essentially, such an exploration could help answer whether activity updates change the design process or quality of the outcome. More interestingly, the relation between metacognition and design rationale could be understood. If one adopts the perspective that design rationale is essentially metacognition about design, subsequent studies can be designed to assess the effects of metacognitive processes on design outcomes.

Our result that activity updates were used in a variety of ways is encouraging in further exploring the generative nature of the predefined activity types. We provided ten activity types, or speech acts (as in the Coordinator). Investigating a broader range of speech acts that continually emerge from the ground up is a research issue worthy of exploration. Some participants who did not find the activity updates useful strongly suggested that these be identified from their chat entries. For example, collaborative filtering mechanisms can be used to extract activity updates automatically that can then be fine-tuned by users. Unlike our design choice, if the activity types are not limited and are allowed to grow over time, these activity types can be suggested to users by recommender systems. Our result that some activity types are used differently during synchronous versus asynchronous communication can be extrapolated to recommend certain activity types, depending on the type of communication users are engaged in. Other attributes in addition to communication type, such as duration of a work session (e.g., short spurt vs. extended period) or the stage at which a group is operating (e.g., divergent vs. convergent thinking), can be also mined to recommend appropriate activity updates.

One limitation of our study was that the participants were undergraduate students, although such a shortcoming is to be expected in controlled settings that pool a large number of experimental subjects. We plan to conduct a field study where participants of a distributed research group are collaborating on a project over several weeks. Such a study would allow us to investigate our results further in a naturalistic setting.

Our general empirical finding that metacognitive abilities affect perceived usefulness of awareness mechanisms should be investigated further. Our finding is based on one study and is limited to one factor of metacognition (metacognitive knowledge). We plan to study how and when metacognition, and both factors of metacognitive regulation and metacognitive knowledge, have an effect on awareness and whether this effect can be controlled. We encourage designers and researchers interested in supporting awareness to incorporate metacognition as a variable in their user studies.

References

Ackerman, M. S. (2000). The intellectual challenge of CSCW: The gap between social requirements and technical feasibility. *Human Computer Interaction, 15*, 179–203.

Brown, A. L., Bransford, J. D., Ferrara, R. A., & Campione, J. C. (1983). Learning, remembering, and understanding. In J. H. Flavell & E. M. Markman (Eds.), *Handbook of child psychology: Vol. 3. Cognitive development* (pp. 77–166). Somerset, NJ: Wiley.

Carroll, J. M., Neale, D. C., Isenhour, P. L., Rosson, M. B., & McCrickard, D. S. (2003). Notification and awareness: Synchronizing task-oriented collaborative activity. *International Journal of Human-Computer Systems, 58*, 605–632.

Carroll, J. M., Rosson, M. B., Convertino, G., & Ganoe, C. H. (2006). Awareness and teamwork in computer-supported collaborations. *Interacting with Computers, 18*, 21–46.

Convertino, G., Neale, D. C., Hobby, L., Carroll, J. M., & Rosson, M. B. (2004). A laboratory method for studying activity awareness. In *Proceedings of NordiCHI* (pp. 313–322). New York: ACM Press.

Dourish, P. (1997, March). Extending awareness beyond synchronous collaboration. Paper presented at the CHI'97 Workshop on Awareness in Collaborative Systems, Atlanta, Georgia, USA. Retrieved July 25, 2011, from http://www.dourish.com/publications/chi97-awareness.html

Erickson, T., & Kellogg, W. (1999). Social translucence: An approach to designing systems that support social processes. *ACM Transactions on Computer-Human Interaction, 7*, 59–83.

Farooq, U., Carroll, J. M., & Ganoe, C. H. (2007). Supporting creativity with awareness in distributed collaboration. In *Proceedings of the international SIGGROUP conference on supporting group work* (pp. 31–40). New York: ACM Press.

Fitzpatrick, G., Parsowith, S., Segall, B., & Kaplan, S. (1998). Tickertape: Awareness in a single line. In *Proceedings of CHI* (pp. 281–282). New York: ACM Press.

Flavell, J. H. (1978). Metacognitive development. In J. M. Scandura & C. J. Brainard (Eds.), *Structural process theories of complex human behavior* (p. 245). Alphen aan den Rijn: Sijthoff and Noordhoff.

Flavell, J. H. (1979). Metacognition and cognitive monitoring: A new area of cognitive-developmental inquiry. *American Psychologist, 34*, 906–911.

Ganoe, C. H., Somervell, J. P., Neale, D. C., Isenhour, P. L., Carroll, J. M., Rosson, M. B., & McCrickard, D. S. (2003). Classroom BRIDGE: Using collaborative public and desktop timelines to support activity awareness. In *Proceedings of UIST* (pp. 21–30). New York: ACM Press.

Greenberg, S., & Rounding, M. (2001). The notification collage: Posting information to public and personal displays. In *Proceedings of CHI* (pp. 514–521). New York: ACM Press.

Gutwin, C., Greenberg, S., & Roseman, M. (1996). Workspace awareness support with radar views. In *Proceedings of CHI* (pp. 210–211). New York: ACM Press.

Kumar, A. E. (1998). *The influence of metacognition on managerial hiring decision making: Implications for management development.* Unpublished doctoral dissertation, Virginia Polytechnic Institute and State University, USA. Retrieved August 15, 2011, from http://scholar.lib.vt.edu/theses/available/etd-62698122255/unrestricted/Diss72698.pdf

Malone, T. W., Grant, K. R., Lai, K., Rao, R., & Rosenblitt, D. (1986). Semi-structured messages are surprisingly useful for computer-supported coordination. In *Proceedings of CSCW* (pp. 102–114). New York: ACM Press.

McEwan, G., & Greenberg, S. (2005). Supporting social worlds with the community bar. In *Proceedings of the international SIGGROUP conference on supporting group work* (pp. 21–31). New York: ACM Press.

Metcalfe, J., & Shimamura, A. P. (Eds.). (1994). *Metacognition*. Cambridge, MA: The MIT Press.

Ocker, R., Hiltz, S. R., Turoff, M., & Fjermestad, J. (1996). The effects of distributed group support and process structuring on software requirements development teams: Results on creativity and quality. *Journal of Management Information Systems, 12*(3), 127–153.

Olson, J. S., Olson, G. M., Storrosten, M., & Carter, M. (1993). Groupwork close up: A comparison of the group design process with and without a simple group editor. *ACM Transactions on Office Information Systems, 11*, 321–348.

Rittenbruch, M., Viller, S., & Mansfield, T. (2007). Announcing activity: Design and evaluation of an intentionally enriched awareness service. *Human Computer Interaction, 22*, 137–171.

Schmidt, K. (2002). The problem with "awareness". *Computer Supported Cooperative Work, 11*, 285–298.

Schraw, D., & Dennison, R. S. (1994). Assessing metacognitive awareness. *Contemporary Educational Psychology, 19*, 460–475.

Smale, S., & Greenberg, S. (2005). Broadcasting information via display names in instant messaging. In *Proceedings of the international SIGGROUP conference on supporting group work* (pp. 89–98). New York: ACM Press.

Strauss, A., & Corbin, J. (1998). *Basics of qualitative research: Techniques and procedures for developing grounded theory*. Thousand Oaks: Sage.

Suchman, L. (1994). Do categories have politics? The language/action perspective reconsidered. *Computer Supported Cooperative Work, 2*, 177–190.

Whittaker, S., Frolich, D., & Daly-Jones, O. (1994). Informal workplace communication: What is it like and how might we support it? In *Proceedings of CSCW* (pp. 131–138). New York: ACM Press.

Winograd, T., & Flores, F. (1986). *Understanding computers and cognition: A new foundation for design*. Norwood: Ablex Publishing Corporation.

Zhao, D., & Rosson, M. B. (2009). How and why people Twitter: The role that micro-blogging plays in informal communication at work. In *Proceedings of the international SIGGROUP conference on supporting group work* (pp. 243–252). New York: ACM Press.

Chapter 13
Studying Humans to Inform Interactive Narrative Technology

Brian Magerko

Abstract This chapter describes the rationale behind studying humans in collaborative story domains to better inform interactive narrative technology practices. It describes two exemplar projects, the study of tabletop gamemasters and improvisational actors. It discusses how these projects point to a potential future direction of interactive narrative technology research.

Keywords Interactive narrative • Improvisation • Games • Cognition.

13.1 Introduction

The field of *interactive narrative*, a subset of AI-based research in the field of *computational creativity*, focuses on building technological solutions to the creation of computer-mediated narrative-based experiences that put users in a meaningful role in a story. Interactive narrative experiences can be viewed as ones that have a heavy technological component (e.g. the AI that controls non-player characters) and a creative/aesthetic one (i.e. the narrative that a user experiences and the impact that experience has on the user). A typical goal of an interactive narrative technology (INT) (e.g. an AI-based approach to creating interactive characters, story direction in a virtual world, or story generation) is to provide the user a high level of *agency* (i.e. they have many possible choices that have meaningful consequences on the narrative progression and content). For example, if the user is at a wedding in a virtual experience, they may show a lot of interest in a particular guest at the wedding,

B. Magerko (✉)
Digital Media Program, School of Literature, Communication and Culture,
Georgia Institute of Technology, Technology Square Research
Bldg. #319, 85 Fifth Street, NW, Atlanta, GA 30308-1030, USA
e-mail: magerko@gatech.edu

J.M. Carroll (ed.), *Creativity and Rationale: Enhancing Human
Experience by Design*, Human–Computer Interaction Series,
DOI 10.1007/978-1-4471-4111-2_13, © Springer-Verlag London 2013

which could lead to a romance story, or find a suspicious looking gift, leading to a mystery story if they follow through with an investigation of where the gift came from. This kind of experience tends to focus on (a) the generation of story content as the user makes choices in the world, (b) the real-time selection of story content from a set of pre-authored story snippets, or (c) a combination of both.

The field has converged on several algorithmic approaches to enabling user agency, such as the "drama manager" agent that observes events in the story world and attempts to affect non-player character behaviors to drive the story a certain way in response or planning agents that can generate and re-edit story plots based on a set of pre-authored, abstract story events (i.e. plot operators) and the events unfolding in the story world. Regardless of the approach being used, the typical design process of creating an interactive narrative experience involves working from either a familiar technology (**engineering centric**) (i.e. using the medium as a means of exploring a computational approach, like for a dissertation) or approach (i.e. formalisms the field or the researcher has used in the past in order to incrementally add on to that approach or apply it in a new way) or, conversely, by reverse engineering a desired experience and deriving the technologies needed to have the experience happen (**experience centric**). There are inherent biases introduced in either of these approaches (e.g. engineering-centric approaches are limited by the capabilities of the technology of interest and design-centric approaches are limited by the ability of the designer to map an experience to a formal system). These biases become a problem when the technology is too limiting or the experience is not well enough understood to reverse engineer. This chapter focuses on the second issue here, when reverse engineering an interactive narrative experience is not possible because the experience is simply not understood formally enough.

There are a handful of human performance/game forms that are idyllic exemplars of real world interactive narrative experiences. Live action roleplay (LARPing) is an immersive experience where participants take on a character to act out for several hours to several days at a time. Participant's characters are typically decided on beforehand (either by self-selection or assignment from the organizers) and represent members of an alternate reality that the participants pretend to be in. Costuming is often a major part of participating in the story world, which is typically a real physical space that is co-opted as pretend space. The narrative aspects of a LARP can be free flowing and emergent or orchestrated by a central storyteller, whose role is a somewhat less powerful version of a gamemaster (described below). Tabletop roleplay is a similar experience, though instead of playing a character in a co-opted physical space, players control small figurines on a tabletop or mentally guided through a pretend space verbally by a gamemaster (GM). A GM typically has a story experience already in mind for the players of the game and has the responsibility of guiding them through that experience. Similar to the approaches in INTs described earlier, GMs can (a) generate story content on the fly, (b) guide players through predetermined content, or (c) do a mixture of both (which seems to be most common). Improvisational theatre (improv) is a performance field that has one major difference compared to these other real world interactive narrative domains. Improv does not typically have a coordinating agent, like a gamemaster, that is part of improvised scenes. Some kinds of improv "games" (i.e. rule sets that dictate how scenes can be created) do allow an outside actor (called the "game host") to intervene in scenes (e.g. ringing a bell that makes whoever spoke last replace the last line they said with something better/funnier/more suitable/wittier/etc.), but they rarely have direct control over story content like a gamemaster does. Improv theatre is a fairly consistent example of what is called emergent storytelling or a "strong autonomy" approach to interactive narrative, where the behaviors of the actors in the scene dictate how the story unfolds (as opposed to "weak autonomy" approaches that rely on a centralized, behind-the-scenes coordinating agent).

Surface analyses of real world interactive narrative domains have been used to inform the construction of INTs. A primary example is the use of "drama managers" in INTs, a common technological practice that is a direct metaphor to gamemasters from tabletop roleplay. Well-known concepts like "status" from improvisational theatre (i.e. the relative high/medium/low social status of a character in a scene) or the reasoning about creating imaginary objects on stage have been used as a primary mechanism in defining agent behaviors in systems (Hayes-Roth and Van Gent 1996; Perlin and Goldberg 1996; Swartjes et al. 2008).

The problem with approaches that are based on canonical improv techniques, naïve observation of improv acting, or how improvisers are taught is that they rely heavily on a surface understanding of a domain that little is understood about formally. The above domains rely heavily on human creativity and narrative reasoning as the main drives for creating a compelling experience – and we do not necessarily understand very well what knowledge and processes are employed in the related creative acts. This lack of understanding of human creativity makes it difficult to build interactive narrative experiences that provide anything similar to what we can create as humans. For example, drama managers work on a functional level like (some) gamemasters do (i.e. taking pre-written story content and player actions as an input and making decisions about the DM-controlled agents in the story world), but that does not mean that they are particularly good DMs. When drama managers became common in interactive narrative in the early 2000s, designers had no formal understanding of what features of players actions were important to attend to, what kinds of actions DMs execute in the world, or what strategies DMs use to inter-weave pre-written story content with completely unfettered player actions. Building technologies that are based on one of these real world exemplars requires a clear, formal understanding of the exemplar so a formal model can be built.

The past several years has shown an increase in the study of real world exemplars for informing INT design and development. Riedl employed improvisational actors as the means of evaluating two different major approaches in interactive narrative systems: weak vs. strong autonomous agents (Riedl 2010). He found by studying this idealized form of interactive narrative that neither approach had a clear advantage in terms of narrative coherence or character believability. Davis et al. (2011) employed a grounded theory approach to analyzing the distributed creative process of machinimators (digital filmmakers who create *machinima*). The end goal of this work is not to create autonomous filmmakers, but intelligent support tools that can intelligently assist in the creation of machinima.

This chapter intends to serve as a call for stronger focus in the field of intelligent narrative technologies on the study of human creativity to better inform the creation of INTs. The field in general can be pushed farther and deeper in building computationally creative systems if we have a better understanding of human creative systems – that, without that better understanding, we are less likely to be aware of the knowledge and processes needed to create systems that yield similar analogues. The kinds of experiences INT researchers want to create have direct analogues in the real world (e.g. tabletop roleplaying, LARPing, experimental theatre, improvisational dance and theatre, etc.); having a rationale for studying these domains and relating the findings to INT practices seems crucial for the longevity of the field. This chapter provides an example of two projects stemming from the work done at Georgia Tech's ADAM Lab that deal with human creative systems: the study of gamemasters and improvisational actors to better inform the design of two common INT approaches, drama managers and synthetic characters.

13.2 Studying Gamemasters

The main role of a drama manager for an interactive narrative system is to mediate between (a) pre-defined/generated story elements, (b) synthetic character behaviors, and (c) the choices a user is making in the story world. A drama manger's typical actions may include: influencing the user's choices to stay within the bounds of the pre-authored content (called the *story space*), changing the effects of executed user actions so the results of actions do not lead the experience outside of the story space, altering the pre-authored content or generate new content to alter the story space to match the effects of user actions, and/or selecting what content should be experienced next (see Roberts and Isbell (2008) for a current overview of the field).

Given the references listed above, we can obviously build technologies to do these things; drama managers have been a staple approach to INTs since the 1990s. However, I would argue that we have not done it exceptionally *well* to date – my own work included (e.g. Magerko 2007); the way we think about building these technologies needs to be reflected on. Drama managers may do the sensible things for mediating stories, but they do not necessarily have the knowledge to do them with the same degree of proficiency, flexibility, and creativity that humans can. We attempted to address this issue by studying the tacit knowledge employed by human gamemasters (GMs) in tabletop roleplaying games to better inform the strategies employed by their computational analogues (Flowers et al. 2006).

There is a myriad of techniques that one could use to elicit knowledge during a task: interviews, observational study, verbal protocol collection (aka "think aloud" collection), controlled experimental study (e.g. changing the conditions of a game to see how GMs behaved differently to support some hypothesis), etc. In our 2006 study of human gamemasters, we opted for a grounded theory approach that combines a retrospective protocol collection with observation (Flowers et al. 2006).

Grounded theory analysis is an important tool for studying human domains like tabletop roleplaying because it encourages a data-driven approach to understanding your data rather than having the analysis being driven by a hypothesis. The existence of a hypothesis indicates some specific view a researcher has about how the world works and is looking to support that view through empirical study. However, the rationale for studying human story creators in the first place is that we do not always have a view that is detailed enough to formally represent (or test!). A data-driven approach that allows us to find meaning from the data collected from people and provides the ability to reach well-supported conclusions without any *a priori* viewpoints to prove.

We opted for the use of retrospective protocol collection for collecting human data (i.e. exposing participants to video or audio recordings of the gaming session and prompting them to comment as it plays) in lieu of interview-only techniques (too much happens in a game session to rely on post hoc reflection without prompting from a recording), observation (would not provide data on why GMs make certain decisions or avoid others), or think aloud protocols (impossible to do for a domain where the participant is actively speaking aloud to others). A retrospective protocol collection provides data that is susceptible to forgetting and fabrication, but does at least provide responses that are cued from recordings (Russo et al. 1989). In other words, jogging the participant's memory after a long gaming session is better than relying purely on what they recall, but they may make things up.

We applied a combination of retrospective protocol collection and grounded data analysis to the study of four different GMs playing their game of choice that could be completed in several hours of gaming. As there are many different kinds of games within the space of tabletop roleplay, the games chosen tended to be more content-heavy as opposed to improvisational in nature. This allowed us to study gamemaster techniques in situations that were most akin to current INT approaches; there is a centralized story manager who has pre-determined content to foster other participants through. Two picked *Dungeons and Dragons v3.5*, one picked a horror-themed game called *Chill*, and another picked a *Star Wars*-based game. The sessions were videotaped, paying special attention to the GM but incorporating all of the players and their actions in the footage. Game sessions typically lasted around 4 h with one of the Dungeons and Dragons sessions lasting approximately 6 h. No more than a day after the game, the GM was brought in for a protocol collection. The GM and researcher reviewed the footage of the game session, and specific questions were asked about moments in the game, what the GM was thinking, and about the way he or she was incorporating the actions of the players.

After the protocol collection, paraphrased transcriptions from the audio interviews were made. The transcriptions were coded, marking what techniques the GM was using at given times. The techniques were matched with techniques mentioned in literature on being a GM. Unexpected techniques were also marked and documented. If the reason for player action or gamemaster intervention was unclear from the audio interview, the tape was matched with the original live game footage for accuracy.

Any time a GM used a particular guiding technique, the technique was marked and coded into one of several categories.

Our study revealed two main axes that describe the space of gamemaster actions with in a tabletop roleplaying session: in-game (i.e. within the context of the game world) vs. meta-game (i.e. outside of the context of the game world) actions and attractors (i.e. enticing a player to do something) vs. detractors (i.e. discouraging a player from a particular action). Our findings cover in-game/meta-game attractors/detractors, plus other in-game and meta-game techniques that do not fit well into the attractor/detractor spectrum. In-game attractors of note could be categorized as:

- *instruction*: have an NPC in the game tell the characters what they should be doing or give them a task. One GM reported that he used an NPC to "(hire the party) to go look at this keep."
- *inverse instruction*: employing reverse psychology to tempt players with what they "cannot possibly do." One GM stated to the players, "The ritual has already begun. … You can do nothing about it."
- *focus*: providing more detail about something to encourage users to approach/examine/interact with it.
- *character hooks*: GMs often use the motivations of characters as the means for having something occur, like having an NPC being mugged in front of a player who's character emphasizes heroism and morality.
- *spontaneous conflict*: spontaneous monsters or mysteries may be forced on the character to give them the opportunity to react.

For a complete description of our findings, see Flowers et al. (2006).

We observed a variety of story mediation techniques that provided excellent insight into the decision making process of GMs. Several techniques emerged that had not been previously documented or considered by us. A major finding of the study was the importance of meta-game techniques, which proved to be as important as in-game techniques for mediating tabletop game experiences. The clear result of this work in terms of its relevance to INT research was a taxonomy of attractor/detractor strategies that could be directly employed in drama manager systems for affecting player behavior. While our work has moved away from building drama managers for the time being, others have recently referred to this study when formulating the gamemaster paradigm (Peinado and Gervás 2007).

While our study of gamemasters uncovered different strategies that could populate the actions of a drama manager agent, the study did not point to major processes that were previously not known of or tried in drama management. We did not uncover specifically *why* a particular strategy is picked over another (this sort of knowledge is difficult to uncover reliably using retrospective protocols), simply the existence of strategies. Part of the issue was the bias introduced into the study; story management strategies were what we were looking for, so that is what we found. This work also did not result in computational models of our findings, so the relationship between data and technology design is only theoretical. Our next project, the empirical study of improvisational actors and the design of technology built on those empirical findings, yielded a more robust approach to INT design and development with a firm grounding in empiricism.

13.3   Studying Improvisers

While our study of human gamemasters was focused on a specific kind of knowledge needed to inform the design of drama managers, the study of human improvisers can be a much broader influence on the construction of a different interactive narrative technology: synthetic characters. Improvisational theatre (also known as *improv*) is a highly group creative domain that has been the inspiration for multiple INT-related projects, such as the works involving models of status (i.e. the relative social strength/ weakness of characters in a scene) by Hayes-Roth, Herger, and Perlin (Hayes-Roth and Van Gent 1996; Perlin and Goldberg 1996; Harger 2008) or the object-creation work of Swartjes et al. (2008). However, as we have argued elsewhere (Magerko et al. 2009), these projects have focused on the surface features of improvisational theatre, on the often-documented tacit knowledge involved in teaching and employing basic improv concepts. This approach has led to INT systems that, while they display some aspect of improv, do not directly tackle the problem of building synthetic characters that can co-construct a scene with each other or a human actor.

Improvisational theatre is an ideal exemplar of a domain of human creativity that is highly relevant to interactive narrative and yet little understood. It involves the real-time processing of information from other actors on stage (and the audience), decision making about your own character, reasoning about narrative construction, physical and verbal portrayal of your character, reasoning about the constraints (called *improv rules*) put on the particular scene being performed, etc. Improvisational theatre is both a difficult performance domain and one highly related to the INT field.

The only serious study of the domain comes from the sociolinguistic work of Sawyer (2003), which is not at a formal enough level to directly inform the construction of intelligent agents. Even if the tacit knowledge of improvisation was well documented and understood, the individual and group cognitive processes that are involved are not understood. Therefore, if we want to build INT systems that do similar things to improv actors – such as agreeing on a setting as a group, negotiating the point of a scene, and reaching a conclusion to that scene all while creating a relatively interesting and coherent narrative performance in real-time *without the use of pre-determined or explicitly coordinated story elements* – we have to better understand the domain. Neither the engineering centric approach nor the experience centric approach mentioned in the introduction will work in this case. We do not understand the domain well enough to reverse engineer it.... and consequently we also cannot employ our favorite algorithms to solve a problem so ill defined.

The *Digital Improv Project* at Georgia Tech is a multi-year project aimed at the empirical study of improvisers with the goal of building synthetic characters based on our findings. The project began with the design of our empirical approach to collecting data from human improvisers with a specific focus on understanding the knowledge and processes, both at the group and individual level, involved in the co-creation of scenes during a performance. We postulate that a better understanding of knowledge and process can be coupled with the observable knowledge from scenes to construct computational models of our formal understanding. In other words, we hope to build improvisational synthetic characters based on our study of human improvisers.

We have relied on a myriad of techniques for gathering data from improvisers. Our initial studies were done in a laboratory setting under controlled conditions (i.e. the games improvisers played were pre-determined as were the constraints/ suggestions for those game by the experimenters). Improvisers were given one of a set of games that we felt mapped well onto the topics of interest we thought would elicit that best data: narrative construction, group communication, and cultural knowledge. A single scene would be recorded. Afterwards, each improvisers would be shown a video of that performance in a separate room for retrospective protocol collection. Finally, the improvisers would be shown the video in a group setting to reflect and discuss the scene as a group. This process was repeated several times through the course of an evening, sometimes with different sets of improvisers concurrently going through the process at different times to efficiently use their time.

The data from our empirical study was then coded using a grounded theory based approach, much like the approach used in the gamemaster study described earlier. While this process proved difficult to elicit accurate intercoder reliability scores (the data was just far too subjective to get accurate codes across coders on a moment-by-moment basis for a 6 min long scene), it did elicit a grounded theory that represented what we see improvisers doing on stage. We cannot make claims about how often they do one thing from another, but we can make existences claims based on our findings. The theory that developed from our data focused on two of the three aspects of improvisation we wanted to study: narrative construction (Baumer and Magerko 2009, 2010) and group communication.

We have proceeded from data collection to analysis to the construction of computational models. Since the domain of theatrical improvisation is so large, we have taken the intentional stance of starting as small as possible in the intelligent agents we build (we call these "just big enough to be interesting" agents *micro-agents* (Magerko et al. 2010)) to help us understand the knowledge representation, user interface, embodiment, and performance issues that arise when building new interactive narrative technologies. We build these small agents with the intent of them informing the next iteration of agents; we have often thrown out the entire codebase of a micro-agent in lieu of building the next bigger and better thing. See Magerko et al. (2011b) for a description of our most complex agents to date, which focus on computationally modeling group communication in a performance game called *Party Quirks*.

Rather than try to derive all of the answers from one data collection, we view the construction of micro-agents as part of the empirical approach. We should be able to build an agent that equals the complexity of our understanding of the aspect of improv we are trying to model. We have yet to claim a complete understanding of any aspect of improvisation, so we are therefore relegated to building incomplete models. However, an examination of these models often points to what kinds of data we are missing, what deeper analysis needs to be done, etc. The process of building agents therefore becomes part of a cyclic process of gathering data, analyzing, building, and then starting over again with the goal of building a more complex agent in the future.

This reexamination of our data through the lens of building computational agents has even led to a change in our data collection techniques. The last collection that was done thus far was executed in an actual performance setting at a local improv troupe's theatre. The purpose of conducting a study this way was to employ semi-structured interview techniques to help "fill in the gaps" of our data, where protocol collection hinted at deeper content but was never elicited during the study. By using semi-structured interview, we were able to directly ask about specific phenomenon. Though this did introduce the reliability issues that come with self-report data, it provided a window into very specific issues in group communication, narrative construction, and the tacit knowledge involved in improvisation.

13.4 Building Agents

The result of our studies of human gamemasters and improvisers has elicited two significant contributions to the interactive narrative technology community. First, we have matured a cyclic process of development that involves the empirical study of human cognition and creativity as a significant part of the technology design process. Conversely, the implementation of the subsequent design can help illuminate future empirical study and analyses (see Fig. 13.1). This process has led us from building very simple micro-agents capable of very little to our current work on an AI/human performance that covers the introduction section of an improvised scene (O'Neill et al. 2011).

Our initial micro-agents were based on our initial data analysis of intermediate and expert performance data (Magerko et al. 2010). They were exemplars of agents

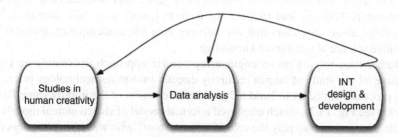

Fig. 13.1 The cyclic relationships between the empirical study of human creativity and the design and development of interactive narrative technologies. *Arrows* indicate ordering in terms of the process we have used in the *Digital Improv Project* to build a deeper understanding of human creativity through the iterative construction of more and more complex agents as we will build a deeper understanding of the improvisational actors we study

that could (a) communicate a character, (b) create a scene in a particular narrative form where one agent tries to solves a problem and the other counterplans to try to create obstacles for the problem being solved, and (c) one agent guessing what character another agent is trying to portray. The systems were non-interactive, done in different codebases, and were used to explore how we might represent concepts in the core knowledge domains we had found in our data: narrative development and the construction of shared mental models.

The micro-agents we constructed pointed out several pertinent problems: (1) "How can we interact with these agents?", (2) "What formal model can be used to encapsulate 'guessing' about a character?", and (3) "How should an agent's knowledge about characters be represented?". With these targeted questions in mind, we revisited our data and, in conjunction with a literature review on research related to shared understandings in problem solving, came to a formal model of shared mental models that could be used both for the 'guessing' process we prototyped earlier and for an abstract menu-based language model that could be used for interacting with the AI actors (Magerko et al. 2011a). The question about character knowledge led us to making a connection between Lakoff's prototype theory (1989) and the way actors reason about characters in our data. For example, an actor reflecting on his portrayal of a video game addict led us to consider how characters can be highly associated with attributes, and those character/attribute associations in turn can be more/less iconic (e.g. having a peg leg is very iconic for pirates):

> With me, I'm not a gamer at all and make fun of my friends that are. So, really, I was just being a ridiculous charicature of my friends who are obsessed with video gamers....or that's what's going through my head...that's...kind of anti-social, don't want....you can only interact on your timetable, you know, which is if you want to pause the game or get irritated when you lose or whatever.

There are elements of the character that are more associated with video game addict than others to this actor, and he portrayed those to get his character across. This fits well with how Lakoff describes how we as people categorize the world where concepts in the world are associated with sets to varying degrees. It also happens to fit well with an AI formalism, *fuzzy logic*, that describes knowledge in terms of *degrees of membership* (from 0 to 1) rather than Boolean (true or false) membership. This has lead us from our data, to Lakoff, to a logic formalism for knowledge about characters that fits both our data and contemporary thoughts in cognitive science about human knowledge.

Rather than relying on an engineering-centric approach to creating an INT, we have let our study of human creativity directly inform our technology practice. This process enabled us to build a digital representation of the improv game *Party Quirks* (see Fig. 13.2), which employed a formal model of shared mental models to enable a human user to play the role of a "party host" who was trying to guess the characters being portrayed at their party (i.e. AI agents who had prototype characters in mind that they could portray) (Magerko et al. 2011a, b).

Reflection on the *Party Quirks* system yielded questions just as the initial micro-agents did previously: (1) How can we interact with these agents in a more naturalistic fashion? (i.e. using shared mental models-based moves in an iPad-based menu was very unsatisfactory in *Party Quirks*), (2) How do we employ the construction

Fig. 13.2 An image of the *Digital Improv Project*'s *Party Quirks* performance game

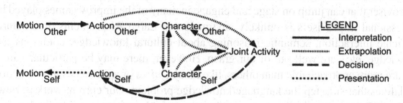

Fig. 13.3 Diagram showing how knowledge is inferred by improvisational actors and our intelligent agents. An observed motion by another actor can be mapped to the semantics of an action (e.g. raising an arm could be mapped to "asking a question"). That action can subsequently be used to infer join activities (e.g. "asking a question" could be mapped to "attending class") or a character (e.g. a student or journalist). Characters and joint activities can be used to infer each other (e.g. if an actor knows they are a student, that allows them to infer likely joint activities they are taking part in and with what other characters, like another student or a teacher)

of shared mental models within a narrative framework?, and (3) How do we expand our representation of character to include elements related to the platform (i.e. knowledge about what characters are in a scene, where they are, what they are doing together, and what their relationship is to each other (Sawyer 2003))? These questions prompted us to do follow up studies with our improv actor population with a more targeted focus on narrative construction. Our subsequent findings have yielded a preliminary design for narrative-based agents that can establish the platform in a scene (O'Neill et al. 2011).

We have extrapolated from the Lakoff-influenced character prototype model to a knowledge model for how actors infer knowledge when another actor communicates knowledge verbally or gesturally about their character, the other actor's character, or the joint activity they are involved in (i.e. the main elements of the platform) (see Fig. 13.3). We anticipate that the next cycle with incorporate elements of building up a scene from the platform to the climax (called the *tilt* of a scene) and its resolution.

13.5 Conclusion

The *Digital Improv Project* can be viewed as using an approach that is a matured version of the one described in the gamemasters study. As opposed to executing a more canonical study of subject matter experts using a verbal protocol collection as the main instrument, our study of improvisers has included the construction of INTs as a core element of a cyclic process that allows our study of humans to influence our construction of agents and vice versa. This cyclic process illustrates the core thesis of this chapter: that there is a space of INT research that can highly benefit from the inclusion of empirical human studies. It is highly unlikely that we would reach the level of complexity that we are currently modeling based solely on reading texts on teaching improvisation, observing performances, or simply thinking really hard. A more cognitively focused study has been imperative in our process. This has consequently led to the most complex computational improv agents constructed to date, which we can build on in the future to continue in deepening their complexity.

The future challenges of this work are myriad. The construction of an intelligent AI improviser that can jump on stage and engage in many of the improv games played by professional improvisers is unlikely anytime soon. Large AI problems, like natural language interaction, semantic reasoning about cultural knowledge, commonsense knowledge, etc., are well out of our grasp. However, there may be particular games that are more approachable than others, like *Party Quirks* or approaches to interaction modalities that sidestep the language/knowledge problem. Our current work is viewing an INT for improvisation not as a "human and AI performance," but rather as a performance between an AI and an AI/human hybrid where the human inputs gestures into the system via a Kinect interface and their AI counterpart uses that gesture as an input into their character's performance. In other words, the AI decides how to map the gesture to some semantic interpretation and outputs dialogue based on that gesture instead of allowing the human actor to speak freely and expect the AI to understand it. Gesture recognition is not an easily solved problem, but is a far better scoped – and more noise tolerant – interaction domain for improv theatre. The final state of this work will not necessarily be to pass an "AI improv turing test" or to readily replace humans in live theatrical conditions, but to create an improv-based experience where humans and AI can co-create scenes together in a satisfying fashion.

The work done on studying gamemasters wound up influencing our theory of drama manager design, though our practical work shifted from implementing drama managers in lieu of the Digital Improv research. However, the path our studies of gamemaster mediation strategies lays out for drama manager design is clear. As opposed to focusing solely on the technology behind how a drama manager models the user or makes decisions, interactive narrative developers should also focus on the *how* and *why* of mediation. Drama managers can have access to the categories of strategies we have uncovered, such as *instruction* or *focus* and employ them for variety, narrative effect, or even as part of a machine learning algorithm that learns what kind of strategies work well with certain kinds of users. For instance, characters who come across as always wanting to make the right decision or as heroes will likely respond immediately to a *character hook* mediation that features a character in distress. On the other hand, *spontaneous conflict* may be a good fallback strategy when other more nuanced strategies have failed. Understanding this vocabulary of story mediation provides INT developers with a much more expressive language to use when creating drama manager-based experiences.

This chapter is not meant to discount the work done by others that are based on introspection. Most approaches in the field have relied on the engineering or design-centric approaches discussed in the Introduction section. If we only based our work on human studies, our progress in the field would likely be much slower. Rather, the purpose of this chapter is to illustrate that INT research can often benefit from human studies and, at times, can only result in very surface level systems without said studies. If one wants to build any computationally creative system – not just those dealing with narrative – it may be helpful to empirically examine the human domain to better inform the computational, such as the work done in cognition and jazz improvisation (Sarath 1996; Pressing 1998; Reinholdsson 1998; Johnson-Laird 2002; Mendonça and Wallace 2004). People are simply good at being creative – and understanding that formally can help us build really weird, difficult, and amazing systems that are similarly creative.

References

Baumer, A., & Magerko, B. (2009). Narrative development in improvisational theatre. In *Proceedings of 2nd international conference on interactive digital storytelling* (pp. 140–151), Guimarães, Springer.

Baumer, A., & Magerko, B. (2010). An analysis of narrative moves in improvisational theatre. In *Proceedings of 3rd international conference on interactive digital storytelling*, Edinburgh.

Davis, N., Boyang, L., O'Neill, B., Riedl, M., & Nitsche, M. (2011). Distributed creative cognition in digital filmmaking. In *8th ACM conference on creativity and cognition*, Atlanta, GA.

Flowers, A., Magerko, B., & Mishra, P. (2006). Gamemasters and interactive story: A categorization of storytelling techniques in live roleplaying. In *Futureplay*, London, Ontario, FuturePlay.

Harger, B. (2008). Project Improv. *Project Improv*. http://www.etc.cmu.edu/projects/improv/

Hayes-Roth, B., & Van Gent, R. (1996). *Story-making with improvisational puppets and actors*. Palo Alto, CA: Stanford University.

Johnson-Laird, P. N. (2002). How jazz musicians improvise. *Music Perception, 19*(3), 415–442.

Lakoff, G. (1989). Cognitive models and prototype theory. In Ulric Neisser (Ed.), *Concepts and conceptual development* (pp. 63–100). Cambridge/England: Cambridge University Press.

Magerko, B. (2007). Evaluating preemptive story direction in the interactive drama architecture. *Journal of Game Development, 2*(3), 25–52.

Magerko, B., Manzoul, W., Riedl, M., Baumer, A., Fuller, D., Luther, K., & Pearce, C. (2009). An empirical study of cognition and theatrical improvisation. In *Proceeding of the seventh ACM conference on creativity and cognition* (pp. 117–126). New York: ACM Press.

Magerko, B., Fiesler, C., & Baumer, A. (2010). Fuzzy micro-agents for interactive narrative. In *Proceedings of the sixth annual AI and interactive digital entertainment conference*. Palo Alto: AAAI Press.

Magerko, B., DeLeon, C., & Dohogne, P. (2011a). Digital improvisational theatre: Party quirks. In *Proceedings of the 11th international conference on intelligent virtual agents*. Reykjavík: AAAI Press.

Magerko, B., Dohogne, P., & DeLeon, C. (2011b). Employing fuzzy concepts for digital improvisational theatre. In *Proceedings of the seventh annual international artificial intelligence and interactive digital entertainment conference*. Palo Alto: AAAI Press.

Mendonça, D., & Wallace, W. A. (2004). Cognition in jazz improvisation: An exploratory study. *Cognitive Science Society annual meeting*, Chicago, IL.

O'Neill, B., Piplica, A., Fuller, D., & Magerko, B. (2011). A knowledge-based framework for the collaborative improvisation of scene introductions. In *Proceedings of the 4th international conference on interactive digital storytelling*. Vancouver: Springer.

Peinado, F., & Gervás, P. (2007). Automatic direction of interactive storytelling: Formalizing the game master paradigm. In *Proceedings of the 4th international conference on virtual storytelling: Using virtual reality technologies for storytelling* (pp. 196–201). Berlin/Germany: Springer-Verlag.

Perlin, K., & Goldberg, A. (1996). Improv: A system for scripting interactive actors in virtual worlds. In *Proceedings of the 23rd annual conference on computer graphics and interactive techniques* (pp. 205–216). New York: ACM Press.

Pressing, J. (1998). Psychological constraints on improvisation. In B. Nettl & M. Russell (Eds.), *In the course of performance: Studies in the world of musical improvisation* (1st ed., pp. 47–67). Chicago, IL: University of Chicago Press.

Reinholdsson, P. (1998). Making music together: An interactionist perspective on small-group performance in jazz. Acta Universitatis Upsaliensis: Studia Musicologica Upsaliensia, Nova Series 14.

Riedl, M. O. (2010). A comparison of interactive narrative system approaches using human improvisational actors. In *Proceedings of the intelligent narrative technologies III workshop*. Monterey, CA.

Roberts, D. L., & Isbell, C. L. (2008). A survey and qualitative analysis of recent advances in drama management. *International Transactions on Systems Science and Applications, Special Issue on Agent Based Systems for Human Learning, 4 (2)*, 61–75.

Russo, J. E., Johnson, E. J., & Stephens, D. L. (1989). The Validity of Verbal Protocols. *Memory and Cognition, 17*, 759–769.

Sarath, E. (1996). A new look at improvisation. *Journal of Music Theory, 40*(1), 1–38.

Sawyer, R. K. (2003). *Improvised dialogues: Emergence and creativity in conversation*. Westport: Ablex Publishing Corporation.

Swartjes, I., Kruizinga, E., & Theune, M. (2008). Let's pretend I had a sword. In *1st international conference on interactive digital storytelling* (pp. 264–267). Berlin/Heidelberg: Springer.

Chapter 14
Improvisation in the Cloud: Devised Theatre in Support of Problem-Finding

Irene J. Petrick, Phillip J. Ayoub, and Matthew J. Prindible

Abstract This chapter provides a conceptual framework for emergent design that is crucial in the cloud environment where the device, the customer relationships and the interactivity of that device with other devices creates the full user experience. The framework draws on improvisational thinking in devised theatre as a basis for incorporating storytelling and problem-finding into the designer's work. The chapter concludes with an example and an assessment of the benefits and the challenges to using this framework.

Keywords Complexity • Cynefin model • Environmental uncertainty • Improvisation • Sense-making

14.1 Introduction

Over the last 10 years, economic conditions have shifted the technology market from a place where consumers buy what business delivers to one where the successful business delivers what consumers will buy (Martin 2010). The shift, from enterprise prioritization to consumerization, has had a profound and disruptive effect on the way organizations approach their innovation processes. The shift

I.J. Petrick (✉) • P.J. Ayoub
College of Information Sciences and Technology, The Pennsylvania State University,
University Park, PA 16802, USA
e-mail: ijpetrick@gmail.com; pjayoub@gmail.com

M.J. Prindible
KIT Digital, New York, NY, USA
e-mail: mattprindible@gmail.com

J.M. Carroll (ed.), *Creativity and Rationale: Enhancing Human
Experience by Design*, Human–Computer Interaction Series,
DOI 10.1007/978-1-4471-4111-2_14, © Springer-Verlag London 2013

has not only given consumers more influence in the design of new products, but the entire development ecosystem and delivery pathways have shifted the balance of power across the value chain. Established organizations (i.e., those with the most resources and the reigning incumbents) that saw creativity and design as in-house tasks are now facing this new environment. These organizations are left questioning their own design rationale and require new approaches to innovation – approaches that rethink the conversation between strategic thinking with creativity and design.

It used to be that innovation was delivered via a stand alone device. Later these devices were bundled with services to increase the barrier to entry to include not only the device and its functionality, but some type of support services that deepened the customer relationship. Today, it is the device, the customer relationship, and the interactivity of that device with other devices that creates the full user experience (UX). As devices become more intelligent, and with sensors everywhere, intelligence converges, and thus is born innovation in (and for) the cloud. This innovation will result from interactive design which emphasizes how humans relate to each other, to the world and to the changing nature of technology and business (Kolko 2011).

Effectively, the cloud separates the backend and frontend, yet never have these been more tightly coupled in delivering the user experience. Established firms such as Intel and Microsoft, are now creating the backend (i.e. hardware and operating system), while holding less control of the software services to general developers, in what has become known as the "app model." In such an environment, the rules of the game have shifted and established organizations must shift their thinking from a predictive state to an emergent state.

In this chapter we argue that the cloud environment represents a changing design environment from one that is complicated to one that is highly complex. Instead of problem solving as might be the more traditional innovation pathway, complex environments require problem-finding approaches. This means a shift in the appropriate model of activity from sense-analyze-respond to a model of probe-sense-respond which for the established organizations looking to facilitate innovation, implies a shift in their current dominant logic. Being the backend player, they must shift their goals from problem-solving to problem-finding. We believe this means designers working in teams must embrace improvisational thinking that is best described by a devised theatre metaphor. This will enable such backend designers to anticipate some of the actions of frontend designers (who are out of their direct influence) as they co-create new emergent applications with users, thus enabling richer user experiences. This shift to a more "strategic" mindset must move hand-in-hand with creativity and design, where the rationale that underlie management and in-house design teams must come to the forefront in order to be able to rapidly and flexibly adjust to the emergent dynamics of the new complex ecosystem.

Our proposed framework is aimed at supporting both strategic management and technology designers. For managers, it explains the importance of designers in the strategy space. For the designer, it provides a broader framework for understanding how design fits into strategy and business economics. The purpose here is for organizations to direct vs. adapt to emergent change (that has become the new norm).

While often not the typical bedfellows, strategic intentionality and creativity and design go hand-in-hand, and it is linked through understanding rationale.

This chapter provides a conceptual framework for emergent design. The framework is the result of over a decade working with industrial new product and service design teams that are dealing with the increasing complexity in their environments ranging from the high tech sector, aerospace, consumer products and medical devices. We begin this chapter by describing the way that environmental uncertainty presents design challenges. We then provide a framework for improvisational thinking in design, and extend this through an example of the way that this supports emergent behavior in the cloud. We conclude with the implications of adopting such a design rationale by identifying benefits and challenges.

14.2 Complexity and the Design Challenge

Successful innovation blends strategy and action in a way that sets the firm's product and/or service offerings apart from its competitors. To achieve this blend, firms must be able to sense changes to their external environment and make sense of these changes. Sense-making beyond the obvious often requires suspension of commonly held beliefs, known as an organization's dominant logic or collective mental model.

The *Cynefin* model (Kurtz and Snowden 2003; Snowden and Boone 2007) identifies four different environmental sense-making states based on the existence of cause and effect relationships and their ability to inform decision making. This model is useful as it highlights differences between complicated and complex states. Additionally this model suggests that the environmental state is best addressed by different strategic approaches to action, including design and innovation. Table 14.1 summarizes the *Cynefin* model and links the environmental states to the design challenges presented therein. In this chapter we are particularly concerned with environments that have shifted or are shifting from a complicated state to a complex one.

With respect to design, Simple environments favor sequential risk reduction and decision-making. A good example of a product in this category would be a PC upgrade, where the change in one model to the next is incremental and aimed primarily at cost reduction. Feature changes are minimal upgrades. In Complicated environments uncertainty increases such that critical knowledge is possessed by a few individuals. Here experts using systems thinking can decompose the inherent risks and can then undertake problem solving. Conversation among experts is critical to overall success since system elements may be interrelated, but in predictable ways. An example of a product in this category would be the Netbook. At the time of its launch, the Netbook represented a smaller and less expensive form factor aimed at primarily the same tasks as the bulkier PC. The key challenges were the interrelationship between manufacturing changes and the need to shrink hardware components to fit into the smaller form factor at a cost competitive

Table 14.1 Cynefin states and their design challenges

	Simple	Complicated	Complex	Chaotic
Cause and Effect Relationships	Repeatable, perceivable and predictable, often in a linear sequence	Separated over time and space and often known by only a small group of individuals	Only coherent in retrospect and not necessarily repeatable	Not perceivable
Approach	Best practices and standard operating procedures	Analytical/reductionist thinking and scenario planning	Pattern management and perspective filters	Stability focused interventions and enactment tools
Sense-making	Sense-categorize-respond	Sense-analyze-respond	Probe-sense-respond	Act-sense-respond
Behavior	Structured techniques with predetermined practice	Learning organization and the adaptive enterprise	Emergent behavior	Courageous action
Design Activities	Risk reduction through empirical analysis and sequential decision-making	Systems thinking with expert input for problem solving	Expert and generalist input for problem finding	Not applicable
Example	PC Upgrade	Netbook	iPad	iPhone and iTunes

pricepoint. The Netbook required significant technology changes including Intel's ATOM processor.

In the Complex environment, feedforward mechanisms create a situation where the actions in one period influence the state under which future actions will be attempted. Here behavior is emergent, and sense making can only be done retrospectively. The expert is no longer able to predict relationships in sufficient detail to properly constrain action. Instead of problem solving, in complex environments the design challenge is problem finding. This often requires both expert and generalist input. An example of a product in this category is the iPad. iPad leveraged the existing infrastructure created for an earlier Apple product, the iPhone (we'll come back to this in the next example). Here the device enabled user experience with its touch based interface, but many of the specific applications the user wanted were unknown at the time of the iPad launch. In point of fact, designers could not predict any but the most obvious tasks that would be accomplished on this device. iPad reflects the emergent behavior of users, particularly in areas such as media consumption, gaming and communication.

Finally in the Chaotic environment, courageous action must be taken without a clear picture of the sources of the uncertainty, of any underlying relationships and without the benefit of comparison events. Pattern matching is not possible and experts have little to offer in terms of decisive action because past successes are not predictors of future success. In this environment, the visionary can only be identified in hindsight. One of the best examples of this is Apple's introduction of the iPhone. This device brought together the power of a communication device with the connectivity of a computer in a mobile form. When eventually combined with the powerful iTunes delivery model, independent developers were able to offer their products – apps – to previously unreachable consumers. The iPhone revolutionized multiple dimensions of the product, services and ecosystem, the scope of which has been evident only in hindsight.

Donald Sull (2009) notes that while uncertainty poses challenges, there is an upside to turbulence for those who can break their mental models of how the world works or the underlying causal factors. Others have argued that the greatest opportunities for innovation are at the "edge of chaos" (e.g. Brown and Eisenhardt 1997, 1998). We believe the cloud represents just such an edge at the present time. In the following section, we briefly summarize two aspects of improvisation – Jazz and devised theatre – and emphasize the way that improvisation can help designers in the Complicated and the Complex environments.

14.3 A Framework for Improvisational Thinking

At its essence, improvisation, regardless of form, is based on call and response. It is this pattern that enables the interplay and communication between artists who, to an audience, create their product spontaneously. Though most commonly associated with jazz, the techniques of improvisation are also used in devised theatre. While

Table 14.2 Improvisational thinking in complicated and complex environments

	Complicated environment	Complex environment
Design metaphor	Jazz	Devised Theatre
Interaction mechanisms	Assertion and openness	Intuition, spontaneity, and accumulation of ideas
Process	Resolving tension in underlying structures and patterns	Freezing to explore "in the moment" experiences to capture nuances of problems
Goal	The underlying structure is preserved, but the responsibility for the preservation shifts throughout the ensemble	Without an end state in mind, create and explore elements of a theme
Expertise of the individual	Technical and intuitive knowledge	Lower barrier to entry enables wider participation

the term improvisation can be used across many different contexts, each specific context has unique associated nuances. Table 14.2 summarizes the role of improvisational thinking in the Complicated and Complex environments which we describe in detail. Later in this section we present our framework for improvisational thinking where we delineate the benefits of each metaphor. From the perspective of designing for the cloud, we believe it more likely that designers will find value in the devised theatre metaphor.

14.3.1   Unique Elements of Jazz and Devised Theatre

Any jazz ensemble can be broken down into its component instrumentalists. The success, or rather the ability of an ensemble to find its groove, begins and, to a high degree, depends on each individual musician's ability to discover, cultivate, and master the technical skills of the instrument, and basic methods of improvisation (Berliner 1994). The bridge between individual talent and performing as a group begins with the technical skill known as ear-training. Ear-training is the ability of a musician to identify, synthesize, and react to complex musical constructs in real time. Recognizing chord progressions, the structural patterns (chorus and verses) of the music, and the improvised musical ideas submitted by other members of the ensemble is an evolutionary skill. In a chapter titled "The More Ways You Have of Thinking," author Paul Berliner (1994) demonstrates how over time, jazz musicians learn to extract (by both listening and playing) patterns and structures from existing music that are used to formulate new improvised, musical ideas. "[Improvisers'] theoretical (technical) and aural (intuitive) knowledge constantly inform one another" (Berliner 1994, p. 146). As this new knowledge is synthesized and abstracted, new tools for the musician to use for improvisation are created.

Arguably the most important skill developed collectively by the ensemble is the ability to create and resolve tension throughout a performance. Paul Rinzler (2008) argues and presents supporting evidence that new ideas emerge as the product of creating and resolving various tensions within the group and performance. One particular contradiction that creates tension is the coexistence of assertion and openness. Within the confines of the inherent musical structure, each musician is free to contribute their own relevant musical ideas (assertion), but, at the same time, must consider the current state of the musical environment constructed by the other members (openness). "Each musician must simultaneously and fully process information going in both directions" (Rinzler 2008, p. 110). In describing the interaction between a bass player and a drummer, for example, Berliner notes that as one explores his musical freedom, the other has to be restricted some-what. The underlying structure of the piece must be preserved, though the responsibility of its preservation can shift throughout the ensemble (Berliner 1994, p. 353).

The resolution of tension and the creation of new musical ideas depends on the ability of each musician to accept exactly what every other musician contributes and use that contribution to complete the performance. "Once something has been contributed musically, it is impossible to take back," notes Rinzler. "The rest of the group has to deal with any individual's contribution" (Rinzler 2008, p. 37). It is the response, derived from intimate musical knowledge, awareness of a surprising amount of structure and rules, and the ability to create and resolve tensions, to an initial call that gives jazz its unique aesthetic.

Devising describes a process by which a theatrical product or script is developed not by writers, but rather created by a group using a series of highly collaborative and improvisational methods. [Within devising,] "there is a freedom of possibilities for all those involved to discover; an emphasis on a way of working that supports intuition, spontaneity, and an accumulation of ideas" (Oddey 1996, p. 1). One unique difference to devised theatre is that, in contrast to jazz improvisation, it is not crucial for each participant to be highly skilled or even classically trained. This lower barrier to entry enables a much wider variety of participants and, consequently, a much wider array of potential results.

The process of devising typically begins by establishing a theme to explore, called a "seed." The seed acts as a way to initially organize, but not determine or limit thoughts and actions. A devising group can choose to build on the seed in a variety of ways; in fact, it is widely accepted that the process of devising is itself improvisational (Milling and Heddon 2005). Developing and exploring personas (sometimes called masking), improvisational narrative, games, contact-based improvisation, and even choreography are several ways of exploring a theme and building on the seed.

Transient, but strong leadership plays an interesting role as members can take turns pushing the group in new directions. In a recent demonstration of a type of devised theatre, participatory theatre-in-education (Oddey 1996), the initial establishment of leadership suspended judgement and allowed the proper space to explore ideas without consequences. Tensions, similar to the tensions created during jazz improvisation can be created in a number of fashions. In the same recent demonstration, "freezing" was used to explore tensions created in scenarios. Each group was tasked with acting out a particular scenario based on the theme. A leader was assigned to yell "Freeze!" at any given moment and the actors were to hold their positions. Frozen in time and place, participants were asked to describe the mental, physical, and emotional tensions they were experiencing.

While each method used in devised theatre is unique in its execution, there is a consistent underlying principle within each method – inquiry. While devising, the goal is not to arrive at an end state, but rather to continue creating and exploring new elements to the theme. As the exploration of the theme continues, a pattern of repetition and revision emerges (similar to jazz's call and response). As the process is repeated, it is expected that new, previously unapparent and perhaps invisible elements to the theme will emerge, be discovered, and be used for the final product.

Devised theatre is a highly emergent process. However, unlike the underlying structure and patterns that are present throughout an entire jazz production, devised theatre's minimalist structure is formed around the introduction of seeds, starting points or ideas, from which the final product emerges.

14.3.2 Sensing, Sense-Making and Problem-Finding

While the prior section outlined two forms of improvisation, we have found that the complex, emergent nature of designing for the cloud is better served by the devised theatre metaphor. In this section, we present a framework for the early stages of innovation and design which uses devised theatre to explore underlying assumptions of the dominant logic, or in design terms, what could be called the design rationale.

The more successful a company is, the more likely its employees are to favor a dominant logic (Prahalad 2004) that includes assumptions about the end user, the business model, the value chain and about the relative role of technology push versus market pull in assessing opportunities. Govindarajan and Trimble (2012) go so far as to argue that it is this dominant logic that has sustained companies in the past but that is endangering future sustainability as the needs of far flung customers distributed in global markets increasingly diverge from traditional developed country-based customers.

The cloud takes the Govindarajan and Trimble argument to new heights. Anticipating the "right" features to bundle into products and services is getting more challenging since anytime, anywhere access means that users in Detroit, Dublin and Delhi could conceivably want similar features. Moreover, with the widely distributed and long tail nature of app developments, designers are further challenged as users mix and match features and services that might once have been offered as a suite.

At the heart of the problem is the need for a deep understanding of the user, their needs and the context in which these needs will be fulfilled. Designers must set aside common assumptions and often misconceptions. For example, when considering context, assuming that the developing world will progress along similar lines as more developed economies have in the past ignores a critical point: while the

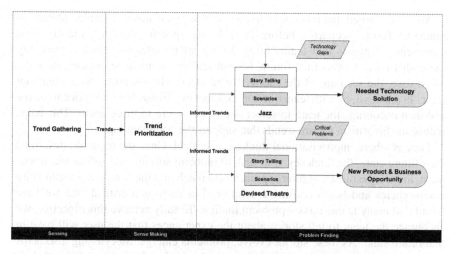

Fig. 14.1 Exploring the rationale of improvisational thinking in design

infrastructure in developing countries may be lacking or absent in many cases, in those cases where infrastructure exists, it is often cutting edge (Govindarajan and Trimble 2012). Thus defining the user experience does not necessarily conform to our expectations when designers take a systems view.

In our framework for bringing improvisational thinking into design, we address the strategic front end of the innovation process. We target three primary outcomes with this model: (1) making explicit the choices that are made in the front end of the design process by identifying underlying assumptions; (2) changing the conversation around the design space by putting the user into context; and (3) refining the designer's understanding of the problem(s) faced by those users in their contexts. It is only when these three objectives are accomplished that designers can truly conceive of elegant designs that delight the user.

Our framework uses a sensing, sense-making and problem finding approach in three stages (See Fig. 14.1). In the first stage, sensing, designers, marketers, and others within the company look externally to their company to identify trends that will shape the design space over time. In our experiences, we are pushing teams to look out to 2020 for these trends. Not all trends, however, are equally relevant to all companies or even to all design teams within a company. Instead, these trends need to be filtered through strategic priorities. In stage 2, the team takes a critical look at the trends and their implications, resulting in a smaller set of trends, which we call *informed trends*. These informed trends become the building blocks of the final stage, problem finding. In this third stage, design teams begin to consider alternative scenarios when two or more trends are combined. Ideally the team is seeking the set of trends that present the "Perfect Storm" opportunity – a unique future state that if achieved will accord competitive advantage to the company while simultaneously constraining other companies' options.

We have learned that it is imperative to push design teams to consider alternative plausible future scenarios before considering specific design tradeoffs. Our experience suggests that teams often do not spend adequate time considering these alternative views of the future, instead settling on the most obvious, or in the worst case, the scenario of the future that most closely resembles their dominant logic. In our sessions with teams, we often select two trends from the prioritized list and then encourage the team to select one or two more to think about. This helps reduce the favoritism toward trends that support the dominant logic.

Here is where improvisational thinking is critical. Once the team has described their future state, the tendency is to rush to problem solving and solution development. In fact, the most common approach is to reach into the company's technology competencies and begin crafting a solution. But there is a critical step we have found that many teams miss – problem finding. To fully achieve this objective, we encourage the team to tell stories about the experiences that the user will have in that future state. As these stories evolve, problems emerge. Storytelling also helps deflect the dominant logic as the team members often have to go beyond their personal experience and the known success factors of past activities.

Our framework breaks down the problem finding activity into two streams that can be differentiated by the strategic intent of the company. There are two primary strategic intents that drive design teams: (1) identifying technology gaps to drive R&D investments, mergers, and acquisitions, and ecosystem partner development; and (2) identifying critical problems that suggest new product, service or business model opportunities. While both of these strategic intents often result in the investment in technology, they tend to have differences that are critical to this discussion. In point of fact, identifying technology gaps reflects a complicated environment, while identifying new products, services and business models is more akin to a complex environment as discussed earlier.

Teams in search of technology gaps tend to be populated with experts who have deep knowledge around core company strengths. These experts each possess a piece to a complicated puzzle and it is in their working together that unique solutions ultimately emerge. Unfortunately, if the experts don't go through the storytelling phase, their solutions reflect what is possible, not necessarily what is needed. In this sense, using the Jazz metaphor in design provides a framework for discussion, interaction, and expected roles. This lessens the reliance on any single individual or discipline, and encourages the discussions to balance the whimsical with the possible. Technology solution development in response to technology gaps that emerge in problem finding, ties strategic intent to action, thus more tightly coupling strategy and design.

On the other hand, teams that are driven by the imperative to grow new businesses through new products, services or business models are often populated by a more diverse set of participants, drawing from technology experts, market experts, finance and other critical areas. Here the Devised Theatre approach provides a framework for storytelling that is user centered, but that evolves through inputs that cannot be anticipated at the start. Moreover discussions are emergent, not necessarily convergent. In these problem-finding sessions, the balance between whimsy and physical possibilities is less at the heart of the discussion. Instead the team is seeking truly new ground. In our experience this new ground often requires a new business model and a different ecosystem than the one in which the company currently participates. The relative importance of one discipline over another depends on the problems that are identified and leadership of the discussion is fluid. We have found that just as "seeds" in devised theatre help the story to develop, carefully placed questions by a facilitator help the team continue to move forward, avoiding those rat hole discussions that go nowhere.

14.4 An Example of Improvisation in the Cloud

This example is drawn from our work with an Intel Corporation business unit focused on automotive technologies that has been using devised theatre and storytelling as a problem-finding method. The team was charged with identifying new products and/or services that would facilitate future experiences in the driving environment. At the outset, the team determined that a technology push solution would not necessarily anticipate the myriad of experiences drivers might be seeking. They also recognized that a multifaceted solution might require new ecosystem partners to achieve. In addition, the team determined that envisioning the platform only as a physical device ignored the cloud based solutions that might extend these devises such as application software, services, and access to real time data. Here is a clear case of the challenge of backend development in light of unpredictable front end partners and uses – the cloud at its best, and its most challenging.

In early meetings, the team invited participants from other areas within the company to help it identify trends that might influence user choices out into the year 2020. Once this team had a full list of trends – and the underlying assumptions that were made in creating them – they were asked to prioritize the trends. A final downselect of trends was assigned to smaller groups on this team by a facilitator with the expressed instructions, "Take these two assigned trends, and choose up to two more trends from the list to consider alternative scenarios of the future." Here the facilitator planted a "seed" that the group could use to begin exploring. To focus the discussions even further, the group was asked to tell a story about this future and to identify the problems from the user perspective. It wasn't until the groups were charged with storytelling and problem finding that truly out of the box thinking emerged.

Designers transitioned their discussion away from "My experience says that …" or "In the past we solved this by …" [problem-solving] to discussions about what the future looked like, what user experiences would be needed and what problems would exist [problem-finding]. Using this framework, discussions centered around user frustrations with increasing traffic congestion, user overload of information and other sensory stimulation in the vehicle, and user desires to have a more productive or relaxing driving experience. Without going into the competitive details of potential opportunities explored and expanded upon, the results of this exercise include previously unanticipated geographies, with widely different potential go-to-market strategies. As of this writing, the team is still exploring its options. The senior leader on this team summarizes the benefits of this process with the following: "[The framework] provided a process that brings order to our chaos. [It] helped bring a diversity of ideas into our group so that we didn't get caught up in our own way of thinking. Some of the trends that have been identified are starting to show up in the way that we communicate our vision [to the rest of the company]".

14.5 Conclusion

Experts have been taught through formal education and experience to anticipate future events based on past events, and to predict future relationships based on past causal factors. As the operating environment becomes more fluid and uncertain, such expertise can be a constraining factor rather than a benefit. Prahalad and Ramaswamy (2003) have suggest that the new frontier of innovation experience will shift the focus from products and services to the user experience which will evolve through the convergence of multiple industries working in a networked world.

We have used the conceptual framework presented here to help teams anticipate what types of conversations they are having at various portions of the design process. A colleague at Proctor and Gamble often comments that there are three questions in the innovation space: (1) questions about opportunities – what are all the things we might do? (2) questions about possibilities – what are all the things we could do? and (3) questions about action – what will we do? All too often teams jump to the question about action before carefully considering the first two questions. This rush to action only reinforces the dominant logic and puts teams at a considerable disadvantage. One of the most important benefits in the proposed framework is that it helps teams focus their discussions in a sequential way, enabling them keep on topic and to table tangential discussions to the appropriate time. We have found that discussions are more focused and more productive. In addition, forcing teams to explicitly articulate their strategic imperatives, tends to help them in filtering trends later on and in ultimately down selecting from among the problems identified to those that are most relevant, given strategic intent.

Overall, we have found that teams that use this framework are better able to articulate the needs of the end user and to translate these needs into metrics that can be measured over time. This improves communication between team members and between the team and others in their company and beyond. However, just as frameworks have benefits so, too, do they have challenges (See Table 14.3).

The primary challenge to using this framework is the time required to develop the trends and to refine the stories around them. Teams spend more time in the early stage innovation development, often requiring two-three multi-day meetings; extensive follow-up fact finding is often required between these meetings. While we believe that this is time well spent, in a fast paced environment where results are expected

Table 14.3 The benefits and challenges of the improvisational framework

Benefits	Challenges
Increases diversity by involving more people in the design discussion	Discussion intensive meetings expand the timeframe for the front end of innovation
Storytelling captures in narrative form the relationship between assumptions and design choices	Does not conform to deductive models of business economics
Improves communication between team members and between the team and the larger organization	Developing a cohesive story is time intensive and often suggests additional fact finding needs
Metrics are consistent with a UX perspective	UX metrics are difficult to translate into ROI

quickly, it is often a difficult tradeoff. In addition, the UX metrics that are so necessary to support design choices are often difficult to translate into the more traditional return on investment (ROI) or other economically derived metrics. Teams choosing to adopt this framework should be advised that the larger organization often pushes back because of the tension between their dominant logic and this design framework. Forewarned is forearmed.

References

Berliner, P. (1994). *Thinking in jazz: The infinite Art of improvisation*. Chicago: University of Chicago Press.

Brown, S. L., & Eisenhardt, K. (1997). The art of continuous change: Linking complexity theory and time-paced evolution in relentless shifting organizations. *Administrative Science Quarterly, 42*(1), 1–34.

Brown, S. L., & Eisenhardt, K. (1998). *Competing on the edge: Strategy as structured chaos*. Cambridge, MA: Harvard Business School Press.

Govindarajan, V., & Trimble, C. (2012). *Reverse innovation*. Cambridge, MA: Harvard Business Review Press.

Kolko, J. (2011). *Thoughts on interaction design* (2nd ed.). San Francisco: Morgan Kaufman Publishers.

Kurtz, C. F., & Snowden, D. J. (2003). The new dynamics of strategy: Sense-making in a complex and complicated world. *IBM Systems Journal, 42*(3), 462–483.

Martin, R. (2010, January-February). The age of customer capitalism. *Harvard Business Review, 88*(1/2), 58–65.

Milling, J., & Heddon, D. (2005). *Devising performance*. New York: Palgrave Macmillan.

Oddey, A. (1996). *Devising theatre: A practical and theoretical handbook*. London: Routledge.

Prahalad, C. K. (2004). The blinders of dominant logic. *Long Range Planning, 37*, 171–179.

Prahalad, C.K., & Ramaswamy, V. (2003). The new frontier of experience innovation. *Sloan Management Review*, Summer, *44*(4), 12–18.

Rinzler, P. E. (2008). *The contradictions of jazz*. Lanham: Scarecrow Press.

Snowden, D. F., & Boone, M. E. (2007). A leader's framework for decision making. *Harvard Business Review*, November, *85*(11), 69–76.

Sull, D. (2009). *The upside of turbulence*. New York: HarperCollins Publishers.

Chapter 15
The Practice Level in Participatory Design Rationale: Studying Practitioner Moves and Choices

Albert M. Selvin, Simon J. Buckingham Shum, and Mark Aakhus

Abstract Most research in design rationale focuses on specific tools, methods, models, or artifacts. There has been relatively little attention to the practice level of design rationale work: the human experience of working with the tools and methods to create rationale artifacts. This chapter explores a particular juncture of creativity and design rationale that is found in the special case of helping groups of people construct representations of rationale within live meetings. Such work poses challenges and requires skills different from those of individuals working alone. We describe the role of practitioners who perform caretaking and facilitative functions in collaborative or participatory design rationale sessions, and present a set of analytical tools aimed at making the practice level more visible. We locate the analysis in a theoretical framework aimed at understanding the experiential dimensions of such practice, including sensemaking, narrative, aesthetics, ethics, and improvisation.

Some of the data analysed in this article were gathered from eScience/robotics field trials funded by NASA (*Mobile Agents* project) and the UK EPSRC (*Collaborative Advanced Knowledge Technologies in the Grid* project), to whom we are indebted.

A.M. Selvin (✉)
Verizon Information Technology, White Plains, NY, USA

Knowledge Media Institute, The Open University, Milton Keynes, UK
e-mail: alselvin@gmail.com

S.J. Buckingham Shum
Knowledge Media Institute, The Open University, Milton Keynes, UK

M. Aakhus
Department of Communication, School of Communication and Information,
Rutgers, The State University of New Jersey, 4 Huntington Street,
New Brunswick, NJ 08901-1071, USA

J.M. Carroll (ed.), *Creativity and Rationale: Enhancing Human Experience by Design*, Human–Computer Interaction Series, DOI 10.1007/978-1-4471-4111-2_15, © Springer-Verlag London 2013

Keywords Aesthetics • Ethics • Facilitation • Grounded theory • Improvisation • Knowledge media • Narrative • Reflective practice • Sensemaking • Visualization

15.1 Introduction

There are a variety of techniques used to foster creativity in design, such as brainstorming exercises and ideation workshops. Other articles in this special issue argue for or against the notion that design rationale techniques can spur creativity in the design process. In this chapter we shift focus away from creativity as something that might be evoked through the collaborative creation of a design rationale artifact, and toward the ways in which creativity can manifest itself in the act of fostering creativity and engagement with such an artifact for others. These can be creative acts on the representation, creative ways of intervening in group process, or reframing participant utterances.

Creating representations of design rationale in collaborative groups requires a set of skills similar to other forms of participatory media practice. Understanding such practices calls for an empirical approach that can illuminate the sociotechnical, as well as aesthetic and ethical, considerations involved in evoking and representing information like design rationale, argumentation, and exploratory discussion within groups of people in live meetings. Our intent is to make this practice, with its particular conditions and challenges, visible and amenable to analysis.

While this approach can help with building better tools and methods for capturing design rationale, that is not our primary goal here. Rather, we aim to focus on the practice aspects of creating complex design rationale (DR) representations in groups. Our principal subject is not the participants in a collaborative DR session, although they are just as interesting in their own right. Rather, we are looking at the experience of people in the role of caretakers or facilitators of such events – those who have some responsibility for the functioning of the group and session as a whole. Collaborative DR practitioners craft expressive representations on the fly with groups of people. They invite participant engagement, employing techniques like analysis, modeling, dialogue mapping, creative exploration, and rationale capture as appropriate. Practitioners inhabit this role and respond to discontinuities with a wide variety of styles and modes of action. Surfacing and describing this variety are our interests here.

Good representations of design rationale do not come for free, and they often do not come easily. Proponents of DR tools and methods have long faced low adoption and even resistance to their approaches from many of their intended audiences (Buckingham Shum 1996). Many researchers have explored this phenomenon, attributing it to factors such as the high cognitive overhead that the approaches seem to instill. For many would-be DR users, it requires considerable effort to move from customary forms of verbal and written argumentation, which seem to pour forth seamlessly, to the ostensibly more abstract forms of DR modeling, such as Rittel's Issue-Based Information System (IBIS; Kunz and Rittel 1970; see Fig. 15.1). Even initially

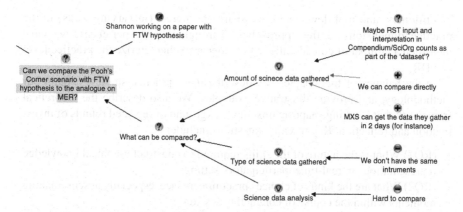

Fig. 15.1 An example of an IBIS summary of a conversation, mapped during eScience field trials described in one of the case studies presented below. This can be contrasted with Fig. 15.4, a much more constrained map largely generated by a software agent

enthusiastic prospective adoptees often run into a variety of difficulties as they try to build their first DR representations, finding the rhetorical moves unwieldy or struggling with the software tools to express and manage things as they would like.

Compounding these challenges by attempting to construct such representations in groups–with the additional interpersonal issues, group dynamics, and usual issues of trying to get things done in meetings—would seem to be a recipe for failure. And yet, successful practitioners of collaborative and participatory DR, issue-based exploration, and argument or dialog mapping do exist. A small but growing community of such practitioners has moved well past the "Can it be done?" phase, and these practitioners have successfully applied their approaches in a wide variety of professional, organizational, and research settings. For such practitioners, further improving their practice involves understanding and deepening the skills required. However, little in the research literature addresses such skills and practices directly, let alone research advanced enough to use them as the basis for developing a body of principles and guidelines, as other professional practices rely on. This chapter aims at supplying some foundational considerations for helping foster increased attention to, and development of, such practices.

A note on terminology: There are many ways to refer to the practices we discuss in this chapter, and the considerations described apply to other sorts of collaborative representations of knowledge besides design rationale. However for our purposes here we will use the abbreviation *PDR* in the rest of the chapter to stand for participatory design rationale.

We authors have spent more than 40 collective years studying, developing, and working with PDR and argumentation approaches, both in individual and group settings. We have trained others to work with such methods, including classes specifically for practitioners intending to facilitate collaborative and PDR modeling sessions. As members of international communities of similar researchers, practitioners, and tool developers, we share an interest (in varying ways) in the practice dimensions of the approaches. Through these experiences, we have identified a number of considerations that appear to characterize the practice level of PDR.

In the balance of this chapter, we describe these practice studies, explain our methodology, and provide illustrative examples. We also describe the theoretical framework that is taking shape against the background of repeated rounds of investigation and reflection. Key research questions include:

- (RQ1) What is the nature of the skills required to construct graphical knowledge representations in real-time, participatory settings?
- (RQ2) What are the kinds of choices practitioners face, especially at sensemaking moments within the course of conducting sessions?
- (RQ3) How does the context of the service being provided affect the choices a practitioner makes?

15.2   An Example of PDR Practice

What do we mean by the practice aspects of facilitating participatory design rationale? In this section we provide an illustrative example.[1]

A committee in a medium-sized public school district (approximately 20,000 students) in the Hudson River Valley region of New York State was tasked with analyzing the alternatives for school building capacity in the district, which has experienced declining enrollment. This highly contentious issue had come up many times before. The district's superintendent of schools was concerned that the discussion would be unproductive, due to tensions and unsurfaced assumptions between the various interest groups (school administrators, teachers, parents, taxpayers, etc.). Every school building has an active, vocal contingent of parents and teachers who have strong interests in keeping their own local school open. Equally strong and vocal are the many local taxpayers who feel that school taxes are already too high. To address this, the superintendent asked two outside practitioners with expertise in conducting PDR sessions to help run the meetings.

The practitioners convened a series of meetings in a library of one of the schools. A committee of twenty parents, teachers, community activists, and administrators met once a week to work through the alternatives. For each meeting, the practitioners prepared an agenda with a hypermedia issue mapping tool.[2] The agenda focused on various alternatives, policy matters, process considerations, and other issues.

---

[1] This case is drawn from an actual project.

[2] For the purposes of this chapter and project, we illustrated with hypermedia knowledge mapping software to capture the design rationale, but the same considerations apply to other sorts of DR approaches and tools.

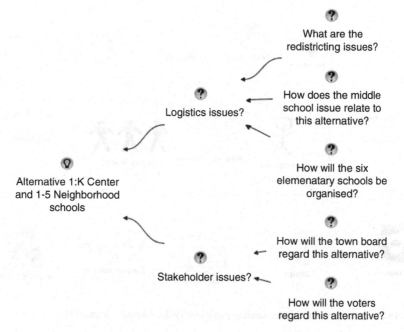

Fig. 15.2 A portion of a meeting agenda, using a template to analyze alternatives

The practitioners employed a variety of approaches. First, they facilitated a general discussion of the issues involved, using a conventional IBIS approach (representing discourse as issues, positions, pros, and cons) to capture and display the discussion as it proceeded. This involved rapid synthesis of what the meeting attendees were saying, thus creating nodes and links in the hypermedia tool that showed the relationship of statements to each other. They also validated the way they captured the statements by frequently asking the participants to look at the maps, asking "Does this capture what you said accurately?" Sometimes participants looked closely and provided detailed feedback (e.g., "Well, not really. What I was really trying to say was this…"). At other times, the heat of the discussion was such that it was difficult for the practitioners to intervene without running the risk of derailing the meeting's momentum. The practitioners had to make moment-to-moment decisions on how much to intervene, and in what ways.

Between meetings, the practitioners analyzed the maps from the general discussion. They looked for recurring themes and questions and, from these, created a template covering the major considerations that would guide choices between the alternatives (see Fig. 15.2). They then facilitated several sessions using the template to structure conversation about each of the alternatives in turn. By the fourth session, the facilitators were able to induce the participants to conduct an analysis according to the template, while still capturing as much of the side discussion and issues as possible. Also between sessions, the district office distributed via mail all of the map output in text form to all the participants.

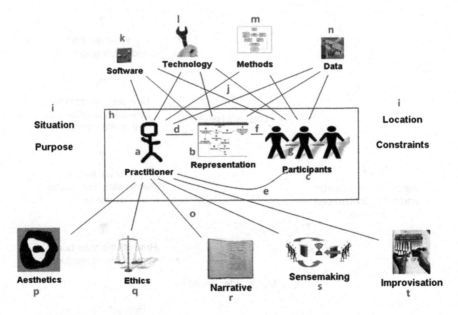

Fig. 15.3 A framework for understanding participatory design rationale practice

At the end of the process, the practitioners held a plenary session for the broader community to understand the final decision. The maps of rationale and templated analysis made the pros and cons for each alternative, as well as many of the comments and points of view, clear and explicit. Even though there was little consensus that the chosen alternative was the best one, the community members completing a postpresentation questionnaire agreed that the process had been conducted in a fair manner, and that the discourse and competing points of view had been made more explicit and comprehensible than in previous years.

15.3 A Framework for Understanding PDR Practice

Understanding practice like that described in the previous section requires taking into account a complex constellation of people, tools, representations, surroundings, and other factors. These have been summarized in the model shown in Fig. 15.3.

The primary elements of the model are the people involved in creating the DR representation, and the representational artifact itself, as seen at the center of the diagram. The practitioner [a], which can be more than one person, orchestrates the participatory event and holds himself or herself responsible for its success. He/she is concerned with the quality and clarity of the representation and the participants' relationship to it. The practitioner takes primary responsibility for the form and content of the representation and the success of the session within its context [i].

As we saw in the example in the previous section, there can be varying levels of intervention. The practitioners are not necessarily the ones with their hands on the equipment: Approaches where the participants themselves do the issue mapping directly are also possible (though often more difficult to carry out successfully). The practitioner interacts with the representation [b] as well as with the participants [c]. The nature of this interaction varies with the context and the specific role(s) that practitioners play in the activity system of the session. We follow McCarthy and Wright (2004) in emphasizing the particularity and situatedness of individual, as distinct from collective experiences of and responses to the tools and methods used in PDR sessions. As such, we look for the unique and creative appropriations practitioners can make, especially in uncertain situations. These often shift in the course of a project, such as the varying ways that the practitioners in the previous section engaged the participants with the representation. Over time they grew to understand both the needs of the different parties involved (parents, teachers, administrators, community members) and the kinds of attention each group was likely to pay to them as outside consultants with a limited franchise to change the accustomed (and contentious) group process. Through extensive "backstage" discussion and work with the materials, they evolved the PDR templates and engaged participants in the representation.

The representation [b] can be any sort of DR or other type of representation, ranging from paper-based argument diagrams drawn on an easel sheet to software-based discourse models, such as the hypermedia representations used in the example above and that we will discuss in our case studies below. There can be multiple types of representation used in a session, including notes and action items. The participants [c] are the people in the room (whether a real or virtual space) taking part in the session. Although the diagram depicts the participants as identical figures, in fact they are quite unique. Being aware of and appropriately dealing with the diversity of participant personalities, relationships, and interests is a key practitioner skill, as well as an ethical imperative. Line [d] symbolizes the interaction of practitioners with the representation, which consists of actions on it (such as creating or modifying it), considering it, planning what to do with it, or even ignoring it. As with that of practitioners, participant interaction with the representation is best understood in a situated manner. Each party in the school capacity example had a unique perspective on the proceedings, the representation, and the other participants. For example, community members whose main purpose for attending was to speak out for lower taxes had to be convinced that a facilitated process would serve their needs, while the administrators who had arranged for the consultants to take part had to balance their anxiousness about both the outcome and the credibility of the process as it played out.

Line [e] shows the interaction of practitioner with participants. This can take many forms, even in a single session, such as facilitative interventions (keeping matters on track, making sure everyone is heard), questions and discussion, and process checks. It is a two-way stream, as participants also interact with the practitioners in various ways. Line [f] is the interaction of the participants with the representation, which ranges from passive to active, from directly engaged with considering it and making changes to it to ignoring it or giving it occasional once-overs. Line [g] shows the interactions of participants with each other, from collegial to disputatious to side conversations.

The three primary elements (practitioner, representation, participants) are contained within box [h], symbolizing the boundaries of the session itself, such as a specific meeting. Some efforts may consist of a single session, where some comprise many sessions (which may include individual DR mapping sessions as well as collaborative ones). The session is in turn located within its surrounding context [i]. The context includes the overall project in which the DR activity is taking place, the specific locations where sessions are held (including whether they are face-to-face, virtual, or a combination); the situation that contains the session, such as the project of which the session is a part, the organizations involved, and the problem domain; the purpose of the session, and the constraints operating in the situation, such as time, budget, attention, or other resource limitations. In the school capacity example, the sessions were the individual meetings held in the library, while the context included the immediate school capacity project, but also elements such as the history of previous attempts to resolve the issue, the relationships of the various participants, and the constraints of producing a report within a limited timeframe.

The lines [j] show the relations between the primary elements and what can be called the set of enablers: software [k], technology [l], methods [m], and data [n]. Each enabler is connected to each primary element, because all interact with each. (Note that methods are not connected directly with the representation; methods are always filtered through a person's actions.) Practitioners use the chosen software [k] to operate on the representation; there can be multiple software packages in use (or none). Participants may also use the software. The software in turn runs on whatever technology platform [l] is in use, such as laptop computers. Technology also includes whatever display tools are being used, such as LCD projectors, virtual meeting or telepresence rooms, and voting keypads (non-computer technology such as flip charts, markers, and whiteboards also count). During sessions, specific methods [m] will be employed, whether formal methods such as IBIS argument mapping or data flow diagrams, or informal methods like brainstorming or round-robin discussion. All of these operate on and draw from the data [n], which is the subject matter for the session, the conversations and ideas put forth and captured during the session, and any supporting material, such as reference information.

Finally, we turn to the dimensions that inform an understanding of practice and the practitioner experience itself. Lines [o] show the aesthetics [p], ethics [q], narrative [r], sensemaking [s], and improvisation [t] associated with the work of the practitioner. These dimensions by themselves do not constitute creativity in the aesthetic and/or improvisational sense, but they help us see how creativity emerges when practitioners respond to breakdowns and anomalies in the course of PDR sessions. In the need to intervene in a session to restore its forward movement, practitioner creativity can result in choice, action, and materials seamlessly coming together to resolve the breakdown. Practitioner creativity can be seen in the ways they draw from these dimensions in the moment of action. Since these dimensions form the basis for the analyses described later in this chapter, we expand on them in the following section.

15.4 Dimensions of PDR Practice

It can be tempting to treat the work of a PDR practitioner as simply one of following established protocols, or unnecessary where it is assumed that meetings and participants can take care of themselves. Yet even when there are no so-called facilitators in a meeting, usually someone, however informally, takes on aspects of the role of ensuring that the meeting reaches its goals. If a knowledge construction task is to be done (as opposed to simply listening to someone else give a presentation), someone will often jump up and take notes on a flipchart or draw a diagram on a whiteboard. This is just as much what we mean by *practitioner* as a paid professional who comes in to run the process and generate the products of a meeting.

In either case, when people act as PDR practitioners in our sense of the word, they inherently make choices about how to proceed [q], give form to the visual and other representational products [p], help establish meanings, motives, and causality [r] and respond when something breaks the expected flow of events [s], often having to invent fresh and creative responses on the spot [t]. These aspects of PDR practice are summarized in Table 15.1 and described in the following subsections. Although we present them as separate entities here for the purpose of description and analysis, in fact in they commingle in the experience of practice, as will be seen in the illustrative example at the conclusion of this section.

15.4.1 Aesthetics [p]

All diagrammatic DR approaches have explicit and implicit rules about what constitutes a clear and expressive representation. People conversant with the approaches can quickly tell whether a particular artifact is a "good" example. This is the province of aesthetics.

Aesthetics has to do with what human beings, in the moments when they are imparting expressive form via some medium (Arnheim 1967), are actually doing: pulling together aspects of experience into a new whole that itself provides a shaped experience (Dewey 1934/2005). The aesthetic dimension of PDR practice is

Table 15.1 Dimensions of participatory design rationale practice

Practice dimension	Definition
Aesthetics [p]	How practitioners shape and craft the representation
Ethics [q]	How a practitioner's actions affect other people
Narrative [r]	Meaning and causality applied to the flow of events
Sensemaking [s]	The ways in which practitioners deal with situations of doubt or instability
Improvisation [t]	The spontaneous, creative moves that practitioners can make

concerned with the shaping and crafting of DR representations in response to both immediate and context-specific imperatives (things that must be done to help achieve participant and project goals), as well as to implicit and explicit concepts of right form. Using the lens of aesthetics offers a unique perspective on the relationship of a practitioner to the participants, emphasizing process, collective and participatory expressive forms, even ethical and political concerns (Cohen 1997). Understanding the aesthetic dimension of a collaborative practitioner's work emphasizes how the encounter between participants, representations, and practitioner unfolds, the extent to which representation-building engages participants, and the ways in which participants are affected by the proceedings.

In explicitly incorporating the idea of aesthetics, we follow Dewey's (1934/2005) argument that aesthetics is not an elite, esoteric, or rarefied concept, even though it is treated that way in common usage. Rather, it is to be understood as the high end of a continuum from prosaic experience; it is a paradigm for "true," unalloyed experience. Aesthetics govern how we would experience any situation if the diluting, dulling, oppressive, or conflictual aspects were stripped away.

Our research investigates what distinguishes form-giving actions from other sorts, looking at the uniquely aesthetic characteristics of such actions in the work of a PDR practitioner. When working with groups, the boundaries of the world of experience are closely aligned with the situation in which they are operating – the people, goals, interests, and constraints of the project or team they are working with. Even within this bounded world, the dimensions and particulars of experience can be vast and diverse, so the problem – and hence the artfulness – of pulling them together into an "integrated structure of the whole" (Arnheim 1967, p. 5).

For example, we look closely at how specific choices regarding form respond to the situation and express something of uniqueness (or fail to). Skilled practitioners can make choices in their actions on the representation that impart a complex of meanings and nuances.

15.4.2   Ethics [q]

The ethical dimension is concerned with the responsibilities of the practitioner to the other people involved, and to their various individual and collective needs, interests, goals, and sensibilities. In some situations, these responsibilities can be weighty in nature—for example, in situations of conflict or dispute, where every action and statement on the part of participants or practitioner holds the possibility of worsening the situation. In less fraught settings, consequences of action or inaction may be less severe, but can still have effects on the concerns of the participants or other stakeholders. Of particular concern are practitioner actions that affect the engagement of participants with each other, with the subject matter of their work, and with the nature and shaping of the representations. These often can take the form of questions: Should I do action x or action y? What effect will it have on these participants if I do x? Should I intervene in their conversational flow? or Should I expend the effort to capture everything that person A is saying at this moment, or is the time better spent in cleaning up the map or preparing for the next activity?

Aakhus (2001, p. 362) advocates research into the communicative actions of facilitators, so as to "advance the normative level of communication practice." He stresses that facilitators' work is not just a neutral enabler of participants' decision-making, or a simple unfolding of a priori processes, but rather contains many instrumental aspects in which practitioner choices directly affect participants and the course of events during sessions of their work. He also examines the "transparency work" performed by communication practitioners in an ethical light (2002). This work, the result of active crafting on the part of the facilitator, is often invisible in accounts of practice. Aakhus (2003) further critiques frameworks that deemphasize the ethical responsibilities of particular mediation and group facilitation practices, arguing that "objectivity" is an inaccurate way to frame practitioner actions. Other researchers also examine choices and dilemmas faced by group support systems (GSS) facilitators (e.g., Yoong and Gallupe 2002). Facilitators do in fact intervene in their clients' situations. Schön (1983) argues for practitioners to take active and conscious ethical stances, recommending reflection-in-action as the means to achieve this. Our research identifies moments when practitioners make choices with such ethical implications. These often arise and pass quickly, such as the momentary shift in attention away from the participants that we see in the example presented below.

15.4.3   Narrative [r]

The narrative dimension concerns the connecting of diverse moments and statements over time, as well as the human experience of causality and consequences. Practitioner actions that have a narrative dimension – that serve to connect elements of the story being built in the DR representations for later telling and reading by others – contribute to the narrative shaping of both the effort itself and the representations that are the primary focus of their actions. Narrative is both a basic human developmental mechanism independent of any particular embodiment (Murray, n.d.) and an aesthetic form that can be represented in verbal, written, performed, or other forms. Narrative functions as a key human strategy for exploring and overcoming unexpected turns of events. Stories and story-making form a key psychological strategy for connecting disparate events. This is particularly so when there is a break or disruption from an expected course of events. "The function of the story is to find an intentional state that mitigates or at least makes comprehensible a deviation from a canonical cultural pattern" (Bruner 1990, p. 49).

The skill of the storyteller lies in the artfulness and effectiveness with which he/she can craft an artifact that makes sense of the "breaches in the ordinariness of life" (Bruner 1990, p. 95). Narrative is a central means by which we are able to glue together bits of experience to construct a new understanding. It is also a key part of human development, a way that we learn to construct and communicate understanding of events and environments. Further, narrative is an intentional form – things that are created, with varying degrees of skill, to serve various purposes. Approaches like scenario-based design employ narratives to capture both concrete detail and the inherent ambiguities in design situations, as well as to create communicative artifacts that can help bridge disciplinary differences (Rosson and Carroll 2009).

McCarthy and Wright (2004) point out that, as individuals, our interactions with technology can be understood through the prism of roles like author, character, protagonist, and coproducer. We are always actively engaging with technology as individuals with our own aims, history, emotions, and creativity, as much as we are also embedded in a sociohistorical context or attempting to perform some kind of task or composite activity.

In our approach, narrative analysis provides a frame for understanding practitioner efforts to maintain the coherence of representations even in the face of interruptions and potential derailments within sessions. Narrative provides a way to understand what coherence means in the context of a particular session (e.g., What is the intended arc of events? How is that arc meaningful to the participants? What roles do the various parties play and how are those important within the surrounding situation?). As well as looking at this encompassing framing of a session, we also look at the ways breaches of the expected occur, and how the practitioner as protagonist reacts to these. Finally, we look at the narrative aspects of the DR representation itself and how changes to the representation relate to the other narrative levels at play in and around a session.

For example, in one of our case studies that took place at a small workshop, the following narrative elements provided key context: There was a pre-existing set of conditions that framed the event, supplying expected causality, reasons for people to be at the event, expected roles, and assumed meanings. Some of the relevant narrative aspects included the ostensible purpose of the workshop, the personal reasons each participant had for attending (e.g., what they hoped to gain from it), the expected trajectory of the facilitated session itself, and the practitioner's own expectation that she would be able to capture and represent the discussion as it unfolded. When the session started to unravel due to a drift in focus on the part of participants (as well as the surfacing of some metadiscussion, like "Why are we talking about this?"), this constituted a breach for which the relatively novice practitioner had no ready-made, unproblematic response.

15.4.4 Sensemaking [s]

Creating DR representations is in itself often a way to help negotiate and construct a shared understanding (Weick and Meader 1993) of a situation or project as a whole. Within this larger frame, the act of representation itself engenders both negotiation as well as confusion, when the tools and discourse lose, if even momentarily, a clear sense of fit. In many design sessions, there are moments where forward progress is blocked because of unforeseen, uncontrolled, or otherwise problematic obstacles. Our research focuses on the sensemaking dimensions of the actions, and their consequences, that take place at such moments. They call for creative and skilled responses from whoever is playing a facilitative representational role, since programmed or prescribed responses and rote actions are rarely sufficient in such situations.

Dervin's (1983) model posits that sensemaking occurs when an obstacle (a "gap" in Dervin's terminology) stops or frustrates a person in their progress through "time-space" and stymies their efforts to continue. In order to resume progress, the person needs to design a movement (a bridge) around, through, over, or away from the obstacle. This can be as simple as asking someone for directions or help, or a complicated set of actions that may have a trial-and-error character. "As an individual moves through an experience, each moment is potentially a sense-making moment. The essence of that sense-making moment is assumed to be addressed by focusing on how the actor defined and dealt with the situation, the gap, the bridge, and the continuation of the journey after crossing the bridge" (Dervin 1992, pp. 69–70). These sensemaking actions can be understood as attempting to answer a set of tacit questions: What is stopping me? What can I do about it? Where can I look for assistance in choosing and taking an action? Weick and Meader (1993, p. 232) define sensemaking as the process of constructing "moderately consensual definitions that cohere long enough for people to be able to infer some idea of what they have, what they want, why they can't get it, and why it may not be worth getting in the first place."

Although in some ways sensemaking can be thought of as a perpetual, ongoing process (Weick 1995), it is also something placed in sharp relief by encountering surprise, interruption, or "whenever an expectation is disconfirmed" (Weick 1995, p. 14). Schön (1987, p. 19) characterizes such moments in professional practice as situations of "complexity, instability, and uncertainty," laden with "indeterminacies and value conflicts." Such moments are further defined by a "density of decision points" (Sawyer 2003, p. 145). In professional practice, the moments where sensemaking comes to the fore can have the character of impasses (Aakhus 2003) or dilemmatic situations (Tracy 1989; see also Aakhus 2001).

PDR practice can include many such moments. Our research looks at the particular character of practitioner sensemaking at those moments, especially as it is expressed through moves on the representations, explorations of and changes to them, and interactions with participants about them (Selvin and Buckingham Shum 2008, 2009). We consider in what ways DR representations, and the practitioners' interactions with them, contain both a source of obstacles and impasses, and a means of resolving or addressing them. In part, we focus on such moments because it is often where practitioner skill and creativity are most clearly manifested. In the example at the end of this section, we see a sensemaking trigger occur when participants discover that the geospatial data they had expected to see was missing from the artifact they were examining. We will see a further example described later in the chapter.

15.4.5 *Improvisation [t]*

As discussed in the previous subsection, practitioners often encounter moments where they must deal with unexpected events in the course of a PDR session. While some aspects of participatory DR practice follow predetermined patterns and draw on techniques and methods planned in advance, skilled practitioners often find themselves switching to alternative sensemaking strategies, or even improvising. It is the degree of creativity employed at this point that distinguishes the *improvisational* dimension of action from other sorts of sensemaking activities. Improvisation can be discerned in the freshness and innovativeness of the response to an event that triggers sensemaking.

Improvisation is difficult to control for, or measure in, laboratory or outcome-based studies of software tool use. Some research into meeting behavior, such as the use of GSS technologies, tends to regularize the practices surrounding the technology, analogous to similar moves to "script" teacher-student interactions (Sawyer 2004) and otherwise de-skill or de-emphasize the creative aspects of many sorts of professional practices (Schön 1983). Yet improvisation is central to understanding what truly occurs in real-world software use situations, especially where there are creative, unpredictable elements at play, such as constructing a representation of design rationale with a group of people in live conversation.

Sawyer (1999) discerns three levels at which to understand improvisation: individual (improvisation on the part of particular actors), group (improvised interactions within a bounded, particular situation), and cultural ("the pre-existing structures available to performers – these often emerge over historical time, from broader cultural processes"; p. 202). The cultural level supplies the elements of a practitioner's repertoire (Schön 1983), the collection of pre-existing techniques and concepts (whether learned in school or from work or other experiences) that contain what the practitioner draws from, combines, and invokes in the heat of an encounter. Practitioners of exceptional skill often possess repertoires of great range and variety (Schön 1983) that they are capable of combining in innovative, expressive, and subtle ways. This kind of characterization is particularly apt when a practitioner is confronted with a situation of confusion or uncertainty, where he or she can no longer continue on with a single pre-existing method or technique (though a return to it later is possible) and must make rapid decisions about what actions to take and ways to inflect those actions, or risk losing the coherence of the session, thus jeopardizing its goals.

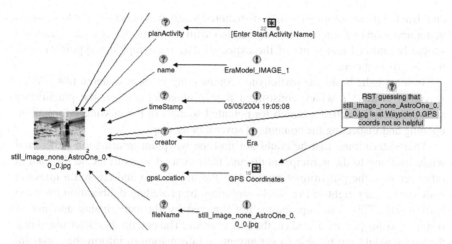

Fig. 15.4 Portion of a screenshot from Mobile Agents project, showing an improvised response to a sensemaking trigger

Maintaining an awareness of the emergent aspects of a situation, however, does not mean that all is left to chance. Sawyer (2004, p. 12) emphasizes the concept of "disciplined improvisation," which juxtaposes improvisational aspects of practice (dialogue, sensemaking responses, spontaneous and creative acts) with "overall task and participation structures," such as "scripts, scaffolds, and activity formats." Skilled practitioners are able to navigate judiciously between moments when they can rely on pre-existing structure and scripted actions, and moments calling for fresh responses and combinations. In a PDR session, improvisation can take many forms, such as sudden shifts in stance or tool strategy. Often these are mini-improvisations that occur and conclude rapidly, unplanned and not referred to verbally in the course of other sorts of actions. This is seen in the example below, which discusses a sensemaking trigger, an improvised response, and the aesthetic dimensions of the response.

15.4.6 An Example

By way of illustrating some of the phenomena discussed above, here we present a highly abbreviated portion of an analysis of one of the episodes from a case study.

Figure 15.4 shows the result of an episode of improvisation on the part of an expert practitioner that took place between 61 min 27 s and 63 min 12 s of a 2 h 15 min session. In the context of NASA field trials (Clancey et al. 2005; Sierhuis and Buckingham Shum 2008), a distributed team was working through auto-generated maps of science data associated with a robotic rover trial. The team suddenly realized that some of the expected data (geographic waypoints) were missing from the map.

As soon as he heard the participants commenting in surprise about this ("What waypoint is this?"), which constituted the sensemaking trigger, the practitioner spontaneously launched a search for potential sources of the missing information, opening and inspecting the contents of several other maps.

After determining that he could not find the waypoint information either, and while listening to the participants discuss their own attempts to locate the data in other records, the practitioner returned to the initial map and created a question node (box on the right in Fig. 15.4) capturing the preceding deliberation from the participants. This was impromptu, not directed by the participants and not in response to any particular coda in the conversation. The practitioner determined that the group would not be able to get any more information to inform the waypoint determination than what they had just said.

The practitioner made several aesthetic choices during this event. He chose an area in the white space to the right of the imported science data nodes, implying or emphasizing by this choice that the new node is a comment on the science data rather than an addition to it: It is outside of the pre-existing imported science data. He also chose to link the node to the main image node, drawing the link across all the other nodes in the view, which serves to make it more dramatic, and possibly effective, emphasizing the disruptive quality of the missing information and the effect it had on the session. He makes a textual aesthetic choice in his use of the gerund *guessing* to imply the unfolding, transitive nature of the comment in the node. If he had used the past tense ("RST guessed"), it would not have conveyed the same process sense of the moment. He also chose to link it to the GPS Coordinates map node, indicating that the node is also commenting on the data contained in that map.

15.4.7 Summary

In our approach, we see the concepts of narrative, sensemaking, and improvisation as providing complementary frames for interpreting instances of practice. Narrative theory provides ways of looking at the container, purpose, intention, and gives the context for the breaches that occur. Sensemaking looks particularly at the breaches and the ways in which actions and representations respond. Improvisation within the context of sensemaking is where we can often most clearly see practitioners demonstrate relative levels of skill and artistry. All of these have both aesthetic and ethical dimensions.

These dimensions are not usually explicit in our source data. Caught up in the proceedings as they are, it is not often that a practitioner or participant in a PDR sessions will directly comment on the narrative framing or aesthetic shaping at work. We have had to develop a number of tools to help us discern and analyze how the dimensions of our framework are manifested in instance of actual practice. These are described in the following section.

15.5   Studying the Practice Level

In this section we describe how we analyzed the ways in which the above dimensions play out in situations of actual PDR practice. As befitting exploratory work in an underresearched domain, we have employed qualitative research techniques to identify themes and hypotheses through close analysis of video and screen recordings of PDR sessions. Qualitative approaches, such as grounded theory (Strauss and Corbin 1990), are generally regarded as appropriate when a field or phenomenon is in its early stages, and when research problems and theoretical issues are not yet well defined. In addition, many of the considerations that the practitioners we are studying must deal with are emergent in character, responding to the unexpected events and anomalies that intrude on even the most carefully planned sessions. Indeed, sensemaking considerations form the core of our analysis here, since being able to resolve the anomalies they encounter is a key success factor for the practitioners we study. The ability to diagnose and repair breakdowns by drawing on a pre-existing "repertoire of expectations, images, and techniques" (Schön 1983, p. 60), as well as fresh creative responses in a near instantaneous fashion, is the hallmark of successful professionals of many kinds, and is no less the case for the practitioners we study.

15.5.1   Source Data and General Approach

We have studied both experienced and relatively inexperienced practitioners. These include several in-depth microanalyses of long PDR sessions, looking at how highly skilled practitioners encounter and solve sensemaking challenges in the course of working with their participants (Selvin 2008). The settings were in situ sessions, often several hours long, held as part of larger projects, where the tasks carried out emerged from the highly contextual needs of those projects (such as a NASA remote science team looking at geological data during virtual meetings over a week-long field trial). We also conducted experiments where teams of mostly novice practitioners planned and carried out a facilitated session for their peers on the theme of space travel. In both types of studies, our primary data are video and screen recordings of the sessions. We analyzed these recordings using a grounded theory approach (Strauss and Corbin 1990), paying special attention to participant and practitioner verbal statements, practitioner actions, and "moves" on the DR representation itself (changes done to the representation, such as adding a node or editing label text).

   The analysis focused on characterizing the choices made by the informants in
their preparation period (what they were trying to achieve, how they organized the
base materials using the software, their intended flow of events, the roles they
assigned, the software aspects they intended to leverage) and in their enacting these
during group sessions. Using critical incident analysis (Tripp 1993), we then selected
moments where practitioners were faced with some kind of anomaly in the course
of a session. We looked at the specific practitioner moves and choices that determined the outcome of the sensemaking moment, focusing on the aesthetic, ethical,
improvisational, and narrative aspects of those moves and how these contributed to
the ways in which participants engaged with the representation, with special emphasis
on the character of the real-time shaping of the representation. Through repeated
viewings and application of a number of analytical instruments (described below),
we built up explanatory concepts, categories, and properties, focusing on the engagement of both practitioner and participants with the hypermedia representation.

15.5.2   Iterative Development of Analytical Tools

The five tools described below emerged from repeated rounds of analysis and
reflection. In each, we started from the data (the recordings of PDR practice) and
identified patterns and concepts that appeared to recur in the moves and statements
contained in the video recordings. Early on, we concentrated on the move-by-move
level and developed a fine-grained instrument with a number of categories derived
from open and axial coding on the contextual meaning of each move and statement
in a session. We identified sensemaking triggers in those sessions, moments where
something disturbed the expected flow of events and forced the practitioner to do
something different, often requiring creative improvisation to resolve the episode
and return the session to its intended track. We then wrote narrative descriptions of
these episodes, starting with the sensemaking trigger, describing the actions within
the episode, and explaining how the episode was brought to closure.

   While this approach produced a large amount of richly described data, several
limitations became apparent. First, it was extremely time-consuming to apply the 18
analytical categories to each move and statement of a 2-h session, which might
contain over 1,300 moves and statements. A grid analysis of a single 2 h 15 min
session required almost 24,000 cells in a spreadsheet. Second, important aspects of
the context itself seemed to recede as we concentrated on the individual moves.
Without losing our focus on the meaning of individual moves, we needed a way to
frame those moves that could more clearly connect them to their context, especially
in ways that allowed us to identify the aesthetic and ethical dimensions informing
the moves. This led us to develop two further instruments. The first provided a way
to characterize the aesthetic "shaping" that both was intended (planned) and actually
occurred during a session. The second was a distillation of the more finely-grained
concepts and categories from the grid analysis that allowed us to characterize
broader timeslots in a session with a more manageable set of three criteria derived

Table 15.2 Summary of tools for analyzing participatory design rationale practice

Analytical tool	Description
Shaping form	Characterizing the representational character of the whole session to delineate the intended and actual shaping that took place
CEU analysis	Mapping the coherence, engagement, and usefulness (CEU) dimensions of timeslots within the session. Aids in identifying sensemaking episodes
Narrative description	Rich description of a sensemaking episode, including dialogue and descriptions of events
Grid analysis	Micro-moment moves and choices during the episode
Framing analysis	Characterizing the practitioner actions during the episode in aesthetic, ethical, and experiential terms

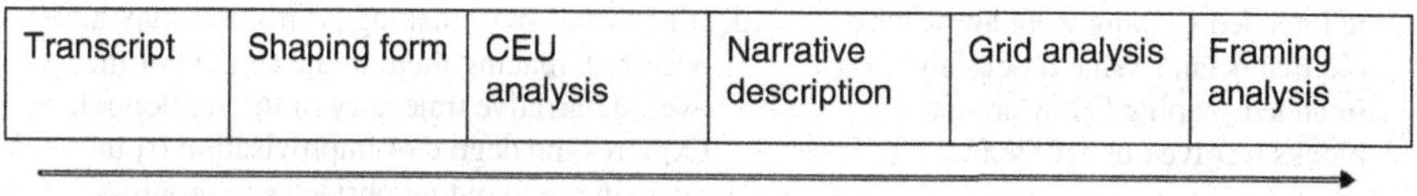

Transcript	Shaping form	CEU analysis	Narrative description	Grid analysis	Framing analysis

Fig. 15.5 Analysis sequence

from our open and axial coding. Both of these processes gave us the means to frame the episodes covered in the other analyses in the context of the session as a whole, in such a way as to highlight our dimensions of interest at all three levels of granularity (session, timeslot, and move).

Finally, we wanted a way to connect the results of these analyses more explicitly to the dimensions of our theoretical framework. This led us to create the "framing" tool. Its categories and questions are derived from the framework, conceived as an ideal, normative model for how a practitioner should act in a PDR situation. This allowed us to compare what actually happened in a session to an ideal model, so as to highlight how practitioner choices moved either closer or farther away from ideal behavior. The full set of analysis tools is summarized in Table 15.2 and described further in the following sections.[3]

15.5.2.1 Analytical Process

For each of the PDR sessions we analyzed, we employed the analytical instruments described above in the sequence represented in Fig. 15.5. By applying this set of tools, we aimed at achieving both qualitative triangulation (Fortner and Christians 1981) and increasing theoretical sensitivity (Strauss and Corbin 1990) by looking at the data through multiple lenses.

---

[3] Analysis artifacts from these studies are available on-line at http://people.kmi.open.ac.uk/selvin/analysis

Table 15.3 Relation of shaping form questions to dimensions of participatory design rationale practice

Shaping form question	Relation to framework
What shaping was intended (how the session was planned to work, what shaping the planners intended to occur, and how it would be accomplished)?	Shaping itself is largely the province of aesthetics [p], the construction of meaningful form. This question refers to the planned or intended sorts of shaping (which may or may not have occurred in the actual session)
What was the level and quality of participant and practitioner engagement (with maps, subject matter, process, environment)?	This question concerns the relationships of participants, practitioners, and representation to each other [framework elements d, e, f, g], as well as to the surrounding context and resources [i, j]
What types of shaping actually occurred during the session?	Means to report what sorts of aesthetic shaping [p] took place in the actual session
If the intended shaping went awry, why did that occur? What blocks an intended shaping? How are the blocks resolved or avoided?	Identifies what sensemaking [s] triggers may have occurred, placing them in the context of the overall narrative trajectory of the session [r]. Explores the degree of improvisation [t] in resolving or avoiding obstacles to progress
Who did the shaping, for what reasons? What contributions to the shaping occurred?	Maps the shaping actions [p] onto the way their performers related to the representation [d, f]
How were decisions about shaping made? What kinds of decisions were they? Who made them, on what basis?	Looks at the choice making involved in both shaping actions and participant inclusion or exclusion in those actions. Often the clearest way to discern the situational ethics [q] of the practitioners
How were these decisions taken up into the representation itself (if they are)? Which are ignored or dropped? Why?	

We started by viewing the video recordings several times and creating a transcript of the entire session. Then, for each of the tools, we viewed the recordings again with the specific lens provided by that tool, which are described below.

15.5.2.2 Shaping Form

The shaping form comprises a set of questions asked about the session as a whole. It aimed at characterizing the representational character of the session. We described what kinds of roles participants and practitioners played in the shaping of the representation, both as a result of planning and intention, and in response to whatever exigencies actually occurred during the session.

The questions included a characterization of the overall ecosystem of the session (the surrounding context, purpose of the session, types of participants), as well as a number of questions designed to put focus on the interaction of people with the representation. Table 15.3 relates the questions to the dimensions of the framework.

The result takes the form of a narrative document (e.g. Fig. 15.6).

If the intended shaping ran off the rails, why did that occur?

> There was no significant running off the rails in this session. Even when the mapper got slightly behind, the facilitator made sure that she provided (or asked again for) material that hadn't been captured. The map was slightly messy by the end, but coherent (well-formed questions, links, and answers).

Who did the shaping, for what reasons? What contributions to the shaping occurred?

> The facilitator and mapper managed the map shaping itself for the most part. Participants contributed ideas verbally throughout but did not question or suggest shaping moves (they appeared to readily accept how the shaping was done). Most participant refinements were verbal rather than map-oriented.

How were decisions about shaping made? What kinds of decisions were they? Who made them, on what basis?

How were these decisions taken up into the representation itself (if they are)?

> See previous. As mentioned above it appeared almost as if the mapper and facilitator had rehearsed and agreed how they would work together. They presented what would look to a newcomer as a nearly seamless front, with the facilitator appearing to prompt the mapper's actions (that she had in fact already started in most cases (e.g. "We're just adjusting the map so we can get a little more space here")), sometimes suggesting that something should be captured differently (e.g. as a question with hanging answers).

Fig. 15.6   Example of a completed shaping form

With the overall character of the representational role described, we now use the CEU tool to zoom into a lower level of detail to characterize the session as it unfolds over time.

15.5.2.3   Coherence, Engagement, and Usefulness (CEU) Analysis

In this analysis, we coded the CEU dimensions of each timeslot to build up a signature (in the sense of a distinctive pattern that indicates the character) for the session. When visualized as a grid, this provides a gestalt view, showing the extent to which the representational artifact being maintained by the practitioner was co-constructed by participants, in a way that seemed to add value.

Coherence involves keeping the information display, and the interaction of participants with it as well as with each other, understandable, clear, evocative, and organized. At any moment, the meaning and organization of the visual and textual elements of the display should be clear to participants (as well as practitioners). *Engagement* refers to the relationship of participants to artifacts in sessions involving any sort of representation, whether a whiteboard, easel sheet, or software projected in front of the real or virtual room. The value of the representation is directly related to the degree that the participants are engaged with it – whether they are looking at it, talking about it, referring to it, and involved in its construction or reshaping. *Usefulness* refers to the extent to which the representation appears to be adding value for the participants and helping to fulfill the predetermined or emergent goals of the session. It is the responsibility of the practitioners to make sure that the representation is a useful part of the proceedings.

We divided the video and screen recordings into 30-s timeslots. For each timeslot, we rated how the session had fared in that timeslot in terms of the CEU of the relationship of the participants to the hypermedia display. There are three ratings: High (three points), indicating a high or strong degree of engagement, coherence, and usefulness; Medium (two points), indicating a medium or average degree of the three criteria; and Low (one point), indicating that there was a low degree during that timeslot. Table 15.4 provides a set of examples illustrating how each rating is derived from the video data. The way we arrived at each rating was derived from the specifics of the session and timeslot itself, and thus vary in what we looked for and were able to discern in the data. Some ratings were assigned based on participant comments or observations of practitioner actions, while others by examining the representational artifact itself at that moment in time in the context of the current participant statements or actions.

For example, the DR representation in a specific timeslot might display a high degree of clarity and "readability"; all the content is legibly presented and laid out, and is faithful to the statements, tone, and purpose of the meeting (at least of its current activity). Thus we would rate both Coherence and Usefulness as High (3 points each). However, at that moment the participants are caught up in a side topic and are not paying attention to the representation, therefore we would rate Engagement as Low (1 point).

By assigning a color to each rating in the spreadsheet, we generate *heat maps* that provide a gestalt visualization of the whole session in terms of the three criteria. Figure 15.7 shows a comparison of CEU heat maps from six different sessions. Such heat maps make it possible to identify the overall tenor of the session, and to point out where sensemaking moments, or breakdowns, may have occurred— typically when the 3 s (High ratings, green shading) drop to 2 s (yellow) or 1 s (red), indicating that the representational artifact seemed to add little or no value at that moment. When a session has High ratings throughout, it can indicate that the preparation and execution of the session (design and realization) were both well thought out in advance and handled in practice. In such sessions, possible breakdowns are avoided, often through the expertise of a practitioner.

Figure 15.7 also shows an overview of the sensemaking character of six of the sessions studied. This visualization shows that three of the Ames sessions contain a fair amount of red cells, indicating Low ratings for one or more of the CEU elements (possibly reflecting the relatively novice level of most of these sessions' practitioners). These are moments in the session when the session went somewhat awry in terms of the practitioners' intentions for having the group

Table 15.4 CEU ratings and exemplars

Criteria	Low	Medium	High
Coherence	The representation is unclear or bears little fidelity to the current focus of interest; e.g., a participant remarks that "I don't see what we're talking about" on the map	Moderate level of coherence, e.g., some confusion about the meaning of the way various nodes on the map are tagged, but generally the representation is clear enough to follow	The representation is a clear reflection of the discussion or exercise, in form, content and organization. All participant contributions have clear places to be entered and linked on the map
Engagement	The participants are paying little or no attention to the map; e.g., some participants are having a side conversation with no reference to the map	An example is when participants start to make side conversation while practitioners are in the midst of making a complicated change to the map, rendering it temporarily less than clear	Participants are looking at, talking about, and appearing to care about what is on a map; e.g., a participant validates that the way the practitioner has captured his/her input on the map is accurate
Usefulness	The representation is not acting as a tool toward the realization of the session's purpose; e.g., the map is no longer keeping up with either the intended exercise or the emergent conversation	This is evident when it is partially, but not completely, clear to the participants how the map will help them complete the exercise	Indicates that the representation is integral to the achievement of the session's purpose; e.g., the structure put in place for the exercise is working efficiently; participants understand the sequence of events and actions

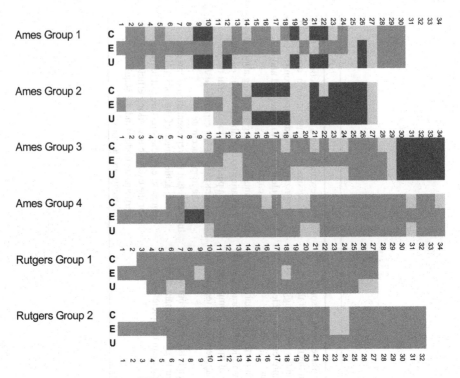

Fig. 15.7 Heat maps from CEU analyses

co-construct the representation. These would be prime locations to look for the sensemaking triggers (what set off the drop in the ratings), as well as what the practitioners and/or participants did to restore the session to better functioning. We can also see that the remaining Ames session as well as the two Rutgers sessions had few or no drops, indicating that the practitioners and participants experienced relatively unproblematic going.

In fact those sessions proceeded very close to plan, whereas the Ames groups 1, 2, and 3 all experienced sensemaking challenges.

Other researchers (e.g., Yoong and Gallupe 2002) apply to electronic meetings similar coherence and engagement constructs as the ones we invoke here. The main difference is one of granularity of analysis. Our primary interest is closer to the brushstroke level – understanding the meaning of the individual practitioner move, when set in context – than the whole-meeting level at which other researchers apply ideas of CEU. At this stage we are not attempting to find inherent relations or patterns among the three criteria, although that may be an outcome of future work.

After reviewing the shaping form and CEU analysis for a session, we selected a particular sensemaking episode for closer analysis. This new analysis started with a narrative description.

15.5.2.4   Narrative Description

The narrative description provides a rich delineation of a sensemaking episode within a session. For this, we identified a starting and ending point for the episode, from the point of the sensemaking trigger (an event or anomaly that initiates some sensemaking behavior) to its resolution or culmination. Sometimes there was no resolution per se, for example, when the practitioners were not able to bring a session back on track after a breakdown. For our purposes, this can happen when participants cease engaging with the representation and just talk to each other without any reference to the representation, as the excerpt below describes:

> In the second episode, the session does not recover from a resurgence of more abstract topics. Here, the sensemaking trigger comes in the midst of a coherent discussion of how to tag the two "surface type" comparison nodes that had come out of the previous few moments. At 13:52, participant E sees an opportunity to ask his recurring (abstract in the sense that it is commenting on the software itself, rather than on the subject matter of the exercise) question again, in a different form: "Well that's—so that's a question …. .so in this tagging exercise are we allowed to have alternative or opposing views?" J jumps right in, echoing this kind of question: "And if you have opposing views how do you do it there in the tag?" At first, E's question is absorbed in the discussion of how to tag the nodes, but then another participant, R, moves the discussion solidly in the abstract direction: "So far, I'm afraid, that we have introduced tags in such a way that you can't question a tag." Unlike the previous episode, however, this time no one jumps in to revert the discussion back to direct engagement with the map. Instead, spurred largely by K, the discussion moves to the relatively abstracted topic of how to think about tags in general.

Our analysis could not capture all of the narrative threads that perhaps were at work in a session. For example, we did not attempt to describe the individual "stories" (professional interests, emotional experiences, project trajectories) that each participant brought to a session, except when such information might have helped to shed light on the narrative framing or construction at work in the practitioner's actions in a sensemaking episode.

Writing out a narrative description in this manner focused the analysis on the place each move or choice has in the way the sensemaking episode unfolds. We drilled down into even a finer level of detail with the grid analysis.

15.5.2.5   Grid Analysis

In the grid analysis for each sensemaking episode, we analyzed each practitioner/ participant statement or representational move according to a number of criteria. This provided a fine-grained understanding of various dimensions of each move, such as the degree and kind of participant engagement with the representation at that moment; the engagement of the practitioner with the participants (e.g., acting in direct response to direction from a participant, or working off to the side to clean up some aspect of the map, or preparing for an upcoming event); the aspects of the setting on which practitioners were focused for that move (participants, maps, text, subject matter, surroundings, or process), and other factors. Mapping each move on

Table 15.5 Move-by-move analysis schema for grid analysis

Aspect	Description
Move type	Assigns each practitioner move to a type in a taxonomy of moves in the *Compendium* software tool (e.g., Node Move-Arranging, Navigate-Map Open, etc.), or Verbal move types (Statement/Announcement, Acknowledgement, Query, Helpful Comment, Exclamation)
Participant engagement with representation	Characterizes the degree to which participants are paying attention to the representation during the move. Possible values: Active, Direct, Delinked, Partial, and Unclear. The Active value, which refers to moments when participants are directing the practitioner to perform particular actions on the representation, has the subtypes Text, Validation, Navigation, and Structure
Practitioner response/ engagement mode	Characterizes the degree to which the practitioner is engaged with the participants during the move. Possible values: Direct, Semi-Direct, Indirect, Delinked. Delinked refers to moves when practitioner attention is focused completely on manipulation of the representation, not interacting or responding to the participants
Practitioner focus	Characterizes what the participant is paying attention to and/or working with during the move. Can be (and often is) multiple. Values: Participants, Maps, Text, Subject Matter, Surroundings, Process

the grid required careful consideration about what that move meant in the context of both the session as a whole and within the particular sensemaking episode, sensitizing the analysis in terms of the meaning to both participants and practitioners. Table 15.5 shows a portion of the taxonomy of concepts used in the grid analysis, derived from open and axial coding through repeated analyses of several long sessions.

The example grid analysis section shown in Fig. 15.8 illustrates six practitioner moves: two verbal statements (at 14 min 47 s and 14 min 51 s) and four actions on the representation, at 14 min 46 s, 14 min 48 s, 14 min 51 s (at the same time as a verbal statement) and 14 min 59 s. Four of these moves were done with simultaneous focus on participants (engaged in conversation with them), maps (working on the form of the map), text (working with the text of the map's icons), and the subject matter of the session, while one (the Link move at 14:59) is a shaping move on the map itself.

The grid analysis required very close inspection and increased sensitivity to nuances of the data. However, the process clearly demonstrated how much is going on when a skilled PDR practitioner is at work, supporting a team with the digital artifacts and rationale it needs as their deliberations unfold. Moreover, the grid analysis set the stage for characterizing practitioner actions and choices according to a set of criteria derived from the dimensions discussed earlier. We call this the *framing analysis*.

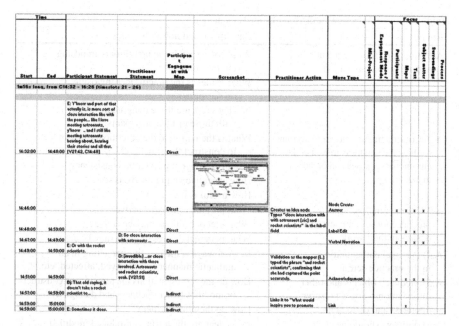

Fig. 15.8   Excerpt from a grid analysis

15.5.2.6   Framing Analysis

The framing analysis characterizes practitioner actions during the session in aesthetic, ethical, and experiential terms. It looks at how the practice and context interweave, and in what ways the aesthetic and ethical dimensions of the practice intertwine (McCarthy and Wright 2004). We use this as the basis for a normative or ideal model against which we can hold up situations of practice (Aakhus 2007; Aakhus and Jackson 2005). Such a model could be used as a diagnostic tool to analyze what factors are preventing a situation from achieving its potential, or at least to characterize a practice situation in potentially useful ways.

The model used in framing analysis provides a set of components, elements, and exploratory questions to help determine how a context of service, the unique set of people, and the goals, constraints, situation, and subject matter can inform the shaping the practitioner performs on the representational object(s), and vice versa. Understanding and characterizing this has both normative (notions of what practice in such settings should be) and descriptive (how do we look at and characterize situated practice in service) aspects (Aakhus and Jackson 2005).

The model contains three columns.[4] The first (leftmost) column shows the major categories or components of the practitioner's stance—his/her orientation toward

---

[4] A full version of the framing analysis model with discussion and citations is available at http://people.kmi.open.ac.uk/selvin/analysis/framing.pdf

Table 15.6 Component A of the framing analysis model

Element	Descriptive and normative questions
(A.1) Imposing their own coherence and values on a situation	What coherence is the practitioner imposing on the situation?
	What values is the practitioner imposing on the situation?
	In what ways are these congruent (or not) with those of the participants?
(A.2) Constructing narratives to account for how the situation arrived at the current pass; causes and breaches in canonicity	What is the narrative the practitioner is using to construct the situation?
	What is its degree of internal consistency?
	How evocative and inclusive is it?
	How useful is it?
(A.3) Eliminating prejudices, preconceptions, and personal desires in their work	What prejudices may be active?
	What preconceptions may be active?
	What personal desires or goals may be active?
(A.4) Personal authenticity in the practice setting	In what ways is the practitioner acting in an authentic manner (vs. received, affected, etc.)?
(A.5) Mediated objects and other interventions should preserve openness and dialogicity	How do the representations the practitioner constructs or modifies foster openness and dialogicity?
	How do they inhibit them?
(A.6) Artifacts should be clear, expressive, and helpful	How clear are the artifacts produced/modified by the practitioner?
	How expressive are they?
	How helpful are they within the context of practice?
(A.7) Perseverance in the face of checks and resistance	What checks to forward progress does the practitioner encounter?
	What resistance from participants, materials, etc. occurs?
	How does the practitioner respond in the face of these?
(A.8) Clear and focused communication	How clear is the practitioner's verbal communication?
	In what ways does the practitioner maintain focus on the aspects of importance in the situation?

various aspects of the situation or practice setting: the practitioner's towards him/ herself and his/her own actions, towards the participants, and towards the situation as a whole. The middle column breaks down each stance into elements, each of which is explicitly related to the body of theory it arose from (largely from Bruner 1990; Dewey 1934/2005; Schön 1983, 1987; McCarthy and Wright 2004). These elements constitute an ideal model of practitioner stance; that is, the model specifies the preferred conduct of a PDR practitioner as maintaining a dialogic orientation, fostering a heightened degree of connection between participants, the setting, purpose, and representation, and so on. The elements in turn generate descriptive (characterizing) or normative (evaluating) questions that can help guide the analysis of a particular setting, found in the rightmost column. The rightmost two columns of Component A of the framing model, which addresses the practitioner's own involvement in the situation, are shown in Table 15.6.

Considering the questions put forward in the framing model involved examining and reflecting on the analytical artifacts produced thus far. Since the framing analysis came last in the analysis sequence, by that time the analyst was very familiar with the specific occurrences in the video recording of the session, and particularly with the nuances of the behavior demonstrated by the practitioners during sensemaking episodes.

For example, in our Ames Group 2 case, we saw the following responses for component A.5, mediated objects and other interventions should preserve openness and dialogicity:

How do the actions of the practitioners inhibit openness and dialogicity?:
The prepared map appeared (and was said by participants afterward to be) too complex/involved for participants to engage with, although the mapping of the "needs" section did seem to invite dialogue (unfortunately shut off by the mapper). The mapper's verbal intervention served to inhibit the nascent discussion about how to map the "needs" section.

In this case the practitioners needed either to be flexible in how the session would proceed, and evolve the map accordingly (with its extensive prestructuring that the participants were not paying attention to), or to intervene again to bring the session back to the course that they had intended. They could have brought the attention of the group to the portion of the map that contained the desired area of focus and created an effective way for the group to engage with it. As it happened, they stood by and waited to see if the conversation would come back to the intended course of its own accord (rarely an effective strategy).

15.6 Case Study

The previous section of this chapter introduced the various lenses we have been developing to make sense of PDR practice, illustrated with examples taken from a range of contexts. We now bring these together around a single design session, presenting brief examples of several of the above analyses to show how they provide different kinds of insight.

15.6.1 Setting

The setting for the session was a workshop for people interested in the Compendium[5] software tool for mapping multimedia information and design rationale (e.g., as IBIS maps), held at the NASA Ames Research Center, in May 2007. (Compendium is the descendant of the Graphical IBIS [gIBIS] design rationale prototype for

---

[5] Compendium Institute: http://compendium.open.ac.uk.institute

Fig. 15.9 Informants working on their materials for the large group exercise

mapping IBIS, questions-options-criteria [QOC], and other argumentation structures; Buckingham Shum et al. 2006; Conklin and Begeman 1988). Half of one of the two days was given to a segment where less experienced practitioners could plan and facilitate a PDR session and get feedback from more senior practitioners. We divided the informants into groups of three to four and gave them the same general assignment and set of materials. We intended the practice task to be one that required neither expertise with real time use of the software, nor in the subject matter, so that the preparation and practice session could occur within a couple of hours without any advance knowledge on the part of the informants. We chose space travel as the subject matter (reasoning that it was a topic of general interest with which participants could be expected to have at least passing familiarity). We provided a set of 127 images inside Compendium that could be used in the exercise. Informants were informed that the sessions would be recorded for research purposes. They were given advance access to the task materials if they wanted to review them before the workshop.

Each group was given about 90 min to prepare (see Fig. 15.9). Some groups included a more experienced practitioner who was allowed to help design and prepare the exercise but not to play an active part during the large group exercise itself.

After the preparation period, each group took turns introducing and conducting their session with the larger group of participants. Typically each group had one person acting as the mapper (hands on the keyboard/mouse to control the Compendium hypermedia knowledge mapping software) and one as facilitator (guiding the discussion from in front of the room). Each group had 15 min to conduct their session, followed by a debrief discussion in which they also received feedback from the larger group.

In the following section we describe what one of the informant groups (Ames Group 1) encountered in their large group session. The process will be viewed through the lenses of the tools presented above.

15.6.2   Shaping Form Analysis

The shaping form analysis of Ames Group 1's large group session described how the practitioner team intended the session to proceed as an IBIS discussion of two central questions, for which they had also supplied seed answers. They also intended that each participant's contribution would be tagged with the participants' names, and that the participants would choose an image to correspond with their answer. There was no set outcome, just discussion mapping augmented with the tags and pictures. Both the facilitator and the mapper stayed directly engaged throughout the session. The mapper tried hard to capture all of the discussion on the map and to perform the ancillary tagging task. Both made interventions in the group process, slowing down the discussion at various times and asking for clarification. Both spoke directly to participants and appeared to be trying to get breadth and depth into the discussion as well as to let it and the map evolve. There were some environment issues having to do with how to use the software for elements like font size, which provided brief distractions. The session did experience some breakdowns, mainly when the mapper fell behind in creating a separate map to handle a rather abstract question that came from one of the participants (who himself was trying to understand why other participants kept steering the discussion away from the intended direction). The mapper was trying to perform a series of operations to do this, but new participant contributions came in while she was doing that and she fell behind.

15.6.3   CEU Analysis

Figure 15.10 shows the full-session CEU heat map for Ames Group 1. It is apparent from the heat map that timeslots 9–12, 19–22, and 26 contain some sort of anomaly or event that caused the coherence and usefulness scores to drop to the Low level.

Figure 15.11 shows a fuller picture of the analytical grid used to develop the CEU ratings for timeslots 19–22 (and the recovery in timeslots 23–24). Here we see a narrative description of the events in each 30 s timeslot, the CEU ratings, and explanations of why each rating was given for each timeslot.

The CEU analysis pictured here provides context for finer-grained analysis of what happened in timeslots 17 through 23, the trajectory of a complete sensemaking episode, starting with a trigger and ending with the resolution.

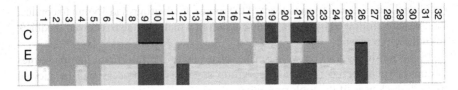

Fig. 15.10 Heat map from Ames Group 1

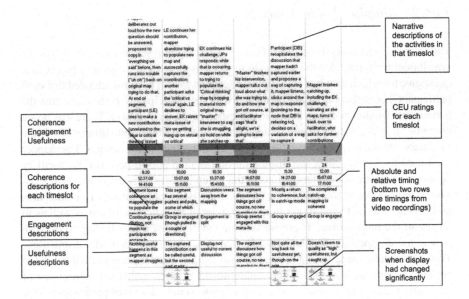

Fig. 15.11 CEU ratings for timeslots 19–24

15.6.4 Narrative Description of the Sensemaking Episode

The instance occurred for about 2.5 min of the 24 min session, starting at 13:36 (timeslot 17) and lasting until 16:58 (timeslot 23). The session had proceeded more or less as planned until, at 13:36, one participant (P1) began to challenge some of the contributions to the overall discussion, questioning why some participants kept asking if others' contributions counted as "critical thinking" or "visual thinking" (illustrated on the screenshot in Fig. 15.12).

The challenge did not fit into the expected flow of events, and the mapper, who up to that point had been able to capture participant contributions within the map quite fluidly, lost her way. This constituted the sensemaking trigger. Trying to make the structure of the representation match the conversation when it veers from the expected course is a frequent challenge in PDR. Often the planned

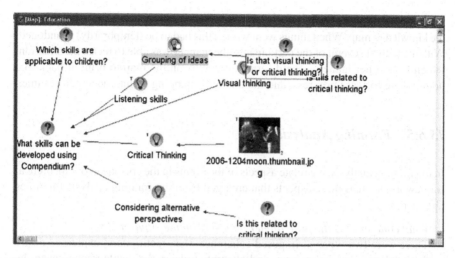

Fig. 15.12   Ames Group 1 session: Map at 13 min 36 s

structure does not seem to contain or fit what people are saying. She began trying to map P1's challenge at 13:49. At 14:42 she was in the midst of doing this when another participant (P2) made a new verbal contribution that did not reference the challenge.

A third participant, P3, asked if P2's comment counted as critical thinking or visual thinking, prompting a further challenge from P1. The mapper was able to capture P2's 14:42 contribution on the fly, but could not map either P3's question or P1's new challenge. In the course of this, the mapper got so far behind in mapping P1's challenge that she became stymied.

She faced two overlapping dilemmas. Firstly the participants' issue about how to frame the conversation itself, and secondly her own attempt to regain her momentum and resume making coherent additions to the map. The argument about critical versus visual thinking itself (and whether it was a fit subject for the session) can be seen as the collision of several competing narratives, some of which preceded the event, such as competing ideas for how such discussions should proceed. In this case, after some further back and forth among the participants, a fourth participant (P4) contributed a possible solution. After some negotiation about how much time was left in the session, the mapper asked the room for help in deciding what should be put onto the map. A fifth participant (P5) provided a helpful summary and suggestion for how to represent the discussion.

From that point until the end of the episode at 16:58, the mapper executed a rapid series of moves on the map, which enabled her to bring the map up to the point where it corresponded to the summary provided by participant P5, and to announce at 16:58, "I'm caught up."

In the excerpt, we see improvised actions that draw on practitioner (as well as participant) repertoires. Up to the point of the breach in timeslot 19, the mapper had followed a straightforward, preplanned dialogue mapping approach in her work on the knowledge map. When things went wrong, this had to be (temporarily) abandoned. With the help of several of the participants, the mapper was able to recast the situation, which helped her launch a rapid series of actions on the map to bring it back to a point where forward progress, and the dialogue mapping technique, could resume.

15.6.5   Framing Analysis

In the framing analysis, we relate aspects of the events in the episode to our theoretical framework, such as these aspects that emerged from the framing analysis for Ames Group 1:

What coherence is the practitioner imposing on the situation?
There were two types of imposed coherence: the practitioners' expressed desire for a "clean" discussion map, and attempts to keep the display coherent in the face of divergent and somewhat problematic contributions (in the sense of being hard to fit in or tending to pull the discussion off the intended course). There was a concerted attempt at coming up with coherent structures on the fly to encompass both the *primary contributions* (the answers to the seed questions) and the *meta contributions* about visual versus critical thinking, such as the participant statements at 13:36 and 14:51.

What values is the practitioner imposing on the situation? In what ways are these congruent (or not) with those of the participants?
There was a value of inclusiveness, of trying to map everything offered, but also a willingness to set some possible directions aside in the interest of cleanly mapping at least some of the contributions. The mapper had to choose between following all of the possible threads – particularly the pull toward the metaquestions about critical thinking – that some of the participants wanted to pursue versus focusing on cleanly mapping a few. Of necessity some participants' interests got shorter shrift as a result, such as a participant comment about "seeing bigger questions" at 14:42.

What is the narrative the practitioner is using to construct the situation?
The practitioners intended that a "clean" discussion would emerge "naturally" from the seed questions. A breach occurred when the actual discussion did not follow the intended form cleanly. The mapper was smoothly capturing the discussion as it happened, but then divergent input came in which required operations that (a) she was not quick enough at doing, or (b) did not seem to fit coherently.

How evocative and inclusive is it?
The preplanned, intended narrative set up a canonicity of a cleanly unfolding discussion, in which participants could provide tagged answers with images in response to the clear questions. However the answers started spawning a meta-discussion that broke down, and the practitioners were not able to be completely inclusive of all the contributions.

How do the representations the practitioner constructs or modifies foster openness and dialogicity?

The seed questions were appropriately open-ended, which lent itself to dialogue (e.g., "What skills can be developed using Compendium?"). The question nodes added during the session were partially so, though some were phrased as yes-or-no questions, which are less open (e.g., "Is this related to critical thinking?"). These were mostly done quickly in response to the metaquestions that were difficult to handle by their nature (e.g., "Is this visual or critical thinking?" or "Why do we keep getting hung up on this question?"). However, by deciding (after some back-and-forth) to link these questions to each answer they pertained to, the practitioners were preserving the opportunity to deal with the metaquestions later, recording them in answer to the concerns of some of the participants, while still keeping the intended discussion course going. A similar dynamic was gained by following the suggestion to open a separate map to address the meta-question "What is critical thinking?" The possibility of exploring that question later remained open.

We see in these excerpts that the practitioner's actions can be characterized along multiple aesthetic and ethical dimensions. She had to make representational and process choices, which ultimately had consequences for which participant interests would be reflected in what ways. She had to temporarily abandon forward movement so that she could catch up, and reach out for help and suggestions for how to proceed. This proved successful, as she was able to get back on track.

15.7   Summary and Discussion

In this chapter we have described research that looks at the practice level of PDR: the wielding of DR tools in service to groups of people in collaborative, real-time settings. We can now revisit the research questions proposed earlier:

- (RQ1) What is the nature of the skills required to construct graphical knowledge representations in real-time, participatory settings?
- (RQ2) What are the kinds of choices practitioners face, especially at sensemaking moments in the course of conducting sessions?
- (RQ3) How does the context of the service being provided affect the choices a practitioner makes?

Rather than evaluating the PDR tools or methods themselves for RQ1, we took them as a given and focused instead on the human activity of creating the representations, especially on the skills needed and obstacles encountered in keeping DR artifacts coherent, engaging, and useful. For RQ2, we proposed a theoretical framework that has proven helpful in characterizing practitioner choices at sensemaking moments, and described the analytical tools that helped us examine video recordings of practice in light of the framework. For RQ3, we presented brief examples from some of our case studies describing instances of practitioner creativity and improvisation, often occurring as short "flashes," and gave examples of practitioners making aesthetic and ethical choices in the course of managing the multithreaded activities of a PDR session, including discussion of how the context and situation of practice informs the choices and moves practitioners make.

How does this kind of analysis advance matters? We propose that by looking closely at how actual sessions unfold, and treating their exigencies with the kind of attention given to other forms of professional practice, we elevate the activity of facilitating collaborative representation-making in groups (whether DR, or any other visual language) into a worthy research subject in its own right. This can provide a way for practitioners to deepen their understanding of their work by giving them a variety of means to analyze and reflect on their own practice, and can contribute to development of practitioner guidelines such as those common to other professional practices, such as the coherence guidelines for GSS facilitators proposed by Yoong and Gallupe (2002). The various analytical tools we have developed can contribute toward a methodology for characterizing the aesthetic and ethical dimensions of participatory media practice. These can lead to development of better approaches to practitioner education, thus "helping a student break into manageable parts what had at first appeared to be a seamless flow of movement" (Schön 1987, p. 112). For example, the framing analysis could be used as a diagnostic tool to analyze what factors are preventing a situation from achieving its potential, or at least to characterize a practice situation in potentially useful ways.

The framework and analysis tools also shed light on the fostering of creativity in design meetings, particularly when rationale is being captured. As we have seen, people taking on the practitioner's role play a key part when teams encounter breakdowns and anomalies in the course of PDR sessions. Such moments, in small and sometimes large ways, can make the difference between success and failure of a design session. Failure can cause frustration and setbacks to a design effort, whereas success in swiftly resolving a breakdown frees up a team to bring their creativity to bear on the design problems rather than on "fixing" the meeting. We have seen how practitioner creativity can emerge when he/she intervenes in a session to restore its forward movement. At its best, practitioner creativity can result in choice, action, and materials seamlessly coming together to resolve the breakdown.

A potential contribution of this research is the development of a typology of dimensions of PDR practice, situations that a practitioner could face and the types of possible actions, such as the partial example in Table 15.7. Practitioners could use such a table to reflect on what did or did not happen in a particular session, considering the pros and cons of the different approaches given the context.

PDR practice is worthy of investigation in its own right and the methods outlined here provide a practical means and theoretical basis for doing so. These methods also point out how practitioners, tool builders, and consumers of PDR services can better understand how the micro, often tacit, dimensions of a practice shape the form and content of the product – namely, the rationale captured. Hence, aesthetics [p], ethics [q], narrative [r], sensemaking [s], and improvisation [t] are consequential

Table 15.7 Some common practice situations and example actions

Situation	Possible actions
Participant topics or statements that do not fit the planned structure	Intervene in the conversation to bring it back to intended topic
	Evolve the structure on the fly
	Engage participants in direct reflection on the structure
Too much information and input coming too fast	Ask participants to slow down; be willing to intervene firmly if needed
	Capture as much as possible in background, wait for an opportunity to ask participants what was missed

for how matters are represented. With the approach described here, we can go much further in understanding how.

In future work we will draw on the foundational considerations outlined in this chapter to develop concrete activities for practitioner education, as well as lessons for supporting tool design. We follow McCarthy and Wright's (2004, p. 62) argument that restoring the "continuity between aesthetic and prosaic experience" can reveal untapped and unexplored dimensions of the human experience of technology, for which more conventional approaches fail to provide tools for understanding. Using felt experience and an aesthetic viewpoint for technology use, they argue, would open up new possibilities for tool design. We will explore what general lessons, heuristics, and guidelines for practice can be drawn from the cases, and develop ways to help practitioners apply them to instances of practice. As a first step, we conducted a session at a gathering of graphic facilitators in August 2009.[6] Participants evaluated an instance of their own practice (a very different approach than PDR) using the CEU constructs, and reported that it helped them reflect in new ways about their actions.

Taking the practice level seriously means looking closely at what it takes to make sessions run well: how different practitioners overcome the experiential challenges involved in bringing a group of people through such an effort successfully. Partly because we have lived these challenges ourselves in many different contexts, and partly because we strongly believe in the benefits and potential of the approaches, PDR for us is already a professional practice deserving of careful study as an ongoing phenomenon rather than a start-up experiment, moving the question from "Can it work?" to "How can it work better?" Better tools and methods alone may help inculcate a broader interest in the practice level, but developing knowledge and expertise in the practice level can help bring about wider and more effective use of the tools and methods.

---

[6] Voices of Visual Practice, 14th Annual International Forum of Visual Practitioners Conference, Montreal, Canada, August 5–7, 2009; http://www.ifvp.org

References

Aakhus, M. (2001). Technocratic and design stances toward communication expertise: How GDSS facilitators understand their work. *Journal of Applied Communication Research, 29*, 341–371.

Aakhus, M. (2002). *Design practice and transparency work in the technological facilitation of collaborative decision making*. Unpublished manuscript.

Aakhus, M. (2003). Neither naïve nor critical reconstruction: Dispute mediators, impasse, and the design of argumentation. *Argumentation, 17*, 265–290.

Aakhus, M. (2007). Conversations for reflection: Augmenting transitions and transformations in expertise. In C. R. McInerney & R. E. Day (Eds.), *Re-thinking knowledge management: From knowledge objects to knowledge processes* (pp. 1–20). Dordrecht: Springer.

Aakhus, M., & Jackson, S. (2005). Technology, interaction, and design. In K. Fitch & R. Sanders (Eds.), *Handbook of language and social interaction* (pp. 411–436). Mahwah: Lawrence Erlbaum.

Arnheim, R. (1967). *Art and visual perception: A psychology of the creative eye*. Berkeley: University of California Press.

Bruner, J. (1990). *Acts of meaning*. Cambridge, MA: Harvard University Press.

Buckingham Shum, S. (1996). Analyzing the usability of a design rationale notation. In T. Moran & J. Carroll (Eds.), *Design rationale: Concepts, techniques, and use* (pp. 185–215). Mahwah: Lawrence Erlbaum.

Buckingham Shum, S., Selvin, A., Sierhuis, M., Conklin, J., Haley, C., & Nuseibeh, B. (2006). Hypermedia support for argumentation-based rationale: 15 years on from gIBIS and QOC. In A. Dutoit, R. McCall, I. Mistrik, & B. Paech (Eds.), *Rationale management in software engineering* (pp. 111–132). Berlin: Springer. Also available at http://oro.open.ac.uk/3032

Clancey, W. J., Sierhuis, M., Alena, R., Berrios, D., Dowding, J., Graham, J. S., Tyree, K. S., Hirsh, R. L., Garry, W. B., Semple, A., Buckingham Shum, S. J., Shadbolt, N., & Rupert, S. (2005, January–February). *Automating CapCom using mobile agents and robotic assistants*. Paper presented at the American Institute of Aeronautics and Astronautics 1st Space Exploration Conference, Orlando, FL, USA. Available from: AIAA Meeting Papers on Disc [CD-ROM], Reston, VA, and as Advanced Knowledge Technologies ePrint 375: http://eprints.aktors.org/375, pp. 1–41.

Cohen, C. (1997). *A poetics of reconciliation: The aesthetic mediation of conflict*. Unpublished doctoral dissertation, University of New Hampshire, USA. Available on-line at www.brandeis.edu/ethics/coexistence_initiative/research_and_scholarship/reconciliation.pdf

Conklin, J., & Begeman, M. (1988). gIBIS: A hypertext tool for exploratory policy discussion. *ACM Transactions on Information Systems, 6*, 303–331.

Dervin, B. (1983, May). *An overview of sense-making research: Concepts, methods, and results to date*. Paper presented at the annual meeting of the International Communication Association, Dallas, TX, USA.

Dervin, B. (1992). From the mind's eye of the user: The sense-making qualitative-quantitative methodology. In J. D. Glazier & R. R. Powell (Eds.), *Qualitative research in information management* (pp. 61–84). Englewood: Libraries Unlimited.

Dewey, J. (2005). *Art as experience*. New York: The Berkeley Publishing Group. (Originally published in 1934)

Fortner, R., & Christians, C. (1981). Separating wheat from chaff in qualitative studies. In G. Stempel & B. Westley (Eds.), *Research methods in mass communication* (2nd ed., pp. 375–387). Englewood Cliffs: Prentice Hall.

Kunz, W., & Rittel, H. (1970). Issues as elements of information systems (Working Paper No. 131). Studiengruppe fur Systemforschung, Heidelberg, Germany.

McCarthy, J., & Wright, P. (2004). *Technology as experience*. Cambridge, MA: MIT Press.

Murray, K. (n.d.). Narrative partitioning: The ins and outs of identity construction. Retrieved May 3, 2006, from http://home.mira.net/~kmurray/psych/in&out.html

Rosson, M. B., & Carroll, J. (2009). Scenario-based design. In A. Sears & J. Jacko (Eds.), *Human-computer interaction: Development process* (pp. 1032–1050). Boca Raton: CRC Press/Taylor & Francis.

Sawyer, K. (1999). Improvised conversations: Music, collaboration and development. *Psychology of Music, 27*, 192–205.

Sawyer, K. (2003). *Group creativity: Music, theater, collaboration.* Mahwah: Lawrence Erlbaum.

Sawyer, K. (2004). Creative teaching: Collaborative discourse as disciplined improvisation. *Educational Researcher, 33*(2), 12–20.

Schön, D. (1983). *The reflective practitioner: How professionals think in action.* London: Basic Books.

Schön, D. (1987). *Educating the reflective practitioner: Toward a new design for teaching and learning in the professions.* San Francisco: Jossey-Bass.

Selvin, A. (2008). Performing knowledge art: Understanding collaborative cartography. In A. Okada, S. Buckingham Shum, & T. Sherborne (Eds.), *Knowledge cartography: Software tools and mapping techniques* (pp. 223–247). London: Springer.

Selvin, A., & Buckingham Shum, S. (2008, April). *Narrative, sensemaking, and improvisation in participatory hypermedia construction.* Paper presented at the Sensemaking Workshop, CHI 2008: ACM Conference on Computer-Human Interaction, Florence, Italy. Available on-line at http://oro.open.ac.uk/19039

Selvin, A., & Buckingham Shum, S. (2009, April). *Coherence, engagement, and usefulness as sensemaking criteria in participatory media practice.* Paper presented at the Sensemaking Workshop, ACM Computer-Human Interaction (CHI) Conference, Boston, MA, USA. Available on-line at http://oro.open.ac.uk/12910

Sierhuis, M., & Buckingham Shum, S. (2008). Human–agent knowledge cartography for e-Science: NASA field trials at the Mars Desert Research Station. In A. Okada, S. Buckingham Shum, & T. Sherborne (Eds.), *Knowledge cartography: Software tools and mapping techniques* (pp. 287–305). London: Springer.

Strauss, A., & Corbin, J. (1990). *Basics of qualitative research: Grounded theory procedures and techniques.* Newbury Park: Sage.

Tracy, K. (1989). Conversational dilemmas and the naturalistic experiment. In B. Dervin, L. Grossberg, B. O'Keefe, & E. Wartella (Eds.), *Rethinking communication* (Paradigm Examples, Vol. 2, pp. 411–423). Newbury Park: Sage.

Tripp, D. (1993). *Critical incidents in teaching: Developing professional judgment.* New York: Routledge.

Weick, K. (1995). *Sensemaking in organizations.* Thousand Oaks: Sage.

Weick, K., & Meader, D. (1993). Sensemaking and group support systems. In L. Jessup & J. Valacich (Eds.), *Group support systems: New perspectives* (pp. 230–252). New York: Macmillan.

Yoong, P., & Gallupe, B. (2002). Coherence in face-to-face electronic meetings: A hidden factor in facilitation success. *Group Facilitation: A Research and Applications Journal, 4*, 12–21. Available also on-line at http://citeseerx.ist.psu.edu/viewdoc/download?doi=10.1.1.125.4454&rep=rep1&type=pdf#page=15

Chapter 16
Managing Conflict in Information System Design Stakeholder Conferences: The Role of Transparency Work

Mark Aakhus

Abstract This chapter examines the management of disagreement and conflict during an information systems design conference that sought agreement on a data-flow-model and design requirements among stakeholders in a new information system. The case identifies micro design practices, such as *fashioning-a-record*, employed in facilitating creativity and capturing rationale during the design conference. The micro-practices reveal the layers of *transparency work* performed by the facilita-tors that involves: (1) setting up the usability and usefulness of the technology and (2) persuading participants about the essence of their interaction. Transparency work draws attention away from the actions of the facilitators and the social-political complications while highlighting any features of the scene reflecting ideals of collaborative decision-making. The persuasion aims to remove doubt about the nature of the activity and trustworthiness of the intervention. The analysis shows how the ethnomethodological principle of the documentary method of interpretation operates in bridging the gap between technology and use, which addresses key matters in the literature on technologically supported facilitation.

Keywords Collaboration • Communication design • Facilitation • Meetings • Meta-structuring • Persuasion

This study is an ethnographic investigation of the technological facilitation of collaborative decision-making. The concern, in this study, lies not so much with how communication technology designed to aid collaboration is employed but with how this technology is made employable. Collaboration is here taken to be a

M. Aakhus (✉)
Department of Communication, School of Communication and Information,
Rutgers, The State University of New Jersey, 4 Huntington Street,
New Brunswick, NJ 08901-1071, USA
e-mail: aakhus@rutgers.edu

J.M. Carroll (ed.), *Creativity and Rationale: Enhancing Human
Experience by Design*, Human–Computer Interaction Series,
DOI 10.1007/978-1-4471-4111-2_16, © Springer-Verlag London 2013

327

belief and quality of participation that is independent of the technology intended to inspire it and thus a quality of interaction to be constructed in the flow of interaction. Using technology to facilitate collaborative decision-making involves two layers of work. The technology must be implemented and the decision-makers using the technology must come to recognize their decision-making as collaborative. This second layer of work involves persuading participants about the essence of their participation in using the technology. As such, it is fundamental to understanding facilitation practice and to theoretical issues in CSCW about bridging the gap between technology design and use. The study reported here focuses on how this second layer of work happens.

A paradigm case from which to investigate the technological facilitation of collaborative decision-making is the work performed by meeting facilitators who use group decision-making technology to manage the disagreement and conflict around the divergence-convergence tension that happens when fostering creativity in group decision-making. The work facilitators perform is often misunderstood and not taken seriously enough as a resource for understanding the technological facilitation of collaborative decision-making. The chapter develops two themes. First, the conventional account of GDSS facilitators work is examined in light of ethnographic observations of the *transparency work* evident in their situated practices. Second, an alternative account of their work as *communication design practice* is developed that has implications for more general understanding of facilitating creativity and rationale in work and decision-making.

16.1 Background

16.1.1 What Do GDSS Facilitators Do?

Central to their work is the fostering of creativity and the capture of rationale in supporting decision-making. GDSS facilitators plan, convene, and run meetings for groups and organizations. Their work is an intervention on the communication between two or more parties to help those parties settle jointly shared problems, choices, or conflicts (Aakhus 2001). A GDSS facilitator, or facilitation team, might be employed, for instance, to help an agency develop a mission statement, to help a firm create design requirements for an information system, or to help the representatives from different companies work out a policy about standards. In most cases, facilitators do not make decisions for the client group but instead provide process support. A common approach facilitators will take in providing support is to foster creativity by enabling divergent thinking and then helping the decision-making group use their divergent thinking to converge on the best acceptable choice. While divergence is typically associated with creativity, creating a path to convergence is yet another kind of creativity. There is a tension, however, between divergence and convergence that facilitators navigate (Aakhus 2000; Nunamaker et al. 1991).

GDSS facilitators support decision-making by engaging the participants in a variety of face-to-face and computer mediated interactions to help the parties make sense of their deliberation and proceed in making decisions and resolving disputes. GDSS technology is designed to provide process support. A GDSS is composed of networked computers and specialized software. The software is designed to aid common decision-making tasks like building lists, organizing ideas, and evaluating ideas and it emulates group process techniques such as brainstorming and nominal group technique (e.g., Baecker et al. 1995; Nunamaker et al. 1991; Poole and DeSanctis 1990, 1992). Importantly, GDSS provide a variety of ways to capture rationale from the group through text based input and visualization (e.g., brain-storming, categorizing, voting). Facilitators make use of these affordances in navigating the divergence-convergence tension.

A key challenge in intervening on decision processes lies in making the GDSS usable and useful. Much research on GDSS focuses on the effects and usability of the system (Nunamaker et al. 1994; Pinsonneault and Kraemer 1989; Poole and Holmes 1995; Seibold et al. 1994). When appropriately implemented, GDSS use leads to higher levels of consensus and decision satisfaction than might otherwise be achieved (Anson et al. 1995; Connelly et al. 1990; Dickson et al. 1996; Ngwenyama et al. 1996). GDSS, however, appear most well suited for small, cooperative groups working on well defined problems (Allen 1993; Grudin 1994; Kraemer and King 1988; Lyytinen et al. 1994; Weick and Meader 1993). Many groups and many of the important choices, problems, and conflicts calling for intervention do not fit what is presumed about decision-making in the GDSS design. Yet, despite the gap between GDSS as designed and the demands of complex decision events, GDSS have been implemented with success (Bikson 1996; de Vreede and de Bruijn 1999; Nunamaker et al. 1991). This is often attributed to the quality of the facilitation that renders the GDSS usable and useful for the end users of the GDSS (e.g., Bikson 1996; Bostrom and Anson 1992; Bostrom et al. 1993; Johansen 1989; Nunamaker et al. 1991, 1994; Poole et al. 1995).

16.1.2 Research on GDSS Facilitation

There is only small stream of research about what GDSS facilitators do that attempts to explain their contribution to successful interventions. The most well developed empirical account is found in Bostrom and colleagues research (e.g., Bostrom et al. 1993; Clawson and Bostrom 1996). Studies in this line have identified particular skills that appear to be critical success factors in successful group outcomes. These include skills such as actively building relationships, planning meetings, directing meetings, and creating an open positive environment (Anson et al. 1995; Clawson et al. 1993; Niederman et al. 1996). The goal of this research is to create an accumulated body of techniques that have been verified to produce certain outcomes (e.g., Clawson and Bostrom 1996). In many ways, this extant research is organized around goals similar to scientific management, which is problematic for understanding what GDSS facilitators do. The problem does not lie in identifying the technical, instrumental dimensions of the work but in framing and investigating facilitators' work as a group or organizational function. This conventional focus renders invisible important aspects of the discretion and the practical knowledge about communication GDSS facilitators exercise, especially their know-how in bridging the gap between GDSS as designed and the complexities of events on which they intervene.

The invisibility of the work performed by GDSS facilitators in rendering technology useable and useful is part of a larger, ongoing issue in understanding the relationship between people, technology, and action. As Orlikowski et al. (1995) point out, much of what is important in bridging the gap between technology design and use is assumed to take place in the way "end users" of the technology use the technology rather than in the ways technology is set up and interpreted for users. This is clearly the case for GDSS facilitators whose influence on the success of GDSS interventions is well acknowledged but the nature of that influence, as it is found in the situated actions performed by GDSS facilitators, is not well documented nor understood.

Two developed theories about GDSS effects that focus on the social/communicative influences that bridge the gap between technology and use are adaptive-structuration-theory (Poole and DeSanctis 1990, 1992; DeSanctis and Poole 1994) and self-organizing-systems-theory (Contractor and Seibold 1993). Both approaches have developed elaborate quantitative models to map out the functions of various influence attempts in the way GDSS is appropriated. Both theories focus almost exclusively on the relationship between the technology and the end user. Neither approach, however, has sufficiently addressed the content of the appropriation moves, structuring norms, or GDSS expertise that both theories claim to be central to the influence that bridges the gap between design and use. The consequence is that "appropriation," which is key to explaining the success of GDSS interventions, remains vague as an explanation for how GDSS as designed is integrated into the complexities of the events in which it is used (e.g., Banks and Riley 1993; Mateosian 1993).

There is a need in GDSS research but also more broadly for understanding the use of information systems to closely examine the influence of the specialists involved in, as Orlikowski et al. (1995) point out, "the shaping of other users' activities of use" or "metastructuring" (p. 425). Orlikowski et al. described mediating activities undertaken to shape how users use newsgroups to manage their project teams. They show how these mediating activities vary with changes in the setting and the rules of the organization. They discuss how mediating activities provide organizations opportunity to adapt electronic media to changing conditions and forms of organization.

The present study not only looks at the techniques for mediating technology and use involved in interventions aimed at fostering creativity in decision-making activities but looks closely at the persuasion involved in articulating the form and quality of communication that render the technology useable and the decision-making acceptable. This is done by articulating the hidden "communication design practice" (Aakhus 2007) in the work of GDSS facilitators to explain the influence they bring to bear in bridging the gap between technology design and use. Their design work involves crafting a line of communicative activity that manages the complexities of the events on which they intervene and it involves persuasion about the credibility of the activity they craft and their trustworthiness in providing this service, and thus the legitimacy of the communicative activity.

16.2   Data and Research Strategy

16.2.1   Data

To understand the work performed by GDSS facilitators and its influence on bridging the gap between design and use, fieldwork was conducted at a university based research and development center specializing in GDSS interventions. The center's clients range from multi-national corporations and governmental agencies designing new information systems and conducting strategic planning to professors teaching classes and local school boards engaged in strategic planning. Ongoing contact was maintained with 14 facilitators associated with the center. This involved observations of actual interventions, attending administrative staff meetings, and engaging facilitators in formal and informal interviews. The materials gathered include ethnographic field notes, audio-visual recordings of some interventions, and follow-up interviews.

There were 11 different interventions observed (see Table 16.1). This included 4 information systems design events, 4 strategic planning events, 2 education events, and 1 training event. Each event had a different duration ranging from a few hours to many weeks and thus involved different lengths of observation. Approximately 200 h of field observations intensively examined the events and the intervention. The observations were conducted to maximize exposure to different types of events, different facilitators, and different intervention goals within the field site. During this time contact was maintained with 14 different facilitators who conducted the interventions. The information system design and strategic planning events involved facilitation teams of two or more facilitators. One of the facilitators usually became the lead person on the team while the others assisted, thus teams reflected the lead facilitator even though their individual styles may have varied (Table 16.2).

16.2.2   Research Strategy

The definition of GDSS facilitation articulated by Bostrom et al. (1993) provides a useful starting point to organize the ethnographic observation, interpretation, and analysis for this strategy. Bostrom et al.'s (1993) definition of practice is grounded in their experience as facilitators as well as their research. According to Bostrom et al. (1993, p. 147), GDSS facilitators perform a "set of functions or activities carried out before, during, and after a meeting to help the group

Table 16.1 Interventions observed by event, client, domains, duration and amount of observation

Event	Client	Domain observed	Duration and amount of observation
Systems design	Private firm	Running the GDSS, Shaping communication outside GDSS	1 day/1 day
Systems design	Government agency	Assisting with meeting design, Running the GDSS, Communication outside the GDSS	1 week/3 days
Systems design	Government agency	Running the meeting, Communication outside the GDSS	1 week/2 days
Systems design	Government agency	Running the meeting, Communication outside the GDSS	1 week/3 days
Strategic planning	Private firm	Assisting with meeting design	1 day/1 day
Strategic planning	Government agency	Assisting with meeting design, Running the GDSS, Communication outside the GDSS	3 weeks/8 days
Strategic planning	University department	Assisting with meeting design, Running the GDSS, Communication outside the GDSS	3 h/3 h
Strategic planning	School board	Assisting with meeting design, Running the GDSS, Communication outside the GDSS	1 day/1 day
Education	Professor	Assisting with meeting design, Running the GDSS, Communication outside the GDSS	1 semester/3 meetings
Education	Professor	Running the meeting, Communication outside the GDSS	1 semester/1 semester
Training	Private individual	Running the GDSS, Shaping Communication outside GDSS	1 day/1 day

Table 16.2 Domain by GDSS facilitator practices identified

Domain	Practice	Design work
Assisting meeting design	Mapping	Establish fit between client needs and GDSS capabilities
Running the GDSS	Tool talk, Running-the-tools	Matches users' ordinary expectations for communication with GDSS
Shaping the communication outside GDSS	Forging-a-record	Manage discussion progress by helping participants shape an electronic record of the discussion

achieve its own outcomes." A GDSS facilitator "works with the group leader (and participants) to establish meeting outcomes. The facilitator then designs the meeting by picking relevant roles, rules, procedures, and techniques to accomplish desired outcomes" (p. 160). Three domains of action are pertinent to what facilitators do: running the computer technology, shaping the communication that takes place outside of the computer technology, and assisting in meeting design (Bostrom et al. 1993; Clawson et al. 1993). As discussed earlier this definition and the research from it, shares a commitment to scientific management especially evident in the use of "design" in the definition. Design is treated as a process of selection—that is, design is an instrumental matching of known meeting facilitation techniques and/or GDSS functions to overcome the obstacles an event presents to accomplishing the goals of the meeting. It is an image of the facilitator as a technocrat where the role involves the neutral administration of techniques and technologies (e.g., Aakhus 2001).

The conventional view provides a definition and serves as ethnographic tool for describing and interpreting the actions of GDSS facilitators. The fieldwork was conducted using the domains of action outlined in the conventional definition. Field notes, audio-video tapes, and interviews were produced to document how facilitators orchestrate the technical communication space so that it fosters collaborative decision-making. The definition, and the studies associated with it, implicate a model, or hypothesis, explaining the work performed by GDSS facilitators. In this study, the definition provided an object for critical reflection. Observations of the work performed by facilitators were compared and contrasted with the definition and its implications for explaining GDSS facilitator work and, in particular, their influence on bridging the gap between design and use. This research strategy follows "grounded practical theory" where the research goal is to rationally reconstruct the techniques, dilemmas, and philosophy of a communication practice (Craig 1989; Craig and Tracy 1995). This research strategy involves gathering "insight into communication problems experienced by practitioners, the specific techniques by which to cope with those problems, and the 'situated ideals' or inchoate normative principles that they employ in normative reflection on their practice" (Craig and Tracy 1995, p. 250).

16.3 Findings

During the fieldwork for this study, it became apparent that much of what GDSS facilitators do is a professional design practice that occupies the space between technical and human systems (e.g., end-users). The design work they perform, however, differs from the technocratic image highlighted in extant research. Their work involves significant discretion and practical knowledge that incorporates a heightened sense of how communication works and ought to work. This aspect of their work, however, remains invisible in part due to the dominance of the technocratic account and focus on GDSS end-users but, more interestingly, due also to the very conduct of the work itself. The purpose in reporting these findings is to articulate GDSS facilitators' communication design practice to better understand what facilitators do.

The findings reported here suggest that using technology to facilitate collaborative decision-making involves two layers of design work. The technology must be implemented and the decision-makers using the technology must come to recognize their decision-making as collaborative. The first layer is articulated here by describing design techniques GDSS facilitators use in conducting their work. What is described here is consistent with the techniques of practice identified in the conventional technocratic literature on GDSS facilitation. The second layer is articulated by showing how GDSS facilitators, through their design techniques, persuade participants about the essence of their participation in using the technology. This second layer is not anticipated by the technical view and points to a deeper communication design practice evident in the work facilitators do. Before developing these points, the idea of communication design practice as it emerged in the gathering and interpretation of the ethnographic data is explained.

16.3.1   Communication Design Practice

The object of GDSS facilitator design practice is the communicative activity of the participants. GDSS facilitators use their actions, and in particular their speech actions, to open up and close down opportunities for people to contribute and, in so doing, they craft particular forms of communicative activity while preventing other forms of communicative activity from taking place. For instance, a facilitator might foster a communicative activity of information sharing while actively preventing the activity of quarreling from emerging. The "materials" facilitators work with are the means of participation, which includes the types of turns, roles, and topics available to the participants (see Aakhus and Jackson 2005). Design practice also involves shaping the principle of relevance for the communicative activity—that is, the facilitator helps set up presumptions about appropriate and effective speech action that participants use to judge what counts as a felicitous contribution at a particular point in time (e.g., Grice 1975; Levinson 1979). The principle of relevance helps participants invent productive action and provides a means for exercising social control over communicative conduct.

Communicative activity is an emergent phenomenon that does not reside in the media designed to support the technology or routine forms—"genres" (e.g., Yates and Orlikowski 1992)—of communicative action. It occurs in the space between technology design and end-user use. GDSS facilitators design it to render the technology employable. Their design tools include concepts, scripts, routines, and ways of speaking to foster or inhibit types of communicative activity participants take up with each other. So, from the perspective of design practice, the GDSS is a facilitator's design tool used to craft or give life to particular forms of participation.

Communication design practice involves discretion in anticipating an appropriate and effective line of communicative activity for the event at hand. Devising opportunities for preferred lines of communicative activity involves practical knowledge about how communication works and how it ought to work. The judgment in design work lies in constructing a credible format of interaction and maintaining the participant's trust in the designer's judgment. GDSS facilitators pay significant attention to the complexities an event presents an intervention so that the complexities do not destroy the quality of the participation facilitator's craft or the participants' belief in it.

The design practice of GDSS facilitators is articulated here in two parts. First, three design techniques, *mapping*, *tool-talk*, and *forging-a-record*, are described to show the layer of design work aimed at crafting communication activity. Second, *transparency work* is described to show the layer of design work that involves persuading participants about the essence of their participation and enabling control to be exercised over communicative action.

16.3.2 Communication Design Techniques

Three techniques facilitators use to implement GDSS within the decision-making of a group are described in this section. The three techniques typify what GDSS facilitators do in each domain of their work activity. The identification of these techniques is not intended to be an exhaustive catalogue of the things GDSS facilitators do to accomplish their work but to illustrate design practice in important domains of their activity that has remained invisible.

16.3.2.1 Tool Talk

Facilitators help run the GDSS for the participants. Tool-talk is one technique central to this domain that typically occurs during actual interventions. Tool-talk happens when the facilitator uses special language to render the communicative expectations designed into the features of the GDSS sensible to the participants and the participants' communicative behaviors sensible to the GDSS. The following example is taken from an audio-visual recording of a GDSS intervention. The example occurs near the beginning of the intervention where the GDSS facilitator describes what will be happening during the session and what participants can expect. Whatever he says about using the GDSS he illustrates on the large projection screens in the room.

> Is there anybody here that hasn't used one of our meeting facilities before? And is brand new to it? So what we're doing is setting up to have conversation on the computer, by typing, it is going to let everybody talk at the same time, and we will step you through it and make sure everything is comfortable and makes sense as we work through it.
> <some intervening talk deleted>
> [A number] is put on the comment to make it easier to have a conversation. So you can say, "comment number three could you explain what you mean about the program in more

detail?" "Comment number four I disagree with you, but here is why I disagree with you." So, it lets you have a conversation, back and forth, even though it is anonymous. That's basically what is involved.

In this example, the facilitator's introduction of the GDSS addresses quite specifically how the participants should take turns. In exemplifying the kinds of comments that can be contributed both with his words and the GDSS, the facilitator highlights what is different about interacting via GDSS and yet how it can be seen as a more advanced form of ordinary communication. Tool-talk bridges the gap between design and use by helping participants understand the pragmatics of communicating in the unique communication environment introduced by the GDSS.

16.3.2.2 Mapping

Facilitators assist in designing meetings. Mapping is one technique central to this domain that typically occurs during planning meetings where the facilitator meets with the client to discuss and plan the event. Mapping happens when (1) the facilitator sees how the client's potential problems with decision-making can be described in terms of what the facilitator thinks the GDSS can do and (2) when the facilitator articulates that vision into a meeting agenda. The following example is taken from an audio-recording of an interview with a facilitator who has just finished a telephone call with a client about some issues for the upcoming intervention. This excerpt highlights what the facilitator says to a client when assisting in the design of meetings and why he says that to the client.

> So my facilitation approach is to [ask], "okay what do you need to know, what are the deliverables that you need to walk out of this session with?" If you're familiar with, you know, your [GDSS] stuff, there are only two types of data structures you can walk out with. You can walk out with text or you can walk out with lists. And, so, you can put your deliverables in the form of lists and texts, you know. I mean an outline is nothing more than a list of lists with some text attached to the outline. So, uh, what is it going to take to get people to produce that and can you get, you know, can you get them to do it easily and comfortably and you know, with minimal, minimal hassle.

In this example, the facilitator expresses how he thinks about a client's "needs" in terms of "lists" and "texts" that can be produced through GDSS intervention. It is basic concepts like these that facilitators use in designing an intervention to make the GDSS useful to the problem faced by the client-group. Mapping bridges the gap between design and use by situating the fe0atures of the technology within the anticipated communicative demands of the event.

16.3.2.3 Fashioning-the-Record

Facilitators help shape the communication outside the GDSS. Fashioning-the-record is one technique central to this domain that typically occurs during the course of an intervention. Fashioning-the-record happens when the facilitator uses the GDSS to create a record of what has transpired in the meeting that creates grounds for moving the discussion forward. The follow example is taken from an audio recording of an interview conducted at the end of an intervention. Note the facilitator's concern with the how he orchestrated the availability of turns and topics to the participants. This reflects an orientation toward making contributions within the GDSS as well as a concern with the quality of the record that is produced. Both are crucial to successful intervention because the record that is fashioned becomes grounds for further discussion and the object of subsequent decision-making activities.

> We had more categories than people and what you get in that case is you get people going and reading the question and answering the question and going on to another one. So it's people interacting with questions but not interacting with each other. If I can keep the number of categories down and there is multiple people in the category and they start interacting with each other. So, it's a question of whether I am promoting knowledge dumping—people just coming and dumping what they—versus conversation. And the needs for this group were more conversational needs and I had to keep the number of categories down to keep the conversation going. [Some intervening dialogue omitted] Yeah and I'm just pulling that number out of the air that number isn't any solid reference and in here we have, because it was two and one half to one, we start with fifteen people, twelve. Six categories. One to. Twelve people. Six categories which is probably too many categories. But the trade off is less categories we have the more focused people are and the more they respond to each other. But in our environment each category represents a thread so the more topic oriented the conversation rather than everybody in the same place talking about different things. So, if I can keep the conversation one thread per one discussion, keep people focused, content oriented and focused, that's good. But then too many discussions is bad so it's a matter of finding an appropriate balance based on the group and topic and the objectives for the meeting.

In this example, the facilitator points out the judgment involved in fashioning-the-record. He expresses his belief about the appropriate relationship between the number of discussion topics (e.g., "categories") and the number of participants. Fashioning-the-record bridges the gap between design and use by shifting aspects of the communication occurring outside the GDSS inside the GDSS, thus editing the informal communication of the group into a formal record for further decision-making.

16.3.2.4 Summary

Facilitator's performance of design techniques shapes the means of communication, such as the turns to be taken, topics to be addressed, and roles to be taken up in interaction, and influences the quality of participation. In crafting communication into particular forms of activity, facilitators use their knowledge of what communication is and ought to be to exercises control over communication in order to manage the complexities of the event.

16.3.3 Design Practice and Transparency Work

The purpose of this section is to more closely examine the design techniques just described to articulate a layer of design work performed by GDSS facilitators to persuade participants about what they are doing. The mere presence of collaboration

technology does not mean that collaboration will happen in a particular event, even
if collaboration is a routine form of communication for a group. There are numerous
complications that can arise to cast doubt on the plausibility that collaboration is
happening or can happen. A key issue for facilitation is to be unnoticed even though
the work can obviously be seen. Central to the design practice of facilitators is their
persuasion that enables participants to see through the actions of the facilitation and
any disruption it may cause. Facilitators persuade participants about the essence of
the participants' participation, even when what the participants are attempting to
achieve (e.g., collaboration) seems implausible or impossible.

The persuasion about what the participants are doing makes the facilitators work
transparent – that is, their work is analogous to a windshield on a car. One cannot
see the windshield but without the windshield it would be hard to see what one is
doing in driving the car. This aspect of facilitation became especially clear when, in
the course of the field-work, the author encountered a veteran meeting facilitator
with 25 years experience, who was learning how to use GDSS and consulting on its
design. During an interview, he explained why facilitation is effective by recollect-
ing a discussion with one of his client groups:

> So at the end this one guy said, you know he said, "I've been going to these meetings for
> years," he said. He said, "I didn't even want to come to this one because I figured this
> organization is dead. Just because it's just too complex." And he says, "this is the best
> meeting. I, I cannot believe we got all this done in two days." And the point of the comment,
> he wasn't saying it to me he was saying it to the group because the process is fairly transparent.
> I mean you know you are using a set of methods, but where the real excitement comes, is
> when the group realizes that it can function as a group and make tough decisions, come up
> with innovative ideas, be creative. You know do all these things and they really realize that
> they did it. So the, so the credit doesn't go to the facilitator, "oh that was a fun meeting,"
> "that was an entertaining meeting." I mean you know people will recognize that and say,
> "well if we hadn't had a facilitator here it wouldn't've worked." People are cognizant of that
> but the process is fairly transparent. People. People. People realize that they're the ones that
> made it work and they're the ones that ought to get the credit because they did the work
> cause you know it's a good process. But if people don't own up, people don't value it, you
> know, you're not going to get good stuff out of it.
> [Interviewer: What gives it that transparency?]
> It's those, it's those, it's those participatory methods. I think that people look back and
> say, "Now this great idea, where did it come from? It wasn't the facilitator because he didn't
> have any good ideas. All he did was say, 'put your ideas on cards'" heheh. And we do this
> process you know, and they'll say it came from several people, "we really worked together
> on that," and "we built a consensus I didn't think was possible," and "I didn't even know, it
> wasn't my idea." You know, a lot of them are saying that. But, it was the way that we
> collaboratively thought and problem solved and creatively planned. So it's, it's the process
> and then the neutral stance, the objective stance of the facilitator that's eliciting the commit-
> ment of the group and the input of the group.

The facilitator's observation points out how collaborative decision-making is a
belief and a quality of participation inspired by the work of the facilitator. It points
out that an overriding demand of their design practice lies in constructing the
believability of the activity in which they are engaged (i.e., what we are really
doing here is "making a decision," "collaborating," or "negotiating" despite potential

indicators to the contrary). The persuasion points to the legitimacy of what is the participants are doing. It is enabled in part by the way facilitators' design practice makes itself invisible so as to draw attention to the actions of those who benefit from the design practice and away from those who perform the design practice. The facilitator's observation points to an aspect of design practice that is referred to here as *transparency work*.

Transparency work is persuasion to confirm and remove doubt about the legitimacy of the communication activity designed to help. Legitimacy involves the credibility of the communication activity crafted by the facilitator (e.g., does the design resonate with participants' routine communication and does the design handle the exigencies the participants face in the event?). It also involves the trustworthiness of the intervention (e.g., can the participants count on the communication activity being sustained despite complications?). Transparency work targets participant's beliefs about what activity they are taking up with each other. It makes visible aspects of the event consistent with the activity the facilitator attempts to craft and makes invisible aspects of the event that would spoil the quality of the participation or belief that what people are doing is the preferred form of activity. So, in the case of GDSS facilitation, it may be that participants behave uncooperatively, attempt to agitate other participants, or interfere with the goals of the intervention, but transparency work hides those aspects of the event while highlighting aspects of the event that would lead participants to conclude that they are engaged in collaborative decision-making. Transparency work also renders design practice as seen but unnoticed.

Transparency work functions in part like Garfinkel's (1967;Heritage 1984; Leiter 1980; Weider 1976) concept of the "documentary method of interpretation" where anomalies and departures from what appears to be happening are made to appear to fit a more fundamental explanation of what is happening. Transparency work is motivated by the sense that the principle of relevance through which people are able to cooperatively interact is always at stake and in need of constant care. In this sense, transparency work also functions like Goffman's (1983) idea of "felicity's condition." That is, even though the background assumptions necessary for understanding what is said and what they are doing may be satisfied, there are still opportunities for slippage between what is said and what is meant. Transparency work aims to prevent that slippage from damaging the legitimacy of the participants' activity and the facilitator's design practice.

The persuasion that happens through transparency work is organized around an ideal model of collaborative communication, design techniques, and the way design techniques are performed to hide and highlight aspects of the event. The persuasion involves a nascent normative idealization about what counts as legitimate communication activity for decision-making. Communicative activity should be organized to maximize opportunities to participate, to preserve informed choice free from coercive influence, and to foster participant responsibility for the choices made (e.g., these ideals of facilitation are discussed in Bostrom et al. 1993; Broome and Keever 1989; Dannelmiller and Jacobs 1992; Kaner et al. 1996; and Schwarz 1994).

The idealized role of the facilitator is to foster collaborative activity by remaining client focused and by managing the process of communication without interfering with the substance of decisions (e.g., these ideals of facilitator action are discussed in Aakhus 2001; Doyle and Straus 1976; Kaner et al 1996; Schwarz 1994; and Weatherall and Nunamaker 1995). The actions performed by facilitators display an orientation toward this idealized concept of participation. Moreover, their actions hide and highlight aspects of the event so that the collaborative essence of the activity is evident and that the ready and relevant conclusion to be drawn about communicative activity is that it is collaborative—even when complexities arise to spoil the sense of collaboration.

The legitimacy of the communicative activity granted through the impression of collaboration can be spoiled in many ways by the complexities of the events on which GDSS facilitators intervene. Four complexities, in particular, stood out in this study. The variation among individual proficiencies in using the software created asymmetries in individual abilities to contribute. The varying expectations about the facilitator's role often put pressure on facilitator's to perform activities outside their neutral, third-party status. The political aspects of choices often exposed latent, unresolved conflict among the participants. Finally, varying disciplinary backgrounds and commitments to different organizations exposed epistemological differences about what counts as a viable problem and an acceptable solution. Each of these complexities puts the principle of relevance at stake and raises doubts about the condition of felicity necessary for participants to sustain a mutual communicative activity.

Transparency work helps prevent slippage between what participants do, what they mean, and the consequences for mutual communicative activity, and to repair it when it happens. This is evident in the design technique of Tool-Talk though which GDSS facilitators formulate a pragmatics for communicating despite the anomalies the GDSS and the intervention present routine expectations about how to interact with others. In the Tool-Talk example presented earlier (pp. 11–12), the facilitator's actions orchestrated the types of turns and the manner of turn-taking. Transparency work was evident in the way the facilitator put a conversational (inter)face on the GDSS interaction and emphasized the democratic quality of the interaction. The odd aspects of tracking the contributions in the GDSS are framed as open communication where everyone contributes, no one is interrupted, there is no waiting for turns, and participants control what they say and when they say it. These are all qualities that index the collaboration ideal described above. Transparency work maintains the participant's orientation toward collaborating as the principle of relevance through which they determine how to contribute and to judge others contributions. Two extended examples of mapping and fashioning-a-record are presented here to explain how GDSS facilitators organize their actions, and in particular their speech actions, to help the participants in the intervention recognize their decision-making as collaborative. The performance of transparency work hides the facilitators intervention while highlighting evidence that the preferred form of communication is happening among the participants.

16.3.3.1 Mapping

The following example of mapping is taken from the author's field notes of a meeting where the facilitator and the client plan a GDSS intervention. It illustrates transparency work through mapping in the way the facilitator's actions emphasize client control over the intervention, distance the facilitator from the politics of the choice to be made in the event, and orient toward complexities that may spoil the impression of collaboration among the participants. The intervention to be designed is intended to organize a diverse collection of professionals with a stake in educational reform into a political action group. The client's goal is to have the group create a document about educational reform that the group can use to influence state education policy. The event involves 30 participants most of whom have never used GDSS. The excerpt picks up following some discussion by facilitator and sponsor about handling the effect of latent disagreements and conflicting professional views on education that might arise among the various professional and political interests in the meeting room. (The numbers represent turns at talk. The italicized words protect identities and fill in missing contextual information. Ed is the facilitator and Art is the client.)

28 Ed: Who uses the information, a committee? You?
29 Art: Currently we are an informed network. We meet in brown bag lunches. We'd like to make it a full fledged collaborative effort. I work in a college of fine arts getting collaboration of arts educators. There will be a meeting where an arts education agenda for (*the state's*) education takes place. We want to take with it an agenda for (*our region*). That meeting is for advising on the delivery and assessment of arts education. Our information that we bring needs to be about processes to move forward an agenda for arts education (*in our state*).
30 Ed: We could use (*a voting/evaluation tool*). Getting a list down to five and not suggest a ranking. We could use yes/no (*a version of a groupware voting tool*). This has been successful as long as everyone agrees to the voting rules. We can look for 80% or above agreement maybe 70 or 75% depending on the room. Let me explain the voting rules. Hopefully a couple items (*on the list of obstacles*) get 80% agreement to remain on the list and some go to 50% or below (*in order to be taken off the list*). What would say 80% be... that's a hammer with 30 (*participants*). What would work for this group?
31 Art: Not sure, need to use your expertise. I don't want it to be so diffuse so we scramble at the end of the meeting. What is your gut level hunch.
32 Ed: I used it with a group with tremendous conflict. In face to face meetings they could never get 80% to come up, but 80% came up for three items (*in that facilitated meeting*). Then they focused on the level of agreement they had and let the differences pan out.

Mapping is evident in this example in the way the facilitator describes the event in terms of GDSS capabilities and how to build those capacities into the meeting agenda. Notice how the facilitator, in turn 29, restates the client's description, in turn 28, in terms of the GDSS tools to be used by the participants in producing the meeting outcomes. Transparency work is evident in the way the facilitator helps the client see how a procedure can be designed to circumvent complexities that might spoil the impression of collaboration among the participants in the meeting. Notice how the client's description of who will use the meeting outcomes, in turn 28, is recast by the facilitator as a potential decision-making problem that can be solved through decision rules and use of the GDSS voting tools. Transparency work is also evident in the way the facilitator's discretion and practical knowledge about intervention design is expressed as group needs and technological demands. Notice how the facilitator, in turn 30, invites the client to request, in turn 31, the facilitator's expertise and how the facilitator, in turns 30 and 32, describes his choice in terms of group needs.

While the mapping proceeds as though the facilitator is simply matching the group's needs with the available GDSS solution, the facilitator is formulating means to legitimately manage what will count as relevant contributions to the proposed communicative activity. The facilitator and the client, in this example, agree that the meeting outcome should be a list of five political action goals accompanied by suggested implementation strategies and that these outcomes are to be secured through group consensus. A key design issue is how to get 30 participants with a wide variety of professional and political interests to agree to five political action goals with strategies in a 2-h time span. The facilitator's solution formulated in turn 30 and elaborated in turn 32 suggests that voting tools can be used to ensure agreement if too much conflict should arise. When the facilitator suggests how voting rules can be used to most effectively map the voting tool onto the meeting problem, he actually defines consensus. It is a solution that directly affects what the meeting content and outcome can be for that intervention.

The facilitator's solution to generate consensus, should there be significant disagreement, reveals an implicit theory about the character of collaborative communication. The proposed procedure is a means for resolving differences of opinion should a decision-making impasse emerge, or be imminent. This procedure establishes some important grounds for technology use by participants prior to their use of the technology. The proposed solution is to guide participant interaction toward developing points of agreement and away from discussing divisive topics. It is worth noting that GDSS tools can be used to explore differences rather than similarities. GDSS tools in this approach are framed as mechanisms for demonstrating consensus to the participants. This strategy can be used to foster the impression that cooperation and progress are made possible in otherwise difficult circumstances, and contributes to the exploration and formation of opinions in the decision context.

16.3.3.2 Fashioning-a-Record

The following example is taken from the author's field notes of a difficult juncture in a business process and information system re-design meeting. During that time, the facilitator handles an escalating disagreement in the talk occurring outside the GDSS through fashioning-a-record. The example illustrates transparency work through fashioning-a-record in the way the facilitator's actions emphasize the maximization of opportunities to participate, preservation of informed choice free from coercion, and participant responsibility for the choices made; and how the actions emphasize the facilitator's management of the process without interfering with the substance of the decision.

The event involved 31 meeting participants from eight different organizations, numerous hierarchical levels, and at least five domains of expertise were brought together to develop system requirements for an information system. They meet in a GDSS meeting room with 30 participant workstations, two facilitator workstations, and three large screens to display content in the GDSS. The participants were brought together because of their functional knowledge of the business processes of their various organizations. The goal of event was to produce a model of how the eight organizations ought to conduct their key business processes so that all the organizations could effectively share the same information system and information. The information system was to improve business efficiencies and cooperation among the eight organizations represented by the participants in the decision room. In the first phase of a weeklong series of meetings, the facilitator's charge was to help the participants build a model that they agreed accurately represented the core business activities of their organizations.

Latent conflict in the broader decisions to be made began to emerge in the early afternoon of the second day of a weeklong series of meetings. Earlier in the day, the facilitator asked the participants to identify as many different business processes for their respective organizations as they could. When the conflict surfaced that afternoon, the facilitator was helping the participants develop definitions of business processes common to all the organizations and the information and forms needed to support that process. The facilitator was leading the discussion from his computer which projected on three large screens an outline of the business processes to be defined. All the participants could see the outline and at the same time use their computer workstation to look through the contributions participants had made to the GDSS earlier in the day. The facilitator led the oral discussion in the room and used his workstation to enter candidate definitions for further discussion and agreed upon definitions.

The oral discussion outside the GDSS, however, began to fragment into many simultaneous discussions in the meeting room between different sub-groups when they were discussing item 4.2 on the outline. The participants were aligning themselves with the particular claims made by different sub-groups in the meeting room. The oral discussion departed from the agenda and grew to reflect deeper political conflicts and professional differences of opinion that. The sub-group discussions would form, disband, and reform around shared identities people have with their organizational membership (e.g., ground or water transportation) or their professional specialization (e.g., engineer or logistics). It got to the point that only 3–5 people contributed to synthesizing the comments in the GDSS to create common definitions while another 10 participants appeared to actively listen to that discussion. Five people seemed to never say anything to the whole group but only whispered and commented to others near them. The remaining 10–13 people were engaged in running commentary about how one group was attempting to gain advantage over another group by the way the business process was being defined. At this point, the event was moving toward impasse. The talk outside the GDSS was taking on a life of its own in direct contrast to the goal of the intervention and the facilitator's attempts to overcome differences of opinion and build common ground among the participants. It seemed that each new definition to be created only presented new opportunities for disagreement. The following exchange among the participants and the facilitator occurred at this point. (The turns at talk are numbered. The italicized words used in parenthesis are used to protect identities.)

01 "The people in *boating* never fill in the form," the *ground transport* leader exclaims.
02 "This form is not done industry wide," counters the *boating* leader.
03 "You are all into a different set of issues not," the *ground transport* leader begins to say.
04 The *boating leader* interrupts with the counter-claim that, "A lot of the sites have tracking from the past." Before he can continue his assertion, the facilitator interjects.
05 "Let's talk about it. I think it is related," says the facilitator in an attempt to show the relevance of their disagreement to the current activity.
06 "I'm less concerned about," the facilitator continues in an effort to keep the discussion from further escalation. The testy exchange of commentary between the two leaders grows.
07 "Okay, listen up. Our defined purpose is to work (*the current format*) in a package that goes to (*each business site*). These (*the new information format*) items should come with other items," the facilitator says while attempting to talk over the testy commentary.
08 "If I have a local system, I should be able to download the information I need," the facilitator continues attempting to regain the group's attention.
09 "Currently what I'm hearing some of you say," the facilitator begins to summarize the discussion when he is interrupted by a number of exchanges spawned by the leaders' disagreement.
10 "Maybe it is a requirement," the facilitator continues his thought while many different people speak at once and he looks towards his workstation.
    [Field notes continue: While the oral discussion escalates toward impasse, the facilitator continues typing at his workstation. The facilitator's primary attention appears to be on rewriting the contents of the outline item 4.2. His attention will momentarily shift to the on-going oral discussion among the participants. He changes the definition of the outline item by adding words like "can include" to the business activity definition, which relaxes the design requirement assumptions. He submits the change to the GDSS. His editing actions are visible to everyone on the large public screen in the room but most participants are caught up in the escalating disagreement. For previous outline items the facilitator would reread the edits he made to the item while continuously displaying his actions on the public screens. He does this to invite comments and further discussion before a definition is finalized. At this time there appear to be only four participants attending to the facilitator's actions. For item 4.2, he displays the rewrite with no extra comments.]
11 "I really think there is an area there for process improvement. Four-point-three, Stores Materials," the facilitator points out that work remains for item 4.2 and then announces the next outline item to be defined.

Fashioning-a-record happens in the way the facilitator attempts to transform the oral discussion into a written record to prepare the ground for further discussion and decision-making. Transparency work happens in the facilitator's uses the electronic record to redirect the conflicted oral discussion around a point of impasse. This design technique can be used to represent common ground among participants, in this example it is used to create the impression of common ground or to at least enable the participants to go forward with their discussion in the face of impasse.

The two faces of fashioning-a-record are evident in the shift in the facilitator's approach between turns 10 and 11. Prior to the surfacing of deeper conflicts and the fragmenting discussion, the facilitator uses this technique to engage the participants in an explicit mutual construction of the record. The record reflects a synthesis of different viewpoints into one account about the ideal information system design. The transformation of the oral into the written is rather straightforward in the routine performance of fashioning-a-record. To ensure this, the facilitator describes his editing of their contributions into unified expression, displays his editing, and seeks confirmation of his editing. When the oral discussion fragments and the disagreement escalates, however, the performance of fashioning-a-record takes on additional purpose. The more the facilitator tries to encourage the participants to reconcile their positions seems only to convince participants of the positions they have taken. The facilitator alters his performance. He produces his own synthesis of positions by editing items using comments and ideas he has heard in the discussion outside the GDSS. Rather than seeking confirmation which will only lead to further disagreement, he enters his changes, suggests that opportunity still exists for that item, and introduces the next outline item.

The practice of fashioning-a-record hides and highlights points of conflict in a way that guides the group discussion through the social and political complexity of their collective choice. Fashioning-a-record sustains an impression of collaboration in decision-making because it provides grounds on which communication can proceed—even in this example where the topic is abandoned for the time. It is, however, substantive grounding shaped by the facilitator. Displaying reformulated messages for ratification by the group emphasizes participant control and de-emphasizes the facilitator's control over what becomes the record while helping transform disagreement and misunderstanding into candidate agreements. Progress built through fashioning-a-record rests on the selective editing performed by the facilitator. It is not a simple reflection of what participants have said or contributed to the GDSS but an active reconstruction of what was said to create an impression of harmony and progress.

16.3.3.3 Summary

Design techniques are not only performed to craft opportunities and constraints for interaction but the techniques are performed in a manner that sustains or repairs the sense of what counts as felicitous contributions. This transparency work highlights the aspects of the event that conform to the idealized sense of activity (e.g., collaboration) while hiding aspects that might spoil that quality of the participation or belief that collaboration is happening. In this way, the facilitation enables the group work to maintain its coherence, which in turn grounds its effectiveness.

16.4 Discussion

GDSS facilitators are a paradigm case for examining what happens in the space between technological design and end-user use. In the case of GDSS facilitators the uses of rationale capture to construct a path through the difficult work of convergence in decision-making. The integration of the technology into the setting illustrated above generated further affordances for moving through the diverse standpoints participants in the meeting continued to advance. In so doing, however, the facilitator continuously repaired the sense that what was happening was moving toward a decision and not a radical breakdown of perspectives (which was an entirely plausible interpretation of the setting). Prior theory and research on GDSS facilitative action is instructive for understanding how to explain the action that takes place to bring people together into mutual activity through technology. Yet, it misses crucial aspects of what GDSS facilitators do, especially how they bridge the gap between technology and its use. In making visible important aspects of GDSS facilitators work, this study articulates the communication design practice of GDSS facilitators to reveal how they craft communicative activity in the effort to create a credible form of participation and a trustworthy intervention. The idea that facilitators design communication provides insight facilitating creativity and rationale and managing the divergence-convergence tension.

16.4.1   The Design Alternative

The findings reported here point out two layers of design work involved in using technology to facilitate collaborative decision-making. First, there is the performance of design techniques that orchestrate the available means of participation into communicative activity. Second, there is the practice of transparency work that sustains and repairs a principle of relevance for the activity that defines felicitous contributions to the activity. Design work, in the case of GDSS facilitators, persuades participants that the essence of their participation is collaborative, and thus legitimate. Collaboration is a belief and quality of participation that is independent of the technology intended to inspire it. The scientific management orientation of GDSS facilitator research overlooks the creative aspect of the design work GDSS facilitators perform by treating design as the neutral administration of procedures. Adaptive structuration theory mystifies this aspect of technology-use by suggesting that the GDSS technology has a "spirit" to be faithfully drawn out by its users. Self-organizing systems theory points to but does not articulate the expertise and norms involved in rendering GDSS useable and useful. Each approach makes significant contributions to understanding the technological facilitation of decision-making, yet the nature of the persuasion that happens through communication design work calls for further examination. The contribution of the present study is its explication of this influence in terms of design practice, design techniques, and transparency work.

The communication design work articulated here helps put into perspective activity that takes place at the boundaries of technical and human systems and that often remains invisible in technological intervention. Communication design work is the crafting of communicative activity—the means of participation—that mediates how people engage each other in decision-making, problem-solving, and conflict resolution. What prior theory and research on the technological facilitation of decision-making misses in whole or in part, that has been addressed here, is that the technological facilitation is a search for a legitimate, and effective, forum for communication—that is, how can communication be designed into a practical means and an appropriate means for decision-making, problem-solving, or conflict resolution. What lies between designed systems and their use are aspects of communication design practice, such as transparency work, that point to the principles that animate design techniques, such as mapping, tool-talk, and fashioning-a-record, performed to construct credible participation. Furthermore, what lies between is the trustworthiness of the intervention—that is, is there someone who can be counted on to sustain or repair the condition of felicity for the communicative activity?

16.4.2 Integrating Prior Research

The approach taken here develops a pragmatics of mediated communication with its focus on how communicative activity is created and sustained (e.g., Aakhus and Jackson 2005). This has implications for integrating and expanding prior theory and research on the technological facilitation of collaboration. The present study expands the possibilities to the technocratic account by articulating the discretion and practical knowledge exercised by GDSS facilitators. This shows the interpretive and moral complexities of the work and how practitioners cope with these complexities. Thus, some basis for why a technique might be performed in a particular way at a particular moment. This also provides grounds for understanding why certain techniques prevail and why other techniques, even though good in principle, are not taken up as the professional practice develops. The approach taken here expands the possibilities of extant structurational theories (e.g., Contractor et al. 1996; Poole and DeSanctis 1992; Yates and Orlikowski 1992). The findings of the present study can clarify the norms and expertise that remain vague in self-organizing systems theory and help to specify the appropriation process vague in adaptive structuration theory. The design practice account developed here further explains how communication functions in the gap between technology design and its use. This evident in how the present study challenges and expands Yates and Orlikowski's (1992) "genre" approach to explaining the structuration of organizational communication.

Yates and Orlikowski (1992) point out a general confusion between medium and genre in understanding the use of communication technology in organizations. Their point is that genres—typified communicative actions taken in response to recurrent situations—are distinct from and interact with media—the physical means for transmitting messages—over time. For instance, the memo genre persists and evolves despite changes in media (e.g., paper and e-mail). The upshot is that the social shaping of media for communicative purposes is a function of the way communicators draw upon the various genres available when using a medium and signal the genre of communication to be used through various strategies adapted to that medium. So, Yates and Orlikowski (1992, pp. 318–320) interpret the lack of opening salutations and closing sign-offs in email to be an adaptation to the memo quality of the email format. When people add greetings and sign-offs they attempt to overcome the memo quality of the email format to invoke alternative genres such as the informal note or formal letter.

What is not clear in this structurational theory, however, is how one genre is invoked over another in the use of a medium. How is it that, for instance, memo-exchange becomes the activity through which people engage each other rather than formal letter-writing? Or, how, relative to this study, communication becomes negotiation rather than quarreling? In answering such questions, it easy to confuse the communicative activity mutually constructed in the flow of interaction with media and genre. GDSS represents a convergence of organizational meeting genres, such as what Yates (1989 pp. 98–100) calls the "committee meeting" and "shop floor meeting" with networked computing. As the medium is not the genre, neither is the genre of communication the communicative activity in which people engage. This is particularly clear in the work performed by facilitators. The articulation of their communication design practice reveals design techniques and the persuasion (e.g., transparency work) that renders the technology usable in end-users ongoing communicative activity. To do this, they rely on the design features of the technology (e.g., the GDSS' tools) and shared knowledge about preferred and dispreferred genres (e.g., collaborative decision-making versus quarreling or positional bargaining) but in the moment the communicative activity must be continuously created and sustained. The design practice, and the model of persuasion entailed in it, shows how one form of activity is crafted and sustained over other potential genres of meeting communication that could be invoked with a GDSS.

The present study builds upon insights of prior theory and research and develops grounds for further understanding pragmatics of communication in bridging the gap between technology design and use. The discretion and practical knowledge about what communication is and ought to be exercised by GDSS facilitators articulated here can, upon further reflection, broaden understanding of the relationship between people, technology, and action.

16.4.3 Limitations and Further Research

The present study was designed to closely examine what happens in the performance of the technological facilitation of collaborative decision-making to better understand the influence of GDSS facilitators. The point, moreover, was to examine this work in light of practitioner actions and not in terms of group and organizational outcomes. As a study of communicative practice, the goal was to gain insight into the relationship between what practitioners take to be problems to be solved, the techniques they find appropriate and effective, and the rationales that justify techniques used and problems addressed.

The study was focused on the skilled performances of experienced GDSS facilitators. No doubt, there are less skilled performances. These are due in part to practitioners not yet to developing the sophisticated orientation toward their work that many of the facilitators in this study displayed. While there was much discussion of facilitators persuading users, the study does not claim that users were always persuaded or even that practitioners understood the persuasion they performed all that well. Further empirical work exploring the relationship between the design practice articulated here and its consequences for technology use and event outcomes must be undertaken.

This study focused on articulating the invisible work of GDSS facilitators and in so doing revealed characteristics of design practice aimed at crafting communication activity. It is presumed here that this design practice is a more general phenomenon. It is particularly interesting in the way its performance constructs the grounds on which people communicate and thus is an exercise in control over the way people communicate. This unique form of influence over the handling of choices and disputes is not that well understood (but see Jacobs and Aakhus 2002; Aakhus 2003). Hinted at but not fully developed in this study was a particular logic in the performance of crafting collaborative communicative activity. It emphasized a "harmony ideology" (Nader 1978) that privileges the demonstration of consensus and openness over justice, rights, and interests. This is most evident in the way interventions appealed to direct, open communication under the control of participants. Whether that is the case, how general such a logic may be, and its consequences for managing decision-making and dispute resolution through technological mediation requires further study. Such investigations would be very enlightening for understanding the forms and consequences of the types of control exercised over communication in the workplace and society at large in technological intervention.

Acknowledgments An earlier version this chapter appeared as: Aakhus, M. (2004). Understanding the Socio-Technical Gap: A case of GDSS Facilitation. In G. Goldkuhl, M. Lind, & S. Cronholm (Eds.), *Proceedings of the 2nd International Conference on Action in Language, Organisations, and Information Systems* (pp. 137–148). Linköping, Sweden: Research Network VITS.

References

Aakhus, M. (2000). Constituting deliberation as "buy-in" through GDSS design and implementation. *The Electronic Journal of Communication/La Revue Electronique de Communication [Online], 10*(1). Available at http://www.cios.org/www/ejcrec2.htm

Aakhus, M. (2001). Technocratic and design stances toward communication expertise: How GDSS facilitators understand their work. *Journal of Applied Communication Research, 29*(4), 341–371.

Aakhus, M. (2003). Neither naïve nor normative reconstruction: Dispute mediators, impasse, and the design of argumentation. *Argumentation: An International Journal on Reasoning, 17*(3), 265–290.

Aakhus, M. (2007). Communication as design. *Communication Monographs, 74*(1), 112–117.

Aakhus, M., & Jackson, S. (2005). Technology, interaction, design. Handbook of language and social interaction. In K. Fitch & R. Sanders (Eds.), *Handbook of language and social interaction* (pp. 411–437). Mahwah: Lawrence Erlbaum.

Allen, J. (1993). Groupware and social reality. *Computers and Society, 22*, 24–28.

Anson, R., Bostrom, R., & Wynne, B. (1995). An experiment assessing group support system and facilitator effects on meeting outcomes. *Management Science, 41*(2), 189–208.

Baecker, R., Grudin, J., Buxton, W., & Greenberg, S. (1995). Groupware computer supported cooperative work. In R. Baecker, J. Grudin, W. Buxton, & S. Greenberg (Eds.), *Readings in human computer interaction: Towards the year 2000* (pp. 741–754). San Francisco: Morgan Kaufman Publishers, Inc.

Banks, S., & Riley, P. (1993). Structuration theory as an ontology for communication research. In S. Deetz (Ed.), *Communication yearbook 16* (pp. 167–196). Newbury Park: Sage.

Bikson, T. (1996). Groupware at the world bank. In C. Ciborra (Ed.), *Groupware and teamwork: Invisible aid or technical hindrance?* (pp. 145–184). New York: Wiley.

Bostrom, R., & Anson, R. (1992). The face-to-face electronic meeting: A tutorial. In R. Bostrom, R. Watson, & S. Kinney (Eds.), *Computer augmented teamwork: A guided tour* (pp. 16–33). New York: Van Nostrand and Rheinhold.

Bostrom, R., Anson, R., & Clawson, V. (1993). Group facilitation and group support systems. In L. M. Jessup & J. S. Valacich (Eds.), *Group support systems: New perspectives* (pp. 146–168). New York: Macmillan.

Broome, B., & Keever, D. (1989). Next generation group facilitation: Proposed principles. *Management Communication Quarterly, 3*(1), 107–127.

Clawson, V., & Bostrom, R. (1996). Research-driven facilitation training for computer-supported environments. *Group Decision and Negotiation, 5*(1), 7–30.

Clawson, V., Bostrom, R., & Anson, R. (1993). The role of the facilitator in computer-supported meetings. *Small Group Research, 24*(4), 547–565.

Connelly, T., Jessup, L., & Valacich, J. (1990). Effects of anonymity and evaluative tone on idea generation in computer-mediated groups. *Management Science, 36*(6), 689–703.

Contractor, N., & Seibold, D. (1993). Theoretical frameworks for the study of structuring processes in group decision support systems: Adaptive structuration theory and self organizing systems theory. *Human Communication Research, 19*, 528–563.

Contractor, N., Seibold, D., & Heller, M. (1996). Interactional influence in the structuring of media use in groups: Influence in member's perceptions of group decision support system use. *Human Communication Research, 22*(4), 451–481.

Craig, R. (1989). Communication as practical discipline. In B. Dervin, L. Grossberg, B. J. O'Keefe, & E. Wartella (Eds.), *Rethinking communication vol. 1, paradigm issues* (pp. 97–122). Newbury Park: Sage.

Craig, R., & Tracy, K. (1995). Grounded practical theory: The case of intellectual discussion. *Communication Theory, 5*(3), 248–272.

Dannelmiller, K., & Jacobs, R. (1992). Changing the way organizations change: A revolution of common sense. *The Journal of Applied Behavioral Science, 28*(4), 480–498.

DeSanctis, G., & Poole, M. S. (1994). Capturing the complexity in advanced technology use: Adaptive Structuration Theory. *Organization Science, 5*(2), 121–147.

de Vreede, G., & de Bruijn, H. (1999). Exploring the boundaries of successful GSS application: Supporting inter-organizational policy networks. *Database, 30*(3–4), 111–130.

Dickson, G., Lee-Partridge, J., Limayem, M., & De Sanctis, G. (1996). Facilitating computer-supported meetings: A cumulative analysis in a multiple-criteria task environment. *Group Decision and Negotiation, 5*(1), 51–72.

Doyle, M., & Straus, D. (1976). *How to make meetings work*. New York: Jove Books.

Garfinkel, H. (1967). *Studies in ethnomethodology*. Englewood Cliffs: Prentice-Hall.

Goffman, E. (1983). Felicity's condition. *The American Journal of Sociology, 89*(1), 1–53.

Grice, H. (1975). Logic and conversation. In P. Cole & J. Morgan (Eds.), *Syntax and semantics, vol. 3: Speech acts*. New York: Academic.

Grudin, J. (1994). Groupware and social dynamics: Eight challenges for developers. *Communications of the ACM, 37*(1), 71–92.

Heritage, J. (1984). *Garfinkel and ethnomethodology*. Cambridge: Polity Press.

Jacobs, S., & Aakhus, M. (2002). What mediators do with words: Implementing three models of rational discussion in dispute mediation. *Conflict Resolution Quarterly, 20*(4), 177–204.

Johansen, R. (1989). *Groupware: Computer support for business teams*. New York: Free Press.

Kaner, S., Lind, L., Toldi, C., Fisk, S., & Berger, D. (1996). *Facilitator's guide to participatory decision-making*. Philadelphia: New Society Publishers.

Kraemer, K., & King, J. (1988). Computer-based systems for cooperative work and group decision making. *ACM Computing Surveys, 20*(2), 115–146.

Leiter, K. (1980). *A primer on ethnomethodology*. Oxford: Oxford University Press.

Levinson, S. (1979). Activity types and language. *Linguistics, 17*, 365–399.

Lyytinen, K., Maaranen, P., & Knuutila, J. (1994). Groups are not always the same: An analysis of group behaviors in electronic meeting systems. *Computer Supported Cooperative Work (CSCW), 2*, 261–284.

Mateosian, G. (1993). *Reproducing rape: Domination through talk in the courtroom*. Chicago: University of Chicago Press.

Nader, L. (1990). *Harmony ideology: Justice and control in a zapotec mountain villavge*. Stanford, CA: Stanford University Press.

Ngwenyama, O., Bryson, N., & Moboluren, A. (1996). Supporting facilitation in group support systems: Techniques for analyzing consensus relevant data. *Decision Support Systems, 16*, 155–168.

Niederman, F., Biese, C., & Beranek, P. (1996). Issues and concerns about computer-supported meetings: The facilitator's perspective. *MIS Quarterly, 20*(1), 1–22.

Nunamaker, J., Dennis, A., Valacich, J., Vogel, D., & George, J. (1991). Electronic meetings to support group work. *Communications of the ACM, 34*(7), 40–61.

Nunamaker, J., Briggs, B., & Mittleman, D. (1994). Electronic meeting systems: Ten years of lessons learned. In D. Coleman & R. Khanna (Eds.), *Groupware: Technologies applications* (pp. 149–193). Upper Saddle River: Prentice Hall.

Orlikowski, W., Yates, J., Okamura, K., & Fujimoto, M. (1995). Shaping electronic communication: The metastructuring of technology in the context of use. *Organization Science, 6*(4), 423–444.

Pinsonneault, A., & Kraemer, K. (1989). The impact of technical support on groups: An assessment of empirical research. *Decision Support Systems, 5*(2), 197–216.

Poole, M., & De Sanctis, G. (1990). Understanding the use of group decision support systems: The theory of adaptive structuration. In J. Fulk & C. Steinfeld (Eds.), *Organizations and communication technology*. Newbury Park: Sage.

Poole, M., & De Sanctis, G. (1992). Microlevel structuration in computer-supported group decision making. *Human Communication Research, 19*, 5–49.

Poole, M. S., & Holmes, M. E. (1995). Decision development in computer-assisted group decision making. *Human Communication Research, 22*, 90–127.

Poole, M., De Sanctis, G., Kirsch, L., & Jackson, M. (1995). Group decision support systems as facilitators of quality team efforts. In L. Frey (Ed.), *Innovations in group facilitation* (pp. 299–322). Cresskill: Hampton Press.

Schwarz, R. (1994). *The skilled facilitator: Practical wisdom for developing effective groups*. San Francisco: Jossey-Bass Publishers.

Seibold, D., Heller, M. A., & Contractor, N. (1994). Review and critique of empirical research on group decision support systems. In B. Kovacic (Ed.), *Organizational communication: New perspectives* (pp. 143–168). Albany: SUNY Press.

Weatherall, A., & Nunamaker, J. (1995). *Introduction to electronic meetings: Informed decisions, better planning, reduced timescales*. Hampshire: Electronic Meeting Services Limited.

Weick, K., & Meader, D. (1993). Sensemaking and group support systems. In L. Jessup & J. Valacich (Eds.), *Group support systems: New perspectives* (pp. 230–251). New York: Macmillan.

Weider, L. (1976). *Language and social reality: The case of telling the convict code*. The Hague: Mouton.

Yates, J. (1989). *Control through communication: The rise of system in American management*. Baltimore: Johns Hopkins Press.

Yates, J., & Orlikowski, W. (1992). Genres of organizational communication: A structurational approach to studying communication and media. *The Academy of Management Review, 17*, 299–326.

Chapter 17
Mining Creativity Research to Inform Design Rationale in Open Source Communities

Winslow Burleson and Priyamvada Tripathi

Abstract Design rationale can act as a creativity support tool. Recent findings from the field of creativity research present new opportunities that can guide the implementation and evaluation of design rationale's ability to foster creative processes and outcomes. By encouraging the exploration of failure through use of analogy, design rationale can foster creative transfer and enable progress in new directions. Open source communities offer an opportunity to observe a form of intrinsically motivated ad hoc design rationale, exhibiting formal and informal information transfer links within forums and allowing access to common tools, expertise, and mentorship. A discussion of a spectrum of implementations of design rationale informs strategies to mitigate conflicts and advance inherent synergies between design rationale and creativity.

Keywords Creativity research • Creativity support tools • Design rationale • Open source communities

17.1 Introduction

The 2003 National Research Council's (NRC) *Beyond Productivity* report examined elements of creativity and the emergence of human–computer interaction in everyday life, emphasizing a need for information technology (IT) to support creativity across domains (Mitchell et al. 2003). It was proposed that adoption of

W. Burleson (✉) • P. Tripathi
School of Computing, Informatics, and Decision Systems Engineering,
Arizona State University, Tempe, AZ, USA
e-mail: Winslow.Burleson@asu.edu; pia@asu.edu

J.M. Carroll (ed.), *Creativity and Rationale: Enhancing Human
Experience by Design*, Human–Computer Interaction Series,
DOI 10.1007/978-1-4471-4111-2_17, © Springer-Verlag London 2013

improved tools that support creativity using IT backbones would yield economic
and cultural benefits. Since then, available technology has matured even further,
making creativity support easier and more productive. The NRC report also
acknowledged that today's IT user has needs that go beyond traditional requirements
for productivity and efficiency. IT has enabled today's user to join and contribute
to new communities with ease, and to engage in creative acts on an everyday basis.
These users, collectively engaged in creation, production, and distribution, demand
that technologies work with them, engage them, and keep them motivated. They
thrive on competition and feedback from peers. They are socially embedded
through IT networks, seek community-level knowledge sources, and revel in
collaborative work. These new generations of users and developers are, in short,
mature users of technology.

A complementary report by the Computing Research Association (2002)
outlined five grand challenges of computer science and information science, including the challenges of creating opportunities for personalized learning, "a teacher for
every learner," and using hybrid teams of humans and software/hardware system
technologies to create a team of one's own (p. 5). By interacting with individuals
and teams to enhance design rationale, these systems act as support tools. When
used to support creativity, these software agents are considered to be creativity
research tools. Systems that allow teams of software agents and humans to collaborate present an opportunity to use design rationale as a creativity support tool,
modulating and communicating process and outcome.

Open source communities present an environment in which users and developers
can take advantage of design rationale to support creativity. Open source simply
means software whose source code is freely available for modification and reuse,
in contrast to the commercial model of software that restricts access to source code
to a firm's employees and contractors. The open source paradigm has given rise to
new organizational structures and practices, allowed for distributed community
management of software, and promoted collaboration among participants. Open
source's mass involvement of highly skilled, intrinsically motivated participants
creates an optimal environment to examine techniques to support creativity and
employ design rationale.

In this chapter, we discuss the use of design rationale as a creativity support tool
in the context of the open source paradigm. The goal of advancing creativity in
software design environments faces at least two issues. First creativity and new
opportunities for creativity must be appreciated within the ongoing cognitive activity
that occurs among software developers. Second, a suitable framework that supports
articulation of these creative processes must be developed and used to enhance the
processes and products of programming. As Hanson, a principal research scientist
at MIT cited in von Hippel (2005), stated,

> Creative programming takes time, and careful attention to the details. Programming is all
> about expressing intent and in any large program there are many areas in which the
> programmer's intent is unclear. Clarification requires insight, and acquiring insight is the pri-
> mary creative act in programming. But insight takes time and often requires extensive
> conversation with one's peers. (p. 124)

Understanding the ways in which the elements of time, attention to detail, expressing intent, clarity, insight, and deep and persistent conversation manifest within the structure, process, and success of open source communities can elucidate ways in which design rationale contributes to creative programming.

As the design community grapples with its understanding of the relationship between design rationale and creativity (Carroll 2010), an exploration of the question, "How can design rationale support creative processes and outcomes?" might allow fuller realization of design rationale's potential. To address this question we will turn to the many possible implementations of design rationale, and the effect that each of them may have on creativity. First, we must ask ourselves how well design rationale plays the role of a creativity support tool, and what strategies can be employed to enhance its efficacy. To understand this in terms of the context of the open source paradigm and the role of creativity in open source communities, we must understand the functions and roles of creativity support tools. Likewise, we must understand what creativity research tells us about the best practices for supporting creativity. This will include wider discussion of the consensual assessment of creativity (Amabile 1983) and the role of transdisciplinary collaboration and metacreativity (Buchanan 2001). We ground this discussion in the evolving nature of human–computer interaction and the opportunities for design rationale to support creativity when design activity spans disciplines, as is seen in hybrid software/hardware development, and process and product development in open source and do-it-yourself communities (Kuznetsov and Paulos 2010; von Hippel 2005).

17.2 Design Rationale

Moran and Carroll (1996) defined design as "the process of creating tangible artifacts to meet intangible human needs" (p. 2). They stated that design seeks to fill the stated and unstated needs of the end user by bridging the gap between requirements and end product. A typical lifecycle of a design project bridges this gap with six phases: the requirement phase, design phase, building phase, deployment phase, maintenance phase, and redesign phase. In some respects, this is similar to models of software development life cycles. In both, design rationale plays an important role because, in practice, these phases and cycles are usually not strictly delineated. The iteration and complexity of their interconnection adds richness and depth to design projects.

Several definitions of design rationale exist, but Moran and Carroll (1996) defined six broad ways in which the term is used. Fundamentally, it is an "expression of relationship between a designed artifact, its purpose, the designer's conceptualization, and the contextual restraints on realizing the purpose" (p. 8). Design rationale could be (a) logical reasons given to justify a designed artifact, (b) a notation for the reasons, (c) a method by which reasons for the design are made explicit, (d) documentation of reasons for the design, (e) steps for the design, or (f) the history of the design and its context. It provides an explanation of why a designed artifact is manifest in the manner that it is. Overall, "design rationale is concerned with systemizing the design process—its tools, techniques, methods, and management—for artifacts and their specifications" (Moran and Carroll 1996, p. 8).

Fischer et al. (1991) stated that the benefits of using design rationale are support for the maintenance and redesign of an artifact, reuse of design knowledge, and critical reflection. MacLean et al. (1996) stated that design rationale aids reasoning and communication. Moreover, design rationale can encompass several tasks (MacLean et al. 1996), including documentation, understanding, debugging, verification, analysis, explanation, modification, and automation (Moran and Carroll 1996). From these perspectives it becomes apparent that design rationale is meant as an explicit effort to promote deeper understanding of the design process and decision making, and to transfer this knowledge within the design team and community. Multiple facets of design rationale have emerged to facilitate and enhance the design process. The question at hand, then, is whether design rationale can be implemented in ways that promote creativity. To address this question, we will explore different implementations of design rationale in terms of their granularity and formality, instantiation, and scale.

17.2.1 Granularity and Formality

Implementation techniques can vary across a range of granularities. Fine-grained approaches detail every step and decision in the process, while coarse-grained methods take a broader, macrolevel view of documentation. Fine-grained design rationale is frequently time-consuming and can be burdensome and disruptive to designers and programmers and their creative processes. Coarse-grained design rationale runs the risk of missing significant events.

Design rationale can also be implemented across a range of formalities. Formal techniques usually track a prespecified set of concepts and categories, but may not fully represent every aspect of design processes. These communication tools can act as accessories to design process deliberation; however it is generally understood that even the most advanced capture tools will fail to completely record all underlying decisions and meanings (Gruber and Russell 1996). This is particularly true when a new audience accesses the recorded design rationale, since the new users' backgrounds, assumptions, and even working vocabulary may have shifted significantly. More positively, formal processes can encourage deliberative processes, reflection, self-explanation, and incubation. The constraints of formal processes make design rationale easy to encode and enhance compliance, which in turn can aid subsequent decision making. Including explicit instruments to formally document creativity within design rationale may help designers to value it within their process.

Informal methods allow considerable freedom but also demand discipline if they are to be a useful compendium. Informal design rationale can be encoded freestyle and later transcribed, or it can be encoded in parallel, where programmers code decisions as they are made. Informal methods can be passive, such as videotaping, or active and explicit in capturing design processes and materials. In design studios, for example, informal compendiums of the design process can include recorded logbooks, Post-it wall and smart board images, concept maps, brainstorming sessions and conclusions, discussions and choices of methodologies, scenario design, and refinement or prototyping processes. In open source software and do-it-yourself communities, informal design rationale compendiums can include information transfer links (von Hippel 2005), for example, logged communication channels and forums, e-mail, chat, and community websites such as www.linuxforums.org, instructables.com, sparkfun, newgrounds. com, or e-how.

To fully understand design rationale's potential to support creativity, a system of evaluation is required. Amabile's (1983) consensual assessment technique can comparatively evaluate diverse implementations of design rationale. Take for example the assessment of design rationale across four conditions of a 2×2 experiment in which individuals or teams engage in a creative task with informal/formal $\times$ fine/coarse design rationale. Programmers who have been selected as judges based on their interrater reliability (the degree to which judges' ratings of creative products correlate with each of the others' ratings) can evaluate the creativity of the processes and products of these teams. The findings would inform the development of best practices for supporting creativity through design rationale.

17.2.2 Instantiation

Implementations of design rationale within a design process can occur at multiple levels. For example, design rationale practices can be structured to occur as a philosophy, protocol, schedule, tool, interface, or system. Different individuals and organizations will place different values on design rationale as a philosophy, from considering it a core attribute to simply ignoring it. Similarly, compliance with the practice of design rationale may be enforced strictly, or followed only on an as-needed basis. With or without a philosophy, design rationale can be implemented as a protocol with guidelines and rules regarding its implementation. As a schedule (which may or may not be an element of a protocol), design rationale can be regulated, either on a time or event (i.e., new idea or change in course) basis. As a tool, interface, or system, design rationale can take a simple form or be mediated through multiple points of view (e.g., from the perspectives of various stakeholders). It can take place through e-mail, on-line activity, or even multiperson interfaces with virtual team members acting as design facilitators and design rationale elicitors. In the context of our considerations of design rationale as a creativity support tool, it is worth noting that creativity and support for creativity can also be considered at multiple levels (granularity, formality, instantiation, organizational, etc.).

17.2.3 Organizational

Regardless of the level of formality and granularity and its instantiation, the essence of the value of design rationale is that it provides a record of the reasons for a particular choice and preserves relevant consideration of alternatives, which in turn enables discussion, revision, reflection, and community building. Implementation of design rationale to facilitate creativity inherently takes place within the context of an organization and/or culture; that context has consequent impact on creativity and design rationale. Recent theory in creativity research has been generated both from large-scale cultural and organizational contexts and from individuals and small teams, while design rationale, at least at the point of its generation, has by and large focused on individuals and small teams. The environments' impact on design rationale can be considered in terms of its adoption and usage, and measured in terms of its benefits and efficacy in supporting creativity and the community. A full discussion of the relationship between design rationale and the context of its implementation is beyond the scope of this chapter. Nonetheless, our exploration of creativity research and its appreciation for organizational influences on creativity can improve understanding of how design rationale can foster creativity.

In terms of organizational scale or complexity, applications of design rationale and creativity research can focus on relatively small organizations, ranging from individuals to small teams, and can extend to the broader issues of larger organizations, such as divisions, companies, and large-scale distributed communities, as are found in open source. Most environments in which design activity and creativity take place have their own forms of ad hoc design rationale that, at least in part, foster creativity. To the extent this is true, there exists the potential to apply lessons from both creativity research and design rationale to further enhance communication, creativity, and design outcomes. Design projects, ranging from architectural or landscape planning to writing a novel to software development, involve sketches (i.e., drafts, prototypes, or templates) that allow for the exchange and development of initial ideas and project requirements. When individuals and small teams work closely together, design requirements and possible solutions are frequently less complicated and more easily communicated across the team than when such projects are developed by larger organizations. Larger organizations must negotiate common agendas and effective strategies to build design rationale into their organizational structures and practices. Take, for example, individual software developers employing class and Unified Modeling Language diagrams to establish system architecture features and objectives as they manage initial requirements. These sketches can be challenging, ambiguous, and cumbersome for small-scale organizations. However, in the context of a large-scale open source design community, project requirements and solutions are often difficult to articulate and agree upon. In order for these larger organizations to make progress, communication and the exchange of ideas and assumptions between peers is necessary. The communal development of this common understanding encoded by information transfer links (von Hippel 2005) is a form of large-scale organizational design rationale, which, in turn, can support organizational progress and creativity.

Beyond the realm of software organizations, emergent hacker spaces and their commensurate on-line communities are an exciting contemporary open source phenomenon, the next generation of physical/digital design and human–computer interaction (Buxton 2007). Increasingly, successful software is the product of integrated development, with well-defined software design attributes that are consonant with the hardware. For example, Apple's Multi-Touch trackpad technology, which allows users to navigate their electronics using various motions and gestures, makes use of both hardware and software affordances.[1] These synergies and designers' understandings between and across hardware and software systems are rapidly evolving within open source and do-it-yourself design communities. These communities develop not only highly creative hybrid physical/digital artifacts, but also expertise and social engagement among their members.

As described above, design rationale covers the spectrum from fine-grained descriptions of all reasoning processes to an organizational structure that provides guidelines to share creativity in the commons. In many contexts, the implementation of design rationale advances the principles and purposes of a creativity support tool.

17.3   Creativity Research

Developing a design rationale that serves as a creativity support tool first requires an understanding of the field of creativity research. Creativity researchers suggest that the quality of creativity can be evaluated based on the value and level of meaning of a new idea product. In this vein, Csikszentmihalyi (1996) claimed that different people and groups experience creativity in multiple ways. Researchers also may distinguish ordinary creativity—small departures, insights, and innovations in everyday life—from the creativity of the few known geniuses, such as Einstein and Van Gogh. Gardner (1994) expressed the former as "little c" creativity as opposed to "big C" creativity. Within creativity research, creativity is recognized as a natural part of ordinary human existence. Shneiderman (2003) described these forms of creativity as everyday, evolutionary, and revolutionary. Since any advancement in society requires some new idea or process, creativity researchers also appreciate that creativity is an important process for societal transformation. Moreover, creativity is an integral cognitive process that is a fundamental part of human makeup.

In creativity research, creativity is considered to be present within any product or process that is novel and appropriate (Sternberg and Lubart 2007), and is a part of everyday life and work activity (Certeau 1984), in contrast to the more popular conception that creativity primarily occurs through "Eureka!" moments. French philosopher Michel de Certeau (1984) was one of the first theorists to propose the concept of everyday anonymous creativity by ordinary people. The many innovative

---

[1] Multitouch is a technology that allows Apple products to recognize when two or more points are in contact with its surface, enabling two-finger scrolling, rotation, zoom, etc.

ways that people recycle, adapt, or transform everyday objects for their own benefit demonstrate everyday acts of creativity and design. This idea has taken hold in interaction and design research as well (Wakkary and Maestri 2007). Photographer Richard Wentworth (1978), for example, created a photo series aimed at reframing our conception of everyday creative acts—using a bottle cap as a makeshift ashtray, or jamming an alarm clock with a half-eaten candy bar. Wakkary and Maestri (2007) reported similar everyday creative acts within families. Amabile (1983) developed the consensual assessment method as a way to rank creative acts. Studying activities such as writing poetry, building block towers, and making collages, she conceptualized a continuous creativity spectrum that ranks degrees of creativity. Her research demonstrated that judges, selected for their high degree of interrater reliability can be used to perform consensual evaluation of the creativity of most processes or products. In a range of studies, this method has been shown to have strong validity and is one of the most widely used and accepted evaluation methods in creativity research. The consensual assessment method could also be used to evaluate creativity in the process of design and compiling design rationale.

Amabile (1996; Amabile and Mueller, 2002) has studied the structure of creativity within individuals and developed the componential model of creativity that identifies three components within the individual that have an effect on creativity: an individual's intrinsic motivation; his/her thinking style; and his/her domain-relevant skills. Intrinsic motivation includes attitudes, perceptions of personal motivation toward a task. Domain-relevant skills include knowledge about the domain, technical skills, and talent. Thinking style includes convergent/divergent processes and implicit/explicit knowledge and appropriate use of heuristics for generating, evaluating, and implementing ideas.

In addition to the componential model's three elements within the individual, Amabile (1983) also identified environmental influences as a fourth component that affects team processes. Her studies of high-tech team collaborations "in the wild" have demonstrated important factors, including the role of affect; time pressure; focused attention; sequestered and prioritized creative activity; motivation; feedback; and actualizing rewards (Amabile et al. 2002; Amabile and Kramer 2003). Actualizing resources and rewards are those that empower individuals to achievements they would otherwise not be capable of. For example, mentorship, tutorials, and on-line forums in open source software and do-it-yourself communities are actualizing resources for their members. Actualizing rewards might be an invitation or resources to attend a conference or lead a team that could assist in furthering already successful endeavors. In a series of studies creativity researchers have found that positive affect promotes creativity both in the moment and from one day to the next. Positive affect may come in the form of a small gift or joke, or as a positive event, breakthrough idea, or actualizing reward for progress in recognition of the creative activity. Open source communities often display elements of creativity support that are consistent with the framework developed by creativity researchers; existing frameworks for identifying and evaluating creativity can inform our discussion of creativity in these communities.

17.4 Open Source Communities

Open source software is characterized by its free availability to be modified and used by anyone, under a few sets of restrictions. The open source agreement restrictions generally prohibit the use of code in commercial ventures. Open source on-line communities have their origins in the hacker culture, which is an example of what von Hippel (2005) called communities of "lead users." Lead users' adoption of toolkits and development of creative projects are core attributes of von Hippel's notions of advancing democratic innovation. In the early 1990s, research laboratories, such as MIT's Artificial Intelligence Laboratory, started licensing their software, restricting access to source code. Some lead programmers of the original source codes were upset by this control over what they felt was community property. In addition, several felt that this level of commercialization severely inhibited the growth of the field. This is an example of what Amabile and Mueller (2002) would call an environment that failed to provide "actualizing rewards."

Stallman proposed the GNU General Public License (GPL) in the 1980s.[2] GPL grants the right to use software, to study and modify the source code, and to distribute or redistribute modified or unmodified versions at no cost. Furthermore, GPL restricts the right to use or incorporate the code into proprietary commercial software. In 1998, the open source software movement was formalized by Perens and Raymond. This movement emphasized benefits of sharing source code as we see today (DiBona et al. 1999; Corbet et al. 2010; von Hippel 2005). The open source movement resonated with individuals who were motivated to be part of the anticorporate culture that was emerging in response to big corporations such as Microsoft and their emphasis on closed system software. In contrast to the restrictive environment (described above), the environment created by GPL could be described as an actualizing one, in which the success of one's creative products were shared and adopted widely and had visible impacts.

The scale of the open source community is significant. As of July 2011, more than 300,000 software projects have been registered on the Website sourceforge.net, a database of open-source software projects. The success of open source communities is largely explained by the intrinsic motivation of its contributors, who code and share information based on their intrinsic interests and domain expertise and act socially to engage in creative activity.

The rights granted by GPL have enabled the open source community to grow; this growth has required concerted conversation about the community's agenda and decision making at the macro (within the structure of the community) and micro levels (within the code). This conversation and the deliberations now present a robust ad hoc design rationale corpus of the community's endeavors. This corpus and the practices of the community around decision making and strategies for progress therefore form a basis for discussion of macrolevel design rationale.

---

[2] The Free Software Foundation is a nonprofit that campaigns for free open source software and drives development of the GNU license. For more information, go to http://www.fsf.org

17.5 Creativity in Open Source Communities

Open source communities are made up of programmers who are engaged in collaborative group activity, making the capture and effective communication of individuals' design process and decision making particularly important. Open source communities use diverse modes of communication, forming unique structures that foster widespread everyday creativity. O'Mahony (Stark 2003) investigated several characteristics of open source communities, finding that open source software developers are intrinsically motivated, value informality, and have distaste for "administrivia" (Stark 2003). These characteristics are in line with a preference for informal and coarse-grained design rationale. However, as O'Mahony (Stark 2003) pointed out, some open source communities have formalized their organizational structures by creating formal boards and designated management roles. Design rationale can be seen to sustain the communal and creative goals of open source communities through a range of granularities, formalities, and organizational elements.

There are parallels between the existing functions of creativity support tools (see below) and the organization of open source communities. To more fully understand the interplay of creativity in open source communities, we now review the roles users play in the process of software coding in open source paradigms. A project is introduced by owners (also referred to as "maintainers" or even "gatekeepers") who are responsible for project management. These project managers also set up an infrastructure for the project that those interested can use to seek help, provide information, or provide new open source code to test and discuss. People download the projects that attract interest and "play" with the code. Some of these people go on to create new and modified code. New code, deemed to be of interest and value by the project maintainers is authorized (von Krogh et al. 2003), and posted back into the infrastructure. In essence this parallels the four-stage process of advancing creativity within information technology contexts, described by Shneiderman (2003) in his book *Leonardo's Laptop,* as a process comprising collecting (domain expertise, information collection), relating (analogical transfer, comparison among works), creating (development, testing), and donating (dissemination, diffusion). In open source communities, the credibility of members is determined through status, experience, and expertise. The roles can also overlap. Typically none of the roles are strictly enforced and most work is voluntary and intrinsically motivated, key parts of Amabile's (1983) componential model of creativity.

O'Mahony Stark (2003) identified three great challenges within the open source software paradigm that both inform our discussion and present opportunities for design rationale to support creativity. The first of these challenges is resources. The effective use of resources as actualizing rewards can be an opportunity for fostering a commitment to design rationale and as a tool for promoting intrinsic motivation and creativity. Second, the tension between creative freedom and need for structure and management is at the crux of the debate about the compatibility of design rationale and creativity (Carroll 2010); the appropriate balance of formality and granularity can be difficult to find. Third, the need for sustaining pluralism in governance presents the classic challenge of individual and shared voices and shared language (O'Mahony and Ferraro 2007). These are common challenges present in what Rittel (1972) termed "wicked problems." Werner and Rittel's (1970/1979) participatory approach to the development of the issue-based information system (IBIS) and its use as a tool for design rationale have advanced approaches to shared dialogue; recent work on computational support and analysis of shared dialogue systems have further advanced these strategies (Conklin 2003). Effective journalism (a record and forum for the communication and debate of multiple perspectives) can lead to effective policy and ultimately toward effective governance of a community, providing an actualizing environment within which to advance creativity. Beschastnikh et al. (2008) studies of organization and governance within Wikipedia support this; they characterized Wikipedia's "policy environment [as]—user editable, reflective of [best] practice, and easily citable" (p. 34). Further, they highlighted the potential for effective policy to foster public deliberation (Beschastnikh et al. 2008). At its core, this is what design rationale, and in turn advancing creativity (especially in open source communities), is about—creating an environment in which shared understanding, decision making, collaboration, and transdisciplinary creativity can occur.

Von Hippel (2005) argued that open source communities are innovation niches that foster widespread group creativity. He defined innovation communities as "nodes consisting of individuals or firms interconnected by information transfer links which may involve face-to-face, electronic, or other communication" (von Hippel 2005, p. 96). These information transfer links are key features where understanding and fostering effective forms of design rationale can be most productive in enhancing creativity. According to von Hippel, innovation in these communities is a distributed process that occurs through both informal (user-to-user) and organized (users interacting within communities) cooperation. The community supplies users with useful tools and infrastructure that are employed to develop, test, and diffuse their innovations. In some important respects, von Hippel's distinction between informal and organized information transfer links recalls the distinction, discussed earlier, of formal and informal approaches to design rationale. In the informal conditions of von Hippel's arguments, and those advanced by this chapter, the ad hoc nature is both useful, since it is spontaneous and responsive to opportunity (e.g., to discuss an important issue or capture, in the moment, salient design rationale), and problematic, since the lack of structure can lead to omission. In the organized or formal condition, the rigid context is productive, in that it allows for organizational progress and the capture of widely agreed upon relevant information; yet the formal condition also runs the risk of missing key information that falls outside of its categorization, such as divergent or minority viewpoints. Luther et al. (2010) suggest that the success of creative collaboration in open source communities relies on leaders with solid reputations and respect from their communities, and that Weber's (2004) principle, "Talk a lot," should be encouraged.

Within open source communities, diverse levels of domain expertise and transdisciplinary collaboration are leveraged to foster what creativity research would describe as fluency and flexibility. Because these "low-cost innovation niches" (von Hippel 2005, p. 79) consist of novel combinations of and within preexisting elements and contexts (the members and organizations that exist within the community and the ongoing development of the source code), members typically draw on their own expertise to advance creative solutions. For example, in the realm of open source and do-it-yourself communities, an individual with a background in mountain biking (a hobby) and orthopedic surgery (a profession) may create a seat suspension that reduces shock to a biker's spine upon landing. Thus, collectively, the community's members are capable of generating a wide range of ideas (fluency) owing to their diverse backgrounds and a broad diversity in the type of ideas (flexibility). Open source communities, therefore, attract people from various backgrounds who are motivated by the same ideals to create or develop upon existing platforms, whether these are source code or electro-mechanical systems, knitting communities, or so on. The different combinations of backgrounds of the participants in the open source communities and their interconnections are aimed at enhancing the potential quality of the final products. This presents opportunities and challenges for design rationale to act as a cross-pollinator, to bridge the expertise and domain gaps, and to foster transdisciplinary communication.

In open source software development, where the transdisciplinary nature of the community is somewhat less diverse than in the open source or do-it-yourself communities, participants still take on a range of roles that allow them to apply their expertise to a wide range of shared interests and problems that serve the communal goals. To support the sharing of their expertise and advancement of their projects, these communities typically utilize various forms of version-control tools that facilitate beta testing and revising processes. In open source software developer communities, the volume of individuals who can test and debug code increases the chances that a bug will be found; as Raymond put it, in a phrase that has come to be known as the Linus Law, "given enough eyeballs, the bugs are shallow" (2001, p. 30). The current paradigms for idea exchange in open source software developer communities are through forums or e-mail lists, forms of asynchronous informal communication that aim to focus on single issues in each thread. The main limitations to the effectiveness of current forms of ad hoc open source design rationale within these communities are the duplication and repetition of ideas. For a new developer, therefore, the onus lies in searching and rediscovering whether or not a certain idea or problem has occurred before and what the possible resolution of that idea might have been. New forms of design rationale or strategies for motivating more constructive implementations of design rationale in open source communities may be able to mitigate these limitations. For example, the Wikipedia community uses "barnstars" to reward their members' effective contributions to articles and commentary (Beschastnikh et al. 2009). One way to interpret the success of the debugging process in open source communities is that users' diverse roles, backgrounds, and expertise allow them to view and discuss issues from multiple perspectives. Collective perspectives and implicit analogies enable them to overcome errors and recover from failure.

It is significant to note that design rational systems should include not only the rejected alternatives, but also, and more importantly, the failed implementations that constitute the valuable experiences needed to form the basis of analogies from which further work, progress, and breakthroughs can be advanced. As Dunbar's (1994) creativity research studies of expert and nonexpert scientific teams show, individuals and teams with more domain-relevant knowledge to draw on can more readily draw parallels between failures and new, more productive domains through analogical reasoning, thus empowering them to overcome setbacks and realize solutions more effectively. In open source communities, users who come from a range of disciplinary backgrounds can use analogies implicitly, both for recognition of bugs as well as for creation of new applications. Advanced design rationale systems have the potential to go beyond their current roles to encourage users to record not just successes and rejected alternatives, but also experiences and reflections of failures as well. This type of design rationale might serve as supporting scaffolding for the development of appropriate analogies and access to generative tools (Gero 1996; Ishikawa and Terano 1996). For example, people who download programs could submit a failed version explaining what problems they encountered, how they tried to solve it, if they failed, and why. This record of failures would allow others developers to either not go the same route or take this up as a challenge and introduce improvements and insightful alternatives.

Individuals engaging in transdisciplinary knowledge sharing in open source communities can discover options that were originally neglected. Members play varying roles in groups that may be different from their own personal background and in turn can influence open source successes in creation and rediscovery. The challenge in realizing improved creativity is perhaps in the realization of these benefits; here, design rationale has a significant role to play. Design rationale can empower members of the group to take on, evaluate, and rationalize decisions from new, diverse, and informed perspectives that challenge and provide the community with paths to move their common agenda forward. One of the biggest challenges is the sharing of unique information that each member possesses in the context of pooling common resources to balance the roles of team decision making. This balance serves both as a means to engender acceptance of, satisfaction with, and commitment to decisions, and to combine disparate points of view, knowledge, and ideas towards better decisions. In contrast to many other group settings, the opportunity to share and capitalize on the benefits of unique information increases with an increase in the number of members in open source communities.

The discussion of creativity and von Hippel's (2005) thesis on democratic innovation within open source communities echoes several of the models of creative processes proposed in decision sciences and creativity literature. For example, according to Cashman and Stroll (1989, p. 136), information technology-based decision processes can be expressed as a "create, communicate, review, and react" action cycle (including awareness management, autonomy, information gathering and dissemination, structuring, modeling options, and execution). Similarly, Shneiderman's (2003) collect, relate, create, and donate stages of creative processes within IT environments and von Hippel's (2005) analysis of open source communities, provide us with insights into the creative processes inherent to these open source communities. As such, these environments provide fertile ground to advance the interplay between creativity research and new forms of design rationale that are fundamentally creativity research tools.

17.6 Creativity Support Tools

In order to advance an understanding of the potential of design rationale to act fundamentally as a creativity support tool for open source communities, it is necessary to review recent developments in the realm of creativity research tools. Over the past decade or so, the goals of fostering creativity at the individual and group levels within the context of computing have evolved, furthering the domain of creativity research tools. The Association for Computing Machinery's Conference on Human Factors in Computing Creativity and Interface Workshop in 2002 focused on opportunities to use interface tools in fostering end-user creativity. Common themes of the discussion included interface elements that offered "exploration, parallel experimentation, generative ideation, media and content pliability, iteration, support for creative mistakes and insights and process assistance" (Burleson and Selker 2002, p. 89). A subsequent National Science Foundation (NSF) Workshop on creativity research tools (Shneiderman et al. 2006) highlighted the potential of creativity research tools as offering "more effective searching of intellectual resources, improved collaboration among teams, and more rapid discovery processes, ... potent support in hypothesis formation, speedier evaluation of alternatives, improved understanding through visualization, and better dissemination of results, ... [to] facilitate exploration of alternatives, prevent unproductive choices, and enable easy backtracking" (p. 62). A set of guidelines for creativity research tools were developed, encouraging a "low threshold, high ceilings, and wide walls" (Shneiderman et al. 2006, p. 70); in other words, easy entry to usage for novices, powerful facilities for sophisticated users, and a small, well-chosen set of features that support a wide range of possibilities, easy exploration of multiple alternatives and powerful history-keeping.

Creativity research tools can take many different forms to support these objectives, encompassing a variety of activities. Shneiderman (2003) demonstrated this in the context of multiple professional domains and organizations, including architects, lawyers, doctors, and the Compumentor and TechSoup communities. NSF's Creative IT (National Science Foundation 2009), a 3-year funding initiative and the community it fostered, further advanced creativity research tools to explore their role in assessing creativity in everyday activities. Following up on Amabile and Kramer's (2003) study of the creative practices of high tech researchers, creativity investigations have advanced multimodal real-time tools that computationally track affect, voice, and motion "in the wild" and relate these to self- and peer-report measures (Burleson and Pentland 2008). Similar tools have been advanced to detect diverse affective states, including frustration at 79% accuracy (Kapoor et al. 2007).

States of frustration and failure in turn present opportunities to promote affective self-awareness and/or algorithmic thinking that have been shown to be instrumental in fostering creative solutions to challenging problems and setbacks (Dunbar 1994).

Just as open source community programmers and do-it-yourself hackers can be encouraged to use design rationale tools to communicate their reasoning process to others who build upon their code and artifacts, design rationale can also act as a creativity support tool to foster reflection. Empowering users at appropriate times, such as times of frustration and failure, to learn from analogies (Dunbar 1994) can be conducted by encouraging them to describe their design rationale choices, both for decisions and practices that were eventually implemented and those more exploratory approaches that were not. Further coupling these with the underlying reasoning as to why they were chosen will allow for design rationale tools to provide the creativity support tool features of a low threshold entry for beginners and a high ceiling for experts to encourage a broader engagement by the community. Although this may sound onerous and fine-grained, we are seeing some initial elements of these types of explanations and design rationale emerging within open source communities, such as Linux developers and the do-it-yourself instructables.com hacker postings and their responsive feedback and discussion groups.

Open source and do-it-yourself communities foster broad participation, expertise development, and communication for novice and experts alike. Within the instructables.com community, we see exciting examples of information transfer links that serve as ad hoc design rationale. Take, for example, robonerd's[3] "Do It Yourself Arduino or 'The DIY-Duino'" (Robonerd 2010) that describes how to make a version of a popular microcontroller from scratch. In response to a community member's interest in minimizing the board size, robonerd augmented the original tutorial's description to provide additional ad hoc design rationale, explaining his appreciation of the anthropomorphic qualities of the spatial layout of the circuit, "… when you look at it vertically, it kinda looks like a face…. I just couldn't change the look on that face!" (March 7, 2011). There is also evidence that the Linus Law (Raymond 2001) helped robonerd with debugging, "I see it, SHOOT! I thought you were talking about the elec caps not the ceramics. Crud, I gotta fix that! Thank you very much for the catch! I appreciate it" (March 7, 2011). The multiple perspectives of the community also offer suggestions for new directions. David97 said, "I want to remote control my arduino useing my xbox controler (bluetooth). how can I do this?" (March 7, 2011). Motivation for expression of rich design rationale can be sustained through positive feedback and extended mentorship: jpr3 said, "This was a GREAT tutorial. Your web site had each and every step documented! Great work!!!!!" (March 9, 2011). Through a detailed dialogue involving 10 posts, robonerd mentored angelovalorreed until his/her microcontroller worked; robonerd then

---

[3] The quotes excerpted from the Do It Yourself Arduino (The DIY-Duino) have been quoted exactly as written. These forum comments took place during March 2010, and the dates of specific comments are included within parentheses.

agreed to update the instructable to include further detailed suggestions: "I'm going to keep the iable as it is though, because if you use the exact components listed, it works like a charm. Though I will add a suggestion to try the caps you used when in use with that crystal" (March 16, 2011). Throughout this and other such communities, elements of design rationale are affected by the organizational structures (tutorials and comments) and by governance policies, which support a range of formality and granularity. There are typically higher levels of formality and granularity in the tutorials than in the comments. Instructables' policy that allows individuals to remove posts (erniehatt said, "I removed the comments because I found a couple of errors"; March 17, 2011) allows community members to alter the history of the design rationale. On the one hand, this allows users to correct errors; on the other hand, it may ultimately inhibit the community from learning from failures. Within these forums, design rationale is not always supportive of creativity; as noted above, there are redundancies, nonsequiturs, and even occasional detractors.

Providing design rationale guidelines that encourage developers to encode design rationale for not only the choices they pursue but also for nonelected choices is likely to encourage others to explore a wide range of alternatives (e.g., through analogy), ultimately leading to more successful and creative processes. Such a process of open source community development and appreciation for broader forms of design rationale is likely in turn to foster the wide walls that are necessary for creative exploration. Studying how design rationale can not only foster its own recording and reviewing processes but also how these can be better understood as synergistic with, and indeed as key elements of, creativity support tools within open source communities will help to advance better choices for the implementation of new design rationale strategies. It also will foster stronger understandings of best practices for encoding and disseminating expert (and nonexpert) deliberation and insight, from which a broader community can learn, and support the development and advancement of their creative endeavors. This can be achieved through the development of a deeper understanding of both the processes and consequences (beneficial and detrimental) of design rationale implementation informed by the perspective of creativity research.

The Creativity and Cognition (C&C) conference[4] community focuses on the nexus of creativity, cognition, design, and emerging technologies. As open source and do-it-yourself communities have emerged, C&C's interests have included understanding design processes and design rationale related to hybrid physical/digital tools for fabrication and collaboration. A study of the design of "egg drop challenge" devices[5] showed that providing designers with tools and resources that foster fluency (lots of ideas) and flexibility (a range of diverse ideas) affected their

---

[4] Creativity & Cognition is an annual conference run by the Association of Computing Machinery, which brings together professionals from diverse fields to discuss the depth and breadth of human creativity.

[5] The Egg Drop challenge is a popular engineering challenge in which participants are given a limited set of materials (often straws, paper, or toothpicks), and asked to create a device that will allow an egg to be dropped from a specified height without breaking.

design rationale practices. Individuals who were provided fewer eggs engaged in fewer opportunities to test their designs. Their explanations of their designs and process (their design rationale) revealed that they were less fluent and flexible in their design process and reflection than were their counterparts who were given many eggs (Dow et al. 2009). Likewise, their products were less effective and less creative. An explicit example of this can be seen where the mental frame in which designers approach problems, and hence expressed design rationale, is affected by the environment, tools, and resources, in ways that impact elements of their creative process and outcome. This demonstrates that broad access to actualizing resources can directly impact design rationale and the creativity of processes and products (Amabile and Kramer 2003; Dow et al. 2009). Related work shows that prototyping in parallel is more creative than prototyping sequentially (Dow et al. 2010). Open source software development environments and gaming worlds also address issues of fluency, flexibility, and prototyping by offering sandbox opportunities that act as "playgrounds" and rapid prototyping environments with which to explore and develop ideas and relationships. Examples of this in the realm of educational gaming include Shute and Becker's (2010) advancement of twenty-first century assessment that places an emphasis on the importance of learning to think creatively through data mining of learners' activities and collaborations in educational gaming environments. Furthering this agenda, Wegerif et al. (2010) have demonstrated the ability to automatically recognize creative reasoning in student e-discussions within in situ dialogue analysis of intelligent tutoring learning environments and their data streams. These examples present opportunities that can inform the development of design rationale implementations as creativity support tools.

17.7 Computational Creativity, Expertise, and Teams

Now that creativity support tools and their potential in design rationale for open source communities have been presented, we explore more recent findings in the area of team and computational creativity research that offer opportunities for future work and development. These should serve as related resources that offer opportunities for the community that is advancing design rationale as creativity support tools.

17.7.1 Team Brainstorming

Smith (2003) proposed that in order to achieve a new way of thinking in a team, members must ignore an existing "fixated" point of view (i.e., sticking with one perspective or idea to the detriment of the overall process) and arrive at a nondominant point of view. The dominant response tends to block minority responses. This characteristic is evident within team interactions when a big idea starts gaining more weight in spite of its possibility of failure or incompatibility with team objectives.

This often occurs due to the familiarity (or safety) of the idea, tendencies of teams to want to agree (groupthink), or individuals' production blocking. Therefore, maintaining and advancing divergent points of view during a large group discussion can be a difficult and daunting task.

In shared brainstorming activities, a high number of ideas often are generated, with one of them subsequently being selected based on discussion of merit with respect to context. A key role of team decision making is to engender acceptance, satisfaction, or commitment to decisions. Smith (2003) suggested that groups should go further, striving to play an important role in combining disparate points of view, knowledge, and ideas towards better decisions. As will be discussed below, open source software communities contend with the interplay of these two roles as they engage in building and generating acceptance for various versions of the open source software code.

One proposed solution is to maintain a log of ideas, avoiding discussion until every idea has been enumerated, such as in electronic brainstorming via individual contributions (Sutton and Hargadon 1996). However, the simple log that this form of brainstorming creates still requires revisiting each idea, thinking it through at both the individual and group levels, and then deciding on the merits of all of this with respect to the group agenda. This latter process typically still requires group-level communication, which again is often confounded by fixation and the effects of interpersonal hierarchy.

Recent work on feedback in group settings has shown that higher individual and/or group self-awareness leads to self-directed adaptation of behavior (DiMicco and Bender 2007). DiMicco and Bender showed that public visualization of group members' verbalization leads to subsequent moderation or improvement of participation, resulting in stronger group outcomes. For example, participants who talk too much will tend to talk less when a bar graph publicly portrays them as an outlier; group members who do not talk enough likewise tend to talk more. For low participating members, talking more fulfills their normative needs, but more importantly provides them with sufficient conversational bandwidth to contribute beneficial information that would otherwise not be available to the group. Such strategies of group self-awareness may also allow higher attention to group processes, goals, and strategies (West 1996). Gersick and Hackman (1990) found that work groups can break dysfunctional habitual routines by self-reflection. Farooq et al. (2007) found that group self-monitoring can enhance the understanding of breakdowns of creativity and lead to prevention of breakdowns.

Understanding team creativity research with respect to the nature of the work a group shares can provide insights into the functioning of open source communities. Tjosvold (1998) showed that creating a common task that requires collective action among members of a team can induce cooperative orientation, thereby promoting resource and information exchanges as well as openness to each other's ideas. Similarly, Wageman (1995) found that teams employing task interdependence increased the need for collaboration and mutual adjustment among members by raising the collective sense of responsibility among team members. Thus, we may conclude that the overall success of team creativity can be ensured by creating conditions of common fate with rewards and/or task interdependence. While the specifics are not well understood, interesting insights about the importance of leadership and active participation are emerging (Luther et al. 2010). These conditions of common fate along with cooperative orientation help to drive today's open source culture.

Thus, a significant opportunity for creativity support in open source communities is to sufficiently reduce sources of inhibition such that each member may engage in adequate expression of ideas. Through the customization and promotion of environments that encourage design rationale expressed through information transfer links, users can be encouraged to share their unique contributions. Tools that support various means to enhance the discussion of individuals' ideas without exacerbating team members' inhibitions are likely to lead to increased team creativity.

17.7.2 Influence of Expertise and Computational Systems

Building on the context of creativity support in teams, we will now discuss expertise with respect to team and computational creativity. In addition, we address how improved understandings of dynamics within their processes might inform implementation of design rationale as a creativity support tool in groups.

Atman et al.'s (2007) research on individual problem solving demonstrated that experts engage in iterative processes—ranging across information gathering, problem definition, modeling, evaluation, reflection, and so forth—that are richer than those of their novice counterparts. Experts engage in activities that allow them to accumulate experience, reflect on them, and transfer their experience and knowledge between diverse stages and activities within design processes; they also engage in significantly more reflection than novices. Here we see that level of expertise impacts both design rationale practices within design process and the outcomes of these open-ended creative activities. Similarly, organizational approaches to design (e.g., organizational processes that pursue iterative design vs. sequential design, sometimes referred to as the waterfall model) impact design rationale and creative outcomes. We have conducted pilot studies applying Atman and colleagues' approach to groups engaged in design processes, exploring the question: If a weaker designer joins a team, does the team become weaker or does the weaker designer rise to the occasion and improve his/her performance (Burleson 2007)? Due to the complexities of conducting team studies, this remains an open question. We also currently are exploring the potential for an embodied agent to participate as a virtual facilitator to prompt shifts in individual or team activities.

Similar processes and questions arise in the realm of efforts to advance computational creativity and its interactions with individuals and integration with teams, for instance in systems aimed at demonstrating expertise and fostering effective team collaboration and creativity. Buchanan (2001) approached computational creativity in terms of metacreativity. He argued, as summarized in Burleson (2005, p. 443), that programs should "provide the ability for the AI [artificial intelligence] to accumulate past experiences and information, reflect on them, and transfer this information throughout the system, as a means for enhancing creative collaboration between machine and user." Even in computational systems that do not yet operate with Buchanan's (2001) metacapacity, there is strong evidence for the potential of creative systems to play a significant role within hybrid teams. Goldenberg et al.'s (1999) "Creative Sparks" research, published in *Science*, demonstrated that a computerized routine (one easily algorithmically implemented by humans) "produces solutions consensually judged to be more creative than those achieved by humans" (Burleson 2005, p. 443). Yet when this algorithm was made available to human teams, they failed to recognize or realize its benefits, opting instead to pursue their task without the aid of the computational creativity system. This example shows that even when computational creativity is highly capable, there is still significant work to be done on the social elements of human–computer interaction to encourage its acceptance by a human team. This example also shows that the team was not sufficiently appreciative of the algorithm as one of its actualizing resources to advance creativity. The creativity process and its outcome could be improved by a design rationale implementation that had sufficient formality and granularity to encourage effectively and persuade the team to record and reflect on the creative resources and concepts at its disposal, and with decision-making support that helped individuals and teams select the most creative ideas (regardless of their origin).

Ultimately, given the advances in computational creativity, humans and computers could work on hybrid teams to foster creativity. Facilitating a frame of collaboration between the creativity support tool and humans is one of the ongoing opportunities for design rationale and creativity support tools, and advances the Computing Research Association's (2002) Grand Challenges. The range of attributes that we find in creativity support tool approaches, if applied to design rationale at the individual and group levels, would arguably have the potential to enable design rationale to serve as a creativity support tool to foster higher levels of creativity, in both processes and outcomes. Since many of the approaches discussed above lay the foundation for enhancing creativity through design rationale at the individual and team levels, they also hold important strategies for implementation of design rationale that supports creativity and acts as creativity support tool within open source communities. Specifically, the creativity support tool guidelines (low thresholds, wide walls, powerful history-keeping, etc.) could be applied throughout open source community information transfer links, within the user or system interface, as a community-level guideline, and as a design rationale philosophy promoted by the community. Merging Shneiderman's (2003) collect, relate, create, and donate approach to systems that foster creativity with Amabile et al.'s (2002) and Amabile and Kramer's (2003) findings from organizational behavior studies— specifically by sensing elements of organizational behavior and understanding positive affect and frustration, time pressure and interruption—could guide, tailor, and refine open source communities' implementation of design rationale as creativity support tool. Open source and do-it-yourself communities that employ actualizing resources and rewards consistent with lessons from creativity research and from individual and team expertise can more effectively use design rationale to enhance the fluency and flexibility elements of creativity. Design rationale can play an important role in understanding better ways to incorporate technological support (computational creativity and creativity support tools) in hybrid teams.

17.8 Conclusion

Applying findings from creativity research and recent efforts that have advanced creativity support tools has the strong potential to realize significant advances to design rationale, both in terms of evaluating diverse implementations of design rationale for their ability to foster creativity and toward transforming existing design rationale tools into creativity support tools. These lessons can and should be used to guide efforts to transform existing design rationale tools into design rationale–creativity support tools. In this manner, a range of organizational practices and innovative interfaces that include appropriate levels of granularity and formality can foster creativity through novel design rationale implementations and enhancements. These might include features that encourage metacreativity and promote users' ability to engage in the expert practices and rich processes that emphasize reflection, transfer, learning, and recovering from failure through analogy. They might also identify times of failure and frustration, and might create sandboxes or equivalent features that foster fluency and flexibility, providing low thresholds, wide walls, and actualizing rewards for creativity. They might minimize time pressure and promote opportunities for positive affect and productive social interaction. While these strategies can be employed throughout programming, design practice, and indeed in any context in which design rationale may apply, they are particularly relevant to open source software and do-it-yourself communities that are highly active in advancing new forms of creative collaborations and creative IT endeavors.

Acknowledgments We thank John Carroll and Siobhan O'Mahony for their feedback and encouragement and Jamie Wernet, Sonia Shah, Margaret Pingolt, and Daniel Davis for their help in preparing this chapter.

References

Amabile, T. M. (1983). Social psychology of creativity. *Journal of Personality and Social Psychology, 45,* 357–376.
Amabile, T. M. (1996). *Creativity in context: Update to the social psychology of creativity.* Boulder: Westview Press.
Amabile, T. M., & Kramer, S. J. (2003, October). *The best (and worst) days in creative project teams: Some preliminary results.* Paper presented at the Society of Experimental Social Psychology, Boston.
Amabile, T., & Mueller, J. (2002). Assessing creativity and its antecedents: An exploration of the componential theory of creativity. In C. Ford & N. Mahwah (Eds.), *Handbook of organizational creativity.* London: Lawrence Erlbaum Associates.

Amabile, T. M., Hadley, C. N., & Kramer, S. J. (2002). Creativity under the gun. *Harvard Business Review, 80*(8), 52–61.

Atman, C. J., Adams, R. S., Cardella, M. E., Turns, J., Mosborg, S., & Saleem, J. (2007). Engineering design processes: A comparison of students and expert practicioners. *Journal of Engineering Education, 96*, 359–379.

Beschastnikh, I., Kriplean, T., & McDonald, D. (2008). *Wikipedian self-governance in action: Motivating the policy lens.* Second International Conference on Weblogs Social Media, Seattle.

Beschastnikh, I., McDonald, D. W., Zachry, M., Kriplean, T., & Borning, A. (2009, May). *Promoting quality in Wikipedia through enculturation.* Paper presented at the Support Amat Workshop at the ACM 2009 International Conference on Support Group Work, Sanibel Island.

Buchanan, B. (2001). Creativity at the metalevel: AAAI-2000 presidential address. *AI Magazine, 22*(3), 13–28.

Burleson, W. (2005). Developing creativity, motivation, and self-actualization with learning systems. *International Journal of Human Computer Studies, 63*, 436–451.

Burleson, W. (2007, May). *Opportunities for ubiquitous design environments in a flat world.* Paper presented at the Harvey Mudd Design Workshop, Claremont.

Burleson, W., & Pentland, S. (2008). *NSF Award 0846148: SGER: Human-centered computing: Creativity in IT research organizations.* Award notification retrieved August 24, 2011, from http://www.nsf.gov/awardsearch/showAward.do?AwardNumber=0846148

Burleson, W., & Selker, T. (2002). Introduction: Creativity and interface. *Communications of the ACM, 45*(10), 88–90.

Buxton, B. (2007). *Sketching the user experience.* San Francisco: Morgan Kaufmann Publishers.

Carroll, J. (2010). The essential tension of creativity and rationale in software design. *Human Technology: Interdisciplinary Journal of Human ICT Environment, 6*(1), 4–10.

Cashman, P. M., & Stroll, D. (1989). Developing the management systems of the 1990s: The role of collaborative work. In M. H. Olson (Ed.), *Technological support for group collaboration.* Mahwah: Lawrence Erlbaum Associates Inc.

Certeau, M. D. (1984). *The practice of everyday life.* Berkeley: University of California Press.

Computing Research Association. (2002). *Grand research challenges in information systems.* Retrieved August 6, 2011, from http://archive.cra.org/reports/gc.systems.pdf

Conklin, J. (2003). Dialog mapping: Reflections on an industrial strength case study. In P. Kirschner, S. J. B. Shum, & C. S. Carr (Eds.), *Visualizing argumentation: Software tools for collaborative and education sense making.* London: Springer.

Corbet, J., Kroah-Hartman, G., & McPherson, A. (2010). *Linux kernel development: How fast it is going, who is doing it, what they are doing, and who is sponsoring it.* The Linux Foundation, San Francisco. Retrieved August 24, 2011, from http://www.linuxfoundation.org/docs/lf_linux_kernel_development_2010.pdf

Csikszentmihalyi, M. (1996). *Creativity: Flow and the psychology of discovery and invention.* New York: Harper Perennial.

DiBona, C., Ockman, S., & Stone, M. (1999). *Open sources: Voices from the open source revolution.* Sebastopol: O'Reilly Media.

DiMicco, J. M., & Bender, W. (2007). Group reactions to visual feedback tools. In Y. de Kort, B. J. Fogg, W. Ijsselsteijn, B. Eggen, & C. Midden (Eds.), *Proceedings of the second international conference on persuasive technology.* Berlin: Springer.

Dow, S. P., Heddleston, K., & Klemmer, S. (2009). The efficacy of prototyping under time constraints. Creativity & cognition. In N. Bryan-Kinns, M. D. Gross, H. Johnson, J. Ox, & R. Wakkary (Eds.), *Proceedings of the 7th conference on creativity & cognition.* New York: ACM Press.

Dow, S. P., Glassco, A., Kass, J., Schwarz, M., Schwartz, D. L., & Klemmer, S. R. (2010). Parallel prototyping leads to better design results, more divergence, and increased self-efficacy. *ACM Transaction on Computational-Human Interaction, 17*(4), 18:1–18:24. doi:10.1145/1879831.1879836.

Dunbar, K. (1994). How scientists really reason: Scientific reasoning in real-world laboratories. In R. J. Sternberg & J. Davidson (Eds.), *The nature of insight*. Cambridge: MIT Press.

Farooq, U., Carroll, J. M., & Ganoe, C. H. (2007, November). *Supporting creativity with awareness in distributed collaboration*. Paper presented at the Intern ACM Conf Support Group Work, Sanibel Island.

Fischer, G., Lemke, A., McCall, R., & Morch, A. (1991). Making argumentation serve design. In T. H. Moran & J. Carroll (Eds.), *Design rationale: Concepts, techniques, and use*. Hillsdale: Erlbaum.

Gardner, H. (1994). *Creating minds: An anatomy of creativity seen through the lives of Freud, Einstein, Picasso, Stravinsky, Eliot, Graham, and Gandhi*. New York: Basic Books.

Gero, J. S. (1996). Creativity, emergence and evolution in design: Concepts and framework. *Knowledge-Based Systems, 9*, 435–448.

Gersick, C. J. G., & Hackman, J. R. (1990). Habitual routines in task-performing groups. *Organizational Behavior and Human Decision Processes, 47*, 65–97.

Goldenberg, J., Mazursky, D., & Solomon, S. (1999). Creative sparks. *Science, 258*, 1495–1496.

Gruber, T. R., & Russell, D. M. (1996). Generative design rationale: Beyond the record and replay paradigm. In T. P. Moran & J. Carroll (Eds.), *Design rationale: Concepts, techniques, and use*. Hillsdale: Erlbaum.

Ishikawa, T., & Terano, T. (1996). Analogy by abstraction: Case retrieval and adaptation for inventive design expert systems. *Expert Systems with Applications, 10*, 351–356.

Kapoor, A., Burleson, W., & Picard, R. (2007). Automatic prediction of frustration. *International Journal of Human Computer Studies, 65*, 724–736.

Kuznetsov, S., & Paulos, E. (2010, October). *Rise of the expert amateur: DIY projects, communities, and cultures*. Paper presented at the ACM NordiCHI Conf, Reykjavík.

Luther, K., Kelly, C., Ziegler, K., & Bruckman, A. (2010, November). *Why it works (when it works): success factors in online creative collaboration*. Paper presented at the Group 2010 conference, Sanibel.

MacLean, A., Young, R. M., Bellotti, V. M. E., & Moran, T. P. (1996). Questions, options, and criteria: Elements of design space analysis. In T. P. Moran & J. Carroll (Eds.), *Design rationale: Concepts, techniques, and use*. Hillsdale: Erlbaum.

Mitchell, W. J., Inouye, A. S., & Blumenthal, M. S. (2003). *Beyond productivity: Information technology, innovation, and creativity*. Committee on information technology and creativity, CSTB, National Research Council. Washington, DC: National Academics Press.

Moran, T., & Carroll, J. (Eds.). (1996). *Design rationale: Concepts, techniques, and use*. Hillsdale: Erlbaum.

National Science Foundation (NSF). (2009). *Creative IT program solicitation*. Retrieved August 1, 2011, from http://www.nsf.gov/pubs/2009/nsf09572/nsf09572.pdf

O'Mahony, S., & Ferraro, F. (2007). The emergence of governance in an open source community. *The Academy of Management Journal, 50*(5), 1079–1106.

Raymond, E. S. (2001). *The cathedral and the bazaar: Musings on Linux and open source by an accidental revolutionary*. Sebastopol: O'Reilly Media.

Rittel, H. (1972). On the planning crisis: Systems analysis of the 'first and second generations'. *Bedriftskonomen, 8*, 390–396.

Robonerd. (2010, March 7–17). *Do it yourself arduino or the DIY-duino*. [On-line forum comments]. Retrieved August 24, 2011, from http://www.instructables.com/id/DIY-Arduino-or-The-DIY-Duino/

Shneiderman, B. (2003). *Leonardo's laptop: Human needs and the new computing technologies*. Cambridge: MIT Press.

Shneiderman, B., Fischer, G., Czerwinski, M., Resnick, M., Myers, B., Candy, L., Edmonds, E., Elsenberg, M., Giaccardi, E., Hewett, T., Jennings, P., Kules, B., Nakakoji, K., Nunamaker, J., Pausch, R., Selker, T., Sylvan, E., & Terry, M. (2006). Creativity support tools: Report from a U.S. National Science Foundation sponsored workshop. *International Journal of Human Computer Interaction, 20*, 61–77.

Shute, V., & Becker, B. (2010). Prelude: Assessment for the 21st century. In V. Shute & B. Becker (Eds.), *Innovative assessment for the 21st century supporting educational needs*. New York: Springer Science + Business Media LLC.

Smith, S. M. (2003). The constraining effects of initial ideas. In P. B. Paulus & B. A. Nijstad (Eds.), *Group creativity*. Oxford: Oxford University Press.

Stark, M. (2003, July 7). *The organizational model for open source: Q&A with Siobhán O'Mahony*. Retrieved August 6, 2011, from http://hbswk.hbs.edu/item/3582.html

Sternberg, R. J., & Lubart, T. I. (2007). The concept of creativity: Prospects and paradigms. In R. J. Sternberg (Ed.), *Handbook of creativity*. Cambridge: Cambridge University Press.

Sutton, R., & Hargadon, A. (1996). Brainstorming groups in context: Effectiveness at a product design firm. *Administrative Science Quarterly, 41*, 685–718.

Tjosvold, D. (1998). Cooperative and competitive goal approach to conflict: Accomplishments and challenges. *Applied Psychology, 47*, 285–313.

von Hippel, E. (2005). *Democratizing innovation*. Cambridge: MIT Press.

von Krogh, G., Spaeth, S., & Lakhani, K. R. (2003). Community, joining, and specialization in open source software innovation: A case study. *Research Policy, 34*, 1217–1242.

Wageman, R. (1995). Interdependence and group effectiveness. *Administrative Science Quarterly, 40*, 145–180.

Wakkary, R., & Maestri, L. (2007). The resourcefulness of everyday design. In: *Proceedings of Creativity and Cognition 2007*. New York: ACM Press.

Weber, S. (2004). *The success of open source*. Cambridge: Harvard University Press.

Wegerif, R., McLaren, B. M., Chamrada, M., Scheuer, O., Mansour, N., Mikšátko, J., & Williams, M. (2010). Exploring creative thinking in graphically mediated synchronous dialogues. *Computers in Education, 54*, 613–621.

Wentworth, R. (1978). Making do and getting by. *Artscribe, 14*, 21–23.

Werner, K., & Rittel, H. (1979). *Issues as elements of information systems*. (Working Paper No. 131). Original publication 1970. Studiengruppe für Systemforschung, Heidelberg.

West, M. A. (1996). Reflexity and work group effectiveness: A conceptual integration. In M. A. West (Ed.), *Handbook of work-group psychology*. Chichester: Wiley.

Chapter 18
Creativity Meets Rationale: Collaboration Patterns for Social Innovation

Aldo de Moor

Abstract Collaborative communities require a wide range of face-to-face and online communication tools. Their socio-technical systems continuously grow, driven by evolving stakeholder requirements and newly available technologies. Designing tool systems that (continue to) match authentic community needs is not trivial. Collaboration patterns can help community members specify customized systems that capture their unique requirements, while reusing lessons learnt by other communities. Such patterns are an excellent example of combining the strengths of creativity and rationale. In this chapter, we explore the role that collaboration patterns can play in designing the socio-technical infrastructure for collaborative communities. We do so via a cross-case analysis of three Dutch social innovation communities simultaneously being set-up. Our goal with this case study is two-fold: (1) understanding what social innovation is from a socio-technical lens and (2) exploring how the rationale of collaboration patterns can be used to develop creative socio-technical solutions for working communities.

Keywords Collaborative communities • Socio-technical systems • Design patterns • Social innovation

18.1 Introduction

Collaborative communities are communities in which there are not only shared practices, but also common goals, such as the joint production of goods or services. Collaboration means much more than mere cooperation. Cooperation means playing

A. de Moor (✉)
CommunitySense, Cavaleriestraat 2, 5017 ET, Tilburg, The Netherlands
e-mail: ademoor@communitysense.nl

J.M. Carroll (ed.), *Creativity and Rationale: Enhancing Human Experience by Design*, Human–Computer Interaction Series, DOI 10.1007/978-1-4471-4111-2_18, © Springer-Verlag London 2013

together in the same game according to agreed rules of interaction. Collaboration, however, also implies creating solutions or strategies, often for very complex, "messy" problems, through the synergistic interactions of a group of people (Denning and Yaholkovsky 2008). In collaborative communities, communication is key, for purposes of information exchange, coordination of (inter)actions, relationship building and collaborative sensemaking (De Moor 2010b). Collaborative communities often require, besides many forms of face-to-face communication, a rich ecosystem of online tools. These include generic communication tools such as e-mail and social media like Facebook and Twitter. However, they also comprise technologies specific to particular types of collaborative communities, such as publication citation and annotation management tools for scholarly communities (Zaugg et al. 2011). Together, these face-to-face and online tools form complex systems, embedded in a rich, situated social context, unique to each community. These socio-technical systems of interlinked social requirements and tools continuously evolve, driven by stakeholders experiencing new requirements and new technologies becoming accessible to and appropriated by the community.

A common misunderstanding about social media and communities is that they automatically trigger a process of self-organization, so that very complex problem solving behaviours will emerge spontaneously. Such emergent behaviours are often limited to much less far-reaching forms of information exchange or coordination on relatively simple issues, however. The often touted "wisdom of the crowds" works best for simple tasks divided up into their smallest possible components, due to a lack of time and attention and diversity of the crowd (Howe 2009). Deeper forms of collaboration needed to address more messy or "wicked" problems do not emerge spontaneously, however (Denning and Yaholkovsky 2008). Furthermore, processes of "social creativity" suffer from spatial, temporal, and conceptual distances between collaborators (Fischer and Shipman 2011). Therefore, concerted efforts are needed to make online creativity work. Such efforts are made by many companies which specialize in providing the technological infrastructure, organization, facilitation, and administrative support of creative communities specifically facilitated for market research, co-created innovation, and corporate idea management.[1] However, such approaches only support highly specialized, constrained forms of creative processes. For more general collaborative communities, with much more widely varying needs, goals, technologies, and cultures, carefully crafted, evolvable socio-technical systems are needed.

For communities to be successfully supported by online technologies, systems designers must translate complex social requirements like freedom, legitimacy, and privacy into technical specifications, thus closing the socio-technical gap (Whitworth 2006). Designing such socio-technical systems, consisting of tool systems that (continue to) match authentic community needs, is not trivial. Like in any requirements engineering process, it is crucial to have key stakeholders identify issues and reach

---

[1] E.g. Redesignme (http://redesignme.com) and InSites Consulting (e.g. http://www.insites.eu)

agreement on substantive issues before moving the project forward (Ocker 2010). Socio-technical design patterns describe in a broad way such agreements on the issues of the interactions between the social and technical systems that need to be built (Dixon 2009). They can be of great value in aiding community members to define customized systems that satisfy their unique requirements, while reusing lessons learnt as much as possible. In this way, they are an excellent example of where creativity meets rationale. A few examples of socio-technical pattern languages exist, for example in the domains of software development (Dixon 2009) and societal change (Schuler 2008). Another example are collaboration patterns (De Moor 2009). These capture socio-technical lessons learnt in optimizing the effectiveness and efficiency of collaboration processes. Collaboration patterns make communication tools actionable by describing how individual community members playing particular collaborative roles could best use particular tool functionalities in a specific work and social context. Of course, what best is depends very much on the purpose of the community, its norms and practices, and its available tools. There is no mathematically derivable prescription for such patterns. Instead, they need to be created from the careful analysis and comparison of cases within and across domains. One domain in which collaborative communities are paramount is social innovation.

Social innovation is a process in which new ideas are generated that not only meet social or economic needs, but also create new social relationships and collaborations (Murray et al. 2010). Balancing creativity with rationale is essential in order to ensure that those new ideas get generated and processed by the right combinations of stakeholders as effectively and efficiently as possible. Rationale as in some form of structure here should be taken not as a straightjacket, but as a "language to improvise", like used by a jazz ensemble (Kane 2005). Some form of rationale is all the more necessary in the design of social innovation as it is not confined to the boundaries of single organizations. Instead, social innovation takes place in webs of collaborative communities permeating and connecting many different individuals, organizations, and networks. Both its potential impact and governance is at least an order of magnitude more complex than the atomic corporate creative communities mentioned above.[2] Social innovation is therefore a very interesting domain for exploring the role that collaboration patterns can play in amplifying creativity by embedding it in relevant networks of stakeholder relations and processes.

In this chapter, we explore the role that collaboration patterns could play in designing the socio-technical infrastructure for collaborative communities. We do so by analyzing the results from a cross-case analysis of three Dutch social innovation communities simultaneously being set up. Our goal with this case study is twofold: (1) understanding what social innovation is from a socio-technical lens

---

[2] For example, the Dutch government has started major research programmes to explore the impact of social innovation on health, learning, and safety (http://www.nwo.nl/nwohome.nsf/pages/NWOP_7ZNHTC_Eng)

and (2) exploring how the rationale of collaboration patterns can be used to develop creative socio-technical solutions for working communities.

The chapter is organized as follows. Section 18.2 introduces the concept of social innovation and introduces a real-world social innovation case from a socio-technical point of view. In Sect. 18.3, we explore collaboration patterns as a way to model the socio-technical systems of collaborative communities and distill lessons learnt from the social innovation cases. Section 18.4 discusses the results. We end the chapter with conclusions in Sect. 18.5.

18.2   Social Innovation – Co-creating New Business

In this section we explore our domain of inquiry – social innovation – by examining a real-world Dutch social innovation case.

18.2.1   *What Is Social Innovation*

Social innovation is essentially about the relationship networks and collaboration processes around new ideas that meet unmet needs (Murray et al. 2010). Mulgan gives a comprehensive overview of what social innovation entails: according to Connected Difference Theory, social innovation concerns (1) new combinations or hybrids of existing elements; (2) cutting across organizational, sectoral or disciplinary boundaries, (3) creating compelling new relationships.

To realize such innovations, they go through different stages: from the generation of ideas through prototyping and piloting, to scaling up and learning. To be successful, social innovation requires effective alliances between small organisations and entrepreneurs ('bees' who are mobile, fast, and cross-pollinate) and big organisations (the 'trees' with roots, resilience and size) which can grow ideas to scale (Mulgan 2007).

The above bird's eye view shows the ambitious scope of social innovation, but also demonstrates the complexity of putting this complex notion into practice. Interpretations abound, but are still vague and contradictory, although satisfactory and comprehensive definitions of the term are of fundamental importance to both guide research and accommodate a significant number of relevant empirical cases (Pol and Ville 2009). In our view, many of the existing definitions are still of too abstract a level to inform more focused theory construction, let alone provide guidance for practice. What seems to be lacking are "meso-level" conceptual models which on the one hand draw from the high-level social innovation theory frameworks and on the other hand are firmly grounded in concepts recognized by practitioners. In this study, we aim to provide such intermediate level theory-meets-practice constructs by distilling some reusable collaboration patterns from a concrete case: the Social Innovation Award Midden-Brabant.

18.2.2   Case: Social Innovation Award Midden-Brabant

Midden-Brabant is the central region in the Dutch southern province of Noord-Brabant. The region does not have many large, heavy industries. Key economic activities include leisure, logistics, care, and industrial maintenance. Midden-Brabant has a strong collaborative and innovative ethos, leading to many tight networks of small-and medium enterprises, woven together into a pluriform service economy. Social innovation, defined as "the creation of new business models and market mechanisms in a community of diverse stakeholders" is therefore high on the regional agenda. Midden-Brabant is the first Dutch region that has declared social innovation as being at the core of it socio-economic development, stimulating collaborative projects between business, education, and government at the regional level. Midpoint Brabant[3] is an organization dedicated to promoting the development of these social innovation projects and the collaborative networks in which they take place.

Awarding prizes can be an important incentive for stimulating social innovation (Pol and Ville 2009). The Social Innovation Award 2010 was given by Midpoint Brabant to three social innovation cases that had demonstrated potential for both a strong business case and thriving social network around the development, promotion, and use of the innovation. The winning innovations were:

- *Genicap*: developing a growing set of practical applications of a mathematical superformula (Gielis 2003) that can be used to very efficiently compress spatial information. These applications range from very efficient antennas for ultrawideband wireless communication to intelligent vision systems for robotics.
- *SafeCity*: developing a mobile app that can be used by both professionals and citizens to report unsafe situations in neighbourhoods and homes, both emergency and non-emergency ones, plus the complex workflow backend of all the organisations that have to act upon the problems reported.
- *Dementia Experience*: developing a simulator for professionals, family and volunteers that need to be trained into what it means to be a gradually worsening patient with Alzheimer's Disease and how to effectively help them.

Together, these cases comprise a wide variation of social innovation needs and approaches. The winners had proven themselves to be innovation leaders and shown a keen interest in expanding their communities and social networks. Facilitated by the author of this chapter, they committed themselves to jointly reflect upon developing a common practical social innovation approach. This exercise thus seemed very promising in eliciting grounded and relevant collaboration patterns related to social innovation. The elicited patterns, in turn, should prove useful in terms of furthering socio-technical theory development and testing in the domain of social innovation. Guiding these analytical effort was an emerging Social Innovation Collaboration model.

---

[3] http://www.midpointbrabant.nl

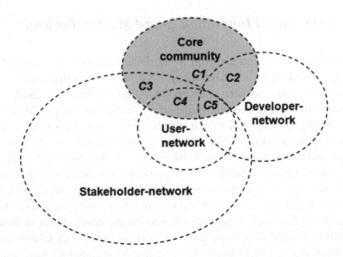

Fig. 18.1 The Social Innovation Collaboration (SIC) model

18.2.3   Social Innovation Collaboration (SIC) Model

The Social Innovation Collaboration (SIC) model aims to capture and link the various spheres of conversations in which social innovation takes place (Fig. 18.1). It was iteratively developed and applied over a period of half a year from January to June 2011. New versions of the model were discussed during monthly plenary meetings with the Social Innovation Award winners and then applied in the analysis of the various cases in subsequent interviews with the case leaders. Iteratively, this conceptual model was calibrated, until it covered all three cases and was deemed sufficiently stable and relevant by all award winners.

The SIC model is based on the premise that social innovations develop around a core idea, and take place in *communicative workflows* within and across several interrelated *conversation spheres*. These communicative workflows range from private conversations in the core and development teams, to very public ones with the stakeholder network, supported by often quite a complex tool system of face-to-face and online tools (sometimes supplemented by interactions with the mass media). The workflows can be further analyzed using the Socio-Technical Conversation Context Framework (Fig. 18.2, see De Moor 2010b). In these workflows, community members play many different roles to accomplish community and individual goals, producing a set of concrete results. Each workflow consists of a "loop" in which one role ("customer") (1) requests another one ("performer") to do something, who (2) after promising (3) produces the result, (4) reports back upon completion, after which the performer (5) evaluates the result. Any of these stages can spawn new workflow loops, leading to a complex web of conversations and commitments. This analytical framework is grounded in Language/Action Theory, which is a natural theoretical approach to modeling emergent collaboration (Denning and Medina-Mora 1995).

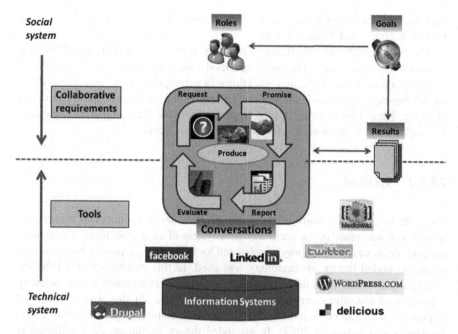

Fig. 18.2 The socio-technical conversation context framework

The SIC model consists of four main connected conversation spheres:

- The *core community*: the initiators of the innovation, often the co-owners of the intellectual property rights, plus the main investors. In the core community, the course for the innovation process is set.
- The *developer network*: the organizations and individuals doing the R&D necessary to go from initial idea to fully implemented product or service.
- The *user network*: the stakeholders using the product or service. In the early stages of the innovation process, often a small group of (future) users is involved as test users.
- The *stakeholder network*: a wide range of stakeholders who directly or indirectly do or could benefit from the innovation. The user network consists of a subset of these stakeholders.

Some conversation spheres, such as that of the core community, are less permeable than others, like that of the amorphous stakeholder-network. Especially the intersections between the spheres require careful attention. From a point of view of design interventions, the core community can affect its own sphere (C1) and the intersections with the other networks (C2-C5). For example, it can decide to have regular face-to-face meetings with its core community members, plus use a private wiki for content management (C1), while it uses regular face-to-face workshops and a closed LinkedIn group as the tool system for communication with the developer network (C2). Still, to communicate with its larger user/stakeholder network, the core community could use a combination of a website, an open Facebook group, and Twitter (C3-4).

The SIC-Model was bootstrapped together with the case representatives in a grounded theory approach. The conceptual model was then used to make a number of observations on roles, tools, and workflows (a subsequent, more detailed analysis would also explicitly include the goals and results of the socio-technical conversation context). These observations in turn form the basis for the collaboration patterns that capture and make available for reuse the lessons learnt.

18.2.4 Method

Using the Social Innovation Collaboration (SIC) model as a conceptual framework, a quickscan was made of the socio-technical system of each case, using a growing – partially cross-case – taxonomy of roles and tools. To this purpose, a basic version of the grounded theory methodology was used. In this practice-oriented theory, concepts and relationships describing and "owned by" a community are extracted by a process of constant comparison of emerging codes. In this way, theories of human behavior can be systematically derived from empirical data (Urquhart 2001; Fernández and Lehmann 2005). In grounded theory formation, data collected is marked with a series of codes, extracted from the text. These codes are grouped into similar concepts, which then are the basis for categories, which in turn are used for deriving hypotheses and theory. In our approach, we started from a set of initial, high-level concepts, drawn from the Socio-Technical Conversation Context Framework: in particular on the *roles* community members play, the *tools* they use and the *workflows* in which they do so. The validation took place by constantly generating with and re-presenting to the case participants the emerging specializations of these concepts, their relations, and derived working hypotheses. As the case participants are leaders in social innovation processes in their respective domains, the emerging patterns should have sufficient validity for the purpose of initial theory formation.

At each monthly iteration, the findings for the various cases were analyzed and where relevant added to the common core. Driving this process was a set of social innovation goals focusing on business case and social network development. Although the goals were partially different in each case, a common goal was how to create relevant conversational "buzz" around each case. Relevant buzz means that the right stakeholders are involved at the right time with the right degree of participation, while simultaneously ensuring that confidential conversations do not "spill over" into spheres were they do not belong. Furthermore, conversations in different spheres need to be connected by social (people) or technical (tool) "linking pins". This means developing a tool system that is sufficiently tailored to the specific conversation norms and practices of the case at hand. In the cross-case analysis, we discovered that there were differences, but also commonalities in how the cases defined and designed their conversation spheres and supporting tool systems. The lessons learnt can form the basis for theory formation as well as guidance in practice.

18.2.5   Lessons Learnt

A number of lessons were learnt with respect to designing the conversation infrastructure for the various cases. Key focus of the analysis were the roles (Appendix 1) and tools (Appendix 2), and how they interact in collaborative workflows. A possible taxonomy of these concept types is presented in Appendix 3.

18.2.5.1   Roles

- The cases vary widely in level of detail of role specification (Genicap: 14 types of roles, SafeCity 32, Dementia Experience 24).
- We distinguish between innovation process roles (based on the SIC model) and stakeholder roles (depending on the domain).
- Core innovation process roles (dark grey) are similar for all cases and derived from the Social Innovation Collaboration model: Core Community Members, Developers, Stakeholders, and Users. From the individual case analyses, additional innovation process roles were elicited, which can help to refine the SIC-model, e.g. Business Developers, Think Tanks, and Consuls.
- Stakeholder roles are candidates for playing the innovation process roles. They can be generic (e.g. Government, Business, Education, Citizens) and more (case)-specific (e.g. Mayors, Housing Associations, Caregivers, Dementia Consultants).
- Some roles act as containers for more specific roles. For example, Municipality in the case of SafeCity can mean Mayor, Security Coordinator, Security Policy Officer or Security House, depending on the context in which it is used. Another example is the role Professional in the Dementia Experience case, which comprises a wide variety of sub-roles, from Nurses to Neurologists (not further specified in the initial analysis).
- Common stakeholder roles (light/dark grey) across different cases (e.g. Researchers, Citizens, Volunteers) could be very interesting linking pins for social innovation, creating new, unexpected connections between innovations in totally different domains, as, for example, suggested by the earlier mentioned Connected Differences Theory of social innovation (Mulgan 2007).
- Organizations are often used in two different role-playing ways. Sometimes, they are considered a stakeholder role (Ministry of Justice), sometimes they are used as containers for the individuals that need to play a particular innovation process or stakeholder role (e.g. a particular organization as a Core Community Member). In general, roles can best be expressed in generic stakeholder role terms instead of specific organizations, to promote the reuse of the patterns in which they are used.

18.2.5.2   Tools

- The cases are quite similar in number of tools used (Genicap: 18 types of tools, SafeCity 22, Dementia Experience 21).

- The average number of tools used is much higher than the amount normally examined in Computer-Supported Collaborative Work and Computer-Mediated Communications studies, which is typically 1–3. This suggest that real-world cases may generate much more complex computer-mediated interaction behaviors than typically studied in lab situations.
- We distinguish between face-to-face (e.g. Consortium Meetings), online tools (e.g. RSS Feeds, Facebook), and mass media (e.g. Newspapers, Magazines). Remarkably, the variation in types of face-to-face tools is very high. This suggests that the usual "face-to-face" category used in many CSCW and CMC studies is underspecified.
- Many of the online tools are the same across cases (e.g. Web Site, LinkedIn, YouTube). Given that the roles of the cases differ widely (as indicated by the few greyed roles in Appendix 1), this suggests that the variability in socio-technical systems of online collaborative communities is caused by the mappings of the roles to the tools, not the tools themselves.

18.2.5.3 Workflows

Roles and tools are combined in very different ways across the cases, leading to a palette of typical interactions which might inspire the construction of explicit, reusable collaboration patterns. The case study did not model those workflows in full detail, but some intriguing examples were collected in this pilot study (numbered here for reference in the next sections):

1. For intellectual property rights reasons, the core community should have a way to privately work together online for internal planning and coordination (C1), e.g. via a closed wiki or LinkedIn group that is not accessible to developers, users, and other stakeholders.
2. A regular series of face-to-face events, should be organized for the core community and developer network to meet (C2). This conversation sphere should have its own, private workspace.
3. Public content about prototypes (C3) should be advertised by the core community as much as possible on the key social media sites where the content of that particular type belongs (e.g. YouTube for videos, SlideShare for presentations) instead of being hosted on company servers. Apart from increasing outreach efficiency, this generates additional conversations on the social media sites, thus attracting new stakeholders. These stakeholders in turn could be recruited as new members of the user and developer networks (C4 and C5). These spheres could have their own private sections on the community portal.
4. The developer network may include many people representing key stakeholders (e.g. physicians in the Dementia Experience case). These stakeholders interact on their own in their own physical and online fora, such as physical meetings, mailing lists and Facebook or LinkedIn groups. One way to involve them is by creating separate social media channels for the project, and then trying to attract overloaded stakeholders to those new channels (core community members then

acting as "ambassadors"). However, it is often more effective and efficient to have stakeholder representatives in the developer network keep their peers informed on their own, existing channels, such as professional society websites and mailing lists (developers then effectively being "consuls") (C5).

5. Typically, a social innovation process takes a long time, often years, from initial idea, via prototype to full product. As an increasing number of developers and stakeholders gets involved, using a growing set of communication tools, collaborative fragmentation can easily occur. The open, fleeting nature of tools like Facebook and Twitter only exacerbates this situation. Rather than trying to control these conversations, they should only be facilitated (trying to create "buzz"). To keep some focus, the core community should ensure that regular updates about project progress are made on a community portal (e.g. a website) they control. These updates should have deep links (their own unique url), so that they can act as "anchors" in the unruly conversation spheres, being referenced wherever possible. Note that the links can be public and shared with all stakeholders (C3), but content referred to may only be accessible to developers behind a login (C2), in case the innovation is protected by intellectual property rights or privacy concerns, for instance.

6. Much content needs both open stakeholder (C3) and closed developer conversations (C2). For instance, a screenshot of a demonstrator could be put on a public Facebook page, where every visitor can leave comments. However, once sufficient feedback has been collected, a selected set of test-users/developers could be led through an "action funnel" in order to accomplish a result (C2, C5). A (Genicap-case) example would be to foster social media conversations around a web server that allows users to experiment with different types of graphical "supershapes", rendered real-time using software based on the superformula. Once a user sees a potential application, she can be funneled through a series of (private) forms to prepare the "create a business application" process.

7. Use a relevant selection of the total tool system to promote desired user and stakeholder interactions (C3-4). For example (in case of Genicap), at a scientific symposium, actionable deep links to specific research publication sections of the community portal could be presented. Afterwards, conference attendees could continue the conversation on the discussion pages of the papers presented at the conference. These scientists would not easily do this on Facebook. In contrast, Facebook would be a natural habitat for the creatives developing graphical applications of the superformula.

18.3   Collaboration Patterns: Sharing Lessons Learnt

Next, we first explore the nature of patterns in general, and of collaboration patterns in particular. We then examine how collaboration patterns can be represented as conceptual graphs and show some examples from the Social Innovation Award-case. We then explore various possible uses of the patterns.

18.3.1 Exploring Patterns

In design, creativity and rationale are co-dependent. Design is a broad, often collaborative human activity about "how things ought to be" (Fischer and Shipman 2011). Design seen as a collaborative activity requires common ground to be built over and over again. Rationale can aid creativity in design through helping designers see their world in alternative ways (Carroll 2010). Design rationale represents and articulates the reasoning underlying the design process explaining, deriving, and justifying design decisions. It provides a forum for airing issues crucial for coordinating group activities (Fischer and Shipman 2011). Patterns, both individually, and by the network of relations they form in pattern languages, can be an important instrument for providing such design rationale.

Patterns are a way of recognizing and describing approaches and structures that are encountered repeatedly in a discipline. They were first popularized by Christopher Alexander in an architectural context. His intuitive definition is worth quoting here: "Each pattern describes a problem which occurs over and over again in our environment, and then describes the core of the solution to that problem, in such a way that you can use this solution a million times over, without ever doing it the same way twice (Alexander et al. 1977, x)". In other words, patterns define relatively stable solutions to recurring problems at the right level of abstraction, making them concrete enough to be useful in a particular case, while also sufficiently abstract to be reusable across cases (De Moor 2006).

With their template structure, patterns provide enough degrees of freedom for situated, contextualized knowledge to be represented, while providing enough structure to help trigger stakeholders in generating such ideas in the first place. Patterns, do not exist in isolation, however, but are organized in pattern languages. These are networks of patterns that call upon one another, patterns being embedded in larger patterns, related to similar patterns and in turn embedding smaller patterns (Alexander et al. 1977, xiii). A pattern language is a living knowledge base that promotes, rather than restrains creativity, collaborative, and critical thinking, integrates theory and action and bridges traditional boundaries (Schuler 2008, 55, 543). Patterns are natural bridges between the unruly world of creativity and the systematic world of rationale. The relationships between patterns in pattern languages furthermore help their users find meaningfully related ideas, which they can then zoom in on to explore the details.

18.3.2 Collaboration Patterns Introduced

Socio-technical design patterns go beyond the more technical-oriented design patterns that focus on interface, interaction, and implementation, which are at the core of human-computer interaction and software engineering pattern languages (Borchers 2000). Instead, socio-technical patterns play an important role at the beginning of social software projects, where they can be used to help scope in application domain terms the overall interactions between the social and technical systems that need to be built (Dixon 2009).

Collaboration patterns as a category of socio-technical design patterns are especially important for helping to create effective collaboration spaces, as they combine the social structures and processes of the communities in which human beings work together with the effective use of the technologies that enable this collaboration (De Moor 2009). Thus, they capture lessons learnt about how to make available functionalities "actionable" by describing how community members playing particular domain roles best use specific functionalities for particular collaborative purposes.

We distinguish five types of collaboration patterns that together can be used to represent and analyze collaborative lessons learnt: goal patterns, information patterns, communication patterns, task patterns and meta-patterns (De Moor 2009). In this chapter, we will not delve into the details of these different types of collaboration patterns and how they are related. Our purpose here is only to illustrate how collaboration patterns could form a language for the formalization of social innovation lessons learnt. Therefore, we only use combinations of two types of collaboration patterns: communication and information patterns. Communication patterns describe acceptable and desirable communicative interactions within communities. Information patterns are conceptualizations of content knowledge essential for the collaboration plus the roles responsible for its creation and maintenance.

As mentioned previously, the conceptual basis for communication patterns is the *communicative workflow loop*, which is the basic unit of coordinating actions in collaborative communities. This loop is grounded in Language/Action Theory, which emphasizes what people do by communicating, how language is used to create a common basis for communication partners, and how their activities are coordinated through language (Winograd and Flores 1986). Each communicative workflow loop consists of three subsequent stages: the initiation, execution, and evaluation of the result. Each stage can be supported by one or more tools. Communicative workflow loops are controlled by three types of roles: domain roles, conversation roles, and functionality roles (De Moor 2010a). Domain roles are the roles somebody plays in the capacity of being a stakeholder member of a collaborative community. Such roles could be played by be the innovation process roles and stakeholder roles we distinguished in the domain of social innovation. Conversation roles are the initiating, executing, and evaluating roles that community members play in controlling the workflow. Functionality roles are the roles that people need to play in effectively using tool functionalities. An example of a functionality role would be the List Administrator of a Mailing List tool. Conversation and functionality roles in turn can be played by domain roles, so role nesting is common.

18.3.3   Representing Collaboration Patterns

Patterns can be represented in different notations. Such a notation can be an informal one, such as the patterns in the Liberating Voices Pattern Language,[4] which are described in English. Here, the only structure is provided by the headings within

---

[4] http://www.publicsphereproject.org/patterns/

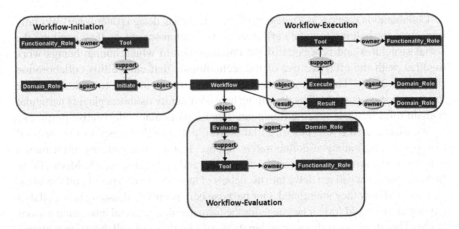

Fig. 18.3 An (enabled) communication pattern template

each pattern: Problem, Context, Discussion, Solution, Related Patterns. However, for the purpose of collaboration design, this lack of structure does not suffice. Sociotechnical systems in the case of social innovation require many detailed design decisions to be made, such as with respect to links between and constraints on workflows, role authorizations, and tool configurations. To be able to represent and (semi-)automatically reason about patterns, ontologies are needed. An ontology is am explicit specification of a conceptualization (Gruber 1994). At the very least an ontology contains the (systematically defined) main concepts and relations agreed upon by the key stakeholders in a particular domain, usually organized in a type hierarchy. Appendix 3 shows a possible type hierarchy for the roles, tools, and workflows distinguished in this chapter. Often, the ontology also includes the rules needed to reason about these representations.

Our ontological formalism of choice are conceptual graphs. Conceptual graph theory is a powerful formalism for knowledge representation and reasoning that is grounded in linguistic principles on the one hand, and formal semantic network representations on the other hand (Sowa 1984). A key feature is that conceptual graph theory allows for generalization hierarchies of graphs, so that more generic (reusable) patterns can be specialized into/derived from more specific (case)-based patterns. Thus, conceptual graphs are very well suited for representing and reasoning about collaboration patterns.

Communicative requirements and enabling tools meet in so-called *enabled communication patterns*. A template of such a pattern is shown in Fig. 18.3. This template says that a workflow is controlled by an initiation, execution, and evaluation process. The agent of each of these control processes is some domain role. Each control process is supported ("enabled") by some tool, owned/controlled by some functionality role. The output of each workflow is some result, owned by some domain role. To prevent confusion: the patterns presented in the following figures are not to be directly used (or even seen) by stakeholders. However, they have been included here to stress that *precise semantics of collaboration patterns are of the essence,* as the devil is very much in the detail. Too much of the collaboration support literature is of the "vigorous handwaving" kind: the broad conceptual models all look very agreeable, until one tries to implement the abstract models, when confusion frequently abounds, and collaboration comes to a halt, if it gets started in the first place. These models need to be translated in different languages for different target groups of users. Technical users like collaboration researchers and systems admins can use them almost directly, to construct hypotheses or configure socio-technical collaboration systems. Domain stakeholders, however, could only see part of these models, presented in natural language or a drop-down box in a web form. For instance, the top-left part of Fig. 18.3 says that some tool is used to support the initiation of a workflow. Translated into a "layman's situation" this could mean that a user being consulted on the design of their community system, could be asked "Which tool would you use to start your [name of the workflow]?", then be presented with a list of all the tools accessible to this community. At the end of this section, we further expand on how to use these patterns.

Note that this template is the most generic form of communication patterns. In realistic settings, enabled communication patterns are contextualized by complex amalgams of other collaboration patterns, such as information patterns to describe the key characteristics of the content produced in the workflow. We will give some examples of such realistic patterns in next.[5]

18.3.4   Social Innovation Award: Distilling the Lessons Learnt with Collaboration Patterns

We are now ready to show how collaboration patterns can be used to distill lessons learnt in our social innovation case. The basis for our analysis are the Social Innovation Collaboration model and the Enabled Communication Pattern template. Domain roles in the latter are played by social innovation process roles, which themselves can be played by stakeholder roles, as we have seen. To illustrate, we show patterns capturing some of the lessons learnt in the list of workflow examples in the previous section.

18.3.5   Recruiting Test Users

In workflow example 3, we saw that new test users can be recruited by sharing prototype visualizations on social network sites, then inviting the most active users to become test users on the community portal. For example, the Initiator of

---

[5] In this chapter, we will refrain from further using functionality roles. These roles especially come into play when optimizing usage of tools across many cases. For example, the book "Wikipatterns" (Mader 2007) gives many examples of functionality roles needed to make effective use of wikis, independent of the particular communities of use. Examples are Champion, WikiZenMaster and WikiGardener.

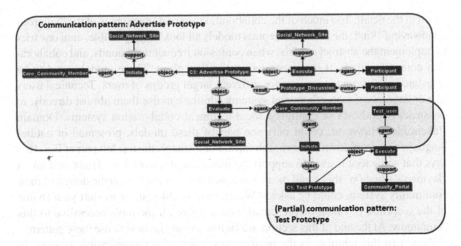

Fig. 18.4 Composite collaboration pattern: Recruiting test users

the C3: Advertise Prototype-workflow could be the (innovation process role) Core Community Member, by virtue of placing prototype visualizations on relevant social network sites, thus starting the advertising process. Next, this or another core community member could select active participants to test prototypes with developers (C5) on the community portal. Figure 18.4 shows the collaboration pattern capturing this lesson learnt.

Note that this is a composite collaboration pattern, consisting of two interrelated (enabled) communication patterns. Active participants are those who are involved in ("execute") the prototype discussion in the Advertise Prototype workflow. In evaluating this discussion, a core community member selects the most promising participants as test users. This selection process is (part of the) initiation of the Test Prototype-workflow that takes place on the (private) community portal. Note that there are dotted lines between the Participant and the Test User concepts. These are "lines of identity" which indicate that these roles are played by the same individuals. Also note that, for instance, the evaluation of "C5: Test Prototype" is not modeled. This is irrelevant from the point of view of recruiting test users, and can be captured by other collaboration patterns, which can then be connected to the current pattern if and when needed.

18.3.6 Reducing Collaborative Fragmentation

Workflow example 5 discussed a strategy using deep links to (public or private) content in order to create "conversational buzz" while reducing the risk for collaborative fragmentation. Figure 18.5 shows a collaboration pattern that captures this strategy:

It is a composite pattern consisting of (partial) communication patterns around two workflows (Developer Conversation and Stakeholder Conversation) and an information patterns stating that content can have deep links. Key to this pattern

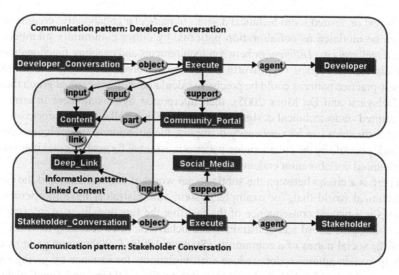

Fig. 18.5 Composite collaboration pattern: Reducing collaborative fragmentation

is the distinction between stakeholder conversations taking place on one or more types of social media (Facebook, LinkedIn etc.) and developer conversations taking place on a (public or private) dedicated community portal. How these conversations are started or evaluated is not relevant here. What both types of conversations have in common are deep links to some form of content. However, and this is crucial, in this case the content itself is private and only accessible to developers in their conversation (as an input in the execution of the Developer Conversation).

18.3.7 Using Collaboration Patterns

Collaboration patterns are conceptual representations of collaboration lessons learnt, in this case with respect to social innovation. We have seen how to distill and formulate them. However, the patterns must be put into practice in order to prove their value. Many applications of these patterns are conceivable:

- Collaboration patterns can be used as best-practice discussion starters for *collaborative sensemaking* by communities. Since the ontology underlying the patterns is expressed in (role, tool, workflow etc.) terms carefully elicited from stakeholders representatives, they provide realistic scenarios related to socio-technical problems and design directions experienced in real world-situations. With a little training, the visual format of conceptual graphs can be understood. Moreover, since conceptual graphs have a well-established linguistic foundation, they can be automatically translated into controlled natural language sentences, creating mini-stories that community members can validate without having to interpret graphical formalisms.

- Current or desired socio-technical designs of particular collaborative communities can be modeled as collaboration patterns, by either community members or external analysts. *Differences* between requirements and enabling functionalities – socio-technical gaps (Whitworth 2006) – and between existing and desired/ best-practice patterns could be precisely calculated with conceptual graph theory (Delugach and De Moor 2005), then interpreted by stakeholders in terms of required socio-technical design interventions. Since collaboration processes and infrastructures can be very easily disrupted, the attention to unambiguous detail made possible by the collaboration patterns is essential for enabling and innovating advanced collaboration endeavors.
- There is a chasm between the subtle social world of communities and the harsh technical world that, for example, system administrators have to operate in. This is a natural consequence of the fact that the functionalities of information technologies afford and constrain social behaviors, often resulting in violations of the social norms of a community (Stamper 1996). Collaboration patterns can help system administrators reduce such violations, for instance by giving clear specifications of role-based access rights to files, folders, and functionalities when configuring the tools used by a specific community.
- Successful collaboration designs, especially in large networks and online communities, cannot be pre-scribed. Instead, they require lots of tinkering and trial-and-error. Typically, fragments of collaboration emerge first and slowly coalesce, often only after many iterations. Collaboration patterns match this *natural evolutionary process*. Initially, only a few, generic collaboration patterns can be selected to kickstart the formation of a collaborative community. Over time, more complex, contextualized collaboration patterns can be added to refine the emerging collaborative infrastructure with increasingly advanced lessons learnt in similar endeavors. The patterns, by using a joint ontology, can be used to circumscribe the boundaries of collaborative workflows at just the right level of detail, and allow for these "collaborative islands" to be linked into a full-fledged "collaborative landscape".
- A major issue for (especially online) collaborative communities is that they often die down after an initial burst of excitement and activity. Furthermore, many social media applications limit themselves to supporting playful social networking, not addressing the larger, more serious applications that could bring larger benefits to society (Preece and Shneiderman 2009). Collaboration patterns, capturing effective collaboration designs, can be used to model necessary conditions for *activating and scaling* collaborative participation that go beyond toy applications. One benefit, for example, is that they provide a language to precisely define the collaborative roles that community members need to play and the tools that they could use in doing so.
- Collaboration patterns also form a bridge between theory and practice. Emerging fields like social innovation have still only rough, high-level (fragments of) theory at their disposal to guide research, development, and implementation efforts. Collaboration patterns like the ones distilled in the case described in this chapter, can be considered "proto-theories". They can be used to formulate socio-technical design hypotheses, to be used in further case studies and empirical testing.

18.4   Discussion

Collaboration patterns are bridges: they span general lessons learnt and situations of specific communities; requirements and functionalities; theory and practice. As we have seen in the previous section, they are multi-faceted constructs, with many potential applications. One main reason for their conceptual power is that they zoom in on the essence of socio-technical systems: systems of tools used in complex, real-world domains like social innovation. In contrast, much related work focuses on single tools (e.g. Twitter, wikis) in more limited contexts of use, such as e-learning by students or knowledge management in professional work situations (e.g. Zhao and Rosson 2009; Witney and Smallbone 2011). Although the results of these studies gives a reasonably good idea about the collaboration (inter)action potentials afforded and constrained by such tools, these insights are not specific enough for the effective design and use of combinations of such tools in realistic usage contexts, such as social innovation cases. Collaboration patterns, built on solid ontological foundations derived from both theory and empirics (e.g. Appendix 1, 2, 3), can help distill reusable lessons learnt, while diversifying the designs of actual tool systems used in particular communities.

Social innovation theory is still in its infancy. Collaboration patterns are at the "meso-level" between formal theory and unruly practice. They provide practical guidance for social innovation (e.g. tool/role selection, systems configuration), but also help in theory formation (e.g. socio-technical design hypotheses). Yet, the patterns can also further social computing theory: designing social innovations contextualizes and conceptually wraps the design of social computing software and methodologies. In the Social Innovation Award case, we adopted a form of grounded theory methodology to try and elicit collaboration patterns of sufficient quality to serve both purposes. Ours is an inductive way of theory construction and testing. Of course, the patterns may not be universally valid, since we have not done controlled, statistical experiments. But then again, a fundamental question is if such statistical generalization is ever possible in the complex, situated reality of the online collaborative workplace. We do not claim to have a fully developed, let alone tested theory. However, the emerging ontology and patterns can serve as an emerging rich language in which to design further hypotheses and experiments. As such, this approach links the design theory paradigm to the "classical" behavior science paradigm. A design theory is prescriptive theory based on theoretical underpinnings which say how a design process can be carried out in a way which is both effective and feasible (Walls et al. 1992). The design theory paradigm is a natural paradigm for information systems research as it seeks to create innovations that define the ideas, practices, technical capabilities, and products through which the study and development of information systems can be accomplished effectively and efficiently (Hevner et al. 2004). Analytical, rather than statistical generalization (Yin 1994) seems to be the appropriate way for such socio-technical pattern theory generation. This does not mean that behavioral experiments are not important. However, the "rich context modeling" taking place in exercises like presented in this chapter can help to provide the meaningful conceptual scaffolding on which more rigorous statistically-based behavioral experiments can subsequently be built. The Social Innovation Award 2011 has just been given to two new innovation cases, in very different domains (construction industry and restaurant/retail business). The monthly plenary meetings will be continued, together with the previous winners, in a Social Innovation Award Academy.[6] This creates a significant opportunity for evaluating, refining, and extending the social innovation ontology and patterns developed so far.

The rise in social computing has led to a shift from passive media consumption to cultures of participation. Coordinating and integrating collective design rationale and social creativity provides new synergies and opportunities in sophisticated socio-technically mediated collaborative communities (Fischer and Shipman 2011). Collaboration patterns unite collaboration rationale and community creativity by acting as "boundary definitions", allowing generic lessons learnt to be uniquely modified, extended, and appropriated by individual communities to match the peculiarities of their own, situated reality. As boundary definitions, collaboration patterns complement process rationale recommendations in upstream requirements engineering and critical conversations by stakeholders and software designers (Ocker 2010; McCall 2010). By "setting the discussion agenda", the patterns can inspire a form of "process composition" (taking into account such process rationale recommendations), through which community members circumscribe rather than exhaustively describe their socio-technical system (Fitzpatrick and Welsh 1995). Advantages of such an approach are that, over time, requirements can be gradually refined and that much flexibility remains in the way collaborative work is done, as only the boundaries of the socio-technical system are delineated, at the necessary – and sufficient – level of detail.

One particular focus of socio-technical interest is "the role of roles" (De Moor 2010a). Roles are important constructs in communities, in which they have structuring, coordinating and supporting functions. The development of roles and their functions takes place by perceiving the repetition of social interaction patterns based on patterns of expectations (Herrmann et al. 2004). Both explicit and informal roles are very important in community governance, as typically organizational hierarchies are lacking, and interorganizational confusion abounds in collaborative communities. Despite their stated importance, role typologies, let alone fully developed ontologies describing how these roles are to be situated in collaborative workflow patterns, are still relatively ill-developed in the literature. With our work, we have started exploring this relatively uncharted territory, by distinguishing between such concepts as domain, conversation and functionality roles; and our initial attempts at empirically grounded domain-specific roles like the social innovation process and stakeholder roles elicited in the Social Innovation Award case, as well as the collaboration patterns in which they "play their natural roles". Even so, there are many other possible role classifications which we have not even touched upon, but might further enrich the mix, such as the facilitation roles needed in virtual teams (Thomas et al. 2007). As more cases get analyzed, and social innovation collaboration theory solidifies, initially case-specific roles might become generic stakeholder or innovation process roles, then possibly even become part of more generic collaborative community role ontologies. One caveat is that nestings of roles can become very complex: for instance, conversation roles can be played by social innovation process roles, which in turn can be played by stakeholder roles, which might be played by an organizational role, which then again might be played by a particular person. Such role nesting is unavoidable in real world collaborative situations. Conceptual graph theory might be of great help here, as nested contexts and pattern/graph hierarchies are among its key research foci.

Finally, to what extent could the results obtained in the domain of social innovation be generalized to other domains? One very related domain that immediately comes to mind is that of open innovation. Open innovation concerns complex, interconnected webs of interacting individuals and organizations focused on producing knowledge-intensive innovative outputs (West and Lakhani 2008). Popular examples include "Wikinomics" and "We-Think" (Tapscott and Williams 2008; Leadbeater 2009), which propose smart combinations of Web-mediated content, social media, context, and conversations to drive and scale mass collaboration forms of open innovation communities. Our approach provides a language and lens for viewing such collaborative problems and socio-technical design solutions with more precision and clarity. It should therefore be applicable to open innovation and other forms of (inter) organizational collaboration networks and communities as well, both in terms of methodology and at least part of the contents of role, tool, and workflow typologies and collaboration patterns.

18.5   Conclusion

Real-world collaborative communities make use of complex systems of face-to-face and online communications tools, tinkering them together into intricate fabrics of tools, roles, and workflows. Collaboration patterns help in the process of weaving these evolving socio-technical systems, by inspiring their design and making it possible to re-use lessons learnt across cases. We studied the use of collaboration patterns in one particular domain, social innovation, by analyzing the results from a cross-case analysis of three Dutch social innovation communities simultaneously being developed. One main result is that we have obtained a better understanding of the nature of socio-technical systems specifically for social innovation. Possibly even more important is that we are pioneering an approach and methodology for using collaboration patterns to develop tailorable socio-technical systems for creative, working communities. We are still at the beginning of a long journey of learning about how to do so, and understanding what are the manifold implications. However, as the Chinese saying goes: "every journey starts with a single step." We are definitely on our way.

Acknowledgments The author wishes to thank all participants in the Genicap, SafeCity and Dementia Experience cases for their many contributions and insights. Also, the support of Midpoint Brabant, the Municipality of Tilburg, and the Tilburg University/Tilburg Social Innovation Lab for making the Social Innovation Award possible in the first place is gratefully acknowledged. The continued and enthusiastic support of all by taking the lessons learnt to the next level in the recently established Social Innovation Award Academy is another great example of social innovation-in-action.

18.6 Appendix 1: Social Innovation Award – Role Analysis

Roles / Cases	Genicap	SafeCity	Dementia Experience
Innovation process roles	Core Community Members	Core Community Members	Core Community Members
	Developers	Developers	Developers
	Stakeholders	Stakeholders	Stakeholders
	Users	Users	Users
	Business Developers		
			Consuls
	Front-Desk		
	Investors		
			(Other) Innovation Projects
		Think Tanks	
Stakeholder roles		Association of Municipalities (VNG)	
	Business		Business
			Caregivers (amateurs)
			Care institutions
	Citizens	Citizens	
		Common Control Room	
			Communications Officers
			Community Representatives
	Creatives		
			Decision makers
			Dementia consultants
		Domestic care organisations	
	Education		Education
	Government		
		Housing associations	
		Insurance companies	
		Lone workers	
			Managers
			Mass Media
		Mayors	
		Ministry of Justice	
		Municipalities	
		Municipal control room	
		Municipality departments	
		Notifiers	
		PACs	
		Police	
		Politics	
			Product developers
		Product owners	
			Professionals (caregivers)
			Professionals (non-caregivers)
		Public task employees	
		Public task organizations	
	Researchers/Scientists	Researchers	Researchers
		Security companies	
		Security policy officers	
		Security coordinators	
		Security demanders	
		Security suppliers	
			Society
		Street coaches	
			Students
	Technologists		
			Visitors
		Volunteers	Volunteers
# of roles	14	32	24

Roles that occur in only 1 case are in white; in 2 cases are in light-grey, in all 3 cases in dark-grey. NB Roles not mentioned in a particular case may still be present, but have not been the focus of the initial analysis.

18.7   Appendix 2: Social Innovation Award – Tool Analysis

Tools / Cases	Genicap	SafeCity	Dementia Experience
Face-to-Face tools			Alzheimer Cafes
	Consortium Meetings		
			Dementia Consultations
			Developer Meetings
		External Events	
		Network Meetings	
	One-on-One Talks		
		"Pasta Talks"	
			Professional Information Points
	Symposia		
			Training Sessions
Online tools	Blog	Blog	Blog
	Delicious (social bookmarking)	Delicious (social bookmarking)	Delicious (social bookmarking)
		Dropbox (filesharing)	Dropbox (filesharing)
	Facebook (social networks)	Facebook (social networks)	
	Flickr (photo sharing)	Flickr (photos)	Flickr (photos)
		Google Docs (co-authoring)	
	Google Forms (forms)	Google Forms (forms)	Google Forms (forms)
		Google Maps (maps)	
		Hyves (social networks)	Hyves (social networks)
	LinkedIn (social networks)	LinkedIn (social networks)	LinkedIn (social networks)
	Mailing Lists	Mailing Lists	Mailing Lists
		Newspapers/Magazines (mass media)	Newspapers/Magazines (mass media)
	RSS Feeds	RSS Feeds	RSS Feeds
			Simulator
	Slideshare	Slideshare	
	Tagging Policies	Tagging Policies	Tagging Policies
	Twitter	Twitter	Twitter
	Websites (Business Portal/Community Portal)	Website	Websites (Own vs. Target Group Sites)
	Wikispaces	Wikispaces	Wikispaces
	YouTube	YouTube	YouTube
	Zotero		
# of tools	18	22	21

Tools that occur in only 1 case are in white; 2 cases are in light-grey, in all 3 cases in dark-grey. NB Tools not mentioned in a particular case may still be present, but have not been the focus of the initial analysis. Also, mass media in the case analysis were grouped under online tools. Strictly speaking, they are a class of their own, which is reflected in the social innovation concept type hierarchy outlined in Appendix 3.

18.8   Appendix 3: Social Innovation Concept Type Hierarchy

An important part of the social innovation ontology-under-construction is the concept type hierarchy. This hierarchy is necessary to interpret, generalize and specialize the growing set of collaboration patterns and helps in theory and hypothesis formation. Inputs are the Social Innovation Collaboration Model, the role and tool types listed in the previous appendices, and the collaboration patterns examples presented in the previous sections.

Concept types from the existing theory (e.g. Conversation Roles) are underlined. The number behind each (newly elicited) concept type indicates how often it was mentioned in the cross-case analysis. The higher the number, the more likely the concept type could become part of the grounded social innovation collaboration theory-under construction.

The concept type hierarchy is far from complete, is merely indicative of the field of social innovation and some of its sub-domains, and is only one out of many possible orderings. The taxonomy presented is only preliminary: for example, is a Public Task Organization part of Government, or its own independent category? The same concept types can be re-organized into very different taxonomies, depending on the (proto)theory being developed. At any rate, the proposed ordering(s) will get more refined and stable over time, in further iterations of the grounded methodology methodology.

Social innovation concept type hierarchy

- Roles
    - Conversation Roles
        - Initiators
        - Executors
        - Evaluators
    - Domain Roles
        - Innovation Process Roles
            - Core Innovation Process Roles
                - Core Community Members
                - Developers
                - Stakeholders
                - Users
            - Candidate Innovation Process Roles
                - Business Developers (1)
                - Consuls (1)
                - Front-Desk (1)
                - (Other) Innovation Projects (1)
                - Investors (1)
                - Think Tanks (1)
        - Stakeholder Roles
            - Business (2)
            - Care Institutions (1)
                - Domestic Care Organisations (1)
            - Citizens (2)
                - Caregivers (1)
            - Community Representatives (1)
            - Control Room
                    - Common Control Room (1)
                    - Municipal Control Room (1)
            - Creatives (1)
            - Decision Makers (1)
            - Education (2)
            - Government (1)
                - Mayors (1)
                - Ministry of Justice (1)
                - Municipalities (1)

- Association of Municipalities (1)
  - Municipality Departments (1)
- Politics (1)
- Housing Associations (1)
- Insurance Companies (1)
- Lone Workers (1)
- Managers (1)
- Mass Media (1)
- Notifiers (1)
- PACs (1)
- Police (1)
- Product Developers (1)
- Product Owners (1)
- Professionals
  - Professionals (caregivers) (1)
  - Professionals (non-caregivers)(1)
    - Dementia Consultants (1)
- Public Task Employees (1)
- Public Task Organizations (1)
- Researchers (3)
- Security Companies (1)
- Security Policy Officers (1)
- Security Coordinators (1)
- Security Demanders (1)
- Security Suppliers (1)
- Society (1)
- Street Coaches (1)
- Students (1)
- Technologist (1)
- Visitors (1)
- Volunteers (2)
- <u>Functionality Roles</u>
- <u>Tools</u>
  - <u>Face-to-Face Tools</u>
    - Cafe Meetings
      - Alzheimer Cafes (1)
    - Consultations
      - Dementia Consultations (1)
    - Consortium Meetings (1)
    - Developer Meetings (1)
    - External Events (1)
    - Network Meetings (1)
    - One-On-One Talks (1)
    - "Pasta Talks" (1)
    - Professional Information Points (1)
    - Symposia (1)

```
      - Online Tools
         - Blogs (3)
         - Co-Authoring Tools
            - Google Docs (1)
         - Filesharing Tools
            - Dropbox (2)
         - Forms Tools
            - Google Forms (3)
         - Mailing Lists (3)
         - Maps Tools
            - Google Maps (1)
         - Microblogs
            - Twitter (3)
         - Photosharing Tools
            - Flickr (3)
         - Presentation Sharing Tools
            - Slideshare (2)
         - Research Annotation Tools
            - Zotero (1)
         - RSS Feeds (3)
         - Simulator (1)
         - Social Bookmarking Tools
            - Delicious (3)
         - Social Network Sites
            - Facebook (2)
            - Hyves (2)
            - LinkedIn (3)
         - Tagging Policies (3)
         - Video Tools
            - YouTube (3)
         - Websites (3)
            - Business Portals (1)
            - Community Portals (1)
         - Wikis
            - Wikispaces (3)
      - Mass Media
         - Magazines/Newspapers (2)
   - Workflows
      - Innovation Process Workflows
         - C1 Workflows (core community)
            - Internal Planning & Coordination (3)
         - C2 Workflows (core community - developers)
            - Involve Consuls (1)
            - Organize Developer Meetings (3)
         - C3 Workflows (core community - stakeholders)
```

```
        - Advertise Prototype (3)
        - Create Buzz (3)
        - Inform Stakeholders (3)
     - C4 Workflows (core community - users)
        - Facilitate Research Conversations (1)
        - Gather User Feedback (3)
     - C5 Workflows (core community - test users -
       developers)
        - Recruit Developers/Test Users (3)
   - Domain Workflows
```

References

Alexander, C., Ishikawa, S., & Silverstein, M. (1977). *A pattern language: Towns, buildings, construction.* New York: Oxford University Press.

Borchers, J. O. (2000, April 2–3). Interaction design patterns: Twelve theses. In *Pattern languages for interaction design: Building momentum, CHI 2000.* The Hague, The Netherlands.

Carroll, J. (2010). The essential tension of creativity and rationale in software design. *Human Technology, 6*(1), 4–10.

De Moor, A. (2006 October). Community memory activation with collaboration patterns. In *Proceedings of the 3rd Prato Community Informatics Research Network Conference (CIRN 2006).* Prato, Italy.

De Moor, A. (2009, November 4–6). Collaboration patterns as building blocks for community informatics. In *Proceedings of Community Informatics Research Network Conference.* Prato, Italy.

De Moor, A. (2010a, October 27–29). Using collaboration patterns for contextualizing roles in community systems design. In *Proceedings of the 7th Community Informatics Research Network Conference.* Prato, Italy.

De Moor, A. (2010b, September 1–3). Conversations in context: A Twitter case for social media systems design. In *Proceedings of I-SEMANTICS 2010.* Graz, Austria: ACM.

Delugach, H., & De Moor, A. (2005, July). Difference graphs. Common semantics for sharing knowledge: Contributions to ICCS 2005. *13th International Conference on Conceptual Structures, ICCS 2005.* (pp. 41–53). Kassel, Germany: Kassel University Press.

Denning, P. J., & Medina-Mora, R. (1995). Completing the loops. *Interfaces, 25*(3), 42–57.

Denning, P. J., & Yaholkovsky, P. (2008). Getting to "we". *Communications of the ACM, 51*(4), 19.

Dixon, D. (2009). Pattern languages for CMC design. In B. Whitworth & A. de Moor (Eds.), *Handbook of research on socio-technical design and social networking systems* (pp. 402–415). Hershey: Information Science Reference.

Fernández, W. D., & Lehmann, H. (2005). Achieving rigour and relevance in information systems studies: Using grounded theory to investigate organizational cases. *The Grounded Theory Review, 5*(1), 79–107.

Fischer, G., & Shipman, F. (2011). Collaborative design rationale and social creativity in cultures of participation. *Human Technology, 7*(2), 164–187.

Fitzpatrick, G., & Welsh, J. (1995). Process support: Inflexible imposition or chaotic composition? *Interacting with Computers, 7*(2), 167–180.

Gielis, J. (2003). A generic geometric transformation that unifies a large range of natural and abstract shapes. *American Journal of Botany, 90*(3), 333–338.

Gruber, T. (1994). Towards principles for the design of ontologies used for knowledge sharing. In N. Guarino & R. Poli (Eds.), *Formal ontology in conceptual analysis and knowledge representation.* Dordrecht: Kluwer Academic.

Herrmann, T., Jahnke, I., & Loser, K.-U. (2004, May 11–14). The role concept as a basis for designing community systems. In *Proceedings of COOP 2004*. Hyères les Palmiers, France.

Hevner, A. R., March, S. T., Park, J., & Ram, S. (2004). Design science in information systems research. *Management Information Systems Quarterly, 28*(1), 75–105.

Howe, J. (2009). *Crowdsourcing: Why the power of the crowd is driving the future of business*. New York: Crown Business.

Kane, B.J. (2005). *The case for improvisational melodic structures. Web resource*. http://www.jazzpath.com/education/articles/melodicImprov.php. Accessed 24 Feb 2012.

Leadbeater, C. (2009). *We-think: Mass innovation, not mass production*. London: Profile Books.

Mader, S. (2007). *Wikipatterns: A practical guide to improving productivity and collaboration in your organization*. Indianapolis: Wiley.

McCall, R. (2010). Critical conversations: Feedback as a stimulus to creativity in software design. *Human Technology, 6*(1), 11–37.

Mulgan, G. (2007). *Social innovation: What is it, why it matters, how it can be accelerated*. London: The Young Foundation.

Murray, R., Caulier-Grice, J., & Mulgan, G. (2010). *The open book of social innovation* (Social innovator series: Ways to design, develop and grow social innovation). London: NESTA/Young Foundation.

Ocker, R. (2010). Promoting group creativity in requirements engineering. *Human Technology, 6*(1), 55–70.

Pol, E., & Ville, S. (2009). Social innovation: Buzzword or enduring term? *The Journal of Socio-Economics, 38*(6), 878–885.

Preece, J., & Shneiderman, B. (2009). The Reader-to-Leader framework: Motivating technology-mediated social participation. *AIS Transactions on Human-Computer Interaction, 1*(1), 13–32.

Schuler, D. (2008). *Liberating Voices: A pattern language for communication revolution*. Cambridge, MA: MIT Press.

Sowa, J. F. (1984). *Conceptual structures: Information processing in mind and machine*. Reading: Addison-Wesley.

Stamper, R. K. (1996). Signs, information, norms and systems. In B. Holmqvist et al. (Eds.), *Signs at work* (pp. 349–397). Berlin: de Gruyte.

Tapscott, D., & Williams, A. D. (2008). *Wikinomics: How mass collaboration changes everything*. London: Atlantic Books.

Thomas, D. M., Bostrom, R. P., & Gouge, M. (2007). Making knowledge work in virtual teams. *Communications of the ACM, 50*(11), 85–90.

Urquhart, C. (2001). An encounter with grounded theory: Tackling the practical and philosophical issues. In E. M. Trauth (Ed.), *Qualitative research in information systems: Issues and trends* (pp. 104–140). Hershey: Idea Group Publishing.

Walls, J., Widmeyer, G. R., & El Sawy, O. A. (1992). Building an information system design theory for vigilant EIS. *Information Systems Research, 3*(1), 36–59.

West, J., & Lakhani, K. R. (2008). Getting clear about communities in open innovation. *Industry and Innovation, 15*(2), 223–231.

Whitworth, B. (2006). Socio-technical systems. In C. Ghaoui (Ed.), *Encyclopedia of human computer interaction* (pp. 559–566). Hershey: Idea Group Reference.

Winograd, T., & Flores, F. (1986). *Understanding computers and cognition: A new foundation for design*. Norwood, NJ: Ablex Pub. Corp.

Witney, D., & Smallbone, T. (2011). Wiki work: Can using wikis enhance student collaboration for group assignment tasks? *Innovations in Education and Teaching International, 48*, 101–110.

Yin, R. K. (1994). *Case study research: Design and methods* (Applied social research methods series 2nd ed.). Thousand Oaks: Sage.

Zaugg, H., West, R. E., Tateishi, I., & Randall, D. L. (2011). Mendeley: Creating communities of scholarly inquiry through research collaboration. *TechTrends, 55*, 32–36.

Zhao, D., & Rosson, M. B. (2009). How and why people twitter: The role that micro-blogging plays in informal communication at work. In *Proceedings of the ACM 2009 International conference on supporting group work* (pp. 243–252). Sanibel Island, Florida, USA: ACM.

Chapter 19
Patterns for Emergent Global Intelligence

John C. Thomas

Abstract This chapter argues that Pattern Languages are an effective way to enhance individual and collective creativity. Several suggested Patterns are presented that are targeted toward making the initial stages of solving complex problems more effective and efficient.

Keywords Collective intelligence • Creativity • Design rationale • Patterns • Pattern languages

19.1 Introduction

Today, humanity faces many challenges such as global climate change that require wide-spread cooperation and creativity. One approach to enhancing individual and collective intelligence is the construction, use and continued evolution of a Pattern Language for emergent global intelligence.

This chapter begins by defining Patterns and Pattern Languages and giving examples of their use in various domains. A few examples of Patterns particularly suited to collaborative creative design will be given. These particular Patterns are chosen because they are especially suited to the early stages of software development. I claim that the Patterns presented here are generally applicable to collaborative creative design although the discussion in this chapter will often be framed in terms of software development. These Patterns are also chosen to represent the range of ways that Patterns arise.

J.C. Thomas (✉)
Software Productivity Research Group, IBM T. J. Watson Research Center,
132 Ridgeview Lane, Yorktown Heights, NY 10598, USA
e-mail: jcthomas@us.ibm.com

J.M. Carroll (ed.), *Creativity and Rationale: Enhancing Human Experience by Design*, Human–Computer Interaction Series, DOI 10.1007/978-1-4471-4111-2_19, © Springer-Verlag London 2013

Every software development project offers two important opportunities. First, a *product* that helps enable people to become more effective and efficient while offering a good user experience provides value. Second, the *process* of software development offers a chance to learn to work together better and in that sense is also potentially a step forward toward emergent global intelligence.

I also claim that the Patterns presented here are useful for individual creativity on one hand as well as for dealing with large scale global cooperation on the other. I use the term "emergent" because what comes from using Patterns on a large scale cannot be specified ahead of time. In fact, the Patterns themselves are not fixed but represent best guesses based on current experience and evidence. The Pattern Language is meant to be an evolving collective effort as well. Next, some advantages and potential disadvantages of Patterns and Pattern Languages will be discussed. I end this chapter by discussing the challenges of attempting to empirically evaluate the effectiveness of a Pattern Language such as this one.

19.2 Patterns and Pattern Languages

This section defines Patterns and Pattern Languages and outlines a brief history of their use in various domains.

A Pattern is the named solution to a recurring problem along with an analysis of that problem. A Pattern Language is an interconnected web of Patterns that attempts to cover a particular field. The concept of Pattern Language was first introduced by Christopher Alexander and his colleagues with regard to the physical architecture for buildings and urban design (Alexander et al. 1977). However, the concept has since been applied to many fields including object-oriented software design (Gamma et al. 1995) change management, project management, community development, pedagogy, human-computer interaction (Bayle et al. 1997; Borchers 2001), socio-technical systems (Coplien and Harrison 2004) and societal change (Schuler 2008).

The potential application of Pattern Languages to the field of human computer interaction was mentioned early by Norman (1988). Since then, there have been a number of workshops at CHI (ACM's Conference on Human Factors in Computing Systems) (CHI 97, 00, 02, 03, 04, 11) as well as the European conference on Computer-Supported Cooperative Work (01, 03), Computer Supported Cooperative Work (02, 11) and Interact (99, 00). There have also been various panels and papers about patterns for computer-human interaction as well as several websites and books spanning issues from interaction design (Bayle et al. 1997; Borchers 2001) to societal reformation (Schuler 2008). Indeed, while *A Pattern Language* (Alexander, *ibid*) primarily deals with city planning and architecture, quite a few of the suggested patterns may be equally seen as patterns of social interaction. Examples include: 10, Magic of the City, 34 Interchange, 40 Old People Everywhere, 41 Work Community, 88 Street Café, 89 Corner Grocery, 90 Beer Hall, 91 Traveler's Inn, 92 Bus Stop, 129 Common Area at the Heart, 148 Small Work Group, 205 Structure Follows Social Space, 251 Different Chairs, and 252 Pools of Light. A number of additional suggested Patterns are even more specifically targeted at fostering creativity and creative interchange including 8 Mosaic of Subcultures, 18 Network of Learning, 43 University as Marketplace, 83 Masters and Apprentice, 151 Small Meeting Rooms, and 253 Things from Your Life. Indeed, taken as a whole, the entire thrust of Alexander's work can be seen as understanding and promoting social life and creativity *through the means of* city planning, architecture, and design rather than treating artifacts at various scales as *ends*. The Pattern Language form as put forth by Alexander is itself intended to promote creativity in that it provides cues, clues, analysis and the *seed* of a solution (as opposed to, say, a formula or a template).

The utility of a Pattern Language is not found so much in the specifics of format but in the spirit of the attempt to capture what is learned at an appropriate level of generality so that it is widely, if not universally, applicable. Consider for example, Christopher Alexander's Pattern 72 (*op cit.*), Local Sports. The Headline states: "The human body does not wear out with use. On the contrary, it wears down when it is not used." In the discussion, a diagram shows the relationship of activity level to mortality. Needless to say, *which* particular sports are popular will vary with culture, geography and time. It would be foolish to try to dictate a particular sport or set of sports as being "best." But, it is claimed, that *some* kind of local sport is desirable and healthy regardless of culture or setting. Variations and constraints in terms of physical terrain, cultural heritage, age, and available money and materials can be seen as providing creative challenges while the Pattern nonetheless provides an inspiration and an overall framework for solving particular problems.

In a similar vein, we may at least hypothesize that socio-technical patterns may also provide some degree of universality and inspiration while still requiring creativity in application. Consider, for instance, the Pattern explicated later in this chapter at some length: "Who Speaks for Wolf?" (Also known as "Voices of the Unheard.") The Pattern basically states that all stakeholders or their proxies should be consulted before design begins. *How* various stakeholders will be brought into the process will obviously vary tremendously from situation to situation, depending for example, on custom and culture. Another proposed Pattern is "Radical Co-location" which proposes that although people may work remotely when they already know each other well and the overall problem can be broken down into somewhat separable sub-problems, when these conditions are absent, it is important for people to be in almost continual contact. How to achieve this in specific cases will require the creative application of this Pattern tuned to the social, material, intellectual, and monetary requirements of the situation.

19.3 Example Patterns Relevant to Collaborative Creative Design

The Patterns below are all particularly applicable near the beginning of the development process. They are chosen because the beginning of development is often where projects go wrong and if they do go wrong, the associated expense and frustration are greatest. Application of the first two Patterns helps ensure that the right issues are actually being addressed. The next three Patterns help ensure that the development process will be as effective and efficient as possible.

19.3.1 Who Speaks for Wolf? (AKA, Voices of the Unheard)

Abstract: Much effort and thought goes into decision making and design. Nonetheless, it is often the case that bad decisions are made and bad designs conceived and implemented primarily because some critical and relevant perspective has not been brought to bear. This is especially often true if the relevant perspective is that of a stakeholder in the outcome. Therefore, ensure that every relevant stakeholder perspective is brought to bear early.

Problem: Problem solving or design that proceeds down the wrong path can be costly or impossible to correct later. As the inconvenience and cost of a major change in direction mount, cognitive dissonance makes it somewhat likely that the new information will be ignored or devalued so that continuance along the wrong path is likely.

Context: Complex problems such as the construction of new social institutions or the design of complex interactive systems require that a multitude of viewpoints be brought to bear. Unfortunately, this is all too often not the case. One group builds a "solution" for another group without fully understanding the culture, the user needs, the extreme cases, and so on. The result is often a "system" whether technical or social, that creates as many problems as it solves.

The idea for this pattern comes from a Native American story transcribed by Paula Underwood (1983). In brief, the story goes as follows. The tribe had as one of its members, a man who took it upon himself to learn all that he could about wolves. He became such an expert, that his fellow tribes-people called him "Wolf." While Wolf and several other braves were out on a long hunting expedition, it became clear to the tribe that they would have to move to a new location. After various reconnaissance missions, a new site was selected and the tribe moved.

Shortly thereafter, it became clear that a mistake had been made. The new location was in the middle of the wolves' spring breeding ground. The wolves were threatening the children and stealing the drying meat. Now, the tribe was faced with a hard decision. Should they move again? Should they post guards all day and all night? Or, should they destroy the wolves? And, did they even want to be the sort of people who would kill off another species for their own convenience?

At last it was decided they would move to a new location. But as was their custom, they also asked themselves, "What did we learn from this? How can we prevent making such mistakes in the future?" Someone said, "Well, if Wolf would have been at our first council meeting, he would have prevented this mistake."

"True enough," they all agreed. "Therefore, from now on, whenever we meet to make a decision, we shall ask ourselves, 'Who speaks for Wolf?' to remind us that someone must be capable and delegated to bring to bear the knowledge of any missing stakeholders."

Forces:

- Gaps in requirements are most cheaply repaired early in development; it is important for this and for reasons of acceptance (as well as ethics!) by all parties that all stakeholders have a say throughout any development or change process.
- Logistical difficulties make the representation of all stakeholder groups at every meeting difficult.
- A new social institution or design will be both better in quality and more easily accepted if all relevant parties have input.
- Once a wrong path is chosen, both social forces and individual cognitive dissonance make it difficult to begin over, change direction or retrace steps.

Solution: Provide automated reminding of stakeholders who are not present. These could be procedural (certain Native Americans always ask, "Who Speaks for Wolf" to remind them) or visual or auditory with technological support.

Examples: As a positive case, some groups make it a practice to "check in" at the beginning of any meeting to see whether any group members have an issue that they would like to have discussed. In "User Centered Design", and "Contextual Design" methodologies, an attempt is made to get input from the intended users of the system early on in the design process.

Resulting Context: When every stakeholder view is taken into account, the solution will be improved in quality and in addition, there will be less resistance to implementing the solution.

Rationale: Much of the failure of "process re-engineering" can be attributed to the fact that "models" of the "is" process were developed based on some executive's notion of how things were accomplished rather than a study of how they were actually done or asking the people who actually did the work how they were done. A "should be" process was designed to be a more efficient version of the "is" process and then implementation was pushed down on workers. However, since the original "is" model was not based on reality, the "more efficient" solution often left out vital elements.

Technological and sociological "imperialism" provide many additional examples where the input of all the stakeholders is not taken into account. Of course, much of the history of the US government's treatment of the Native Americans was an avoidance of truly including all the stakeholders.

A challenge in applying the "Who Speaks for Wolf" pattern is to judge honestly and correctly whether, indeed, someone does have the knowledge and delegation to "speak for Wolf." If such a person is not present, we may do well to put off design or decision until such a person, or better, "Wolf" can be present.

Related Patterns: Radical Co-location (Provided all stakeholders are present in the radical co-location, this tends to insure that their input will be given at appropriate times).

Known Uses: As a variant of this, a prototype creativity tool has been created (See www.research.ibm.com/knowsoc/prototypes_directors.html). The idea is to have a "board of directors" consisting of famous people. When you have a problem to solve, you are supposed to be reminded of, and think about, how various people would approach this problem. Ask yourself, "What would Einstein have said?" "How would Gandhi have approached this problem?" And so on.

19.3.2   Reality Check

Abstract: In developing complex systems, we often monitor effectiveness based on ersatz measures of what we are really interested in assessing and controlling. This is expedient in the short term but often leads to serious problems and distortions. Actions based on these measures or models of reality rather than on reality itself result in negative consequences. The solution is to perform regular "reality checks" to insure that measures or indicators of reality continue to reflect reality.

Problem: In developing complex systems, it is often expedient to develop feedback loops based on ersatz measures of what we are really interested in assessing and controlling. While this seems expedient in the short term, it often leads to serious problems and distortions, particularly in times of crisis or transition when the correlation between ersatz measures and actuality substantially drifts or even suddenly disconnects. Actions can be based on these measures or models of reality rather than on reality. This can result in negative consequences.

Context: Many problems were partly responsible for the disaster at the Three Mile Island. One crucial problem in particular arose from the design of a feedback loop. A switch was supposed to close a valve. Beside the switch was a light that was supposed to show that the valve was closed. In fact, rather than having the light actually go on as the result of feedback from the valve closure itself, the signal light was merely a collateral circuit to the switch. All it actually showed was that the switch had moved position (Wickens 1983). Under normal operation; that is, when the valve was operating normally, these two events were perfectly correlated. At a critical point in the meltdown, however, the valve was not operating properly and an operator believed that the valve was closed even though it failed to close. The resulting actions, taken on the basis of the assumption that the valve was closed, exacerbated the problems.

In running an application program recently, I was given a feedback message that a file was posted. In fact, it wasn't. The programmer, rather than checking to see whether the file was actually posted, merely relied on the completion of a loop.

In advertising campaigns, it is difficult to measure the impact of ads on sales. Instead, companies typically measure the "recall" and "recognition" rates of ads. This may often be correlated with sales changes, but in some cases, the ad may be very memorable but give the customer a very negative impression of the company or product and decrease the chances of actually selling a product.

Historically, monarchs and dictators often surrounded themselves only with people who gave them good reports and support no matter how their decisions impacted the reality of their realm. Eventually, the performance of such people tended to deteriorate over time because their behavior was shaped by this ersatz feedback rather than reality.

During the "oil crisis" in the 1970s, oil companies relied on mathematical models of continually increasing demand. Year after year, for 7 years, they relied on these models to predict demand despite the fact that, for 7 years, demand actually went down. The results are purported to have cost them tens of billions of dollars (Van der Heijden 1996).

Forces:
- Organizations are often hierarchically decomposed and bureaucratic. Therefore, it is often simplest to communicate with those close to us in the hierarchy and to build systems that rely for their model of reality only on things within the immediate control span of our small part of the organization.
- While more comfortable to limit system design and development to those things within one's own team or department, it is often precisely the work necessary to capture more reality based measures that will reveal additional challenges and opportunities in business process coherence.
- The measure of reality is often more time-consuming, more costly, or more difficult than the measure of something more proximal that is often correlated with reality.
- It is likely to be exactly at times of crisis and transition that the correlation between proximal ersatz measures and their referent in reality will be destroyed.
- It is likely to be exactly under times of crisis and transition that people will tend to simplify their cognitive models of the world and, among other things, forget that the proximal measure is only ersatz.

Solution: Therefore: Whenever feasible, feedback in any process should be based on reality checks, not on ersatz measures. When this is too costly (as opposed to merely inconvenient or uncomfortable), then at least design systems so that the correlation between proximal measures and their referent in reality is double checked periodically.

Examples: Rather than rely solely on a circle of politically minded advisors, Peter the Great disguised himself and checked out various situations in Russia in person.

Known Uses: Richard Feynman (1997), during the Manhattan project, noticed that the bureaucracy was worried about the possibility of accidentally stockpiling a critical mass of uranium. To prevent this, each section chief was required to insure that their section did not have a critical mass. To insure this, each section chief instructed each sub-section chief to insure that their sub-section didn't have a critical mass and so on, down to the smallest level of the bureaucracy. Upon hearing this plan, Feynman observed that neutrons probably didn't much care whose sub-section they "reported to"!

In another incident, various bureaucrats were each trying to prove that they had better security than their peers. In order to prove this, they escalated the buying of bigger and thicker safes. The bigger and thicker the safe, the more they felt that they had made their secrets secure (and by implication, the more important their secrets and the associated work). Feynman discovered that more than half of the "super-safe" safes had been left with the factory installed combinations of 50-50-50 and were trivially easy to break into.

19.3.3 Radical Co-location

Abstract: When small to medium teams of people need to solve a problem or design a novel solution and there are many highly interactive parts, it is useful for the people to work in one large room where people have easy access to each other and shared work objects can be easily viewed, modified, and referred to when necessary (Teasley et al. 2000).

Problem: Some problems are amenable to decomposition; that is, the overall problem can be broken down into a series of sub-problems and when each of the sub-problems is solved, the overall problem will be solved, possibly with slight modification to some of the sub-solutions. In other cases, especially problems that are relatively novel, complex, or "wicked", such decomposition is not possible *a priori*. If decomposition is attempted and each of the sub-problems is solved, the resulting composition of sub-solutions will not be anything close to an overall solution. Under these circumstances, people working alone on their sub-problem will become frustrated because all the progress they thought they had made will prove illusory. Morale will suffer. Management will become upset that the apparent progress has not been real and typically attempt a variety of counter-productive measures such as requiring more frequent reports and adding new personnel to meet a schedule (cf. Brooks 1975).

Context: In the design of complex systems with many interacting parts, it is often the case that understanding how best to "decompose" a problem cannot be determined ahead of time. Examples include complex software systems, especially where the overall system includes human-human and human-computer interaction, new machinery, novel nuclear power plant designs, and complex military operations.

In such a context, handing out separate "assignments" to various individuals or small teams will at first seem to produce progress as each individual or small team carries out their assignment. Unfortunately, when an attempt is made to compose or integrate these sub-solutions into an overall solution, the result doesn't work because of unanticipated interactions.

For instance, suppose that a software development team is designing an integrated office support package. Independently, various teams or individuals design various functions. Each of these may be well designed in itself. However, the combination will be flawed on at least three counts. First, numerous functions will have been duplicated in separate modules. Second, some functionality that would have been useful for the whole package will not have been implemented at all because it would have been too much work for any one team. Third, the user experience will be scattered and inconsistent as separate designers make independent choices about what the user experience will be. In addition, it is quite likely that hard bugs will also be in the design due to the inconsistent treatment of data objects, deadlocks, infinite loops, etc.

There are two main general solutions common in the software development community. First, there may be an attempt to set "ground rules" or "style guides" that everyone is supposed to follow. These will help ameliorate the problem but cannot solve it entirely. Second, there may be overall project meetings where people report on progress or even do mutual design reviews. Again, this helps but even if problems are found and resolved, the resolution will require considerable rework.

Forces:
- People are naturally gregarious.
- People can concentrate better on difficult mental tasks when it is quiet and when there are a minimum of interruptions.
- Some problems are amenable to decomposition into relatively independent sub-problems; others are not.
- Social cues can be used to guide how interruptible are others.
- Having work-related shared artifacts that can be viewed and understood by others continually leads to productivity.
- Shuffling work artifacts in and out of view in a small space takes time.
- Space costs money and is therefore limited.
- A group will tend to develop useful social conventions when they are co-located.
- Noticing and resolving conflicts among sub-solutions early will result in minimizing rework.
- Noticing common problems and solving them collectively as soon as possible will result in maximum efficiency.
- Human performance often shows a "social facilitation" effect; that is, people perform better in the presence of others.

Solution: When small to medium sized teams work on non-decomposable problems, it is useful for them to be radically co-located in one large room. This room should provide each person some private space and individual work tools (e.g., a computer, a drawing table) as well as numerous spaces for public display of large scale work artifacts (e.g., designs, work plans, diagrams, decisions, group rules, etc.).

Examples: In the Manhattan Project, people from all over the United States were relocated to a relatively remote and isolated area. There they had large workrooms to work on complex problems together.

Recently, automobile companies have empirically compared software work teams that were radically co-located with traditional software development and found the former to be significantly more productive. Interestingly, although before the experience, people thought that they would hate working in a single room, afterwards they said they preferred it.

Resulting Context: Prior to the experiments at the auto companies, developers were afraid that they would be too distracted by noise and interruptions to get much work done. In fact, social cues can be read fairly well and a potential interrupter can gauge the time to interrupt. In radical co-location, a person might have to wait minutes or hours to resolve an issue by conversation and mutual problem solving. In traditional software development, they may have to wait for a weekly meeting or not discover a problem until integration testing. People working under conditions of radical co-location tend to develop common vocabulary and artifacts quickly and can easily and efficiently refer to these artifacts. Motivationally, it is also easier to see where the individual's work fits into the larger whole.

Rationale: In a complex problem solving process, it is most efficient to solve the most difficult constraints first. Similarly, the sooner potential design conflicts or potential design commonalities are discovered, the more efficient the global optimization. Social groups that work together can rely on subtle cues about whether to interrupt or not. Being alone in the office may seem more conducive to concentration but is still amenable to a knock on the door or a phone call; in this case, the person interrupting generally does not know the state of concentration of the person being interrupted. When we work separately, it is easy to imagine that others are "slacking off." If we actually see all of our colleagues working, it tends to motivate us to work harder as well.

19.3.4 Small Successes Early

Abstract: Some problems require large teams of relative strangers to work together cooperatively in order to solve the overall problem. Yet, people generally take time to learn to trust one another as well as to learn another's strengths and weaknesses and preferred styles. Plunging a large group of strangers immediately into a complex task often results in non-productive jockeying for position, failure, blaming, finger-pointing, etc. Therefore, insure that the team or community first undertakes a task that is likely to bring some small success before engaging in a more complex and challenging effort.

Context: A complex undertaking requires the interaction of many people with various backgrounds, skills, and temperaments. Often, whether in an industrial setting or a community building effort, many of these people have not worked together before. The group wants to get started and wants to be successful. Although their diversity is a potential source of strength, at first, there is likely to be natural confusion about how to proceed because people will have different experiences about the best way to organize and proceed.

Forces:
• Problems are often too complex for all aspects to be addressed simultaneously.
• If a problem is understood, it is logically better to deal with the hardest constraints first.

- The structure of complex problems often becomes clearer as one tries to solve the problem.
- A part of any complex problem solving process requiring more than one person is the interaction and relationship among the people.
- People in a new team need to learn about each other's skills, working styles, and trustworthiness.
- When people get frustrated because of non-success, they tend to blame each other.
- As people work toward a goal, the goal tends to become viewed as more valuable and therefore people are willing to work harder to reach it.

Solution: Therefore, when bringing new teams or organizations together, it is useful to begin with a small success. In this way, people begin to learn about each other and trust each other. People learn more about the nature of the problem domain. This makes tackling more difficult problems later relatively easier.

Example: At the kick-off to a new software development project, rather than having the people be invited to "attend" an event that is "thrown" for them, encourage them to organize a party, cook-out, pot-luck, song-fest, or storytelling event among themselves. In the process of organizing and carrying out this activity, they will learn about each other's styles, learn about the trustworthiness of others, and be encouraged by having a success.

Alternatively, the team might simply work on an aspect of the problem to be solved, provided it is something fairly clear that will result in "success" quickly. For instance, the team might initially work profitably on a short presentation about the project, a poster, or a scenario but not immediately jump into working on a systems design or a requirements document.

Rationale: As people experience team success, they tend to view the others in the team more positively. Teamwork is often hard under the best of circumstances. In highly complex problems, when people come together from different cultures, backgrounds, or agendas, it often becomes so difficult as to seem impossible. Rather than having people simultaneously attempt to solve a complex problem *and* at the same time learn to work together as a team, it is often more effective to separate the otherwise tangled problems.

First, have the people solve a tractable problem where it is clear that they have a common agenda. A successful experience working together to solve that simple problem will help people learn each other's styles, strengths, weaknesses and so on. With this knowledge and trust, they can now move on to try to solve more difficult problems.

The human factors psychologist James Welford was called in as a consultant to deal with what appeared to be a very large age effect. People over 35 were having a tremendous difficulty learning new hand weaves. The difficulty, as Welford discovered, was in two tangled problems. On the one hand, it was hard to see the actual threads and second, it was hard to learn the patterns. What Welford did was introduce a short training segment with very large, quite visible cords. Once people had mastered that, they were transferred to the much smaller production size. This eliminated the "age effect" and in fact, both older and younger people learned much more effectively and efficiently.

In similar fashion, we argue that trying to solve a complex problem with virtual strangers, especially when there is reason to believe there may be a difference in agendas, is a "tangled problem." Untangling the getting to know people from the complex task will help insure ultimate success.

Some care should be given to the task and setting. The "small successes early" task should allow some degree of give and take, some opportunity for expressive, not just instrumental communication. People should have the opportunity and space for doing something creative, for sharing stories, for physical interaction.

19.3.5 Narrative Insight Method

Abstract: Experts learn valuable lessons from their experiences that could help guide less experienced people. In small trusted groups, a natural, effective, and traditional way for experts to share their knowledge is to trade stories with each other while novices listen. A challenge for large organizations is to extend this method to larger groups and non-co-located personnel. Writing stories is a possibility; however, in many cases experts are too busy to write stories and find the process difficult and unnatural. In addition, when the number of stories in a story base is large, it becomes difficult for a user to find the ones most relevant to the particular case at hand. We suggest a method that minimizes the time of the expert, allows them to tell stories in a natural setting and organizes the knowledge in a useful manner.

Problem: Experts have valuable knowledge based on their experience. However, experts in organizations are typically very busy people. They are willing to share stories informally and orally but do not necessarily have the skill or patience to write stories. Moreover, it can be difficult to find stories relevant to a specific situation.

Context: Less expert people in a large organization or community of practice want to learn from more experienced people. This is beneficial for the individuals as well as for the larger organization or community of practice. Some of the people who have relevant knowledge may be far away physically from the people who need the knowledge. In many cases, much of the most valuable knowledge of experts is tacit knowledge. There are likely to be people available who may not be expert in the subject matter but have relatively more expertise in writing stories and organizing educational materials. The experts in a given subject matter are typically very busy and in most cases, may lack the skills to produce good written stories.

Forces:
- The time of experts is valuable
- Subject matter experts may not be experts in producing educational materials.
- People expert in producing education materials need to gain access to high quality content.

- In many fields, much of the most important knowledge that experts gain through their experience is in the form of tacit knowledge.
- Tacit knowledge is not well communicated by formal methods but is well communicated by stories.
- Experts telling stories orally to small groups that contain other experts as well as some novices, is a natural way for experts to share experience.
- Storytelling occurs only when the social situation is right.
- Telling a story increases the probability that someone else in a group will tell a story.
- Producing written stories requires special skill.
- Finding stories relevant to a given situation requires thoughtful metadata.
- Experts who have experience relevant to novices may be remotely located from them.
- Different learners learn best at different rates, by different media, and in different styles.

Solution: Provide an informal setting conducive to storytelling; this is encouraged by several factors. (1) Provide non-standard seating arrangements with easily movable chairs. (2) Conduct in a room with an informal atmosphere. (3) The structure and content of the invitation should be friendly but make clear the importance of the activity. (4) Gather a commitment to participate, making sure people know their time commitment is for one hour only. (5) Provide friendly but clear reminders near the time of the session with an additional check on the commitment to participate. (6) Provide refreshments at the beginning of the meeting. (7) Limit participation to a group of 8–20. (8) Groups should include experts as well as people knowledgeable in the topic but less expert. (9) Set expectations both prior to and during the session that people will be sharing stories, (E.g., "We find that when a group of experts get together like this, they generally end up telling stories about their experiences."). (10) Make the recording clear but not obtrusive, and model storytelling at the outset.

During the session itself: (1) Greet people warmly and thank them for coming. (2) Break people into 3–4 smaller groups. (3) Each group should include a facilitator/recorder. (4) Digitally record the sessions with separate high quality tape recorders for each subgroup. (5) Tell the subgroups that they will be sharing stories based on their experiences and that then the group will choose one story from each subgroup to share with the larger group. (6) Implement this plan. (7) Facilitate to gently guide people back to telling stories of concrete instances. (8) After each subgroup shares its story with the whole group, allow discussion to continue, encouraging but not insisting on storytelling.

Examples This methodology was used to provide learning materials in the form of stories for NOTES 5, focusing not on how to invoke specific functions but rather on how to use NOTES to enhance the user's work practices or enhance team coordination and communication. We have also used this methodology to develop stories about "boundary spanning skills." Finally, we have also used this method to develop learning materials for the IBM Patent Process.

19.4 Discussion of the Application and Formation of Patterns and Pattern Languages

The particular Patterns chosen for this chapter are meant to show the range of ways in which Patterns arise as well as the wide range of ways that they can be applied. For example, "Small Successes Early" can be applied at many levels of organization from thinking about reducing international conflicts to large scale software development projects to an individual writing code in a new area. Similarly, "Reality Check" can be applied at the level of wondering whether Gross Domestic Product is the best "metric" of national economic health to considering whether salary is the best indicator of which job an individual should taken. In general, the Patterns presented here may be applied at the level of individual creativity, group interaction, setting organizational context or for influencing the larger societal context to support and promote creativity.

Patterns may also provide a relatively low-cost and succinct way of providing (partial) design rationale. In the case of Human Computer Interaction Patterns and Object-Oriented Programming Patterns, such rationale applies primarily to the design *product* and would be referred to by user experience professionals and programmers respectively. The Patterns suggested in this chapter refer more often to the *process* of design. They might be referred to by development managers, for example, as a rationale for why they are doing what they are doing in terms of governance.

Pattern Languages also provide an interesting case of an attempt to generalize. Clearly, good design depends to a great extent upon the particulars of users, tasks, and context as well as what technologies are available. Yet, it seems odd to suppose that *nothing* can be generalized across situations. Patterns attempt to do this in a way that is more specific than general principles; e.g., "consider the users" and less specific than, say, cognitive modeling (e.g., Bellamy et al. 2011). They are a way of communicating knowledge which often incorporates both literary and artistic representations as well as argumentation and reference to empirical results. They are a way of knowing that is integrative among not only explicit symbol-based cognition but also includes perceptual and empathic ways of knowing. Pattern Languages also provide a way of knowing that is neither overly concrete nor overly abstract and therefore may offer a convenient way to generalize lessons learned among case studies involving a range of types of users, tasks, and technologies. Of course, exactly how widely to generalize for best results is not specifiable ahead of time. It is the attempted application of a Pattern that teaches how and when to apply it and, in some cases, points to a need for re-writing or reconsideration.

Pattern Languages in Human-Computer Interaction, as well as in the above-mentioned domains, may play a role *throughout* the development process. That is, they help one not only *solve* problems, but also help *find and formulate* problems. Unlike traditional scientific theories, suggested Patterns are not typically tested against each other (though that is sometimes possible); rather, suggested Patterns may be aggregated and combined, refined, or split as well as discarded. This means that the Pattern Language approach is particularly suitable to community development and tends to foster cooperation rather than competition.

While many HCI techniques such as empirical studies or modeling may require considerable educational effort before other stakeholders in a complex development process understand, let alone admit any credence to them, Pattern Languages may be stated in ways that are more immediately understandable to parties with different values, backgrounds, and interests and may therefore serve as a kind of *lingua franca* (Erickson 2000). Patterns can address the whole spectrum of HCI-related issues from the specifics of interaction design and user interface to the utility and aesthetics of applications and the broader social issues implied by decisions about the design of tools, work, and the workplace.

Patterns can be sourced in many ways. Specific experimental results may inspire Patterns. For example, "Radical Co-location" is closely related to Olson and Olson (2000) and Teasley et al. (2000). New inventions may be expressed or lead to Patterns; for example, the Pattern "Abstract Social Proxy" is the concept of social translucence exemplified in Babble (Erickson and Kellogg 2000) put into Pattern form. Patterns may be suggested based on metaphor from other domains. For example, many of Christopher Alexander's Patterns in physical space may well have analogues in on-line social spaces; for instance, "Gradients of Privacy" makes sense in many on-line contexts as well as physical ones. In some cases, Patterns may be gleaned from the traditional wisdom of other cultures ("Who Speaks for Wolf?" Thomas et al. 2002). While inspired by that story, I would not have written it in the form of a Pattern unless the story also resonated with many of my own personal experiences and lessons learned. One of the Patterns in this chapter, "Small Successes Early" was inspired by an example from *Peopleware* (Demarco and Lister 1999) which similarly resonated with many of my own personal experiences leading an artificial intelligence lab (Thomas 2008) as well as some of the suggestions in *How to Solve It* (Polya 1945). In the case of "Reality Check", the suggested Pattern is based on my own experience in managing groups, in observing issues in corporate governance and in observing roadblocks in individual problem solving (Thomas 1974). As these examples indicate, the initial inspiration for Patterns can come from many kinds of sources but are generally retroactively tested for generality against personal experience. Additional sources of cross-checking include what I know of the business literature, the software development literature, the literature on human computer interaction and computer supported cooperative work and the literature on creativity. I do not do, nor know do I know how to do, an exhaustive check of the entirety of such literatures for examples and counter-examples. It is possible that the interpretation of my own experience leads to a personal bias which in turn impacts my choice of, say, business books that reinforce the value of diversity. Patterns, however, are meant to be understandable and accessible to a wide audience. The point of publishing them is to gain feedback on how they work in practice as well as whether they seem to contradict knowledge in any domain.

Patterns and Pattern Languages however, may not appeal to everyone. If we look at the biographical data of people who have been highly successful in creative fields, we see that they use a wide variety of methods. In the realm of poetry, we have reported cases such as the "composition" of the *Xanadu* fragment by Cooleridge which he claims to have "transcribed" from an opium dream. At the other extreme, we have the supposedly (though not universally accepted) deliberative process of

Edgar Allen Poe in writing *The Raven* which gives a design rationale for virtually every decision (Poe 1846). An analogous contrast has been made between the compositions of Mozart and Beethoven respectively. It is perhaps then not surprising that with respect to Pattern Languages, one finds both enthusiastic supporters and those who not only do not find them personally useful but object to their potential usefulness on *a priori* grounds as being antithetical to creativity.

This controversy about the potential usefulness of Pattern Languages as a design and creativity tool naturally leads to the question of empirical validation. While on the surface such a question seems quite reasonable, in practice, attempting to "prove" or "demonstrate" the effectives of Pattern Languages as a tool is fraught with difficulties as outlined below.

Pattern Languages are potentially useful at many stages in the overall process of creativity and further, at least some of their value is in being able to use such Pattern Languages *throughout* the design process. This tends to make evaluation a lengthy process. Second, the value of a Pattern Language come partly after being familiar with the complete language and having some practice with it. This long familiarization period means that evaluation requires a long preparation phase. Third, as hinted above, it may well be the case that a Pattern Language is particularly well-suited only to certain types of creative people, groups, or situations. It may well be too structured to suit some and too ill-structured to suit others, inviting instead a middle-ground of abstraction based on previous experience. Fourth, the proposed benefit of Pattern Languages is on the effectiveness of resulting designs. The effectiveness of designs is not an easy thing to measure. For example, in the domain of HCI Patterns, one would ideally compare the interfaces that resulted from groups of people either using or not using an HCI Pattern Language. But if there were as few as 15 people in each group, one would ideally then do a subsequent usability evaluation on 30 different designs!

It is also of some note that the difficulties inherent in the empirical validation of the usefulness of Pattern Languages are not unique. In most cases, the general practice of a field changes over time despite the lack of any definitive empirical evaluation that the new practice is better than the old practice. Despite these caveats and difficulties, there have been some attempts to demonstrate the effectiveness of Pattern Languages. In particular, Dearden and Finlay (2006) provide an extensive critical review of HCI and Pattern Languages. Their review shows only one study of the effectiveness of Patterns in HCI (Chung et al. 2004) and none in object-oriented software design. Subsequently, however, Koukouletsos et al. (2007) show a significant difference in student design performance favoring Patterns over Guidelines.

19.5 Conclusion and Summary

In this chapter, I have explored the premise that Patterns and Pattern Languages are one useful way to help enhance group creativity. Further, a number of specific Patterns that could prove useful in various situations have been outlined and two

Patterns have been presented in detail. It seems unlikely that the potential utility of such an approach to real world problems will be settled by detailed empirical comparisons. More likely, practice will gradually evolve to include the greater use of Patterns and Pattern Languages – or not.

References

Alexander, C., Ishikawaa, S., & Silverstein, M. (1977). *A pattern language*. New York: Oxford University Press.

Bayle, E., Bellamy, R., Casaday, G., Erickson, T., Fincher, S., Grinter, B., Gross, B., Lehder, D., Marmolin, H., Potts, C., Skousen, G., & Thomas, J. C. (1997). Putting it all together: Toward a pattern language for interaction design. Summary report of the CHI'97 workshop. *SIGCHI Bulletin, 30*(1), New York: ACM.

Bellamy, R. John, B. E., & Kogan, S. (2011). Deploying CogTool: integrating quantitative usability assessment into real-world software development. In *Proceeding of the 33rd International Conference on Software Engineering (ICSE '11)* (pp. 691–700). New York, NY, USA: ACM.

Borchers, J. (2001). *A pattern approach to interaction design*. West Sussex: Wiley.

Brooks, F. (1975). *The mythical man-month: Essays on software engineering*. Boston: Addison-Wesley.

Chung, E. S., Hong, J. I., Lin, J., Prabaker, M. K., Landay, J. A., & Lin, A. L. (2004). Development and evaluation of emerging design patterns for ubiquitous computing. In *Proceedings of DIS 2004* (pp. 233–242). New York:ACM Press.

Coplien, J. O., & Harrison, N. B. (2004). *Organizational patterns of agile software development*. Upper Saddle River: Prentice Hall.

Dearden, A., & Finley, J. (2006). Pattern languages in HCI: A critical review. *Human Computer Interaction, 21*(1), 1–71.

DeMarco, T., & Lister, T. (1999). *Peopleware: Productive projects and teams*. New York: Dorset House Publishing.

Erickson, T. (2000). Lingua franca for design: Sacred places and pattern languages. In *Proceedings of DIS 2000*. New York: ACM.

Erickson, T., & Kellogg, W. A. (2000). Social translucence: an approach to designing systems that support social processes. *ACM Transactions on Computer-Human Interaction, 7*(1), 59–83. doi:10.1145/344949.345004 DOI:dx.doi.org.

Feynman, R. P. (1997). *Surely you're joking Mr. Feynman: Adventures of a curious character*. New York: Norton.

Gamma, E., Helm, R., Johnson, R., & Vlissides, J. (1995). *Design patterns: Elements of resusable object-oriented software*. Reading: Addison-Wesley.

Koukouletsos, K., Khazaei, B., Dearden, A., & Ozcan, M. (2007). Teaching usability principles with patterns and guidelines. In *Proceedings of HCI educators*. Berlin: Springer.

Norman, D. (1988). *The psychology of everyday things*. New York: Basic Books.

Olson, G. M., & Olson, J. S. (2000). Distance matters. *Human Computer Interaction, 15*, 131–178.

Poe, E. A. (1846). *The philosophy of composition*. Philadelphia: Graham's American Monthly.

Polya, G. (1945). *How to solve it*. Princeton: Princeton University Press. ISBN 0-691-08097-6.

Schuler, D. (2008). *Liberating voices a pattern language for communication revolution*. Cambridge, MA: MIT Press.

Teasley, S., Covi, L., Krishnan, M. S., & Olson, J. S. (2000). How does radical collocation help a team succeed? *CSCW proceedings of the ACM Conference on Computer-Supported Cooperative Work*. New York: ACM.

Thomas, J. C. (1974). An analysis of behavior in the hobbits-orcs problem. *Cognitive Psychology, 6*, 257–269.

Thomas, J. C. (2008). Fun at work: Managing HCI with the peopleware perspective. In T. Erickson & D. McDonald (Eds.), *HCI remixed*. Cambridge, MA: MIT Press.

Thomas, J., Lee, A., & Danis, C. (2002). *Who speaks for wolf?* (IBM research report 2264). Yorktown Heights: IBM.

Underwood, P. (1983). *Who speaks for Wolf? A native American learning story*. San Anselmo: Tribe of Two Press.

Van der Heijden, K. (1996). *Scenarios: The art of strategic conversation*. Chichester: Wiley.

Wickens, C. (1983). *Engineering psychology and human performance*. Columbus: Merrill.

Chapter 20
Collaborative Design Rationale and Social Creativity in Cultures of Participation

Gerhard Fischer and Frank Shipman

Abstract The rise in social computing has facilitated a shift from consumer cultures, focused on producing finished media to be consumed passively, to cultures of participation, where people can access the means to participate actively in personally meaningful problems. These developments represent unique and fundamental opportunities and challenges for rethinking and reinventing design rationale and creativity, as people acclimate to taking part in computer-mediated conversations of issues and their solutions. Grounded in our long-term research exploring these topics, this chapter articulates arguments, describes and discusses conceptual frameworks and system developments (in the context of three case studies), and provides evidence that design rationale and creativity need not be at odds with each other. Coordinating and integrating collective design rationale and social creatively provide new synergies and opportunities, particularly amid complex, open-ended, and ill-defined design problems requiring contributions and collaboration of multiple stakeholders supported by socio-technical environments in cultures of participation.

Keywords Collaborative design • Creativity • Cultures of participation • Design • Design exploration • Design rationale • Domain-oriented design environments • Envisionment and Discovery Collaboratory • Incremental formalization • Metadesign • Science of design • Social creativity • Spatial hypertext • Visual Knowledge Builder

G. Fischer (✉)
Center for LifeLong Learning and Design (L3D), Department of Computer Science and Institute of Cognitive Science, University of Colorado, Campus Box 430, Boulder, CO 80309-0430, USA
e-mail: gerhard@colorado.edu

F. Shipman
Center for the Study of Digital Libraries, Department of Computer Science, Texas A&M University, College Station, TX 77843-3112, USA
e-mail: shipman@cs.tamu.edu

J.M. Carroll (ed.), *Creativity and Rationale: Enhancing Human Experience by Design*, Human–Computer Interaction Series, DOI 10.1007/978-1-4471-4111-2_20, © Springer-Verlag London 2013

20.1 Introduction

Most of the pressing and important design problems of today's world are systemic problems that make collaboration supported by new technologies not a luxury but a necessity. These systemic problems—including the design of policies to address environmental degradation, economic disparity, and the disappearance of local cultures in the age of globalization, to name a few—are complex, open-ended, and ill-defined (Rittel and Webber 1984; Simon 1996), requiring

- contributions of many minds, particularly from the people who "own" problems and are directly affected by them;
- the integration of problem framing and problem solving, where the understanding of the problem co-evolves with the activity of designing a solution (Schön 1983);
- communication and collaboration among people from different disciplines and educational levels (Clark and Brennan 1991); and
- intelligent use of technologies and resources that support collective knowledge construction where multiple people contribute to a shared knowledge representation (Arias et al. 2001).

These problems need contributions from people with a wide range of experiences and perspectives, including stakeholders representing all those affected by the design results. The problems also often evolve over time, providing unique new challenges for design rationale and creativity research.

In this chapter we first describe our understanding of the cultures of participation that are becoming more common on the Web, where volunteers share design activities with professional designers. We then discuss design and design rationale, and use our past work to articulate some of the challenges of supporting collaborative design to be addressed by the following sections. This is followed by arguments for the social nature of creativity and discussion on how metadesign and the seeding, evolutionary growth, reseeding model support collaborative design rationale and social creativity. Then three case studies are presented, describing (a) the Envisionment and Discovery Collaboratory, a long-term research platform exploring conceptual frameworks for social creativity and democratizing design in the context of complex design problems; (b) the Design Exploration Builder and Analyzer; and (c) the Visual Knowledge Builder that illustrates incremental formalization. These demonstrate how the more general ideas were pursued in specific contexts. We end the chapter by presenting implications and conclusions.

20.2 Cultures of Participation

While initially a space where anyone could publish almost anything, the World Wide Web in its first decade led to a separation between designers and consumers for many forms of content. New technological developments, such as Web 2.0 architectures and infrastructures (O'Reilly 2005), have emerged to support a social or participatory Web, where people use comments, annotations, blogs, and so forth to converse with others about topics of interest. These developments are the foundations for a fundamental shift from consumer cultures, in which people passively consume finished goods produced by others, to cultures of participation, in which all people are provided with the means to participate actively in personally meaningful activities.

Consumer cultures go hand in hand with professionally dominated cultures characterized by a small number of producers and a large number of consumers. The traditional information cultures surrounding the systemic problems introduced above (e.g., policy design) are traditionally based on strong input filters (e.g., editorial boards deciding what gets published, low acceptance rates for conferences and journals), where relatively small information repositories are created. The advantage is the likelihood that the quality and trustworthiness of the accumulated information is high, and that relatively weak output filters are required. The disadvantages of this model are that it greatly limits that "all voices can be heard"; that most people are limited only to accessing existing information; and that potentially relevant information (which may be of great value not at a global level, but for the work of specific individuals) may not be incorporated into the information repository.

Cultures of participation can be characterized by weak input filters that allow users to become active contributors engaging in informed participation (Brown et al. 1994). Cultures of participation provide a framework to rethink design rationale and creativity from the following perspectives:

- by enabling users to innovate, they can develop exactly what they want, rather than relying on developers to act as their agents; this democratizes innovation by putting the owners of problems in charge (von Hippel 2005);
- by breaking down many of the distinctions between designers and users through metadesign (i.e., designing tools so that they can be redesigned by the end users and designing tools for use by designers; Fischer and Giaccardi 2006) many more voices can be heard and social creativity can be supported (Fischer et al. 2005);
- by decentralizing design (Benkler 2006), the power of the long tail (Anderson 2006) and the wisdom of crowds (Surowiecki 2005) can be exploited.

We are exploring numerous themes in our efforts to understand, foster, and support cultures of participation with social computing, including

- Models of community (Fischer 2001; Wenger 1998): how the shared knowledge and common ground necessary for effective communication are created to support mutual learning and collaborative problem solving;
- Distributed intelligence (Salomon 1993): the idea that intelligence is not located in a single mind but is distributed among people and tools that work together, and emerges in the process of problem solving;
- Reflection: helping individuals and communities intelligently monitor, assess, and adapt their work through such processes as "reflection-in-action" and "reflection-on-action," where conscious evaluation of an action's effects occur during or after design (Schön 1983);

- Sociotechnical design (Mumford 2000): with emphasis on the evolutionary creation of effective learning and problem-solving environments made possible with new media and having interacting social and technical components; and
- Exploiting knowledge sources from the "Long Tail" (Anderson 2006): engaging learners in self-directed learning activities about which they feel passionate.

20.3 Design and Design Rationale

Design is a ubiquitous activity that is practiced in everyday life as well as in the workplace by professionals (Cross 1984; Schön 1983; Simon 1996). It is not restricted to any specific discipline, such as art or architecture, but instead is a broad human activity that pursues the question of "how things ought to be," as compared to the natural sciences, which study "how things are" (Simon 1996). It is a fundamental activity within all professions: Architects and urban planners design buildings and towns, educators design curricula and courses, people in the creative practices design new artifacts with new media, citizens from around the world contribute 3D models to be displayed in Google Earth, and software engineers design socio-technical environments for people with cognitive disabilities (Fischer 2010).

Design problems can be framed in different ways and they have no unique answers. A core activity of design is not only problem solving but also continual problem finding and problem framing, the selection of a framework with which to discuss and/or model the problem (Rittel 1984). It is a process of dealing with the kind of "messy situations" (Rittel and Webber 1984) that are characterized by uncertainty, conflict, and uniqueness, and it can best be characterized by creativity, judgment, and dilemma handling, rather than by objective scientific methods.

Design rationale (or *argumentation*, which will be used as a synonym) represents and articulates the reasoning underlying the design process that explains, derives, and justifies design decisions. A complete account of the reasoning relevant to design decisions is

- not possible because some design decisions and the associated reasoning are made implicitly by construction and are not available to conscious thinking (e.g., decisions based on tacit knowledge). Some of the rationale must be reconstructed after design decisions have been made; and
- not desirable because many design issues are trivial; their resolution is obvious (Schön 1983) to the competent designer, or the design issue is not very relevant to the overall quality of the designed artifact. Accounting for all reasoning is not desirable because it would divert too many resources from designing itself.

The promise of design rationale is achieved if it helps designers

- to improve their own work;
- to cooperate with other people holding stakes in the design;

- to understand existing artifacts (i.e., to communicate with past designers); and
- to trigger critical thought (i.e., writing an idea down allows designers to make the transition from simply creating that idea to reflecting about it).

Collaborative design is a necessity rather than a luxury because most important design problems are complex, requiring social creativity in which stakeholders from different disciplines must collaborate. Design rationale can serve as a memory aid not only to individuals but also to groups (Conklin and Begeman 1988) by providing a forum for airing issues crucial for coordinating group activities. It is useful for triggering and focusing discussion among members of a project team. By making the processes of reasoning public, it extends the number of people who can participate in the critical reflection on decisions, thereby reducing the chances of missing important considerations.

20.3.1   Our Past Design Rationale Research

In an article titled "Making Argumentation Serve Design" (Fischer et al. 1996), we argued that construction is essential for design, for no design project can be completed until the construction is done. Based on Schön's (1983) work, we conceptualized design not primarily as a form of problem solving, information processing, or search, but as a kind of making and creating environments in which design knowledge and reasoning could be expressed in designers' transactions with materials, artifacts made, conditions under which they are made, and manner of making.

These ideas led to the development of a class of systems called *domain-oriented design environments* (DODEs; Fischer 1994). A prominent example was JANUS, a DODE for kitchen design (see Figs. 20.1 and 20.2).

The short messages the critics presented to designers did not reflect the complex reasoning behind the corresponding design issues. To overcome this shortcoming, we initially developed a static explanation component for the critic messages. The design of this component was based on the assumption that there is a "right" answer to a problem. However, the explanation component proved to be unable to account for the deliberative nature of design problems. To enrich the "back-talk" of the situation, argumentation about issues raised by critics must be supported and argumentation must be integrated into the context of construction.

The core ideas relevant for design rationale and creativity that we developed and analyzed in the context of our DODEs research were:

- to make argumentation serve design and to support reflection-in-action and reflection-on-action (Schön 1983), we had to link action (construction; see Fig. 20.1) with argumentation (reflection; see Fig. 20.2); this was achieved with critiquing systems (see "messages" pane in Fig. 20.1; Fischer et al. 1998);
- to avoid designers being taken off-task with elaborate design rationale recording activities, incremental formalization (Shipman 1993; Shipman and McCall 1994;

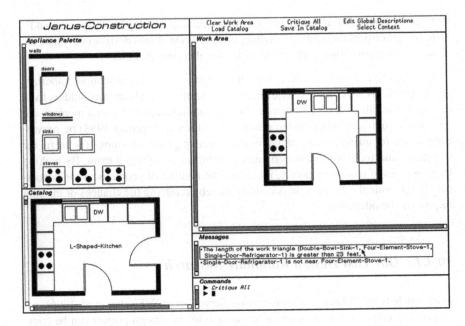

Fig. 20.1 JANUS-Construction: A DODE for kitchen design

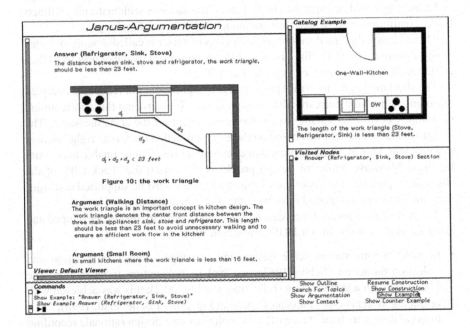

Fig. 20.2 JANUS-Argumentation: A DODE for kitchen design

see more below) was developed as an important technique to allow designers to leave reminders in the environments to be developed at later points of time;

- to contextualize/illustrate argumentation with concrete, specific examples, the Argumentation Illustrator was employed (see "Catalog Example" pane in Fig. 20.2).

We explored and supported the following issues for effective documentation and use of design rationale:

- a rationale representation scheme was used to organize information according to its relevance to the task at hand;
- argumentative and constructive design activities were explicitly linked by integrated design environments; and
- the reusability of the argumentation was supported.

20.3.2 Collaborative Design

Design projects may take place over many years, with initial design followed by extended periods of evolution and redesign. In this sense, design artifacts typically are not designed once and for all, but instead they evolve over long periods of time (Fischer et al. 1992). In such long-term design processes, designers may extend or modify artifacts designed by people they actually have never met.

In extended and distributed design projects, specialists from many different domains must coordinate their efforts despite large separations of time and distance. In such projects, long-term collaboration is crucial for success, yet it is difficult to achieve. Complexity arises from the need to synthesize different perspectives (Fischer 2001), exploit conceptual collisions between concepts and ideas coming from different disciplines, manage large amounts of information potentially relevant to a design task, and understand the design decisions that have determined the long-term evolution of a designed artifact.

An important objective to support collaborative design is the externalization of tacit knowledge (Polanyi 1966). Externalizations (Bruner 1996) can support creativity in the following ways:

- They cause us to move from a vague mental conceptualization of an idea to a more concrete representation of it, which creates situational back-talk (Schön 1983), making thoughts and intentions more accessible to reflection;
- They produce a record and rationale of our mental efforts, one that is outside us rather than vaguely in memory;
- They provide a means for others to interact with, react to, negotiate around, and build upon an idea; and
- They are critically important for social interactions because sometimes a group has no "head" leading to the artifact becoming the focus of social activity (Reeves 1993).

20.4   Creativity

20.4.1   The Social Nature of Creativity

The power of the unaided individual mind is highly overrated (John-Steiner 2000; Salomon 1993). Although creative individuals (Gardner 1993; Sternberg 1988) are often thought of as working in isolation, much of our intelligence and creativity results from interaction and collaboration with other individuals (Csikszentmihalyi 1996). Creative activity grows out of the relationship between individuals and their work, as well as from the interactions between individuals. In other words, creativity does not only happen inside people's heads, but in the interaction between a person's thoughts and a sociocultural context (Engeström 2001). Situations that support social creativity need to be sufficiently open-ended and complex so that users will encounter *break-downs* (Schön 1983). As any professional designer knows, breakdowns—although at times costly and painful—offer unique opportunities for reflection and learning.

Social creativity includes the exploration of computer media and technologies to help people work together. It is relevant to design because collaboration plays an increasingly significant role in design projects that require expertise in a wide range of domains. Software design projects, for example, typically involve designers, programmers, human–computer interaction specialists, marketing people, and end-user participants (Greenbaum and Kyng 1991). Information technologies have reached a level of sophistication, maturity, cost-effectiveness, and distribution so they are not restricted only to enhancing productivity; they also open up new, creative possibilities (Mitchell et al. 2003).

Despite the rhetoric of collaboration, however, the prevailing perspective in the US on design work advocates within universities, schools, offices, and communities a culture in which people need to distinguish themselves as individuals (Bennis and Biederman 1997). As already mentioned, collaboration in today's world is not a luxury but a necessity. We need not only reflective practitioners (Schön 1983), but reflective communities. We need to understand how individual and social creativity (Fischer et al. 2005) interact with each other, and how we can exploit distribution and diversity in design teams, communities, and tools that support reflective communities.

20.4.2   Multiple Distances in Social Creativity

The social nature of creativity establishes the fundamental objective for design rationale that is constructed collaboratively. The goal seeks to support collaboration and integration of many minds and many artifacts across multiple distances: spatial, temporal, and conceptual.

Spatial Distances. Bringing spatially distributed people together by supporting computer-mediated communication allows the shift that shared concerns rather than shared location become the prominent defining feature of a group of people interacting with each other. It further allows more people to be included, thus exploiting local knowledge. These opportunities have been employed successfully by the open source communities (Scharff 2002). Transcending the barrier of spatial distribution is of particular importance in locally sparse populations, enabling a critical mass of interest in a topic to form when it otherwise would not.

Temporal Distances. A design strategy for making creative contributions is to master as thoroughly as possible what is already known in a domain. The ultimate goal is to transcend conventions, not to succumb to them (de Paula and Fischer 2004). Design processes often take place over many years, with initial design followed by extended periods of evolution and redesign. Design artifacts and systems (such as reuse environments; Ye and Fischer 2002) are not designed once and for all, but instead evolve over long periods of time (Dawkins 1987).

Much of the work in ongoing design projects is done as redesign and evolution, and often the people doing this work were not members of the original design team. To be able to do this work well, or sometimes at all, requires that these people collaborate with the original designers of the artifact, through artifact or media support for indirect collaboration. In ongoing projects, long-term collaboration is crucial for success, yet difficult to achieve. This difficulty is due in large part to individual designers' ignorance of how the decisions they make interact with decisions made by other designers. A large part of this, in turn, results from simply not knowing what has already been decided and why.

Long-term collaboration requires that present-day designers be aware of not only the rationale (Moran and Carroll 1996) behind decisions that shaped the artifact, but also any information about possible alternatives that were considered but not implemented. This requires that the rationale behind decisions be recorded in the first place. A barrier to overcome is that designers are biased toward doing design, not toward putting extra effort into documentation. This creates an additional rationale–capture barrier for long-term design (Grudin 1987).

In the context of long-term, indirect collaboration (Fischer et al. 1992), *incremental formalization,* where structure is added over time to content initially captured in a less structured form (Shipman 1993), is an attempt to achieve two conflicting goals: (a) assuring that design rationale recording does not take too many cognitive resources away from the primary task to be done; and (b) assuring that the rationale is (at least partially) formalized so that computational support makes it easier to retrieve later when needed.

Conceptual Distances. Diversity is not only a constraint to deal with but also an opportunity to generate new ideas, new insights, and new environments (Basalla 1988; Mitchell et al. 2003). The challenge is often not to reduce heterogeneity and specialization, but to support it, manage it, and integrate it by finding ways to build bridges between local knowledge sources and by exploiting conceptual collisions and breakdowns as sources for innovation. Our own research efforts have focused on supporting diversity based on the conceptual gap between stakeholders from different practices (conceptual distances between different domains). Rather than being focused on homogeneous communities of practice (CoPs; Wenger 1998), we have been particularly interested in heterogeneous communities of interest (CoIs; Fischer 2001) that bring together stakeholders from different CoPs to solve a particular (design) problem of common concern. CoIs can be thought of as "communities-of-communities" (Brown and Duguid 2000) or communities of representatives of communities. Fundamental challenges facing CoIs are found in building a shared understanding (Resnick et al. 1991) of the task-at-hand, which often does not exist at the beginning but evolves incrementally and collaboratively and emerges in people's minds and in external artifacts. Members of CoIs must learn to communicate with and learn from others (Engeström 2001) who have different perspectives and perhaps different vocabularies to describe their ideas, and to establish common ground (Clark and Brennan 1991).

Boundaries as they exist in CoIs are the locus of the production of new knowledge and therefore an important source of creativity. They are where the unexpected can be expected, where innovative and unorthodox solutions are found, where serendipity is likely, and where old ideas find new life. The diversity of CoIs may cause difficulties, but it also may provide unique opportunities for knowledge creation and sharing. Boundary objects (Bowker and Star 2000; Star 1989) are objects that serve to communicate and coordinate the perspectives of various constituencies. They serve multiple constituencies in situations where each constituency has only partial knowledge and partial control over the interpretation of the object. Boundary objects perform a brokering role involving translation, coordination, and alignment among the perspectives of different CoPs coming together in a CoI. For example, a building floor plan may act as a boundary object between the constituents concerned with plumbing and those concerned with electrical issues in the design.

20.5 Collaborative Design Rationale and Social Creativity in Cultures of Participation

Creativity and innovation are being democratized (von Hippel 2005): Users of products and services are increasingly able to create and innovate for themselves (in the sense of psychological creativity, i.e., new to the person, rather than historical creativity, i.e., new to the world; Boden 1991). Democratizing design is necessary because users' needs are highly heterogeneous in many fields and therefore cannot be anticipated by designers; users' expertise and talent also is widely distributed. Although the existence and availability of tools are necessary, they are not sufficient to support social creativity and democratizing design. Access to these environments is a first step, but we need to create sociotechnical environments (Mumford 2000) that allow people to acquire the technical knowledge and social skills necessary to use them and adapt them to their needs.

In CoPs, collaboratively constructed design rationale can bring social creativity alive by

- allowing participating stakeholders to express themselves by combining different perspectives and generating new understandings, thus avoiding being entrenched in "group think" (Janis 1972);

- making all voices heard and exploiting the symmetry of ignorance (Fischer 2000) as a source for new insights rather than as limitations; these two concepts are specifically important in dealing with complex, systemic problems that require more knowledge than any single person possesses (e.g., in software design, domain experts understand the practice and system designers know the technology);
- supporting distances and diversity in multiple dimensions (Fischer 2005) and creating boundary objects understandable across different domains (Star 1989) will allow users to develop common ground and shared understanding.

We have developed metadesign and the seeding, evolutionary growth, reseeding model as frameworks to foster and support CoPs by providing all people with the means to participate actively in personally meaningful problems.

20.5.1 Metadesign: Creating Opportunities for Creativity

To bring social creativity alive with collaboratively constructed design rationale, media and environments can be supported by metadesign. Metadesign (Fischer and Giaccardi 2006) characterizes objectives, techniques, and processes that allow users to act as designers and be creative. The need for metadesign is founded on the observation that design requires open systems that users can modify and evolve. Because problems cannot be completely anticipated at design time, when the system is developed, users will discover mismatches between their problems and the support that a system provides during use time. These mismatches will lead to breakdowns that serve as potential sources for new insights, new knowledge, and new understanding. Metadesign advocates a shift in focus from finished products or complete solutions to conditions for users to fix mismatches when they are encountered during use.

Metadesign supports informed participation (Brown and Duguid 2000), a form of collaborative design in which participants from all walks of life (not just skilled computer professionals) transcend the information given to incrementally acquire ownership in problems and to contribute actively to their solutions. It addresses the challenges associated with open-ended and multidisciplinary design problems. These problems, involving a combination of social and technological issues, do not have "right" answers at the start, and the knowledge to understand and resolve them changes rapidly. Successful coping with informed participation requires social changes as well as new design rationale that provides the opportunity and resources for social debate and discussion rather than merely delivering predigested information to users.

20.5.2 The Seeding, Evolutionary Growth, and Reseeding (SER) Model

The SER model (Fischer et al. 2001) characterizes the lifecycle of large evolving systems and information repositories. The lifecycle starts with a seed that is developed by a design team composed of domain experts and software designers and provided to domain users. At this point the system or repository alternates between periods of activity and unplanned evolutions made by domain users, and periods of deliberate (re)structuring and enhancement by the design team. The SER model requires the support of users as designers in their own right, rather than restricting them to only passive consumer roles. It provides a framework that supports social creativity through supporting individual creativity. Users of a seed are empowered to act not just as passive consumers, but also as informed participants who can express and share their creative ideas. System design methodologies of the past were focused on building complex information systems as "complete" artifacts through the large efforts of a small number of people. Conversely, instead of attempting to build complete and closed systems, the SER model advocates building seeds that can be evolved over time through the small contributions of a large number of people. The SER model provides a framework to analyze and support environments that are evolved by CoPs.

Many design activities can be characterized by the SER model. Even before the introduction of Wikipedia and other Web 2.0 applications, activities ranging from the design of operating systems (e.g., UNIX), document preparation systems (e.g., MS Word), and the development of university courses (de Paula et al. 2001) involved alternating phases of the gradual introduction of new features or ideas and phases of reorganization to enable further enhancement.

20.6 Case Studies

This section describes three case studies. They are based on the experiences with our previous work and informed by the frameworks discussed in the previous sections.

20.6.1 The Envisionment and Discovery Laboratory (EDC)

The EDC (Arias et al. 2001) is a long-term research platform exploring conceptual frameworks for social creativity and democratizing design in the context of complex design problems. It brings together participants from various backgrounds to frame and solve ill-defined, open-ended design problems. The EDC provides contextualized support for reflection-in-action (Schön 1983) within collaborative design activities (see Fig. 20.3).

In many cases, the knowledge to understand, frame, and solve complex design problems does not already exist (Engeström 2001), but is constructed and evolves during the solution process—an ideal environment to study social creativity. The EDC represents a sociotechnical environment incorporating a number of technologies, including tabletop computing, the integration of physical and computational components supporting new interaction techniques, and an open architecture supporting metadesign.

Fig. 20.3 The EDC showing action space (*horizontal board*), reflection space (*vertical board*) and multiple stakeholders interacting with computationally enhanced physical objects

Our work with the EDC has demonstrated that

- more creative solutions to urban planning problems can emerge from the collective interactions with the environment by heterogeneous CoIs than homogeneous CoPs (Wenger 1998): The EDC avoids group think (Janis 1972) by supporting open representations that allow for deeper understanding, experimentation, and possibly refutation;
- participants are more readily engaged if they perceive the design activities as personally meaningful by associating a purpose with their involvement (Brown et al. 1994): A critical element in the EDC design is the support for participation by individuals whose valuable perspectives are related to their embedded experiences (e.g., neighborhood residents) rather than on any domain expertise;
- participants must be able to naturally express what they want to say (Myers et al. 2006): The EDC employs the use of physical objects and supports parallel interaction capabilities and sketching to create inviting and natural interactions; the interaction mechanisms must allow participants to record design rationale with a reasonable effort: Figure 20.4 shows one system component that we developed to integrate design rationale into the EDC.
- visualization of conflicting actions and decisions lead to lively discussion among participants and helps them reach consensus or explore further alternatives (Rittel 1984); and
- the representations of decisions and their consequences should be easily shared with other users so they can reflect upon others' decisions (Ye et al. 2004).

Fig. 20.4 The association of design rationale with buildings in the EDC

Fig. 20.5 Visualization and incremental formalization in the EDC

Figure 20.5 illustrates two aspects:

- *Visualization support:* The EDC allows stakeholders to sketch new buildings, associate a height with them, and analyze their impact on the surroundings (e.g., Do they block a neighbor's view of the mountains?). An integration with Google Earth is used to create the visualization shown from different locations.
- *Incremental formalization:* The two panes illustrate how we support incremental refinement and formalization in this context. The left pane shows very crude sketches of new buildings created with a minimal effort to explore height limitations. The right pane shows versions based on the crude images that are refined to resemble more closely the buildings that will be eventually constructed by taking advantage of existing 3D models from Google's 3D Warehouse. The gradual progression from rough concepts of a design to more detailed designs (e.g., the 3D model) is an example of incremental refinement and formalization.

The answer to the question shown in the Figure is that the architects wanted to allow in more natural light from the streets between the buildings and therefore designed the buildings so that higher floors were set back in comparison to lower floors.

20.6.2 Increasing Participation Through Design Exploration

Design Exploration (DE) is a process formulated to collect and make use of creative input from a larger number of stakeholders than is traditionally included in design (Moore and Shipman 2008). We explored this process in the context of interface design. DE democratizes design by asking stakeholders to generate partial designs, using the program DE Builder (a deliberately rough-hewn GUI builder) for the domain of widget-based interfaces. DE Builder supports the creation of windows and the layout of widgets on these windows. Additionally, each window and widget can include free-form text (annotations) explaining the graphic design. In this way, stakeholders can choose between visual and textual modes of expression based on individual preferences and the concepts in question. Annotations can combine description of the design choices with explanation for why those choices were made (i.e., rationale).

While the DE Builder attempts to minimize the effort for stakeholders to express design ideas, it potentially increases the effort required to make use of these ideas. Therefore, a second tool supports the DE process: The DE Analyzer provides an environment that aids interface designers in browsing and making sense of a collection of annotated partial designs. The DE Analyzer includes textual analysis of the annotations and text components of widgets and windows, as well as spatial analysis of the layout of widgets in windows. In Fig. 20.6, the designer is examining the main window of an application for locating housing in a college town that was created by one of 75 undergraduates who created annotated partial designs in a study of the system. In this case, the designer can navigate to other designs based on similar terms and concepts, similar spatial structure, or by browsing or searching the vocabulary of terms used by the students.

Studies of the effectiveness of the DE process and tools have occurred for both the collection phase and the analysis phase (Moore 2007). In a study collecting annotated partial designs, we divided participants into three groups: those having only textual forms of expression or only visual forms of expression, and those having both forms of expression. This provided several insights regarding textual and visual design expression:

- There are clear individual preferences for modes of expression when designing interfaces. Some stakeholders will work around the limitations of the system, for example, by generating window layouts in formatted text and using button or other widget text to explain the operation or reasoning behind a design.
- Visual expression motivated stakeholders. Stakeholders in the visual and both visual and textual conditions were more satisfied with their activity and spent

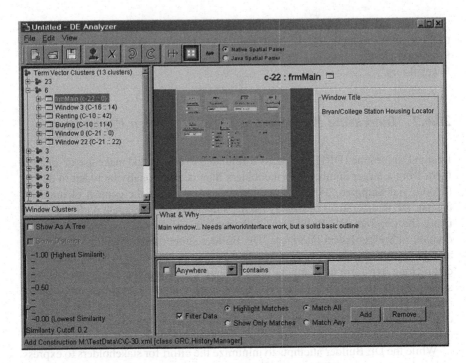

Fig. 20.6 DE Analyzer showing reduced view of design and associated text

longer times generating their feedback than did the stakeholders in the text only condition. In addition, the stakeholders in the visual and textual condition provided more text than the stakeholders in the textual condition.

- Providing tools that limit stakeholders to generating rough designs (e.g., no alignment and distribution options, no snap-to-grid, coloring, or shading options) was frustrating to some stakeholders. These few spent time trying to beautify designs rather than explain or expand the scope of their designs.

A study involving the use of the DE Analyzer pointed to a number of features and issues with interpreting collections of partial designs:

- Designers liked to navigate by vocabulary. Finding all the interface windows involving *apartments* or *condos* aided in locating alternative design ideas around single or related concepts. Designers commented that the ability to navigate through a variety of means meant they could follow different lines of reasoning or investigation while exploring the collection.
- Designers asked to locate design concepts from a collection of annotated partial designs generated a similar number of design concepts as those designing without access to partial designs (e.g., brainstorming). The negative interpretation of this result is that the number of concepts was not greater, although many more stakeholders were represented by the overall design process. The positive interpretation is that the two sets of designers had the same time limit for their

work. Thus, those browsing the collection of partial designs generated a similar number of design concepts while using a complex system to browse a large information space and giving voice to the design ideas of a number of stakeholders.

The DE process was meant as an intermediary between participatory design, where a few stakeholders provide input through rich communication channels, and surveys and questionnaires, where many stakeholders provide input through less expressive forms. It democratizes design in the sense that end users create and explain potential designs. Moving ahead, it is natural to support design groups and to include mechanisms for stakeholders to comment on and share aspects of their annotated partial designs.

20.6.3 Supporting Incremental Formalization in Spatial Hypertext

The need for incremental formalization became evident in early efforts to merge hypertext systems with knowledge representations systems. Both hypertext and frame-based or object-based knowledge representations require expression in nodes that are connected via associations. We, and others, saw this similarity to be an opportunity to integrate discussions about domain activities with knowledge engineering by domain experts. What became clear was that systems integrating these activities were fine for authoring human-readable and navigable content but did not result in the creation of formal knowledge structures required by knowledge representation engines (Shipman and Marshall 1999).

An analysis of the representations shows that the node and association representations were not as similar as originally thought. In hypertexts, the internal representation of a node is in a natural form of communication (natural language, image, video, etc.) while knowledge representations require the internal representation of nodes to be structured in a form interpretable by the computer (e.g., attributes with values and methods). Associations in hypertexts are generally navigational links although some hypertext systems, including design rationale systems, allow or force the assignment of a type to the link. These associations imply a relationship exists between the nodes but say little about the semantics of that relationship or its effect on the semantics of the nodes. On the other hand, associations in knowledge representations encode specific semantic relationships that can be acted upon by production rules or other forms of automatic interpretation.

Users of these systems created navigational links between authored chunks of information. They were less willing to assign specific semantics to the link. More generally, systems that included both natural and formal modes of communication found unexpected use of natural forms of communication in order to avoid use of the formal modes of communication. One such example comes from the use of Aquanet shown in Fig. 20.7. Aquanet, developed by Catherine Marshall and colleagues at Xerox PARC (Marshall et al. 1991), included the ability to define relation types and constraints on the object types that could fill roles in relations. It also

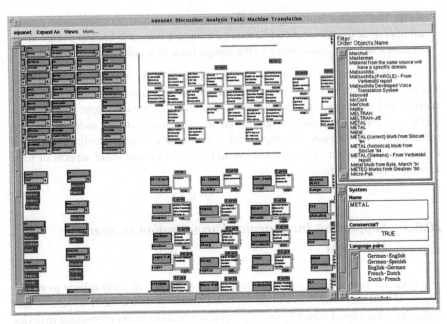

Fig. 20.7 Visual structures expressing semantic relations between people, companies, publications, and software systems in Aquanet

provided for relatively freeform visual expression through modifications to object shape, color, and layout. Here the user has developed a color scheme for classifying information objects concerning machine translation software, such as people, companies, publications, and software systems. The user's layout practices indicate specific relationships between the objects, such as relations between objects identifying a researcher in the field and their software projects and publications.

People make use of natural forms of communication when possible. In our study of systems that allow for visual expression, people often engaged in the opportunistic development of visual languages to match their activity. These languages have several advantages over the formal relationship models found in knowledge representation systems. They are easy to initiate: They start as simple categorizations. They evolve over time, not only in terms of the complexity of expression but also in terms of their meaning to their authors. The original classifications often change, becoming more semantically rigid as users' understanding of their task increases.

To enable the system to understand these emergent visual languages, we developed spatial parsers meant to recognize the object types and associations that people see when looking at these layouts (Shipman et al. 1995). In VIKI (Marshall et al. 1994), the resulting relations were used to suggest formalizations, including the creation of templates for common association types and the creation of collections (i.e., subspaces) for regions containing coherent forms of expression.

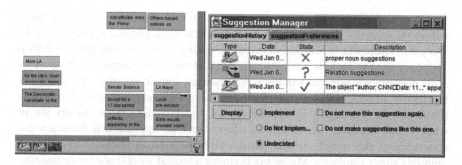

Fig. 20.8 Suggestions in VKB aim to decrease effort required to capture semantics. (*left*) Icons at bottom indicate new suggestions while (*right*) dialog shows suggestion details

The Visual Knowledge Builder (VKB) expanded on these suggestions by combining the results of spatial parsing with text analysis to generate term vectors for each of the structures recognized in the workspace. These term vectors were then used to make recommendations for where to place new information objects (Shipman et al. 2002). VKB also combined the spatial parsing results with temporal analysis to disambiguate interpretations of spatial structures. By keeping track of each edit to the workspace, it is possible to compare the structures recognized in prior states of the workspace to those recognized later. VKB used these differences to determine whether gaps in lists were likely to be semantically meaningful or a side effect of manipulations (e.g., removing an object from a list leaves a gap that would be meaningful if deliberate).

A lesson from earlier efforts to actively support incremental formalization is that users do not want to be interrupted from their main activity to address potential formalizations. Earlier versions of VKB included a Suggestion Manager that presented suggestions through progressive exposure. When a formalization suggestion was available, an icon would appear in the bottom area of the window and would gradually fade away (see Fig. 20.8a). Several suggestions could be visible at once. The user could mouse over the suggestion icon to gain more information about the suggestion. By clicking on the suggestion the user brings up the Suggestion Manager in order to implement suggestions or to tell the system to quit making specific suggestions or classes of suggestions (see Fig. 20.8b). Because users may not be ready to evaluate or make use of a suggestion when the system initially generates it, the Suggestion Manager retains a history of suggestions so users can explore them later, when they have the time.

While we learned a number of lessons about the generation and presentation of suggestions for formalizations, one problem remained. Most uses of VIKI and VKB do not require formal representations. While they could theoretically benefit from the generation of a formal representation, the cost–benefit trade-off was never favorable for that to occur.

Today, VKB and other spatial hypertext systems do not attempt to expose the formal structures to the user, instead using the results of spatial parsing, text analysis, and temporal analysis to generate formal representations only used within the systems. The DE Analyzer mentioned earlier uses a spatial parser to recognize structures of widgets in interface window constructions (Moore 2007). These are used to provide navigational opportunities to structures intermediate in scale between widgets and windows. A somewhat similar use of spatial parsers is to identify structures in order to apply transforms for adaptive spatial hypertext (Francisco-Revilla and Shipman 2004). By understanding what objects are in what visual structure, geometric transforms can be applied that maintain the coherence of the layout. Spatial parsers also are used as evidence of people's opinions about similarity. MusicWiz includes a spatial workspace for organizing the elements of a music collection and visual expression is used as one of many components in calculating the similarity between two pieces of music (Meintanis and Shipman 2010). Finally, application of spatial parsers to Web pages has been used to provide access to visual structures to the visually impaired (Francisco-Revilla and Crow 2009).

One lesson from these experiences is that people will use natural means of communication to express information that could be more valuable if formalized. Another lesson is that formalization must be in support of a real problem. Many times information does not need to be formal, at least in terms of how users interact with the information. In design, formalization is a necessary part of specification and can be valuable in task decomposition, assignment, and tracking. For some uses of rationale, designers do not need to formalize the rationale by encoding it in a particular representational framework. Much like with the end use of the results of the spatial parsers, relations between design information can be inferred and tracked by the system in order to provide useful services without requiring designers to ever acknowledge or commit to these relations.

20.7 Implications

As the previous sections document, we have explored a variety of themes related to the synergy of collaborative design rationale and social creativity made feasible in cultures of participation. Numerous other challenges remain, including (a) learning environments to become a contributor (Preece and Shneiderman 2009), (b) minimizing the effort required to learn how to contribute in order to avoid participants being taken off-task and not getting their work done (Carroll and Rosson 1987), (c) the role of curators in organizing large living information repositories, (d) rating mechanisms for identifying the quality of information, and (e) tagging mechanisms to allow all stakeholders at all times to provide more design rationale.

One of the most important challenges for design rationale research has been the question, What motivates participants to contribute (Grudin 1987)? To motivate participants to contribute design rationale, the following questions need to be answered: (a) from an individual perspective, Am I interested enough and am I willing to make

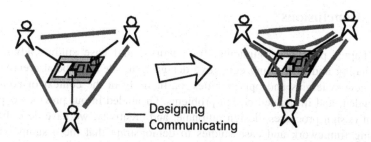

Fig. 20.9 "Storing the Artifact" versus "Mediating Design and Communication" architectures

the additional effort and time so my voice is heard? and (b) from a social perspective, How can we encourage individuals to contribute to the good and progress of all of us? These questions indicate the importance of motivation and rewards in persuading people to make their voices heard and create the following objectives:

- change making must be perceived as within the skill and experience level of users (creating the requirement of systems with a low threshold and high ceiling, and learning and performance support (Shneiderman 2007));
- changes must be technically possible (by supporting interaction mechanisms suited for end-user development); and
- benefits must be perceived (creating the requirement that participants must perceive a direct benefit in contributing that is large enough to outweigh their effort).

Since human beings try to maximize utility, increasing the value and decreasing the effort of contributing design rationale is essential. Utility can be defined as the relationship between *value* and *effort*, or the difference between effort expended for value gained. A sufficiently high utility factor can be obtained through a combination of

- *increasing the value* for being an active contributor, including mechanisms and rewards, such as allowing people to be in control, mastering a tool in greater depth, making ego-satisfying contributions, and acquiring social capital;
- *decreasing the effort* in making a contribution by creating support for learning to become an active contributor, extending metadesign to design communities by allowing local developers and gardeners to emerge (Nardi 1993), and automatically collecting design rationale by channeling as much as possible of communication between participants through the computational environment.

Figure 20.9 illustrates this objective as we have pursued it in the EDC. The left diagram shows that all communication between the participants takes place outside the computational environment (and therefore is not available as design rationale), whereas in the right diagram as much communication as possible is channeled through the environment, gets captured, and can be used as design rationale.

20.8 Conclusions

This chapter provides arguments, frameworks, and case studies advocating coordinating and integrating collective design rationale and social creativity to create new synergies and opportunities, particularly in the context of complex, open-ended, and ill-defined design problems. Grounded in our previous explorations of design processes, design rationale, and creativity, we have described an emerging framework and case studies to demonstrate that the assumption that design rationale and creativity are at odds with each other is misleading. Cultures of participation, supported by sociotechnical environments, have the potential to exploit the opportunities provided by the synergy of collective design rationale and social creativity.

Acknowledgments The authors thank the members of the Center for LifeLong Learning & Design at the University of Colorado and the Center for the Study of Digital Libraries at Texas A&M University, who have made major contributions to ideas described in this chapter. Ray McCall and Andres Morch have been collaborators in our research on design rationale for a long time. Ernesto Arias and Hal Eden were the major designers of the Envisionment and Discovery Collaboratory and have made numerous contributions to the ideas and developments discussed in this chapter. J. Michael Moore was the designer and developer of the VKB Suggestion Manager and the Design Exploration tools. The research was supported in part by (1) grants from the National Science Foundation, including: (a) IIS-0613638 "A Metadesign Framework for Participative Software Systems," (b) IIS-0709304 "A New Generation Wiki for Supporting a Research Community in 'Creativity and IT,'" (c) IIS-0843720 "Increasing Participation and Sustaining a Research Community in 'Creativity and IT,'" and (d) IIS-0438887 "Design Exploration: Supporting a Design Process for Engaging Users"; (2) a Google research award, "Motivating and Empowering Users to Become Active Contributors: Supporting the Learning of High-Functionality Environments"; (3) a SAP research project, "Giving All Stakeholders a Voice: Understanding and Supporting the Creativity and Innovation of Communities Using and Evolving Software Products"; and (4) by SRA Key Technology Laboratory, Inc., Tokyo, Japan.

References

Anderson, C. (2006). *The long tail: Why the future of business is selling less of more.* New York: Hyperion.

Arias, E. G., Eden, H., Fischer, G., Gorman, A., & Scharff, E. (2001). Transcending the individual human mind: Creating shared understanding through collaborative design. In J. M. Carroll (Ed.), *Human-computer interaction in the new millennium* (pp. 347–372). New York: ACM Press.

Basalla, G. (1988). *The evolution of technology.* New York: Cambridge University Press.

Benkler, Y. (2006). *The wealth of networks: How social production transforms markets and freedom.* New Haven: Yale University Press.

Bennis, W., & Biederman, P. W. (1997). *Organizing genius: The secrets of creative collaboration.* Cambridge, MA: Perseus Books.

Boden, M. (1991). *The creative mind: Myths & mechanisms.* New York: Basic Books.

Bowker, G. C., & Star, S. L. (2000). *Sorting things out: Classification and its consequences.* Cambridge, MA: MIT Press.

Brown, J. S., & Duguid, P. (2000). *The social life of information.* Boston: Harvard Business School Press.

Brown, J. S., Duguid, P., & Haviland, S. (1994). Toward informed participation: Six scenarios in search of democracy in the information age. *The Aspen Institute Quarterly, 6*(4), 49–73.

Bruner, J. (1996). *The culture of education.* Cambridge, MA: Harvard University Press.

Carroll, J. M., & Rosson, M. B. (1987). Paradox of the active user. In J. M. Carroll (Ed.), *Interfacing thought: Cognitive aspects of human-computer interaction* (pp. 80–111). Cambridge: The MIT Press.

Clark, H. H., & Brennan, S. E. (1991). Grounding in communication. In L. B. Resnick, J. M. Levine, & S. D. Teasley (Eds.), *Perspectives on socially shared cognition* (pp. 127–149). Washington, DC: American Psychological Association.

Conklin, J., & Begeman, M. (1988). Gibis: A hypertext tool for exploratory policy discussion. In *Proceedings of the conference on computer supported cooperative work* (pp. 140–152). New York: ACM.

Cross, N. (Ed.). (1984). *Developments in design methodology.* New York: Wiley.

Csikszentmihalyi, M. (1996). *Creativity: Flow and the psychology of discovery and invention.* New York: HarperCollins Publishers.

Dawkins, R. (1987). *The blind watchmaker.* New York: W.W. Norton and Company.

de Paula, R., & Fischer, G. (2004). Knowledge management: Why learning from the past is not enough! In J. Davis (Ed.), *Knowledge management and the global firm: Organizational and technological dimensions* (pp. 21–54). Heidelberg: Springer.

de Paula, R., Fischer, G., & Ostwald, J. (2001). Courses as seeds: Expectations and realities. In P. Dillenbourg, A. Eurelings, & K. Hakkarainen (Eds.), *Proceedings of the European conference on computer-supported collaborative learning* (pp. 494–501). Maastricht: McLuhan Institute.

Engeström, Y. (2001). Expansive learning at work: Toward an activity theoretical reconceptualization. *Journal of Education and Work, 14*(1), 133–156.

Fischer, G. (1994). Domain-oriented design environments. *Automated Software Engineering, 1*(2), 177–203.

Fischer, G. (2000). Social creativity, symmetry of ignorance and metadesign. *Knowledge-Based Systems Journal, 13*(7–8), 527–537.

Fischer, G. (2001). Communities of interest: Learning through the interaction of multiple knowledge systems. In *24th Annual Information Systems Research Seminar in Scandinavia* (IRIS'24, pp. 1–14). Ulvik, Norway: University of Oslo.

Fischer, G. (2005). Distances and diversity: Sources for social creativity. In *Proceedings of creativity & cognition* (pp. 128–136). London: ACM.

Fischer, G. (2010). End-user development and metadesign: Foundations for cultures of participation. *Journal of Organizational and End User Computing, 22*, 52–82.

Fischer, G., & Giaccardi, E. (2006). Metadesign: A framework for the future of end user development. In H. Lieberman, F. Paternò, & V. Wulf (Eds.), *End user development* (pp. 427–457). Dordrecht: Kluwer Academic.

Fischer, G., Grudin, J., Lemke, A. C., McCall, R., Ostwald, J., Reeves, B. N., & Shipman, F. (1992). Supporting indirect, collaborative design with integrated knowledge-based design environments. *Human Computer Interaction, 7*, 281–314.

Fischer, G., Lemke, A. C., McCall, R., & Morch, A. (1996). Making argumentation serve design. In T. Moran & J. Carroll (Eds.), *Design rationale: Concepts, techniques, and use* (pp. 267–293). Mahwah: Lawrence Erlbaum and Associates.

Fischer, G., Nakakoji, K., Ostwald, J., Stahl, G., & Sumner, T. (1998). Embedding critics in design environments. In M. T. Maybury & W. Wahlster (Eds.), *Readings in intelligent user interfaces* (pp. 537–559). San Francisco: Morgan Kaufmann.

Fischer, G., Grudin, J., McCall, R., Ostwald, J., Redmiles, D., Reeves, B., & Shipman, F. (2001). Seeding, evolutionary growth and reseeding: The incremental development of collaborative design environments. In G. M. Olson, T. W. Malone, & J. B. Smith (Eds.), *Coordination theory and collaboration technology* (pp. 447–472). Mahwah: Lawrence Erlbaum Associates.

Fischer, G., Giaccardi, E., Eden, H., Sugimoto, M., & Ye, Y. (2005). Beyond binary choices: Integrating individual and social creativity. *International Journal of Human Computer Studies, 63*, 482–512.

Francisco-Revilla, L., & Crow, J. (2009). Interpreting the layout of web pages. In *Proceedings of 20th ACM Conference on Hypertext and Hypermedia* (HT'09, pp. 157–166). New York: ACM Press.

Francisco-Revilla, L., & Shipman, F. (2004). Instructional information in adaptive spatial hypertext. In *Proceedings of ACM conference document engineering* (pp. 124–133). New York: ACM Press.

Gardner, H. (1993). *Creating minds*. New York: Basic Books, Inc.

Greenbaum, J., & Kyng, M. (Eds.). (1991). *Design at work: Cooperative design of computer systems*. Hillsdale: Lawrence Erlbaum Associates, Inc.

Grudin, J. (1987). Social evaluation of the user interface: Who does the work and who gets the benefit? In H. Bullinger & B. Shackel (Eds.), *Proceedings of Interact'87: 2nd IFIP conference on human-computer interaction* (pp. 805–811). Amsterdam: IFIP.

Janis, I. (1972). *Victims of groupthink*. Boston: Houghton Mifflin.

John-Steiner, V. (2000). *Creative collaboration*. Oxford: Oxford University Press.

Marshall, C., Halasz, F., Rogers, R., & Janssen, W. (1991). Aquanet: A hypertext tool to hold your knowledge in place. In *Proceedings of hypertext'91* (pp. 261–275). New York: ACM Press.

Marshall, C., Shipman, F., & Coombs, J. (1994). VIKI: Spatial hypertext supporting emergent structure. In *Proceedings of 1994 ACM European Conference on Hypermedia Technology* (ECHT'94, pp. 13–23). New York: ACM Press.

Meintanis, K., & Shipman, F. (2010). Visual expression for organizing and accessing music collections in Musicwiz. In *Proceedings of European Conference on Digital Libraries* (ECDL 2010, pp. 80–91). Heidelberg, Germany: Springer.

Mitchell, W. J., Inouye, A. S., Blumenthal, M. S. (Eds.), & the Committee on Information Technology and Creativity, National Research Council. (2003). *Beyond productivity: Information technology, innovation, and creativity*. Washington, DC: National Academy Press.

Moore, J. M. (2007). *Design exploration: Engaging a larger user population*. Unpublished doctoral dissertation, Texas A&M University, USA.

Moore, J. M., & Shipman, F. (2008). Combining spatial and textual analysis to support design exploration. In *Proceedings of the IEEE Automated Software Engineering Conference* (p. 35). New York: IEEE Press.

Moran, T. P., & Carroll, J. M. (Eds.). (1996). *Design rationale: Concepts, techniques, and use*. Hillsdale: Lawrence Erlbaum Associates, Inc.

Mumford, E. (2000). A socio-technical approach to systems design. *Requirements Engineering, 5*(2), 59–77.

Myers, B. A., Ko, A. J., & Burnett, M. M. (2006). Invited research overview: End-user programming. In *Human factors in computing systems* (CHI 2006, pp. 75–80). New York: ACM Press.

Nardi, B. A. (1993). *A small matter of programming*. Cambridge, MA: The MIT Press.

O'Reilly, T. (2005, September 30). *What is Web 2.0: Design patterns and business models for the next generation of software*. Retrieved July 8, 2011, from http://www.oreillynet.com/pub/a/oreilly/tim/news/2005/09/30/what-is-web-20.html

Polanyi, M. (1966). *The tacit dimension*. Garden City: Doubleday.

Preece, J., & Shneiderman, B. (2009). The reader-to-leader framework: Motivating technology-mediated social participation. *AIS Transactions on Human-Computer Interaction, 1*(1), 13–32.

Reeves, B. N. (1993). *The role of embedded communication and artifact history in collaborative design*. Unpublished doctoral dissertation, University of Colorado at Boulder, USA.

Resnick, L. B., Levine, J. M., & Teasley, S. D. (Eds.). (1991). *Perspectives on socially shared cognition*. Washington, DC: American Psychological Association.

Rittel, H. (1984). Second-generation design methods. In N. Cross (Ed.), *Developments in design methodology* (pp. 317–327). New York: Wiley.

Rittel, H., & Webber, M. M. (1984). Planning problems are wicked problems. In N. Cross (Ed.), *Developments in design methodology* (pp. 135–144). New York: Wiley.

Salomon, G. (Ed.). (1993). *Distributed cognitions: Psychological and educational considerations*. Cambridge: Cambridge University Press.

Scharff, E. (2002). *Open source software, a conceptual framework for collaborative artifact and knowledge construction*. Unpublished doctoral dissertation, University of Colorado at Boulder, USA.

Schön, D. A. (1983). *The reflective practitioner: How professionals think in action*. New York: Basic Books.

Shipman, F. (1993). *Supporting knowledge-base evolution with incremental formalization*. Unpublished doctoral dissertation, University of Colorado at Boulder, USA.

Shipman, F., & Marshall, C. (1999). Formality considered harmful: Experiences, emerging themes, and directions on the use of formal representations in interactive systems. *Computer Supported Collaborative Work, 8*, 333–352.

Shipman, F., & McCall, R. (1994). Supporting knowledge-base evolution with incremental formalization. In *Human factors in computing systems, InterCHI'94 conference proceedings* (pp. 285–291). New York: ACM.

Shipman, F., Marshall, C. C., & Moran, T. P. (1995). Finding and using implicit structure in human-organized spatial layouts of information. In I. Katz, R. Mack, & L. Marks (Eds.), *Proceedings of ACM CHI'95: Conference on human factors in computing systems* (Vol. 1, pp. 346–353). New York: ACM Press.

Shipman, F., Moore, J. M., Maloor, P., Hsieh, H., & Akkapeddi, R. (2002). Semantics happen: Knowledge building in spatial hypertext. In *Proceedings of the ACM conference on hypertext* (pp. 25–34). New York: ACM Press.

Shneiderman, B. (2007). Creativity support tools: Accelerating discovery and innovation. *Communications of the ACM, 50*(12), 20–32.

Simon, H. A. (1996). *The sciences of the artificial* (3rd ed.). Cambridge, MA: The MIT Press.

Star, S. L. (1989). The structure of ill-structured solutions: Boundary objects and heterogeneous distributed problem solving. In L. Gasser & M. N. Huhns (Eds.), *Distributed artificial intelligence* (Vol. II, pp. 37–54). San Mateo: Morgan Kaufmann Publishers Inc.

Sternberg, R. J. (Ed.). (1988). *The nature of creativity*. Cambridge: Cambridge University Press.

Surowiecki, J. (2005). *The wisdom of crowds*. New York: Anchor Books.

von Hippel, E. (2005). *Democratizing innovation*. Cambridge, MA: MIT Press.

Wenger, E. (1998). *Communities of practice: Learning, meaning, and identity*. Cambridge: Cambridge University Press.

Ye, Y., & Fischer, G. (2002). Supporting reuse by delivering task-relevant and personalized information. In *Proceedings of 2002 International Conference on Software Engineering* (ICSE'02, pp. 513–523). Orlando, FL, USA: IEEE Computer Society.

Ye, Y., Nakakoji, K., Yamamoto, Y., & Kishida, K. (2004). The co-evolution of system and community in open source software development. In S. Koch (Ed.), *Free/open source software development* (pp. 59–82). Hershey: Idea Group Publishing.

Subject Index

A

Action, 12, 13, 19, 23, 24, 28, 29, 34–37, 54, 58, 61, 63, 67, 75, 77, 81, 87, 90, 124, 138, 139, 176, 216, 226, 239, 260, 263, 264, 269, 275–277, 282, 284, 288, 293, 294, 296, 297, 299, 300, 324, 332, 335–337, 342–344, 348, 350, 367, 372, 384, 389–391, 397, 399, 427, 429, 436, 437

Adaptive structuration theory, 332, 348, 349

Aesthetics, 8, 73, 77, 294–296, 306, 324, 421

Affordances, 4, 6, 31, 32, 71, 81, 85, 86, 88, 90–93, 101, 185, 331, 348, 361

Alternative functionality, 123, 127, 134, 136, 139

B

Boundaries, 7, 65, 100, 110, 149, 158, 203, 217, 294, 296, 348, 381, 390, 396, 398, 434

Brainstorming, 19, 89, 99, 101, 110, 111, 115, 116, 178, 224, 229–231, 241, 246–248, 288, 294, 331, 359, 371–373, 440

Business process, 344, 345, 413

C

Claims, 6, 17, 30, 43, 50, 54, 58, 59, 61, 80, 86, 88, 91, 92, 94, 95, 99–101, 105–116, 121, 123, 124, 166, 172, 173, 175–177, 189–191, 200, 202, 230, 266, 332, 345, 346, 351, 397, 407, 408, 421
claims analysis, 198

Cognition, 12, 13, 22–35, 42, 46, 59, 60, 62, 65, 98, 172, 173, 244, 253, 254, 267, 271, 370, 420

Collaboration, 5, 35, 61, 101, 107, 134, 200, 225, 238, 329, 339–340, 342, 343, 347–349, 356, 379, 426

Collaboration patterns, 393–395

Collaborative communities, 379–381, 387, 391, 396, 398, 399

Collaborative decision, 179, 329, 330, 335, 336, 340, 341, 348, 350

Collaborative design, 8, 9, 29, 207, 425–446

Communication, 15, 42, 66, 113, 132, 153, 204, 223, 240, 266, 277, 297, 329, 330, 332, 334–342, 344, 347–351, 358, 379, 418, 426
design, 341, 348
design practice, 330, 332, 336–337, 348–350
design techniques, 337–339

Communicative activity, 333, 336, 337, 341, 342, 344, 348–351

Comprehensiveness, 7, 206–211, 215–220

Computer-supported cooperative work (CSCW), 162, 238, 239, 253, 330, 387

Conceptual graphs, 389, 392, 395, 398

Conflict resolution, 348, 349

Conversation with the situation, 13, 24, 67, 123

J.M. Carroll (ed.), *Creativity and Rationale: Enhancing Human Experience by Design*, Human–Computer Interaction Series, DOI 10.1007/978-1-4471-4111-2, © Springer-Verlag London 2013